A *Backwoods Home* Anthology:

The Fourteenth Year

Published by
Backwoods Home Magazine
P. O. Box 712
Gold Beach, OR 97444
www.backwoodshome.com

A Backwoods Home Anthology

Copyright 2003, 2008 by Backwoods Home Magazine

All rights reserved

Editor: *Dave Duffy*

Senior Editor: *John Silveira*

Art Director: *Don Childers*

Contributors:

Jackie Clay, Edward King, Massad Ayoob, Dr. Roger W. Grim, D.C., Rev. J.D. Hooker, Habeeb Salloum, Gary D. Kirchmeier, Tom R. Kovach, Alice B. Yeager, James O. Yeager, Jeffrey R. Yago, P.E., CEM, Linda Gabris, Clay Sawyer, O.E. MacDougal, Don Fallick, John Silveira, Don Childers, Gary F. Arnet, D.D.S., Nancy Pierson Farris, Sylvia Gist, Charles A. Sanders, Tom and Joanne O'Toole, Brad Rohdenburg, Anita Evangelista, Beverly Mettot, John Kallas, Ph.D., Dorothy Ainsworth, Dr. Bill Glade, Marcia E. Brown, Pete Earl, Phil Nichols, Ilene Duffy, Chuck Davis, Bill Wilson, Claire Wolfe, Steve Gregg, Edna Manning, Jon Stram, Donn Rochlin, Grace Brockway

Introduction

The publication of this 14th Year Anthology is an auspicious occasion because it has been a couple of years since we published one of our big 360-page anthologies, and because this is only one of four big anthologies we intend to publish during the next six months. Numbers 15, 16, and 17 will follow shortly.

As we go to print with this book, Congress has just approved a $700 billion plus bailout package for Wall Street and the banks over the objection of a majority of the American people. The bill, which essentially bails out Wall Street and bank gamblers with taxpayer money, will fuel the inflation that is already damaging the American economy. Time will tell how things actually play out, but I predict this is the beginning of the unraveling of capitalism in America. Many Americans, particularly those who don't grasp the idea of being self-reliant, will simply be condemned to a lower standard of living.

That's why I've decided to publish four anthologies in such a short span of time. I think people need this self-reliant information to help them cope with a less affluent future. I believe America is headed for some hard times, but I'm certain each of us can take care of ourselves and our individual families just fine, so long as we are willing to act on the self-reliant information given in this anthology and our other anthologies.

We all have the ability to control how well we live. These books are full of ideas to help you live well, no matter what stupid laws our Government passes.

Dave Duffy
Publisher/Editor

Contents —

Issue Number 79

- ❑ *My view: The attack on Colin Powell prompts questions I'm not supposed to ask* — **10**
- ❑ *Use Wallo'Water and gain a month of growing season* — **11**
- ❑ *A packing crate mini-barn* — **15**
- ❑ *Harvesting the wild: acorns* — **16**
- ❑ *Ayoob on Firearms: Firearms and cold weather considerations* — **21**
- ❑ *How to butcher a chicken in 20 minutes or less* — **25**
- ❑ *Want more fruit from less space? Espalier your trees!* — **28**
- ❑ *Pemmican* — **30**
- ❑ *Mane and tail tools* — **31**
- ❑ *The vanishing outhouse* — **32**
- ❑ *Caring for spices and herbs* — **33**
- ❑ *Preparing garden soil in winter* — **34**
- ❑ *Living with wildlife* — **37**
- ❑ *Sell your home: get a good price and sell it faster* — **38**
- ❑ *Install a mobile, solar powered toilet* — **42**
- ❑ *Cracklin's—an irresistible snack that you can't stop sneakin'* — **46**
- ❑ *Portable fence panels: the homesteader's friend* — **49**
- ❑ *Hingeless gate* — **52**
- ❑ *Preserving fish* — **53**
- ❑ *The gee-whiz! page* — **55**
- ❑ *The irreverent joke page* — **56**
- ❑ *Mountain and winter driving* — **58**
- ❑ *Ask Jackie* — **64**
- ❑ *The last word—A proposal for ending violent crime* — **68**

Issue Number 80

- ❑ *My view: Smallpox—it's worth worrying about* — **70**
- ❑ *Keeping your heart healthy* — **71**
- ❑ *Ayoob on Firearms: A 24/7 backwoods handgun* — **82**
- ❑ *The irreverent joke page* — **86**
- ❑ *A comfortable base camp* — **88**
- ❑ *Home canning equals fast, easy, tasty meals* — **95**

- ❏ *The gee-whiz! page* — **98**
- ❏ *Growing cauliflower* — **99**
- ❏ *My garden: A springboard of food, pleasure, and history* — **102**
- ❏ *Harvesting the wild: greens* — **106**
- ❏ *Brooder in a box* — **112**
- ❏ *Growing and using blueberries* — **114**
- ❏ *A pleasant surprise: the asparagus bean* — **117**
- ❏ *Mosquitoes outnumber us and no one likes them* — **120**
- ❏ *Leaves of three, let them be!* — **122**
- ❏ *Ask Jackie* — **124**
- ❏ *The last word—Do we really need Yuppies?* — **126**

Issue Number 81

- ❏ *My view: Confronting the enemy* — **128**
- ❏ *What can you do to protect yourself against chemical, biological, and nuclear terrorism* — **129**
- ❏ *Dark winter—A simulated terrorist attack on three American cities using weaponized smallpox* — **138**
- ❏ *How safe is smallpox vaccine?* — **144**
- ❏ *Think of it this way...Biological and chemical weapons through history* — **150**
- ❏ *Preparedness for travelers* — **159**
- ❏ *Jackie Clay's basic "grab & git" emergency kits* — **162**
- ❏ *The irreverent joke page* — **164**
- ❏ *Ayoob on Firearms—In time of war: The Israeli answer to terrorism* — **165**
- ❏ *Traditional trail foods—transportable calories* — **170**
- ❏ *The home citrus orchard* — **173**
- ❏ *Companion planting* — **176**
- ❏ *The gee-whiz! page* — **179**
- ❏ *Ask Jackie* — **180**
- ❏ *The last word—Is television still a wasteland?* — **182**

Issue Number 82

- ❏ *My view: Gulf War II opened the eyes of Americans to the UN and the media* — **184**
- ❏ *Making dandelions palatable* — **185**
- ❏ *Dandelion facts and history* — **189**

- ❏ *Tomato canning tips* — **190**
- ❏ *Dandelion recipes* — **191**
- ❏ *How to select the right backup generator* — **192**
- ❏ *The informed juror—How an informed jury helps safeguard liberty* — **198**
- ❏ *Growing & storing herbs* — **203**
- ❏ *The amazing yogurt* — **205**
- ❏ *Successful cold storage* — **207**
- ❏ *Chokecherries* — **212**
- ❏ *Alternative lifestyles* — **215**
- ❏ *Homemade cottage cheese, rhubarb pie, lemon custard pudding cake, pasties, beef stew, biscuits, butter, grouse breast* — **217**
- ❏ *The irreverent joke page* — **221**
- ❏ *A simple backwoods hay baler* — **222**
- ❏ *Diagnosing appendicitis* — **224**
- ❏ *The gee-whiz! page* — **226**
- ❏ *Ayoob on firearms: Shooting left-handed* — **227**
- ❏ *Ask Jackie* — **232**
- ❏ *Making wild nuts into nut oil, nut meal, and nut butter* — **235**
- ❏ *The last word—The "curse" of oil* — **236**

Issue Number 83

- ❏ *Publisher's Note: Mousers and cat loonies* — **238**
- ❏ *My view: "I stink!" but that's okay* — **239**
- ❏ *Battery powered weekend retreat* — **240**
- ❏ *Lyme disease—a little tick can cause a big problem* — **244**
- ❏ *Piccalilli—a late summer bonus* — **250**
- ❏ *Ayoob on Firearms—1911: The classic homeland security pistol* — **251**
- ❏ *Creating your own job* — **256**
- ❏ *Venison burger chow mein* — **260**
- ❏ *Harvest your own firewood* — **261**
- ❏ *The gee-whiz! page* — **264**
- ❏ *The art of wood splitting* — **265**
- ❏ *Standby battery charging techniques can ensure engine startups* — **270**
- ❏ *Keeping cats out of the garden* — **273**
- ❏ *For health, pleasure, and relaxation gardening rules!* — **274**
- ❏ *Harvesting the wild: Flower buds* — **279**

- Black walnut warning — 281
- Sew a baby quilt in two days...for a lifetime of memories — 282
- Grouse hunting...the ultimate joy of autumn — 284
- Life in a chicken coop — 287
- How to make money from storage building auctions — 289
- Living the outlaw life: Credit card monte: Finance flim-flam & how to foil it — 292
- Ask Jackie — 296
- The last word—Gun control, race, and rotten politicians — 302

Issue Number 84

- My view: Animal rights loonies save the chickens but ruin the County Fair — 304
- Your wild neighbors — 305
- Ayoob on firearms: On a quiet holiday, a cop gives thanks — 312
- Shaving with a straight razor — 316
- The irreverent joke page — 318
- Rattlesnake bite — 320
- Keep those gadgets working after the power goes out — 327
- Recycled bicycles — 330
- Skunks — 333
- Cultured milk: Food of centenarians — 334
- Small Town America: Thorne Bay, Alaska — 336
- Woolen winter mittens in minutes — 341
- Ask Jackie — 343
- Hey! Sandwichman! Selling sandwiches for an income — 348
- The joys of making soap — 350
- Wind chill factor makes it colder than you think — 353
- Hypothermia—a real winter danger — 355
- From weasels to chocolate bars—it all came to naught — 358
- Qawarma—a food since antiquity — 359

The NEW O.E. MacDougal Report - See page 29

Backwoods Home magazine

Jan/Feb 2003
No. 79
$4.95 US
$6.50 CAN

practical ideas for self-reliant living

Questions we're not supposed to ask ...page 7

Start your garden in winter
Sell your home QUICK
A solution to violent crime
Solar-powered mobile toilet
Make pemmican and cracklin's

www.backwoodshome.com

My view

The attack on Colin Powell prompts questions I'm not supposed to ask

What's wrong with black Americans?

Provocative question, isn't it, especially when it's being asked by a white guy like me. We white guys aren't supposed to question what blacks do, because it automatically makes us a racist. Which brings up another obvious question: How come blacks can criticize whites, calling them honkies and racists at the drop of a hat, but whites can't criticize blacks?

Let me break my first question down into some smaller, more obvious questions:

How come when Harry Belafonte recently called Secretary of State Colin Powell "a house slave" for serving in the Bush administration, few blacks came to Powell's defense? Is it because they resented Powell's heroic climb from the slums of New York to chairman of the Joint Chiefs of Staff, then to the inner circle of the White House, without asking for any special treatment along the way?

How about when Congress was interrogating Clarence Thomas some years back during his confirmation hearings for the Supreme Court. When a lone woman accused Thomas of sexual impropriety, black leaders joined in the attack with a fury. But later, when Clinton was accused of the same thing and worse, by many women with many corroborating witnesses, blacks came to Clinton's defense? When Thomas was exonerated and confirmed, his accuser, Anita Hill, went on the speaking circuit for years attacking Justice Thomas, but few blacks criticized her. Clinton was impeached over his improprieties, but just the other day he became the first white man to be inducted into the Arkansas Black Hall of Fame as an honorary member.

What gives? Is it because Clarence Thomas was another black heroic figure who broke ranks and rose to the pinnacles of the justice system by his own determination and hard work, and Clinton has always been the white crusader wanting ever more free federal dollars for downtrodden blacks?

How about the O.J. Simpson affair? Simpson brutally murdered two innocent people. DNA tests proved it, and overwhelming evidence proved it. Yet a mainly black jury voted him "not guilty," and we all witnessed the TV scenes of crowds of blacks cheering wildly when the verdict was announced. Did they cheer because Simpson had killed two whites and got away with it? Sure looked like it!

Why did 85% of black congress people vote against America going to war with Iraq 10 years ago, and why do Congressional blacks now hold rallies against us going to war with Iraq again? They claim it's because blacks represent a larger percentage of the armed forces so it is they who will be asked to die. But I think that's just cover for the real reason, namely that they think America is the villain in this showdown. They empathize with Iraq as the underdog, just as they perceive themselves as the underdog in America. It's America they hate, not Iraq.

And here's a really racist question: Why haven't blacks assimilated completely into American society, even after the federal government has spent more than $700 billion dollars on the poor—largely on poor blacks—since former President Lyndon Johnson vastly expanded welfare with his War on Poverty nearly 40 years ago? Irish people like me have assimilated, and my immigrant ancestors were valued below slaves when they arrived on the boats in places like New York and New Orleans at the height of their great flight from Irish hunger a century ago. And millions of Mexicans are assimilating right before our eyes. Is it really because racism continues to keep blacks down, or is it their own fault, a fault that mainly has to do with their desire—or lack of it—to stand on their own two feet?

These are all terrible questions for a white man to ask, I know. I must indeed be a racist to bring these things up.

But I can't help it. When I watch Colin Powell, one of the greatest Americans of my lifetime, being viciously attacked by activists like Belafonte, with people like Jesse Jackson and Spike Lee joining in, I feel like screaming: What are you fools doing?

Powell is a black man who has lived the American Dream. He didn't do it with the federal handouts that have done nothing for blacks but make them a permanent underclass in America. He did it by himself. Why aren't you rising in outrage against Belafonte and the rest of the attackers. Isn't this what the War on Poverty was all about, to make sure poor people, especially poor black people, could take part in the American Dream?

Of course we all, in our bitter, racist, heart of hearts, know the answer to all my questions. Black heroes like Colin Powell and Clarence Thomas believe in the wrong ideology. They believe in self-reliance. They are renegades from a liberal ideology that says blacks can't take care of themselves. Rather than criticize those blacks who have made themselves a success, blacks should feel ashamed that they, as a race, have wandered in the wilderness from one type of slavery only to find another: the new nanny state of black slavery, with Jesse Jackson and a host of white bureaucrats directing how all the welfare freebies are to be divied up. But step out of line, as Powell and Thomas did, and they'll be after your ass with a vengeance, accusing you of every crime in the book and calling you the white man's house slave. That's about as ironic as it gets!

My Irish immigrant mother has some advice for black Americans: She gave it to me in the 1950s when I was a boy in all Irish South Boston. I had been boasting about how great it was to be Irish. She told me curtly: "You are not Irish, you are American. Act like it!" — *Dave Duffy*

Use Wallo'Water and gain a month of growing season

By Jackie Clay

If I had to choose one season extender over all the rest, it would be Wallo'Water, hands down. And I have absolutely nothing to gain from this "endorsement," not even free products. While all plant protectors, such as hot caps, cut off plastic milk jugs, cloches or floating row covers, offer both some degree of freeze and/or frost protection, only the Wallo'Water offers radical freeze protection. I've had tomatoes planted in Wallo'Water when the temperature suddenly plummeted to 19 degrees with over a foot of snow blowing in. The temperatures remained below freezing for two days and nights. I didn't even look in at my plants. I was sure they were history.

Then on the third day, I brushed the snow off the row of tomatoes and grimaced as I peered into the first little plastic tipi. The tomato had not only survived, but had actually grown and was happy. I was sold.

What the heck is a Wallo'Water, anyway? It's a series of approximately 1½ by 18-inch flexible plastic tubes, fastened together forming a circle. This circle is just a little larger in diameter than a five-gallon white plastic bucket. You'd be surprised that all those tubes hold several gallons.

And it is this large amount of water, coupled with solar gain, that provides the protection for that baby plant, nestled comfortably in the soil beneath its protective "wings." The water heats up, which in turn heats the soil and the plant. Even with constant temperatures below freezing, the water and soil provide enough warmth to protect the plant for many hours. (Wallo'Water doesn't need direct sunlight to work, they'll work even on cloudy days, so don't wait for sunny days to set them out.)

After springtime temperatures climb dependably above freezing, those same neat little plastic tipis act as a miniature greenhouse, encouraging the plant to really get busy and grow.

So what does all this mean to the serious gardener? It means that you can gain over a full month of great growing season. To those of us with northern gardens, or gardens in higher elevations in other areas, it is nearly a Godsend. When we lived in northern Minnesota, we were lucky to have a 90-day frost-free period, and some of those were pretty darned chilly at that. I couldn't set unprotected tomato and pepper plants out before June 16th for fear of that sure-to-come late killing frost. But with Wallo'Water, I could put them out May 16th or earlier, and have plants growing out of the plastic tipis by the end of June. I credit Wallo'Water with giving me a highly productive garden, even when the climate attempted to dictate otherwise.

Our Montana mountain homestead enjoys plenty of tomatoes and peppers with help from Wallo'Water.

Wallo'Waters being set out a full five weeks before the last spring frost

Setting plants out

Till your soil and work in plenty of good rotted compost. Lightly rake the row. Mark off your row after you decide how far apart your plants should be and carefully rake a two-foot square pretty flat. This is especially important if you, like me, have a hillside garden. You want your little tipi village to sit level, or the first good wind will blow them downhill.

Pick out any sharp rocks or roots. Wallo'Water are made of plastic and will puncture.

I usually wait until the spring weather has settled quite well before I plant my plants. (But the manufacturer has said to set the Wallo'Waters out even earlier than I do while the temperatures are still freezing, as the Wallo'Waters actually warm the soil and allow you to plant that much earlier. In a few days the soil is warm enough to plant and sprout your seedlings, even though the surrounding landscape is still frozen.)

To plant, I dig out a nice hole and set my plant in, firming the soil nicely around it. Then sit an upside down four or five-gallon plastic bucket over the transplant, centering it over the plant. I slip the Wallo'Water sleeve over the bucket. I line up the seams of the sleeve with the places the bail attaches to the bucket. It's easier to lift the bucket off later on. With a garden hose or watering can, fill the tubes. A helper at this point is really handy. If one person opens the tubes, it's easy to insert the hose (without sprinkler nozzle) and fill the tube. It's harder to open the tubes and run the hose by yourself.

Fill all of the tubes, nearly to the top. You won't gain anything by filling them all the way full, as some water will spill when you pull the bucket out. With two hands, reach into the Wallo'Water and grasp the sides of the bucket and gently haul it straight up and out. As you pull the bucket, the tops of the cylinder will collapse against each other, making a tipi instead of a cylinder. This provides even more plant protection.

I use both overhead sprinklers and drip irrigation in my gardens. I use the sprinklers when the plants are young and small. This allows me to thoroughly weed around each plant so the rows are weed-free when we put the drip system into place. If you want to use your drip system from the start, simply lay it out on your row after it has been tilled and raked. Then when you plant your transplant, simply take a finger and dig a shallow trench on both sides of the Wallo'Water to keep the bottom flat on the ground, despite the drip pipe.

Care of Wallo'Water

The old Wallo'Water were clear plastic. Most of mine are. The only drawback to these is that they sometimes grow a nice crop of algae in the tubes along with the garden plants. This is easily controlled by adding a few drops of chlorine bleach to each full tube.

The new Wallo'Water are light green, which still allow light transmission. The color change was done primarily for eye appeal

As I've said, the Wallo'Water will puncture fairly easily. All plastic does. Sharp rocks, roots, rototillers, rakes, and hoes all take their toll. Eventually you will have a leaking tube. You need to fix it as soon as you discover it. If you don't, the strength of the tipi will be breached and the first thing you know, it will simply collapse. I never have had a collapsed Wallo'Water hurt a plant, though.

Each Wallo'Water package contains three units. You can also buy a repair kit which contains several "repair tubes." These are simply single sleeves. By slipping a yardstick in the repair tube, you can easily slip it down inside the leaking tube and you are instantly ready to refill. Pretty darned slick, I'd say.

I now have over 52 Wallo'Water—and wish I had more. Most of them are over 10-years-old. As my gardens are often in wild areas, with plenty of rocks and roots, it's only reasonable that I come up with leaks once in a while. So I've taken the repair sequence one more step to self-reliance. When one Wall springs more than two leaks, I mark it, while full, with a permanent marker. X is for good cells and 0 for leakers. Then

Day one: It's 19° F and snowing in May. Will the tender plants survive?

I drain the Wall. With a pair of scissors, I carefully cut along both sides of all of the X cells I can salvage. Lots of my "repair cells" are fashioned from a "throwaway." I've even used plastic freezer bags in a pinch.

You have to keep the cells full of water. If one or more tubes gets too low, there's a good chance that a strong wind will collapse the whole thing as it's not fully supported. And sometimes, even without a wind, such a tipi will simply go "whoosh" and collapse. By simply going down the row once a week with a hose, you can add water here and there as needed, keeping them all quite full.

After the plant has grown up through the top of the tipi, we carefully squeeze the Wallo'Water, dumping off about half of the water. We then grasp the tops of each side, and the whole thing is gently lifted upward off the plant. By laying the Wallo'Water on its side, the water can be emptied. I let the plastic dry in the sun and if I don't reuse it on another crop right away, I fold it, along with all the others, and store them in a large cardboard box until next season. Don't leave them on the plant for the whole growing season or take them off and leave them in the garden. You'll never get it untangled from the plant once it reaches full growth and the sun will eventually weaken the plastic, shortening its life. So use them when you need to, then put them away. They'll last for years.

By the way, the manufacturer says he leaves his Walls on his plants through the entire growing season, right up to Thanksgiving.

Other uses for Wallo'Water

Besides using Wallo'Waters to start tomato and pepper plants, I usually use several to jump start watermelon, muskmelon and other "long-season" seedlings. Instead of starting these seeds indoors and then transplanting them, which really slows down their growth, I set out full Wallo'Water on each prepared hill or basin I plan on planting. This raises the soil temperatures quickly, and weeks before it would reach melon-friendly temperatures on its own.

Then, after the Wallo'Waters are in place for a few sunny days and moderate nights early in the season, I plant five seeds in each tipi, as far apart as reasonably possible. These are then watered well with hot water. The seeds sprout very quickly and grow even faster. I thin out the hill/basin to three of the most vigorous seedlings and water with weak manure tea. You wouldn't believe how fast they grow. No set-back, whatsoever. I keep them in the Wallo'Waters until they are starting to bush out and vine. By then, the weather is dependably warm and all danger of frost is long gone.

You can use similar strategy for a lot of different seeds: okra in northern climates, cucumbers, tender flowers, and even hills of extra early sweet corn.

I often recycle the same Wallo'Waters, first starting my tomato plants and a few peppers, then moving them to melons, cukes, and geraniums to get them growing *fast*.

You'll see them on my front porch in the early spring. And then in the fall, protecting my geraniums and begonias from sneaky frosts. I even use Wallo'Water around some of my smaller pepper plants, which I dig up before cold weather to plant in two-gallon pots for winter. With the Wallo'Water around the plants in the pots, they continue to grow happily, scarcely realizing they have been transplanted. And, of course, the fall frosts never bother them at all, even when frosts turn to freezes, which blacken the rest of the tender garden vegetables. Then, into the house they go to produce all winter.

The manufacturer suggests that Wallo'Water can be used to protect tomato plants in the fall, but I don't

The same tomato plants a month and a half later

Can you grow tomatoes on a Montana mountain? Sure you can!

growing I get from them, and how long they last, I consider them a bargain.

Not quite convinced yet? Let me tell you about a "trial" I ran inadvertently this past spring. I have 52 Wallo'Waters, and I had 100 tomato plants and 26 peppers of different varieties. I planted what I needed in the Walls. The rest I simply planted "normally" when the weather was suitable. They were in the same gardens, fertilized the same, were the same varieties, and were watered and cared for exactly the same.

The plants started in the Wallo'Waters were exactly twice as big, twice as stocky, and more than twice as productive. Made a big believer out of some of my friends, for sure.

Why don't you pick up a pack, or a dozen packs, and give this nifty product a trial in your garden. No gimmick here—just plain common sense. They'll boost your tomato and other vegetable harvest so you'll have lots to eat and put up come fall. You'd think I was getting paid to say this. But I'm not; I'm just a true believer.

Wallo'Water is available through many garden supply houses, local farm and garden stores, and seed catalogs. Δ

think this is much of an idea, unless you are growing very small patio type tomatoes. My average determinate (non-vining) tomato plant is four feet tall, and spreads out to about two feet in diameter. The average indeterminate (vining) tomatoes, even staked, go five feet tall and drape down stakes over about four feet in diameter. Needless to say, these tomato plants would not receive much protection from an 18-inch high Wallo'Water. Oh, well, nothing is perfect.

But after using these plastic tipis for years and years, I can truly say they add at least four weeks of aggressive growing season to our northern short-season garden. This, in itself, is a major miracle.

Now Wallo'Waters are not cheap, averaging about $9 to $9.50 for three, though you may find them even cheaper at some of the large discount stores. And they are cheaper, yet, in bulk. But considering just how much

Restore the Bill of Rights with Fully Informed Juries

Find out how ordinary people, as trial jurors, can repair years of legislated special-interest damage to our rights, simply by saying *No* to bad laws!

Phone: 1-800-TEL-JURY for a free Jury Power Information Kit!

The Fourteenth Year

A packing crate mini-barn

By Edward King

Need an extra storage building for all those things that are too good to throw away, but not good enough to keep in the house? Need a place to keep your lumber out of the weather, stacked neat and dry? If you're like me, you can probably use more storage space all the time, but you don't have the money to invest in a metal barn or one of those wooden prefabs.

The problems of need and cost could be answered through the use of some free lumber in the form of packing crates available from many businesses.

I guess I've always been what you'd call a pack rat of sorts. Whenever I drive by a pile of trash that has useable material such as boards, plywood, sheet metal, or pipe, a little voice in me says, "Pick it up." And I usually do. So, it was only natural when I drove by a dealer for motorcycles and ATVs and read the sign that said "Free Wood," that I had to take advantage of the situation.

After hauling away and disassembling a dozen or so 3 by 8-foot packing crate bases made of 2x4s, I began to amass a considerable amount of lumber that needed a proper cover. As I had already hauled away 23 of the smaller packing crate bases made of 2x4s and 1x3s, measuring 4 by 6 feet, I decided it was time to put them to some good use and provide a shelter for the 2x4 lumber. I had already attempted to separate the lumber from the smaller crate bases without much success. Since the bases are stapled together, removing the boards often results in destroying the base. What few boards you are able to salvage are too cracked to be of use.

I decided that whatever I used these small bases for, they would have to be kept intact. Since they were already about 4 feet wide and 6 feet long, I combined them with some cedar logs I found locally on my 32-acre plot of heaven, two 2x4s, and seven 2 by 10

The roof joists were fitted into notches atop the cedar posts.

corrugated steel panels to produce a wood shed for under $100.

The shed ended up 12 feet wide and 8 feet deep. I used four cedar poles, two 9 feet long and two 8 feet long. The longer ones went in the front. With 2 feet of them sunk in the ground they gave me a 7 foot height. The shorter ones went in the back and with their 2 feet sinking they gave me a 6 foot height.

The roof was made of seven 2 by 10-foot corrugated economy steel sheets. For the cross support, I used two 2 x 4 x 14-foot beams.

Not only did these 4 by 6-foot sections make great wall frames but I took two more of them to make support for the lumber I was to store in the shed. Using old lumber and scrap sheet metal, I covered much of the walls against blowing rain and covered the forward portion of the floor.

Since I finished my shed several months ago, I've yet to have any problem with wet lumber. In the future I plan to build a bigger outhouse and a photographic darkroom using these 4 by 6-foot crate bases. ∆

The crate bottoms make great wall sections. The 1 x 3-inch boards will support an outer skin, while the 2 x 4s comprise the wall frame.

Harvesting the wild: acorns

By Jackie Clay

When I was just a little girl, I used to collect acorns by the boxful as they fell in the fall. I didn't know why. They just felt nice in the hand and somehow a big bunch of them felt satisfying. Could that be because somewhere in my ancestors' time, acorns were a very important food? Native Americans all across oak-growing North and South America harvested acorns, which were nearly as important a food as corn or beans. Such tribes as the Cherokee, Apache, Pima, and Ojibwa routinely harvested and used the acorn. These Indian gatherers taught early settlers how to harvest and use acorns in their cooking, as they did corn and other traditional foods. Even today, many Indians gather acorns, both to use themselves and to sell in Mexican markets.

And those bright, shining round acorns are very good for you, besides tasting great.

Health benefits of acorns

Acorns have been tested and found to be possibly the best food for effectively controlling blood sugar levels. They have a low sugar content, but leave a sweetish aftertaste, making them very good in stews, as well as in breads of all types.

They are rich in complex carbohydrates, minerals, and vitamins while they are lower in fat than most other nuts. They are also a good source of fiber.

An additional benefit from eating acorns is in the gathering. Acorns,

Ground, leached acorn meal, ready to dry. The bitterness is gone.

although they "fall from trees," must be picked and processed before eating, which requires a walk, then bending and picking up. All of these are good exercise. In fact, that is why many "primitive" foods are so healthy. They require exercise just to put them on the table, not just a short trip to the convenience store or fast food joint.

But acorns taste bitter!

One of the first things I learned as a little girl harvesting acorns was that they tasted awful. Unfortunately, many acorns do taste bitter. This is because they contain tannin, a bitter substance in oaks which is used to tan leather. Real pucker power here. Some varieties of acorns contain more tannin than others. They range from the Emory oak of the southwestern United States and northern Mexico, which is so mild it can be used without processing, to some black oaks with very bitter acorns, requiring lengthy processing to render edible.

Generally, the best acorns to harvest are those of the white oaks, such as the swamp oak, Oregon white oak, and burr oak, as they contain less bitter tannin. Luckily, nearly all acorns can be made usable with natural processing which renders them nutty and sweet.

From the mighty oak

Acorns are one grain that literally grows on trees. Even a small oak tree can produce a bushel or more of tasty, nutritious acorns. And that grandaddy oak out in the pasture could produce nearly a thousand pounds. Now that is a lot of eating from a small area.

There are now several varieties of grafted oak trees, which bear nearly double the harvest of wild trees. These trees are available for purchase from specialty nursery companies.

Not only are acorns great food for us, but for many birds and animals as well. Any deer hunter can tell you that one of the best spots to ambush a wily buck is on a trail to a big oak tree. Deer and wild turkeys harvest these nutritious acorns to fatten up for winter.

Early settlers must have noticed this, as they soon began to turn their hogs out into the oak woods to fatten on the bounty of acorns. I accidently had this happen to two of my own pigs. I had a litter of weaner pigs, six in number in an outside pen. While we were in town, a stray dog came by and had great fun, chasing the little porkers around the pen. None were injured, but two of them vaulted the pen wall next to the shed and took off for the woods as fast as their little legs would run.

My son, Bill Spaulding's hunting "shack" sits right in the middle of white oaks, which produce "grain from trees," as some Indian tribes refer to acorns, and also lure big deer, which come to feed on sweet, fat acorns.

We hunted, called, and scoured the woods for days. Weeks. No piggies. By then, we figured a black bear, which were numerous in our woods, had a midnight snack of pork on the hoof.

Then one November, I was riding my horse down one of the wooded trails through huge old oaks, when I noticed turned-up fresh soil. Bear? Nope, my "bear" had left pig tracks. I tied my horse and scouted further, discovering seemingly acres of ground dug up underneath those bounteous oak trees. My lost piggies were found. But those tracks looked pretty big.

To make a long story short, we corralled those errant porkers and hauled them home. On putting them in the pen next to their brothers and sisters, we were shocked. Out in the woods, they really looked big, but now they looked huge. They were a third again as big. On butchering, the woods raised hogs weighed 290 pounds, while the grain fed hogs barely made

Nice fat, ripe acorns, ready to be used for acorn meal or flour

200 dressed. So much for "modern feeding." Of course the pigs had access to roots, grasses, insects, and more. But I credit much of their hearty size to those fat acorns they were gorging themselves upon.

As acorns hold a long time under the tree, the hogs were feasting on last year's crop all summer, then the fresh crop come fall. Not a bad natural feed.

Harvesting

First of all, you'll have to check out your local oaks during the spring when the leaves and underbrush are not as dense. Get a little pocket tree book and try to identify the oaks you find. In many areas, there are several varieties of oaks available to the acorn harvester. Some are quite mild and sweet and others pretty darned bitter. If you have a choice, try to find a variety with mild meat and only a little initial tang of tannin.

You may have to simply nibble and check, come fall. Different varieties of oak have different shaped acorns. Crack a nice fat acorn with no worm hole. Examine the meat. It should be yellowish, not black and dusty (insects). Now, simply nibble and chew up a part of the nut. If it is very bitter, spit it out and try another kind of acorn. When you find a grove of relatively mild acorns, note this for next year and harvest away.

As the understory is usually very thin below a decent sized oak tree, the acorns are quite easy to pick up. Depending on the variety of oak, your acorns will drop between late September and October, more or less, depending on your climate zone. The best way I've found to pick up acorns is to simply pick a nice dry, sunny day as soon as the acorns begin to drop and take baskets and sacks to the woods and sit down and pick them up. If you wait too long, the handy dandy squirrels and other wild critters will beat you to them, leaving only the worm-riddled hulls behind.

Processing

The term "processing" brings to mind machines and chemical additives. With acorns, processing simply means making them ready to eat.

When I get home with my bounteous haul, I spread them out a layer thick on an old sheet which I have laid on a roof, corner of the yard, or some other out-of-the-way dry, sunny place. This lets them sun dry and prevents any possible molding before I get them shelled. It will also kill any insect eggs or larvae, which might be inside. If you cannot lay the acorns out in the sun, spread them in a single layer on cookie sheets in a very slow oven for an hour.

Some acorns, such as those of the Emory oak, require no more processing than cracking them open and eating them. Like most nuts, acorns of all types benefit from toasting on a cookie sheet in an oven at 175° F. Stir to prevent scorching.

However, most acorns do contain enough tannin to make leaching this bitter substance out necessary. To do this, simply sit down and crack a big bowlful of acorns, carefully examining each nut for black holes, which indicates a worm is inside rather than a wholesome plump yellowish-beige nut. Acorns are very easy to crack. The shell is pliable and quite thin. Pop the cap off, then simply grasp it with a pair of pliers and give a squeeze. Don't mash the kernel. Simply crack the shell. Then peel it off and toss the kernel into a bowl.

When all are done, get out your food grinder. Put a fine knife on the grinder and run the shelled acorns through it. This makes a coarse meal. Place this in a large crock or glass bowl. Then add boiling water to cover and let stand an hour. Drain and

Author grinding shelled acorns in a hand grinder

throw away the brownish, unappetizing water. Repeat. Then taste the meal. It should have a bit of a bitter tang, then taste sweet as you chew a piece. Continue leaching out the tannin as long as necessary.

When the acorn meal is mild tasting, it is ready to dry. I usually lay out a piece of old white sheet in a basket and pour the wet meal on it. Then, gathering up the edges, jelly bag style, I press and squeeze, getting out as much of the water (and tannin) as possible.

One caution—don't let wet acorn meal lie about for hours, or it will surely mold. Keep at the leaching process.

Spread the damp meal out in a shallow layer on a cookie sheet or on sheets of your dehydrator. Then begin to dry it. In the oven, you only need the pilot light or the very lowest oven setting. As it begins to dry, take your hands and very carefully crumble any chunks which hold moisture. Slowly your meal will begin to look quite good.

When the meal is completely dry, run it through a fine setting on your grain mill. The traditional method was to use a stone (mano in the southwest) hand grinder to crush the meal on a large, flat stone (metate). It is now ready for use in your recipes. If you produced more meal than you need right now, you can store the meal in the freezer or refrigerator in an airtight bag or jar. The dry, ground meal will last a week or so, stored in an airtight jar on the shelf. But, because of the oil, the meal will begin to go rancid, as will whole wheat flour and homeground cornmeal.

You can also grind your meal in a food processor or blender a little at a time. I smile, thinking of the vast difference between grinding acorns between stones and using a food mill. What would our ancestors think?

Using acorn meal

Some Native Peoples called acorns "grain from the tree," indicating the use they had for it as a grain in cakes, breads, and thickening for stews and soups. Today folks use "cream of this and that" soups for the same thing.

I think processed acorns taste like a cross between hazelnuts and sunflower seeds, and I often include acorn meal in my multi-grain bread recipes. Adding half a cup of acorn meal to a two-loaf bread recipe and reducing the flour, as needed, works quite well. Because the acorn meal is a natural sweetener, I only use a bit of honey to feed the yeast while softening it, relying on the acorn meal to give sweetness to the bread. No complaints yet.

As acorn meal is very dense, you will have to take care to get your bread to rise when adding it. One way to ensure this is to use hot liquid and beat in your flour, making a batter. Then cool so you can add the yeast and the rest of the ingredients. This helps release wheat gluten to let the bread rise, despite heavy ingredients. Indian bread was always very dense and heavy, as there was seldom, if ever, wheat or yeast added to the recipe. It takes wheat gluten, as well as yeast, to make bread rise properly. Indian breads were often small, thin cakes baked before the fire on large, reflecting rocks. They were not puffy, large loaves as we are accustomed to today.

While camping some time, why not tuck your food grinder into your kitchen pack and try making some old-time Indian bread out of acorn meal. It really puts you in contact with past ways in a hurry. Here is an Apache recipe for acorn cakes.

Apache acorn cakes:

1 cup acorn meal, ground fine
1 cup cornmeal
¼ cup honey
pinch of salt

Mix the ingredients with enough warm water to make a moist, not sticky dough. Divide into 12 balls. Let rest, covered, for 10 minutes or so. With slightly moist hands, pat the balls down into thick tortilla-shaped breads. Bake on an ungreased cast iron griddle over campfire coals or on clean large rocks, propped up slightly before the coals. If using the stones, have them hot when you place the cakes on them. You'll have to lightly peel an edge to peek and see if they are done. They will be slightly brown. Turn them over and bake on the other side, if necessary.

These cakes were carried on journeys dry and eaten alone or with shredded meat. We cheat and add homemade butter, too. But then, we are spoiled.

Multi-grain bread with acorn meal:

Let's take a look at one of my mixed grain breads with acorn meal to see how it differs from the Indian cakes above.

1½ cup rolled oats
½ cup cornmeal
½ cup coarse ground, leached acorn meal
1 cup lukewarm water
2 Tbsp. dry granulated yeast
2½ cups boiling water
1 Tbsp. salt
¼ cup vegetable oil
2 eggs, beaten
About 8 cups whole wheat flour
½ cup honey
butter

Pour boiling water over oats, cornmeal, and acorn meal. Set aside. Dissolve the yeast in lukewarm water. In a large mixing bowl, beat the hot oatmeal mixture with the rest of the ingredients, except for the yeast and butter, adding the flour a cup at a time until you get a medium batter. Cool to lukewarm. Then add the yeast. Mix well and add enough flour until you have a spongy dough that is not sticky. Knead, adding flour if necessary to keep from being sticky. Place in a greased bowl and grease the top of dough, then cover it with a moist, warm kitchen towel and set it in a warm place until it doubles in size. Punch down, knead several times, and let rise again. Shape into loaves and place in greased bread pans or on a greased cookie sheet.

This also makes great rolls, so you can use a cake pan, making golf ball sized rolls. Cover and let rise again until almost double. Preheat the oven to 350° F and bake for about 35 minutes or until the tops are golden brown. Brush with butter and cool.

You can also make this bread in camp, using smaller loaves and a reflector oven or forming ½ inch thick by 1 inch wide by 8 inch long sticks and twisting the dough around a green stick and gently baking over medium coals—never a fire.

So far, we've talked about using acorn meal as a grain. But the acorn is so much more versatile. Most Native Americans and early settlers used acorn meal as either an ingredient in mush, which is sort of a thick, mealy soup, or pounded with meat, fat, and berries, making pemmican. In a survival situation which requires lightweight, high calorie foods, pemmican would be a good choice. (But, of course, many of us really don't need the extra fat in our diets.)

Here are a couple recipes for these uses of the acorn. When I say "acorn meal," I mean ground, leached-till-mild acorn meal, not raw.

Cornmeal and acorn mush:

```
4 cups water
1 tsp. salt
½ cup acorn meal, ground
about 1 cup cornmeal
```

Bring salted water to a boil and sprinkle the acorn meal into the boiling water, stirring briskly with a wire or twig whisk. Then add the cornmeal. Add just enough cornmeal to make a thick, bubbling batch in which a wood spoon will stand up fairly well. Place the saucepan in a larger container holding two inches or more of boiling water. (Use a double boiler, if you have one.) Simmer the mush until quite thick, about 45 minutes, stirring occasionally to keep it from lumping.

Cornmeal and acorn mush is very good for breakfast on a cold morning. It can be served with sweetened milk and a dab of wild fruit jam or homemade butter. But it is also great as a main course lunch or dinner. You can also add salsa or bacon bits and grated cheese on top to get great variety. This mush is very filling and will stick to your ribs.

I often make a double batch and pour the "extra" in a greased bread pan. When cooled in the fridge overnight, it becomes quite solid and can be sliced in half inch thick slices, dipped in flour and fried in oil, first one side, then turn and fry the other. Fried acorn and cornmeal mush is one of our absolutely favorite camp (or at-home) breakfasts. Serve it with butter, salt, and thick fruit jam or maple syrup. Of course, David likes his with catsup.

You might want to try your hand at a "modern" type of pemmican. It doesn't keep on the trail for months, but it is pretty good.

Modern pemmican:

```
1 lb. lean stewing meat, cut quite
   small
½ cup dehydrated wild plums
½ cup acorn meal
```

Boil the lean stewing meat. When it is tender, drain and allow it to dry in a bowl. Grind all of the ingredients together in a meat grinder using a fine blade. Grind again, mixing finely, distributing the ingredients very well. Place in a covered dish and refrigerate overnight. (Or you can eat right away, but like many foods, the refrigerating allows the flavors to blend nicely.) You can serve this on any flatbread, such as a tortilla. It is best served warm, or you can reheat it in the pan in the oven like a meatloaf.

Acorn meal can also be used in place of a good portion (or all) of the nuts in most desserts, from brownies to cookies. It does depend on the variety of acorn you have available and the taste after leaching. Some acorn meal never gets "nutty," only mild, while the meal of other acorns, such as those of the Emory oak, are so sweet that you can eat them without leaching, or with very little leaching.

You will have to experiment a bit here. But the end results are usually surprising.

Oh gee! You say oak trees don't grow where you live? Well, just because they aren't "native" doesn't mean you can't plant some. No matter where I go, I always plant a big bunch of food producing trees, shrubs, and perennial plants. And a lot of them certainly aren't native to the area. Of course, you can just plant acorns or buy seedling trees from a nursery. From an acorn or small seedling, you can usually figure you'll begin to get a decent amount of acorns in about 10 years.

Want faster results? Several nurseries are carrying grafted oak varieties, meant for food production. And at least one nursery has a very good hybrid of the burr oak that produces mild acorns requiring no leaching. You can write to St Lawrence Nurseries, 325 State Hwy. 345, Potsdam, NY 13676 or find them online at www.sln.potsdam.ny.us. They have a free catalog which includes many very hardy fruits and nuts.

Oaks don't grow where we will be moving, but you can darned betcha I'll be planting them so I can enjoy those fabulous acorns. Until then, I'll just have to drive down to my son Bill's place near Oak Lake and pick a few baskets so we can enjoy all those good acorn recipes. Δ

Get The Whole Sheebang!
www.backwoodshome.com

Ayoob on Firearms:

Firearms and cold weather considerations

Many of our readers have established their abodes in places which, during the winter months, do not exactly draw the beachgoers. The older I get, the less the longest season of the year seems like "winter wonderland" and the more it seems like "frozen wasteland." Cold weather, particularly in its extreme, changes our approach to everything from starting our vehicles to planning long hikes. With weaponry, it is no different. Some changes have to be made there, too.

Cold, bare hands are dangerous when applied to complicated machinery that requires a dextrous touch to operate properly and safely. Firearms certainly fit that category. The logical solution is to warm those hands with gloves or even mittens. Alas, those layers of unfeeling fabric will blunt your sense of touch. This pretty much brings back the same problem.

Deep cold requires thick layers of warm clothing. That reduces the body's range of mobility.

Bitter cold can quickly become so overpowering to the senses that it is all you can think about. This means that in particularly bad episodes of inclement weather, we can be distracted from the task at hand. This is dangerous when operating any sort of powerful equipment, and it is particularly dangerous when the equipment being operated is a potentially lethal weapon.

Long guns

Cold weather generally means thick layers of clothing. This can affect the way a rifle or shotgun mounts to your shoulder. Good news: the fabric of the winter garb can act as a cushion to help dampen recoil. Bad news: the gun's butt is pushed forward away from your shoulder.

This means that the telescopic sight whose eye relief (distance from the eye) was adjusted for your vision on a nice sunny day when you were wearing light clothing is now farther forward than it should be. You may not be able to get a proper target image. When you sight in a scoped deer rifle, sight it in while wearing the same clothing you'll have on when you aim it at a deer.

Practice mounting the gun to the shoulder with your winter gear on. The added thickness of the warmer clothing may force you to push the gun a little bit out forward and away from you, then tuck it back in to get it at the right spot.

You may find that the upper rear portion of the stock's butt snags on heavy winter upper body garments. If so, there's time now for you to round off that edge.

With more clothing material between your body and the long gun's butt, it's the same as if you had put on a longer stock. You may have to cantilever your shoulders back to compensate. If you do that, your body weight is no longer leaning into the gun. That in turn is likely to accentuate the muzzle jump that occurs in recoil with a powerful long gun. If the shoulders are back, the gun muzzle is likely to jump enough to block your view, which will make it harder for you to hold the gun on target long enough to monitor the strike of the bullet.

How to fix? If cost is not an object, you can have a shorter stock fitted for winter use, and change the stock when the season changes. If for any

Massad Ayoob

reason that is not practical, go with the shorter stock for all purposes. It's easier to adapt to a shorter stock than to a longer one. This will also make the gun more suitable for smaller-statured people you have authorized to use it. Remember the rule: bigger people can adapt to smaller firearms more easily than smaller people can adapt to larger guns.

Remember that lose-lose situation of frozen fingers or gloved hands. Most rifles and shotguns have relatively short-stroke triggers. Bear in mind that an unfeeling hand—whether it has been numbed by the cold, or its sense of touch has been interfered with by gloves—is much more likely to cause a premature or unintended discharge of the gun.

The best combination of tactile sensitivity and adequate warmth will be found in gloves made of high-tech materials such as Thinsulate. You can always try the old arctic outdoorsman's trick of making a slit lengthwise in the trigger finger pocket of the gloves or mittens, through which you can extend your index finger just long enough to make the shot and then bring the digit back to its warm place if that is necessary. Downside: I found that snow tended to get into the glove through the slit.

When I toured Anchorage, Alaska, in the company of local city and state law enforcement officers, I learned their approach to "deep freeze shooting situations" insofar as gloves. Most, when they were outdoors long enough to have to worry about it, knew that in the Alaska winter the cold would be so savage that they would need substantial, serious-size gloves that could get in the way of manipulating their rifles and shotguns. They learned to fit the gloves just snugly enough to stay in place, but loosely enough that they could be flung clear, or the officer could at least raise the hand, sink his teeth into the end of the glove fingers, and jerk a bare hand clear to operate the gun.

It is always important to keep the finger completely clear of the trigger guard until such time as the decision to immediately and intentionally fire has been made. This is even more starkly necessary in cold weather, where hands numbed by cold or blocked from touch by fabric can start applying pressure to the trigger without the person holding the gun actually feeling it. I know one deer hunter who made a habit of letting his index finger stray to the trigger of his 7mm Magnum Remington Model 700 hunting rifle. One frigid late afternoon in the remote wilds of Utah, his finger rested on that trigger, and began to contract. He didn't notice it was happening until he was jolted back to reality by the deafening roar of his hunting rifle. Fortunately, nothing but his pride was hurt. Since that accidental discharge, he has become scrupulously careful to keep his finger away from the trigger area until he is certain that the time to fire has come.

John Kapson makes sure his heavy winter coat won't alter eye relief factor with the Weaver K2.5 scope on his Winchester Model 94 .32 Special deer rifle. Note how action lever accommodates his gloved hand.

There are special "hunter's mittens" or "shooter's mittens" designed for Arctic-level cold that have separately articulated finger pockets for the trigger finger. Whatever your handwear, it is critically important that you log some practice time with it on, handling and shooting your firearms. The gun will feel bigger when held in a gloved hand. If your firearm has a very small trigger guard, such as the old Winchester Model 1897 pump shotgun, a glove thick enough to be really warm may also be thick enough to fill the trigger guard to the point where the glove material is putting pressure against the trigger without you realizing it.

Exposed entirely to the weather, the rifle or shotgun wants to have minimal lubrication, nothing that's likely to become gel-like in sub-freezing or even sub-zero weather and prevent the mechanism from operating. When the hands are cold, simpler guns work better. For more than a century, the lever action rifle has been popular from ice floes to frozen woods because mittened hands could easily lever a shell into the chamber, or cock back the exposed hammer of a Winchester 94 or Marlin 336. With shotguns, the sliding thumb safety seen on makes like the Mossberg is easier to manipulate in extreme cold than a push button safety on the trigger guard as is standard on some other brands. As a young hunter in northern New England, I found the hammerless double barreled shotgun the easiest of all to manipulate.

Ammo? Nickel-plated cartridge cases, as found on premium hunting ammunition such as Winchester Fail-Safe, seem a little more friction-free and may give a small edge in operating smoothness and reliability when cold weather concerns force you to keep gun lubrication to a bare minimum. Shotgun ammo? For home defense, remember that in this sort of weather, most intruders will be heavily clad. The traditional 00 (double-aught) buckshot load will often send four or five of its nine .33 caliber pellets through and through an average-size human male who is lightly clad and takes a face-on torso shot. This dangerous over-penetration is less likely on a heavily clad man. This is why in the winter, I always changed out my warm-weather #1 buckshot (sixteen .30 caliber pellets per shot) for 00 in my home defense 12 gauge. Some of my colleagues prefer the even deeper penetrating 000 (triple-aught) buckshot in winter, throwing eight .36 caliber pellets.

Handguns

The good news about cold weather garb is that it discreetly hides larger handguns. The bad news is that the thick, heavy padding of Arctic clothing can restrict your mobility and range of movement in terms of reaching for a location like a shoulder holster hanging beneath the opposite side armpit. You also have to worry about getting the reaching hand through the fastened clothing to the gun underneath.

Practice, practice, practice. Work out a gun carry system that will be comfortable and also accessible when dressed for bitter cold. The practice will be hot and sweaty when you do it months ahead of time, but if you ever need that handgun one cold dark night, it will pay for itself.

I have night sights on most of my carry guns now. What does that have to do with winter gun-handling? Only that in the winter there's a helluva lot more dark than in the summer, and a "shot in the dark" is proportionally more likely to be required.

Do you have a system that lets you reload quickly with cold or gloved hands? Fumbling loose cartridges out of shell loops or spill pouches will be next to hopeless under those conditions. A speedloader will be a better answer if your preferred handgun is a revolver. Once again, the heavy winter clothing will help to hide the bulkier accessories. You'll find that reloading a fresh magazine into a semiautomatic pistol will be much easier than reloading any kind of revolver in the sort of weather conditions we're talking about here.

You want a secure holster. In ice and snowdrifts, we're simply a lot more likely to take a fall in wintertime. You want the gun to stay in place. A holster with a simple thumb-release safety strap may suffice, and releasing it with the thumb is so easy that a gloved hand or a nearly frozen bare hand can manage it.

I noticed an interesting thing with Alaskan cops. The great majority carried their service handguns in high-security holsters, for just the reason cited above as well as the danger of a suspect snatching at their exposed duty weapon. However, the great majority of these officers also carry their spare magazines in open top, friction tight pouches. The reason: cold, gloved hands can retrieve the magazines faster without fumbling for a pouch flap. Besides, with the pouch generally underneath the winter coat, the magazines are protected from inclement weather and in any case, no perpetrator would try to snatch the spare ammo instead of the gun.

Gun design is a factor. Single action, frontier-style revolvers tend to have very small trigger guards. As with that old Winchester '97, the glove material can fill the trigger guard to the point where the trigger is inadvertently pressed backward, causing an unintentional firing. Double action revolvers, for the most part, don't have a lot of space between the front of the trigger guard and the frontal surface of the trigger. This won't cause an accidental discharge by itself, so long as the gun has not been cocked. However, if you have to fire more than one shot, you may find that a thickly-gloved index finger blocks the trigger's return, converting your six-shooter to a single-shot at what could be the worst possible time. The sharp edge at the top of most double action revolver triggers can also snag on glove material as the trigger begins to return forward under spring pressure to re-set.

The 1911 style single action semiautomatic pistol, especially one with a long trigger, also leaves very little room for a gloved finger. You can once again end up with unintentional pressure being put on the trigger before you actually want to fire the shot.

With all these "gloved finger on trigger" elements, we have to keep

SIG P-220, a traditional double action .45 auto loaded with nine rounds of Federal Hydra-Shok, is an excellent choice for winter use in a gloved hand.

something in mind. We all know—or should know—that the finger should never be inserted into the trigger guard until we have determined that we are immediately going to fire the gun. However, we also know that under stress a lot of people insert their finger into the trigger guard prematurely.

Even if you have perfect trigger finger discipline, consider this scenario. You have had to fire a shot in self-defense, wounding the opponent. He drops his weapon and falls next to it; you keep your gun on him, your finger still on the trigger. The cold-numbed finger or the thick padding of the glove material now cause an unintentional second discharge. Witness

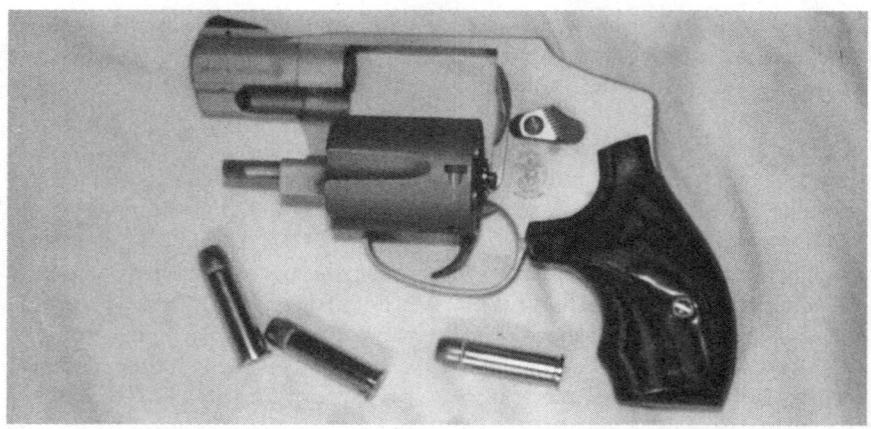

Trying to reload a revolver with loose ammunition in extreme cold weather is a daunting task; you at least want speedloaders. This is Smith & Wesson's AirLite Ti Model 342, a 5-shot .38 Special weighing less than 11 ounces.

testimony will be that you fired the second shot into a downed man who was separated from his weapon and who, at that moment, did not deserve to be shot. You may spend your next winter behind bars.

This is why what is currently called the "traditional double action" semiautomatic pistol is an excellent design for use in a gloved hand. The long, heavy double action trigger pull required for the first shot minimizes the chances of a cold-desensitized finger pulling it unintentionally. After the first shot, the gun cocks itself to single action mode for subsequent shots, so the trigger stays to the rear of the guard and does not return all the way forward. This eliminates the chance of the gloved hand blocking trigger return and preventing subsequent shots from being fired. A thumb-operated decocking lever is not hard to use even with gloves on. Beretta, Ruger, SIG, and Smith & Wesson traditional style double action autos all work well in cold weather conditions.

Another excellent semiautomatic pistol for cold weather use is the Glock. It is by far the most popular service pistol in Alaska. City police from Fairbanks to Anchorage issue it, and the Alaska State Troopers have recently adopted the .40 caliber Glock 22. There are no decocking levers or safety catches to manipulate, and the Glock's trigger guard was intentionally made large for use by ski troops in European alpine warfare scenarios.

Handgun ammunition

Hollowpoint handgun bullets tend to plug with wool, Fiberfill, and whatnot as they pass through the heavy winter clothing of a criminal assailant. When plugged with inert matter, they usually won't expand. This fact makes larger caliber bullets popular in cold climes. The two times I had to pick a single standard-issue sidearm for Northern New England police departments we wound up with traditional double action .45 caliber semiautomatics. If the bullets were going to turn into non-expanding ball projectiles, we wanted them to turn into *big* non-expanding projectiles. That said, high-tech hollowpoint designs like the Federal Hydra-Shok, Remington Golden Saber, Speer Gold Dot, and Winchester SXT in .45 caliber are likely to open up even after passing through heavy clothing.

A semijacketed hollowpoint .357 Magnum slug weighing 125 grains and traveling at some 1400 feet per second velocity will probably open up irrespective of heavy clothing. Ditto the soft all-lead 158 grain +P .38 Special hollowpoint known colloquially as the "FBI load." So will the fastest 9mm bullets, 115 grain hollowpoints in the 1300 foot-second velocity range. In .40 caliber, the Winchester Ranger SXT 180 grain, 155 to 165 grain hollowpoints going 1150 to 1200 feet per second, and Pro-Load Tactical (driving a 135 grain Nosler bullet at some 1300 feet per second) all seem to mushoom reliably despite thick clothing barriers.

Preparation

I learned early to practice intensively in drawing from underneath heavy outerwear. I spent lots of time manipulating rifle, shotgun, and handgun with heavy gloves on. I discovered that my favorite handgun shooting stance (the isosceles position, with both arms locked straight out forward toward the threat) often would not work with restrictive heavy coats. I learned that the isometric bent-arms Weaver stance worked better for me when so dressed.

Practice drawing and holstering, loading and reloading. Practice mounting, slinging and unslinging the rifle and/or shotgun, and don't neglect loading and unloading practice with these guns too. Make sure your gloved hand has the right interface with safety mechanisms and trigger guards when you have to bring the gun into action quickly in these weather conditions.

I find shooting to be a helluva lot less fun in cold weather. But big game season is more likely to be in chilly weather than hot weather, and violent criminal attacks upon the innocent are not restricted by season. With careful planning and lots of practice, you'll be able to adroitly handle your firearms in the coldest and nastiest weather that any frozen wasteland can throw at you. Δ

The Fourteenth Year

HOW TO BUTCHER A CHICKEN IN 20 MINUTES OR LESS...

...while leaving the carcass and feathers intact!

By Dr. Roger W. Grim, D.C.

When I was 12 years old Grandpa would let me help him pluck whole chickens after we had dipped them in scalding hot water in a washtub. That was the way he sold whole chickens to stores with his family business.

One day I asked Grandpa, "Isn't there an easier way to dress out a chicken?" He showed me a method with no need to pluck feathers and no smelly stench from a wet chicken. It's just a fast, easy way to put meat on the table.

Things you will need

1. **A sharp knife, axe, meat cleaver, or machete** for cutting off the head.

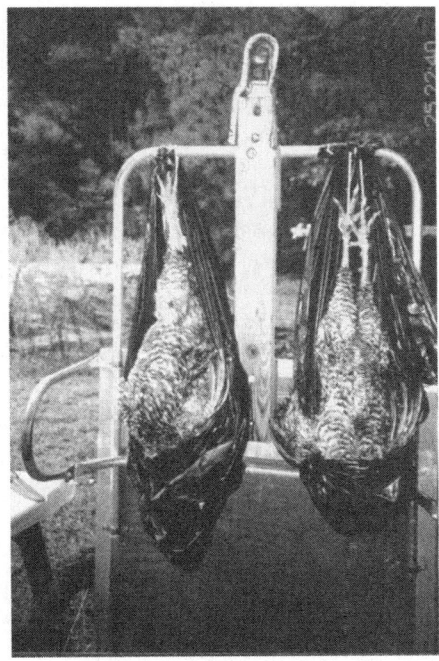

Figure 1. With a trash bag properly fitted around the chicken, clean up will be easy.

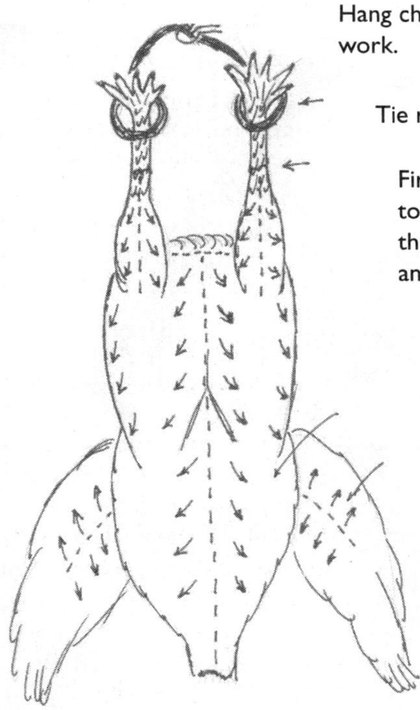

Hang chicken at a comfortable height to work.

Tie rope tight around feet.

First cut around joint just enough to pull skin down and away so that the leg and thigh are free of skin and feathers.

Cut and pull breast skin away from breast and wing.

Also pull skin and feathers away from wing bone.

= Cuts
= Direction of cuts and pulling skin

Figure 2. Front view showing where the cuts are made and how the skin is peeled away

2. **Rope.** Cut 3 or 4 pieces of ¼-inch rope 12 to 18 inches long. One is to tie the chicken's legs together tightly before you cut the head off; otherwise you will have a headless chicken running about the yard. The other is to tie the chicken's legs onto your hook on a tree or cart.
3. **A bowl.** I use a stainless steel one but any large bowl or pan will do. Put your chicken in it once you cut it away from the carcass.
4. **A large bowl of water.** Again I use a stainless steel one. It's to keep my hands and knife clean while skinning the chickens.
5. I use **two sawhorses** for a table base, over which I placed a **sheet of ¾-inch plywood** 24 x 48 inches. If you have a small folding table you could use it.
6. **A clean sheet of plastic or butcher's paper** big enough to cover your work table top. Tape it on or tuck it under the table top.
7. I use my trusty **cart,** setting it up on end. The handle bar is just the right height for me to hang the chickens from and skin. I

25

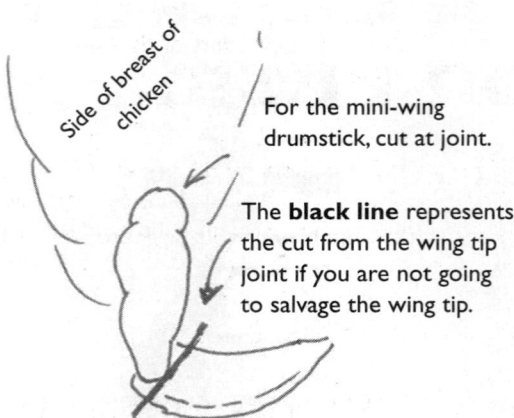

Figure 3. A view showing how to cut away the mini-wing drumstick

put a concrete block in it while I'm pulling the skin downward so the cart will not fall on me.

8. **A garden hose** is handy to clean your knives and to pre-clean the chicken of any dirt or feathers before they are taken into the house for final cleaning and freezing preparation.
9. **A large black garbage bag** with two twist ties that hold the garbage bag on the cart. Cut the garbage bag two-thirds of the way down so that anything you cut off while skinning, such as the feathers and carcass, goes into the bag (Figure 1).

The process

Now you are ready to butcher and skin the chicken.

Tie the chicken's legs together and cut off its head. Then hang the chicken up by its legs (see Figure 2) with the breast of the chicken facing you. Make the first cut around the yellow part of the leg joint only deep enough to separate the skin, but not deep enough to cut the leg tendon.

Cut and pull down the skin from the leg, cutting just deep enough that the skin will come loose from around the meat. Pull the skin of the chicken down laterally to each side, all the time cutting away the other skin to reveal the leg meat that you will cut off later.

Continue to cut and pull the skin all the way down and backwards around the upper thigh. Continue to cut and pull the skin down around the breast and cut the wing loose at the first joint of the wing (Figure 3). Some people may want to continue to clean and cut around the feathers of the wing for the small tip of the wing bones, but for me there is so little meat it is not worth it.

It's as easy as 1, 2, 3

Now we are ready to strip the skinned carcass (Figure 4).

First, cut the wings, or mini-drumsticks, off at the joint near the breast. By forcing them backwards and cutting as close to the breast and joint as possible, you will expose the wing joint and you can cut through and around it.

Next, cut the breast out. Lay your knife at an angle, starting the cut as close to the breastbone as possible. Take your knife and stay close to the rib cage while cutting downward and backward in an arcing direction as shown in Figure 5. Repeat the process on the other breast.

You are ready to claim the legs and thighs all in one piece. If you want to separate them later you can do so. Go up to the ankle joint at about ¾ to 1 inch above the "leggin's" (that's what I call the scaly yellow part above the feet on the chicken), and cut through and around the joint so that each leggin' and foot falls free. While holding the drumstick and thigh in the left hand, take your right hand and hold the carcass while at the

Figure 4. The skinned carcass, ready for you to take the meat

Figure 5. Side view showing where to cut the meat

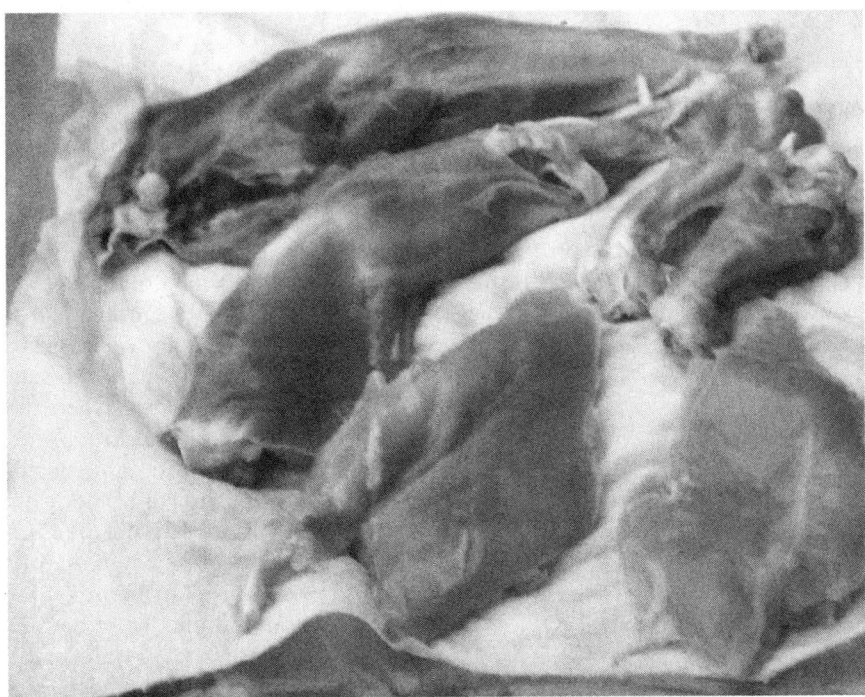

Figure 6. The results of a freshly skinned and butchered chicken.

same time pushing the thigh and drumstick backwards. This is like opening a set of French doors. You will both see and hear the thigh joint pop loose from the hip joint. Cut as close to the round point as possible (Figure 5).

To separate the thigh from the carcass, make the next and final cut at the back upper part of the thigh, just about 1½ to 2 inches next to the anus. You now have a complete thigh and drumstick.

Some folks might say that you are not getting all the meat, that you are leaving the two small bony pieces on the wing tip, the two little scraps of meat on the backbone, the liver, and the neck. I say if you like those parts, go for it.

100+ years in our family

With this method, I have butchered chickens for more than 40 years, just like my grandfather did for 60 years before me. I can remember that Grandma's chicken fried in a cast iron skillet beat Col. Sanders by a mile.

Raising your own stock, whether it be young chicks to fryer size, rabbits, goats, or beef cattle can be a family affair. Children gain knowledge, learn responsibility, and the necessary basics of self-sufficiency. Δ

GET IN THAT KITCHEN AND RATTLE THOSE POTS AND PANS!

- breads • casseroles • beverages
- canning • jams, jellies & preserves
- salads • soups • vegetables • appetizers
- pasta, rice & beans

GET BACKWOODS HOME COOKING

Only $21.95

(plus $4.95 S&H)

Send a check or money order to
BHM, P.O. Box 712, Gold Beach, OR 97444.
Or order online at www.backwoodshome.com

Call 1-800-835-2418 to order.

Want more fruit from less space?
ESPALIER YOUR TREES!

By Rev. J. D. Hooker

After originating in the semi-arid regions of the middle east, espaliering (is-`pal-yer-ing) became a commonly employed fruit tree growing method of the Greco-Roman world. Later, during the so-called "Dark Ages" after Rome's fall, these techniques were kept alive in isolated monasteries.

Once you realize just how minimal the space requirements are, and how productive the results, you'll understand why espaliered fruit trees were so common along the inner walls of castle courtyards and walled cities.

Today, these techniques remain just as popular over much of Europe, yet oddly, except among a few high grade landscapers and orchardists, these techniques are rarely used in the U.S.

Aside from regular pruning and shaping of the growing fruit trees (which you do to fruit trees anyway), the only real requirements are a minimum of six hours of daily sunlight throughout the growing season, and sufficient water. This makes south or east facing walls ideal growing locations.

Horizontal espaliering

The horizontal method involves nothing more than training the trees to do most of their growing horizontally. Normally this is done using spaced horizontal supports fashioned of wood, wire, or metal in much the same manner as grape vines are grown. I've had equally good results using nothing more than stakes and soft string.

A simple horizontal multibranch fan that would grow flat along a wall

Beginning about 15 inches above the ground, run each horizontal support about 14 inches above the last, until you've reached a height of about 6 feet. Next, plant one-year-old fruit tree "whips" (preferably dwarf or semi-dwarf varieties) about 15 feet apart along the line of supports. Using very sharp pruners, snip off the top of each whip, right at the lowest support.

With frequent waterings it should only take a few weeks until the young trees begin vigorously branching off, right at the point where you've cut it off. Once these sprouting branches are about an inch long, select three of the most vigorous, and trim away the rest. After they reach a length of three or four inches, select two and use strips of soft cloth to fasten them horizontally along the bottom support. The third branch is simply allowed to grow vertically until it reaches the next support, where the snipping, branching, and training process is repeated. Once the growth of the tree's main trunk has reached the topmost support, use only two of the branches that sprout, training them both to grow horizontally along the top wire. After the trees have become established, prune away every branch that tries growing forward or backwards away from the supports. Each year after the fruit ripens, but before the leaves start to fall, prune off all the new branches at a point three leaf-groups away from each of the main limbs. Keep the limbs pruned off at a point seven inches away from the main trunk.

Palmette espaliering

A second espaliering method which uses these same basic techniques ensures an equally productive, but dramatically more eye appealing, planting of fruit trees. In order to produce palmette (fan shaped) espaliers, you'll need to place your first horizontal support about 30 inches above the ground. Again, using year old whips of the desired varieties, plant one every 15 feet along the supports. Prune each one off 20 inches above the soil's surface. Allow only the two best budding branches to grow. Attach pieces of wooden lath solidly to the supports at 45-degree angles, and use strips of cloth to attach each of these branches to one of the laths.

Later, branches are removed, pruned to length, allowed to grow, trained, and supported until each tree has filled up its allotted space. From that time on, they're simply pruned regularly using the same methods already explained for horizontally grown espaliers.

Cordon espaliering

The third technique, cordon espaliering, is also quite dramatically eye catching. My experience with this method comes from seeing the meticulously perfect work of my sister's fiance.

He starts with sturdy upright supports spaced 20 inches apart, and attaches horizontal strands of heavy galvanized fence wire at 2, 4, and 6-foot elevations. Next, every 30 inches he wires a sturdy 8 or 10-foot length of bamboo pole (1x3 furring strips work just as well) to these horizontal wires, leaning each pole at the same 35-degree angle. He plants a single one to three-year-old dwarf fruit tree at the same 35-degree angle at each pole. Using cloth strips or soft jute cord, he then ties each tree loosely at several points along the angled support.

Through the entire first summer's growing season, he does no pruning whatsoever, simply using more strips of cloth to fasten the main trunks to the supports as they continue to grow. Next, all upward growing branches are pruned off at a point three leaves away from the central trunk, while downward and sideways growing branches are pruned off two leaves away from the trunk. Each year after the fruit ripens, these branches are pruned in the same manner. Once the trunks have reached the top wire, they're kept trimmed to that height.

He uses this cordon espaliering technique to form edible and picturesque living fences around smaller properties and estates. When planting small orchards he spaces rows of trees trained in the fashion either six feet apart (as done in Europe) which is perfect spacing for a hand cart, or nine feet apart, which is ideal for driving a pickup between the rows during harvesting.

Horizontal or palmette espaliers can readily be grown in rows with this same row spacing, and in fact are often grown that way in much of Europe.

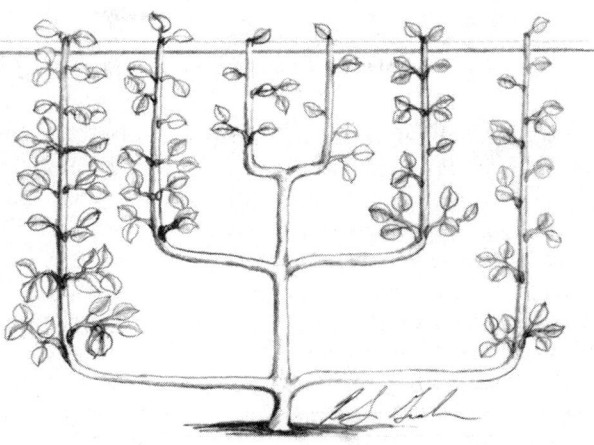

Six-Armed palmette verrier espalier growing along a wall

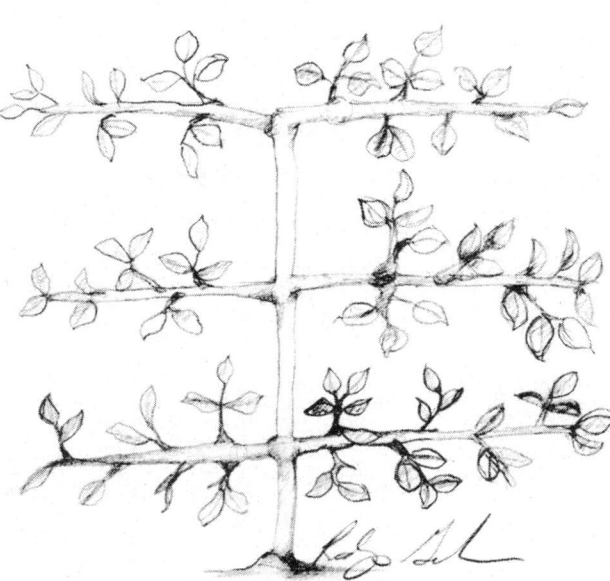

Triple horizontal cordon

I prefer using these growing techniques right along the house walls, or porch edges, as these plantings made 6 to 24 inches away from the walls not only guarantees an abundance of ripe fruit in close proximity to the kitchen, but during the summer's heat the deciduous leaves provide some cooling shade.

Forcing fruit trees to grow more horizontally greatly increases the number of fruiting spurs, while reducing both sucker and leaf growth. We've found that once your trees are well established, the area between the trunks provides an ideal location for plantings of low growing herbs and vegetables. ∆

Chat with other self-reliant people in Backwoods Home Magazine's popular forums: www.backwoodshome.com

Pemmican

By Habeeb Salloum

The first time I heard of pemmican was in the 1940s when a Native Indian friend in Regina, the capital of Canada's province of Saskatchewan, invited me for a meal. Among the dishes on which we feasted was this food par excellence of the prairie natives, which before the advent of the Europeans was their most important staff of life. It also became the mainstay of early explorers, and today it is an ideal provision for trappers and Arctic travelers. From that initial familiarization with pemmican, I developed a taste for its somewhat exotic flavor.

Perhaps my love for a similar Syrian dish, qawarma (meat cooked in fat for preservation purposes), led me to appreciate this aboriginal creation. With no refrigeration possible on the prairies during the Depression years, our family had thrived on qawarma, this ancient Middle Eastern method of preserving meat.

In later years, I often searched for pemmican but could not find it for sale. The few times I had it in the homes of friends and acquaintances only increased my yearning for this close relative of meat jerky, the South American charqui, and South African biltong. Eventually, I developed my own version of this flavored dried meat.

Pemmican, whose name is derived from the Cree pimikon (manufactured grease) was a Native Indian invention found on the menus of all prairie Indian tribes and some of their northern neighbors. It was an exceedingly valuable nourishment which sustained the tribes, especially during their yearly migrations and in times of shortages. One of the first forms of highly condensed food, it was an excellent portable life-saving ration for people who were always on the move.

In Canada's north, extending to the Arctic region, the Indians and Inuit dried the meat of caribou, moose, fish, and other animals, then stored it in accessible caches for use as needed in winter. Only rarely was it made into pemmican, mostly by the Chipewyan, the forest people in the eastern part of the Canadian Territories.

In Alaska, the Inuit made a type of pemmican by mixing chewed venison with deer-suet or seal oil. Also, some Inuit allowed their meat or fish to decay slightly, then buried it in permafrost pits. Even though these forms of preservation would not be appreciated by modern man, it appears that these products were considered palatable by the Inuit. Only occasionally was fish made into pemmican, but with sturgeon oil instead of fat. And then it was mainly used as a food for children.

The pre-European peoples on the western plains usually made pemmican from the flesh of buffalo or deer, and after the white man came, from cattle. Bison meat was considered to have the finest flavor, but when buffalo and deer were not available, it was made from the flesh of antelope, bear, and any other hunted mammal available.

Making pemmican

To make pemmican, the meat was cut into very thin strips, then hung on racks to dry in the hot sun for about two days or until it hardened. At times, the strips were attached to the inside top of a tepee to dry above a slow-burning fire. The smoke gave the meat an enhanced flavor, making it much more tasty.

The dried meat was then pounded into powder and mixed with hot melted fat. To enrich the taste and cut down on the greasiness of the fat, dried vegetables, herbs, or fruits such as cranberries, huckleberries, saskatoons, and wild cherries were added. If fresh bones were plentiful, a superior type of pemmican was made by substituting bone marrow for the fat obtained after boiling broken bones.

When the mixture cooled, it was tightly packed into rawhide bags, often with hair and pebbles mixed with the pemmican, then firmly sewn. Or the mixture was placed in various types of skin containers and sealed. At other times, the pemmican was poured into casings of animal intestines or allowed to solidify and then cut into cakes or loaves. These were then made air tight by dipping the cakes or loaves into melted wax.

The finished product, if protected from moisture, would remain edible almost indefinitely. However, in most cases it was usually consumed within four to five years. Of maximum nutritional value, it required a minimum amount of space which made it a perfect sustenance for travelers. In times of war and to supplement short winter rations, there was no better food. An ideal strength-giving unique meat preservative, it served as the main staple for the tribes in lean times and as almost the only nourishment for hunters and warriors.

It was after their arrival to this continent and their contact with the native peoples that the Europeans came to learn how to make pemmican. A perfect food for long journeys, it became a significant factor in the development of the interior communication and transportation systems of both the North West and Hudson Bay Companies. It was ideal to take on lengthy expeditions where it was inconvenient to carry large quantities of provisions.

These newcomers adopted it as their own, and in the ensuing decades many newly arrived explorers and pioneers thought of it as a white man's invention. It became very important in their daily lives. The fur trade and the many exploration expeditions, like that of Alexander Mackenzie in the Northwest Territories, would have encountered serious difficulties of survival had it not been for pemmican.

Nourishing, easy to carry, and virtually unknown to spoil, it became of great value in times of war. There was even a conflict which carried its name, "The Pemmican War," a struggle between the hunters and traders of the Northwest Fur and Hudson Bay Companies from 1812 to 1821 in the Indian controlled territory of the West.

Mostly, pemmican was eaten raw, but at times it was made into a soup called rubaboo by adding a little flour, sugar, and any available vegetable. In spite of being tasty and nourishing, like corn beef fed to soldiers, it became monotonous and new ways of serving it were often concocted.

Today, a form of pemmican is commercially manufactured, usually from beef with the addition of dried currants or raisins and a little sugar. Providing the most nourishment for the least amount of weight, it is heaven-sent for mountain climbers, Arctic travelers, hunters, surveyors, and others who journey in the wild.

This recipe is a simple modern method of making a tasty pemmican.

---

2 lbs. round beef steak
¾ cup hot melted margarine
1 Tbsp. brown sugar
1 tsp. salt
1 tsp. thyme
½ tsp. pepper
½ tsp. ginger
1 cup dried currants

Cut beef into very thin strips, then place in a greased pan. Dry at lowest oven heat possible until the meat turns hard.

Place in a food processor with the remaining ingredients, then process into a paste, adding more margarine if needed. Place in a plastic container with a tight lid if taking along on a journey, or store container in a cool place and serve as needed. ∆

Mane and tail tools

By Gary D. Kirchmeier

All too often horse owners make the mistake of feeling they have to cut off a nice mane because it gets too tangled. Frustration causes hasty action. That is too bad because it takes a long time to grow a mane or tail. Tangles can be a headache, especially on long manes such as many Arabian horses tend to have. Combs are prone to break hair and hang up. A superior tool for manes and tails is an inexpensive human hairbrush. They break very little hair and don't catch like a comb. Use the type with natural bristles and avoid the kind that have single stiff plastic teeth with little balls on the ends.

The second tool worth considering is a can of WD-40. This product comes in an aerosol can and is great for squeaky hinges. Few people would agree to put a common lubricant on their horse, thinking it would leave a terrible residue. I, for one, insisted on being shown on someone else's horse. It is quite surprising to find that there is no detectable residue and the tangles slip right apart. The spray emulsifies any oil and lubricates the hair. It leaves it feeling clean and dry. A lot of people are already putting it on their horse inadvertently, by using it as a blade wash for their clippers.

It also becomes an inexpensive aid for teaching horses that are leery of aerosol sprays. Spray-on medications can be expensive training aids. When the time comes to spray on medications, your horse needs to be accustomed to it already.

Should your horse be nervous about the spray can, try this procedure. Stand at your horse's left (near) shoulder and tip his nose toward you slightly with the lead rope. Touch him on the shoulder with the can and hold it there if you can. If he tries to move away he can only do so with his hindquarters pivoting around his forequarters. If he is not able to avoid the can touching his shoulder he will soon understand it isn't going to hurt him. It is a strange phenomenon that a horse will ordinarily accept frightening things quickly if you are able to hold it against him for a few seconds and if they cause him no pain. When he is able to move away and avoid the touch, that behavior is reinforced. Try not to let that happen. Move with him and stay in contact.

Gentle persistence is the key here. No one is encouraged to proceed beyond their individual skill levels if a horse violently resists.

To untangle the tail, start at the tip and work towards the base. The same is true for the mane. Spray on a little WD-40 when tangles are encountered and brush. A little experimentation will reveal the right amount of lubricant to use. Frequent grooming should alleviate most severe tangles if your horse is isolated from other horses. Horses kept in groups are inclined to groom each other, causing chewed or knotted manes and tails. Keep the WD-40 handy and you can fix all those tangles, lubricate the clippers, or silence a squeaky hinge. ∆

The vanishing outhouse

By Tom R. Kovach

A person recently wrote to a large Midwest newspapers' advice column asking for information about outdoor privies. It seems that this person's family inherited a log cabin from out of the 1930s and it came with no indoor plumbing. Instead there was an outhouse. But the problem with the outhouse was that the hole was starting to fill up. What to do? The family began talking to a lot of folks, but nobody knew anything what-so-ever when it came to outhouses. They were told that the building and care of outhouses appeared to be a "lost art."

Apparently they're right, when it comes to dealing with outhouses there is no longer any common knowledge to be shared with the new generation.

But it certainly wasn't always that way. I can personally vouch for that. I was born in 1945 and our farm didn't get indoor plumbing until after I joined the army almost 20 years later. And believe me, growing up in northern Minnesota, the old outhouse wasn't something to look forward to on a night when the temperature outside was sinking to 40 degrees below zero. Even when it is a "mild" 0 degrees, those wooden seats could get mighty frosty.

Until around the time of the Civil War, every American household had one or more pit privies. Then they began to disappear with the advent of indoor plumbing. But even as recently as the 1930s, the old familiar outhouse was the most common way to deal with human waste. During the Great Depression, the Works Progress Administration (WPA) built two million pit privies.

There are a lot of jokes about the good old outhouses. When I was growing up kids were always trying to sneak up on someone's outhouse on Halloween night in an attempt to tip it over. I was no better than the rest. But we seldom succeeded. Most of the old farm bachelors in the neighborhood kept a close eye on their privies on Halloween day and the day before and the day after. (Some of these kids were tricky and

tried to accomplish their foul deed when the outhouse owner was unsuspecting).

I remember two brothers whose father refused to let them go out trick or treating. As revenge, they tipped over their own outhouse. Of course their father caught them and sitting down became a problem for them for the next few days.

The basic design for the outdoor toilet hasn't changed for hundreds of years. Basically it's a shack sitting over a hole in the ground. The inside has a bench with holes cut into it. Besides being notorious in the winter for the cold drafts that chilled one's bare flesh and raised the goose bumps, outhouses in the summer were hot, smelled bad, and drew a lot of flies. In winter or summer, one did not dally long in the outhouse. Visits were as short as possible.

But some outhouses are quite comfortable and don't smell bad at all. *BHM* Publisher Dave Duffy says the outhouse he built next to his first backwoods home sat on a small hill with a beautiful view of a creek. He had put a Dutch door on it with a screen so he could leave the top half of the door open and keep out flies. A scoop of lime thrown down the hole after each use eliminated all odor. He even installed a small magazine rack on one wall, and a foam seat that didn't get cold in winter.

The crescent moon cut into the door has become a cliche signifying the outhouse. But it had a definite purpose and the moon was only half of the story. A moon or sunburst (often looking like a star) in the door provided light and ventilation, and differentiated the men's and women's privies. The moon, or luna, is an ancient symbol for women, while a sunburst stood for men. These symbols were necessary at a time when very few people knew how to read.

Pit privies aren't commonly used in my home state of Minnesota. According to Sara Christopherson of the University of Minnesota's Extension Service, "About a third of Minnesotans are using onsite sewage treatment systems, but only five percent or less of these are pit privies."

But if you're thinking about adding an indoor plumbing system to your cabin, think twice says Christopherson. Before you tear down that old outhouse, bear in mind that there is a growing movement in North America, especially in New York and Nevada, to preserve this vanishing icon. At a recent Canadian auction, an outhouse sold for $5,600.

The friends I hunt deer with have a nice outhouse next to the hunting shack. And it serves us quite well. We've even got scenic wall-paper inside. And as far as dealing with the filling up hole, simply dig a new hole and move the outhouse over it. The old hole is covered with dirt and any plants or grass you plant there should do quite well. Great for flowers!

If you want more information on how to deal with pit privies, you can contact the Minnesota Extension Service's website at: http://www.bae.umn.edu/septic. ∆

Need more information?

Find hundreds more articles at *Backwoods Home Magazine's* extensive website, and even chat with other self-reliant people on the *Reader's Forum*.

www.backwoodshome.com

Caring for spices and herbs

By Tom R. Kovach

A lot of people use spices to enhance their meals. And it helps to keep your spices and herbs fresh. According to McCormick & Company, producers of spices, there are three ways to determine whether or not spices and herbs are fresh... sight, smell, and taste. Visually, you can check your spices and herbs to make sure that their color has not faded. Loss of color is an indication of flavor loss. A fragrant, intense aroma is characteristic of fresh spices and herbs. Crush the spices and herbs in your hand. If you don't smell the aroma, or if you taste them and the flavor is not apparent, it's time to replace them.

Spices and herbs will keep for a long time if they are stored in airtight containers, away from heat, moisture, and light. For optimum flavor, properly stored whole spices can be used within four years and ground spices within three years. The green leafy herbs will last from one to three years depending on the herb. Members of the red pepper family (capsicums), such as paprika and chili powder, should be refrigerated to help retain color and guard against infestation. This is important especially during the summer months and in particularly hot climates.

General shelf-life guidelines:

Ground spices, 3 years
Whole spices, 4 years
Green leafy herbs, 1-3 years
Seeds, 4 years
Extracts, 4 years
Seasoning blends, 1-2 years

Spices and herbs don't spoil, but they do lose their intensity over time. Old seasonings will not flavor your food the way they are intended to. Here are some tips that will assist you in preserving the flavor and quality of your spices and herbs:

• Replace the lid on containers right after use.

• Do not sprinkle spices and herbs directly from the container over a steaming pan or kettle. Steam introduced into a spice and herb container will hasten the loss of flavor and aromas. Measure your seasonings into a bowl, then add the seasonings to the pot.

• Make sure the measuring spoon is completely dry when you dip it into the spice or herb container. Moisture introduced into the container will also result in deterioration of the contents.

Freezing does not extend the shelf life of dried spices and herbs. If spices and herbs are stored in the freezer and are constantly removed for use, condensation may form in the containers and accelerate the loss of flavor and aroma.

Spices and herbs should be stored in airtight containers away from heat, moisture, and direct sunlight. These elements advance the loss of flavor and aroma. Therefore, avoid storing your spices and herbs over the stove, dishwasher, sink, or near a window. ∆

Preparing garden soil in winter

by Alice B. Yeager
(photos by James O. Yeager)

We have to prepare for everything whether it's for a career, a city council meeting, a country fair, junior's first day at school, a well stocked pantry, or anything else. It's the same with gardening. You can't expect to reap much of a crop if you throw your seeds out on the ground with nature's wildflowers, weeds, and debris. There has to be more preparation than that.

Ancient gatherers moved about taking whatever nature provided. Those folks were dependent on the wild to see them through thick and thin. Gradually some of the ancients began to till the soil with sticks and such and they began to learn how to grow certain grains and vegetables, save seeds for the next season, and so on. They found that certain areas were good for growing food plants and others were not.

Let's fast-forward to our time and see if we're not following the same pattern when we select a gardening spot and begin to enrich and till it.

The first thing we do is to pick an area open to the sun and with a slight slope to it if possible. All vegetable gardens need sunlight—a bare minimum of six hours. Even so, lots of plants won't reach peak production, as they really require more sunlight than that. Peppers, okra, tomatoes, and other summer crops only reach their potential if given eight hours or more of sun.

We all love our shade trees, particularly in the summer when old Sol beams down and tries to wilt everything in sight. However if there are shade trees nearby the garden site, you can bet they're not only going to cast shade part of the day but they are also going to "sap the soil." Their roots are not gathered up neatly near their trunks. Instead, they are roaming underground away from the trunks seeking moisture and nourishment for the trees. Where better place to find their requirements but out there in a nice garden spot that is being organically tended and watered? This is the reason we often find long, live roots showing up in odd places in our gardens if there are trees just beyond the garden spots.

Preparing the soil

When you have found what you believe is the best location for your garden, then the soil factor comes into play. If you luck out and select a spot where someone has diligently tilled a garden before you came, you'll probably find that the soil may need some attention, but it will be feasible to garden there again. You can go about the chore of clearing off the spot getting rid of weeds, grass, etc.

There is always the possibility, even with existing gardens, to find that the soil is too acid or too alkaline for the plants you want to raise. To be absolutely sure you have the soil pH you need, it is well to ask your county extension agent about a soil test and be guided as to how to go about this. Generally speaking, soil samples need to be taken from several spots in the garden. Brush aside any surface debris and insert a sharp trowel into the ground for a few inches to obtain a small sample of the soil. (The agent will tell you how much is needed for a test.)

After receiving the results of the test, you will then be advised as to how to go about changing the pH of your garden soil if need be. The term "pH" is used to indicate the degree of acidity or alkalinity of the soil. pH values from 0-7 indicate acidity and 7-14 indicate alkalinity. pH 7 is regarded as neutral.

Most good garden soils will have a pH of 6.0-8.0 which will accommodate many of our vegetables—tomatoes, okra, turnips, lettuce, cabbage, asparagus, etc. There are others, however, that prefer a lower pH. Lima beans do best in a soil with pH of 5.5-6.5. Potatoes like pH 4.8-6.5 and strawberries produce better if soil has a pH of 5.0-6.0. A handy book to have is the *LaMotte Soil Handbook*. It lists many shrubs, trees, flowers and vegetables giving the soil preference for each.

To illustrate the importance of the proper pH, here is a little story about a problem some friends of ours had with their blueberries. They had planted several blueberry bushes in a

Rose bushes require maintenance. Why not grind up these clippings, put them in the compost bin and make further use of them as mulch for your garden?

very good location—good drainage, sun most of the day, etc. These folks also owned some poultry houses and disposed of the litter by distributing it on their pastures and vegetable garden. The pasture was green and the garden was flourishing. All was going well except for the blueberries. They definitely looked like they were on the way out.

"I can't understand it. Everything else is doing so well. We have watered these plants and fertilized them. Look at them! We don't know what else to do for them. Could it be the soil?"

The bushes looked like they were planted at the right depth and the soil seemed moist enough. I asked what they were using for fertilizer.

"Oh, we're using the same litter we use on everything. You know poultry fertilizer is one of the best fertilizers around. That is, if you apply it in the cool season."

They were amazed that one of the best fertilizers around, was not good for everything. It's poison for acid lovers like blueberries, azaleas, and many varieties of trees and berries, etc. The end result was that they had to dig up the blueberry plants, remove the soil and start all over with new plants. The new blueberries were given plenty of leaf mold and mulched with a mixture of leaves and pine needles. Last accounts I had was that they were doing fine and the owners were happy with their blueberry harvest.

Not only does the pH enter into gardening, but the quality of soil is a big plus or minus for gardeners. However all soils may be improved by the addition of organic matter such as grass clippings, pine needles, leaves,

Weeds in their young growing stage can be used in the compost pile. Don't wait until they have produced seeds, as the seeds will come back to haunt you.

and so on. Be diligent about trying to improve your soil and one day you'll realize a good garden spot was worth all the effort. Avoid using chemicals in your garden and cater to creating a habitat for earthworms. If you have any by-products of black walnut trees (leaves, twigs, walnuts) dispose of them away from the garden as they are toxic to many plants.

We'd all like to have perfect gardening soil, but sometimes we come across obstacles, particularly if we're beginning to garden in a new place. Clay is probably the worst of the soils with which to work. A garden rarely contains pure clay, but there can be enough of it to stymie one's best efforts. A test for clay is to rub some of the wet soil between your fingers and notice the extremely fine particles that actually have a greasy feeling to the touch. When clay soil is dug or plowed, it produces big clods which, when dry, are almost as hard as bricks. When clay soil dries out on a level spot such as a yard, it produces large cracks through which any sub moisture escapes. Grassy areas are in peril during drought as the runners from the grass are actually stretched to the breaking point when the cracks enlarge.

If you want to make clay soil productive, you can begin by the addition of plenty of organic matter. Provide good drainage and work, work, work. If your problems with clay are severe, I'd suggest you find another garden spot.

Sandy loam is probably the best soil for gardening as long as there is plenty of humus and not too much sand. A nice balance is ideal for most food plants. Too much sand and it's like gardening in a sieve as water doesn't linger long in sand. You'll find yourself spending far too much time watering the garden between showers if your soil is too much on the sandy side.

After all the spring and summer effort, the time arrives when the last possible vegetable has been gleaned from the garden. Maybe some fall greens remain, but winter is soon going to take its toll on them. Here in the Southwest Arkansas part of Zone 8, fall is a good time to take stock of your failures and successes and plan ahead for next year.

Fortunately, gardeners in our area can do quite a bit while the garden is resting. We can remove old bean vines and supports, pull up stalks of plants that were cut down by Jack Frost, and generally tidy up the place. We can almost work at this at our leisure, as our really foul weather usually occurs from mid-December through January.

We have raised beds and after removing any dead plants or debris, I like to give them a nice thick layer of organic matter to decompose during the winter. This will make a home for the earthworms that will till our soil in the spring. Nothing with a lot of seeds attached is put on the beds or in the compost bin. Seeds will only come back to haunt us in the spring. You can count on nature to keep a liberal supply of weed seeds in reserve.

Stalks of tall plants such as sunflowers, Jerusalem artichokes, and okra all make good places for certain garden pests to harbor over until warm weather begins again. However these stalks may be crushed in a shredder along with twigs, vines, etc., and added to the compost bin where they will be of use. Shrub clippings and rose bush trimmings may be ground up and put in the compost bin where they will make mulch and be ready to apply to the garden when spring rolls around.

Some folks rake up their leaves and put them in bags for the local trash hauler to cart away. Then they buy fertilizer for their plants. What better fertilizer than the organic matter they paid the trash hauler to remove? Yard rakings can almost always be used around shrubs and trees to a good advantage. Want to cut down on the summer water bill? Try mulching.

The cold season is also a good time to check one's gardening tools with a view to sharpening some, replacing handles in others, and discarding those that are of no further use. When spring comes, you'll be glad your tools are prepared for it. If you have a greenhouse, chances are you could use the room now occupied by some things that belong in the trash bin. In our case, we are making plans to remodel our greenhouse with a view

Picture perfect baskets of vegetables require some preparation. Soil pH, quality of soil, mulch...they all add up.

to cutting down on some of the work connected with handling large plants. After all, there does come a time.

The Scout motto, "Be prepared" can certainly be applied to gardening. There's no point in beginning the gardening season by having to clear the place of debris, tough perennial weeds, matted vines, and other tripping hazards. That sort of thing makes one wonder if Mama raised a fool. Gardening should be a pleasant experience wherein gardeners look forward to tending their plants and harvesting those picture perfect vegetables that make them the envy of the neighborhood. Δ

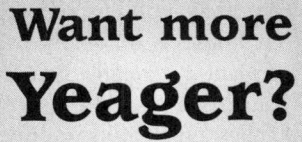

Living with wildlife

By Tom R. Kovach

As the human population grows and spreads out to other areas, there appears to be a huge increase in human and animal confrontations. Some wildlife encounters are merely nuisance experiences. Others can be costly and dangerous.

There are reports from all over the United States concerning the increase of coyotes who have an uncanny ability to adapt to populated areas. There have been more than a few reports of coyotes attacking young children. And with mountain lions protected in just about every state, the population of these big cats has increased to the point where there have been several fatal human/mountain lion incidents.

The same holds true for bears, especially black bears which have been on the increase in a number of states. A mother black bear with her cubs nearby can be a very dangerous creature.

Wildlife officials have a number of suggestions for homeowners and others who live in areas populated by nuisance animals and also those of the more dangerous variety. Here are some ideas put forth by those who deal with wildlife on a regular basis. These tips can help keep the creatures we live with at a safe distance:

• Feeding birds and squirrels is just fine. But feeding larger animals like bears, raccoons, etc., is just asking for trouble. Feeding wildlife can make these creatures less afraid of man. And that can be dangerous.

• Bring in pet bowls in the evenings. Most wild animals really enjoy the food we put out for cats and dogs. Once they know the food is there, animals will keep coming back for more.

• Garbage is a big attraction for wildlife. They love an easy meal. Keep your garbage in cans with tight-fitting lids and keep them chained or tied down in some way. Keep outside grills clean and pick up any food that might have fallen on the ground after outdoor meals such as picnics.

• Pick up any fallen fruit if you have fruit trees in your yard. Animals love fruit. I'm told that coyotes even have a taste for watermelons. Gardens should be fenced in whenever possible.

• Keep your pets inside at night or in a building or enclosure that offers them protection. Keep an eye on your pets during the daytime hours. Mountain lions can take down even the biggest dog.

• Deer seem to have an appetite for almost any sort of greenery, from garden goodies like cabbage and sweet corn to popular ornamental shrubs such as azaleas. Try planting some deer-resistant plants. Your local garden center might have some suggestions.

• If you're going to be gone for a long period of time, it would be a good idea to cap your chimney. Raccoons often use open, uncapped chimneys as nests. And once they're in there, they can also get into your house. And while they may look like neat, little creatures, they can be very destructive and costly in a house.

• Raccoons and skunks, often make use of areas under out-buildings, or inside of them if they have a way to get in. Try to close off crawl spaces and other little crannies where these animals can crawl in and make themselves at home. Skunks and other creatures in these places not only cause a lot of bad odor, but they can also transmit disease.

• Wildlife biologists also suggest that you make your yard as park-like as possible. Keep it free of brush and low branches that make for good hiding spots.

• And if you have neighbors close by, get their help. If even one resident in a neighborhood decides to feed deer, raccoons, or other critters, the wildlife problem will be the same for everyone. Δ

Sell your home:
get a good price and sell it faster

By Jackie Clay

Few of us backwoods folk were born rich or have made a bundle somewhere along the way. We work hard and have big dreams, but unfortunately, little cash. Home ownership can be a ladder to those dreams, but like a ladder, sometimes you have to start at the bottom.

If you buy wisely, with creative financing, and immediately begin remodeling and dressing a place up, you'll be able to increase your buying ability when your family feels ready for the next step in that dream.

Dress that place up

So many times it seems that home sellers just hang a FOR SALE sign and that's that. Bad move. How about doing a little to perk up the looks and sales possibilities?

No one should move into a new place and just let it sit. Not only is this depressing to you, the owner, but if a place is not improving in looks it will slowly decrease in value. Simple things, such as maintaining fences, building new ones, adding a barn, gardens, putting a needed addition on the kitchen, fixing the broken window in the garage, etc., do a lot.

Work on the appearance of the yard. Establish flower beds, permanent landscape plantings, add trees, a rock garden, even a pond or trickling fountain. Encourage the birds to feed and inhabit your yard. Nothing beats the beauty and fragrance of bright, cheerful flowers and the soft birdsong all about.

Keep the house painted, washed, and clean. We spent $40 on four gallons of quality house paint on sale and completely changed the feeling of our little stucco home in New Mexico. It went from a plain, white, isolated ranch house stuck out on the plains to a comfortable, soft adobe home, radiating warmth Spanish-style as soon as the neutral adobe rose-tan was rolled on. The change was amazing.

Likewise, when we pressure washed our log cabin in Montana, faded grey from time, then brushed on a comfortable glowing stain and sealer, everyone who saw it was amazed. It went from "plain-Jane" to "log-lodge" in three days.

Such dramatic changes are common, and each dramatically increases the sale value of your home.

Don't neglect the barns, shed, garage, or even outhouse. A little paint and a few days' work can pay big dividends, quickly adding thousands to the value of your property.

If your home is on a large lot or acreage, plant a vegetable garden and some fruit trees. You'd be surprised at how many other folks are interested in grow-your-own food. My garden has always been a big factor in selling a place when we were ready to move on to another step on our dream ladder.

Don't go overboard in remodeling the interior of your home, but don't let it stagnate, either. You don't have to be rich to do wonders for a

The kitchen of our New Mexico home was done in a warm "chili pepper" motif.

"boring" home. Pick a theme for the rooms: apples, chickens, cows, or whatever. So far, I've had a "chicken" kitchen, where I simply removed cracked 1960's plastic from the kitchen cabinet doors and put in pieces of masonite, on which I painted hens sitting on nests of eggs, covered by real chicken wire—an instant oak-framed farm picture. Cost: $6 for the entire kitchen.

Then it was elk when we moved to the mountains above Jefferson City, Montana. I used pieces of elk antler for drawer and door pulls, hung some from a light fixture, stenciled bull elk shadows marching across lamp shades and the 1x6" finished pine border in the living room. Cost: $4.99 for the paint.

Your home can be "Indian," "Farm," "Wilderness Lodge," or "High Fashion," Sticking to a theme will definitely make it stand out to prospective buyers in the future. You can't just decide to sell on Monday and develop a look. It takes time.

Keep the inside painted, clean, and functional. If a sink trap leaks, fix it. Door hard to close? Take a few minutes and repair the problem.

Things to do when you are ready to sell

Make a detailed pass around your home with notebook in hand. Jot down every little bitty thing that turns you off. Then ask your friend, relative, or neighbor to do the same. And fix the problem spots.

Pick up any trash, hay strings, little bits of plastic or paper in the grass. Mow any weeds or unsightly brush around the buildings. Rake the yard and keep it mowed and watered as needed. If it is winter, make sure the walks are easily accessible and buyer-friendly.

Wash the windows inside and out. Then do the drapes, curtains, and carpets, if necessary. Don't bother recarpeting the floors, as most buyers will change the flooring to suit their tastes, anyway. The only exception would be if one is so shabby that it just plain looks tired, giving a dingy appearance to the room.

If the walls need washing or repainting, do it. Wash the light fixtures, and clean out the dead bugs.

A lot of experts recommend putting any "extra" furniture or boxed "junk" in storage. I agree. The more furniture and boxes around, the smaller and more cluttered rooms seem.

The same house in New Mexico as it was when the Clays bought it.

Pay special attention to the front walk, flower beds, porch, and front door of the house, as this is where the buyer will get their first impression of your home. You can make it or break it here. Paint the front door and hang a nice wreath next to it. Hang some potted plants on the porch or set some next to the steps. You only have one chance for that vital first impression, so make the most of it.

A warm, comfortable home...with a lot of work that increased its value.

When your home is at its best, take a couple of rolls of film of the house or homestead, inside and out, on a beautiful morning. When you are satisfied, get reprints of several of the best to show or send to interested buyers.

Pricing

Decide what price you need to sell your home for. Take into account a realtor's commission (if you decide to use a realtor), closing costs and any money you still owe on the home. Shop around and see what similar properties are selling for. Get a couple of estimates from realtors. You don't have to list with them. If their estimates seem to be in line with your idea, you have your price.

Don't get hung on a low estimate if you have a unique property. For instance, when we sold our farm in northern Minnesota, it was a very developed homestead (I'd been there 17 years.). There were three gardens, hay fields, pastures, an old hay/cow barn, a new horse barn, a pretty yard, a 40' log greenhouse, lots of flowers, shade trees, woods for lumber, firewood, and hunting, etc. The bank told me I'd be lucky to get $40,000 for the 120-acre "farm." I sold it quite quickly to a happy buyer for $67,000. (I even won a $10 bet with the banker!)

How did I pull that off? I'm no financial whiz, but I am very attuned to self-reliant living, and what folks are looking for in this line. I may be ready to move on up my dream-ladder, but the step I was on was just right for a whole lot of other folks. I realized this, but "traditional" realtors and bankers didn't have a clue. So I "earned" an extra $27,000 by having informed confidence.

There is a buyer for every home; it is up to you to decide just who your buyer might be and target them with your sales approach.

Even if you use a realtor (which we have done twice), you can still sug-

Bright flower beds quickly beautify a home.

gest places he or she might advertise your place. We have carried it a step further, insisting on the right to advertise ourselves, even if a property was listed with a realtor.

By the way, you certainly do not have to list a property with a realtor in order to sell it. Most attorneys will gladly handle the legal end of a real estate sale for a very reasonable fee. But if you decide to sell it yourself, be prepared for much extra work, answering phone calls, showing the property, talking to prospective buyers, etc.

Realtors have the advantage of having a listing instantly available on the internet for out-of-town buyers looking for a property in the area.

You have the advantage of intimately knowing your home, neighborhood, and locale. And with increasingly user-friendly computer programs, you can easily list your property yourself on the internet. We did our place in New Mexico, which we sold in December. It was listed through a small-town Chamber of Commerce and through *Rural Property Bulletin*. We had good responses to both.

Regardless of whether or not you choose to use a realtor, you should aggressively advertise. This can cut the time it takes to sell a home in half or less. Target your buyer, then go after them.

Is your place a first-buyer home? A ranch? A homestead? A backwoods home? There are magazines and advertisers for every market. We advertised in *Backwoods Home Magazine, Countryside and Small Stock Journal, The Mother Earth News*, and *Rural Property Bulletin*, and sold property, through the years, from each of them.

Don't neglect your local "free shopper" paper, the Sunday paper of the nearest large city, ads on the feed store bulletin board, or whereever you think a potential buyer might access your ad.

Answering questions

The phone rings. It's the first inquiry on your property. Choke down that racing heart and make a friendly, intelligent impression. But what do you say?

It's helpful to make a short list of your property's good points: the square feet of your home, how many bedrooms, how deep the well is, and those really neat things about your home and area. Don't gush, just tell them about your property and answer any questions honestly.

If the buyer is from a ways off, and seems interested, offer to send a packet including a few photos for their convenience. Be aware that you'll probably send many such packets before an inquiry turns to a "looker," let alone a buyer. It can be a long process.

If such a person calls back with more questions, do all you can to help, including sending a larger packet with such things as maps, local Chamber of Commerce flyers, fishing

A producing garden is a good selling point.

information, or whatever seems to interest the buyer.

Never lie or gloss over obvious (or not-so-obvious) detractions to your property: a dirt access road, a drive that floods, poor winter access, etc.

Showing your property

The day arrives. Your first "buyer" has made an appointment to view your home. Hopefully, you've had time to pick up, clean up, and mow the lawn. It doesn't hurt to bake a batch of bread or a couple of pies just before you expect the buyer. Don't laugh! I've had two buyers tell me later that those wonderful loaves of bread and that cherry pie made my home seem so nice. Neither was an on-purpose bait, but hey, it works!

If your place is listed with a realtor, most prefer that you discretely fade away and let them show the property, as most realtors feel that having the owner around makes buyers shy about asking questions.

If you are selling the home yourself, make the buyer feel welcome, and take them for the tour. Honestly answer any questions they pose. How are the neighbors? Is the well good? What can you grow in your garden? Where do the kids go to school?

Never ask, "Well, what do you think?" If they are interested, they'll tell you. Some need to look, then go home and think about it. Let them.

But don't quit trying to sell the property or take it "off the market" until you have it SOLD. We made that mistake recently. We had very interested out of state buyers who wanted our ranch in New Mexico. They signed a contract, and put down several thousand dollars. They were real gung-ho folks. We signed a contract on a neat remote homestead in Alaska, then began to have our animals tested for the trip through Canada. We contracted with a friend to buy his tractor and equipment and my oldest son even bought plane tickets to fly down to help us drive. We were that sure.

Then our buyers just dropped out. OUCH!

We lost the place in Alaska, due to the seller's needed time frame, Bill lost his $1,200 in unused plane tickets, we inconvenienced our friend with his tractor, and we had to start all over again, selling the ranch while spring turned to summer.

We should have kept in contact with the other four potential buyers who had expressed much interest in buying the place. Instead, we told them it had been sold. By the time our deal fell through, they had found other properties to buy.

Don't really quit selling until you have cashed the check and have moved. Instead, develop a portfolio of back-up buyers; buyers who have been very interested when the contract to buy was signed. Instead of saying, "It's sold," say, "We think we have it sold, but we'll be glad to give you a call if the deal falls through." That is less permanent-sounding, and gives some hope to the second-place buyer.

And, as we found out, it is a darned good idea. Sort of like carrying a spare tire when you drive, just in case.

The legal stuff

When the happy day comes and your buyer says he'll buy, meeting the terms you have decided on, offer to drive them to your attorney to sign a buy-sell agreement. At this time, they will probably put down earnest money (usually $500-$1,000), which goes into an escrow account, binding the deal until the title search, if required, has been done, guaranteeing a clear title to the buyer. At this time, the closing is done and the purchase price or down payment is paid to the seller.

Out of this amount are taken a portion (usually half) of the attorney's or realtor's fees, taxes due (usually prorated), any money still owed on the property, and the cost of the title insurance, if required.

There can be other miscellaneous expenses, such as home inspection for such things as termites, radon, structural problems, etc.

With a little luck (and a lot of work on your part), you'll walk out with a check in your hand and smile on your face, knowing that you're soon stepping up on that next rung of the dream ladder, and on to that backwoods home. Δ

Want more Clay?

www.backwoodshome.com

Get The Whole Sheebang!

www.backwoodshome.com

Install a mobile, solar powered toilet

By Jeffrey R. Yago, P.E., CEM

When our solar business started to really increase, I found myself spending more and more time in my truck traveling down the highway to very remote job sites. My first investment was to buy a good quality parts trailer when I outgrew the back of my truck. Unfortunately, I soon learned that when mother nature calls, I was either working on houses still under construction that did not have a working plumbing system, or on the road many miles from the next drive-thru.

Although I do not own an RV, I have watched RV owners go through their daily routine of connecting temporary drain pipes, emptying holding tanks, flushing gray water tanks, and refilling a fresh water tank just to have a working toilet. Since I am basically lazy, I knew the solution to my problem would definitely not involve installing a typical RV flush toilet in my work trailer.

After extensive research (net surfing) with my trusty laptop, I found several suppliers of toilets that did not require water connections, sewer connections, septic tanks, or holding tanks. This seemed too good to be true, but there was a catch: to eliminate any odors and increase liquid waste evaporation, most of these units include a small exhaust fan that must operate continuously. In addition, during cold weather or higher use rates, most models include a small thermostatically controlled heater plate to prevent freezing of the damp mulch and to increase liquid evaporation.

So the question is, can this type of toilet operate satisfactorily without having the convenience of a grid connected 110-volt AC wall outlet? I decided that I would not need the auxiliary electric heater plate due to my limited weekly usage. If this ever became a problem, I could temporarily power the heater plate from an extension cord to the garage when parked at home. This leaves the small exhaust fan that must be powered full time. Further research found that almost all manufacturers of self-contained remote cabin toilets have modified versions for mobile applications like boats and RVs which replace the standard 120-volt AC fan with a 12-volt DC fan.

Brief history

The first non-traditional water flush toilets were developed in Europe in the 1960s for small rural mountain cottages. These operated on the principle of incinerating the waste. Although this technology is still in use today, the high electric consumption needed for operation makes this design not very practical for solar power or mobile applications.

Today there are several manufacturers for composting toilets which are available in many different sizes, styles, and capacities. Some high capacity units are as large as refrigerators laying on their side, and they are usually installed under the bathroom floor or in a basement. Smaller versions are self-contained and include special mounting hardware for installation in RVs and boats. Some models still utilize limited water flushing toilet seats in their operation, while others do not. Several have a manual hand crank to turn the compost drum and some use an electric motor.

Installation

I decided to purchase the Sun-Mar Ecolet Mobile toilet and was very surprised when it was delivered. I was expecting to receive just a toilet, and like most products requiring installation, I was dreading the multiple treks to the building supply store to purchase the missing odd sized pipe fittings, special mounting hardware, and hard to find supplies. Instead, the shipping box included the toilet, all required three-inch vent piping, a one-inch pipe drain pipe, flex exhaust pipe, all mounting bolts and brackets, a large bag of mulch, and initial start-up supplies.

All mounting and venting hardware was included with the Sun-Mar kit.

The Fourteenth Year

First I built a plywood divider wall inside the work trailer to create a small bathroom area with access from the side door. Unpacking the 50-pound toilet and mounting it in the work trailer took less than 30 minutes. It took another two hours to install the vent pipe because I had to cut a 3-inch vent hole in the metal trailer wall, which I finished with a plastic exhaust grille I found at a marine supply store. The toilet vent pipe extends up to the exhaust fan using the 3-inch PVC pipe, then it is routed at an angle to the upper side trailer wall using the various vent pipe fittings and flex duct provided. The instructions recommended a more vertical pipe route with minimum turns, but I wanted to avoid making a roof penetration. Now that the toilet installation was complete, how could I power this thing?

Solar power system

The 12-volt DC exhaust fan for the mobile version of the Sun-Mar toilet consumes 4 watts of power and must operate continuously, which equals 96 watt-hours per day (4 x 24 hrs.). Assuming there will be several days per week of cloudy weather, I decided to use a larger 75-watt solar photovoltaic panel to provide the fan power, which leaves more than enough solar energy for battery charging. Since most locations in this country receive at least 4 to 5 hours of peak sun per day, this should provide 300 watt-hours per day (75 watts x 4 hrs.) which is three times the exhaust fan daily load.

A battery allows storing the excess solar energy collected during the day so the fan and light can continue to operate at night and during periods of inclement weather. I chose two 6-volt gel cell golf cart size batteries which are designed to handle the daily deep charge/discharge solar cycle that would soon destroy a standard car battery. The gel cell version of this battery eliminates the need for periodic water refilling and does not require a liquid electrolyte that could spill, which is perfect for mobile applications.

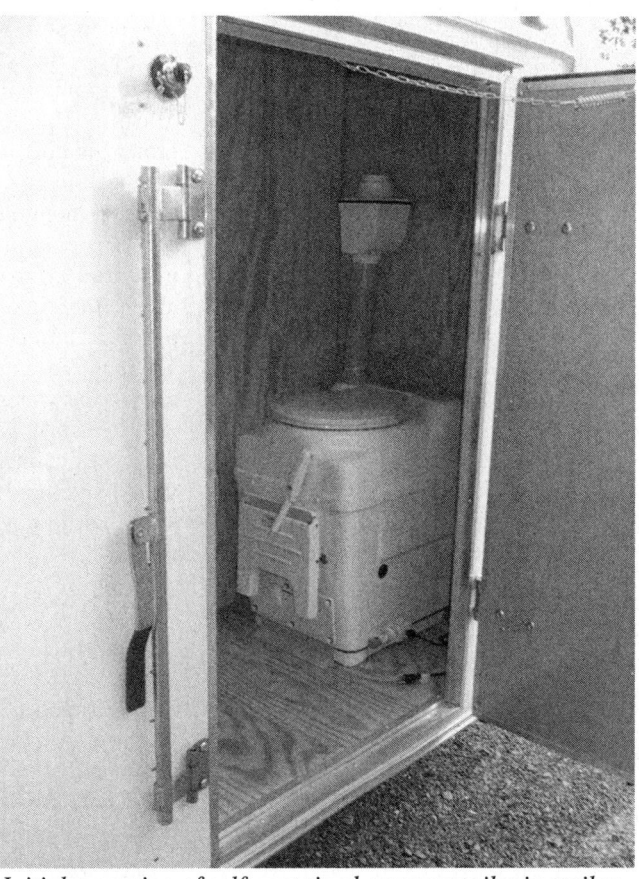

Initial mounting of self-contained compost toilet in trailer. A plywood wall was installed to create the restroom.

The two 6-volt batteries wired in series provide the 12-volts needed for the fan and lights. A solar module should face south in the northen hemisphere to maximize solar collection, which is a problem for a mobile application that could be facing any direction while parked or moving. Mounting the module flat on the roof would produce the same solar energy collection regardless of which way the vehicle is turned, but the flat mounting angle would greatly reduce winter performance due to the low sun angle. I decided to mount the 75-watt module on the side of the trailer that faces south when parked next to my house. This provides a fully charged battery for the next trip or project.

You cannot wire batteries directly to a solar module without a solar charge controller, as this would overcharge the battery during a sunny day and discharge the battery at night. I purchased a Morningstar Model 55 photovoltaic 12-volt charge controller with low voltage disconnect option. This is an excellent controller designed to charge both liquid and gel cell batteries, and its low voltage load disconnect will keep the exhaust

Three 75-watt solar module installed on the side of a 12-foot storage trailer

43

12-volt DC exhaust fan and 3-inch vent piping after installation

fan from totally discharging the battery during long periods of cloudy weather. It has many built-in safety features and a small LED light to indicate charging status. I added a switch and in-line automotive type fuse between the controller and the exhaust fan. This allows shutting off the fan for extended non-use periods, which greatly increases battery life.

Since the trailer now had a fully functioning solar charged battery system of its own, it seemed a waste to only power a tiny toilet exhaust fan, so I disconnected the interior dome lights from the trailer hitch electrical feed and rewired these to the new solar power system. This is really convenient when you need to find a tool or part inside and the trailer is not connected to the tow vehicle for power. I also added a small 12-volt fluorescent light that includes its own switch and produces much more light than the small dome light, and a 120-volt AC battery charger to plug in when parked for extended periods as a backup for the solar charging system.

To complete my bathroom on wheels, I installed a standard vanity sink base and a very deep sink basin. The deep sink will hold a large volume of water without splashing out when moving if I am parked where draining the soapy water onto the ground is not acceptable. I purchased a 15-gallon RV fresh water tank and exterior mounted hose fill plug from a marine supply store, which I mounted near the ceiling directly above the sink. At this elevation, a pressure pump or expansion tank is not required. Opening the sink faucet allows the water in the tank to drain into the sink. Although the water is not heated, it does allow washing your hands and face at job or camp sites that do not have restroom facilities.

So where's the smell?

After the installation was complete and in use, I was expecting what I usually smell (and unfortunately see) in those portable fiberglass johns everyone rents for fairs, races, and large public events. However, a composting toilet is very different. First,

Initial filling of the rotating drum with compost

Placing the bags of Zeolite and activated charcoal in the fan box

the seat is higher above the floor, so a small fold down step increases comfort. This increased height is necessary to accommodate the large rotating drum and various internal chambers, but this design also increases the visual distance down which almost completely blocks your view of what you may prefer not to see.

The exhaust fan is mounted inside a fiberglass box having a removable lid. During installation and setup, two nylon mesh bags (also included with the supplies) are placed in this fan box. The first bag contains what looks like limestone rocks, but are actually Zeolite. This natural mineral is a virtual "sponge" for ammonia, a common by-product of urine. The second bag contains activated charcoal pellets, a material that can remove most other objectionable contaminates except ammonia from the exhaust air. Together these materials filter and remove all "smell" from the toilet exhaust air, so the odor is completely gone even if you were standing right next to the exhaust outlet. Since this fan runs continuously, room air is drawn down through the lid and into the toilet, meaning there

The Fourteenth Year

Dual 6-volt gel cell golf cart batteries and backup AC battery charger

is no possibility of foul air floating up and out of the interior chambers prior to being filtered and exhausted.

How it works

During initial setup, several cubic feet of peat mulch is added to the rotating drum through a small flip door that lines up with the opening under the toilet seat. A small packet of harmless bacteria and a half-gallon of warm water is also added to get the bacteria-driven compost process started. After every few uses, you dump in a scoop of mulch from a closed storage container normally located next to the toilet. After adding the mulch, a front-mounted crank is turned several times which rotates the compost drum inside the toilet. A mechanical latch prevents the drum from stopping out of line with the top opening. This drum rotation covers the waste and mixes everything together much like you do with a compost pile. When the drum is rotating, the small flapper door closes to keep the composted material from falling out the bottom. Just below this rotating drum is a removable drawer that holds any already composted waste, which at this point is virtually organic dirt. The drum also includes a screen that allows any excess liquid to drain into an evaporator tray located at the bottom of the toilet below the removable drawer. Although completely sealed thanks to the one piece molded construction, this tray includes a one-inch plastic safety overflow pipe which prevents any spillage if the toilet is used by far more people than it was designed to handle. The small 120-volt AC heating element and automatic thermostat are located directly under this evaporator tray. This heater greatly speeds up waste liquid evaporation when the toilet is used on a daily basis.

Assuming the toilet is not used by more people and more often than it was designed for, the finishing or holding drawer may only need to be emptied once or twice each year. When the rotating drum is almost full, you turn the crank "backwards" for several turns which causes the flapper door to open and some of the composted material to fall down into the drawer where it will finish its composting and drying. Although at this point I have not

Books and websites on composting toilets

Oikos Bookstore
www.oikos.com

Compost Basics Library
www.wastenot-organics.wisc.edu

Compost Resource Page
www.oldgrowth.org/compost

The World of Composting Toilets
www.compostingtoilet.org

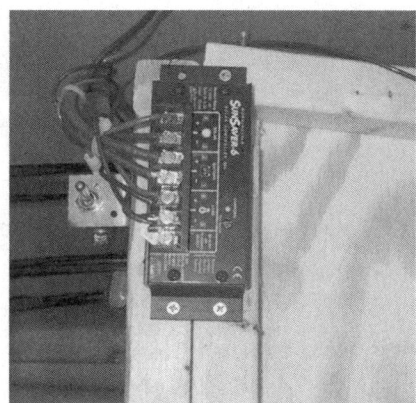

Closeup view of solar charge controller and fan shut-off switch

needed to empty this drawer, the manufacturer assures me this material is harmless and can be used as garden fertilizer. As for me, I'm thinking garbage bag into the trash can when that time finally comes.

Conclusions

Whether you are building a remote weekend cabin and do not or cannot install a conventional flush toilet and septic system, or looking for a toilet for your RV or boat that does not require daily draining, there is a compost toilet available in a size and configuration to meet almost any application. Δ

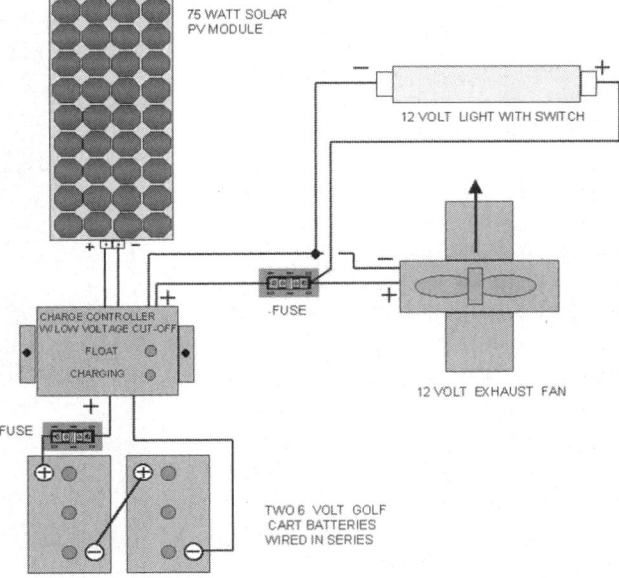

Wiring diagram

45

Cracklin's

An irresistible snack that you can't stop sneakin'

By Linda Gabris

When I was a girl growing up in the backwoods, one of my favorite times of the year was autumn when grandpa would butcher a pig to put up for winter. Regardless of the sadness I felt as the time drew near for our specially chosen oinker to meet his impending waterloo, I still looked forward to the season with much mouth-watering anticipation.

On pig butchering day, grandpa would rise long before daybreak and by the time grandmother and I had the morning fire lit and a kettle of dandelion coffee perking, the most unpleasant part of the job would be over. The plump porker that I had spent the summer fattening up for the larder with armloads of pig-weed and buckets of swill had, almost magically, turned into two sides of pork ready to be made into all kinds of good eats to enjoy over the long winter months ahead.

After blessings were given, grandpa, grandmother, and I would set about putting up the pig, which meant a long day's work making good use out of every part of the animal, from the snout to the hoofs. As much as I liked pickled pigs feet, salted belly, headcheese, smoked hooks, and bacon, my favorite treat was, and still is, the cracklings, or as we called them—*cracklin's!*

Cracklin's are crispy, tasty tidbits of pork that are left over from the lard-making process. Since my grandparents were very self sufficient—putting up most of their own provisions—homemade lard was an important staple for our household as grandma never had options of cooking with expensive store-bought butter or fancy vegetable oils. Even if she had, I'm sure she would still have preferred homemade lard above all else.

To this day I, too, prefer to use homemade lard for all of my frying and baking needs. Even though I don't raise a pig every year in the old manner like my grandparents did, keeping with tradition I still indulge in the age-old craft of making lard and, in turn, ending up with a delightful mess of cracklin's to boot.

Making lard is a fun activity that can be enjoyed in all seasons since most butcher shops these days have a ready supply of pork fat that is inexpensive and can be purchased not only in fall, but throughout the entire year! Because I like cracklin's so much, I often make a batch of lard even when my supply isn't running low in order to render the special treat. When I have a craving for cracklin's and my lard pot isn't yet empty, I melt down a kettle of fresh lard and treat the birds to my old batch. Making suet for the birds is a delightful way to put excess or old lard to good use.

Even though animal fats have—in the past number of years—gained a bad reputation as being cholesterol-makers, I believe that when eaten in moderation by healthy folks, with active lifestyles, it can still be enjoyed just as it was by our ancestors. My grandparents both lived long into their nineties with no fear what-so-ever of pork fat being bad for their health!

All of grandmother's recipes for biscuits, pies, fried fish, and birds called for the use of lard and I can vouch for the fact that her pastries were light and flaky and her grouse as finger lickin' as any chicken. And grandpa and grandmother—even in

Cracklin's, fresh lard, and buttermilk biscuits—what a treat!

old age—were a fast-footed pair hard to keep up with.

Since cracklin's are a by-product of lard, in order to end up with a special treat of these munchies, you'll have to first make a batch of creamy smooth, fragrant lard. To do this, go to your butchershop and ask for a couple slabs of pork fat or you can contact a local pig farmer to see if they have any available fat fresh off the farm. My supplier sells pork fat in rolls of about 3 to 5 pounds. One of these rolls will melt down into about one or two quarts of lard. From this, you will get an ample plateful of cracklin's.

There are different kinds of pork fat and the very best for pastry lard is said to be that which comes from the layer next to the bacon strips, known as leaf fat. Usually leaf fat is harder to obtain so if you're not picky, like me, you'll be happy with shoulder, loin, or back fat which, in my opinion, are all great for lard. The caul (stomach) and ruffle (from around the intestines) fats can be used for lard too, but they will produce a slightly stronger flavor and darker grease more suitable for frying than for baking. However, if cracklin's are your number one concern, then go with whatever you can get. The grease from all these fats is equally delicious and, as far as I'm concerned, work well in all recipes.

When you purchase fresh pork fat, you can ask for skinless slabs or that which still has on the rind. Personally, I like pieces that come with the rind on as this makes the best cracklin's for eating out of hand—ones with lots of crunch. Rindless fat produces a softer, puffier cracklin's which are excellent when crumbled and added to biscuit dough or sprinkled on cornbread.

Once home from the market, chill the fat until it is firm, as cold fat is much easier to handle. If the fat has been previously frozen, wrap in a tea towel and thaw in refrigerator. When ready to use, pat well with paper towels to remove all traces of moisture.

Fresh pork fat ready to melt down for lard and cracklin's

Using a sharp knife, cut the fat into uniform cubes a bit plumper than the size of playing dice. Put a handful into a large, heavy kettle—do not use aluminum or glass, as they might not be able to withstand the extreme heat—and melt until the bottom of the pan is well greased. Add the rest of the fat, making sure the kettle is never more than 2/3 full as it could boil over and splatter.

Over medium heat, stir with a long handled wooden spoon until the fat begins to fry down. As the fat melts, the grease level will rise. Be extremely careful when stirring as the hot liquid can cause severe burns if splashed on the skin. Never allow children near the stove when making lard! As the grease fries out of the cubes, the cracklin's will begin to rise to the top of the kettle. Once they have all turned a golden brown and have surfaced, it is time to remove the kettle from the heat. Again, be sure to handle very carefully.

Using a metal strainer or sieve, strain the grease into another heavy-bottomed kettle, catching the cracklin's in the sieve. Using a wooden spoon, force the remaining grease out of the cracklin's by pressing against the sieve. DON'T use plastic strainers, as they will surely melt.

Once strained, spread the cracklin's on a clean tea towel or several thickness of paper towels to help absorb remaining grease. While hot, season with salt, pepper, and cayenne—if you like your snacks with extra kick.

After the lard has cooled down it is ready to be ladled into your lard pot. If you don't have an earthen lard pot as I do, then a sterile canning jar or a coffee tin makes suitable lard tubs. The lard can be stored in the refrigerator or frozen. My grandmother kept a handy pot of lard at room temperature in the cupboard as we didn't have a fridge or freezer and it saved very well. Every so often she would send me to the root cellar to get a refill from her big earthen lard crock.

When using the lard for dessert pies or pastries, scoop from the top of the pot as this is the purest. Lard scraped from the bottom of the lard dish will contain traces of cracklin's. This tasty sediment is great when used as fat for biscuits or savory meat pies. The specks also taste mighty good when spread on top of golden cornbread. My grandparents and I used the "bottoms" of the lard pot as spread for fresh baked bread and topping for baked and mashed potatoes.

Once the cracklin's have finally stopped crackling—and they really do snap and crackle as their name implies—the time has come for tasting. Try one. But let me warn you—you can never stop at just one! If you're like me, you'll be sneaking and snacking til there's nothing left but a lick of salt!

Whether you enjoy a couple cracklin's and a biscuit for lunch or tote a pocket full to munch on as you hike your favorite trail, nothing makes a better bite! Cracklin's can be made into a delicious trail mix sure to become a family favorite. A snack that's guaranteed to give you energy to burn...

Cracklin' trail mix

This is a delicious pocket treat that is not only nutritious, but saves exceptionally well and is quite cheap to make.

Mix together:

```
2 cups cracklin's
3 cups raisins
1 cup dried apricots
1 cup sliced dried apple rings
3 cups nuts (peanuts or mixed
    nuts, whichever you prefer)
1 cup dried cranberries (or a mix
    of dried berries if you do your
    own. I dry my own blueberries
    and add to this mix. If you don't
    have home-dried blueberries,
    then currants work well in their
    place).
```

You can add any other dried fruit or vegetable you fancy to the above. Divvy up into little zip lock bags. Store in a cool, dry place.

Buttermilk biscuits

```
4 cups flour
pinch of salt
3 tsp. baking powder
½ cup homemade lard (scoop from
    the bottom)
1¼ cup buttermilk
```

Mix dry ingredients. Blend in lard. Stir in the buttermilk until dough can be formed into a ball (You may need a little more or less buttermilk than above). Pat on floured board and cut into circles. Place on baking sheet and bake at 400°F until golden brown. For a wonderful lunch, serve these biscuits with a few cracklin's and a crisp sour pickle.

Pie crust

```
2 cups flour
pinch of salt
½ cup lard (from the top of the
    pot)
¼ cup cold water
```

Mix dry ingredients. Cut in lard. Sprinkle with cold water (using more or less as needed) in order to form a ball. Roll out on floured board and use in your favorite recipes for pie.

Homemade suet for birds

When your hankering for cracklin's lands you with more lard than you need, you can always make a special treat for the birds out of excess or old lard.

```
lard
peanut butter
wild bird feed (a mix of seeds and
    grain)
corn meal (if you wish)
```

Mix above ingredients not bothering to worry about measures. What you want is a combination that you can form into balls or shape into cakes. A neat idea is to take this mixture and, using your hands, press it into pinecones. These hang very nicely from your backyard trees and the birds seem to fancy them.

The best eggs in the world are those that are fried in homemade lard. The only way to prove this is by testing for yourself! Chicken, liver, steak, potatoes, onions ... almost any fryable is so much tastier when done in lard. Just try it! Δ

Portable fence panels: the homesteader's friend

by Jackie Clay

It seems that things are always changing on our homestead. Last year, the biggest garden was 100 by 150 feet. This year, we doubled its size. And because we have plenty of deer and free-range poultry, this garden must be fenced. In it, we grow our most critter-prone vegetables: sweet corn, broccoli, cabbage, cauliflower, tomatoes, and peppers. (They pretty much leave the other crops alone.)

You can see why we don't put up a permanent wire fence around the garden. There are other places a portable fence is needed: the chicken yard, hay stack and strawberry beds, for instance.

For years, we monkeyed around with Mickey Mouse fencing, and were always disappointed. Even high electric fence did not keep the deer out, and it certainly didn't bother the chickens. Finally, after hauling home a large truckload of "firewood" from a post and pole mill, I had a great idea.

A good part of that load was 12-foot long, two-inch diameter poles that were too thin for the debarking machine to peel. And I certainly wasn't about to cut all those nice poles into stove wood.

These poles were the basis for our niftiest invention yet—portable fence panels. These panels can be as wide as your poles, but 10 and 12 feet seem to work out best. Wider and they tend to be heavy and flimsy. Narrower and you need too many fence posts on the fence line.

Uses for portable fence panels

The thing I like about portable fence panels is the variety of applications they can be used for. With livestock, they are excellent temporary fencing for goats, sheep, and calves. Poultry can effectively be kept in—or out with this fence.

We fence around our haystack in the fall to keep out deer, bighorn sheep, and elk, and around the gardens in the spring and summer for the same reason.

Portable fence panels work well as temporary gates or pens in a shed.

I also use the panels to trellis up beans, cucumbers and other vining crops. Lean them together at the top, and you have a temporary support for plastic, in case of an unexpected freeze.

I'm confident that you can think of other uses for these portable panels. They are truly versatile and nearly free.

Construction materials

You can use just about any straight poles but they should be of two inches in diameter at a minimum. Of course you can use heavier poles, but the panel will be heavier and cease to be portable. If you use thinner poles, the panel will not last as long because it will break more easily.

We've used lodgepole pine, but cedar, oak, and even aspen or poplar would work.

By peeling the bark off the poles, they will rot much slower and therefore last much longer than unpeeled poles which collect moisture. Likewise, if you take the time to slap a coat of sealant stain on them, you will add several years to their life.

I use 6-foot poles for the uprights on either end. If it's leaping deer that you want to fence out, I'd suggest going another foot higher. Our deer don't bother jumping the 5½-foot fence, but we could tack a wire on the top if one decided to become airborne.

We tack the panels together with 16-penny nails. This gives good strong joints and the nails don't poke through the uprights.

Panel construction

We quickly learned that we needed a pattern to speed up building. Without the pattern, we spent way too much time measuring and marking. Therefore, the first fence panel we made that met our satisfaction became our pattern. The others became garden trellises, etc.

Take two poles and lay them out 8½ feet apart if you are going to use 10-foot cross poles or 10½ feet if you are going to use 12-foot poles. You want from 5 to 10 inches of "overlap" which sticks out past the uprights for the most utility when you put them up.

Our panels have the cross poles nailed on from the bottom up in this order: 8, 10, 12, and 18-inch spacing between the poles, not on center. Make one up and take a look, deciding on what you will be using it the most for, then either use that for the pattern or change it to suit your needs.

One nail (or screw) in the center of each pole is adequate; two will split the pole. Take care to keep the entire panel square as you nail on rails. One or more helpers, along with a large square is more than useful. Things bounce around and get out of square as you pound.

You'll notice that this panel is very flimsy. That is why it is necessary to nail on two brace poles as an inverted V from halfway down the "leg" of the upright post to the center of the top rail. We use the same diameter poles for the entire panel, including these braces.

To add the diagonal braces, have your helper get hold of one side of the panel and you take the other. Carefully turn it over and square it again.

Mark the center of the panel on the top rail and lay a pole in position. Then, taking a chain saw, trim the angle needed for the bottom of the brace. Have your helper hold the brace in place at the top, then spike the leg to the bottom of the brace pole. Then go around and do the top, followed up by a nail through the brace into each of the five cross poles. Again, take care that the whole panel stays square. It's easy to mess up by getting in a hurry at this point.

The reason that I don't trim the top off before I nail it is that if you do this, the pole will usually split when

These panels are so quick to build. My husband, Bob, and I do three in one hour.

you drive a nail through it. (Using screws with a battery-powered drill will cause fewer splits.)

Repeat with the other diagonal brace, completing the upside-down V and your panel. Again, be sure to keep the panel square when you nail (or screw) the second brace in place.

Now you are ready to trim the panel to fit. I don't bother to trim each pole before I build the panel. It's much quicker and easier to trim it afterward. Do make sure that all uprights are the same height. When laying out the panels, I always keep the "feet" the same length, for ease of measuring for the cross poles.

Voilà! You have just made a portable fence panel. The first will take awhile, but remember, this is your pattern, which will make all the others go so much faster.

These panels work. This is me in my critter-free garden.

So go at it again, only this time lay out your poles on top of your pattern panel. I've found that if you tack each upright pole to a center cross pole on a diagonal so you don't get the nail in your way, it greatly helps keep things square.

In less than 15 minutes, you and a helper can spike together the next rough panel, less the braces. Now pull those temporary nails and carefully pick up the panel and carry it end-for-end and set the "feet" on the ground. Carefully lay the panel down on top of the pattern. In this way, you'll get the diagonal braces exactly the same. This looks much nicer on a fence than random measurements. And it ensures that each panel is as strong as the next.

Unless you have two helpers, it's best to again temporarily spike the upright to the upright beneath it in the center. I put these nails about two inches from a cross pole, which lets me use the pole as a block to pull out the nail nice and straight. (I reuse my nails—like I do almost everything else.)

Critter-proofing

Deer, bighorn sheep, moose, and elk do not jump or crawl through these fence panels. But chickens or cottontail rabbits would simply duck and walk under. So we add a two foot high strip of two inch chicken wire to the bottom of each panel. Of course this would not deter a very determined woodchuck or raccoon (more on that later), but it will keep out most any poultry or bunny—and also your pet dog who might tramp on the garden plants. Notice, I said keep your dog out. This fence will not contain a dog, as chicken wire is not strong enough.

To re-enforce these fence panels for goats or sheep, you need to add a four foot strip of 2 x 4 heavy-gauge welded or woven wire. By stapling the wire to each individual panel, you will keep them portable, and thus, much more useful than if you staple the entire roll of wire to, say 100-feet of fence.

But, say you have persistent varmints (or even neighbor pets) that you need to keep out. You can further reenforce this fence with one or more strands of electric wire. For small critters, add a wire five inches up from the bottom. A stand-off wire three feet high will keep stray goats and sheep from trying to push through or climb on your fence. This fence is made by nailing plastic stand-off insulators to the fence, which holds the wire about five inches out from the poles. Therefore, the animal contacts the wire before getting on or near the fence panel.

Add a top hot wire if your neighborhood deer are prone to leaping. Tie a few white, fluttering bits of plastic or cloth to it, so they realize there *is* a wire way up there.

Putting up your fence panels

In small areas, it is usually best to anchor each end of your portable panel to a six-foot heavy duty T-post, driven well into the ground. The smaller the area, the more stress to the fence, especially if you are fencing a critter in, rather than out. I use a heavy, but bendable electric fence wire to wire each panel tightly to the T-posts' top, middle, and bottom and never yet have had an animal escape.

On longer runs, such as in my garden, I often pound a T-post at the end of a panel, then a sharpened 3-inch wood post at the other end, fastening

We have just finished this panel. (It's upside-down.) It shows the pattern panel underneath.

the next panel to that, then another steel post on the other end of that panel, so your posts are in this order: steel, wood, steel, wood, etc. It makes a strong fence, yet is half the cost of an all T-post fence. If you are short, like I am, you may have to stand on the tailgate of your pickup or on a sturdy ladder to pound those wood posts with a maul. You can't use a T-post driver on them.

When erecting portable panels to protect a haystack, use all steel posts, and make your "corral" large enough that animals won't try to reach through to nibble on the hay. That spells doom to lightweight fence panels. If necessary, you can either make haystack panels out of heavier posts and rails or add a stand-off electric wire about four feet high, all around the fence.

But I have no power

No problem. We don't have power, either, and have an electric wire inside most of our existing fence to strengthen it and make it last longer. One of the best investments we've made has been a solar electric fencer. Not only does it protect our fence, but also our garden, and it keeps stray cats and raccoons out of our bluebird houses. It's amazing what a little strand of hot wire will do. Ask at a farm and ranch supply store. Our fencer cost $100 on sale and has worked faithfully year-round without any maintenance or trouble. A neighbor has had his (same model as ours) for years with great luck.

Using portable panels as garden trellises

While heavier vines will climb the portable fence panels without support, we've found that adding some sort of netting (nylon, old field fence, or even twine) pays big dividends on the growth of plants up the trellis.

Use a steel T-post on either end of the trellis, as wind will blow it down if you don't. All those plant vines and leaves will create a "wall" for the strong wind to blow against.

By using these trellises, you will be able to grow more in the same space. Even cukes love to be trellised, even if you have to "help" them by gently tying them here and there. And they'll reward you by hanging clean and straight. Right where you can easily pick them.

These portable fence panels make such great trellises, as they are so sturdy, they will hold a bounty year after year with no wear and tear. You may have to replace a twine net on one, but the poles are good to go for years. And, being portable, you can change your garden to suit your needs and yank all your trellises in 15 minutes.

Whatever material you have at hand, I hope you'll give our portable fence panels a try. We've scarcely anything else on the place that is so versatile, long lasting...or *cheap*. I figured it out that each panel cost us 28¢. Not bad, huh? ∆

Hingeless gate

By Clay Sawyer

Build an easy "no cost" gate using your hardwood and black polypropylene pipe. (Don't use PVC pipe as it will degrade in sunlight.) No poly pipe on hand right now? Empty coffee cans can be used temporarily.

First cut poly pipe into sections using a hacksaw, then predrill all holes as shown in the diagram. The length of the poly pipe section will depend on the tree or post used. I would suggest making them as long as possible for stability. Screws should be at least 2½" long. Once the poly pipe sections are secured, measure and cut hardwood lengths so that at least one foot overhangs on each end, the width determined by the circumference of the poly pipe used. Every two years or so the hardwood will need replacing, but the poly pipe will last indefinitely. ∆

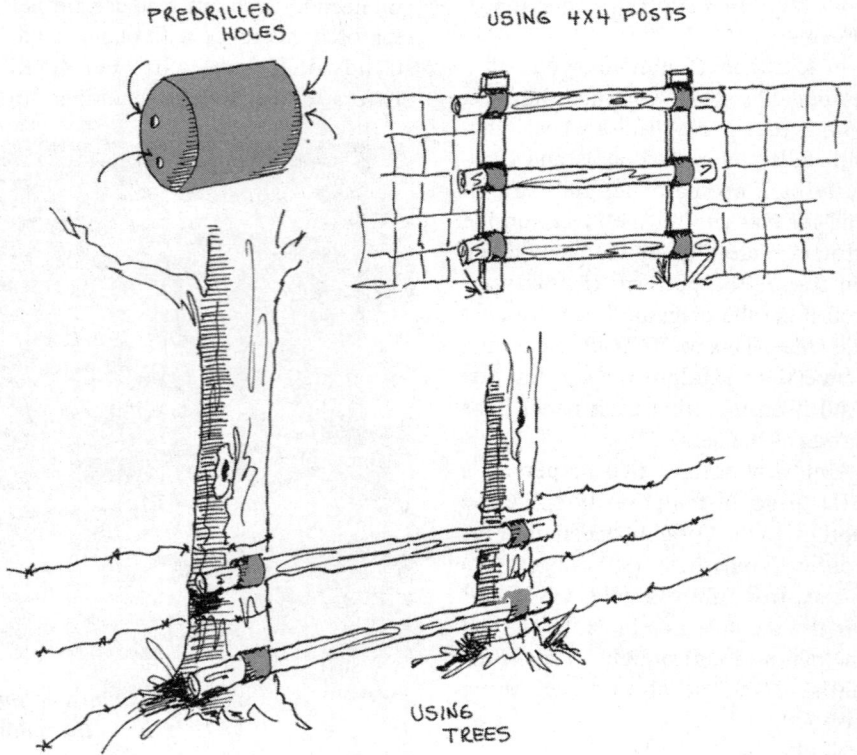

Preserving fish

By Tom R. Kovach

The four most popular methods of fish preservation are freezing, canning, pickling, and smoking. Here are some tips for each.

Remember, top quality fresh fish are essential for fish prservation. Of all flesh foods, fish is the most susceptible to tissue decomposition, development of rancidity, and microbial spoilage. Keep freshly caught fish alive as long as possible. Fish begin to deteriorate as soon as they leave the water. To delay spoilage, clean the fish as soon as possible. Thorough cleaning of the body cavity and chilling of the fish will prevent spoilage.

Freezing

This is the simplest, most convenient, and most highly recommended method of fish preservation. A good quality frozen product requires careful handling of the fish after catching, wrapping in material that is airtight, and a freezer storage temperature of 0° F or lower.

To freeze fish: Remove the guts and thoroughly clean the fish. Prepare the fish as you would for table use. Cut large fish into steaks or fillets. Freeze small fish whole.

Wrap the fish in heavy-duty aluminum foil, plastic wrap, or heavy-duty freezer bags. Separate layers of fish with two thicknesses of packaging material for easier thawing. Store at 0° F or lower. Thaw in refrigerator when ready.

Small fish (pan fish or small servings) can be frozen in ice. Place the fish in a shallow pan or watertight container, cover with ice water, and place in freezer until frozen. Remove block from container, wrap, and store in freezer.

The storage life of good quality frozen fish held at 0° F or lower: Northern pike, lake trout, and smelt: four to six months. Bluegills, bass, crappies, and sunfish: seven to nine months. Walleys and yellow perch: nine months or more.

Canning

Fish is a low acid food and can be processed safely only at temperatures reached in a steam pressure canner. Failure to heat process fish at 240° F or higher may allow spores of the dangerous heat-resistant bacteria, *Clostridium botulinum,* to survive, germinate, and grow. The poison produced by botulinum bacteria causes botulism, a deadly food poisoning. The addition of small amounts of vinegar, or packing in tomato juice or tomato paste, does not remove the requirement for heat processing fish in a pressure canner.

Use standard heat-tempered canning jars. All processing times mentioned here are for 1-pint containers. Do not use quart jars because of slower heat penetration.

The general USDA method for canning fish without sauce includes blue, mackeral, salmon, steelhead, trout, and other fatty fish except tuna.

Clean and gut fish within two hours after catching. Keep cleaned fish on ice until ready to can.

Note: Glass-like crystals of magnesium ammonium phosphate sometimes form in canned salmon. There is no way for the home canner to prevent these crystals from forming, but they usually dissolve when heated and are safe to eat.

Remove head, tail, fins, and scales. Wash and remove all blood. Split fish lengthwise, if desired. Cut cleaned fish into 3½-inch lengths. Fill pint jars, skin side next to glass, leaving 1-inch headspace. Add 1 teaspoon of salt per pint. Don't add liquids. Adjust lids and process.

Recommended processing for a dial-guage pressure canner is 100 minutes at 11 PSI. For a weighed-guage pressure canner, 100 minutes at 15 PSI.

Remove jars from canner. Place jars upright on a dry, nonmetallic surface (towels, board, or newspaper may be used). Heat fish to boiling temperatures for 10 minutes before tasting.

Pickling

Pickling is an easy method of preserving fish, but remember to refrigerate the fish during all stages of the pickling.

Ingredients:

Fish—use only fresh, high quality fish

Water—avoid hard water, as it causes off color and flavors

Vinegar—use distilled, white vinegar with an acetic acid content of at least 4% (40 grains)

Salt—use high grade canning or picling salt

Spices—best results when fresh, whole spices are used

General method for precooked pickled fish:

Soak fish in a weak brine (1 cup salt to 1 gallon of water) for one hour. Drain the fish, pack in heavy glass, crock, enamel, or plastic container in a strong brine (2½ cups salt to 1 gallon of water) for 12 hours in the refrigerator. Rinse the fish in cold water.

Combine the following ingredients in a large pan or kettle:

¼ oz. bay leaves
2 Tbsp. allspice
2 Tbsp. mustard seed
1 Tbsp. whole cloves
1 Tbsp. pepper, ground
½ Tbsp. hot, ground dried pepper
½ lb. onions, sliced
2 qt. distilled vinegar
5 cups water

Bring to boil, add fish, and simmer for 10 minutes until fish is easily pierced with a fork.

Remove fish from liquid, place on a flat pan. Refrigerate and cool quickly to avoid spoilage. Pack cold fish in clean glass jars, adding a few whole spices, a bay leaf, freshly sliced onions, and a slice of lemon. Strain the vinegar solution, bring to a boil, and pour into jars until fish is covered.

Seal the jar immediately with two-part sealing lid.

Smoking

Smoking has long been used as a means of temporarily preserving fish. The steps in the smoking process are necessary not only for safe preservation, but also to produce good flavor and aroma. Carp, suckers, buffalo catfish, salmon, trout, and chubs may be sucessfully smoked.

Use the correct amount of salt in the brine. Use enough brine for a given amount of fish. The temperature must be no higher than 40° F. Use similar size and kinds of fish.

There should be uniform heat in the smoking chamber. Fish flesh should be maintained at 180° F for the total smoking period.

Steps for safe smoking:

- Use freshly caught fish, whole or filleted. Wash fish. Fish for smoking must be brined.
- 1½ cup salt to 1 gal. water for 12 hours in the refrigerator, remove the fish *then* place in a mixture of 4 cups salt to 1 gal. cold water for 15 minutes.
- Remove from brine, rinse. Place short stem of meat thermometer in thickest portion of flesh of largest fish. Put fish in smoker when air temperature is 100° F (you need a second thermometer to measure this). During smoking, air temperature should rise to 225° F. Fish flesh should reach 180° F and be kept there for 30 minutes. Fish flesh must be stored in refrigerator. Use within one month. Δ

The Fourteenth Year

the gee-whiz! page
By O.E. MacDougal

Heroes of the Old West

Bat Masterson, legendary gun fighter, gambler, and friend of Wyatt Earp, was a Canadian. At the end of his life he lived in New York City where he was a respected sports writer for the New York Morning Telegraph. He died of a heart attack at his desk in the offices of the Telegraph in New York City at age 65.

Doc Holliday, another of Earp's friends and also a gunfighter who accompanied Earp and his brothers in the gunfight at the OK Corral, was by profession a dentist. He "died with his boots on" succumbing to tuberculosis in a Denver sanitarium at age 37.

Wyatt Earp himself, a legendary lawman, was actually a lawman for only 6 of his 81 years. At various times in his life he was wanted for murder, running a confidence game, cattle rustling, and horse theft. Later in life he appeared as an extra in at least one Hollywood movie and when he died, movie legends Tom Mix and William S. Hart were among his pallbearers.

Right and left

People are not only right or left-handed, they're also right or left-footed and right or left-eyed. Being right handed doesn't necessarily mean you're right-footed or right-eyed. Such a condition is known as "crossed dominance." (I'm right-handed and right-footed, but I'm left-eyed.)

The world's highest mountain

What's the highest mountain on earth? The answer depends on what you mean by "highest."

The peak with its top furthest above sea level is Mt. Everest, at 29,035 feet. But Mt. Everest and all of the other mountains in the Himalayan range sits on land that is already well above sea level. The highest mountain from base to peak is Alaska's Mt. McKinley.

Everest isn't even the "highest" point on earth. Little known Mt. Chimborazo, an extinct volcano in Ecuador, is the highest, although it is only 20,561 feet high. The reason is that the earth is widest at the equator where Chimborazo sits. This places its peak 10,560 feet further from the center of the earth than Everest's.

But all we've been talking about here are mountains above sea level. To many, the highest mountain of all is Mauna Kea, which is the highest mountain in Hawaii. When measured from the ocean floor it is 33,476 feet high.

Things that can get you sent to hell

Until the Italian inventors, Gasparo Berti and Evangelista Torricelli, independently invented the barometer, and in doing so created the first sustained man-made vacuum, it was thought that a vacuum couldn't exist. The belief was that "nature abhors a vacuum" and the concept was so strong it became part of Catholic doctrine. In fact, the Church excommunicated anyone who defended the idea that a vacuum could exist or that one could be produced by man.

David vs Goliath

We all know the biblical story of David and Goliath. Their confrontation has become a cliché for a little guy, David, in contest with a giant, Goliath. But the fact is, David was always the favorite in that confrontation. What we don't understand about slings today is that in the hands of a trained slinger, a sling was a weapon of certain destruction.

Slings used in ancient times had nothing in common with the slingshots young boys make today, and slingers were as accurate with their weapons as archers were with theirs. Until the development of the compound bow, slingers could hurl their missiles beyond the range of an archer. Roman slingers trained to throw their stones at a distance of 200 yards, but ranges of a quarter mile were possible and enemy troops were often in more danger from slingers than from archers.

And what they hurled were not "pebbles" but stones that ranged in size from as small as a golf ball to as large as your fist; they were thrown faster than Randy Johnson can throw a baseball and with deadly accuracy that's hard to appreciate today. The larger stones could smash skulls, break bones, penetrate the body, and even penetrate much of the armor used in ancient times. Some "stones" were even cast from dense clay and others from lead to establish uniform size and weight which ensured consistent range and accuracy.

So, on the day they met, Goliath may have been almost 10 feet tall, carried a sword, and worn armor, but the smart money was on the guy carrying the sling.

THE IRREVERENT JOKE PAGE

(Believing it is important for people to be able to laugh at themselves, this is a continuing feature in *Backwoods Home Magazine*. We invite readers to submit any jokes you'd like to share to *BHM*, P.O. Box 712, Gold Beach, OR 97444. There is no payment for jokes used.)

A man requested a female blonde painter to paint him in the nude.

"No," the talented blonde artist said. "I don"t do that sort of thing."

"I'll increase your fee two times," he said.

"No, no thanks."

"I'll give five times as much as you normally get."

She thought about this. "Okay," she finally said, "But you have to let me at least wear my socks. I need somewhere to place my brushes."

A lawyer awakened after a serious operation only to find himself in a room with all the blinds drawn.

"Why are all the blinds closed?" he asked the doctor.

"Well," the surgeon responded, "They're fighting a huge fire across the street, and we didn't want you to wake up and think the operation had failed."

Once there was an explorer lost in the deepest part of the Amazon. After a few days, he finds himself suddenly surrounded by hundreds of bloodthirsty natives.

He looks up to the sky and says, "Oh my God, I'm screwed!!"

All of a sudden, the sky opens up, and then there is a beam of light streaming down on him, and a voice booms out, "No, you are NOT screwed. Pick up that stone at your foot, and smash it onto the skull of the chief."

So the explorer looks down, and sees the stone. He picks it up, and bashes the life out of the chief, who is standing right in front of him. And he stands on the chief, triumphant, huffing and puffing, with the bloody stone in his hand.

And the chief is down on the ground, bleeding and lifeless, with his tribesmen in shock and disbelief.

Now, the sky opens up once again, and the voice booms out... "NOW, you're screwed."

ATM INSTRUCTIONS

To enable customers to use this new facility the following procedures have been established. Please read the procedure that applies to your own circumstances and remember them when you use the machine for the first time:

MEN
1) Drive up to the cash machine.
2) Lower your car window.
3) Insert card into machine and enter PIN.
4) Enter amount of cash required and withdraw.
5) Retrieve card, cash, and receipt.
6) Raise window.
7) Drive off.

WOMEN
1) Drive up to cash machine.
2) Backup to align car window to machine.
3) Set parking break, lower the window.
4) Find handbag, remove all contents on to passenger seat to locate card.
5) Turn the radio down.
6) Attempt to insert card into machine.
7) Open car door to allow easier access to machine due to its excessive distance from the car.
8) Insert card.
9) Re-insert card right side up.
10) Dig through handbag to find diary with your PIN written on the inside back page.
11) Enter PIN.
12) Press cancel and re-enter correct PIN.
13) Enter amount of cash required.
14) Check make up in rear view mirror.
15) Retrieve cash and receipt.
16) Empty handbag again to locate wallet and place cash inside.
17) Place receipt in back of checkbook.
18) Re-check make-up.
19) Drive two feet forward.
20) Back up to cash machine.
21) Retrieve card.
22) Re-empty hand bag, locate card holder, and place card into the slot provided.
23) Give appropriate one-fingered hand signal to irate male drivers waiting behind.
24) Restart stalled engine and drive away.
25) Drive for 2 to 3 miles.
26) Release parking break.

The Fourteenth Year

How to be a good liberal

1. You have to believe the AIDS virus is spread by a lack of federal funding.

2. You have to believe that the same teacher who can't teach 4th graders how to read is somehow qualified to teach those same kids about sex.

3. You have to believe that guns in the hands of law-abiding Americans are more of a threat, than U.S. nuclear weapons technology in the hands of Chinese communists.

4. You have to believe that there was no art before Federal funding.

5. You have to believe that global temperatures are less affected by cyclical, documented changes in the earth's climate, and more affected by yuppies driving SUVs.

6. You have to believe that gender roles are artificial but being homosexual is natural.

7. You have to be against capital punishment but support abortion on demand.

8. You have to believe that businesses create oppression and governments create prosperity.

9. You have to believe that hunters don't care about nature, but loony activists who've never been outside of Seattle do.

10. You have to believe that self-esteem is more important than actually doing something to earn it.

11. You have to believe the military, not corrupt politicians, start wars.

12. You have to believe the NRA is bad, because it supports certain parts of the Constitution, while the ACLU is good because it supports certain parts of the Constitution.

13. You have to believe that taxes are too low, but ATM fees are too high.

14. You have to believe that Margaret Sanger and Gloria Steinem are more important to American history than Thomas Jefferson, General Robert E. Lee, or Thomas Edison.

15. You have to believe that standardized tests are racist, but racial quotas and set-asides aren't.

16. You have to believe Hillary Clinton is really a lady.

17. You have to believe that the only reason socialism hasn't worked anywhere it's been tried, is because the right people haven't been in charge.

18. You have to believe conservatives telling the truth belong in jail, but a liar and sex offender belongs in the White House.

19. You have to believe that homosexual parades displaying drag, transvestites, and bestiality should be constitutionally protected and manger scenes at Christmas should be illegal.

20. You have to believe that illegal Democratic Party funding by the Chinese is somehow in the best interest of the United States.

21. You have to believe that this piece is part of a vast right wing conspiracy.

Half a lawyer

Two women came before wise King Solomon, dragging between them a young man in a three-piece suit.

"This young lawyer agreed to marry my daughter," said one.

"No! He agreed to marry MY daughter," said the other.

And so they haggled before the King until he called for silence.

"Bring me my biggest sword," said Solomon, "and I shall hew the young attorney in half. Each of you shall receive a half."

"Sounds good to me," said the first lady.

But the other woman said, "Oh Sire, do not spill innocent blood. Let the other woman's daughter marry him."

The wise king did not hesitate a moment. "The attorney must marry the first lady's daughter," he proclaimed.

"But she was willing to hew him in two!" exclaimed the king's court.

"Indeed," said wise King Solomon. "That shows she is the TRUE mother-in-law."

A group of hunters, sitting around the campfire, got to talking about the worst pain they had ever experienced. One listened quietly as the others told their tales of woe. Finally, it was his turn. He said:

"Well, the second worst pain I ever experienced happened a few years ago. I was hunting then too, and I really had to go to the bathroom. I looked around and seeing no one, I went behind a tree, pulled my pants down and squatted. But I didn't realize I was right over a bear trap and, suddenly, it snapped shut on my testicles."

The other men winced and one said, "Oh, that must have hurt. But if that was the second worst pain you've ever experienced, what was the worst?"

"When I hit the end of the chain."

Mountain and winter driving

By Don Fallick

Every year, many people die needlessly while driving in the mountains. It's a shame; a little bit of forethought could prevent most of these tragedies. Mountain driving is different. It's always colder in the mountains than it is down on the flatland. Fall and winter come early at higher elevations, spring comes late, and summers are short and cool. In many parts of the mountains the snow never leaves, while others are subject to snowstorms, even blizzards that would be unseasonable anywhere else. So it's important to always be prepared for an emergency when driving in the mountains.

Light snow flurries, with an inch or less of snow on the ground, call for driving techniques very similar to rainy weather. Turn your lights on, slow down, allow extra room for stopping, and be very courteous to other drivers. Serious snow is deeper, thicker, icier, or wind-driven and drifting. If cars are sliding around on the road, or sliding off it, it's time to chicken out and find a motel. If you have never driven in serious snow or ice, get someone with experience to teach you. Learning by yourself is often learning the hard way, and it's never fun.

Of course, you may not have much choice. If you get caught unexpectedly in serious snow conditions, you may just have to cope with them anyway. There are four main dangers in snow driving. You may lose control, you may get stuck, your vision is certain to be restricted, and the other drivers on the road share these problems.

Maintaining control

Losing control poses the biggest immediate danger. You can slide into other cars, into ditches, even off cliffs. Driving too fast for conditions and inadequate traction are the main culprits. If you have a pickup truck, make sure there is enough weight in

If you start to spin out, immediately remove your foot from the accelerator and steer the car in the "direction of the skid."

the bed to hold the rear wheels down. A load of firewood is about right. Don't try to brake on slippery surfaces. Unless you are going perfectly straight, you are sure to swap ends. Even if you are going perfectly straight, hitting the brakes on snow or ice can cause you to spin out. So can applying the accelerator pedal abruptly, or shifting to too low a gear. If you have a manual transmission, try starting in second gear to reduce torque, and stay in as high a gear as you can. With an automatic, stay in Drive. If you do start to spin out, immediately remove your foot from the accelerator pedal and steer the car in the "direction of the skid." You may find that your car is going the way you want it to, but not pointing exactly the way it's going. Don't worry about it. It's much more important for the car to be under your control than to look like it. More on skids later.

Busting drifts

Leave lots and lots of stopping room between you and any cars ahead, even if you have to just creep along. The one exception to such slow speeds is when the snow is drifting across the road. If you go slow, the drifts will stop you, and you will not be able to get out. You would then face a serious winter survival situation. The way to beat drifting snow is to keep up enough speed to bust through the drifts. There's an art to it. The drifts will be thinner on the downwind end than on the upwind end, so it's usually a good idea to try to bust through the downwind end. But be aware that the snow will tend to "suck" the car in toward the center of the drift. If the drift angles across the road at a sharp angle, with the downwind end closest to you, it may be safer to try to bust the upwind end, where you will be

The Fourteenth Year

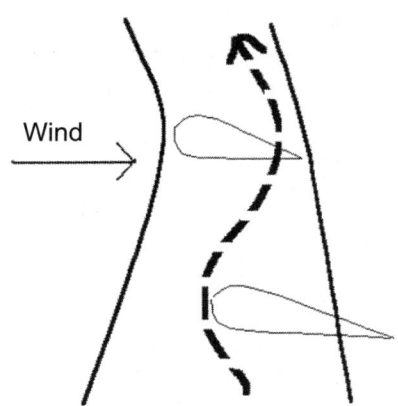

Busting snowdrifts in normal conditions: Avoid the upwind (deep) ends of the snowdrifts.

Chains

Not all cars are fit for snow tires or "serious" chains. The auto parts dealer who sells chains will tell you what sort are appropriate for your car. Carry a set of the proper size and type of chains whenever you travel in snow country. After the snow storm hits it's too late to buy them. You may not be able to drive to the store, and if you can get there, they will likely be sold out. There are three basic types of chains. So-called "cable-chains" are light weight, light duty devices suitable only for city driving. They don't work well, or last long, but they are the only kind of chains that will fit on most un-modified passenger cars without beating the wheel wells to pieces. They won't get you out of really deep snow, but may help keep you from getting stuck in snow up to two inches deep.

Regular chains, with cross-chains of real chain and elastic side-chain tighteners, are made for trucks, vans, and other vehicles with higher clearance around the wheels. They are heavy, take up lots of room, and are difficult to put on. They cost about twice as much as cable chains, but can handle deep snow up to six inches, depending on the size of the chain links. They generally last for years of seasonal use.

Whichever kind you have, you will want a pair of Channel-lok pliers to put them on with, a piece of cardboard or a tarp to lie on in the snow while putting them on, and some light-gauge wire for temporary repairs. If your chains require elastic side-chain tighteners, keep a spare or two, with hooks. Elastic tighteners are always breaking, and hooks are always getting lost. You will probably need to work bare-handed in putting on and taking off chains, so keep a pair of warm gloves or mittens for warming up afterward.

All chains go on the same way. Lay them out neatly behind the drive

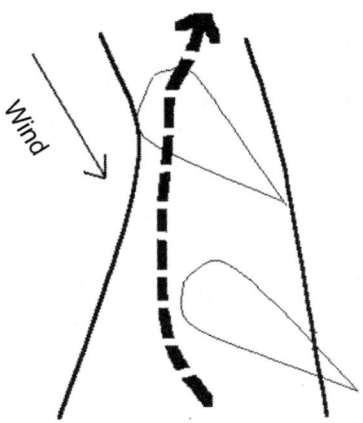

If drifts are angling toward you, it may be best to hit the deep end to avoid getting "sucked into" the entire drift

wheel tires (rear-wheel drive) or in front of front-wheel drive tires and drive onto them. Grab the rear ends of the chain and bring them over the top of the tire, until you can hook the inside chain. Then work the chains around until they will allow you to hook the outside chain. Try to get the inside and outside chains equally tight. Then do the other wheel. If you have cable chains, you will not have elastic tighteners to worry about, but if you have regular chains, put the tighteners on, hooking as many hooks into the outside side-chain as necessary to pull it tight. Drive a half a mile or so and re-tighten, regardless of which kind you have. Thereafter, check tightness every five or ten miles. If you end up with loose chain ends banging against the wheel well, tie them down with the light-gauge wire so they can't flop around.

Remove chains as soon as you are not driving on snow any more. Driving on hard pavement is a surefire way to stretch, or even ruin, any kind of chains. Let them dry, and store them where they can be reached easily. You will probably need to remove and replace them several times in one trip. Don't worry if you have a hard time putting them on or taking them off. It doesn't get much

past most of the drift by the time you hit snow. Even drifts that appear small and flat can be nearly a foot deep and 10 or 15 feet across. You have to hit them quite hard to carry you all the way through the drift. Speeds of 45 to 50 miles per hour may be required. You are taking quite a risk, because speeds like that are enough to get you very thoroughly stuck if you fail to bust a drift, or if one sucks you off the road. Do not even attempt to bust snow drifts without snow tires or chains.

Snow tires are more than just "all season radials." They are made with big, deep treads that look much like off-road tires, but they are made of special rubber that remains flexible at cold temperatures. They may not help much on ice. One of Mother Nature's meanest tricks is "black ice." It is completely invisible, and does not look icy, but is slipperier than calf snot. Most people cannot even stand up on black ice. Even snow tires will not help. If you hit black ice at even one or two mph you will not be able to stop. Studded tires, siped tires, or walnut-shell recaps may give you some purchase on black ice. But they may not help much on serious, deep snow. Only four-wheel drive, chains, or both are likely to help in real deep snow.

59

easier with practice, either. Nobody likes chains.

Stuck in the snow

If you drive in snow very much, sooner or later you will get stuck. If you are on a major highway, you can call a tow truck and pay the driver $50 to pull you out. If the storm struck suddenly, you may have to wait a long time. While you are waiting, see if you can dig yourself out. Any time you drive in snow country, you should have a shovel in your trunk. A snow shovel works best, but any kind will do. A short-handled, flat-nosed garden shovel fits easily in the trunk without taking up much room, and works equally well in snow, sand, or mud.

Clear snow away from each of the tires, and shovel paths for the tires to the nearest clear pavement. Usually, this will be behind the car, but not always. There will probably be hard-packed snow under the car too. It will hold the drive wheels off the pavement, so you have to remove it too. A relatively narrow shovel like the garden shovel mentioned above works well for excavating under the car. People who live in the country often carry a regular snow shovel as well as a very narrow post-hole shovel, for under-car excavation.

The road may be icy beneath the snow. If it is, sprinkle some traction sand (sold in ten-pound bags at grocery stores in snow country) on the pavement. Kitty litter works even better, and costs less, and it won't add much weight to your trunk. Then try to drive out of the snow. If you can't, see if someone with four-wheel drive can pull you out. It's helpful to have a tow chain, tow strap, or at least a stout rope in the trunk for this purpose. Start the car and try to drive it out while the other driver pulls. It's polite to offer a tip, but they will probably refuse it. Have your exhaust system tested as soon as possible. You may have knocked something loose, allowing carbon monoxide gas into the car. It is colorless, odorless, and deadly.

Winter emergency

If you are in a real blizzard, you may not be able to get out, or even get any help at all. Getting stuck in the snow can be an adventure, a nuisance, or a life-threatening catastrophe, depending on your state of preparedness and how long you are stuck. If you are beyond quick help, you have only two options: abandon your car or prepare to spend the night. **Do not** abandon the car unless you are certain that you can reach shelter right away. If a four-wheeler or snowmobiler comes to your rescue, that would qualify. So would walking to a nearby house that you can see clearly through the snow, if you know the path is clear. The rule in a blizzard is, "If you can't see it, don't go looking." Drifting snow can change the landscape in less than five minutes, making it totally unrecognizable and getting you hopelessly lost. People die every year this way. **Stay with your car**.

If you wait out a blizzard in your car, dig out the snow around your tailpipe before you settle in. You may need to run the engine to keep warm part of the time, and the engine won't run if the tailpipe is plugged with snow. Try to find some way to protect it from blowing or drifting snow. Also, clear snow from at least one of the car doors, so you can get out. If you have warm clothes and blankets in the car, it's best not to run the engine for heat at all. You could have knocked part of the exhaust system loose when you got stuck. Running the engine could fill the car with deadly carbon monoxide. You'd never even know it. If there is more than one person in the car, huddle together for warmth. One "space blanket" can keep two people warm enough to survive this way. If you absolutely must run the engine for heat, run it just long enough to warm up the car, then shut it off. There won't be enough gas to run it all night anyway. You might as well conserve gas and minimize the carbon monoxide danger too. Don't play the radio more than a few minutes when the engine is not running. You want to be able to start the motor after the blizzard quits.

Melt snow to drink by putting it in a cup or other container inside the car. Eating snow will make you thirstier in the long run, as you lose precious body heat. You'll do much better if you have some hard candy or other source of energy on hand. Beef jerky is not good for winter survival. It makes you thirsty. Even if you have plenty of water handy, you will have to pee a lot, losing body heat in the process. If you don't have food, plan to sleep a lot. Remember the Eskimos' saying, "Sleep is food."

The worst danger in winter survival is not snow, but wind. Snow is actually a pretty good insulator. Stay inside the car and out of the wind as much as possible. Nevertheless, you do not want to get buried. Check every two

> **What to carry**
> *Inside the car:*
> Snow brush/scraper
> Space blankets
> Fresh water
> Container for melting snow
> Hard candy
> Warm gloves or mittens
> Cell phone
> Flashlight
> *In the trunk:*
> Snow shovel & narrow shovel
> Jumper cables
> Tow chain or rope
> Kitty litter or traction sand
> Chains, tighteners, hooks, wire
> Channel-lok pliers
> Tarp or cardboard

or three hours to make sure you are not completely covered. Let someone know where you are. If you have a cell phone, call 911. If you do get buried, at least they will know where to look.

Vision and visibility

Even if you don't get stuck in the snow, it can restrict your vision by piling up on your windshield, windows, and lights. Keep a combination snow brush/ice scraper in the car. If you get caught without one, any broom will do for brushing snow. A credit card often makes an acceptable emergency ice scraper. If the ice is thick or hard, it may ruin the credit card, so use an old one. Never use metal for scraping glass.

Be sure to clear snow from your headlights and tail lights, too. When it's snowing, drive with the headlights on in the daytime, so other drivers can see you better. Stop every so often to clear snow from the headlights. The heat of the bulbs usually is not enough to keep them clear.

A blizzard not only reduces your vision, it also tends to make you invisible to other drivers. So does fog. If either is thick enough, other drivers may be stopped right in the travel lane of the road. Do not over-drive your lights. Go slow enough that you can come to a complete stop in the distance that you can see. Don't use your high beams. The light will reflect back into your own eyes and blind you. "White-out" conditions, whether caused by blowing snow or fog, are extremely hazardous. If you cannot see the road or tell where its edges are, there is no way you can steer straight. Stop immediately on the road and wait for conditions to clear enough to drive off the road to park. Stay well off the road until conditions clear enough to drive. There are always idiots who go 50 mph in fog so thick they can't see their own hood ornaments. Don't get in their way.

Overheating

Air is denser at lower elevations and less dense at higher ones. Any time that you change elevation in either direction by 3000 feet or more, the air setting on your carburetor will be wrong. Your engine will not produce as much power as it used to, and may even run rough. If you are just passing through, it's probably not worthwhile adjusting the carburetor. But if you will be staying at a higher or lower elevation than normal for several days or longer, and you notice a change in your engine's performance or gas mileage, a simple, inexpensive carburetor adjustment will probably fix the problem. Any mechanic can make the adjustment in about 10 minutes, and there are no parts to buy, so charges should be minimal. You will need to have the carburetor readjusted when you get home.

Sometimes when driving up steep slopes, the engine can heat up high enough to vaporize the fuel in nearby fuel lines. The coolant contains alcohols and similar chemicals to prevent freezing in low temperatures. These chemicals also have relatively low boiling points, especially at low air pressure. When the engine is laboring hard, as in climbing a steep hill, at high elevations where the air pressure is lower, the engine can get hot enough to boil part of the coolant solution. This condition is called "vapor lock," and is more common in carbureted engines than in fuel-injected engines. The engine will begin running very rough, then will quit altogether.

The solution is to allow the engine to cool off, so the vaporized fuel in the lines can re-condense. Some drivers try to hurry the process by pouring cold water on the fuel lines or packing snow around them. **Don't do it!** It is very easy to spill cold water on the hot engine block, causing it to crack, and ruining the engine. A small crack may not make itself felt right away, but will allow engine coolant to contaminate the oil, destroying its lubricating ability and causing the internal engine parts to rust. A new engine costs several thousand dollars. It takes less than an hour for the engine to cool off by itself. Few people's time is that valuable.

If the vapor lock persists, **wait until the engine block is cool enough to rest your hand on**, then cool it further with cool water. The idea is to cool the vapor until it condenses. But remember, **NEVER pour water on a hot engine**. Be careful not to soak the spark plugs and other ignition parts, or the motor may not start. One highly-recommended trick to fix or prevent vapor lock is to clip ordinary, spring-type, wooden clothes pins to the hot fuel lines, to "draw the heat." I've never heard a satisfactory explanation of why this works, but it does.

Fuel-injected engines do not have carburetors to adjust. Nevertheless, they still need to be adjusted for altitude. And contrary to popular opinion, they are subject to vapor lock, though it is much less likely to occur in a fuel-injected engine. The solutions to these problems are the same as for carbureted engines—have the fuel/air mixture adjusted to compensate for major elevation changes, and let the engine cool off by itself.

Cooling help

The heater in your car is essentially just a second, small radiator. Hot coolant from the engine is forced through thin, flat tubes in a "heater core" while a fan blows air past them. The air thus heated is ducted into the passenger compartment of the car, and the coolant continues to the radiator, where it is further cooled before returning to the hot engine block. By opening the heat control to the "full hot" position and turning the fan to "high," you can assist your radiator's cooling ability by 20% or more. Overheating often happens in summer, when you don't really want extra heat. Nevertheless, do not run the air conditioner at the same time to cool off. Running the air conditioner places added strain on the engine, making it run hotter. The best strategy is to roll down the windows and run the heater as long as you can stand it, then stop the car and cool off.

Your engine is not the only part of your car that can overheat. If you are planning to pull a trailer over mountains, and you have an automatic transmission, it's a good idea to have an auxiliary transmission cooler installed as part of your towing package. The extra work of towing a heavy trailer up a steep hill makes the transmission heat up. Transmission fluid can get so hot that it bursts the seals. You lose all your fluid at once. The effect on your transmission is very much like what would happen in your engine if you lost all your oil at once. Melt down. But you have engine temperature and oil pressure gauges and warning lights to warn you of imminent engine problems. There is no instrumentation in your transmission. Prevention or risk are your only options. An auxiliary ATF cooler works and looks like a small radiator. It costs about $100, and can prevent thousands of dollars of damage to your automatic transmission. Any transmission shop can install one.

Driving techniques

There are techniques to mountain driving that cannot be taught in a book. Watching someone use them to safely negotiate the curves and switchbacks of a mountain pass at high speed can give you the idea that they are driving like maniacs. They are not. Locals buy special, high-altitude equipment and engines so they can drive in these conditions without trouble. They know the roads intimately, they know just how far they can see around each curve, and they know where to look to scan the road ahead. You do not know these things, so do not attempt to keep up with the natives. Of course, it's also dangerous to go twenty mph on a two-lane road where everyone else is going fifty. Here are a few mountain driving techniques that you can safely teach yourself. They won't allow you to drive like the natives, but they should keep you out of their way.

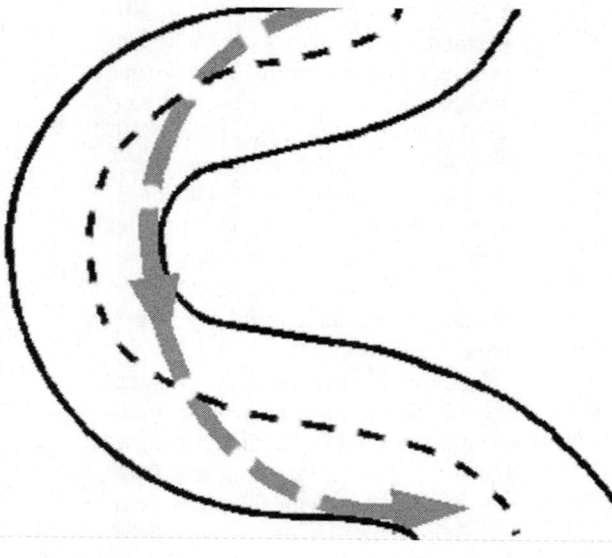

To "straighten out a curve," Use both lanes when you can see them. Begin each curve as far to the outside of the curve as you can safely get. Aim to pass as close to the inside of the curve as possible just at the middle of the curve, and end at the outside again.

1. Gear down going downhill. It can save your brakes. The lower gear or drive range produces more torque, gives you better control in turns, and allows quicker stopping. It's safer to gear down at the top of a grade before your speed builds up dangerously.

2. On a winding road, slow down going into each turn, and use extra power to pull out of it. Smoothly adding power as you come out of the turn adds torque to the wheels, giving you better control. Done correctly, it feels like the car is on rails, and you come out of the turn going faster than you went in. Avoid braking while turning. You can lose control and skid. Brake only when the front wheels are straight.

3. Use the entire width of the road, including both lanes **when you can see them**, to "straighten out" the curves. Begin each curve as far to the outside of the curve as you can safely get. Aim to pass as close to the inside of the curve as possible just at the middle of the curve, and end at the outside again, regardless of the lines separating the lanes of two-way traffic. You can do this legally where the center line is broken to allow passing. Just be sure there is no oncoming traffic.

Gradually add power after you pass the midpoint of the curve. Plan each curve so you begin and end in your own lane, going at a comfortable rate of speed. **Caution:** your heavily-loaded car, truck, or van is not a sports car.

Once you start through a downhill curve this way, you are committed, as it will be difficult to negotiate the curve at high speed without crossing the centerline. If you cannot see the entire curve plus enough of the road to know that no traffic will get in your way, it's best to slow down before the curve and drive it normally. If you get caught partway through a curve and have to slow down to pull out of the way of oncoming traffic, back off on the accelerator and shift a manual transmission to a lower gear to slow down. Avoid braking if you can. If you must use the brakes, modify your line through the curve to allow a brief straight stretch for braking.

Be especially careful going downhill in curves. That's where you are most likely to skid. How you get out of a skid depends on which wheels are skidding, whether you have ABS (Anti-Lock Brake System), and whether your car is front-wheel drive or rear-wheel drive. If you have anti-lock brakes, brake normally and steer the way you want the car to go.

Without ABS, it gets more complicated. Rear-wheel drive cars are better for getting out of skids because you have more options. The brakes work mostly on the front wheels, while the engine works on the rear ones. If the front wheels are skidding, gear down and back off on the accelerator. Stay off the brakes! The rear wheels will slow the car from the back, allowing the weight of the car to pull it straight. Steer in the direction the car is skidding until control is established, then apply brakes gently.

If you are not stopping fast enough, apply the parking brakes, which work only on the rear wheels. Hold the brake release "ON" all the time to keep the brakes from locking. If you have a lever type parking brake, with a button in the end for release, just hold the button in while using the lever as a hand brake. If you have a pedal-type parking brake, pull out on the brake release handle while pressing down the parking brake pedal with the left foot.

If the rear wheels are skidding, ease the pressure on the accelerator and steer in the direction the car is skidding. Stay off the brakes! Once the skid is corrected, gear down and apply the brakes gently.

If you have front-wheel drive, press down hard on the accelerator to increase steering effectiveness. Then apply the parking brake with the brake release held "ON" to slow down. Don't try to recover just by backing off the accelerator. That will only increase the skid.

Use common sense

Limited visibility caused by curves in the road and hills can also create problems. Be alert for signs warning of falling rocks and wildlife. Slow way down in areas where deer occur. You will see them most frequently in the hours around dusk and dawn, but they may be present any time. Deer will usually run away from cars, but if they get scared, they may bolt right in front of you. Hitting a deer can damage your car as much as hitting a tree. Natives often purchase "deer repellers"—wind-powered, ultrasonic whistles that mount on the front bumper. You can't hear them, but the deer can. If you are going to be in the area, they're good to have. Buy them at sporting goods shops and local auto parts stores.

The lower oxygen content of the air at high altitude will make your engine burn gasoline less efficiently, producing less power. So you will get less gas mileage in the mountains. Gearing down for braking also burns more gas per mile. And, of course, pulling up steep hills makes the motor strain and use even more gas. Plan on more frequent fuel stops in the mountains.

Your motor is not the only thing that needs more air at high altitude. You will tire more quickly too. If you smoke, the effect will be compounded. Change drivers very frequently. Your driving ability will deteriorate significantly *before* you feel tired. Ask the passengers to help watch for deer, fallen rocks, and snow slides.

Pay attention to avalanche warnings. Often, mountain roads will have signs prohibiting stopping between certain dates. That's avalanche season. Obey the signs; they mean it. If you must stop, to fix a flat tire or let an overheated engine cool, keep all passengers inside the car, buckled up, and quiet. Loud noises can start an avalanche, dumping an entire mountainside full of snow on the road in seconds and burying your car under yards and yards of hard-packed snow. It can carry you and your car off the road and down into the valley far below, pounding you with huge boulders and full-size trees along the way. There is nothing funny or gentle about an avalanche.

Actually, the mountains are no more dangerous to drive through than big-city freeways, but the dangers may be unfamiliar and unexpected. If you carry the right equipment and don't try to drive in conditions beyond your experience and ability, mountain driving can be fun and relaxing. ∆

Ask Jackie

"Retiring" in the backwoods, canning cabbage, green tomato pickles, grape jelly & grape juice, rolled oats, canned cheese, cleaning up cat puke, and storing eggs

Jackie Clay

Have you considered your options for maintaining your lifestyle into your "golden years"? Self-reliant and off-the-grid are great, but are they always doable or even practical as one gets older and less physically able to handle the associated workload? I like living in the country. However, I also like much of today's modern medical technology and want to have it available to me if needed. For instance, I'm all for natural childbirth, but I want to be in a hospital where there's access to ventilators and neo-natal equipment in case of an unplanned situation. I don't know if I could feel comfortable knowing that emergency medical help was two hours away and only by helicopter (if the weather would allow).

T "Jane"
jzee@2ki.net

Yes, we have considered maintaining our lifestyle into old age. Both my husband, Bob, and I are 56, so that is natural. But it is not much of a decision for us, as neither of us could ever consider living anywhere but on a wild, unspoiled homestead. Simply living in the country would never work for us; it's something in the soul, not simply a conscious decision. For us to be happy, this is a necessity.

For you, or many other readers, this is probably not the case. One does not have to live in the wilderness to strive for a self-reliant lifestyle. Each and every one of is different, and thank God for that.

We feel that we would rather live a self-reliant lifestyle off grid, instead of opting for the "safety" of having medical care close by. Both of us have medical experience and supplies for sudden emergencies. But the bottom line is the quality of our life, verses living in total safety. Personally, I would rather live 20 more years (or two, or five), content and satisfied, than 30 years near facilities, and be unfulfilled and miserable.

Consider Helen and Scott Nearing, who were still homesteading when she was in her 80s, and he until he was 100. In fact, they built their last homestead in their "golden years" by hand.

We hope to be as active and will continue our lifestyle until death claims us. Of course, we will slow down. Everyone does. But we also learn easier and less strenuous ways of doing things as we go. As my dad says, "Too soon old, too late smart!" When I was 30, I canned 60 quarts of corn in one 24 hour day. Today, I can 16 pints a day, and can for a week, a little at a time.

We also learn what tools will accomplish the results we need with less work. Instead of hoeing two acres of garden, we've bought a Mantis tiller, which is like having a gasoline powered mad weasel weighing in at only 20 pounds. It lets us plant less garden by planting rows closer together, yet it quickly and effectively cultivates in a manner that is very easy on our bodies.

We used to do most of our wood cutting with a powerful but heavy Husqvarna chainsaw. It still is a good saw, but too hard on us over the hours. So we bought a new, much lighter, yet still powerful Stihl saw and can do the same work with much less strain on our backs.

I am quite sure that as we age, we'll opt for more raised beds and intensive gardening to ease the "ups and downs" as well as the total size of our sustainable garden.

And, if it comes to it, we are willing to pay for "grunt work" should we become unable to do it, rather than give in and move to a more "convenient" locale. We feel very strongly that our home-raised food is the best for our bodies and we could never switch to "storebought" food, simply for its lack of taste.

Another help for us is that we plan our next, imminent move as our last, and hope to have our "heavy" new homestead building chores done before we are much older. Maintaining the lifestyle is, of course, much easier than beginning anew. There is a house to build, barns, chicken coops, orchards, new soil to break and make fertile, weeds to tame, fences to build, etc., etc. And, as we build our homestead for *us*, we will, of course, keep an eye to the future. There will be no long, steep stairways. Much of the home's living space will be on the ground floor. The outbuildings will be clustered, for ease of choring, especially in the winter. The barn aisles will be wide enough for a small tractor or team of horses and manure spreader to pass through daily. You get the picture.

Even today, our lifestyle does not require tremendous strength or energy. Bob is an agent-orange (Vietnam, again) diabetic, with heart disease because of it. I've got a bad back (horse wreck, long ago), and other assorted ouchies. We do our work in little bites. The key is to keep on until a job is done. In this way, we usually out-work most young homesteading couples. We just get out there and do it. By not pushing our bodies severely, but keeping very active every day, the work gets done, and we aren't done in. When we need a break, we say so and simply take one, with no reproaches from the other, then get back at the task.

Right now, we don't live a "primative" life even off grid, seven miles from a blacktop road. We have running spring water, hot and cold in the house, a generator and battery bank for power for my word processor, the washing machine and television/vcr, power tools, etc. We waste no time (or energy) watching television, as there just isn't anything we want to watch on it anymore. We have a flush toilet and septic system. A decent forest road runs past our quarter-mile-long driveway, which is drivable year-round. We also have a large propane refrigerator, which is very economical, and better than most electric models. Life here is truly very easy.

Unfortunately, many people equate living off grid as pounding clothes on rocks in the creek, lugging water in buckets, using a smelly outhouse, and struggling to read by kerosene light. Put together correctly, off-grid living is nothing of the kind. We have friends living off the grid, who have satelite TV, a dishwasher, microwave, propane clothes dryer, electric freezer, and more.

We miss the adventure of beginning a remote off grid homestead. Living in such a spacious, finished home with everything in place, there is little adventure. I actually envy friends who are living in small cabins, lugging water, using an outhuse and reading by kerosene lights. Some of us are just built that way. After all, where would we be without the Lewis and Clarks?

I *never* expect everybody to be like me. (Boy would that be scary.) Each of us has his or her own decisions to make. We should live where we will be happy, whether it be in the city or in the remote central Alaskan wilderness. One thing I've learned, though, is that most of us can do much, much more than we ever thought possible, if we have the will and inclination to do it, whether we are 20 or 70.

Jackie

Do you have a recipe for canning cabbage, not sauerkraut?
Emmett Nelson
dewlds@msn.com

You bet, Emmett. I can a lot of it. While cabbage will keep a long time in the root cellar or even in a dark corner of a cool basement, there comes a time when it begins to soften and go bad. Before this happens, I can it up and it stays good nearly indefinitely. Cabbage does get a little strong flavored in the jar when canned, but I offset this by dumping out the canning liquid at the time of use, and either boil the canned cabbage in fresh water or milk with a little butter, salt, and pepper. This takes care of things 100 percent.

Canned cabbage:

Choose tight, firm heads. Trim off any wilted leaves, cuts, or bad spots. You can either can your cabbage in chunks, such as quarters, or cut it up as you would for sauerkraut. I prefer the cut cabbage the best. Boil in salted water for five minutes, which wilts it a bit enabling you to pack more cabbage into each jar. Drain. Pack cabbage into jars to within one inch of the top of the jar. Add 1 teaspoon salt to each quart, or ½ teaspoon to each pint if desired. Fill jar to within 1 inch of top with boiling water. Wipe the rims clean. Place hot, previously boiled lid on each jar and screw down the rings firmly-tight. Process quarts 60 minutes and pints 50 minutes in a pressure canner at 10 pounds pressure, adjusting pounds of pressure for altitudes above 1,000 feet above sea level if necessary. See your canning book for more directions.

Jackie

Can you tell me a recipe for pickling sweet green tomatoes? How long does it take to process in the jars in a boiling water bath?
Rosa
BBRA82@aol.com

I sure can, Rosa. In the fall, there are always so many green tomatoes that are not needed to ripen indoors for sauces. I make green tomato pie (fake apple), dill green tomato relish, sweet tomato pickles, dilled half green tomatoes, and fake mincemeat with green tomatoes, to mention only a few. Here's a simple sweet green tomato pickle.

Spiced green tomatoes:

6 lbs. small hard whole green tomatoes
1 pt. white vinegar
½ Tbsp. cloves
4 lbs. sugar
1 Tbsp. cinnamon
½ Tbsp. allspice

You may scald and peel the tomatoes or not. Make a syrup of the other ingredients and bring to a boil. Drop in the tomatoes and simmer until they take on a somewhat translucent appearance. Dip out onto a cookie sheet or shallow bowl and cool rapidly. Pack cold into jars. Strain syrup and heat to boil. Pour over tomatoes and seal jars. Process in hot water bath for 15 minutes, counting from the time the canner reaches a rolling boil. Be sure that the boiling water covers the jars by at least one inch. Makes about 4 pints.

You may alter the spices to suit you, but this recipe makes a quite sweet, spicy tomato pickle that is nice and crunchy.

Jackie

My mother used to make homemade grape jelly and grape juice. She recently passed away and I do not know where her recipes are for these items. I do know that she used Sure Jell in her jelly and she used so many cups of sugar to so many cups of juice, cooking for so long. She also used to put wax on top of the jelly before putting on the lid.

Would appreciate it if you could supply me with any recipes or at least direct me to where I might obtain them. Your consideration will be appreciated.

Linda Linderman
Winter Haven, FL

My grandmothers and mother also used to make lots of homemade grape jelly and grape juice. We even used to have a large grape arbor (which you seldom see any more which is too bad) in our side yard, from which baskets and baskets of succulent, sweet grapes were harvested every fall. Grape jelly and grape juice are very easy to make at home. You can get a box of Sure Jell at the grocery and find a very good list of common jelly and jam recipes inside using the product of course. Here are the basics for both juice and jelly. I'm sure it will be just about what your mother made.

Grape juice:

Stem and wash ripe grapes. Cover them with water and heat slowly. Do not boil hard; only simmer. Cook slowly until grapes are very soft, then strain through a bag as you would for jelly. Do not press, or the juice will be cloudy instead of clear. To each quart of juice, add half a cup of sugar (or to taste). Mix well. Pour into clean jars to within half an inch of the top. Wipe rim of jar clean and place hot, previously boiled lid on jar and screw down ring firmly tight. Process jars for 15 minutes in a water bath canner, counting from the time that the canner comes to a full rolling boil. Be sure that the water covers the jars by at least one inch.

As well as using a jelling agent such as Sure Jell, you can simply add juice and sugar and boil it until it reaches the jelling point which is when a teaspoon full of the hot jelly will slide off a spoon in a sheet, not drip off. Here's such a recipe.

Grape jelly:

Extract grape juice as above. Measure and bring to a boil in a very large kettle. For each cup of juice, add three quarters of a cup of sugar. Boil hard to jelly stage. Pour into jars, seal, and water bath for ten minutes.

As your mother did, I used to use the old method of pouring melted paraffin on top of the jelly or to coat the top of the jar and lid with it. As we used to use "odd" jars for jellies, we usually used the paraffin to seal the jelly. This was okay, but really not so hot. Any movement would often crack the seal loose, resulting in leaking jelly or moldy jelly. The mold was completely harmless, but ugly. It can be spooned off, but no one feels like eating the jelly after seeing the mold. Also, mice would nibble through the wax and sample the jellies which was unhealthy and very unappetizing, especially when they left little rodent "presents" on top of the wax.

Today, I use standard pint and half pint jars with new lids. These are sealed in a water bath canner as above. No leaks. No mold. No mice. Much more economical as you don't lose processed food. And because our home canned jams and jellies are so good, who wants to lose even one jar?

Jackie

I want to grow oats to produce my own rolled oats. I plan on using hullless oats. How do I process the oats to make the rolled oats?

Mary Crabtree
Springfield, OH

It is very easy to make rolled oats from your own home raised oats. Before the new hull-free oats, it was nearly impossible. But now it's easy. All you need is a rolled oat mill. They are not expensive and will last a lifetime and more. They are like a hand grain mill only they squash the oats flat, instead of grinding them into flour. Lehmans carries them or you can pick one up from most any company selling grain mills. Not only is it easy to roll your own oats, but it's fun. Even the neighbors beg to be allowed to "squash oats."

Jackie

I read with great interest how you can cheese and how someone tried butter. My question is how do you get the cheese out of the jar? Does it stay soft, like a spread? Can you take a slice off for a sandwich? Maybe I missed something, but I can't visualize how once melted in the jar, you can get it back out, except maybe in small pieces, dug out with a knife.

**Rick Murphy
Boise, ID**

Good question Rick. But you haven't stumped me yet. I can my cheese in wide mouth pints and half pints. To release the cheese, I simply heat the jar in a pan of water up to the cheese level until the outside barely melts. Sort of how you release Jello from a mold. Then quickly slip a thin knife in alongside the cheese to release the vacuum and dump it out on a plate. Stick it in the cold for a few minutes and you again have firm, cold cheese.

Slice or grate as you wish. I put leftovers in a plastic baggie in the fridge. This cheese isn't quite as good as fresh cheese, but it is better than store cheese, and the canned cheese is a good way to save homestead crafted cheeses over time.

Jackie

There MUST be an easier way to clean up pet messes than using a paper towel. Last night my cat got sick and threw up in the hall, which I discovered by stepping in it barefoot. Paper towels soak through and you get your fingers in the disgusting mess. And me, with a delicate stomach. Any ideas?

**John Silveira
Brookings, OR**

I gave up paper towels years ago. Instead, I cut a stiff paper plate in half and scoop up an accident with that. It gets nearly all of it. The rest, you can mop up with a dampened rag. No more fingers in the mess. This also works great for broken jars of jam, tomato sauce, catsup, relish, kiddie (and adult) messes of all kinds. In fact, I keep a stack of paper plates mostly for just this use.

Jackie

How can I store fresh eggs when egg production is down and have fresh eggs during the holiday baking time?

Also, my husband has a tobacco habit. Where can I find seeds and what kind is best? He likes to dip snuff. I remember reading an article out of BHM about this, but after reading the article, I read another article that said the flowering tobacco seeds are harmful to use. Do you know what is true? I would like to know if they are safe to use.

**Lois Hutson
Jackonville, TX**

First of all, you can encourage your hens to lay longer in the season by keeping extra light in the coop. Sometimes this is only adding a west facing window. Other methods include keeping a light in the coop. I know people living off grid who bought solar walk lights and place them in the south and west windows of the chicken coop to charge, then they come on at dark, keeping the hens active and laying all evening. If you have electricity, keep a 40-watt light bulb burning in the coop using a cheap timer for four hours after sundown, and you'll find your hens lay more eggs and lay them longer in the year. Also, keeping your coop windproof and warm will encourage laying.

When your "girls" begin to slow down, gather all the fresh clean eggs to store. Eggs are protected, naturally, by a thin external membrane. Therefore, when you wash or scrub the eggs, the membrane is washed off and the eggs will store for shorter periods of time. Store only naturally clean eggs. By storing them in a cardboard egg carton in the refrigerator, you can keep them quite a long time.

When we lived way remote and snowmobiled in and out seven months out of the year, we gathered up eggs in November which was as late as the girls produced. Storing them as above, the eggs generally lasted nearly until spring production kicked in. Of course, the older eggs should be broken first into a cup, as once in a while, you'll get a bad one. You can tell these by the runny yolk, watery white and ugly look.

You can keep eggs in waterglass, which is a solution of sodium silicate and water. The sodium silicate clogs up the pores of the egg and helps keep them for longer periods of time. Likewise, rubbing fresh, clean eggs with lard or shortening will help keep them longer. As keeping eggs is not much of a problem by using the above methods, I do not bother with these ways, as they are messy and there is not much nastier feeling than reaching into a crock of waterglass solution for an egg or two.

Now, to the tobacco. All tobacco is poisonous. Period. It contains nicotine, which is so toxic that you can kill chicken lice and mites by shredding up some tobacco and putting it into the nest boxes. But smokers don't want to hear that.

You can raise your own tobacco by buying smoking/chewing tobacco seeds for such a variety as burley, from a number of seed houses, such as Henry Field's. Their website is mySEASONS.com or write to them at 415 North Burnett, Shenandoah, IA 51602-0001.

This tobacco is not the same as flowering tobacco, although it does have flowers. Flowering tobacco is not used to smoke or chew. There are Native American tobaccos which are basically wild tobaccos available, but these tobaccos are more toxic and should not be used for everyday smoking. Indians used tobacco mainly for ceremonial use.

Jackie

Want more Clay?
Go to:
www.backwoodshome.com

The last word

A proposal for ending violent crime

It was an interview I caught just a part of back in the '70s. I can't remember who the interviewer was; it's not important. He was interviewing a diplomat from Saudi Arabia just after the price of oil went to dizzying heights and Western money began to pour into Arab coffers changing Arab economics. The interview went something like this:

The interviewer said, "Your country is trying to leap from a 13th century feudal society into the 20th century on this oil money..."

"Yes, we are," the Saudi conceded.

"...and yet you retain a lot of barbaric ways."

The Saudi looked perplexed. "What do you mean we have barbaric ways?" he asked.

"Well, if a man is caught stealing, you cut his hand off, don't you?"

The Saudi thought about this for a moment. "You consider cutting off a hand barbaric?" he asked.

The interviewer said, "Of course."

The Saudi said, "We don't cut the hand off for the first offense. A man has to commit two or three offenses before we do that. Each year we cut off six or seven hands, but we have almost no crime in our country. In your country, every year you throw people in jail for awhile, or worse, you put them on probation, and every year you turn hundreds of thousands of criminals out of prisons and back onto the streets, knowing full well that hundreds of thousands of these criminals are going to continue to murder, rape, rob, steal, and molest children. Do you think this is more civilized? We don't.

"In my country the guilty suffer the punishment and the stigma that goes with it. But men, women, and children can walk our streets in safety. Can you say that in America? The way you turn criminals back out into the general population is like loosing packs of wild dogs into the streets. We consider Americans the most barbaric people in the world."

The interviewer was embarrassed and quickly changed the subject, never again coming back to the question of "barbarism." And though those weren't the exact words exchanged, that was the gist of it, and 30 years later the Saudi's response is still on my mind.

There is no doubt that there is an ongoing crime problem in this country that all the prisons and all the social workers are incapable of fixing. But I think there is a solution. Here's my proposal: We change the Constitution, amending the prohibition against "cruel and unusual punishment" and we institute some exceptions.

The punishment? Those now regarded as either career criminals or criminals who are both violent and incorrigible, would have their right arms and left legs cut off—or left arms and right legs, but the dominant arms go. And they're sent home right afterward. No prison, but also, no welfare and no state aid of any sort.

Think of the impact of such punishment. If Bubba raped two women, or he's a hit man for the Mob, or he got caught once too often robbing liquor stores, and he's tried and convicted, it's off to the hospital, *whack, whack,* and he goes home minus an arm and a leg. His life of crime is over. No long-term prison costs, and he becomes a walking—hobbling—billboard for how crime *really* doesn't pay.

Street gangsters who admire members who spent some time in the Big House aren't going to look up to or respect Bubba when he's a pathetic invalid sitting on his porch all summer with nothing to do except swat flies away with his one good arm. Kids aren't going to admire him, women aren't going to give him those sidelong glances they reserve for the tough and the powerful. Sexual predators aren't going to have to register anymore. We'll know who they are.

Again, it would only apply to violent crimes. Not drug crimes, not adultery, not speeding, but murder, armed robbery, burglary, rape, child molestation. For most crimes, the sentence would be carried out only after two or three offenses. For a few, like murder or child molestation, there would be exceptions; one offense and *whack, whack.*

The recidivism rate for violent crimes in this country now stands at about 60 percent in three years. This means that 60 percent of offenders who have been through the system will eventually be caught and convicted again—in three years or less. But before they're caught again, they'll have committed dozens and sometimes hundreds of crimes. And that's just the ones who get caught.

How many of the people we read about who have abducted, raped, and murdered little girls turn out to have been repeat offenders? How many women have been raped and how many store owners murdered by career criminals who already have a string of convictions behind them? What are these people doing on the streets?

Crime wouldn't completely disappear. There would still be the psychotics. But my prediction is that murder, robbery, burglary, and all other violent crimes would soon drop more than 95 percent. People would begin to feel safer in their homes. They'd feel they could walk the streets at night. Gun control advocates could take solace because the general population would feel less need for guns.

For those who would want to argue that it was still cruel and unusual? Don't worry, soon it would almost be unneeded, as cutting off the right hand is almost unneeded in Saudi Arabia, because there'd be almost no crime.

But who'd take care of them? I don't care. Their families can, charities can, churches can, but no public money.

And what if they still commit a violent crime after that? Well, they still have one arm and one leg left so, *whack, whack,* then send them home again. Let me see them commit a crime then. Δ

— *John Silveira*

Backwoods Home magazine

Mar/Apr 2003
No. 80
$4.95 US
$6.50 CAN

practical ideas for self-reliant living

The smallpox threat...
It's time to worry!

Keep your heart healthy

Foraging wild greens
Build a "temporary" home
Home canning = tasty meals
Grow cauliflower, asparagus beans,
& blueberries

www.backwoodshome.com

My view

Smallpox—it's worth worrying about

Is a smallpox epidemic brought about by terrorists something to worry about? After all, it is a horrible disease, killing 30% of its victims and terribly disfiguring, sometimes blinding, those who survive.

We've all read or heard something about smallpox, how Bush has ordered the vaccinating of the military and a half million medical "first responders," and how he's ordered more smallpox vaccine be ready for the general public by early 2004. Does he know something we don't?

And there's been a lot of discussion on how terrorists might attack us with smallpox: infected jihad volunteers walking among us, aerosolized containers containing weaponized smallpox placed surreptitiously on the walls of shopping malls and airports.

Most media pundits have concluded that it's a very small threat. Jihad volunteers would be too sick, and too noticeably ill, if they had smallpox to be able to walk around infecting people, and getting hold of weaponized smallpox would be about as hard to do as winning the lottery.

But I am a media pundit who has spent the last two months reading everything I can about smallpox, and I am very worried that a smallpox attack is *the threat* we should all take seriously. For one, I think getting hold of weaponized smallpox will be a lot easier than most people think; after all, someone got hold of weaponized anthrax and sent it though the mail shortly after 9-11.

But I also have another reason, a fact that has been overlooked in the media, it being perhaps too deeply embedded in the literature detailing the 12,000-year history of this greatest of all human plagues: a person previously vaccinated with the smallpox vaccine, then exposed to smallpox, can get a mild case of smallpox if his vaccination is so old it doesn't give him full protection. He may not even know he's sick, he will be able to walk around fine, he will have few symptoms, perhaps a light rash, but he will then be capable of passing on full blown smallpox to someone else, especially to our children who, almost without exception, have never been vaccinated.

This disturbing fact is one of the reasons why the "ring method" of controlling smallpox outbreaks was used back in the 1960s and 70s to finally eradicate the disease. With the ring method, all contacts of a smallpox victim were closely watched, vaccinated, and forcibly isolated if necessary until it was certain they had not contracted smallpox, even a mild form. Then a second ring of people who had had contacts with the first ring was established to make sure they hadn't been infected.

They took no chances. They knew that smallpox was persistent. It could remain alive in the clothing and bedding of infected patients, even lay dried but alive in the dust of a patient's room, for months after the patient had either died or recovered. That's why disinfecting a smallpox patient's room was critical. Smallpox had already killed 300-500 million people in the 20th century, which is three to five times the number of people killed in all that century's wars combined. The final defeat of smallpox, the only disease to ever have been eradicated, is an achievement at least as significant as landing a man on the moon.

But if enough jihad volunteers with waning smallpox vaccinations (and that includes half the human race since most vaccinations stopped in the 70s) were to expose themselves to smallpox so that a few of them got a mild but contagious case of smallpox, they could then walk among us and bring smallpox back again to plague humanity. And here in the U.S., we wouldn't even know we had been attacked until two weeks later when our symptoms started showing up. By that time the jihad attackers could have travelled to dozens of cities in America and infected hundreds. The "ring method" of controlling the disease would not work because the jihad volunteers would not cooperate. They would be like so many Typhoid Marys. And the attackers wouldn't even have to commit suicide; they would recover and escape. We wouldn't even know how we had been attacked.

It is an impossible attack strategy to defend against, except if we resort to mass smallpox vaccinations. But that may be a very difficult strategy to sustain in light of the fact that data from the 1960s and 70s smallpox eradication program indicates that the vaccinia vaccine itself, which is made from cowpox, will kill one or two Americans per million vaccinated, and gravely sicken at least another 2,000. And that data does not take into account our modern day situation: millions of Americans with eczema-related skin conditions, AIDS, and other immune system problems who absolutely should not be given the vaccine unless they are in imminent danger of contracting smallpox.

Even an attack of this type that produced only a handful of smallpox cases would virtually shut down our society.

That's a big problem on a grand scale I hope the nation never has to face. But it is definitely worth worrying about.

At the individual level, it's less of a problem. If you're not among those in the "at risk" group, you can get vaccinated when the vaccine is made available to the public early next year—or earlier if there is an actual attack. The vaccine will protect you for up to four days after exposure to smallpox. If you're in the "at risk" group (I am because I've got an eczema-related skin condition) and we do get attacked, you can formulate a plan now, as I have, to isolate yourself and family (I'll also vaccinate my kids) with lots of food and survival stuff until the threat passes.

What are the odds of such an attack? What were the odds of them flying planes loaded with people into the WTC and Pentagon? — *Dave Duffy*

The Fourteenth Year

Keeping your heart healthy

By Gary F. Arnet, D.D.S.

"I'm sorry, Doctor Arnet, but you must have immediate cardiac bypass surgery. Your coronary arteries are 95% blocked."

"That can't be, doctor," I replied. "I am only 38, I have no symptoms, I exercise, and I don't smoke. Besides I have patients to see, young children to care for, and have to provide for my family."

"I'm sorry. We will do the surgery Thursday. Get your affairs in order because you will be off work 12 weeks," he answered.

Your life stands still when you get the news that you need cardiac bypass surgery. As I found out, all of the important things on your "to do" list don't matter anymore. The places you need to go, the people you need to meet with, your family activities, your job, all of these things no longer are important. You are in a struggle for your life. While a safe, routine operation today, devastating or fatal complications can still occur and there is a long recovery period.

Whether you are 38 or 75 years, all sorts of worries go through your mind. You wonder how your family is going to manage while you are recovering, how you will pay your bills, what will happen to your job, and what will happen if you have a stroke or die during surgery. What type of lifestyle changes will you need to make afterwards? How will you learn about these? If you live by yourself, who is going to take care of you while you are recovering? You think about all the ways heart surgery will affect your life.

My oldest child was in second grade and my two youngest were in pre-school when I had heart surgery. I worried about how would my wife take care of them if something happened. Would they even remember me if I died? Heart surgery was certainly not something I wanted to deal with.

Author and his sons while hiking on a 90-mile backpacking trip that reached elevations of 12,000 feet. This trip was taken 10 years after author's cardiac bypass surgery.

Yet, I was one of the lucky ones. For many people with heart disease, their first symptom is death. They have no warning until they collapse one day and die.

Heart disease is the leading cause of death in the United States. About 1.5 million Americans have a heart attack each year and about 500,000 of them die. About 2 million men are estimated to have significant coronary artery disease that they are not aware of because they have no symptoms.

Healthy heart living is not just for older adults. Autopsies of young men killed in the Vietnam War showed that many had coronary artery disease and lifestyles have not improved in the past 30 years. Many of our youth today are overweight and don't exercise. We are raising our next generation of heart attacks. It is important to teach young children healthy heart living as they are growing up.

The good news is that many advances in the understanding and prevention of heart disease have occurred in recent years. With better knowledge, testing, and medications, people are living longer, healthier lives.

All of the information in this article is current and is taken from established medical recommendations and medical literature. It is intended for general knowledge on the subject, not as a substitute for proper medical evaluation and care. If you have any of the risk factors listed or any heart symptoms, you should see a physician and follow a plan for healthy heart living.

The heart

Ancient Greeks thought that the heart was the source of intelligence. Others throughout time believed it to be the seat of emotions. Most of us, however, don't even think of our heart unless it beats hard or skips a beat.

The heart is actually a muscular pump located in the chest behind the sternum (breastbone) with its lowest point pointing to the left. About the size of a fist, it weighs less than a pound. The right side of the heart pumps the blood returning from the body to the lungs, replacing carbon dioxide waste products with oxygen. The left side of the heart is more muscular and pumps the oxygenated blood from the lungs to all the tissues of the body.

71

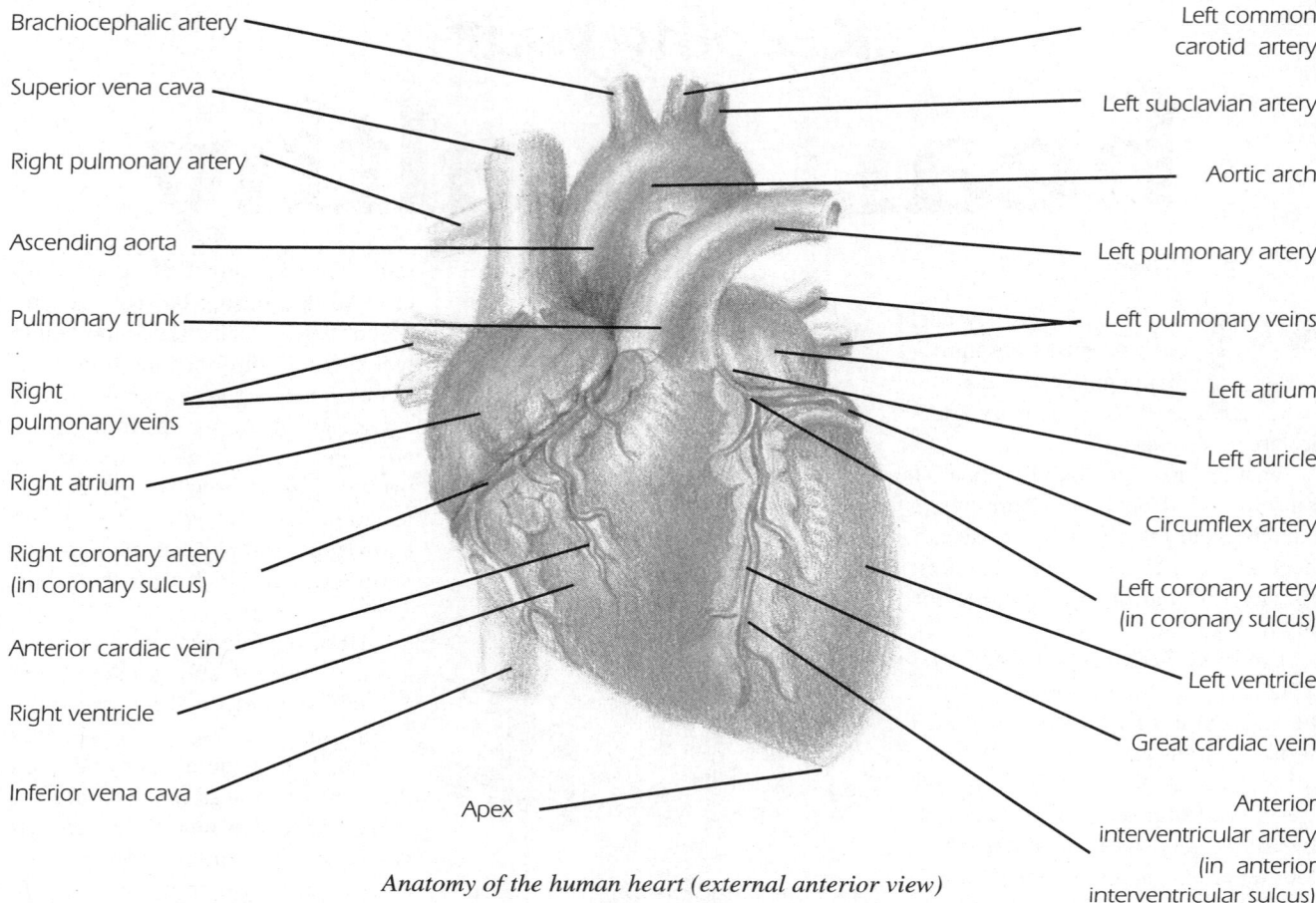
Anatomy of the human heart (external anterior view)

The heart itself does not receive blood for its own use from the blood that flows through its chambers. Rather, it receives blood from the coronary arteries, blood vessels that arise from the aorta immediately as it exits the heart. The left coronary artery begins from the left side of the aorta and branches into two main branches, the anterior interventricular artery and the circumflex artery, providing blood to the middle and left sides of the heart. The right coronary artery branches off the right side of the aorta and splits into the marginal artery and posterior interventricular artery supplying blood to the right side of the heart.

The blood supplied by the coronary arteries nourishes and provides oxygen to the muscle tissues of the heart. An interruption of coronary artery blood flow, as seen in coronary artery disease, can cause injury or death of the heart muscle supplied by the affected blood vessel.

What is heart disease?

Heart disease can include problems to the coronary arteries, heart muscle, heart valves, or the conduction system. This article will deal only with coronary artery disease, the disease that leads to heart attacks.

Commonly called "hardening of the arteries," atherosclerosis and arteriosclerosis are medical terms used to describe a buildup of fatty deposits in the inner lining of the blood vessels of the body. When the arteries of the heart are affected it is called coronary artery disease. Blood vessels are partially blocked, blood flow to the heart is diminished, and the heart muscle does not receive the amount of oxygen it needs. A common symptom of this is angina pectoris, or chest pain, due to low oxygen causing temporary injury to the heart muscle cells. This often occurs during exercise, when oxygen requirements of the heart are increased.

If blockage of the coronary arteries is prolonged or more complete, a heart attack (myocardial infarction) can occur as the lack of oxygen causes heart muscle cells to die. If the myocardial infarction is severe, an individual can die due to extensive loss of heart muscle tissue (a weakened heart) or electrical conduction disruption (arrhythmia).

Most people with symptoms of angina or heart attack have chest pain that stimulates them to seek medical care. Through diet and lifestyle changes, medications, or surgical intervention they can restore the blood flow to the heart and live a nor-

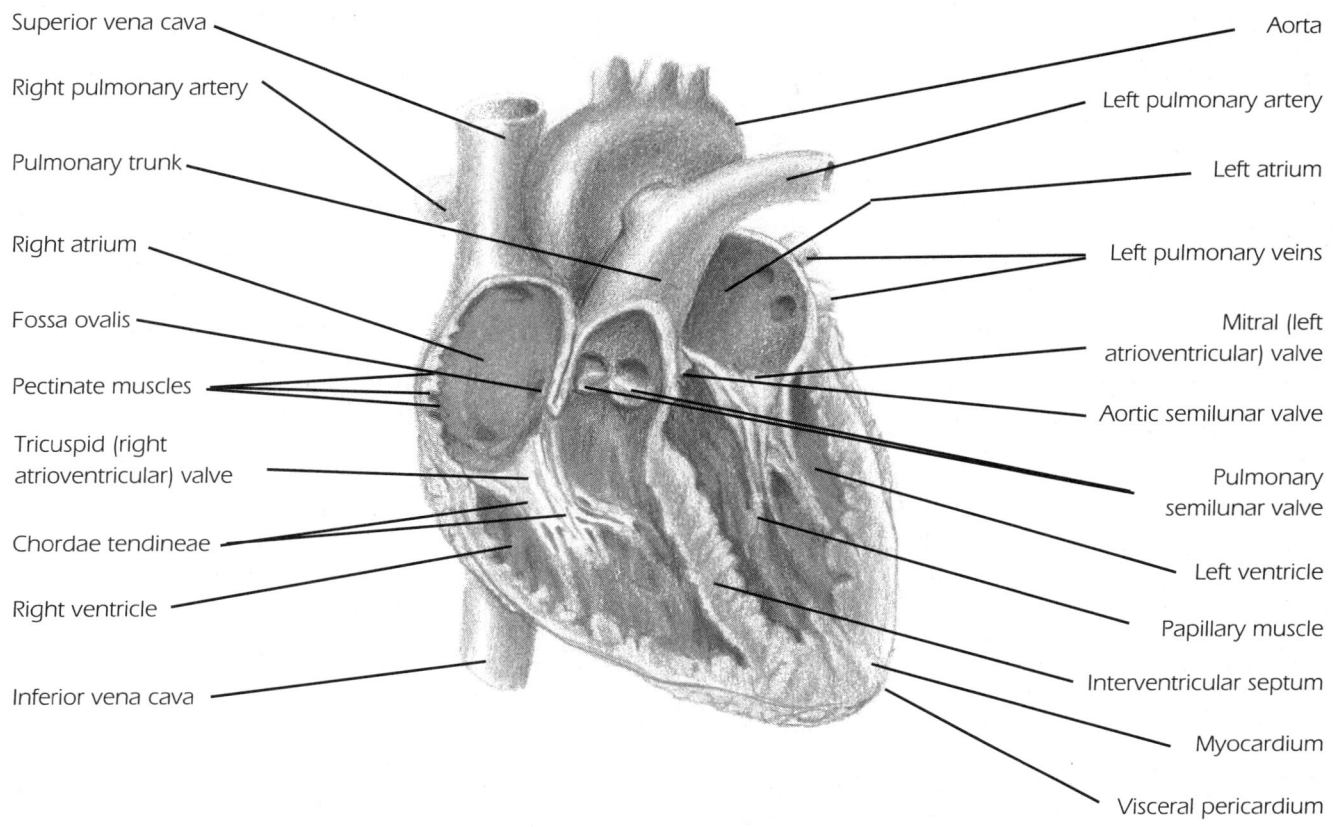

Anatomy of the human heart (frontal section)

mal life. Surgical intervention can include an angioplasty, where a balloon is inserted inside the artery and it is stretched open, or bypass surgery, where other arteries or veins are grafted from the aorta to the heart to "bypass" the obstructed section of the coronary artery.

Unfortunately, the first warning some people have is death. They have silent ischemia, a condition where blood flow through the coronary arteries is diminished, but without causing pain to warn them. They can suffer a fatal heart attack and die suddenly without warning.

The good news is that coronary artery disease is largely preventable.

What causes coronary artery disease?

Long-term studies have clearly identified certain risk factors for coronary artery disease, heart attack, or stroke. Some factors, such as heredity, sex, race, and age, cannot be changed. Others, such as diet, cholesterol level, cigarette smoking, high blood pressure, diabetes, exercise, and stress, can be altered through lifestyle changes or medications.

Risk factors that cannot be changed can be used to determine the likelihood of developing heart disease. A family history of heart disease is a strong clue that children may develop disease. Family history would include a heart attack or sudden death of a father or male sibling occurring under the age of 55 or mother or female sibling occurring under the age of 65. Men over the age of 45 and women over the age of 55 with normal menopause or over the age of 45 with early menopause and no estrogen replacement are at higher risk.

Millions of Americans begin unhealthy living habits at a young age. Children overeat, eat unhealthy foods high in cholesterol and fat, and do not exercise enough. Rather, they tend to be "couch potatoes" in front of the television, computer, or electronic games. This carries over into adolescence, where many add the habit of smoking. By the time they reach adulthood, many Americans are already obese, lead sedentary lifestyles, and smoke heavily.

A recent study in the Journal of the American Medical Association found that over 60% of American adults were considered overweight and 5% extremely obese. We don't need studies to show that is true. Just look around when you are with a group of people.

Most individuals reach their adult weight by age 21 to 25. After this age, fewer calories are needed to maintain the same weight. Unfortunately, most people in their

30's and 40's eat at least as much as they did in their 20's, if not more, and are usually less physically active. The calories eaten in excess of those burned by metabolism and exercise are stored as fat.

Individuals who are significantly overweight (over 30% greater than normal weight) have a shorter life span than those who are normal weight. For example, middle aged men who are overweight have a three times greater chance of having a fatal heart attack as men the same age who are not overweight. Studies are indicating that individuals who reduce their calorie intake by 20 to 40% may prevent or delay heart disease, even when they start doing so at middle age.

Diet is important not only in managing weight, but also the amount of fat and cholesterol in the blood. Cholesterol is both manufactured by the body and taken in through diet. Excess cholesterol is deposited in the inner lining of arteries, causing atherosclerosis. It is thought that cholesterol needs a chemical reaction called oxidation to form pockets of disease known as plaques. Vitamin C and vitamin E are anti-oxidants and are sometimes recommended as it is thought they may help reduce plaque formation.

Individuals with increased risk of LDL cholesterol, to be discussed later, of over 130 mg/dL or HDL cholesterol of less than 40 mg/dL are at greater risk. The risk of having a heart attack doubles when the total cholesterol rises from 200 to 250.

Cholesterol management is somewhat dependant on the natural production of cholesterol by the body. Occasionally, individuals can eat virtually cholesterol-free diets (such as strict vegetarians) and have very high natural cholesterol levels. Many other people can have dramatic lowering of their cholesterol with only moderate dietary changes.

High blood pressure (hypertension) is associated with an increased risk of heart attack. The increased pressure on artery walls seems to set up an inflammatory reaction that causes heart disease. Blood pressure exceeding 140/90 mmHg can damage the heart, kidneys, and other organs and increases the risk of heart attack, stroke, or kidney failure.

Smoking currently or within the past 5 years raises the chance of many diseases including heart disease. The younger an individual is when they begin smoking, the greater the future risk. Individuals who quit smoking have a lower death rate from heart attack than current smokers.

Diabetics almost all have high cholesterol and have up to four times more than the normal risk of heart attack. Aggressive treatment of diabetes with diet, weight management, and medication is important to minimize heart disease and other debilitating complications.

A sedentary lifestyle may lead to a higher risk of heart disease. Exercise tones muscles and the heart, stimulates circulation, and helps maintain normal weight. Strenuous exercise or work in someone unaccustomed to such activity may cause a heart attack in an apparently healthy individual with undiagnosed heart disease, so a physician should be consulted before starting an exercise program.

Other known factors that lead to heart disease include a Type A personality, especially in hostility prone individuals, depression, and lack of a supportive primary relationship. It is also known that job stress in individuals who have other cardiac risk factors can trigger heart attacks. Individuals who felt they had high demands at work with little opportunity for advancement and a feeling that their job was not rewarding were twice as likely to have a heart attack, according to a study in the British Medical Journal.

Our understanding of heart disease is changing rapidly. Medical researchers are constantly identifying other risk factors that cause heart disease.

Inflammation is emerging as a major factor in the development of coronary artery disease. It appears that in some individuals the immune system attacks the coronary arteries in response to inflammation or infection. A recent study of 28,000 women at Boston's Brigham and Women's Hospital has conclusively shown that inflammation by itself can cause heart attacks in women with normal cholesterol levels.

Doctors believe that a chemical necessary for fighting infection, C-reactive protein (CRP), is produced by the body and does damage to the blood vessels of the heart by weakening plaques in the linings of the arter-

A healthy lifestyle is important beginning at a young age. Eat right, exercise, and minimize your risk factors for heart disease. Finding some physical activity that you enjoy makes it easier to exercise on a regular basis. In the winter, my daughter, Sonja, cross-country skis for relaxation and exercise.

It is easy to forget how many calories you are eating. This typical fast food meal consisting of a Big X-tra hamburger with cheese, super-sized fries, chocolate shake, and apple Danish has 2120 calories. For many people, this one meal alone exceeds the calories recommended for an entire day.

ies. When plaques weaken enough, they burst releasing a chemical that causes the blood to clot and block blood flow through the artery, causing a heart attack.

In the Boston study, women with high levels of CRP had a greater chance of heart attack even when they had low cholesterol levels. High CRP levels combined with high cholesterol levels made the risk even greater.

Inflammation that raises CRP levels can be caused by anything from a lingering infection, smoking, high blood pressure, or obesity. Bacterial or viral infections that can linger in your body for years are also being looked at as a source of inflammation. A respiratory infection due to Chlamydia pneumoniae is known to be associated with an increased risk of heart attack. It can be tested for in the blood and treated with antibiotics. Even low-grade gingival (gum) infections are suspected as a source.

Both aspirin and "statin" drugs used to treat high cholesterol, such as pravastatin (Pravachol), lovostatin (Mevacor), or atorvastatin (Lipitor), have been shown to lower C-reactive protein levels.

C-reactive protein in the blood can be tested with a simple blood test. It is probably a good idea for everyone who has their cholesterol checked to also have their CRP checked. Doctors are still debating which individuals should be checked and what to do if CRP levels are high. The American Heart Association is currently discussing recommendation guidelines for testing. As this may completely change the way we think about and manage heart disease, until they decide, it is probably a good idea to pay attention to inflammation as a risk factor.

An amino acid called homocysteine can be found in elevated levels in some individuals. Doctors feel this can irritate the inner lining of blood vessels and be a source of inflammation that can trigger a heart attack. Recent studies have shown that lowering the homocysteine levels by 25% will lower an individual's risk of heart disease by 10%. Adequate levels of folic acid and vitamins B-6 and B-12 in the diet or in dietary supplements will reverse high homocysteine levels.

Metabolic syndrome affects one in four Americans and is considered a risk for heart disease. It is a syndrome that includes three or more of the following conditions: heavy around the waist, low HDL, high triglyceride levels, borderline or high blood pressure, or elevated blood sugar. Each of these can be treated.

A cholesterol product called lipoprotein (a) is another risk factor that is thought to contribute to formation of blood clots in coronary arteries. Up to 30% of individuals with early heart disease have high levels of lipoprotein (a). Levels are largely hereditary and can be tested with a simple blood test. Estrogen or high doses of niacin can lower these levels.

As you can see, there are many factors involved in heart disease and there is no question that understanding it all is complex. In fact, the health of the coronary arteries has been shown to be so important that a new specialty in medicine is in the process of developing. Endotheliologists (named after the inner lining of blood vessels) will be physicians that manage all the conditions that affect artery health.

Fortunately, it is not necessary for us to understand why everything works in order to make the lifestyle changes that can reduce the risk of heart disease.

Assessing your risk

My physician saved my life. While having a routine annual physical, I mentioned a vague shoulder pain I had while swimming. He suggested I have an exercise treadmill to make sure it was not coming from the heart. "I think it is bursitis," I said. "I exercise regularly and don't have chest pain."

He convinced me to do it and after a few additional tests, I was on the operating table. I was lucky he was suspicious and didn't just assume it was bursitis. I could have been one of the many who die suddenly.

The first thing to do to assess your risk of heart disease is to see a physician to evaluate your risk factors and develop a plan for healthy heart living. Laboratory studies (blood work) should be obtained. Depending on your situation, other heart studies might be recommended. Your physician can also help you safely start an exercise program.

For those individuals who have been determined to have no risks of heart disease, following a healthy heart lifestyle is all that is needed. Individuals with cholesterol, blood pressure, or diabetes problems can be

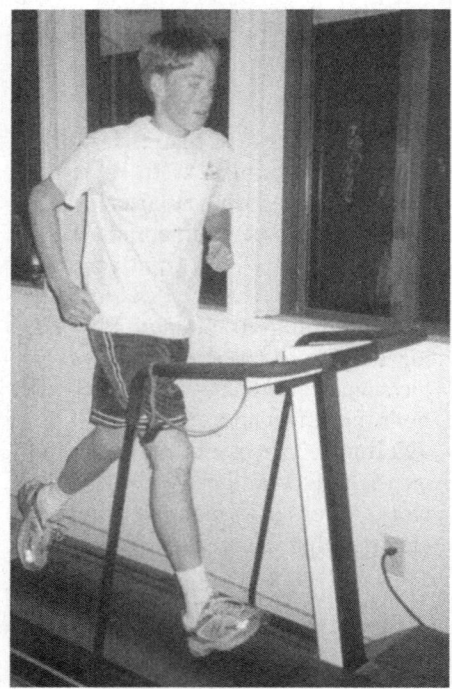

Aerobic exercise decreases the risk of heart disease by lowering cholesterol, triglycerides, and blood pressure. Swimming, dancing, walking, jogging, bicycling, or similar activities are good activities. Treadmills have been found to be the most effective indoor exercise equipment.

helped with medications in addition to a healthy heart lifestyle.

Laboratory studies

Cholesterol is a type of fat, called a lipid, which the body uses to build cells and certain hormones. It is produced by the body and is also absorbed through our diet. When the level of cholesterol in our blood is more than is needed, it may build up along artery walls.

Cholesterol molecules in the blood attach to a protein as they travel throughout the body. This molecule is called a lipoprotein. Lipoproteins are classified as to how much fat is attached to the protein. Ones with more protein than fat are called high-density lipoproteins, or HDL, while lipoproteins with more fat than protein are called low-density lipoproteins, or LDL. Triglycerides are another type of lipid (fat) measured in the blood.

The risk of heart disease is commonly assessed by simple blood tests that evaluate the amount of lipids in the bloodstream. The National Cholesterol Education Program recommends a routine fasting lipid analysis (lipid panel) for adults every 5 years, starting at age 20. A typical lipid panel will evaluate the total cholesterol, LDL, HDL, and triglycerides.

Total cholesterol

Total cholesterol is typically used as a screening to determine the total amount of lipids in the body. Levels below 200 mg/dL are recommended. A middle-aged man who has a level of 250 mg/dL has twice the risk of having a heart attack as compared to what it would be it was 200 mg/dL. Since coronary artery disease takes years to develop, a high total cholesterol level in a young individual definitely needs to be taken seriously.

Total cholesterol can be lowered by diet (reducing saturated fats while increasing fiber and complex carbohydrates), weight loss, and exercise.

Disposable home cholesterol tests can be obtained without a prescription. They test total cholesterol and can be as accurate for screening as tests used by physicians. Costing about $10 to $20 they are performed by an individual by sticking their finger to obtain blood and placing it on a thermometer-like test strip. Results are given not in numbers, but in according to risk of heart disease: normal, borderline-high, and high. They may be useful as a screening, but, if elevated, one should see a physician for a complete lipid panel.

LDL cholesterol

LDL is commonly called the "bad cholesterol" because it is the cholesterol that accumulates on the inner lining of arteries. LDL cholesterol is calculated (vs. being measured) from the total cholesterol, HDL, and triglyceride measurements. When the triglyceride level is high, this can give an inaccurate LDL level.

Low levels of LDL help prevent heart diseases. LDL levels of less than 130 mg/dL are recommended in individual with no history of heart disease. Individuals with a history of heart disease should have levels of LDL below 100 mg/dL.

Besides a high-fat diet or heredity, high LDL levels can be caused by medications, including some diuretics, corticosteroids, androgens (male sex hormones), tranquilizers, and birth control pills. Diabetes, anabolic steroid use, and a number of diseases also raise LDL.

Lowering LDL cholesterol can be done with a low-fat diet, exercise, or medications.

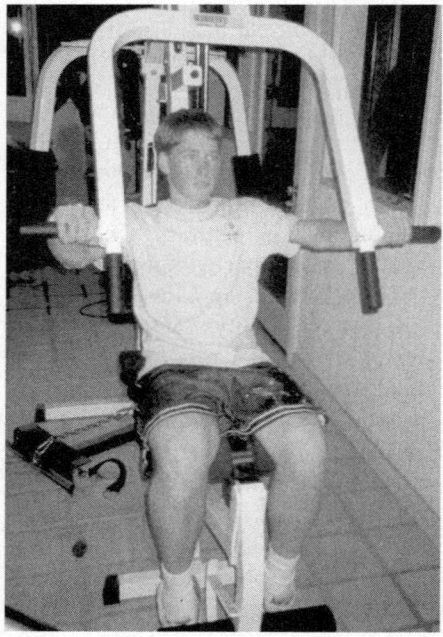

Strength and resistance exercises (muscle toning) using free weights, weight-training machines, or elastic tubing is an effective way to build lean muscle tissue. Increasing lean muscle mass helps reduce weight and reverses the natural progression of muscle loss that occurs with age.

HDL cholesterol

HDL is commonly called the "good cholesterol" because it removes LDL cholesterol from the blood by binding with it in the bloodstream and transporting it to the liver where it is disposed. A high level of HDL lowers an individual's risk of coronary artery disease.

An HDL level should be as high as possible. A level of greater than 40 mg/dL is preferable. Lower than this and an individual is at risk of coronary artery disease. Low HDL levels are largely determined by genetics, however, they may also be caused by diabetes, smoking, excessive weight, lack of exercise, or high triglycerides.

HDL can be increased by vigorous physical exercise, losing weight, and stopping smoking. As much as a 5 pound loss of weight can increase HDL. Moderate alcohol use (1 ounce per day) may be beneficial and increase HDL, but may also have the negative effect of raising triglycerides and contributing to liver problems or alcoholism.

Ratio of LDL/HDL

An individual with a low HDL is at less risk if their LDL is also low because there is less circulating LDL to attach to the artery walls. Conversely, an individual with a high HDL can tolerate higher levels of LDL without developing coronary artery disease.

Triglycerides

A type of fat used by the body to store energy, triglycerides are found in only small amounts in the blood. Still, they are a type of fat that can also build up in the walls of arteries. High levels of triglycerides, with or without high levels of LDL, are a risk factor for coronary artery disease.

Triglyceride levels are considered normal if they are below 150 mg/dL. Borderline high are 150 to 199, high 200 to 500, and very high is above 500.

High triglyceride levels can be caused by diet, weight gain, alcohol, diabetes, kidney disease, and heredity. Triglyceride levels can be lowered by a low-fat diet, losing weight, increased exercise, and medications. A 5-pound weight loss is enough to help lower triglycerides.

It has been clearly established that triglycerides can also be lowered with omega-3 fatty acid, therefore decreasing the risk of cardiac disease. A study of 11,000 individuals who had heart attacks found that sudden cardiac death was reduced 45% when patients took 850 mg of omega-3 fatty acids per day.

Omega-3 polyunsaturated fatty acid can be obtained through diet. Commonly referred to as "fish oil," it is found in fish and some plants. Fish sources, including albacore tuna, salmon, Rainbow trout, Atlantic cod, and some other fish, are a source of EPA and DHA, two types of polyunsaturated fatty acids. Plant sources include almonds, walnuts, raw soybeans, and flaxseed and are a source of ALA, the third type of polyunsaturated fatty acid. Note that flaxseed also causes a huge increase in the risk of prostate cancer, so it is not a good idea for men to use this as a source of omega-3.

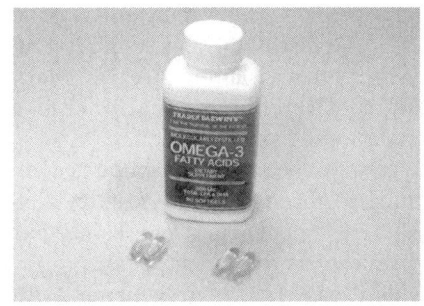

Omega 3 fatty acids, found naturally in fish and some plants, can help lower elevated triglyceride levels. Dietary supplements, as shown here, are a way to include enough omega 3 fatty acids in the diet daily.

Another source of omega-3 fatty acid is a dietary supplement. It is recommended that four capsules each containing 300 mg of EPA and 200 mg of DHA be taken daily. Trader Darwin's Omega-3, available at Trader Joe's, and Omega Caps, available at health stores, are two brands that contain the correct amount. Take 2 capsules twice a day.

Other blood tests

After initial screening of the lipid level in the body, a physician may recommend additional blood tests. These may be include checking levels of VLDL (very-low-density lipoprotein), homocystine, C-reactive protein, or lipoprotein a. As mentioned previously, it may become common to have C-reactive protein tested with the initial lipid testing.

Heart studies

Depending on symptoms, history, and cardiac risk factors, other tests may be recommended by your physician to screen for coronary artery disease. These may include an EKG, exercise EKG (treadmill), heart scan, or angiogram.

What you can do

Health heart living is following a healthy lifestyle that will reduce your risk of heart disease while

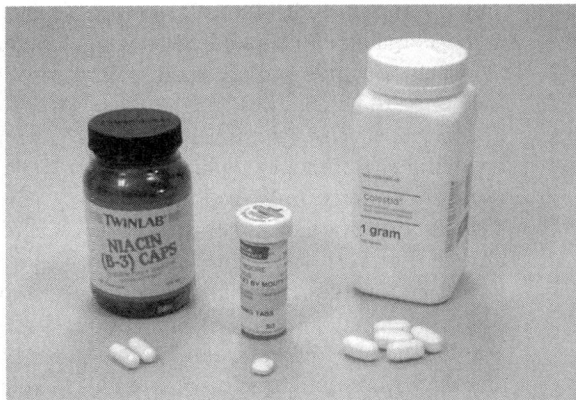

Medications prescribed by a physician can lower cholesterol levels when diet and exercise alone are not enough.

also helping to prevent a stroke, other vascular disease, diabetes, and a number of other disabling diseases. Many of these recommendations also reduce the risk of cancer.

Healthy heart living can be accomplished through your lifestyle, diet, dietary supplements, and, as needed, medications from your doctor.

Is it easy to change your lifestyle? It hasn't been for me. We are so accustomed to eating a certain way, living a certain way, and to our daily routine. Our social life also partially determines our activity and what we eat. I have lived a healthy heart lifestyle for the 12 years since my surgery and I still struggle with it at times. It doesn't mean we shouldn't try, however.

Diet

A diet low in fat is recommended. Current guidelines recommend the total calories from fat in a diet be 25 to 35%, from carbohydrates 50 to 60%, and from protein 15%. Saturated fats, such as found in cheese, whole milk, and red meat, should be less than 7% of the total calories.

Practically speaking, this means to go light on meat and eggs, use low-fat dairy products, watch the amount of fat and oils, eat fruits and vegetables, and use low-fat breads, cereals, and grains.

Meats should be limited to 5 to 6 ounces per day of lean meat, poultry without skin, or fish (not fried). Coldwater fish have fish oil, unsaturated omega-3 fatty acids, which have been shown to decrease triglycerides.

Egg yolks should be limited to less than 2 to 4 per week, substituting 2 egg whites for one whole egg in recipes. Many egg substitute products are available at the market and in many restaurants.

Two to three servings of low-fat dairy products per day are recommended. These could include skim milk, low-fat yogurt, low-fat cheese, low-fat cottage cheese, or frozen yogurt. Use low-fat creamer and low or nonfat sour cream.

Unsaturated oils are healthier than saturated oils. Unsaturated oils include safflower oil, sunflower oil, olive oil, canola oil, and oils in seeds and nuts. Saturated oils include coconut oil, palm oil, and milk chocolate. Watch the amount of oils used on salads. Three tablespoons of olive oil on a salad or in food is the same amount of calories as eating three, four-ounce scoops of ice cream.

Six or more servings of breads or cereals per day are recommended. These should be low-fat breads, cereals, and grains, including whole grain bread, oats, wheat, or corn, low-fat crackers, rice, and pastas. Avoid high fat pastries, croissants, and granola.

Fresh vegetables should include 3 to 5 servings per day, especially including green vegetables. Avoid fried vegetables, cream sauce, or cheese sauce. Include 2 to 4 servings of fruit per day, avoiding fried fruits, cream sauce, or butter sauce.

Soups tend to be high in calories, fat, and sodium. When choosing soups, avoid ones containing whole milk, cream, fats, or skins.

Desserts and sweets taste so great because they are full of fat and saturated oils. It is easy to add a lot of calories and fat to your diet by eating milk chocolate, doughnuts, cream pies, commercial pies and cakes, and desserts containing coconut oil, palm oil, or palm kernel oil.

Instead, eat low-fat cookies, pies, or pudding containing egg whites or egg substitutes, skim milk, and unsaturated oil or margarine. Angel food cake, fig or fruit bars, and ginger snaps are good alternatives. Frozen yogurt, ice milk, sherbet, and sorbet are good replacements for ice cream. Candy made with sugar, syrup, or honey, such as candy corn, gum drops, and hard candy, is a better alternative than chocolates.

I found that changing my diet was actually one of the easiest changes to accomplish. It is mostly being aware of what you are eating and choosing healthy alternatives. It is not as hard as it seems.

Exercise

Exercise, on the other hand, is harder to incorporate into your lifestyle. It takes time and it takes effort. If it is not something you already do regularly, it means finding the time and energy to exercise in your already busy schedule. Its benefits, however, are not some vague "improvement of future health." Exercise makes you feel better, sleep better, and have more energy. It makes you more productive and happier.

Physical exercise is the greatest way to keep weight off and strengthen muscle, yet most adults in the United States perform little or none. Twenty-five percent are completely sedentary and over 60% are physically active less than 30 minutes per day. Among Americans over 65 years old, 75% are sedentary.

Exercise builds healthy muscle. Aerobic exercise, such as walking, running, and swimming, increases the heart rate and is necessary for heart health. Strength and resistance exercises build and preserve lean muscle tissue. An exercise program should provide both and it is not as hard as one might think. It simply requires an exercise plan that you enjoy and will follow.

Aerobic exercise decreases the risk of heart disease, decreases cholesterol and triglycerides, lowers blood pressure, reduces risk of colon, breast, and prostate cancer, decreases osteoporosis, reduces obesity, and improves the immune system, among other things. Daily, it is recommended that an individual have 30 minutes or more of moderate physical activity, such as a brisk walk for 30 minutes or three ten-minute walks. Three or more times per week, more intensive exercise that brings the heart rate to 60-80% of maximum for 20 to 60 minutes is recommended. This could include swimming, dancing, walking, jogging, bicycling, or similar activities.

For years I tried various indoor exercise programs using treadmills, stationary bikes, and more. I struggled every day with exercise because I hated it and would make any excuse not to make time to exercise. I'm too tired, too busy, I have to go here, I have to go there, my muscles still hurt from last time—I used them all. And I knew better. I had already been through heart surgery.

Then, I figured out I love to exercise outdoors. I don't care if it is hot, raining, or snowing, I would rather do something outdoors than stay inside. So, for me, bike riding, hiking, swimming, and snowshoeing are ways I enjoy getting aerobic exercise.

Many of my friends are the opposite. They like to watch television while exercising or enjoy the social interaction of sports clubs, so they use exercise machines indoors. Actually, treadmills have been found to be the most effective indoor exercise equipment, requiring more energy use than Stairmasters, rowing machines, Nordic track, or exercise bikes. Exercising indoors is also better when it is dark or bad weather outside.

Outdoors or indoors, it doesn't matter. What is important is that you find something that you enjoy doing and will work with your schedule. If it is fun, you will do it without making excuses.

Speaking of schedules, if you don't include exercise in your schedule, it is never going to happen. You will never just "find time" in your day. Plan exercise into your daily schedule.

Some other practical exercise tips include walking instead of driving when possible, parking your car at a distance from a mall or office, using stairs instead of an elevator, playing golf without a cart, and exercising while watching television.

After age 20, an individual loses seven-tenths of a pound of muscle mass per year. Not only does strength decrease, but lean muscle mass uses energy. The more muscle mass an individual loses, the fewer calories their body burns in a day. Their metabolism decreases and they gain weight while eating the same amount of calories.

If you are trying to lose weight, gaining muscle mass will increase your metabolism and burn more calories. For every pound of lean muscle mass a body increases, 50 calories more are used per day. Just one

> **Here are the key things you can do to live a healthy heart lifestyle:**
> - Eat a proper diet
> - Exercise
> - Lose weight
> - Manage lipids
> - Blood pressure control
> - Stop smoking
> - Aggressively treat diabetes
> - Dietary supplements

pound of increased muscle mass will burn 18,250 calories more per year, or 5.2 pounds of weight loss. Five pounds of increased muscle will cause 26 pounds of weight loss per year!

Aerobic exercise does not build lean muscle mass. Strength and resistance exercises (muscle toning) performed twice a week are the most effective way to build muscle tissue. A muscle is challenged to perform above its current strength level by free weights, weight-training machines, elastic tubing, or an individual's body weight, stimulating production of lean muscle.

Forget the image of body builders or weight lifters. That is not what most of us need. A simple program using elastic tubing at home is as effective as "pumping iron" at a club. Strength and resistance training has even been shown to improve health and reduce injuries in elderly individuals living in retirement homes.

The key is to exercise regularly doing exercises that do not cause injury to joints or back. Start slow and avoid overdoing it with heavy weights. Increase weight or repetitions as time goes on. In his book, "Business Plan for the Body," author Jim Karas, shows with descriptions and photographs a low-impact strength and resistance program using elastic bands at home. Sports and exercise clubs also have trainers who can help develop a plan for an individual.

Lose weight

If you are one of the millions who are overweight, losing pounds can help your health tremendously. Despite hundreds of diets, exercise machines, and pills available, Americans are still grossly overweight. Most know that being overweight is not good for health, but it is hard to do anything about it.

Weight-loss is a major industry in our country, often based on the fact that we want quick fixes. The problem is that many of the products or diets don't work, or when they do, we regain the weight rapidly when we go off the product. It can take months of work to lose 20 pounds and a few weeks to put it back on.

I know this is true. Realizing I would be hiking at elevations as high as 10,000 to 12,000 feet, I trained for 6 months to go with my sons on a rugged 90-mile backpacking trip at Philmont Boy Scout Ranch in the mountains of New Mexico. I lost 30 pounds between the training and the trip. I felt great when my pants were too loose on the way home, but not so great when they were tight again a mere three weeks later.

The answer to weight-loss is actually pretty simple, but most of us don't want to hear it. If you eat fewer calories than you use, you will lose weight. Period.

This can be accomplished by eating less, by exercising more, or by doing both. If you eat right and exercise, you will lose weight. It is impossible not to lose pounds.

This does not mean it will be quick. After all, it took time to gain the extra pounds and it will take time to lose it. However, losing weight requires a permanent lifestyle change. It has to be more than just a temporary adjustment.

Individuals do differ and some lose weight easier than others. Genetics and metabolic conditions certainly are a factor. Twenty-five percent of an individual's weight is determined by genetics and the rest is determined by environment and behavior. For most of us, eating is 20% physical and 80% emotional. We eat without thinking when we are stressed, tired, or in social situations. Women typically lose weight slower than men since they frequently have less lean muscle tissue.

The first thing to do to lose weight is to determine what your body needs to survive, your basal metabolic rate. The basal metabolic rate is the amount of energy your body needs to function if you were to do nothing but stay in bed awake for 16 hours and asleep for 8. Add to this your activity per day and this is the amount of calories you need to maintain the same weight.

The formula for calculating your basal metabolic rate (BMR) is:

Instead of doing the calculations yourself, you can also go to the website www.fpnotebook.com (click on "Dietician in a Box") and let them do the calculations.

As an example, a 35 year old woman who is 5'5" tall and weighed 145 pounds would have a BMR of 1,416 calories per day. A man of the same age, height, and weight would have a BMR of 1556 calories per day.

To this, add the calories expended by activity and exercise. Multiply the BMR by 1.15 for a sedentary lifestyle, 1.3 for normal, everyday activity, 1.4 if you exercise 3 to 4 times per week, 1.6 for exercise 4 to 5 times per week, and 1.8 for exercise 6 to 7 times per week.

If our 35 year-old woman's daily activity is limited to normal, everyday activities with no other exercise, she could eat 1,416 calories x 1.3, or 1840 calories, per day to maintain her current weight, while our 35 year-old man could eat 2023 calories. If they ate more, they would gain weight. If they ate less, exercised more, or both, they would lose weight. For every 3,500 calories that you exercise in excess of the calories you eat, you will lose one pound of weight in the form of fat. So, if you burn 500 calories a day more than you eat, you will lose 1 pound in 7 days.

It is very easy to eat more than we should. Awareness of how many calories we are eating is the most important part of weight-loss. For example, a typical "healthy" dinner at an Italian restaurant might include 2 pieces of bread, a Caesar salad, a tomato, basil and olive oil pasta, 2 glasses of wine, and a few bites of dessert. This "healthy" dinner is approximately 2,300 calories, almost the total caloric intake for the entire day for our above man and woman.

If our woman exercised four times a week, her daily caloric needs increase to 2,265 calories, an increase of 60%. She can eat 849 calories more a day in addition to her BMR and not gain weight or eat the same and lose weight at a rate of about 1 pound every 4 days. Our man also increases 60% to 2489 calories, an increase of 934 calories over BMR. He could lose a pound every 3.5 days. It is certainly easier to exercise four days a week than it is to cut 800 to 1000 calories from out diet.

To lose weight, it is important to really pay attention to the portion size and calories. This can be done through self-determination or with support groups such as Weight Watchers. Recording the calories you eat daily in a notebook is a useful way to help watch calories. It is surprising how fast they add up.

A impressive website called Family Practice Notebook, a site intended for physicians, but available to anyone, has a unique, free analysis that can also help get you started. When you enter your age, weight, height, food likes and dislikes, and types of exercises you would do, it will calculate your metabolic rates, caloric needs, and give you a detailed print-out of recommendations for diet, ideal calories per day to eat, exercise, and weight-loss using the foods you like (or are at least willing to eat) and the exercise you like to do. It can be accessed by going to www.fpnotebook.com and clicking on "Dietician in a Box."

Lipid management

Diet, exercise, and weight loss may take care of high cholesterol for many individuals. Minor changes in diet and weight make major changes in cholesterol levels for many people. For others, diet changes alone won't work. If it does not, then there are numerous cholesterol-lowering medications available through your physician.

The morning I entered the hospital for my surgery, I ate a high-fat diet of Eggs Benedict and ham, knowing I would never eat these foods again. A few hours after eating this meal, I had a non-fasting cholesterol test that showed me to have a cholesterol level of 200. After one year of being a complete vegetarian, eating no dairy, no eggs, and a very low-fat diet, my total cholesterol was 200. No change despite all that effort. Despite all my diet changes, I have a body that produces its own high cholesterol and medications are the answer.

High blood pressure

High blood pressure is a silent killer. You cannot feel when your blood pressure is high, so have your blood pressure checked by your physician. If you are prone to high blood pressure, buy an automatic blood pressure cuff, widely available at department stores and drug stores, and keep a record of your blood pressure.

While there are many causes of high blood pressure, some known and some unknown, it is usually controllable. Treatment includes weight loss if overweight, elimination of smoking, modifying stressful living habits, and increasing exercise. When these are not enough, medications to lower blood pressure can be prescribed by a physician. This will eliminate the harmful effects caused by high blood pressure.

Smoking and diabetes

If you smoke, stopping is important. Just as with weight loss, it is not easy for some people. Talk to your physician. They will be able to help with medications and information on local stop smoking groups that may help.

Diabetics need to aggressively control their diet and medications in order to prevent complications to all of the blood vessels of the body, including the coronary arteries.

Dietary supplements

Several dietary supplements and vitamins available at most markets and pharmacies are recommended by physicians for patients at risk of coronary artery disease. A multivitamin with vitamin B-6 and B-12 and a tablet of folic acid 400 micrograms per day helps decrease homocysteine levels which irritate linings of arteries. Vitamin C, 500 mg per day, and vitamin E, 400 IU per day, act as antioxidants. Two capsules twice a day of omega-3 fatty acid containing 300 mg of EPA and 200 mg of DHA may help reduce triglycerides.

Do it now

Is it easy to make these lifestyle changes? For most of us the answer is no. I have lived them for the 12 years since my heart surgery, so I understand.

However, they are necessary for all of us whether or not we have been diagnosed with heart disease. Healthy heart living can make you feel better and give a better quality of life.

For Women:
661
+ (4.38 x weight in pounds)
+ (4.38 x height in inches)
- (4.7 x age)
= BMR

For Men:
67
+ (6.24 x weight in pounds)
+ (12.7 x height in inches)
- (6.9 x age)
= BMR

Although it can seem overwhelming at first, all you have to do is to set your mind to it and make the changes. If it seems like too much, work at it a little bit at a time. See your physician, start doing some exercise, improve your diet, lose some weight, or stop smoking. Then, gradually improve other areas. Many hospitals offer education in healthy heart living, often associated with their cardiac rehabilitation or community education programs.

Can you make all of the changes at once? Absolutely. Many people "see the light" when they have heart problems and are forced to make all the changes at once. They are scared into making changes. If they can, so can you.

The key is to start today to do something towards a healthy heart lifestyle. Not only will you feel better, I can guarantee that you don't want to hear, "I am sorry, you need immediate heart surgery." Δ

Ayoob on Firearms:
A 24/7 BACKWOODS HANDGUN

A handgun can come in awfully...well...*handy* at a backwoods homestead. You're puttering in the garden when a squirrel suitable for the pot makes his presence felt, or the weasel that's been raiding the henhouse pokes its head out of the bushes. There isn't time to go back in the house for a long gun. If only you'd had a sidearm on your hip…

There are more compelling moments. A female jogger is pounced and killed by a cougar. A man who has doubtless read in the books that black bears don't attack humans is attacked and killed by a black bear who apparently does not read. Some of our readers have much bigger bears than that in their neighborhoods. Some share their turf with poisonous snakes. More are probably bothered by feral or outlaw dogs than any other dangerous four-legged beast. And there is always the two-legged predator to worry about. A gun in the house won't help you if you can't get to it. The rural Clutter family was said to own rifles and shotguns. If so, they couldn't get at them when they were massacred by the murderers Truman Capote made infamous in his book "In Cold Blood."

Resolved: It can make sense for responsible adults in locations remote from assistance and possibly infested with lethally dangerous life forms to have a loaded handgun on their person where they can reach it.

Different authorities have taken different approaches. The great hunter and rifleman Jack O'Connor said that if he could own only one handgun, it would be the graceful .22 caliber target revolver known as the Smith & Wesson K-22. Good for putting the turtle in turtle soup, but a bit light for the more dangerous fauna. Another great shooter and hunter, Elmer Keith, said the handgun he'd keep if he could have only one would be a Smith & Wesson .44 Magnum with four-inch barrel. Now, that's a tune I can march to. If I won the lottery and retired to a remote cabin, my daily wear would include my favorite version of Keith's pet revolver, the S&W Model 629 Mountain Gun.

However, like Keith, I've become habituated over decades to wearing a full size handgun at my hip during virtually all my waking hours. An outdoor person new to the armed lifestyle is likely to find the big .44 too heavy and bulky to wear 24/7. Most cops carry lighter guns than that, and can't wait to get the weight off their hips at the end of an eight to twelve hour shift. Therefore, the "always" gun for the backwoods person should be light and compact enough for constant carry.

There is also the matter of discretion. For people like Keith or me who have carried a gun for a living, the people we associate with us are used to us being armed. Your visitors from the city, the rural postman, and the yuppie who bought the parcel of land next door to yours may freak at the sight of a handgun worn openly on your hip. There's also the matter of going into town on errands and to catch up with neighbors over a cup of coffee. A century or so after the phrase was first uttered, we know that it's still bad taste to "frighten the horses." Therefore, the 24/7 backwoods handgun needs to be concealable in all circumstances where it is legal for the wearer to carry it so.

Massad Ayoob

Which leads me to a recommendation some might find unconventional.

The nominee is…

When you look at the job description above, it's hard to come up with a better "always" gun than the Ruger SP101, caliber .357 Magnum. I would choose the version with the 2¼-inch barrel. This will fit nicely in the pocket of jacket, pants, or overalls. It fits in the glove box of the smallest farm vehicle. It's compact enough for an ankle or boot holster.

No, you won't be dropping deer at a hundred yards with it. But if you've learned to shoot it well and you get a shot at a deer standing broadside to you at a quarter of that distance, you should be able to kill it cleanly with a lung cavity shot. We're not talking handgun hunting, here. We're talking an emergency utility handgun that's always with you. Hence, the short barrel.

The Fourteenth Year

Both for snag-free drawing from concealment and for civil liability reasons, author favors spurless hammer "double action only" model as issued by his police department (right) to conventional model (left).

Gun experts have long touted the .357 Magnum as the most versatile of handgun calibers, because a gun chambered for that round can also fire the .38 Special or, for that matter, the .38 Long Colt cartridge that the sport of Cowboy Action Shooting recently resurrected from obsolescence. Just how versatile is that? Let's take a look.

.357 versatility

Start with the .38 Special mid-range wadcutter, a flat-nose bullet weighing 148 grains and trundling out of the short barrel at something like 700 feet per second. Its sharp edges chop a clean hole in the full bullet diameter. There are those at the International Wound Ballistics Association who think that makes it just fine as a self-defense load against criminal assault. Certainly, it's the lightest kicking load you can put in a .38 Special or .357 Magnum revolver.

It's also hell for accurate. When the SP101 came out (in 1988, as a .38 Special) gun expert Wiley Clapp tested one with a Ransom machine rest. He put ten consecutive shots into a group that measured 1.33 inches, center to center. "This is superlative accuracy," he wrote at the time in Guns & Ammo. Who would argue?

The ammunition Wiley used that day was Federal Match. While preparing this article I shot some of the same stuff through my snub-nose SP101. Five shots, double action, two-hand standing went into an inch and three-quarters. The best three measured three quarters of an inch. The group wasn't as good as the machine rest's, obviously, but it was damned impressive for a short barrel revolver that requires a long pull of the trigger for each shot. Some guns have great inherent mechanical accuracy, but don't let the shooter deliver it because the sights or the trigger pull aren't good enough. The little Ruger has a smooth double action trigger stroke, and big sights that are easy to hold on target. It's a user-friendly revolver in more ways than one. Within ten paces, the SP101 loaded with .38 wadcutters lets you nail a bushytail in the head for a painless kill that doesn't waste the key ingredient of squirrel stew.

Jack the power up a notch, to .38 Special defense loads. In a standard pressure round with mild recoil, experience tells me that you can't do better than the 125 grain Federal Nyclad. It's nowhere near as accurate as the wadcutter, but much more dynamic in flesh. It's the defense load of choice for people sensitive to "kick."

Next up on the scale is +P .38 Special ammo. The 125 grain full- or partially-copper jacketed hot load has gotten rave reviews in some quarters, but I'm one of many old-timers who prefer the FBI load conceptualized in 1972, a 158 grain all-lead semiwadcutter hollowpoint at the accelerated velocity delivered by the +P pressures. With no tough copper jacket to peel back, the soft lead bullet almost always mushrooms, even when fired through short barrel guns and after passing through clothing. It kicks more than the lighter bullet +P loads, but I think the superior street-proven performance is worth it.

Then we get all the way up to the .357 Magnum. A 125 grain bullet that would be under a thousand feet per second in a +P .38 Special is running at 1400 to 1450 feet per second in the full Magnum loading when fired from a full size service revolver. Out of a snub, velocity drops to 1220 to 1300 foot-seconds or so. A generation of bad guys shot with this ammo out of the snub-nosed revolvers of detectives and off-duty cops never knew the difference. The 125 grain Magnum semi-jacketed hollowpoint earned a reputation for putting the bad guys down with a single hit better than any other load or caliber, irrespective of the barrel length of the revolver used.

This 125 grain Magnum load is what I would (and do) personally carry in the SP101 most of the time for defensive purposes. It's also devastating on vicious dogs. A friend of mine recently needed six fast shots with his .45 automatic to stop a charging German Shepherd, and another had to empty his high capacity 9mm into a big Chow that was attacking him before the beast gave up the ghost. But the combination of a hollow-nosed bullet about .357 inches in diameter, weighing 125 grains and traveling 1200 to 1400 feet per second has earned a reputation for fast, one-shot stops of the biggest and most vicious canines.

Those bullets go into flesh about ten to twelve inches and stop, with a dramatically wide wound channel along the way. That's what makes them ideal for anti-personnel work against facing, erect bipeds, or for a shot through the brisket of an oncoming Hound of the Baskervilles, or to put through the breastbone of a mountain lion that's on top of you. If you're in big bear country, though, you'll need something that penetrates deeper.

In 1935, when Smith & Wesson introduced the .357 Magnum cartridge, the only available load was an all-lead semi-wadcutter bullet at a red-line velocity of 1500 feet per second. No responsible manufacturer loads that bullet to that high a velocity now. At the time, though, it went deep enough to kill the biggest grizzly and Kodiak bears, which admittedly was something of a stunt.

Father Hubbard, the legendary "Glacier Priest" of Alaska, killed many a large critter to help feed native families and his own group. He guided S&W's Douglas Wesson on the hunts in which both men shot enough big bears and moose with .357 Magnums to prove that they could cleanly kill such huge game. However, both used guns with barrel lengths ranging from 6 to 8 3/8 inches; remember that in a short barrel "pocket gun," you lose some velocity and therefore lose some power.

It takes a lot to ruin a bruin, and a .357 Magnum revolver is on the light side no matter how you cut it. Today's jacketed soft-nose 158 grain bullets will penetrate much deeper than any hollowpoint, and some specialty loads are available that go deeper yet. On an animal this big, with a skull this hard and thick, penetration is what you want. In my forays to Alaska thus far, I've been doing police training stuff or shooting trial stuff in the cities, and carried one or another .45 auto. When I go for myself and travel the boondocks, the .44 Magnum will be at my side…and my backup gun will be this SP101, loaded with deep-penetrating .357 Magnum GameStopper ammo by Pro-Load.

You'll have to look far and wide to find a more hard-headed creature than the Cape buffalo of Africa. Legendary international big game hunter Elgin Gates was treed by one, and saved his life by shooting it through the brain with armor-piercing bullets from his Smith & Wesson .357 Magnum. I believe it had a four-inch barrel. Today, such ammunition is forbidden to private citizens, but a load like the GameStopper should punch through the skull of the toughest animal that's likely to come after you in the United States.

Now, let's go back down the scales. Down the power scale, down the evolutionary scale, and down from critters that tower over you like bears to the ones that slither up and bite you on the calf. If you're in poisonous snake country, there is a very limited range at which you are likely to employ a firearm against said serpent.

If you see the snake at a distance, avoid it unless it's a matter of keeping your children safe and proactively destroying the creature. If a poisonous snake is close enough to bite you, you're going to have to get your gun out quick and hit a small target very fast. At snakebite range, the logical thing to have in the gun is snakeshot, which sends a cloud of tiny birdshot pellets out in a fan that is highly likely to nail the rattler before the rattlesnake nails you. Speer's .38/.357 snakeshot load is what I would have in the first one or two chambers in line to come up under the firing pin if I was carrying the SP101 in poisonous snake country.

Short barrel revolver advantages

One thread runs repeatedly through tales of survivors mauled by bears and the great cats. Many were holding their rifle or shotgun when the animal took them down, and could

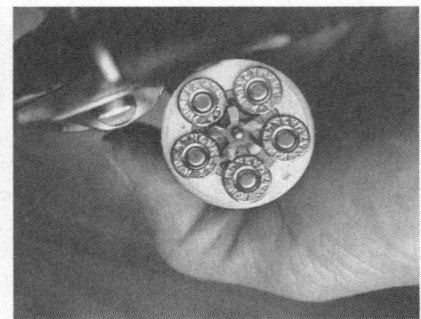

The size of the little Colt Detective Special .38, the Ruger SP101 carries five rounds of powerful .357 Magnum. Note ample steel between chambers in cylinder for maximum safety.

not bring the muzzle to bear on their four-legged tormentor because the long gun was trapped between their body and that of the beast. Even a long barrel handgun could be hard to get out and into action.

The short barrel revolver is faster to clear from holster or pocket. It is faster to get pointed at the vitals of the creature on top of you. In a great many animal attack cases, the defender or protector has to shove the gun muzzle right up against the critter's body. If you do this with most semi-automatic pistols, it will push the barrel slide assembly rearward and "out of battery." That is, the parts are pushed out of the alignment in which they must be for the gun to fire. This won't happen with the revolver, whose barrel is rigidly fixed to the frame and ahead of the firing mechanism.

Something else can happen with a muzzle contact wound. As the muzzle blast roars into the soft tissue of the body, a "blowback" effect occurs in which tissue, fur, and viscous blood can be blown into the open mechanism of the pistol in the instant in which its slide is cycling. This matter can block the slide from returning to battery, and prevent the auto pistol from firing subsequent shots if needed. This does not, of course, occur with the revolver. A friend of mine, a

Good, better, best. From bottom up: Federal Nyclad standard pressure .38 hollowpoint, author's preferred defense load for the recoil-sensitive; +P .38 Special, which hits harder; and the decisively fight-stopping 125 grain Magnum hollowpoint.

CIA agent who has had to do more "wet work" than he would have liked in the service of his country, knows how that term came about. After the first time he had to shove a gun muzzle into an opponent's body and pull the trigger, the backblast taught him to always use a powerful revolver for this sort of work.

It happens with animals, too. A friend of mine was attacked by a Briard, a rare variation of the huge Bouvier des Flandres. As the dog's open jaws approached his crotch, he shoved the muzzle of his Colt Commander against its neck and fired. The bullet killed the creature instantly and saved my friend from injury, but fur and blood and tissue blasted back into the muzzle/barrel bushing area of the .45 auto as it cycled, jamming the gun. He was using the Glaser Safety Slug, a lightweight, pre-fragmented projectile at very high muzzle velocity.

It can even happen beyond contact distance. Some years ago, I had occasion to put down a large beef critter. A 190 grain Super Vel .45 hollowpoint to the brain killed it instantly, which was a good thing. The backsplash of blood and brain matter out of the entry wound not only soaked me but adhered to the exposed barrel of my Colt Government Model autoloader as it cycled from the recoil, and jammed the gun. A quick slap with the heel of my support hand's palm on the back of the slide compressed the tissue and drove the gun back into battery, but I had learned a lesson.

Suffice to say that if a living thing is on top of you and trying to kill you and your only chance is to shove your gun muzzle into that thing and pull the trigger several times, a revolver has a distinct advantage over an autoloading pistol.

The SP101 in particular

There are lots of small .357 Magnum revolvers available today. What's so special about this one in particular?

It's no secret that I had a hand in convincing the late, great Bill Ruger to make this gun in .357 Magnum instead of just .38 Special. If you're interested, you can read about it in R.L. Wilson's superb book *Ruger and His Guns* (Simon & Schuster, 1996, page 193) or in *Complete Book of Handguns 2003*, which should be on the newsstands about the time you read this or shortly thereafter. However, ego investment in the gun isn't the reason I recommend it. Practicality is.

The SP101 was the first successful "baby" .357 Magnum, small enough for pocket or ankle carry. It was not the last. Rossi, Smith & Wesson, and Taurus have all since produced short barrel, five shot, small frame .357 Magnums. Most of them are lighter and kick much more viciously, however, and none of them seem to have quite the deliverable accuracy, the mix of user-friendliness and inherent mechanical ability to get those powerful bullets delivered not only fast but straight. The Colt Magnum Carry came closest, but has been out of production for some time.

At slightly over 26 ounces in weight, the Ruger is a solid little gun that absorbs recoil well. It is aided in this by well thought out forward balance and particularly by Ruger's trademark "live feel" grips, which tend to soak up the kick to a degree that has to be felt to be appreciated. Bill Ruger told Shooting Times staffer Jim Bequette, in one of the last interviews he granted before his death, that the secret to the SP101's success was that "Those damned cushioned grips make it the easiest small-frame .357 to shoot."

How good is the SP101? Good enough that in 2002, my police department adopted the spurless hammer double action only version with short barrel and issued it to all sworn personnel for backup and off duty use. Each officer is issued Black Hills 125 grain Magnum ammunition and an Alessi hideout holster. I had often carried one of these little guns for backup anyway. I feel good to know that my brother officers have backup as solid as this.

It would feel good to know that you had it too. Δ

Want more Ayoob?

www.backwoodshome.com

A Backwoods Home Anthology

THE IRREVERENT JOKE PAGE

(Believing it is important for people to be able to laugh at themselves, this is a continuing feature in *Backwoods Home Magazine*. We invite readers to submit any jokes you'd like to share to *BHM*, P.O. Box 712, Gold Beach, OR 97444. There is no payment for jokes used.)

Did you hear about the teacher who was helping one of her kindergarten students put on his boots? He asked for help and she could see why. With her pulling and him pushing, the boots still didn't want to go on. When the second boot was on, she had worked up a sweat.

She almost whimpered when the little boy said, "Teacher, they're on the wrong feet." She looked and sure enough, they were.

It wasn't any easier pulling the boots off than it was putting them on. She managed to keep her cool as together they worked to get the boots back on—this time on the right feet. He then announced, "These aren't my boots."

She bit her tongue rather than get right in his face and scream, "Why didn't you say so?" like she wanted to. Once again she struggled to help him pull the ill-fitting boots off. He then said, "They're my brother's boots. My Mom made me wear them."

She didn't know if she should laugh or cry. She mustered up the grace and courage she had left to wrestle the boots on his feet again. She said, "Now, where are your mittens?"

He said, "I stuffed them in the toes of my boots..."

Her trial starts next month.

Dear Abby:
I have been engaged for almost a year. I am to be married next month. My fiancée's mother is not only very attractive but really great and understanding. She is putting the entire wedding together and invited me to her place to go over the invitation list because it had grown a bit beyond what we had expected it to be. When I got to her place we reviewed the list and trimmed it down to just under a hundred ... then she floored me. She said that in a month I would be a married man and that before that happened, she wanted to have sex with me. Then she just stood up and walked to her bedroom and on her way said that I knew where the front door was if I wanted to leave. I stood there for about five minutes and finally decided that I knew exactly how to deal with this situation. I headed straight out the front door... There, leaning against my car was her husband, my father-in-law to be. He was smiling. He explained that they just wanted to be sure I was a good kid and would be true to their little girl. I shook his hand and he congratulated me on passing their little test. Abby, should I tell my fiancée what her parents did, and that I thought their "little test" was asinine and insulting to my character? Or should I keep the whole thing to myself including the fact that the reason I was walking out to my car was to get a condom?

Three Irishmen, Paddy, Mike, and Sean, were stumbling home from the pub late one night and found themselves on the road which led past an old graveyard.

"Come have a look over here," says Paddy, "It's Michael O'Grady's grave, God bless his soul, he lived to the ripe old age of 87."

"That's nothing," says Mike, "here's one named Patrick O'Toole. It says here that he was 95 when he died."

Just then, Sean yells out, "But here's a fellow who died when he was 145 years old!"

"What was his name?" asks Paddy.

Sean lights a match to see what else is written on the stone marker, and exclaims, "Miles, from Dublin."

A man was walking in the city, when he was accosted by a particularly dirty and shabby-looking bum who asked him for a couple of dollars for dinner.

The man took out his wallet, extracted two dollars and asked, "If I gave you this money, will you take it and buy whiskey?"

"No, I stopped drinking years ago," the bum said.

"Will you use it to gamble?"

"I don't gamble. I need everything I can get just to stay alive."

"Will you spend the money on greens fees at a golf course?"

"Are you MAD? I haven't played golf in 20 years!"

The man said, "Well, I'm not going to give you two dollars. Instead, I'm going to take you to my home for a terrific dinner cooked by my wife." The bum was astounded.

"Won't your wife be furious with you for doing that? I know I'm dirty, and I probably smell pretty bad."

The man replied, "Hey, man, that's OK! I just want her to see what a man looks like who's given up drinking, gambling, and golf!"

Once upon a time there were three little pigs. The straw pig, the stick pig, and the brick pig.

One day this nasty old wolf came up to the straw pig's house and said, "I'm gonna huff and puff and blow your house down." And he did. So the straw pig went running over to the stick pig's house and said, "Please let me in, the wolf just blew down my house." So the stick Pig let the straw pig in. Just then the wolf showed up and said, "I'm gonna huff and puff and blow your house down." And he did. So the straw pig and the stick pig went running over to the brick pig's house and said, "Let us in, let us in, the big bad wolf just blew our houses down!" So the brick pig let them in just as the wolf showed up. The wolf said, "I'm gonna huff and puff and blow your house down."

The straw pig and the stick pig were so scared. But the brick pig picked up the phone and made a call. A few minutes passed and a big, black stretch limo pulled up. Out stepped two massive pigs in pin striped suits and fedora hats. These pigs went over to the wolf, grabbed him by the neck and beat the stuffing out of him. Then one of them pulled out a gun, stuck it in is mouth and fired, killing the wolf. Then they got back into their limo and drove off. The straw pig and stick pig were amazed!

"Who the heck were those guys?" they asked.

"Those were my cousins from Jersey ... the Guinea Pigs."

Two men working in a factory were talking. "I know how to get some time off," said one.

"How are you going to do that?"

"Watch," he said, and climbed up on a rafter. The foreman asked what he was doing up there, and the man replied. "I'm a lightbulb."

"I think you need some time off," the foreman said, and the first man walked out of the factory. After a moment, the second man followed him.

"Where do you think you're going?" the foreman shouted.

"I can't work in the dark," he said.

At 2:00 a.m. a cop saw a man, obviously drunk, walking down the street. He pulled over, stepped out of his vehicle and confronted the drunk.

"Where are you going?" he asked the man.

"To a lecture," the drunk replied.

"And who," the officer asked looking at his watch, "gives lectures at 2:00 a.m.?"

"My wife."

Nearly every man is a firm believer in heredity until his son makes a fool of himself.

Q. Why do women close their eyes when they kiss?
A. They can't stand to see a man having a good time.

The Ant and the Grasshopper—CLASSIC VERSION:

The ant works hard in the withering heat all summer long, building his house and laying up supplies for the winter. The grasshopper thinks he's a fool, and laughs and dances and plays the summer away.

Come winter, the ant is warm and well fed. The grasshopper has no food or shelter, so he dies out in the cold.

The Ant and the Grasshopper—MODERN VERSION:

The ant works hard in the withering heat all summer long, building his house and laying up supplies for the winter. The grasshopper thinks he's a fool, and laughs and dances and plays the summer away.

Come winter, the shivering grasshopper calls a press conference and demands to know why the ant should be allowed to be warm and well fed while others less fortunate are cold and starving. National News shows up to provide pictures of the shivering grasshopper next to a video of the ant in his comfortable home with a table filled with food. The nation is stunned by the sharp contrast. How can this be, that in a country of such wealth, this poor grasshopper is allowed to suffer so?

The opposition parties stage a demonstration in front of the ant's house, where the news stations film the group singing, "We Shall Overcome."

A local member of government rants in an interview with a celebrity news reporter that the ant has gotten rich off the backs of grasshoppers and calls for an immediate tax hike on the ant to make him pay his "fair share."

Finally, the Government drafts the Economic Equity and Anti Grasshopper Act, retroactive to the beginning of the summer. The ant is fined for failing to hire green bugs for help and, having nothing left to pay his retroactive taxes, his home is confiscated by the government.

The story ends as we see the grasshopper finishing up the last bits of the ant's food while the government house he is in, which just happens to be the ant's old house, crumbles around him because he doesn't maintain it.

The ant has disappeared in the snow. The grasshopper is found dead in a drug related incident and the house, now abandoned, is taken over by a gang of spiders who terrorize the once peaceful neighborhood.

A comfortable base camp
while building your backwoods home

By Jackie Clay

It would be nice if we could find a "pre-built" self-reliant homestead when we decided it was time for a move to a safer, more quiet, saner lifestyle. There would be a dependable water source—developed, of course. Gardens would flourish on the gentle, south-facing slopes. A picturesque, sturdy fence would contain pastures for our livestock. There would be a chicken coop, barn perhaps, and other outbuildings. And there would be a home. Not just any home, mind you, but a true independent home, built for the self-sufficient family, complete with huge pantry, off-grid power, country kitchen, and roomy enough for the whole family to spread out and enjoy life.

Unfortunately, these places are very rare, seldom for sale, and if you should find one, it's not likely to be affordable. So for most folks their off-the-beaten-path-homestead home starts out as acres of bare, totally undeveloped land. Hoping to build their dream homestead on this raw land that they could afford, these families face tremendous challenges, especially if they must move onto this bare land while they build. (It's much easier to drive out to the new homestead on weekends and vacations, building as you can afford and moving onto the land when the place is comfortably established and ready to run.)

Challenges come in the form of living in cramped "camping-out" quarters for months or even years, while building a home. You might have to adjust to living without the so-called modern conveniences that were previously taken for granted. You may have to get used to being wet, cold, frightened by nature so close at hand, and living with very little money.

Over the years of living very remote ourselves, we've seen folks come and go. Like us, they had big dreams and plans. But unfortunately, their dreams and plans were not often realistic, given their experience in roughing it and hard living. I've seen them try to live in poorly built straw bale and sheet plastic huts with dirt floors, and I've seen them try to live in tipis, travel trailers, buses, and tents, complete with five or more dogs, small children, and memories of city living.

Wait! Am I saying you have no chance of making it on a raw piece of wild land? Most definitely *not*. We've also seen folks with very little money and those same dreams succeed beyond their wildest expectations. All over the country are huge success stories from new homesteaders who built their dream homestead from scratch and are now living out their fantasies of raising their own fresh food, making cheeses and other dairy products, putting up the harvest of their bountiful gardens and fields every fall, and watching their children and grandchildren grow into reliable, loving, happy young men and women.

The difference between the failures, who end up going back to the rat race and that hated job, and these successful families usually lies in one word. Preparation.

And the most important part of that preparation is developing a plan on how your family will live while you build your home. Too often, a family does not realize just how long it actually takes to build your own home from scratch, to the point it is ready to move into. Nearly everyone figures

My son, Bill's, new log home under construction, and to the left the "shack" he lived in while he built his home

The wall tent is always pitched first in a new camp. Here, my mom and son, David, help unpack the kitchen gear.

one good summer's work will do the job. But, usually, this is a very optimistic guess, unless the family is skilled in construction, has good tools, and enough money to see the job through.

Most of us do not have enough money to hire a contractor and sit by while they build our new home. Nor do many of us wish to go that route, much preferring the do-it-yourself, hands-on, sweat equity way of building.

And many new back-to-the-landers are not skilled in construction, and must learn as they go, guided by good books and experienced friends and relatives.

So, what is a realistic time frame in building a home on the land? For a small, frame home, we would allow at least a full year, two if it was not possible to build during the winter. A log home, built from your own logs from the woods will take longer, often three years unless you have much experience and lots of help.

My oldest son, Bill, whose log home was featured in previous issues of *BHM*, is just putting the finishing touches on the inside of his gorgeous home. So far, he's spent over three years on it, doing much of the work himself, while working full-time at another job. He is an experienced builder, from cement work through woodwork. An inexperienced builder, working full-time on the same home would probably not be as far. Now this is a large home, being 3,500 square feet, but again, building just takes time. Usually much longer than most folks allow for.

Some families do somehow survive, while building their home, living in a tipi, yurt, tent or bus. But this is like playing Russian roulette. You may make it, but most do not. True, Indians lived their lives in tipis, Mongols lived in skin tents. One of my best friends in northern Minnesota, Nels Speese, came from a family who homesteaded in South Dakota. One of the first black pioneers in that area, his folks raised a family of 16 in a sod shack. And those kids grew up to be lawyers, doctors, and musicians.

But most people today are spoiled, just plain spoiled, and used to having money and all that money can buy. Today's average urban home is over 2,000 square feet. Three bedrooms and two baths is the low-norm. Nels' family had an outhouse, no bedrooms and a whole lot of happy kids.

It's culture shock for most city people to move from a three bedroom, two bath home with all the conveniences, to a tipi in the woods. And after a few weeks, the shock sets in with deadly force.

We feel that it is much, much better to plan on more permanent living quarters while building your home, something that your family can actually function in and remain comfortable. For us, the answer is a "shack," our humorous name for a small cabin which can be built in a few weeks' time for little cost and will let you live in comfort during the time it takes to build a home.

Later on, the shack can be used for a guest house, office, mother-in-law quarters or whatever else you can imagine. The main thing is that you have stable, warm, dry quarters in which to function normally.

We have taken this a step further, and bought a fixer-upper travel trailer in tough shape for $700 and fixed it up over a year, equipping it for camping in bad weather while building our shack, with the trailer being temporarily attached to the shack for more living space. In this way, when our present homestead sells, we will be ready to go onto our raw wilderness land, no matter what time of year it is, no matter what the weather. (Even if we must have a dozer or snowcat haul our trailer in to our building site, through deep snow.) No leaky tents for us. We're past thinking that's much fun.

Our old homestead way in the bush. It was our first shack.

The fixer-upper travel trailer

Some people planning to move to the land from the city may think, "Why not just buy a new travel trailer or RV to live in?" Even if you could afford it, we feel this is not in your best interest. For even during the summer, a nice travel trailer or other recreational vehicle, doesn't function the same on raw land as it does in a campground or in your city backyard. There is seldom any electricity available, and running a generator 12-7 is not only expensive, but a pain in the butt. And you do need power to run the water pump for a shower and the toilet, the fan for the furnace, the air conditioner, etc.

Of course, you can equip the RV with solar panels to do these things for you, but that's getting deep into your pocketbook.

We prefer to use the older, "beater" travel trailer as a sort of hard sided tent that we are not afraid to track construction dirt into in the evening or at lunchtime. This means using a solar shower instead of a 12 volt pump, using Coleman lamps at night for light and a bit of heat if necessary, keeping the sewage tank and grey water tanks empty (so they will not freeze) and hauling water in barrels so that our water lines do not freeze

Now used as a bunk house, this is where the folks who built our home lived while building the main house.

and break, as they most definitely *will* in cold winter weather no matter how much heat you run.

I heat water on the kitchen stove in tea kettles and a canning kettle so the water heater can remain drained in cold weather. We put a T in the waste line so we can run the sink drain water outside into a hole in the ground.

For refrigeration, we have a large propane unit. A single solar panel and occasional generator charging will let us use the 12-volt lights for occasional TV/VCR use, as we have a small DC unit to watch an occasional movie. TV is not worth watching. It will also do away with much flashlight use for night time potty trips.

There is a toilet in the trailer, but we used an outhouse so we wouldn't have to depend on dump stations.

We do have a nice propane kitchen range with a large oven, a comfortable double bed, and a sofa sleeper. There is a small dining area in the kitchen and quite a lot of storage, including added pantry for my bulk dry supplies.

With a tarp hung outdoors, we'll have a snug picnic area to rest in during drizzly weather. I think this will be a very comfortable first base camp for our family of three and a couple of dogs while we put up our stick-built shack.

Priorities when moving onto raw land

We believe the first thing new homesteaders need to do when getting ready to move onto raw land is to have a good, hard, realistic look around their land for the ideal spot to site their home as well as that cozy shack they're going to live in while their home is being built.

Is there a good spring available, preferably uphill from the building site? Having running water, even to the shack, is a definite plus, reducing much of the work during the camping out stage. It is a simple matter to develop a spring and run black plastic

Older, beat-up travel trailer before complete remodel job

water line downhill to the buildings. This provides instant running water, under pressure of sorts (depending on how much higher the spring is than the home site). It may just run out the faucet, if the spring is only five or ten feet above the camp site, or blast out, if it is more than thirty feet above the lower end of the water line.

But if the spring (or other live water source) is at or below the best home site, the water can still be brought up to a storage tank by means of a small gasoline, 12-volt pump (such as a cheap bilge pump for boats) or even an electric sump pump run off a generator. Relatively inexpensive poly water tanks all the way up to 1,000-gallons, are available at most farm and ranch stores. Not having to bucket water is a huge plus. Of course, never drink untested water unless you have filtered it with a good quality filter that will remove bacteria and giardia cysts, or boiled it first.

When deciding on your future home site, consider the availability of

Our new garden is always one of our first priorities on new raw land. It feeds us.

Bob and David (two, at the time) till up a spot for a new garden on the first day we moved in.

relatively flat land for ease of construction, the later addition of gardens and orchards, support outbuildings, such as barns or chicken coops, and their network of fencing.

You may want your shack right next to the spot you plan on building your home. After all, it is convenient and you will spend little time "commuting" back and forth between the shack and your home site.

But you may want it a bit further off as we plan. In this way your home site will be free of the camp clutter, making it easier to get equipment and trucks to and from the area. Then, once your home is finally completed, you may want to use the shack as a guest house, art studio, or home for another family member. It might be best to have a little distance between the two for privacy and to ease the clutter of buildings crammed into one area.

Before building anything, check to see what, if any building permits are necessary in your area. You don't want to build, then be told you are in violation, and must tear down what you have already built, then rebuild to code. You might find it easier if you are building a "hunting shack", instead of a homestead cabin.

Once you mentally lay out your homestead, haul in your camp trailer (or tent, if you prefer). Next, locate a privy spot at least 100 feet from your water source. It should be private, on a small rise or gentle slope, and as rock-free as possible. Dig a deep hole. Four feet is a general minimum. A labor saver is to dig a hole for a two seater and only use one seat. When that part of the hole becomes filled up, simply move the seat over to the next area. Another hint is to deposit your toilet paper into a paper bag, not down the hole. This paper is later safely burned. This will save more than a year's worth of hole.

A good outhouse can be easily built in three days, and is a "must" when camping out.

Once the outhouse is finished, take time to straighten your travel trailer, even with the way your shack will be sited, and level it very well. Some folks even remove the tires and lower the trailer, blocking the axles with concrete blocks. If winter is coming, you might take the time to stack straw bales around the perimeter, as the floor will get cold enough to freeze mop water if you don't.

Once you have taken care of the water, outhouse, and trailer/tent camp, you are ready to begin work on your shack.

A good spring, located 50 feet above the outlet, will provide good pressure without a pump.

The shack

Now a shack can be many things or anything you desire, need, and can afford to build quickly. My son, Bill's, "shack" was a roomy two car garage, built on a slab out of "second" lumber and OSB (wafer board). Sided and painted, Bill divided the garage in two. Half was for storage, and the other half he made into a very comfortable apartment. He had no spring available, so he had a well drilled. The apartment has an indoor bathroom, kitchen, and living room/dining area, which also doubles as a bedroom. It is very cute and comfortable.

We also have friends who built small shacks on cement piers and even bought wooden storage buildings to live in while building their home. Remember there is truth to the old "cabin fever" stories. Winter is long, and when camping in a small shack, everybody tends to get on everybody else's nerves, especially when you throw in a teen who didn't really want to move to the backwoods, a bouncing three-year-old or a dog who doesn't wipe his feet when he comes in—of course, my husband, Bob, doesn't either.

Ideally, the shack should be as large as you can afford and be able to build within a few weeks' time. This lets people have their own "space," and greatly reduces conflicts. Our shack will be 16 by 22 feet with the trailer being parked very close to it, giving another 32 by 8 feet of living space. The shack will have an 8-by-22-foot loft for storage and bedroom/play area for our 12-year-old son, David. After the shack is finished, complete with a stiff foam "airlock" between trailer and shack, we will add an 8-by-16-foot porch on the south side which will be enclosed and glassed. This will be a dining area and a place where I can start my garden plants in the spring.

Yes, we could get by in much less space. And if we need to we will. But this sized shack, planned out carefully, will let me have a small office space so I continue to work at my writing in relative comfort, provide two bedrooms, enough storage space that we will not have to rent a storage unit, have all our food conveniently inside and give us enough elbow room to be comfortable for the time it takes us to build our new log home.

We have even talked about adding a large log addition onto our shack and then siding the shack with log siding to blend perfectly with the log work. There are many options available to building a shack.

There are a few considerations for shack living. One of the most important is insulation. Be sure you insulate the shack as well as you would your home. In such a small area, you'll heat with either propane or a small wood burner. There simply isn't room for a big wood stove, due to the safety space of at least two feet (with a back-board of heat-safe material, plus two inches of air space, behind that) behind the stove and three feet clear on both sides of the stove. The typical wood stove would require nearly one third of our planned shack just to heat it.

Instead, we will do as Bill did and hang a small wall propane heater on the shack wall and use our wood burning kitchen range for the primary heater. The wood kitchen range only needs about a foot behind it, as it does not get as hot behind it as a woodstove does. Nor does it require three feet on both sides, but only the side on which the fire box is located. Most kitchen stoves are positioned so that the fire box side is next to a door opening, neatly avoiding the use of additional space for safety.

Cooking with a wood kitchen range is nothing short of wonderful once you get the hang of it. (For instance, it takes about half an hour to pre-heat the oven for baking.) And the stove not only heats a room well in subzero cold, but provides enough space to keep two or more canning kettles full of water hot at all times, ready for showers, dish washing, or washing a load of clothes in a wringer washer, stashed out of the way in the corner pantry.

During the summer, you will want your wood burning kitchen range outside, under cover, or on the front porch. This is known as a summer kitchen, and eliminates heating up the shack during hot days and nights. When the weather turns cool, you can slide the stove into the kitchen, where you will again appreciate the heat.

A wringer washer is a must for shack living, as it uses only a few gallons of water, while getting the clothes cleaner than any conventional washer on the market. I use one every week, doing five loads of wash on six gallons of water. By starting out with the whites, then washing the cleaner lighter colors such as sheets, then T shirts and long johns, then heavier shirts, then "cleaner" jeans, work jeans, then rugs, all in the same water.

All laundry is hung on the lines, year around. At first they will freeze in the winter, but if left on the line for several days, they will freeze dry nicely. If you are in a hurry, you can bring in stiff laundry to finish drying on wooden racks or on lines inside.

When designing your shack, it's a good idea to allow for additions. Make sure there are adequate windows and at least two exits in case of fire. The windows are necessary, not only for light and ventilation, but also for mental well-being. Without adequate light, people become short-tempered and depressed. One thing your family does not need, when building your dream homestead, is feeling down and hopeless.

Tips for shack living

When you build your shack, cover the floor (insulated from below) with a sheet of vinyl flooring or at least paint the floor with a minimum of three coats of sturdy basement and floor paint. This is a *must* in order to keep the floor clean while you are working on your new home, tracking in construction dirt and Mother Nature's snow and mud. You just can't keep a plywood floor clean, especially in the kitchen where grease spots and other cooking spills quickly muck up the floor.

Adding an enclosed front porch is a great idea, as it gives you a place to sit down and take off muddy clothes and boots, greatly saving on cleaning time. It also gives you a convenient place to store your kitchen wood while keeping it nice and dry. The enclosed porch also serves as an air lock, keeping drafts from chilling the whole cabin, every time someone opens the door.

If you don't have a travel trailer with a propane refrigerator, consider

A 200-gallon Poly water tank makes hauling water to remote locations a snap. Bob is watering the horses.

buying a used RV propane fridge instead of using coolers. During the summer, it costs over a dollar a day, plus gas to the nearest store where you can buy your ice and the travel time to get the ice just to maintain one cooler. And that cooler will not cool food as well as a refrigerator. You'll have more milk and meat spoil in the cooler. The propane fridge is very easy to operate and very economical, using only a small pilot light-sized flame to cool. And the small freezer compartment sure comes in handy at times.

One reason I like shack living is that I can easily and quickly cook meals my family is used to having, bake when I need to, and even process food for home storage. While we build, I'm sure I will be putting up wild foods, such as blueberries, mushrooms, and venison.

Keep a clean camp, especially during the building time. Separate paper and plastic trash from unburnables. You can burn the paper and plastic (which you should try to keep to a minimum), a little at a time, in your kitchen range. Yes, I know, plastic generates toxic smoke. But in the landfill, it is not exactly a godsend, either. We feel that Mother Earth can better handle small bits of toxic material, rather than huge loads, dumped all in one spot.

The cans should be kept in a container, indoors, until they can be taken to the dump. If bagged up and stacked outdoors, you'll be inviting bears and other critters to raid your camp. And they sometimes don't stop with outside bags.

Remember, you will probably be living in your shack for at least two years, during which time, you'll have to do all the mundane "normal" things you did back home: laundry, care of sick family, showers, baths, canning, jelly making, hobbies, such as putting puzzles together on rainy days, etc. It's nice to have things under control, with enough room to function.

Other assorted tips on moving back to the land

Finances: Today, there is hardly anything such as "living off the land." We all try to be self-reliant, but you'll always need a source of cash for things you can not grow or barter for. The doctor, dentist, lumberyard, feed mill, county tax office, and gas station will all expect cash for their services and merchandise.

So be sure you have at least a moderate savings or a way to make at least a modest living on your new homestead. And remember, many very rural areas have a pay rate that is half or less, of that back in the city rat race. Also expect a lengthy commute to that lower paying job.

Of course, there are many ways you can earn money from home, especially if you are skilled in some useful craft. Carpenters, stone masons, electricians, plumbers, small engine repairmen, heavy equipment operators, teachers, and other professional people can usually find work nearby with little problem.

The absolutely biggest problem we see in new back to the landers is flagrant misuse of money. This is a real *biggie*. We've seen it in literally hundreds of new homesteaders, and constantly watch for it in our own situation.

Number one is Mr. and Ms. Newcomer buying one expensive "toy" after another; ATVs, horses, boats, computers, satellite TV systems, composting toilets, new this and that. And soon, the money's gone, and the stress begins.

So much time has been spent with the new toys that the shack didn't get built and the people are freezing in an RV or tent. And back to the city they go. It's all so sad. And unnecessary.

Financial priorities simply must be established and discussed openly with the whole family. Even children can understand how money must be used, if it is explained carefully and often.

And high on that list of priorities is a warm, dry, comfortable shack, in which to live while that new home is built. Remember, it may take years to finish a home, especially if one or more of the family members must be working full time or is going to public school. We deeply feel the loss of our son, David, while he is in school, as even at 12, he is simply a lot of (usually) enthusiastic help at home.

Resist the temptation to get every animal your family ever dreamed of having, at least until you get facilities to keep them right. We've seen dozens of chickens, goats, dogs, and horses on new homesteads, with absolutely no facilities, housed in hay and board shelters which leaked and were freezing cold, tied to trees, or simply let run. You can't enjoy homestead animals like this and will get little use from them. Better to build a small chicken coop, then get a few chickens, fence a pasture and build a shelter, then get livestock.

Beginning the garden while living in your shack: One of my absolutely first priorities while moving onto a new homestead is to get the garden going. I don't care what time of year it is, there is always something you can do to improve the harvest of your future garden. Only in the deepest part of winter are you slowed down, and then you can build portable fence panels to keep the critters out of your garden in the future.

Even if you move onto the land during late summer or fall, there is plenty of time to plot out the gardens and clear them of stumps, branches, rocks and weeds. Then get that soil tilled up so that you can begin working in organic material to make the soil more workable and fertile.

This first working of the new garden lets you get a good feel for the soil. Is it black and deep? Or solid clay? Of course, we'd all rather have the former, but I've turned red clay, eight feet deep into fertile, fluffy black loam in a few years, simply by working in tons of organic material, such as leaves, livestock bedding and manure, green manure (which is a crop, such as rye, grown and turned under to enrich the soil), compost, and even grain elevator wastes, such as chaff and moldy grain.

I try to till the new garden plot at least three times before my spring planting, each time removing any debris and adding good organic amendments to the soil.

It's best to have at least two gardens, one for annual vegetables such as tomatoes, corn and potatoes, and another for perennial plants such as berries, rhubarb, asparagus, and horseradish.

On site storage: When planning on moving to raw land, living in a shack, it's best to get rid of as many "extras" as you can. When we first moved to Montana, we had a huge sale and sold all our furniture and much of our "stuff," keeping mainly our pantry, home-canned food, clothes, and tools. We crammed all we owned into a pickup truck and 16-foot stock trailer. A friend hauled our livestock for us separately. We've used that closed in trailer for storage while we set up camp—and longer. With careful packing, we could find much of what we needed, using the side and rear doors for access.

Our new camp set-up will have storage in a pantry and above in the loft. We will also use our wall tent which we salvaged from the dump as a tool storage building. A wall tent is a heavy canvas tent meant to take inclement mountain weather including heavy snow. We used one for two years and it performed very well. It is extremely unwise to pay for storage buildings just to house stuff that is not possible to store on the building site, especially for things that will not be valuable on the new homestead.

With a lot of future planning, the move to the new raw land will not only be successful, but a grand adventure and plenty of fun, too. And I love to tell people we'll once again be living in a shack. It sure gets a conversation started. Δ

Get The Whole Sheebang!
www.backwoodshome.com

Starting Over
Chronicles of a Self-Reliant Woman
Our latest compilation of articles by one of our favorite writers, Jackie Clay.

1-800-835-2418
www.backwoodshome.com

home canning equals fast, easy, tasty meals

By Jackie Clay

Even if canning wasn't easy (which it is), I still would spend the effort, simply because it gives me easy, home-cooked meals in minutes. In modern times with so many folks using "instant" and microwave this and that, no wonder why the vast populace is always dieting. I've tasted that instant "wonder food!" Yuck. Tough, stringy, grizzle, in place of tender, lean meat, chicken lips and mystery meat in soups, woody or soggy, tasteless vegetables in every dish, potatoes that taste like wallpaper paste.

If I fed my family that, Bob would cook. Not a pretty picture.

Now I often don't have time to spend lots of time fixing meals, as I get out there and saw wood, fence, till the garden and do other time consuming things with Bob and David. But, through home canning, I'm able to sneak away for a few minutes, then call the boys in for a meal that actually tastes like real food, because it is.

Barbecued beef on a bun

Dump a pint of beef (venison, moose, or elk) in a heavy sauce pan. With a fork, shred the meat, removing any fat or grizzle. There will be enough natural juice to begin simmering the meat on low. Add to this 1

Tomatoes—the base for lots and lots of quick yummy eating

A pantry full of home-canned food equals hundreds of quick, easy tasty meals.

Tbsp. dehydrated onion and ½ pint of home-canned or other barbecue sauce. Simmer on low until well heated and meat absorbs much of the sauce. Serve on warm buns.

Nachos with corn, bean, and tomato salsa

Dump out half a large bag of corn chips on a cookie tin or fry your own quartered corn tortillas until crisp. Shred ½ pound of your favorite cheese over, place in oven at 300° until cheese is melted and bubbly. We like sliced olives on the chips, along with the cheese.

Mix ½ pint canned, drained black beans, ½ pint canned, drained sweet corn, 1 fresh jalepeño, 1 Tbsp. oil, 1 Tbsp. lemon juice, ½ pint fresh or canned, drained tomato, 1 small chopped onion, and 1 tsp. chopped cilantro .

The salsa is best if the canned vegetables have been refrigerated, then is mixed and used fresh. If your family likes hotter salsa, you can vary the pepper content to taste.

Alphabet chicken soup

Pour out 1 quart of home-canned chicken with broth (small boneless pieces, mostly broth) into large saucepan. Begin simmering. Add 1 shredded carrot, 1 small chopped onion, ¼ tsp. dried, powdered sage, ¼ tsp. black pepper, enough salt to taste

Organized, neat shelves help to make healthy meals.

and 3 oz. (more or less) of alphabet macaroni. Simmer until tender, covered. Cool a bit and watch the smiles.

It's fun to serve this with a cottage cheese salad that's simply a leaf of lettuce with a large spoonful of cottage cheese and half a peach, hollow down. It looks like a big egg, and the kids love it; chicken soup and an egg!

Creamed new potatoes and garden peas

Gently fry crisp four strips of lean bacon. Remove bacon & add to grease 1 Tbsp. butter. Over low heat, stir in 2 Tbsp. flour until well blended. Add 1 cup milk slowly while stirring. As it thickens, add 1 pt. small new potatoes canned with skins on. (You can simply pinch each potato and the skin will slip off!) Do not add water in which potatoes were canned in.

Add ½ cup fresh, frozen, or reconstituted garden peas. Do NOT use canned peas....the taste is NOT the same. While warming, add more milk, as needed to make a medium cream sauce, blending well, but not breaking potatoes.

Crumble the bacon and add it to the mixture along with salt and pepper to taste. I like to add ½ tsp. dehydrated lemon.

Note: I can every small potato at harvest time, from quarter size on up to nearly golf ball size for such use. Most folks just leave 'em in the garden or feed them to the hogs. We really love this mid winter "fresh garden" treat!

Apple pancakes

Make your favorite plain pancake recipe, then add ½ pt. of chopped, canned apples and ½ tsp. cinnamon. Use a little extra grease and fry, rather than bake them. They'll be a little crispy at the edges. You can sprinkle them with powdered sugar if you wish. I like to serve them hot with a swirl of whipped cream on top.

You won't have many left on the plate, GUARANTEED!

You'll be quick to notice that none of my recipes are "fancy" or take long to make. With home canning, cooked ingredients are always at hand, and the quality is excellent. You know that because you can it yourself. There's seldom any "nasty" stuff to sort through, as you only can the best for your family....not like big commercial canning plants that shovel "whatever" into hoppers, to be deposited eventually into sterile-looking cans to line grocery store shelves.

My home-canned foods are made up of the cleanest, chemical free ingredients humanly possible. This allows anyone who eats at my table to relax and enjoy the meals, knowing that they are not ingesting any "weird" stuff.

Home-canning tips for easy, quick meals

Put up many pint and half pint jars, no matter what your family size is. This allows you to use smaller amounts of each food in a recipe. This leaves no "leftovers" to refrigerate (a bonus to those of us with small...or no propane refrigerators), minimizing the chance of waste.

Put up pints and quarts of mixed vegetables. This is convenient for use in soups, stews and casseroles. The combinations can vary with those you most frequently use.

Can many quarts of broth and soup stock. With these you can add vegetables, meat, noodles or pasta, as needed, for instant homemade soups.

Remember, when canning multiple ingredient jars to always process the jars the longest time any one ingredient requires. This is usually meat or meat broth.

While you must heat to boiling all home-canned vegetables and meat, never boil away endlessly. If you do, you'll end up with vegetables that taste little better than store-bought food. A slow, gentle simmer for fifteen minutes is what you want. This is recommended to kill any possible pathogens surviving in the jar. (But, for the life of me, I can't figure out why they aren't lurking in store-bought cans, as well.....)

Meat which is raw packed in jars tends to be a little dry and stringy when used. You can offset this by simmering it for over an hour at very low temperatures in broth, then slicing large chunks of beef/venison/elk across the grain at serving.

The more you use home-canned foods in everyday cooking, the more inventive and creative you'll become in canning and then using foods. I've been canning for over forty years and every week I think up or learn something that makes my life easier and my meals quicker and better. And that gives us more time to enjoy the lifestyle on our backwoods home. Δ

Jackie, Jackie, and more Jackie

Everybody's favorite writer. Get the Jackie Clay CD-ROM and find information on gardening, preserving the harvest, self-sufficiency, recipes, building, livestock, and harvesting the wild.

Only $12.95 plus $4.95 S&H

www.backwoodshome.com
1-800-835-2418

GET IN THAT KITCHEN AND RATTLE THOSE POTS AND PANS!

- breads • casseroles
- beverages • canning
- jams, jellies & preserves
- salads • soups
- vegetables • appetizers
- pasta, rice & beans

GET BACKWOODS HOME COOKING

Only $21.95
(plus $4.95 S&H)

1-800-835-2418
www.backwoodshome.com

Send a check or money order to
BHM, P.O. Box 712, Gold Beach, OR 97444

the gee-whiz! page
By O.E. MacDougal

Photography

If you go through old history books, you'll find photographs that include family portraits, politicians, outlaws, lawmen, all with dour faces. It's easy to imagine that the grim look most of them wore was a sign of hard lives and the times they lived in.

Nothing could be further from the truth. The reason people are unsmiling is because of the long exposure times of the photographic plates. Exposures could take anywhere from several seconds to a minute or more. No one was expected to hold a smile that long. The fact is, rather than smiling your objective was not to move anything at all because with such long exposure times, almost any movement would cause a blur.

To prevent movement, many photography studios had metal braces along the walls. The idea was that you would back up to one of the braces and let it hold your neck still. Then you tried not to move any other part of your body. Blinking was okay because your eyelids would move so fast they didn't blur the film. But you had to make it a point to *stare* at a fixed object across the room and not move your eyes at all, because if your eyes moved too much your pupils wouldn't show and in the resulting photograph you'd look like a zombie.

Hence, the stern look on the faces in the photos taken by Matthew Brady and his contemporaries. Otherwise, those people were just as happy and smiling in their lives as you and I are in ours.

Roads of wood

Roads are among the most common sights of civilization. They are, in fact, so common that we take them for granted. But the history of commerce, warfare, and the spread of civilization are closely linked to the existence of roads. And paved roads go back at least 4500 years to ancient Egypt.

The Romans were the great road builders of their time and they held their Empire together by the construction of roads over which commerce and armies could move. Many of their roads, though rebuilt and resurfaced, are still in use today.

Road construction is part science and part mathematics. Curves on modern roads are segments of circles, so we don't have to keep readjusting the steering as we drive on the curve, and hills are shaped like parabolas, to ensure a smooth transition from the upside to the downside.

Modern roads have deep bearing layers to accommodate the weight of traffic and wearing surfaces that protect the bearing layer beneath. The current multilane highway system in the United States is built so the first and second lanes have a deeper bearing surface than the other lanes. By having only one or two of the several lanes with deep substrata, money is saved in construction. It's the real reason large trucks are confined to these lanes except when passing.

Through history, roads have been paved with dirt, sand, gravel, cobblestone, bricks, and today with asphalt and concrete. But what many don't know is that one of the time-honored materials used to pave roads was wood. Such roads were called "corduroy" roads because the logs lying parallel across the roads recalled the image of corduroy fabric. Gravel, brick, and stone were the preferred materials, but in swampy and low, wet areas, where stones settled and disappeared and wheels would sink and become almost impossible to move, logs were used because they "floated" on the mud.

Sometimes the log "paving" ran less than 100 feet, just enough to cross some muddy ground. Other times they went on for miles and miles.

Traffic, including horses and wagons, microbes, insects, and the elements wore the roads away. However, with some maintenance, many corduroy roads, particularly, those made with cedar, lasted for decades. But they had other drawbacks. Travel was slow and extremely bumpy. And horses could break legs if their hooves slipped between the logs. Sometimes, the ends of the logs sprouted and, if not cut back, would grow into full-sized trees.

To make them a little more hospitable, the roads were often covered with a layer of sand—never dirt which would start the logs to rotting. Other times they were even covered with planks to smooth out the ride.

Corduroy roads were a common sight in many parts of America. But gradually, all of them rotted away or were dug up and replaced with sand, gravel, and finally the modern paving surfaces.

Though once there were thousands of them, today hardly anyone even realizes roads that were paved with wood were an integral part of the system of highways that holds America together.

Growing Cauliflower

by Nancy Pierson Farris

Whether you like to eat it raw with dip, or in a salad, steamed with a taste of butter, or smothered in cheese sauce, cauliflower is a low-cal, low-carbohydrate source of fiber, calcium, and Vitamins A and C. You can grow it in spring or in fall, if you provide for its specific needs.

Cauliflower goes through three stages of growth: plant development, curd formation, and leaf growth. Since the curd is the part usually eaten, it makes sense to provide optimal conditions for curd development.

The best curd forms during cool weather, but too much cold causes the plant to form buttons rather than large, succulent heads. High temperatures cause curds to form rapidly, but they are small and bitter. The window of opportunity for cauliflower is a small one, especially in my area of South Carolina, where weather can turn brutally hot as early as mid-May.

I start my own plants. Most seed companies sell packets of about 75 seeds. Since I don't want that much cauliflower all at once, I plant what I need, and store the leftover seed in a glass jar in a bottom shelf, where they stay cool and dry. They will remain viable for up to four years.

Another reason to start my own: I can spread out the harvest by using a few plants each of two or more varieties. *Silver Cup* matures in 40 days, *Milkyway* is ready in 45 days, *First White* needs 50 days and tolerates cold, *Amazing* needs 75 days.

If I want a touch of color, I can grow *Cauli-Broc* which produces pale green heads in 60 days, or *Shannon* which produces pale green florets in 70 days.

Most companies offer at least one self-blanching variety. *Self-Blanching Snowball* matures in 70 days and *Avalanche* matures in 75 days.

I sow the seed in late January in my cool greenhouse. I keep the temperature above freezing at night, cool (about 50°) in the day, and provide seedlings with plenty of light.

When plants have at least one set of second leaves, I transplant them into 4" pots. I will hold plants in the greenhouse for about 6 weeks.

On cloudy days in February, I use cool white fluorescent tubes to provide at least 8 hours of light. Without adequate light, plants grow spindly and weak.

I feed the plants weekly with fish emulsion (5-1-1). The high nitrogen

I plant cauliflower seedlings into 4" pots so the roots can become well developed.

gives me sturdy plants with dark green leaves and well-developed roots.

In early March, three weeks before my last frost date, I prepare hills 20" apart. Cauliflower prefers a soil Ph of about 6.0 to 6.5. If soil is too acid, plants may develop clubroot.

I place a trowelful of compost in each hill to warm the ground under the plant. I don't use fresh manure or kitchen scraps because this could encourage black rot. I could use a tablespoonful of 5-10-10 fertilizer, as recommended by the USDA for cole crops. At this point, a high nitrogen formula would encourage plant growth rather than curd formation.

After plants are set into the garden, the main needs are lots of water—those big leaves transpire a lot—and protection from cabbage worms. Those cute little yellow or white butterflies flitting around the plants will lay eggs on leaves of any cabbage-related vegetables.

In early morning, I check the plants for egg clusters. These are located under the leaves and look like bunches of tiny yellow grapes. If I find any, I crush them. They'd hatch into hungry green cabbage worms. If I find a worm, I am merciless—I pull it off the plant and step on it.

We also use *Bacillus thurengiensis*. This biological control is not toxic, but causes any kind of caterpillar to develop fatal indigestion. My husband prefers the dust (*Dipel*), but I'd rather use liquid *Thuricide* in a spray bottle. We apply this once a week.

During the spring, my husband uses a rotary tiller to keep the aisles between rows weed free. I prefer to pull weeds by hand and use a hoe to keep soil loose around plants.

Depending on the variety you plant, you should see tiny heads forming in the leaf rosette within ten days after you set out the plants. If you are growing a variety that is not self-blanching, the heads may turn a dirty white color as they mature. To prevent this, pull 3 or 4 leaves together at the top and tie loosely with soft twine or a strip of fabric.

You can harvest cauliflower at any stage—if you're anxious to enjoy the fruits of your labor, go ahead and cut a small head. Bear in mind that cauliflower does not produce any side shoots. You get one head per plant and that's the crop.

> Here's a recipe that we like using with raw cauliflower:
>
> ### Curds and carrots
> ½ cup cauliflower, broken into florets
> ½ cup shredded carrot
> ¼ cup grated cheddar cheese
> ¼ cup thinly sliced celery
> Moisten with your favorite salad dressing, Add a handful of chopped parsley or dillweed if you wish.

As weather warms, check the cauliflowers daily. When the curd begins to "rice" (it will appear loose on top) cut it. If you leave it, it won't get bigger, only separate and become tough and perhaps acquire a bitter flavor.

In the kitchen, look over the head carefully, because sometimes a tiny green worm will get down into the curd. You can stand the curds on their heads in a shallow pan of lukewarm water with salt dissolved in it—about ½ tsp. of salt per pint of water. Leave the cauliflower for about 20 minutes. Resident worms will "scrunch up" making them easier to see—and some will give up their hold and float out into the water.

I use a hoe to remove weeds and loosen soil around the plants.

Cauliflower will retain good quality if stored in the vegetable drawer of your refrigerator for 3 or 4 weeks.

If you wish to freeze cauliflower, blanch it for 3 minutes in a small amount of boiling water, or steam 4 minutes. I use just enough water to prevent scorching. when the water boils, I stir so all pieces are moistened, then turn to low heat. After 4 minutes, I dump it into a shallow bowl, and set a plastic bagful of ice on top. After the food cools, I pack it into freezer containers. Never add salt to food you plan to freeze.

Some growers recommend cauliflower as a fall crop. Since plants grow well in warm weather, curds develop in cool weather, and light frost may improve the flavor, cauliflower may produce a better harvest in fall.

Seeds can be sown directly into the garden, about 3 months before the first expected frost date. Either space seeds about 20" apart, or thin seedlings when they have second leaves. You can transplant thinned-out seedlings to an adjacent row.

I start my fall crop in flats on a screened porch, protected from insects and hot summer sun. I set the plants into a row where a summer crop, such as tomato plants, are finishing their job for the year. The mature plants shade the young cauliflower and I think the smell of tomato plants may help confuse the cabbage butterflies.

We have charts showing expected frost dates, but the reality is uncertain. Though cauliflowers will tolerate a light frost, a hard freeze will damage the plant cells and any curds that form will be small and tough. So when the weather forecaster says, "Hard freeze tonight," cut your curds.

We can't always beat the weather. In spring of 2001, I kept my cauliflower plants in the greenhouse til late March, waiting for weather to settle. I thought I had out-guessed Mama Nature. Wrong! We got a record cold night in early April. Even though my transplants had been well-developed, and I tried to protect them from that late freeze, the heads were not good quality. I did get a head from each plant, but the largest was about 3" across—maybe half the size I usually expect from cauliflowers. However, I figured that my fall crop would be better—and there's always next year! Δ

Seed sources for cauliflower varieties mentioned in this article:
W. Atlee Burpee & Co.
300 Park Ave.
Warminster, PA 18991-0001
Gurney Seed & Nursery Co.
110 Capital St.
Yankton, SD 57079
Harris Seeds
355 Paul Road
PO Box 24966
Rochester, NY 14624-0966
Geo. W. Park Seed Co., Inc.
1 Parkton Avenue
Greenwood, SC 29647-0001
Pinetree Garden Seeds
PO Box 300
Gloucester, ME 04260
Vermont Bean Seed Co.
Computer Operations Cntr
Vaucluse, SC 29850-0150
Johnny's Seeds
184 Foss Hill Road
Albion, ME 04910

**hope for the best
plan for the worst**

Both for $27 plus $4.95 S&H

Emergency Preparedness and Survival Guide
• food
• water
• fuel
• warmth
• medical
• electricity
• vehicles
• firearms

300 pages

The Book
• 300 pages of practical preparedness information.
• The best of 14 years of BHM expertise.
• Comprehensive, accurate, and exciting to read.
• This is an exhaustive analysis of what needs to be done and how to do it. $21.95 plus $4.95 S&H

The CD-ROM
• Even more comprehensive than the book. Dozens of articles comprising hundreds of pages. A preparedness library on CD-ROM. $12.95 plus $4.95 S&H

1-800-835-2418
Backwoods Home Magazine
P.O. Box 712, Gold Beach, OR 97444
www.backwoodshome.com

Visit the
**Backwoods Home Magazine
CHAT ROOM**
at the BHM website:
www.backwoodshome.com

My garden: *A springboard of food, pleasure, and history*

By Habeeb Salloum

"You mean that from this postage-size garden you grow enough vegetables and herbs to last you all year?" my friend asked in disbelief as he watched me plant my tomato plants in early May. "Not all, but many of the vegetables that we eat year-round, I grow in this garden. However, my garden is also for me a work of pleasure and a reminder of my family's history." I grinned as I went about my task.

I was not surprised that my friend was amazed that on this small 25 by 12 feet plot of land, I could grow a good part of our family's vegetable larder. I even feel astonished myself when, at the time I am planting my tomatoes in spring, our family is still eating frozen tomatoes from the previous year's harvest. Yet, there is no magic in my garden's abilities. My success in growing a fine garden year after year goes back to my family's history.

My parents emigrated from Syria in the 1920s and by the early 1930s were farming on the arid western Canadian prairies. For over a half dozen years, almost nothing grew, but we survived well, mostly from the produce of our yearly garden. Unlike some of our neighbors who barely could subsist and moved away one after the other, our hand-watered garden made sure that we were never hungry.

In Syria, my parents were peasants and had inherited from their ancestors the art of survival in an arid land. When our neighbors' fields were bare, we grew chickpeas and lentils which needed little moisture. Hence, they were perfect for the dry prairie climate.

Leek pies

Some of the chickpeas, we ate as a delicacy—green or roasted green. However, almost all the chickpea and lentil crops, we reaped ripe and they formed the main basis for our meals. For herbs and tasty greens, in spring my mother would scour the countryside around our garden. Those she did not use fresh, she dried for the winter months.

Our vegetable garden, which we hand-watered from a well, produced enough vegetables and herbs to last us a whole year. All summer we ate the produce fresh and for future use, we canned, dried, or pickled a portion. Others we preserved in our earth

Radishes, tomatoes, and basil

The Fourteenth Year

Tomato and coriander salad

cellar—beets, carrots, potatoes, and turnips, covered with soil. With the few bushels of wheat, which even in the driest years we harvested and made into burghal (wheat that is cooked, then dried and ground) and a few chickens, our family ate well the whole year. We barely had any clothes and virtually no luxuries, but our garden produced gourmet meals.

During these Depression years, the taste for green chickpeas and the great dishes my mother prepared from our garden produce never left me. Today, even though I live in the middle of Toronto, the largest city in Canada, year after year I still plant a micro replica of our Depression years' gardens, growing some of the same produce I relished in my youth.

Every year in early spring, I prepare the soil, except a portion reserved for a half dozen perennial leek and onion plants and two tiny patches of mint and sweet oregano, by adding cattle or sheep manure. Around the first of May, I plant from seed, beets, kohlrabi, turnips, a few cabbage plants, a small patch of chickpeas and a few climbing bean plants at the bottom of an edging tree. A week or so later, I plant one or two eggplant, a few hot pepper and a dozen tomato plants—six ripening early and six later in the year.

In between the tomatoes, I plant a few radish seeds and a number of herbs like basil, caraway, dill, parsley, thyme, and every year without fail, coriander—my favorite herb. A week later I complete the planting with usually three cucumber and three zucchini plants, hugging the edge of the garden. In order to give them room as they grow, I train them to flow away from the garden.

If the weather is fine, the garden quickly begins to flourish, but if there is a cold spell and the temperature dips below zero, I replant the frozen plants and this tends to retard the progress of my garden. In the main after the first planting, the garden takes off.

Beginning in May, we are making leek pies and in early June herb salads from fresh coriander, onions, mint, radish, and sweet oregano. Thereafter, as the herbs grow, I harvest them and what we do not eat, I dry or freeze for winter use. In the ensuing days, the dishes we cook from our garden produce are never ending. Soon the quick-growing herbs and the cooked green tops of the beets, kohlrabi, radishes, and turnips are gracing our table. Not long after we add fresh tender cucumber, cooked green beans, and zucchini dishes.

All summer long I pick tender cucumbers, green beans, and the zucchini when they are about six inches long—mostly to be stuffed. However, the garden produces more zucchini than we can use. The extra ones we hollow, then freeze for future use. The scraped-out inner hearts are not wasted, we utilize them in omelets, soups, and stews.

What I always look forward to are the ripe tomatoes about mid-July. They not only beautify the garden but

Herb salad

are delicious. Tomato salads in endless varieties, especially with herbs like fresh basil, coriander, and caraway, are now on the daily menu. Always there are more ripe tomatoes than we can use. The extra ones we wash, then place in plastic bags and freeze.

At the same time when the tomatoes begin to ripen, every day I relish a few of the green chickpeas and a few pieces of raw kohlrabi. Usually, by the time autumn rolls around, the chickpeas are finished, but if there are any remaining chickpea pods, I roast them in the oven—for me a heavenly treat.

In August, we pickle the remaining small cucumbers with dill from our garden into dill pickles; and the large ones become bread and butter pickles. This time also, I pick the remaining hot peppers and dry them—our yearly supply. From mid-August to frost time, beet and turnip dishes are frequent. By the time the cold grips the land, I pick the eggplants and make them into one or two jars of garlic-eggplant pickles for the winter months. I then harvest the cabbage and in the ensuing days our family enjoys a number of cabbage roll meals. Shortly thereafter, I pick the remaining beets, kohlrabi, and turnips to complete our yearly supply of pickles.

Pickles made from these vegetables are only prepared in the Middle East, but in my view they outdo pickled cucumbers. The beets, kohlrabi, and turnips are peeled and sliced, then the kohlrabi and turnips are placed in jars. Along with the pickling solution, a slice of beets is placed in each jar. In a few weeks bright red pickled vegetables will always beautify the surrounding dishes being served.

In autumn, when I hear the first rumor of frost, I pick the remaining green tomatoes and wrap them with paper, then place them in a cool place in the basement. As they ripen, we either freeze or eat them. At times we are eating fresh tomatoes from our garden until December.

Almost every year, my garden produces enough of the herbs and vegetables which I plant to last us the whole year—fresh in summer, and dried, pickled, or frozen the remaining months of the year. Yet, this is not all my gardens' attributes. Even though it produces much of our family's vegetable needs, it is also to me a springboard of pleasure and enshrines the history of my family.

Recipes from my garden

Tomato and Coriander Salad
Salatat Banadura Wa Kuzbara
Serves about 6

- 5 medium sized tomatoes, quartered, then thinly sliced
- ¾ cup chopped fresh coriander leaves
- 1 tsp. salt
- ½ tsp. pepper
- ⅛ tsp. cayenne
- 3 Tbsp. lemon juice
- 3 Tbsp. olive oil

Place tomatoes and coriander leaves in a salad bowl, then gently toss and set aside.

In a small bowl, thoroughly mix remaining ingredients. Pour over tomatoes and coriander, then toss just before serving.

Herb Salad—*Salatat Tawabil*
Serves about 8

- 1 small bunch dandelion, thoroughly washed and chopped
- 1 cup finely chopped stemmed parsley
- 1 cup finely chopped fresh coriander leaves
- 2 medium tomatoes, diced into ½-inch cubes
- 1 large clove garlic, crushed
- 4 Tbsp. olive oil
- 4 Tbsp. lemon juice
- 1 tsp. salt
- ½ tsp. pepper
- ¼ tsp. cumin
- about 10 pitted black olives, sliced in half

Combine dandelion, parsley, coriander leaves, and tomatoes in a salad bowl, then set aside.

In a small bowl, thoroughly mix remaining ingredients, except olives, then pour over salad bowl contents. Toss, then decorate with olives and serve.

Leek pies
Leeks, which are not used much in cooking in North America, make an excellent-succulent pie.

- 1½ pounds frozen dough
- 4 heaping cups of thoroughly washed, chopped leeks
- 4 medium onions, chopped
- 4 cloves garlic, crushed
- 1 small hot pepper, very finely chopped
- 2 Tbsp. sumach (purchased in Middle Eastern food markets)
- 2 Tbsp. finely chopped fresh coriander leaves
- ¼ cup olive oil
- ¼ cup lemon juice
- 1 tsp. salt
- ½ tsp. pepper

Allow the dough to thaw, then set aside.

Make a filling by thoroughly combining all remaining ingredients, then set aside.

Form dough into 20 balls, then place them on a flowered tray. Cover with a damp cloth, then allow to stand in a warm place for 30 minutes.

Roll balls into 5 to 6 inch rounds, then place 2 heaping tablespoons of filling on each round, stirring the filling each time. (Preferably the filling should be divided into 20 equal parts.) Fold dough over the filling, then close by firmly pinching edges together into half moon or triangle shape.

Place pies on well-greased baking trays, then bake in a 350°F preheated oven for 20 minutes or until pies turn golden brown. Remove from the oven, then brush with olive oil. Serve hot or cold.

Fried Zucchini with Pomegranate
Serves from 4 to 6

¼ cup olive oil
1 medium sized zucchini (about 8 inches long and 3 inches diameter), cut into half then sliced into ½-inch thickness
1 Tbsp. pomegranate concentrate, diluted in 2 tablespoons water
2 Tbsp. very finely chopped fresh coriander leaves
½ tsp. garlic powder
½ tsp. pepper
½ tsp. paprika
⅛ tsp. cayenne

Heat oil in a frying pan, then fry zucchini slices until they turn golden brown, adding more oil if necessary. Remove and place on a flat serving platter.

Prepare a sauce by combining remaining ingredients, then spoon sauce over zucchini slices. Allow to stand for an hour before serving.

Fried zucchini with pomegranate

Moroccan Mint Tea
Serves 4

The preparation of this tea, called *atay* by the Moroccans, is Morocco's most popular drink. It is consumed at all times of the day by people from every stratum of society. Whether served in a humble café, an elaborate restaurant, or in the home, this drink is the refreshment most loved by the Moroccans and the other peoples of North Africa.

4½ cups boiling water
3 tsp. green tea (if not available, Indian tea may be substituted)
½ cup of pressed fresh mint leaves with stalks (2 teaspoons finely crushed dried mint leaves can be used if fresh mint is not available.)
3 tsp. sugar

Rinse out a teapot with hot water, then add tea. Pour in ½ cup boiling water, then, to remove bitterness, swish around in the pot quickly. Discard the water, but make sure not to throw away tea. Add mint, sugar and remainder of boiling water, then allow to steep for 3 minutes. Stir and taste, adding more sugar if necessary before serving. Note: For second helpings, leave mint and tea in pot; then add a teaspoon of tea, several mint leaves, and some sugar. Add again the same amount of boiling water. When mint rises to surface, the tea is ready. Stir and taste for sugar, then serve.

Eggplant Salad
Serves about 8

Very tasty, this dish native to Palestine can be served as an appetizer or as a salad.

1 large eggplant
about 2 lbs. oil for frying
4 cloves garlic, crushed
1 small hot pepper, very finely chopped
4 Tbsp. lemon juice
2 Tbsp. olive oil
1 tsp. salt
½ tsp. pepper
1 small piece of tomato
sprigs of parsley

Peel, then dice eggplant into about ¾-inch cubes. Place in a strainer in a sink, then place heavy weight over top of eggplant cubes. Allow to stand for an hour in order to drain.

Heat oil in a frying pan to about an inch deep, then fry eggplant cubes until they begin to brown. Remove with slotted spoon, then drain on paper towels.

In the meantime, combine remaining ingredients, except tomato and parsley, then set aside.

Place eggplant cubes on a serving platter, then decorate with the tomato and parsley and serve. ∆

Moroccan mint tea

Harvesting the wild: greens

by Jackie Clay

Winter's dreary end seems to drag on and on into early spring. We itch to get planting the garden, poring over seed catalogs and babying those tiny light green tomato, pepper, and other infant plants in the south windows. How lucky we are that the very first delectable greens that our bodies crave are already growing in sunny, protected areas around the homestead, planted for us by God, himself.

More than a few mothers have taken a basket and paring knife, desperately scrounging around the south sides of buildings, trying to find enough tender, nourishing greens to feed their family during hard times. This was especially common during pioneer years and during the lean Great Depression. Such common "weeds" as dandelion, purslane, pigweed, and lambs quarter are very nourishing. And they are extremely tasty, to boot.

Each year, our family forages for and harvests many local wild greens to enjoy with simple meals. And we like them so much that I can and dry several varieties to use year-around. One benefit of eating "weeds" is that they grow exceedingly well, as we all know from weeding the lawn and garden. While we struggle to get that row of spinach to grow during warm weather, the pigweed and lambs quarters simply shoot up. (Did you know that no one can tell my home-canned spinach from these weeds when canned as well?)

Let's take a look at some of the more common and easily identified wild greens. Of course, as with any wild foraging, we must be sure of the plants we pick as there are some poisonous little buggers out there that we sure don't want to serve for dinner. And take care not to harvest any plants from an area that might have been sprayed with insecticides, chemical fertilizers, or orchard sprays.

Pigweed (wild amaranth)

The coarse, lowly pigweed is one of our most favorite wild greens. Most folks call pigweed a blankety-blank weed. But they've never actually cooked up a mess or they would realize what a jewel they have clogging up the garden rows. When we first looked on our New Mexico homestead, walking over the abandoned cow yard with shoulder-high pigweed and waist-high lambs quarter among other edible wild plants, I thought to myself, "Well, here we could never starve to death!"

Pigweed ready to pick. Pigweed is an amaranthe—a better known edible.

The most common pigweed is the red rooted pigweed. It is a coarse weed—even when young—vigorous and quick growing. The leaves are oval and come to a point, with distinct ribs and wavy or scalloped edges. The leaves grow in a widely branched rosette, with the new growth tighter and held above the older leaves. The leaf stems are a pale greenish pink, and the root a distinct red. You will seldom find only one pigweed; it is a prolific reseeder. This fact makes it a nasty garden weed, but ensures that it is also an abundant vegetable. (One plant can have over 100,000 seeds.)

This fact is also important, as the seeds are not only edible, but very good. Pigweed is wild amaranth which is an important food to many Native Peoples all across North and South America.

Pigweed is nutritious in all forms, being high in vitamins A and C and high in iron and calcium. There is one caution. In farmland and in some Western American areas, pigweed can store up dangerous amounts of nitrates. This does not mean you should not eat pigweed. Be moderate, varying it with other forms of greens.

We begin to pick pigweed when it is about six inches tall and very tender, continuing the harvest through summer when the plants shoot up. With larger plants, harvest only the tender leaves and stems, including the growing rosette at the top. Once it begins to flower, we either pull the plant or cut off the top to encourage new growth. The main stem and larger side stems become woody and inedible, as do sunflowers. (The stems of our New Mexican cow yard pigweeds became so large that we literally had to cut it with a chain saw.)

Cooking pigweed is simple. The most common use is to simply rinse the leaves and steam or boil until wilted and tender. A dab of butter and a sprinkle of salt and vinegar and you have real good eating.

You can substitute pigweed greens for any recipe calling for spinach. The raw leaves are a bit rough, so if you use the most tender leaves in salads, you probably will choose to add only a few until you see how your family likes the mixture.

One of our favorite recipes for pigweed is piggy quiche, your basic spinach quiche, only using abundant and tasty pigweed.

Piggy quiche:

- 1 unbaked flaky pie crust
- 6 large eggs, separated
- ¼ cup mushrooms
- 1 red bell pepper, sliced
- ½ tsp. salt
- pinch rubbed sage
- 1 tsp. butter
- 1 cup slightly wilted pigweed leaves & tender stems
- 1 small onion, chopped
- ½ cup grated sharp cheddar cheese
- ¼ tsp. Tabasco Sauce
- ½ tsp. roasted, mashed garlic (optional)

Rub unbaked pie crust with butter. Whip egg whites until stiff, then fold in the beaten egg yolks. Mix gently. In sauce pan, sauteé chopped onion, sliced mushrooms, and green pepper until barely tender. Mix in slightly steam-wilted pigweed leaves and tender stems. Add seasonings and cheese to egg. Mix gently. Add vegetables. Pour into pie crust. Bake at 375° until a toothpick inserted in the center comes out clean. Serve at once. This simple quiche can be put together including making the pie crust in half an hour and tastes like it took all day. (Never tell 'em they're eating weeds.)

The seeds of the pigweed are very good. In fact, amaranth is very well known, especially south of the border, as a grain. There are many varieties of domestic edible amaranth available, bred especially for their tasty seed production. As I've said, an amaranth plant can produce over 100,000 seeds. And all of them are tasty.

To gather the seeds, wait until the plants mature and die in the fall, turning brown and brittle. Then, before the wind sows billions of potential weed seeds right in your garden, gently clip the seed heads off into a paper bag such as an empty feed sack that is clean. Do this on a dry day when the plants are quite dry to avoid mold problems during curing. Fill the sack with seed heads, but do not pack them down, allowing for air circulation. Store the sack in a warm, dry area, protected from birds and rodents. In about a week, the seeds will shatter out quite easily.

I tie the sack shut with stout twine, then simply walk on the bag quite briskly, even stomping gently on it. Turn the bag over and repeat. Shake the bag. You'll begin to hear lots of little seeds rattling happily in the bottom. Repeat again, until you think you've threshed the seeds out pretty well. Then untie the twine and gently pull out one seed head over a newspaper. Examine it, rubbing the hulls between your fingers. I'd recommend wearing gloves as amaranth seed heads are picky. More than one Indian tribe refers to pigweed as "that which picks the fingers."

When the seeds have been mostly threshed free, I pour the sack's contents a little at a time into a screen or basket with smaller holes between weaves, held over a large, clean, dry container such as a canning kettle. Shake the sieve and watch the little seeds trickle through into the kettle.

Throw the spent heads into another paper sack to burn, as there are always some seeds that never thresh out and you sure don't want to add them to your compost pile.

Now you have a kettle with a good layer of tiny seeds mixed with chaff. On a fairly windy day, winnow out the chaff by simply pouring the seeds from one container to another on the ground, with a foot or so between them. The wind will carry the light chaff away, and let the heavier seeds fall to the lower container. **Do not** do this in a heavy wind, as amaranth seeds are small and fairly light and will blow away in a stout wind.

You may now toast the seeds by spreading thinly on a cookie sheet in an oven set at 250° and baking for about 15 minutes, stirring occasionally to prevent scorching. Toasting gives the grain a nutty flavor.

The raw or toasted seeds may now be ground with a mortar and pestle or blender and added to any multi-grain bread. To each five cups of wheat flour, you can add a cup of amaranth flour.

Red-rooted pigweed, or wild amaranthe, makes an excellent green and also a wild grain.

Or you can make a traditional "mush" by simmering 1 cup of water with 1 cup of ground amaranth seeds. The toasted seeds work best for this unusual breakfast food. Adding dried fruit improves the flavor to those accustomed to more zesty fare.

Lamb's quarters

Another wild green that is a favorite of ours is lamb's quarters. Also a common garden weed, plentiful in most areas of the country, this wild vegetable is easily gathered in the spring and early summer. In some parts of the country, lamb's quarter is called pigweed, but is not a true pigweed or amaranth, but a chenopodium.

Lamb's quarters has triangular, notched leaves that look sort of like a goose's foot. This is why, in some parts of the country, folks call it "goosefoot."

The veins of the leaves are whitish, and the undersides and tops of new leaves are sparkling with white "fairy dust." We pick lamb's quarters when it is about eight inches to a foot tall. When it gets too large, the stems become woody and tough.

Lamb's quarters leaves are quite good in a salad or just for a snack on cool mornings with dew still clinging to them.

Like pigweed however, don't go overboard eating this green exclusively, as it can harbor nitrates in heavily farmed and fertilized areas. And lamb's quarter contains oxalic acid, which can be harmful when consumed in bulk over quite a lengthy period.

But when eaten in moderation, as one would any garden vegetable, there is scarcely any better green, domestic or

Common lamb's quarter is easy to spot with its scalloped oval and pointed leaves. Pick when young and tender. In the photo on the first page of this article, the author's son, David, sits in his favorite patch of lamb's quarters.

wild. We use a lot of it, off and on, all year, for I home can pints and pints of lamb's quarter to use during the winter.

Besides being very tasty, the lamb's quarter is extremely nutritious, being high in vitamins A, C, riboflavin, thiamine, and niacin. It's easy to see why this green was a staple of many ancient cultures, from Europe to North and South America.

While we were in New Mexico, many of our Spanish neighbors carried burlap feed sacks into pastures and abandoned homesteads to pick "quilites" or "greens," namely the succulent lamb's quarters. And we were right there with them with our own sacks. Then the next day, the greens were rinsed, boiled in salt water just enough to wilt them, and packed into canning jars and processed to ensure that we had enough lamb's quarters to last until the next spring's crop was abundant.

One of my favorite recipes for lamb's quarters is to fry a slice of ham, then add a tablespoon of butter to the frying pan when the ham has been removed. Then sprinkle handsful of fresh, rinsed lamb's quarter into the pan, stir frying until just wilted and tender. Sometimes I add a small chopped onion or mellow mild red chile pepper, which has been seeded. Served hot, along with the fried ham, you have a pretty darned good lunch. (For those of you who do no eat pork, a slice of smoked venison ham works equally well.)

Like pigweed, the seeds of lamb's quarter are also tasty. They are tiny, but we find they thrash out quite easily, just as do those for pigweed seed. You may toast the seeds and/or grind them to make mush or flour. It's fun to add wild seed ground grain to your homemade breads. Try sprinkling toasted lamb's quarter seeds on the tops of buttered, baked rolls and bread as you would poppy or sesame seeds. Pretty darned good.

Dandelion

The dandelion is one weed which needs little introduction. Many of us grew up, digging this tenacious weed out of our folks' lawns and gardens. With its cheery bright yellow flower, we think it's as pretty in our lawn as planted crocus and daffodils. And at the Clay homestead, it is very seldom ever pulled as a weed.

The dandelion is very nutritious, perhaps *the* most nutritious garden vegetable. Pretty darned impressive for a weed. It is very high in vitamins A, B1, B2, B3, C, D and many minerals, such as calcium, zinc, selenium, magnesium, iron, manganese, phosphorous, potassium, and sodium.

Nearly every part of the plant is not only edible, but delectable and different tasting than the others. The flowers, twisted and pinched off the stems are sweet and when steamed just enough to make them less "fuzzy" to the mouth, they are wonderful drizzled with butter and sprinkled with vinegar and salt.

The leaves are a bit bitter but still very good, both raw and cooked. The steamed or boiled leaves are more

The edible bracken fern shoot, often called "fiddleneck" for obvious reasons, is gathered early in the spring.

mild than the raw ones, and when more bitter leaves are boiled in two waters they become milder. Never over-boil dandelion or it loses its health benefits.

The crown, or smaller rosette of leaves, and small, unopened buds just at and barely below ground level are like a separate vegetable, being mild and succulent to the taste.

Even the slender, parsnip-like root of the dandelion is good to eat. I scrub the larger roots well with a pot scrubber, then lay them in a shallow baking dish. If the root seems woody or stringy, I scrape or peel it, depending on the root. Then bake the roots in a moderate oven until tender. Serve with a dab of butter or chill and add to cold salads.

You can even toast the roots in an oven with the very lowest temperature or only the pilot light on until crisp, but not scorched. Then run through a grinder or your blender. Now you have a coffee substitute which can be brewed just as you would coffee. (I hate coffee and think roasted dandelion root tastes *much* better.) This could come in handy as a survival drink for those of you who just need that morning cup of java. Unfortunately, you won't get a caffeine fix, as dandelion is caffeine free.

One problem for many people is that the dandelion grows so low to the ground that it is often gritty with blown dirt. This makes it hard to rinse clean enough to get the grit out completely. I find that a salad spinner does a great job. Or lacking that tool, rinsing the plant vigorously, under strong running water will do quite a good job.

Cattail

Nearly everyone is familiar with the cattail, especially its round, cigar-shaped fuzzy seedheads. Besides being fun to whack each other with (as kids we would watch the fuzzy seeds blow about in the wind,) the cattail plant is a storehouse of good eating. From the very top (the yellow pollen), to the mucky bottom (fleshy roots), the cattail provides a wide variety of edibles for the wild forager. And you don't have to get very "wild," either, as the cattail is common in farm ponds, along streams and lowlands nationwide.

Do not pick cattails from polluted bodies of water, or those having high-nitrate run-off from farm fields. Also be careful about harvesting from heavily traffic areas, due to auto pollutants.

Be sure of the plant you pick, as the wild flag or wild iris, which has a blue-purple flower, is toxic to consume, lives in the same habitat as the cattail and has quite similar leaves. Generally, the cattail leaves are wider and more hollow. The wild flag's leaves are iris-like and flat down to the bottom, where the cattail shoot is rounded right down to the root.

Like many other wild foods, the cattail is extremely nutritious in all forms.

Our first spring foraging trips always include a side trip to a remote mountain marshy creek, where abundant cattails grow. As a child canoeing with my parents, we would pull tender white cattail shoots from the water to eat as a snack on each trip. These taste just like a mild cucumber. Simply grasp the green cattail leaves of young plants and pull upward. The shoot comes up easily, with the lower portion being a very succulent, tender white.

Dipping these in your favorite vegetable dip or simply sprinkling with vinegar dressing as you would a garden cucumber, and you have a wild salad deluxe. I've even made wild pickles by using sliced cattail shoots in place of cucumbers for fresh refrigerator pickles, from dill to bread and butter types.

This same blanched, tender shoot can be steamed for ten minutes and served with butter or a cream sauce and you have a tasty vegetable that tastes kind of like mild parsnips.

Likewise, in the spring for a short period of time, the spike on top of the plant above the more familiar green "hot dog" that later becomes the brown seed head, can be eaten for a delectable treat. This is sometimes called cattail corn on the cob. Like corn on the cob, you prepare it by dropping it in boiling water for about five minutes. If not tender at this point, simply let it sit in the boiled water for five or ten more minutes until it is. Then dribble butter over the spikes and sprinkle with salt and you have an excellent vegetable.

This male spike quickly goes from green (corn on the cob) to yellow. This yellow powder is the pollen, and once the spike loses its green color, it is no longer good as corn on the cob. But this yellow pollen is quite easily collected and is a flour substitute (use about half domestic flour and half pollen). To collect the pollen, simply stick the pollen spike into a paper sack and shake or beat the head inside to release the pollen.

You will get quite a bit of chaff as well, but this can be sifted out with a common flour sifter or fine screen. Once you have sifted your pollen, it is ready to use as flour. We often make pancakes or cornbread using cattail pollen, especially when out camping. It is a bit slow to absorb water, so you need to make your batter, then let it rest for half an hour, stirring occasionally, until all is evenly moist.

And finally, the root can be dug to eat as a starchy flour substitute. This is a messy job, as you can't simply pull the cattail plant. You need to get down and dirty. We wade barefoot in cattail marshes, digging down around the base of the cattail with bare toes and a pointed digging stick. The toes locate the rhizomes and the digging stick helps pry them out of their mucky bed.

Once cleaned, the rhizomes can be slowly roasted until dry. Then grind the roots between two smooth large stones to release the starchy powder. These roots contain a net of fibers, which can be picked out and the flour sifted. This flour is good to add to stews and soups or to add to your bread or pancakes. As well, they really aren't too bad roasted and eaten with salt and butter, mashed with your fork or fingers and the good part sucked off the fiber.

Not bad at all, for this common weed of marshy places.

Purslane

Our 12-year-old son David's very favorite wild plant is purslane. This is a very common garden weed and grows nearly everywhere including waste land. This is a portulaca, related to the garden flower and is easily recognized. It is low-growing, forming a large mat. The leaves and stems are succulent and fleshy. They are smooth and reddish in color, with the stems being more highly colored than the greenish oval leaves, which like the garden flower, are broader at the tip than the stem end.

The plant is easy to pull, having roots small for such a hearty plant. We like purslane so much that we scarcely ever pull it from the garden.

And it is very nutritious, more so than most domestic vegetables. It is high in vitamin A, C, E, folic acid, containing fatty acids, sterols, calcium, potassium, iron, and magnesium, to name only a few nutrients.

Besides, it is very tasty. David often just plucks leaves and stems to snack on as he weeds the garden. He calls it "my weed," and rejoices when the young plants dot the garden paths in the late spring.

After it is thoroughly rinsed, I snip up tender stems and leaves, adding it to garden salads. Or you can simply drop large pieces into boiling water for a few minutes and serve with a bit of butter or drizzled with herb vinegar. I also often stir fry it with a little smoked meat. Or dip hand-sized pieces of purslane in deep frying batter and fry until golden brown.

The tiny black seeds can be harvested in the late summer and ground to add to breads. The numerous seeds do take awhile to gather. (One reason hunter-gatherers were seldom over weight.)

Home canning wild greens

These wild greens, with the exception of the cattail, can be easily home-canned, allowing us to enjoy them year-round. In fact, I generally can more wild greens than domestic greens. Not only do the wild cousins out-produce their domestic brothers—which can be finicky to grow some years—but they just plain taste better.

Wild greens **must be canned under pressure**, as they are low-acid vegetables. It is not safe to can them in a water bath canner, as they require a higher temperature to kill possible harmful bacteria. But this is easy to do using a pressure canner.

Simply harvest and rinse your wild greens well to get rid of all grit and dirt. Pick through them, discarding any insect-chewed leaves or dry leaves. Then dip them into a large pot of boiling water for just long enough to wilt them. A large amount of greens will wilt down to an appreciably smaller amount.

Dip the greens out of the pot and fill clean canning jars to within one inch of the top. Then dip up the boiling water, in which they were cooked, filling the jar to within an inch of the top with the water. Add one teaspoon of salt to quarts or one half teaspoon to pints, if desired.

Wipe the rim of the jar clean and place a hot, previously boiled new lid on the jar and screw down a ring, firmly tight. Place in warm canner. Process the jars (all types of greens) at 10 pounds pressure for 90 minutes (quarts) or 70 minutes (pints). Adjust pounds of pressure, as needed for altitudes above 1,000 feet, if necessary. See your canning book for directions.

Wild greens, canned in this way, will stay wholesome and tasty, nearly indefinitely. Be sure to mark the jars, regarding what type of green you have canned. I neglected to do this and can never tell what type of greens I am serving at a meal; we play "guess the green" while we eat. Is it spinach? Pigweed? Lamb's Quarters? Oh well, they are all great eating.

While these and more wild greens are great eating, one more of our favorite spring wild food is not really a green, but appears at the same time.

Fiddleneck ferns

In the early spring, the tender shoots of ferns poke up suddenly through pine needles and debris of the forest floor. The shoots of bracken fern and ostrich fern are edible and very good. While the bracken fern is toxic when mature and eaten in bulk, the new shoots are edible and taste like asparagus.

Fiddlenecks (fern shoots that have a small curl at the top, resembling the neck of a violin) are covered with a fuzzy, papery sheath. They must be picked before the leaves appear, or the stem becomes woody and tasteless.

Like asparagus, pick the youngest shoots, just after they emerge, cutting off just below the surface with a sharp knife. Wipe the papery and fuzzy membrane off as well as possible, then simply steam or boil until just tender. Remove from the pot and wipe off any clinging membrane or fuzz. Serve with butter or a cream sauce as you would asparagus and you have truly delectable eating.

Fiddlenecks can be home-canned to enjoy during the winter. In some parts of the country, they are harvested heavily just for this use. Process as you would asparagus after you have cleaned the stalks of their fuzz and membrane.

Some folks regard wild greens as a "survival" food. This is not giving them enough credit. While hundreds of wild foods are edible, these wild greens are truly scrumptious eating, deserving of being added to regular homestead meals. I hope you, like us, never quite regard a "weed" in the same light again. Δ

Brooder in a box

By Sylvia Gist

It's spring and the farm store has a tempting variety of baby chicks begging for you to take them home. Or the breed you've always wanted has been marked down. If you plan ahead a little, you can take advantage of the situation. Last spring, a local farm store was desperate to rid themselves of some roosters. Because I had the materials for the following brooder stored for just such an occasion, I took the chicks and within an hour, they were enjoying their new home. The inexpensive brooder described below will provide your chicks with a snug, happy home for several weeks.

The idea began when we had no place to put our first order of chicks, certainly nothing that resembled the setup pictured in the book we had borrowed from the library. In desperation, we decided to use a large cardboard box with a brooder lamp. It worked out so well for us here in northwest Montana that we make one every spring for our new batch of chicks.

Materials

To set up the brooder, you will need a large cardboard refrigerator box, some baling twine, a 250 watt brooder lamp (preferably with infrared bulb) and a chain to suspend it, and a stick or dowel about 6 feet long. Make it chick ready by adding a 1x6 board to set the feeder on, the top of a plastic 5 gallon bucket (or something of similar size and shape) to set a waterer on, a few optional boards to put under the box, litter for the floor (with a top layer of paper toweling the first two days), and chick waterers and feeders.

Setting up the box

First, get a large cardboard refrigerator box from an appliance dealer (Ask early if you want to be sure to get one.). The best ones are the ones on which the end was removed by cutting the strapping, not the cardboard. Select a location with accessible electricity in the building where you want to keep your chicks. This location should have a hook or something above the middle of it from which to hang the heat lamp. Take the empty box and reassemble it, replacing the missing strapping securely with baling twine. Then lay the box on its side, placing the largest surface on the floor. We found that slipping a few boards under the box at evenly spaced intervals provides air circulation and helps keep the bottom of the box dry.

Now you are ready to cut openings in the box. First mark the top. Draw one line across the box approximately in the middle, but always directly under the spot from which the light will hang. Then draw 2 more lines from side to side, one at each end about 10 or 12 inches from the end of the box. At the front of the box, draw a line to connect all three of the crosswise lines, keeping the connecting line 6 or 8 inches from the front edge. (See illustration.) Next, without bending any cardboard, cut the line across the front (a box cutter or utility knife works well). Then cut each of the three lines which go from front to back, stopping 6-8 inches from the back.

You will have what looks like a split door. Next bend each door at the back to hinge upward. A long stick or a dowel can be laid lengthwise under the flaps to keep the flaps from falling into the box. The flaps can be raised by simply propping them up, or a length of twine can be strung through a puncture in the flap and secured to something at the back of the box. The need to adjust the flaps will depend primarily upon the temperature of the building.

The box will most likely be too high for the average person to reach into using the top flaps, so we cut a window flap in the front. We like the flap to hinge at the top; it is easier to keep it closed if the weather is chilly. But we have to prop it open to care

Why buy a more expensive brooder, when this box brooder works just as well?

for the chicks, the main reason for the flap. It also serves to ventilate the box on warm days. Be sure to make the front edge at least 12 inches high to keep the chicks from walking or jumping out.

Finishing touches

The next step is hanging the 250 watt heat lamp from a chain passing through the middle slit in the top flap, allowing the bulb to be about 18 inches above the floor. In order to get the chain to hang straight, you may have to put a notch in the roof flap of the box. Using S-hooks to connect the lamp with the chain allows us to adjust the height of the lamp to get the temperature right for the chicks. We usually have a safety chain, too, to make sure the light does not fall to the floor; any secure tie will do the job.

To complete the interior decor, we spread a two inch layer of pine wood shavings (locally available for us) on the bottom of the box, lay down a 1x6 board to put the feeder on, and install a plastic lid to set the waterer on. We have found that a plastic lid (from a 5-gallon plastic bucket) with a rim of some kind to put the gallon waterer on prevents spills on the floor, thus keeping the bedding drier. Putting the feeder up on a board seems to slow the accumulation of shavings in the feeders.

Now you are ready to install your baby chicks. The refrigerator box brooder will hold 25 chicks for 4 to 5 weeks (the larger the breed, the sooner they outgrow the box) if the box is large, or 50 for a shorter time. With more chicks, you can expand by adding a second box of some sort. We have had 2 brooder boxes, end to end, (both with lamps if heat was needed) going at the same time, connected by a large hole cut in the end of the box. You have to experiment and adapt to the situation you have.

This brooder is cheap, convenient, and disposable. It enables us to raise

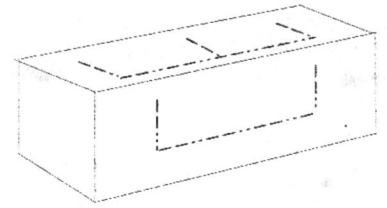

Diagram of cutting lines

chickens without having a lot of special brooder equipment or housing. When we are done with the box, it can be sent to the dump, burned, recycled, or used for mulch.

Making the chicks comfortable

1. Preheat the box. The temperature should be 95 degrees 2" above the floor at the outer edge of the lamp. Adjust lamp to reduce the temperatures about 5 degrees per week. While the glow from the infrared bulb discourages the chicks from picking other chicks, the heat can be intense, so monitor the temperatures in confined areas.

2. Put down paper toweling to keep chicks from eating the litter. Change often enough to keep it clean and remove on the third day when chicks are eating well.

3. Supply adequate fresh, clean water, about 1 quart per 25 chicks to begin. Disinfect waterer daily.

4. Provide enough feeder space: 1 slot per chick or 1" per chick in open feeders. For non broilers, keep feed available at all times.

5. Put some feed on the paper toweling, a paper plate, cardboard, or even plastic lids for a few days to make sure all chicks find food right away.

6. Dip each chick's beak in water and make sure he drinks as you put him in the box.

7. Check frequently to make sure you have the temperature right and flaps on the box opened or closed appropriately. Happy chicks will wander freely, make musical sounds and sleep side by side. If they crowd under the lamp, they are cold; if they stay around the edges of the box, they are hot; and if they huddle to one side, the box is drafty. If your box is in an unheated place, the outside temperatures will affect the inside. Watch the chicks and they will let you know if they are comfortable. We often closed them up completely on cold nights, but opened the box on warmer days. Δ

Growing and using blueberries

By Charles A. Sanders

The rich taste of blueberries is one of those special and all too rare garden treats. But that doesn't have to be so. Blueberries can be grown on your place in a relatively small area with good results.

Blueberries (Vaccinium species) are erect woody perennial bushes belonging to the Heath family. I first became acquainted with blueberries when I found small wild varieties growing high atop the bluffs and rocks on the sharp ridges around my home area. Later, a canoe trip into the wilderness of Minnesota found me gathering bunches of the prolific wild fruit to go with pancakes. Finally, I started a few of my own bushes here at home, to have my own dependable supply of the sweet dark fruit.

Generally, blueberries can be grown if your winter temperatures are mostly above -20°F. You will also need a growing season of about 160 days or longer and at least 1000 hours of temperatures under 45°F during the winter. For southern growers, some species of Rabbiteye blueberries and southern species hybrids require less winter chilling. Those varieties can be grown as far south as the Gulf Coast. Blueberries are rather shallow rooted and do best where the water table is about 14 to 22 inches below the soil surface. Don't attempt to grow blueberries unless you can supply needed water when the rainfall is not adequate.

Most of the major tree and seedling suppliers sell blueberry starts. When purchasing your plants, try to get two-year-old plants that are 10 to 15 inches tall. Be certain not to let the roots dry out prior to transplanting. Keep them moist and covered. Dig a hole the size of a five-gallon bucket or larger and mix in some good organic material such as sphagnum or peat moss with the soil. (As the mail order fruit tree suppliers used to state: "Dig a twenty dollar hole for a ten dollar tree.") Put about half the mixture in the hole, set the plant, and fill the hole with the rest of the soil mix. Blueberry plants should be spaced about 5 to 8 feet apart. If placed in rows, space the rows about 8 to 10 feet apart or wide enough to get your particular tractor, mower, etc. between the rows. Remember that the mature bushes themselves will get to be from 3 to 8 feet in diameter, so be sure to allow for that.

Blueberry bushes can make an attractive screen when planted in a row along a roadway or property line. They are also often planted in maintained rows, as indicated above.

It will take three or four years for your transplants to begin producing fruit. It is also a good idea to remove most or all of the first year blossoms. This will encourage vigorous plant growth instead of fruit growth during that important first year.

Blueberries are not very self-fertile. That means that two or more different varieties must be planted in the same area to insure good pollination and good fruit crops. Blueberries require moist, yet well-drained acid soils. There are several commercially available soil amendments which can get your soil in the 4.8 to 5.2 pH acid range. I give my plants an annual dose of common 10-10-10 fertilizer in addition to any acidic soil amendments. With good fertilization and soil management, it is not uncommon for your cultivated bushes to reach 5 to 10 feet in height.

Blueberries require a good mulch as far out as the drip line of the plant. A thick mulch of sawdust or crushed corncobs is good. Oak leaves are also very good and help to supply the acid needed by the plants. I often use plain old pine needles around my plants. They are good mulch and also supply the acid that blueberries love. I head over to the nearby state forest and use a scoop shovel to gather piles of them that accumulate along the roadway that runs through the forest property.

When it comes to blueberries, I have found that insect pests are few. However, birds can wreak havoc in

A colander full of blueberries

your blueberry patch. Catbirds, Brown Thrashers, and similar songbirds love blueberries and seem to nail them just before you get out to pick them. One remedy I have had good success with is to purchase some simple toy pinwheels at your local dime store or Wally-World. I fastened a piece of ½-inch PVC pipe to a nearby fence post and just dropped the pinwheel in. The loose fit enabled the pinwheel to turn into the slightest breeze. The motion created by the shiny spinning toy has worked well in keeping the berry bandits at bay. While this works well for my few bushes, you may need to consider fine net coverings if you have a row of several bushes. I have used net coverings over rows of raspberries and they are very effective in reducing destruction of the fruit by birds.

Blueberry bushes will need to be pruned after about their fourth year. Don't be bashful with the pruners. You will need to prune out two main types of growth to encourage prolific fruit bearing—the very slender stems which do not bear much, and the oldest and largest branches which are probably bearing mainly at the tips.

On a healthy, mature blueberry bush, you may expect to harvest about 12-14 quarts of fruit each year. With a half dozen or more bushes, this can translate into some extra money for you. Depending upon your area, you should be able to easily earn $2 to $4 a quart for the fruit. However, if you only have two or three plants, you will be likely to use all the berries yourself. There are a variety of tasty ways to preserve and use blueberries. Let's look at a few.

Picking and preserving

If possible, it is best to let the blueberries hang on the bush for about a week after they turn dark blue. This will give you the sweetest, ripest berries that just roll off the stem into your hand as you pick. The downside of this is that the birds may give you a run for your money and beat you to the fruit. The kids may also keep the easy berries picked for you…and stuffed into their mouths. For picking, I just cut the top front out of a plastic milk jug and tie a long piece of binder twine through the handle. I then hang the loop over my shoulder and go to picking.

Blueberries may be frozen, dried, or canned. Freezing the fruit is perhaps the easiest way to put them up. We just wash and drain them, put them in freezer bags and throw them in the freezer.

Blueberries are also dried easily. Simply remove all the stems then quickly blanch the fruit just to break the skins. Dry until the berries are sort of chewy and leathery, like raisins. They are good eaten dried or may be reconstituted by using equal parts of berries and water and soaking for 10 to 15 minutes. Then, use as you would fresh berries.

Canning blueberries is not difficult. The hot pack method works well with them and is recommended. Wash the berries and drain them well. Add about a quarter cup of sugar for each quart of fruit. Cover the pan and bring the fruit to a boil. Pack the berries in jars to within ½-inch of the top. If the berries have not made enough juice, cover them with syrup. Process pints for 15 minutes, quarts for 20 minutes.

Season	Variety	Quality	Comments
Early	Earliblue	Good	Good producer. Freezes well.
Early	Collins	Good	Attractive large berries.
Mid	Berkeley	Fair	Big berries, productive. Cans well.
Mid	Bluecrop	Good	Large berries. Slightly earlier than Berkeley. Cans and freezes well.
Mid	Blueray	Good	Large berries. Cans well.
Mid	Jersey	Fair	Produces large crop. Freezes well.
Late	Coville	Good	Good variety to extend season. Berries tart until ripe. Cans well.
Late	Herbert	V. good	Productive. Large fruit.
Very late	Lateblue	Good	Large, productive.

Blueberry recipes

Using blueberries is a pleasure. Simply tossing a handful into a bowl of pancake batter can turn breakfast into a tasty and aromatic pleasure with the resulting blueberry pancakes. Another time-tested favorite is sweet blueberry muffins.

Blueberry muffins

2 cups all-purpose flour
½ cup sugar
2 tsp. baking powder
½ tsp. salt
¼ tsp. cinnamon
¾ cup milk
½ cup butter or margarine, melted
½ tsp. vanilla
1 egg, slightly beaten
1 cup fresh (or frozen, thawed and drained) blueberries
1 tsp. sugar

Heat the oven to 400°. Grease the bottoms only of 12 medium muffin cups, or line with paper baking cups. Mix the flour, ½ cup sugar, the baking powder, salt, and cinnamon in a large bowl. Stir in the milk, butter, vanilla, and egg just until blended. Fold in the blueberries for a lumpy batter. Divide the batter evenly among the muffin cups. Sprinkle each muffin with ¼ tsp. sugar. Bake for 25 to 30 minutes or until nice and golden brown. Cool for 5 minutes; remove from pan. Makes 1 dozen muffins.

Blueberry jam

This is one of my personal favorites. Blueberry jam on a hot buttered biscuit is hard to beat. This recipe works well using a standard hot water bath.

4 cups crushed blueberries
2 Tbsp. lemon juice
1 pkg. Sure-jel pectin or equivalent
4 cups sugar

Have your jelly jars ready in hot water. Add the berries and lemon juice to a saucepan. Add the pectin and bring the mixture to a full boil over high heat, stirring it constantly. Add the sugar and return it to a full boil for one minute. Keep stirring the whole time. Remove the mixture from heat and skim any foam which has formed if necessary. Take the jars from the hot water, one at a time and ladle the hot jam into the hot jars. Leave about ¼-inch headspace. Wipe the jar rims and threads and apply the lids-fingertip tight. As each jar is filled, place it in the canner of hot water. Once the canner is full, add hot water as needed to cover the lids a couple of inches. Put the lid on the canner and bring to a gentle boil for 10 minutes (You may need to adjust the time for altitude, adding 5 minutes for every 3,000 feet elevation.). After processing, remove the jars and place on a towel to cool. They should each seal themselves shortly. After each jar has sealed and cooled, remove the bands, wipe the jars clean and store.

Fresh blueberry pie

Probably one of the most popular uses for blueberries is to make a rich thick blueberry pie. You may want to try this quick and easy recipe:

1 baked 9-inch pie shell
4 cups fresh or frozen blueberries
1 cup sugar
3 Tbsp. cornstarch
¼ tsp. salt
¼ cup water
1 Tbsp. butter or margarine

Line the baked pie shell with 2 cups of blueberries. To make the sauce, cook the remaining berries with sugar, cornstarch, salt, and water over medium heat until thickened. Remove the mixture from heat; add butter and cool. Pour over the berries in the shell. Chill and serve with whipped cream.

Another blueberry pie recipe

Here is another great blueberry pie recipe using your favorite pie crust recipe.

To the pie crust, add the following ingredients:

4 cups blueberries
1 cup sugar
3 tsp. flour

Mix all the ingredients and add to the pie shell. Add the top pastry, crimp the edges and pierce the crust in a few spots. Now here is a trick. Using 3-inch strips of aluminum foil, cover the crimped edge of the pie crust. Now bake the pie for 25 minutes at 350°. Then remove the foil strips and bake the pie for another 25 minutes. This will result in a nicely browned, yet not overdone pie crust edge.

Blueberry syrup

Maine is probably known as the Mother of all blueberry-producing regions. Here is a simple recipe from that area to make Maine blueberry syrup.

Simmer together the following ingredients:

2 cups blueberries
½ cup sugar
½ cup water
1 thin slice of lemon

Simmer for about 10 to 15 minutes. Makes about 2 ½ cups.

I hope this article encourages you to try your hand at growing and using blueberries. Once you get your bushes established and begin harvesting and using the dark blue fruit, you will wonder why it took you so long to get to know this gourmet treat. ∆

The Fourteenth Year

a pleasant surprise: the asparagus bean

By Alice Brantley Yeager
Photos by James O. Yeager

The year 2000 was not what one would call a great gardening year at Yeager Acres. We had hardly recovered from the spring rains when summer hit with high humidity and temperatures that soared until we thought Nature's thermometer had stuck. Drought settled in all over our area; ponds became mud holes, and trees began to shed their leaves long before fall. Add hordes of blood thirsty mosquitoes to these conditions and you don't have a pretty picture. TV weather forecasters became more apologetic with each passing day and there was talk of hunting up those folks who claim they can seed the clouds and produce rain. You might say our summer was an endurance test.

Near the end of July when we ordinarily plant fall beans, greens, etc., most of the vegetables in gardens hereabouts had succumbed to the ravages of our unpleasant summer. We gardeners who were bold enough to plant fall crops in spite of the weather did so with a mixture of fear and hope, our reasoning being that unfavorable weather does not remain the same forever.

I had on hand some asparagus bean seeds which I had meant to plant in the spring, but I ran out of space, so had put the seeds aside until "later." Early one morning before the day's searing heat began, I removed some spent cucumber vines from one of our

Asparagus bean, also known as Yard Long bean, is a good yielder and thrives in hot weather.

117

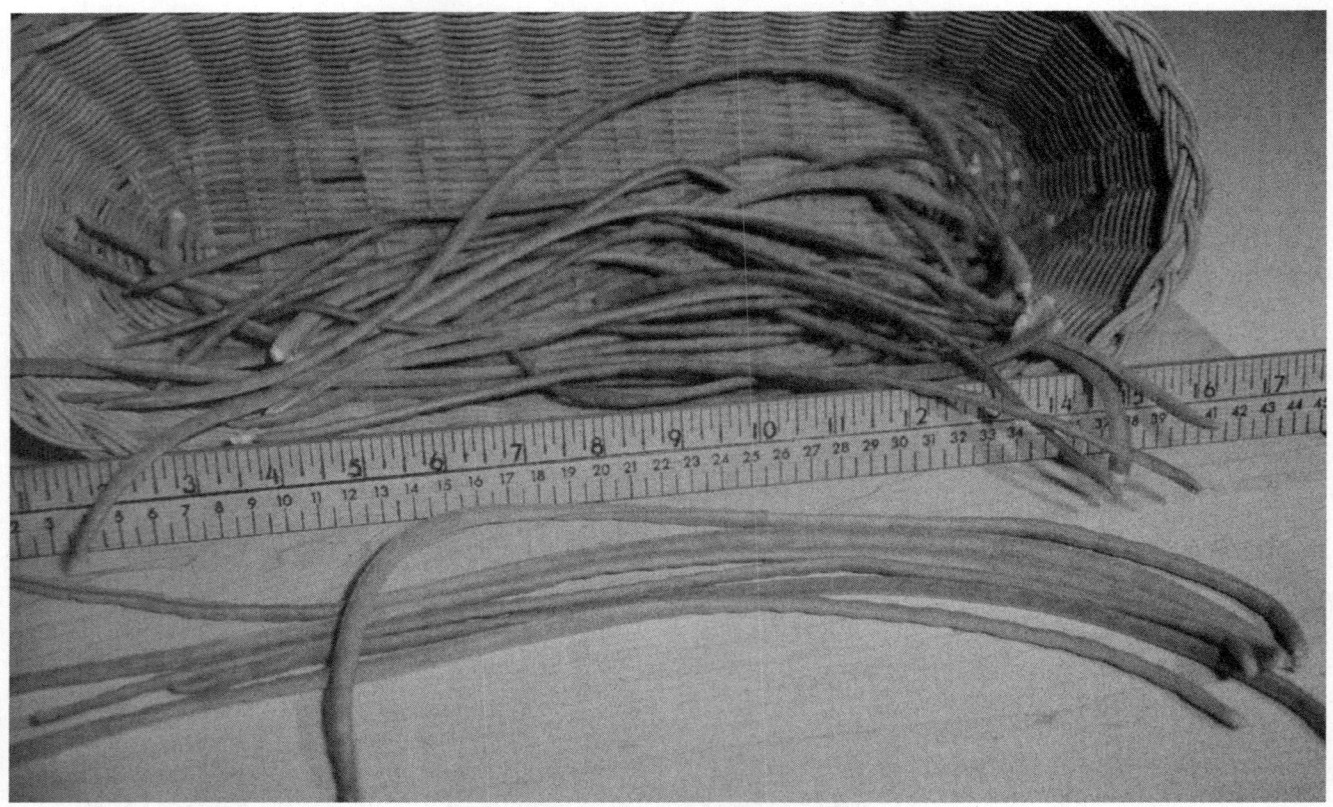
The first picking of asparagus beans gave us a nice sampling of a vegetable new to us. The delicious flavor is more like black-eyed peas than any beans we have tasted.

raised beds and put in the asparagus beans. Support racks were already in place and mulched ground was easy to work, so I finished before the sun had a chance to make life miserable. A good soaking with the water hose completed the project.

The seedlings began to pop up in only three days. Within about ten days most of the plants were ready to reach up and climb. Once the runners came in contact with the racks, there was a race to the top. I have always thought one of the joys of raising any pole bean is to visit the young vines each morning and see how much they have grown overnight. The asparagus beans were exceptionally fast climbers.

We were anxious to see the first beans. About the time the vines had reached the tops of the six foot racks, tiny flower buds appeared and they opened into small, creamy-pink, pea-like flowers. Then came the very slender beans that grew longer and longer. We found that the beans were at their best quality for snapping when they were about a foot long. Beyond that the pods toughened and the beans reached more of a shelling stage. However we shelled the larger beans and cooked them right along with the snapped pods.

I'm not quite sure why the asparagus bean is called a bean. The flowers and beans both more closely resemble those of a black-eyed pea plant than they do a regular bean such as *Kentucky Wonder* or *Romano*. The flavor is definitely enhanced black-eyed pea and delicious. Maybe something suffered in translation as the asparagus bean is not native to this country, but apparently hails from the Orient.

Like pole beans, the asparagus bean likes a sunny spot in the garden but will tolerate some afternoon shade. Tall supports are a must. We use a variety of supports for climbing plants—racks made from reinforcing wire, hog wire strung between posts, etc. We have access to plenty of bamboo, so it's easy to make A-frame or tepee towers from bamboo. When you make your supports, keep in mind that you want supports that will make harvesting easy. Don't erect something that you will have to maneuver through to reach the beans. Also, don't have rows so close together that vines weave back and forth and become a trap for dead leaves. Allow adequate space between rows so air may circulate freely and plants may receive plenty of sunshine.

Soil should be well cultivated—no clods or weeds. If you have raised beds covered with mulch, as we do, so much the better. We don't need our old garden tiller anymore. We just use a garden fork or spade now and then. We make a shallow trench-row and plant seeds about 5 inches apart. If planted closer together, plants will have to be thinned when they come up and who wants to throw away healthy seedlings? It's a good idea to put your support down when you finish planting to avoid damaging roots later.

When seedlings have several leaves and are about 4-5 inches high, it is wise to lay down a good organic mulch of grass clippings, straw, pine needles, etc. This will protect the young plants from losing dirt around their roots during heavy rains, cut down on weeding and help retain moisture in the soil. As a fringe benefit over the long term, the breakdown of the mulch will add nutrients to the soil and make it easier to cultivate.

If your garden soil is already loamy, well-drained and easy to work, chances are it's okay for most vegetables—squash, cucumbers, beans, etc, However if you have had trouble with some plants getting off to a poor start and you suspect the soil could be the problem, a soil test might be in order. Your county extension agent should be in a position to give you some good advice and also run the soil test. This is usually free-of-charge—a taxpayer's perk.

The development of asparagus beans is fun to watch as each day the pods lengthen. I am sure under ideal climatic conditions they would reach their yard-long potential, but, 2000 not being a banner year, the longest bean we harvested was about 22 inches. As said above, however, the best quality stage is a foot or less.

We found the asparagus bean to be relatively pest-free. There were a few ants that seemed to be drawn to the vines, but we knocked those off with a stream of water from the hose. We lost no small plants to cutworm as cutworms are non-existent in our garden. I believe we wiped them out years ago by putting a tiny bit of 10% Sevin Dust at the base of plants that often fell prey to cutworms. However I don't urge the use of much Sevin Dust, as it also destroys the good along with the unwanted.

It's strange how some vegetables grown as oddities can be quite delicious despite negative statements by seed companies. Makes you wonder if they have ever actually tried them. One company says asparagus beans produce an astonishing crop but the beans are slightly stringy. Another states the beans are grown more as a curiosity and that the plants produce more vines than food. Well, our asparagus beans endured the heat, out-produced the struggling regular pole beans and earned themselves a future in our garden.

With a botanical name like Vigna sesquipedalis, the asparagus bean has to be good!

Hoppin' John with fresh asparagus beans

1 cup uncooked rice (not instant)
1 pound pork sausage broken into small pieces
3½ cups water
1 pound asparagus beans, rinsed and snapped.
1 medium onion, chopped
1 green bell pepper, chopped
⅛ tsp. cayenne pepper
1 tsp. salt
1 tsp. dried sweet basil

Cook rice according to directions on package. (Directions will vary with different types of rice.)

While rice is cooking, saute sausage to a light brown in a large iron skillet. Drain off most of grease, but leave a bit for flavor. Add the rest of the ingredients and simmer, covered, for 30-40 minutes or until asparagus beans are tender.

Combine sausage mixture with cooked rice and serve hot. A dash of Tabasco (hot) sauce is in order for those who enjoy the Cajun touch.

Served with a salad and drink, this recipe should serve 4-5 people.

TIP: Want something different in a stir-fry mixture? Try putting in a few snapped, fresh asparagus beans!

Cooked fresh asparagus beans

1 pound asparagus beans, rinsed and snapped. (If some have grown beyond the tender snapping stage, shell the beans and discard the pods.)
2 slices cured bacon, fried and cut in small pieces. Reserve bacon drippings.
1 small onion, chopped
¼ tsp. salt
1/8 tsp. freshly ground black pepper

Put beans in 2 quart pot and cover with water. Bring to a boil and reduce heat to simmer. Add other ingredients, including one tablespoon of bacon drippings, and cook about 25-30 minutes or until beans are tender. Avoid overcooking as beans could become mushy.

Serve as a side dish with other food or serve as a main dish with your favorite bread or cornbread, a salad, and hot tea or coffee.

Freezing asparagus beans

We have found that asparagus beans freeze quite well. Simply wash and drain the beans thoroughly in a colander and snap them into desired lengths. Any that have gone beyond the snapping stage may be shelled and pods discarded.

Put snapped beans and any shelled beans on a cookie sheet and place in freezer. When frozen, put beans into freezer bags, label and date, and store in freezer for future use.

Seed Sources:
The Cook's Garden, P.O. Box 535, Londonderry, VT 05148
Gurney's, 110 Capital Street, Yankton, SD 57079
Pinetree Garden Seeds, Box 300, Gloucester, ME 04260 Δ

MOSQUITOES
outnumber us and no one likes them

By Tom and Joanne O'Toole

Mosquitoes are responsible for irritating bites, cause itching welts, can spread diseases, are a constant aggravation at picnics, and are ear-tormenting little beasts. No wonder they are so disliked.

Like many other things in nature's cycle, there are thousands of different species of mosquitoes around the world, all with varying flight habits, food and climate preferences, and breeding requirements. Only two things are constant. The females need a blood supply to lay their eggs, and water in which the eggs must hatch.

These vicious blood-sucking buggers are hearty and adaptable, surviving freezing temperatures and hundred-degree heat. The mosquito "season" is year around in hot, humid parts of North America, while in other areas the cycle begins and ends at different times of the year depending on the climate. Usually, wet, warm, spring and summer months are peak times when the critters are hungriest. The northern fringes of the United States and all of Canada have the shortest mosquito seasons.

So where's the heaviest concentration of these creatures? You'd think some place like the Florida Everglades. Well, the experts say the Alaskan and Canadian tundra are the most infested areas. In fact, in the arctic, mosquitoes hatch in such multitudes that they can turn the sky gray.

If you want to get technical, the pesky mosquito is a member of the fly family, having the mouth parts elongated into a proboscis equipped for piercing and sucking. They have scales on their wings and antennae which are markedly hairy in the male, but less hairy in the female. They are also one of the most irritating insects known to man, always managing to buzz their way into our otherwise peaceful lives.

Only the adult females bite, as they need a protein blood meal to develop the eggs before they can reproduce. In fact, females can sip almost twice their own weight in blood. The male has different mouth parts, and must be content to be a vegetarian, supplementing his diet with nectar and plant juices.

Mosquitoes find their victims—both human and animal—by flying into the wind and picking up sensor beams which they follow to their meal. These beams include the concentration of carbon dioxide which is emitted with exhaled breath, and lactic acid which is produced by muscle movement. Moist skin and a warm body is an immediate target, and the female is able to detect the slightest change in temperature. They know when you're near!

These heat-seeking insects are drawn to dark colors, hair, and fur, but are also drawn to people because of scented grooming products like after-shave, perfume, cologne, and body lotions, as well as perspiration and body odor. Yet humans and animals are not their only victims. They also go after birds, frogs, turtles, and even snakes.

Thankfully, other wildlife that share the same habitat, such as dragonflies, water insects, fish, water and insec-

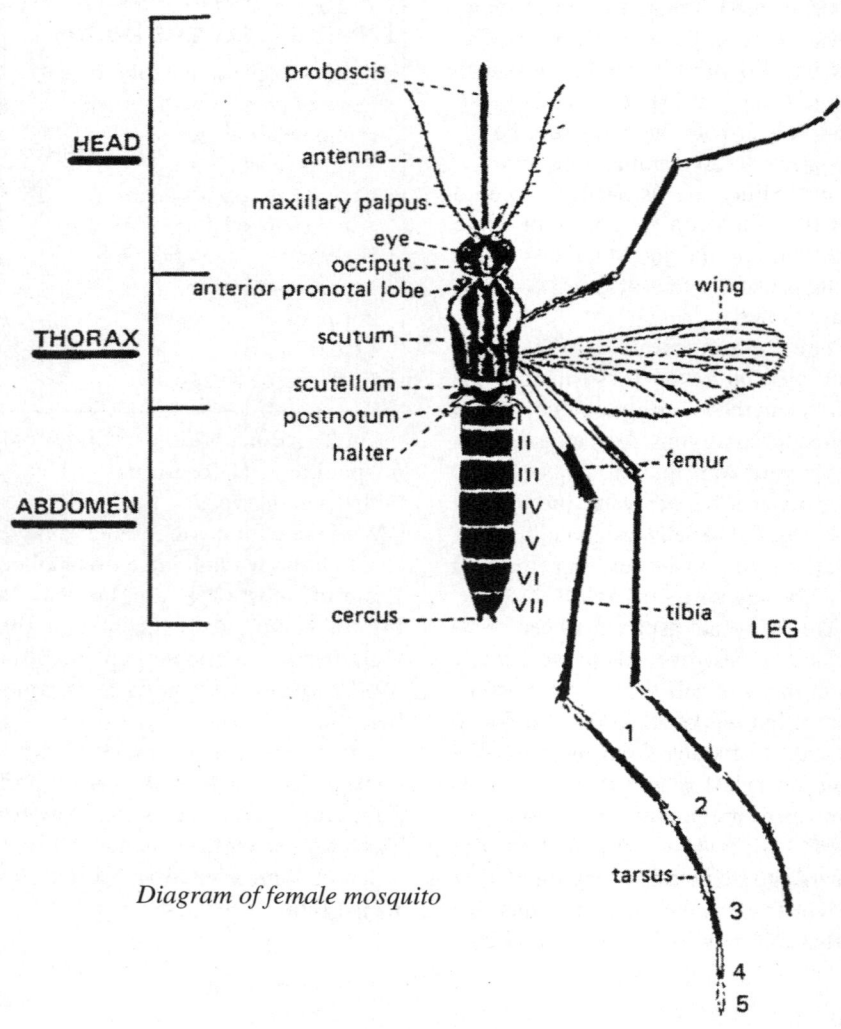

Diagram of female mosquito

tivorous birds, and bats prey on mosquitoes. Although it's of little comfort, mosquitoes have pests bothering them too, in the way of tiny mites and midges.

While the biting female appears to have a simple tube-like snout, it is actually a protective sheath around a hollow, flexible canal up which blood is drawn, a saliva duct that carries anti-coagulant into the wound, and four cutting stylets to penetrate the skin as they work alternately up and down—sort of sawing or stabbing their way through.

When a mosquito penetrates a victim, it injects saliva to ease the blood flow which also acts as an anesthesia on the skin in order for the insect to bite without being initially detected. The substance then creates an allergic reaction on the skin, it itches, we scratch, and this develops into a welt.

Worse, some types of mosquitoes are capable of carrying and transmitting a variety of diseases, including malaria, yellow fever, dengue fever, as well as four major types of encephalitis (a viral disease causing inflammation of the brain). However, organized mosquito control in North America has greatly reduced the incidence of these diseases.

With a mate and a blood supply, the female needs only water in which to hatch her eggs—the smaller and less disturbed the better. In her 60-day life cycle, she can lay thousands of eggs in puddles, birdbaths, watering troughs, rain barrels, and pet dishes—in clean or foul water, it makes no difference. Eggs thrive in stagnant water, as well as in a humid swamp or marsh. Breeding sites are as diverse as depressions in the woods, gutters and flat roofs that hold water, sewage pipes, discarded tires, old tin cans, and basins in city streets. For some species the life cycle begins in a week to 10 days, or eggs can lie dormant for several years just waiting for water.

After hatching, mosquitoes quickly go through the larvae and pupae stages before reaching adulthood. Just hatched larvae—known as "wigglers" because they squirm like worms in the water—are equipped with a breathing tube opening near the end of the abdomen. They eat constantly, feeding on bacteria, pollen, and microscopic plants. Some species also eat other mosquito larvae.

The pupae is known as a "tumbler" because it rolls and tumbles through the water, staying near the top so it can breathe. Usually within two weeks the adult mosquito emerges for its seasonal existence, with the male living about half as long as a female.

After a couple of weeks the female is looking for its blood supply, and is ready to reproduce. Humans are also ready to whack them whenever they land on their skin, but that age-old method of swatting the biters is only effective in eliminating that one particular insect.

There are trillions of mosquitoes all over North America, and experts predict the ratio of people to mosquitoes each season at about 1 to 41,000.

Ouch! Public agencies in the United States and Canada spend millions of dollars annually trying to eliminate them or at least control them.

Methods of control are numerous, ranging from destroying habitats, draining breeding places, spraying, treating surface water with kerosene, to lighting smudge pots.

As each individual has a different level of attractiveness to mosquitoes, so every hiker, camper, hunter, fisherman, boater, and other outdoor enthusiast has a favorite personal remedy for warding off the annoying insect.

Early man spread mud and animal fat on his skin to prevent bites. As we became more sophisticated mosquito-deterrents included pine oil, camphor, citronella, pennyroyal, cedarwood, eucalyptus, wintergreen, turpentine, and oil in any form. Orange peels worn around the neck were also believed to be effective.

Today there is a wide variety of repellents (sprays, creams, and lotions), but these do not drive mosquitoes away, they merely confuse the insect's sensors so they aren't able to recognize you as a potential meal. The repellents keep the pests from biting (rather than killing them), and when they start buzzing around again, it's time to re-apply to all exposed skin, and sometimes even your clothing.

There are endless remedies to ward away mosquitoes, and Avon's Skin-So-Soft Bath Oil seems to work wonders. There's also OFF, Cutter's, Ben's, Repel, Ben's Max, and other products with DEET (N, N-diethyl-meta-toluamide). If you want to avoid DEET-based repellents, look for Tender's Natrapel. These come in a variety of uses—non-aerosol pump sprays, liquids, squeeze bottles, aerosol cans, single-use foil packets, towelettes, and lotions. To keep a yard mosquito-free, Raid Yard Guard seems to have a proven track record. Remember, these are all temporary solutions.

However, when mosquitoes do get through the defenses, and you are bitten, there are a few things you can do to help stop the itching. It is recommended the bite be swabbed with household ammonia every hour or so; calamine lotion can be dabbed directly on the bite; and if the itching persists, take a cool bath or shower.

But wait! Not everything works as it is meant to. Some years ago a British publicity stunt for a new repellent backfired when 3,000 starved mosquitoes—released into a booth with a model slathered with the new product—escaped and attacked the audience of businessmen and journalists who were there for the demonstration. Wonder if that same firm is going to demonstrate a new shark repellent? ∆

Leaves of three, let them be!

By Tom and Joanne O'Toole

If you've ever had poison ivy dermatitis you're among millions of others who have had the same distressing experience. It's probably the most common skin allergy in North America. It is also the most aggravating, frustrating, and tormenting of rashes.

Statistics suggest about half the population is allergic. Being immune one year is no guarantee you won't be sensitive the next. Showing little partiality, it affects people of all ages, and both sexes equally. Estimates are that each year poison ivy causes about two million cases of skin poisoning serious enough to require either medical attention, or at least a day of restricted activity. There are another 18 million annual cases that cause weeks of itching and unsightly blisters.

While people are susceptible to poison ivy any time of the year, it is much more prevalent in spring and summer when the leaves are in full bloom, and people are involved in more outdoor activities.

So what is this irksome pest? Knowing the enemy by sight can be a big help in avoiding it. The green leaves have the distinctive characteristic of always appearing in clusters of three (remember the old adage, "leaves of three, let them be"), often shiny on top, slightly hairy underneath, with either smooth or slightly toothed edges, and each with a pointed tip. The middle leaf at the end of the stalk is slightly longer than the other two which have no stems.

Drooping clusters of small green flowers grow at the base of the leaves, and by fall, hard little whitish waxy berries ripen, and last into winter. Birds love the berries, and drop the seeds for new growth far and wide. As autumn arrives the leaves turn a bright scarlet, orange, and yellow, adding to the colorful fall landscape.

The most common form of poison ivy is the climbing vine variety, and it thrives in woods, fields, thickets, along fences, wrapping itself around trees and telephone poles, and growing up walls. It can climb the sides of houses, up and over fences, find a home in flower beds, as well as in hedges and shrubbery. This woody vine climbs by means of its aerial roots and has a remarkable capacity for survival under the worst conditions.

When there is nothing to attach itself to, it takes the form of a shrub or bush, and can live in dry areas, pastures, around rocks, and near water. In this form it's frequently

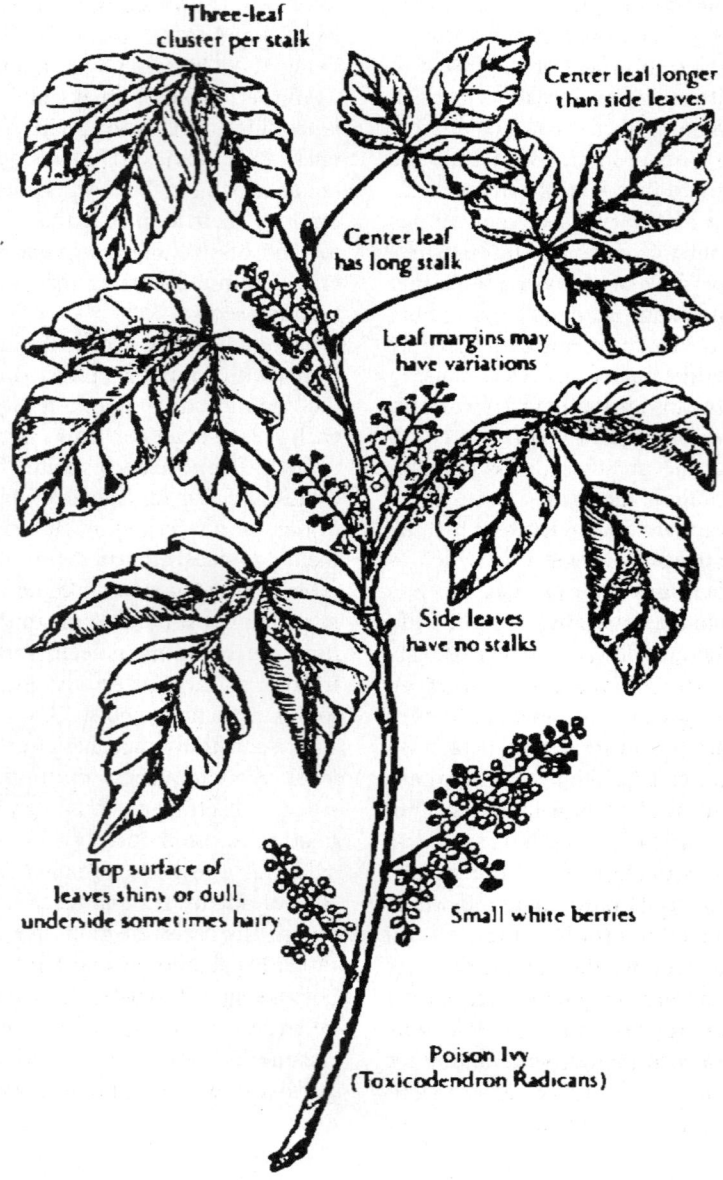

Poison Ivy (Toxicodendron Radicans)

referred to as poison oak, and is predominant in the west and southwest part of the U.S. In other areas it is called poison sumac when it becomes a small tree.

What causes the violent skin reaction is the yellowish resin (cardol) found in the leaves, stems, bark, roots, flowers, and berries. The plant is saturated with this volatile oil. A chemical found in the resin is the phenolic poison urushiol (yoo-ROO-shee-ol) which actually causes the rash.

The milky-to-clear sap is not on the surface of the leaves, but appears whenever the plant is broken, cut, or bruised. It takes very little of it to cause a severe inflammation, and the slightest brush can result in a painful irritation.

While you must come in contact with urushiol to get the poison ivy rash, the sticky resin can be carried to your skin from domestic animals that bring the misery to you on their fur, from clothing, outdoor equipment, walking sticks, firewood, garden tools, or any object that has touched a broken or bruised poison ivy vine or plant.

The urushiol vaporizes when burned, and is then carried in the air. Inhaling the smoke of brush fires containing this cursed plant can be toxic, causing internal blisters and serious lung infections.

Initial symptoms of the rash are reddish streaks, blotches, and clear blisters—sometimes appearing within a few hours, or delayed for several days, but usually within 12-24 hours. The signs are often accompanied by oozing, scaling, scabbing, and the ever-present itching.

Lasting 10-24 days, there are sometimes lingering effects to areas of the skin—especially the forearms—that seem as though they will never heal.

Fortunately the rash itself is not contagious. Although you cannot get it by touching someone who already has it, the rash can be transmitted from another person if the oil is still on their skin.

Spreading poison ivy to different parts of the body is usually the result of touching one area with another soon after exposure while the resin is still on the skin. Once the rash develops, the urushiol has already penetrated, and it will not spread.

There are, of course, myths connected with the poison ivy plant. Although some people are immune, eating the poison ivy leaves isn't going to make you immune. Eating the leaves can result in a serious reaction, and even death. Another fallacy is that one or more attacks renders you less prone to get it. Often, it's just the opposite.

Like the common cold, there is no sure cure for poison ivy, but there are ways to achieve some relief. Sometimes the rash can be minimized if the exposed skin is washed with a strong alkali soap soon after contact. Fels naphtha seems to be a recommended favorite.

Another remedy is to swab the affected area with a mixture of equal parts of vinegar, buttermilk, and salt. This dries the skin and prevents the blisters from oozing.

Home remedies like calamine lotion, Benadryl, and witch hazel can help relieve some of the pain and itching, as will washing the rash areas with a strong solution of baking soda. Analgesic-anesthetic medicines like Rhulispray or Rhuligel can ease itching and lessen scratching. Rhuli medicines in poison ivy country are excellent itch insurance. Do all you can to avoid scratching the rash, as it can lead to infection.

For severe reactions, see your physician. He can prescribe a cortisone cream or antihistamine to help relieve the itching discomfort.

A new quick-drying lotion is the USFDA-approved Ivy Block. However, this product must be applied before you come in contact with poison ivy. It forms a barrier, and is a preventive measure.

If you get caught up in poison ivy, you should also wash your clothing, gear, and anything else you suspect of contamination.

There are several ways to rid your property of poison ivy. If the soil is loose enough, you can lift up long sections of roots with a garden fork. The best time is after a rain when the soil is soft.

Another tactic is to apply an herbicide in spring or summer when the vine is in full leaf, covering as much of the plant as possible.

Recommended preparations include Amitrol-T, Ammate, Roundup, Kleenup, Weed-B-Gone, Ortho Poison Ivy Killer, 33-Plus, and other selected products.

Perhaps the best way to avoid that all-too-common woodland nemesis poison ivy is to be able to recognize it, then keep your distance. Δ

Ask Jackie

Home canned bologna and corned beef, homemade sun dried tomatoes, sweet potato butter

Thank you for answering my questions on smoked fish and baked beans canning. You mentioned you can bologna and corned beef. Would you please share the recipe?

James R. Coffey
Elkton, MD

Jackie Clay

Glad I was of help. That's what I'm here for, after all. And the more people I can help out, the better, as far as I'm concerned. As for the recipes, here are two that work for us:

Home canned bologna:

25 lbs. fresh ground meat
1 lb. Morton's tender quick
1 tsp. garlic powder
4 tsp. liquid smoke
½ tsp. saltpeter
¾ cup brown sugar
1 oz. coarse ground black pepper

Grind the meat twice, adding spices etc., as you grind, and mix well. Put in an enameled turkey roaster, covered, and let set in a cool place for three days. A refrigerator works fine. Grind again and pack into wide mouth pint jars to within an inch of the top. Wipe the rims clean and place a previously boiled, warm lid on the jar and screw down the ring firmly tight. Place in a pressure canner and process for 90 minutes at 10 pounds, adjusting the pressure as needed to allow for altitude. (Check your canning book for these adjustments.)

This bologna is very good and doesn't taste like "store" bologna (which we hate). It kind of tastes like a cross between good liver sausage and corned beef. We like it sliced from the jar and fried. I hope you'll like it, too.

Home canned corned beef:

To corn the beef, choose well-chilled beef and remove all the bones. You may use the brisket, rump, or chuck roasts. Cut the meat into uniform pieces and weigh the entire pile. Allow 2 to 2½ pounds of salt for each 25 pounds of beef. Sprinkle a layer of salt on the bottom of a crock. Place a layer of meat in the crock and add more salt. Continue packing in this manner until all the meat has been packed. Cover the top layer with a good layer of salt.

Allow the packed meat to remain in the salt for 24 hours, in a cool place, covered to prevent debris and insects from falling into the crock. Then cover the salted meat with this solution:

2 lbs. sugar
2 oz. saltpeter
1 oz. baking soda
2 gallons of water

Make a spice bag containing 1 ounce pickling spices and two or more (to taste) crushed cloves of garlic. Place the bag in the brine with the meat. Be certain that all the meat is completely covered with brine. Place a China plate on top and weight it down to keep meat submerged.

The meat is cured for 30 days at 38° to 40° F. If the temperature gets warmer, the brine will get ropy, which means that it feels snotty and stringy when you dip your finger into the brine. If this should happen, immediately drain all the brine and rinse the meat it well. Throw away the old brine and make new brine and cover. Be sure to check your pickling meat often, especially if the temperature fluctuates and could go above 40°.

At the end of the brining period, remove the meat from the brine, rinse well and drain. Pat it dry with a clean towel.

To can the corned beef, soak the meat for two hours in clean water, then boil it slowly in clean water for 30 minutes. Remove the meat from the boiling water and cut it into pieces that will pack into wide-mouth pint or quart jars. Pack the jars to within an inch of the top of the jar. Add liquid, in which the meat was boiled, to within an inch of the top. Wipe the rim of the jar clean. Place previously boiled jar lids in place and screw down ring firmly-tight. Process in your pressure canner for 90 minutes at 10 pounds pressure, adjusting pressure, if necessary to make allowances for altitude. (See your canning book for instructions.)

This corned beef is very good and tender. I hope you will like it.

Jackie

Can you tell me how to make sun dried tomatoes like they sell at gourmet shops? We like them on pizza and pastas.

Carol Williams
Santa Barbara, CA

Actually, sun dried tomatoes are simply dehydrated tomatoes, usually tomato halves. And tomatoes dry very well at home. The trick to "gourmet" dehydrated tomatoes is to use a thick-meated, thin skinned, quite sweet variety. I dehydrate two main kinds, an extra-sweet yellow cherry tomato, Sungold, which tastes almost like a dried apricot when dehydrated, and a largish, red cherry-plum type, Principe Borghese. Principe Borghese is an Italian heirloom developed especially for sun drying, where the entire vine was pulled and draped over the garden fence to dry the tomatoes naturally in the sun.

While this method does work very well in some climates, many folks have a damper climate and the tomatoes dried in this manner would mold before drying. I prefer to simply harvest the ripe tomatoes, pull the stem out, and slice them in half, drying them cut side up on a cookie sheet in my gas oven with only the pilot light on or on racks in a dehydrator. They are done when shriveled and tough-leathery. The dehydrated tomatoes can be stored in any airtight container such as a gallon glass jar. Be absolutely sure they are dehydrated well or they can mold.

You can find Principe Borghese seed at several seed houses, including Pinetree Garden Seeds, Box 300, New Gloucester, ME 04260. Sungold is a common yellow tomato found in most seed catalogs.

To use the dehydrated tomatoes, simply add to any moist tomato (or other) sauce. They rehydrate rapidly and retain their exceptional taste.

Jackie

I'm looking for a recipe for sweet potato butter. The sweet kind that would be spreadable on muffins, toast, etc. I have found several recipes but none with canning directions. As I would like to put them up, I would like help. Would any recipe I might find that says to pack in canning jars be okay to water bath them, and how long for?

Nancy
jazzy@dnet.net

I have an old, old sweet potato butter recipe for canning that I have used and I would assume one could use any spice or variation, as long as the sugar to sweet potato ratio remained about the same, since the sugar preserves the low acid fruit, just as it does for pumpkin butter. Now I can't "recommend" that you can this preserve as it isn't approved or tested by experts. But the ratio of mashed, cooked sweet potatoes to sugar is to every cup of mashed sweet potatoes add three quarters of a cup of sugar and a pinch of salt and spices (cinnamon, cloves and allspice) to taste. I use brown sugar, but that is a matter of taste. Pack the hot butter in hot, sterilized pint or half pint jars and process in a boiling water bath for ten minutes, counting from the time the water begins to boil with the jars in it.

Jackie

The last word

Do we really need Yuppies?

Yuppies: they're the folks we love to hate. Snobs and show-offs, the whole bunch of them. They're the first on your block with cell phones, 2.5 GHz PCs, Segway scooters, Palm Pilots... What purpose or benefit do these people, who run out and suck up the latest fad toys, serve? The world would be a whole lot better off without them. Right?

Wrong. Without them we'd still be in the Dark Ages.

Am I kidding?

What if I told you the rise of modern western civilization can be attributed to the Yuppies of the 15th century? It was the middle class, what was then the merchant class, that drove the Renaissance and the Age of Discovery. They were the Yuppies of their time. Before the rise of that class, which started in Italy and spread throughout Europe, there was little nonreligious art and literature, even less in the way of science and technology, and almost no trade between Europe and the rest of the world. Because there was no trade, there were almost no spices, tea, or anything else Europeans couldn't produce for themselves. Only the Church, royalty, and the nobility had money to buy anything and there were very few of them—certainly not enough to support artists, research, or prosperous trade routes. There were too few to pay for these goods. So tea and silk stayed in China. Spice stayed in the East Indies. Most of the would-be Rembrandts, Mozarts, and Dantes had no one to whom they could sell their wares and were consigned to their plows, or chopping wood, or herding sheep. How many geniuses were lost to humanity because there was no one there to pay them for what they could have done best?

It was after the first Yuppies emerged in Europe that the printing press with movable type came along. It was used to print and sell books, including the Bible, to others in this rising middle class. It was because this middle class kept the printing presses busy that, ultimately, poor folks could afford a family Bible, or the works of Milton, or their own copy of Shakespeare. Before that, there were no books except in the Church, and therefore, almost no literacy. Until that time books had been laboriously copied by hand making their costs so prohibitive that only the rich could own them. Had it not been for the Yuppies of their day, almost all of us would be illiterate because the printing press would have rusted away in Gutenberg's barn, its production unsold and unused.

And it's been Yuppies driving progress ever since. In the century we just bade goodbye, it was the Yuppies of their generations who ensured that the rest of us would one day afford cars, televisions, computers, telephones, air travel, and all the other things that are hallmarks of our times.

If Yuppies and Yuppie-like consumers hadn't bought products and services like these when they were first introduced and still expensive, most, if not all, would have died like unripened fruit on the vine.

Sure, there were tinkerers who would have bought them. And some would be the domain of other large businesses or the rich, as with mainframe computers and yachts. But just as with PCs, geeks and businesses buying them wasn't enough. It takes Yuppies, buying en masse and waiting in line to buy each new generation of faster computer with more storage and better graphics to create a market that eventually brought the prices of PCs down, drove the quality up, and made them mainstream. Without Yuppies, the computer on my desk simply wouldn't be there. Cell phones would be all but nonexistent.

One of the reasons many poorer countries have problems tapping their native geniuses and creating new, affordable products to bring to market is that they don't have a Yuppie class that nurtures that genius or supports the producers at a time when products are new, primitive, and expensive to produce. In the 1930s Stalin, then dictator of the Soviet Union, invited Henry Ford to come to Moscow. He asked Ford to give him some advice on how to build the fleets of trucks and farm equipment the Soviets needed to march into the 20th century. Ford gave the old Ruskie the secret to building an empire with which he could have conquered the world. He told Stalin to build cars first and turn the Soviet Union into a nation of drivers. Of course, the only way to sell the first cars off the assembly line would have been to sell them to...you guessed it, the Soviets would have had to build a Yuppie class, first. It wasn't the communist way. The Evil Empire fell further and further behind the West until now it has crumbled—because it did not coddle its Yuppies.

I imagine that when the first of our ancestors climbed out of the trees to hunt on the ground, or skinned an animal and wore its fur to keep warm, or said, "I'm sick of sleeping in the rain," and built a hut, it was the Yuppies of their day who said, "Wow, what are you doing there?" and next thing you know, they—we—were all doing it.

Just recently, it was Yuppies flocking to the Internet who fueled Internet service providers so we could all get on. And it is they who are fueling what is going to be the next great economic boom when e-commerce takes off. When they're done there, stand back, because the Yuppies will be, as always, somewhere else, spending their money and dragging the rest of us, kicking and screaming, into the future.

So, give the Yuppies a break. For centuries they've supported genius and innovation while the rest of us stood back and watched—and waited—until it was safe to jump in. Without them the rest of us would still be living in caves. Δ

— **John Silveira**

DEFENDING AMERICA ISSUE

May/June 2003
No. 81
$4.95 US
$6.50 CAN

Backwoods Home magazine

practical ideas for self-reliant living

TERRORISM

- **Its Bloody History**
- **The Current Danger**
- **How to Protect Yourself**

www.backwoodshome.com

My view

Confronting the enemy

I got a lot of criticism a couple of issues ago from liberals when I pointed my finger at black Americans and asked why they had their heads screwed on so backwards when it came to politics. Some insinuated I was a racist. What a laugh. You always know a liberal is squirming under the glare of the truth when they lash out that you must be some kind of a racist.

Well now I've actually discovered someone to hate: terrorists. And I'm going to describe how Americans, all Americans, black and white, brown and yellow, are going to root them out from the sewers where they hide, and kill them, one by one, despite the fact that liberal whiners like the United Nations, France, and the Democratic Party will try to block us.

The question of whether or not we can do it should have been settled conclusively with Afghanistan. You know, that "graveyard of empires" as the liberals were calling it when we first went in after the Taliban and bin Laden. It's a quagmire, they insisted. It's hopeless—the mountains, the bitter winters, the lawless tribes, on and on. Yet within a few months the Taliban were gone and Al Qaida was on the run. The Afghan people embraced us as liberators.

And do we have the determination and the will to persevere? Ask the dictator of Iraq and all the third rate has-been powers of the UN who supported him. Ask Cuba's Castro if we have perseverance. And ask their former Soviet friends if we have the will to hold the course until even the most formidable foe is history.

The American species is unique in all of history. Not because of our race—we are a blend of races, after all—but because of our achievements which are a direct result of our freedoms. We are free to do what we want like no race on earth has ever been, and we rule the Earth because of it—economically, militarily, any way you can measure it. We are free, therefore we are powerful. It's a simple equation. We taught it to the European powers like France and Germany after World War II, but they have forgotten freedom in their late love affair with socialism. We haven't, and we'll pursue terrorists to the ends of the earth because we have no intention of giving freedom up.

Every step of the way the Ted Kennedys and Dianne Feinsteins of the world will say we are engaging in racial profiling, or we are flailing around like an out of control brat beating smaller countries over the head with our power. The United Nations with its assortment of dictatorships and socialist regimes will complain we are acting outside of international law. So what. If it were up to them, every Arab muslim terrorist in Guantanamo Bay would have an American tax payer-paid high priced New York lawyer defending him.

America won't listen to the naysayers in this war.

The naysayers will say we haven't proven countries like Iraq guilty of anything, and besides their people will suffer if we act against them. But we will crush them like the cockroaches they are if our intelligence shows they are working with or selling weapons to terrorists who target the U.S. We'll spare their innocent civilians if we can, but not at the expense of American freedom fighters.

They'll tell us that countries like North Korea are poor and need to be negotiated with and helped financially so that they give up their nuclear arms and their reckless behavior. If we determine they pose mainly a danger to their part of the world, we will ignore them and tell their neighbors to solve the problem, but if we determine they are supplying arms to terrorists who target the U.S., we will destroy them too.

And they will tell us that Islam is a peaceful religion despite the fact that nearly all terrorists who have targeted the U.S. have been militant Islamists. But if we find, as we well may, that there is a profound Islamist element to the terrorists' actions, that a certain percentage of Mohammed's followers take seriously his commandment to conquer the world by the sword if necessary, then we will hunt these Islamists down by the hundreds until Islam's leaders, especially those in America, condemn this antiquated commandment and put a stop to the religious aspect of terrorism.

At home in America, the ultra liberals in the Democratic Party, and the leftists and socialists on our college campuses, will tell us to stop, stop, stop the hunting down and killing of terrorists because we might be violating someone's rights. And we might be on occasion, but that won't stop our slaughter of terrorists. They picked this fight with us, and just like we did with the Japanese and Germans of World War II, we'll finish it, while frail and afraid countries like France lie in the mud with their shame and lack of action.

Make no mistake about it. This is a war about America's freedoms. The terrorists may not see it that way, but Americans do. And we will kill anyone to keep our freedoms, to keep our streets free to walk without fear of being blown up by some slimeball, to keep our neighborhoods free from the fear that some piece of human trash may try to inflict death on us with chemicals or disease.

If terrorists wanted a fight to the death, they picked the perfect country. We're going to take you one by one as you ooze out of your sewers and crush you into the slime you are. And when you're too much of a coward to come out of your sewer, we'll make the sewer and everything in it your grave.

Now how's that for racism!

— *Dave Duffy*

The Fourteenth Year

What can you do to PROTECT YOURSELF
against chemical, biological, and nuclear terrorism

By Gary F. Arnet, D.D.S.

"DUE TO RECENT INFORMATION WE HAVE OBTAINED, THE STATE OF ALERT IN THE NATION IS BEING RAISED TO CODE ORANGE. TAKE APPROPRIATE ACTION. EVERYONE SHOULD HAVE PLASTIC SHEETING AND DUCT TAPE." — HOMELAND SECURITY SECRETARY TOM RIDGE

Television news programs showed lines of people swarming stores buying up every roll of duct tape, every roll of plastic sheeting, and leaving with armfuls of gas masks. Bottled water, food, and other needed supplies flew off the store shelves. This was followed by scenes of people sealing up rooms with plastic and even wrapping the entire outside of their house in sheets of plastic.

Homeland Security Secretary Tom Ridge is now warning people to be prepared for terrorist attacks. "Make a kit, have a plan, get informed," he says. This is good advice. Despite years of previous warnings to prepare for natural disasters, this recent panic proved people had not stored emergency supplies, creating predictable chaos when they were needed. If this had been a terrorist attack, instead of a warning, things would have been even worse. Even when they had supplies, people didn't know what to do with them.

Weapons of mass destruction are chemical, biological, or nuclear weapons developed by countries for war, but now being sought by terrorists for use against civilian populations. Some in the government agree that their future use against the civilian population within the borders of the United States is almost guaranteed.

Despite the horror this will cause, it is possible to protect yourself and your family from the effects of many of these attacks by using common sense, avoiding panic, becoming informed, and preparing ahead of time. This article is intended to help you start doing just that.

Chemical terrorism

NATO defines a chemical weapon as a chemical substance intended for military use to kill, injure, or incapacitate people. Not only do they cause death and injury, they can have devastating psychological effects, crippling not only the affected population, but the nation in general. Depending on

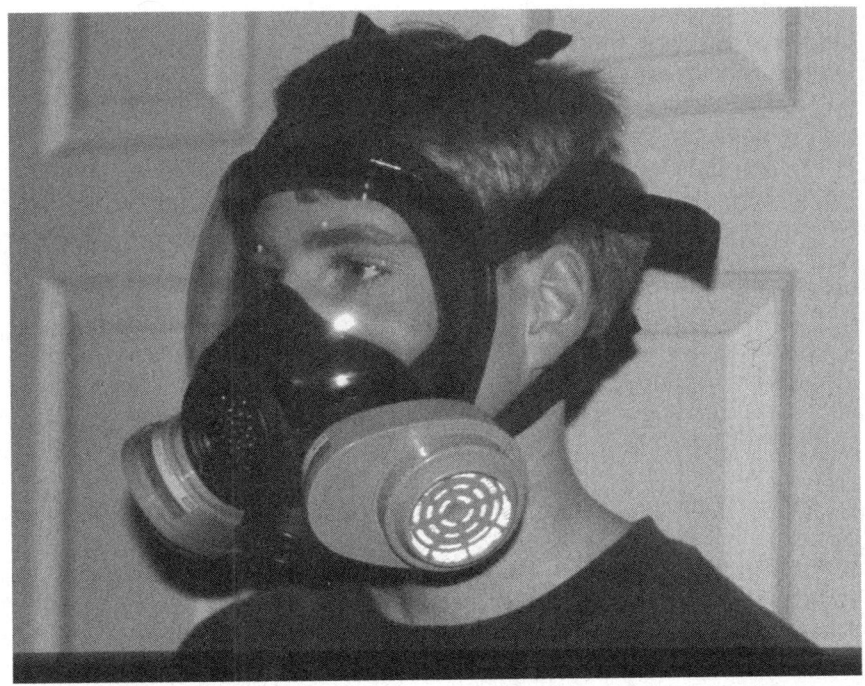

Chemical protection masks (gas masks) have been issued to 23,000 workers at the Pentagon and to Israeli citizens. Most Americans will probably not need them, but those who may live or work in areas that could be targets of chemical attack may want to obtain their own.

the chemical used, the weapon will affect the nervous system, lungs, skin, eyes, nose, throat, or a combination of these.

Relatively inexpensive to produce or obtain, it is fairly certain that terrorists have access to such chemical weapons which they would use against civilian populations without hesitation. This was proven on March 20, 1995, when the Aum Shinrikyo religious cult attacked the Tokyo subway with sarin nerve gas, killing 12 and injuring more than 5,000.

Unfortunately, chemical attacks against a civilian population is a reality today. Israeli civilians have been living with this possibility for some time. Civilians are issued gas masks and chemical "safe rooms" are being built in new homes. American civilians must be prepared also.

Just as we could not believe that terrorists would fly airplanes into buildings, we cannot begin to think of all the ways terrorists might use chemical weapons. Logic says that confined areas with large numbers of people would be likely targets. Subways, tunnels, office buildings, hotels, apartment building, and airports seem to be potential targets.

However, nothing is to stop terrorists from spraying football stadiums, parades, or any other large gathering of people with chemicals from aircraft or chemicals released upwind. For military applications, chemical weapons are also dispersed via missile, rocket, bombs, artillery shell, and land mines and it is possible these could be obtained for use against civilians.

To understand the actions to take during a chemical attack, it is important to first understand the chemicals and their effects. Thousands of poisonous chemicals are known, but only a few are suitable as weapons and have been stockpiled for war. While about 70 different chemicals have been produced as weapons, two main types of chemical agents are currently available, poison gases, and nerve agents.

Mustard gas is felt by experts to be the most likely gas used in a terrorist attack, although Iraq also has cyanide gas weapons. Germany introduced and effectively used mustard gas during World War I, causing thousands of casualties. Since then, it has been used many times, including by Iraq against the Iranians and Kurds in the 1980s. It is widely available in Third World countries and former Warsaw Pact countries. The United States still has a stockpile in its arsenal that is awaiting destruction.

The population downwind of a chemical attack may be advised to "shelter in place" by authorities. If so, go indoors and create a "safe room" that is isolated from outside air. Turn off air conditioning, heaters, and fans that can draw outside air into the room. This would be the time to use plastic sheeting and duct tape to seal cracks around the door, air ducts, and any vents into the room.

In a class called vesicants, mustard gas does not immediately kill people, rather taking hours for symptoms to develop. Vapors of mustard gas penetrate most fabrics quickly and the chemical is absorbed into the skin. A sunburn appearance of the skin develops within 2 to 48 hours, with itching and stinging pain often present. After this, small blisters on the skin can form, eventually enlarging into very large blisters called bullae. Eyes can develop a mild inflammation (conjunctivitis) or severe ulcerations of the cornea, causing blindness. Death from mustard gas is most often from inhaling the gas. Irritation of the nose, throat, and sinuses is the first sign of inhaled gas, followed by laryngitis, nose bleeds, and a cough. The cough worsens as damage to the lower lungs leads to respiratory failure and death.

The Germans used cyanide gas during World War II in their gas chambers and it was used by Iraq against the Kurds in the 1980s. Deadly when used in enclosed spaces, cyanide gas is lighter than air and rapidly dissipates outdoors. It causes death by starving the body's cells of oxygen, being especially toxic to heart and brain cells.

Nerve agents are some of the most potent chemicals known to man and are a more likely terrorist threat than poison gases, often killing the victim within minutes of exposure. German scientists developing pesticides in the 1930s observed that chemicals called organo-phosphate compounds affect transmission of nerve impulses and kill humans rapidly. Although 12,000 tons of chemical weapons were made for the German military during World War II, they were not used on the battlefield. Although many countries have the ability to produce nerve agents, the only time they have been used in war so far was by the Iraqis in the Iraq/Iran war.

Early types of organo-phosphate weapons are classified in American nomenclature as "G agents" and include tabun (GA), sarin (GB), soman (GD), and cyclohexyl methylphosphonofluoridate (GF). In the 1950s, while researching insecticides, the most toxic nerve agents ever known to man were developed by American and European scientists. Called "V agents," they are 10 times more deadly than sarin. VX is the most common V agent.

Nerve agents are all colorless liquids. Sarin easily vaporizes and may be inhaled into the lungs as well as absorbed through the skin. An area contaminated by sarin decontaminates itself within a few days because of this easy vaporization. VX is more of a thick oil that does not vaporize as rapidly and is, therefore, mostly absorbed through the skin. VX may remain on the ground for several weeks. The effectiveness of tabun, soman, and GF contamination are somewhere between those of sarin and VX.

Nerve agents kill people by inhibiting acetylcholinesterase, an enzyme in the body that stops conduction of nerve impulses. When a nerve impulse gets to a junction, called a synapse, a chemical called acetylcholine allows the impulse to move to the next nerve cell. Acetylcholinesterase then degrades the acetylcholine so the nerve impulse will stop. When nerve agents block acetylcholinesterase, the muscles of the body continue to be stimulated by acetylcholine until they fatigue and breathing muscles no longer function.

The effects of exposure to a nerve agent depend on the dose and route of exposure. When exposed to a low dose, symptoms may include a runny nose, excess saliva, constriction of the pupils of the eyes, headache, or tightness of the chest. Slurred speech, tiredness, nausea, and hallucinations may occur.

Exposure to high doses of nerve agent, especially when inhaled, lead to muscle twitching, convulsions, and loss of consciousness. In large exposures, this may happen so quickly that symptoms previously mentioned may not have time to develop. Paralysis of the muscles of respiration and effects on the breathing centers of the brain cause death by suffocation. High doses of inhaled agent can cause death in two minutes, while exposure through the skin only takes longer for symptoms to develop.

Protection from chemical attack

We have all seen news photos of our soldiers in chemical protection gear, but what can we as civilians do? First, remember that an attack anywhere in the United States will bring nationwide panic, which is one of the goals of the terrorists. An attack in one city will be a local disaster, however, affecting only those in immediate contact with the chemical agent. If it is an airborne attack where wind could spread the agent, there could be an effect to the downwind population.

Signs of a possible chemical attack include many people suffering from watery eyes, coughing, choking, twitching, or having trouble breathing. Large numbers of dead or sick birds, fish, and small animals may be present.

There are three main ways to protect against chemical weapons: physical protection, medical protection, and decontamination. At the first sign of a chemical attack, quickly determine where the chemical is coming from and get away. When the chemical is in the building in which you are located, leave the building without passing through the contaminated area. If you can't get out, get as far away from the chemical release as possible.

Physical protection involves protection of the body and respiratory system. Military and front-line civil-defense rescue units who will need to be in the contaminated area will have full body suits and respirators that are not going to be available to the civilian population.

Civilian exposure to chemical agents will be mostly during the time that they are evacuating the attacked area. When doing so, individuals should make sure all areas of their skin are covered and they are wearing a protective mask.

Protective masks provide barriers preventing the chemical agent from being inhaled through the nose or mouth. While useful in chemical attacks, they are also useful in biological attacks and after major explosions that release fine dust and debris

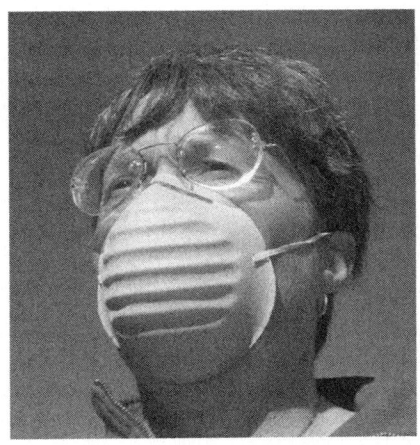

Surgical or dust masks prevent inhalation of biological agents or fine dust and debris caused by explosions that can damage the lungs, but will not adequately protect against chemical agents.

that can damage the lungs, such as the September 11 attacks on the Trade Center. They may also protect against smoke and chemicals released from attacks using conventional explosives on oil refinery or other industrial targets.

Surgical masks or masks made of dense-weave cotton that tightly cover the nose and mouth work to prevent inhalation of biological agents or dust, but will not adequately protect against chemical agents. Still, they are better than nothing in a chemical attack.

Protective chemical masks (gas masks), such as those issued to the Israeli civilian population, are available for adults and older children. In February, 23,000 workers at the Pentagon were issued chemical masks by the Department of Defense, so the government is taking the threat seriously.

Protective masks are not something that we can expect the government to be able to provide in an emergency. Those individuals who live or work in an area where a chemical attack is a possibility might want to have their own mask. For most people, they probably are not necessary. To be

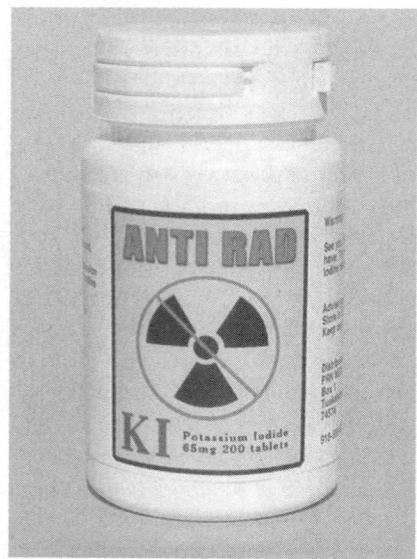

Potassium iodide is useful in preventing thyroid cancer from radioactive fallout. The National Pharmaceutical Stockpile program has large amounts stored, but many individuals prefer to have their own supply, which is inexpensive to purchase and does not need a prescription.

effective, they would need to be immediately accessible at all times.

Protective masks are available through stores that sell emergency preparedness or industrial safety supplies, as well as some military surplus stores. Since your life depends on it, purchase a new one designed for this

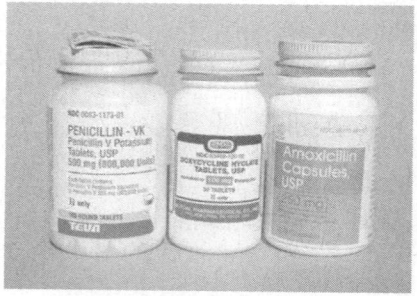

Antibiotics are used to treat bacterial infections caused by biological weapons and are being acquired by the National Pharmaceutical Stockpile program for use throughout the country. Authorities do not recommend that individual store antibiotics, although some are doing so with the help of their physicians.

purpose, not a used "army gas mask." Costs vary, but expect to pay as much as $190 for a good quality mask.

The population downwind of a chemical attack may be advised to "shelter in place" by authorities. If so, go indoors and create a "safe room" that is isolated from outside air. Turn off air conditioning, heaters, and fans that can draw outside air into the room. This would be the time to use plastic sheeting and duct tape to seal cracks around the door, air ducts, and any vents into the room.

Since some chemicals are heavier than air, they may seep into basements even if windows are closed, so a room above ground level is best. Listen to information provided by authorities over radio or television. Further actions depend on the type of chemical weapons used.

Medical protection

Since nerve agents work very rapidly, any medical treatment must be immediately available. The military provides kits with auto-injectors of antidote to those personnel at high risk of exposure to nerve agents. While these are not available to civilians and are reportedly not on the surplus market, these antidotes are standard pharmaceutical drugs. It may be possible to obtain them through a friendly physician or pharmacist if you believe you are at high-risk for exposure to chemical attack. For most of us, this is probably not the case.

Atropine is an anticholinergic compound that reduces the effect of excess acetylcholine and should be injected when exposure to nerve agent has occurred or is imminent. Pralidoxime chloride (Protopam chloride or 2-PAM), restores normal activity of acetylcholinerterase, blocking the effects of the nerve agent. Each combat soldier in the military is issued three MARK I kits, each containing an auto-injector with 2mg of atropine and 600 mg of pralidoxime chloride.

Diazepam (Valium) is an anti-seizure drug that is used as a pre-treatment drug or at the onset of severe symptoms from a nerve agent. As a pre-treatment, it is taken when an exposure is expected. A tablet is taken at least 30 minutes prior to exposure, with the best effect two hours later. Treatment can be repeated every eight hours for several days, if necessary. U.S. soldiers carry an auto-injector containing 10 mg of diazepam to be injected in case of severe nerve agent symptoms.

Decontamination

Once exposed to a chemical, rapid decontamination is important before it can be absorbed through the skin. Because decontamination works best within the first few minutes after exposure to chemical agents, self-decontamination is a priority. Strip off any contaminated clothing and wash with any source of water, using soap if available.

Flush contaminated skin with large amounts of water to remove or dilute the chemical agent. A wooden stick can be used to scrape off chemical agents, as can absorbent materials such as dry powders, soil, flour, and soap detergents. It is reported that applying flour and wiping with tissue paper is particularly effective in removing VX and soman, although all methods work for all agents. You don't need to know what you are dealing with to decontaminate.

Soap and water hydrolyze and inactivate VX and nerve agents, while chlorine can be used to oxidize mustard gas. The military recommends using a 0.5% solution of sodium or calcium hypochlorite solution (diluted bleach) for skin and a 5% solution for equipment. Household bleach is generally 4-6% chlorine and can be diluted for use.

Biological terrorism

Biological weapons are bacteria, viruses, and toxins that cause disease in humans, livestock, or crops. Attractive to terrorists because they are relatively inexpensive compared to nuclear, chemical, or conventional weapons, they can be manufactured with readily available scientific equipment and biological cultures.

Projections on the casualty rate from bioweapons are staggering. A government study estimated if 200 pounds of aerosolized anthrax was released over Washington D.C., there would be up to 3 million deaths. Smallpox killed over 500 million people in the world during the 20th century before it was eradicated in 1977.

Biological agents are odorless, colorless, and tasteless, and can be distributed by crop duster aircraft, boats, or trucks. With low wind speeds and inversion conditions, they can be sprayed upwind of the intended target, increasing the number of casualties.

Bioweapons must be inhaled, eaten, or enter through a cut in the skin. Some, like smallpox, are contagious and are spread from person to person, while others, like anthrax, are not contagious. Terrorists would likely prefer inhaled agents, since they can be spread rapidly and a large number of individuals can be infected before anyone is aware of the attack.

Of twelve different agents mentioned repeatedly in biological warfare literature, six are considered most likely to be used: anthrax, smallpox, botulism toxin, plague, tularemia, and hemorrhagic fevers such as Ebola. Anthrax and botulism toxin have already been weaponized and are likely to be available to terrorists.

Smallpox is highly contagious and can be easily made in large quantities. The secret Soviet program of the Cold War reportedly made tons of weaponized smallpox. Since a good portion of the population has never been vaccinated, it is considered an ideal terrorist weapon.

Ricin is also something that has been in the news lately, having been found in an apartment in London.

Volumes of information have been written about all known biological warfare agents and detailed information can be found on the Internet and in medical books. Since the precautions we can take are the same no matter the biological agent, I will review only the few most likely agents.

Anthrax is a bacterial infection that causes diseases that affect the skin, gastrointestinal system, or respiratory system (inhalational anthrax). Inhalational anthrax is most severe and begins 3 to 5 days after inhaling anthrax spores. Respiratory symptoms begin slowly and then rapidly progress to shortness of breath and lack of oxygenation of the blood. Shock and death occur within 2 to 3 days after respiratory distress begins. Treatment with antibiotics is usually not effective once symptoms begin.

If exposure has occurred or is imminent, antibiotics are advised. Cipro 500 mg twice a day or doxycycline 100 mg twice a day are used. Vaccine is given to those not previously vaccinated.

Botulism toxin (Botox) is produced by Clostridium botulinum bacteria. It is the strongest toxin known, being 100,000 times stronger than sarin nerve gas. Working by blocking nerve transmissions, botulism toxin causes muscle paralysis and respiratory failure. Symptoms may appear 2 to 3 days after exposure and death occurs in as little as 24 hours after the first symptoms.

No medicines are available to reverse this toxin and extensive hospital care is required which could take weeks or months. While this was fatal 60% of the time in the 1950s, medical care today has reduced the death rate to less than 5%. However, it should be expected the death rate would increase after a terrorist attack, as it would be difficult for hospitals to provide intensive care for hundreds of victims who might become simultaneously infected.

Smallpox is a virus that was eradicated from the world in 1977. Only two secure facilities in the world were supposed to have stored virus samples in case it was needed for a vaccine. One was in the United States and one in the Soviet Union. It is known the Soviet Union did research to weaponize smallpox pox, and to combine smallpox and Ebola viruses to make a weapon. A 1998 intelligence report concluded that smallpox for military use was possessed by Iraq, North Korea, and Russia.

Should potassium iodide be needed on a large scale in the United States, it is likely that enough would not be available. Since it is cheap, safe, and does not require a prescription, it may be a wise idea to have some available as part of a disaster preparedness plan.

Spread by coughing, sneezing, or dust on clothing and bedding, smallpox is highly contagious. After an incubation period of 12 days, fever, vomiting, and headache begin, followed by rashes and blisters of the skin. Smallpox kills about 30% of its victims and scars and sometimes blinds the survivors..

A smallpox pox vaccine recently has become available for first responders and health care workers, and will be offered to the public in the future. Vaccination after exposure will protect if it is taken within four days..

Ricin is a deadly poison in the form of a powder, mist, or pellet that can be made by amateurs from the waste of castor beans. It was found recently in Afghanistan while searching Al-Qaeda caves and is suspected of being used in the Iran/Iraq war. Within hours of exposure, the victim starts coughing and their lungs fill with fluid. There is no antidote and treatment is aimed at supporting respiration until the victim recovers or dies. Death occurs within 3 to 4 days of exposure.

Protection from biological attack

A biological attack may not be immediately obvious, as biological agents cannot be detected until people become sick. Usually, hospitals will notice an unusual pattern of disease or there will be a large number of people seeking help.

Once a biological attack is suspected, local public health officials will notify the public via radio, television, and, possibly, door-to-door advising the public what steps to take. Expect mandatory quarantines of infected victims, possibly the entire civilian population.

Travel may be stopped with any significant biological attack on the United States. Long-term disruptions to the infrastructure of the country could affect the economy and food supply. This is another reason to consider a long-term preparedness plan, with three months to a year supply of food, water, and essentials.

It doesn't hurt to protect yourself if you become aware of a suspicious release of an unknown substance. Move away rapidly while covering the nose and mouth with a cotton filter, such as a handkerchief, towel, or T-shirt. Once safe, wash with soap and water, and contact authorities.

If a biological emergency is declared for a contagious disease, such as smallpox, follow health department instructions, use common sense, and practice good hygiene to avoid spreading the disease. If you have Internet access, www.cdc.gov has extensive descriptions of possible terrorist agents and decontamination procedures. Depending on the severity, this might be a good time to consider a self-imposed quarantine, avoiding contact with others. Definitely, it would be a time to wear a mask when in public. If a family member becomes sick, be suspicious, but do not automatically assume it is a result of the attack since symptoms of many common illnesses overlap with symptoms of biological weapons.

The National Pharmaceutical Stockpile program has stockpiled antibiotics, vaccines, and medical supplies that can be rapidly sent anywhere in the country for use in biological attacks. If antibiotics or vaccines are recommended, public health officials will give information about who should get them and where they are being offered.

Nuclear terrorism

A nuclear disaster, called a "nuclear emergency" by government agencies, is any accidental or intentional large-scale release of radioactive material. This could occur from any number of terrorist attacks in the United States or from fallout from a nuclear war in Iraq, Korea, or between India and Pakistan.

A relatively small nuclear bomb detonated in New York City could kill over 100,000 people and spread radiation over much of the east coast. Authorities worry that nuclear weapons could be bought, stolen, or built by terrorists or obtained by the fall of a nuclear power, such as Pakistan. Nuclear bombs, missiles, and "suitcase" bombs are all in demand by terrorists and Third World countries.

Nuclear power plants are also potential terrorist targets. An attack on one of the 103 nuclear power plants in the United States using a commercial jet or large bomb would have some of the same effects as the detonation of a nuclear weapon. A meltdown of the core or dispersal of spent fuel waste would spread radiation in lethal doses over large areas.

Nuclear waste material is transported by ship, truck, and rail throughout the United States. Radioactive waste from Asia actually is transported by rail through heavily populated areas of California to be stored in the West. Terrorist attacks against such largely unguarded rail transportation could spread radiation locally.

"Dirty" bombs are the most accessible radiological weapons available to terrorists. Islamic terrorists placed, but did not detonate, such a weapon in a Moscow park in 1996.

Relatively easy to make, "dirty" bombs are conventional explosives wrapped with radioactive waste material. Upon detonation, radiation is scattered widely. Cars, trucks, or shipping containers can easily hide such a bomb. It is estimated that forty percent of the inbound shipping into the United States could be affected if such a bomb were detonated at a major shipping port.

Many disaster preparedness experts suggest having enough food and water to last several weeks or more. Foods stored can be a combination of everyday foods that are rotated every six months and foods designed to be stored for years.

A nuclear disaster brought about the detonation of an actual atomic bomb would affect us in three ways. First, the population in the immediate area affected by the thermal effects (fireball), shock wave, and intense radiation would have to deal with death, injuries, and radioactivity.

Second, those living downwind would have to deal with radioactive fallout. Fallout is radiation that is scattered into the atmosphere and carried by the wind until it settles to the ground or is washed to the ground by rain or snow. Plant crops and animals used for food are contaminated and unusable, as are exposed sources of drinking water.

Third, there would be general panic throughout the United States and possible disruption of transportation, food, and supplies. Everyone, whether or not affected by radiation, will be affected by a major nuclear disaster in the United States. Understanding the effects of a nuclear explosion allows us to develop a rational plan of what to do if faced with a nuclear disaster.

Detonation of a nuclear weapon would cause a fireball of blinding light and heat, causing blindness, burns, and death. Everything nearby would catch fire and burn. Superheated air would cause a shock wave with winds traveling at supersonic speeds and blowing over every building, train, vehicle, or person in their path. Such winds travel several hundred miles per hour and cause damage over a mile away.

Severe radiation will cause immediate death and injury to those in the area of detonation and radiation sickness to those somewhat further away. Radiation sickness can cause hair to fall out, nausea, vomiting, diarrhea, bleeding, or infection. An individual can be shielded from the initial radiation blast by being sheltered by a concrete or dirt structure. Nuclear weapons also produce an electromagnetic pulse, causing localized disruption of electrical equipment, communications, and computers, but not injuring humans.

Fallout is the least serious consequence of a nuclear explosion, however it affects many more people than the initial blast since, depending on the winds, it can travel hundreds or thousands of miles. It causes deaths in the future due to cancer or birth defects.

Radiation exposure from fallout is either external or internal. External exposure occurs when radioactive material contaminates the skin or clothing and internal exposure occurs when radioactive material is swallowed, inhaled, or absorbed through open wounds. Most of the victims from the Chernobyl accident received internal radiation from drinking milk produced by cows that ate contaminated grass.

The human body normally produces hormones in the thyroid gland from iodine in our diet. One of the byproducts of a nuclear explosion is a form of radioactive iodine that is also absorbed and can cause cancer of the thyroid gland, especially in children, years later. Thousands of cases were reported after Chernobyl.

Time, distance, and shielding are factors that minimize exposure to radiation. Most radioactive fallout loses its strength rapidly and the farther from the source of radiation, the less radiation exposure. Concrete, dirt, and other dense building materials will block out radiation. For radioactive fallout, staying indoors may be all the shielding needed.

Protection from nuclear attack

Depending on the amount of notice that you have and the distance from the nuclear disaster, you will either need to stay put in a sheltered place or evacuate.

In the case of nuclear power plant disasters, the Federal Emergency Management Agency (FEMA) has plans in place and residents within 10 miles of nuclear power plants are given information on what to do in such an emergency.

After a nuclear device explodes, move quickly away from the explosion site, going home or to a protected indoor site. If you are advised to "shelter in place" by authorities, go indoors and bring pets with you. Protect the inside of your home or business from fallout by turning off air conditioning, heating, vents, and fans, closing and locking windows and doors, and closing fire place dampers.

Cover air conditioners and vents with plastic, aluminum foil, or waxed paper taped in place to prevent radioactive dust from entering the room. Cracks around windows or doorways should be closed with duct tape or wet towels. Fill sinks, bathtubs, and containers with water and shut pipes off as a protection in case reservoirs become contaminated. If possible, go to a basement or other underground area, as these areas would give more protection from radiation.

When coming inside after exposure to fallout, remove clothes and shoes worn outside, place them in a sealed plastic bag, shower, and put on clean clothes and shoes. Stay indoors until authorities report that the level of radiation outside has subsided enough to be safe.

When going outdoors after it is safe, remember that fruits and vegetables in home gardens will be contaminated. Safety information on eating farm and home garden products should be provided by public health authorities, but, if you must use home grown products that have been exposed to radiation, wash and peel vegetables and fruits.

Use water that has been stored, or comes from underground sources, such as a well. Make sure water from exposed sources, such as rivers, open reservoirs, or lakes, is deemed safe by

Red Cross and government agencies recommend everyone have food, water, and supplies to take care of themselves for at least 72 hours. A "72 hour kit" should be able to be easily loaded into a car in case evacuation is necessary during a terrorist attack or natural disaster.

authorities before drinking. Normally, collecting rainwater is a pure source of drinkable water during a survival situation, but in this case rain may wash radioactive particles out of the atmosphere.

Potassium iodide is used to prevent thyroid cancer after exposure to radioactive fallout. It blocks the radioactive form of iodine from being absorbed by the gland by filling up the thyroid gland with normal iodine. It prevents only thyroid cancer, not the other effects of radiation.

After the Chernobyl accident, thousands of cases of thyroid cancer occurred years later in children in Russia, which did not give its population potassium iodide. Poland was also subjected to radioactive fallout but gave potassium iodide to over 17 million people and did not suffer increases in cancer rates.

During the Three Mile Island crisis, the U.S. government found itself without potassium iodide for the population and scrambled to find some from manufacturers. It turned out that it was not needed for that incident and the stockpile was discarded when it became old.

On September 11, although it wasn't needed, it turns out that the U.S. government again had no stockpile. Since then, the National Pharmaceutical Stockpile program has purchased large quantities of potassium iodide and people who live near some nuclear power plants have been issued pills to have available.

Should potassium iodide be needed on a large scale in the United States, it is likely that enough would not be available. Since it is cheap, safe, and does not require a prescription, it may be a wise idea to have some available as part of a disaster preparedness plan.

The FDA recommends adults and children over one year of age take one 130 mg tablet per day for 10 days. One-half tablet (65 mg) is the dose for children under one year of age. Individuals allergic to iodide should not take this product as it can cause severe allergic reactions. If you are considering having potassium iodide as part of your survival kit, you should talk to your physician to make sure it is safe for you and check the FDA web site for additional information. It is widely available over the Internet or through your pharmacy.

Radiation monitors are available to test for the presence of radiation. It is questionable if they are necessary or worth the cost. A nuclear disaster today is likely to be localized in one or several parts of the country and nuclear response teams will be equipped to monitor the environment. Waiting in a sheltered place until local authorities report it is safe is probably the best thing to do. Still, for those interested, information and radiation monitors are available through the Internet or surplus stores.

Preparation

The current government buzzword for "hunkering down" in your house or place of work after a chemical, biological, or nuclear attack is "Shelter in place." Basic preparations are the same for any terrorist act, as well as any natural disaster.

FEMA and the Department of Homeland Security advise people to have enough food, water, and supplies on hand to take care of their family for three days "until help from the government can arrive." Preparing the "72-hour kit" that they recommend is a good idea and can be used for immediate evacuation or as part of your overall home disaster supply kit.

However, in a major terrorist attack or disaster it is unlikely that government relief agencies will be able to help everyone within three days. They will be overwhelmed by disaster and the massive job of caring for the number of people who failed to prepare ahead of time.

It is not unreasonable to expect to have to take care of yourself for several weeks or longer. Some scenarios in which the economy or infrastructure is damaged by biological or nuclear terrorism suggest the need to care for your own needs for a year or longer. Be prepared by storing needed water, food, first aid materials, tools, emergency supplies, and special needs items.

One can live a while without food and comfort items, but cannot live long without water. The body needs at least two quarts of water per day to avoid dehydration, with exercise, hard work, and hot weather increasing the need to as much as four to five quarts per day.

It is recommended that at least a gallon of water per person per day (two quarts for drinking and two for food preparation and sanitation) be stored in food-grade plastic containers. Plastic water containers, empty two-liter soda bottles, or thirty to fifty gallon containers all work well. Two-gallon bottles of water available at markets are a convenient size to move and use. Water supplies should be rotated every six months to maintain freshness.

Non-perishable foods requiring minimal water to prepare, no refrigeration, and no cooking are ideal for part of your food supply. It is good to have a variety of ready-to-eat canned foods including canned meat, tuna, chicken, stews, beans, fruits, and vegetables, along with canned juices, milk, and soups. Canned foods don't require cooking and can be eaten unheated right out of the can, if necessary. Have a mechanical-type can-opener available in case there is no electricity to run electric ones.

Peanut butter, crackers, granola bars, trail mix, or energy bars are easy to store and are high-energy foods. Cookies, hard candy, coffee, or tea are nice comfort foods that will help brighten spirits in stressful times.

A good way to start out buying a supply of emergency food is to visit a large warehouse distributor, such as Costco or Sam's Warehouse, or some of the suppliers who advertise in this magazine. By buying in bulk, a large quantity of food can be purchased at a great discount. At Costco, a 25-lb. bag of rice sells for as little as $3 and a 25-lb. bag of pinto beans for $7. So, while it may get boring eating only beans and rice, you can feed a family for a long time during an emergency for only $10.

Stored food should be rotated every six months. To keep costs down and food fresh, store foods that you normally would buy and use these food supplies for your regular meals. Replace food used with newly purchased food.

Emergency foods packaged to last for 5 to 10 years are available from many sources. Their advantage is you don't need to remember to rotate food on a regular basis, they are convenient in evacuation situations, and they can be stored in a vehicle. Military MREs (Meals Ready To Eat) have a long shelf life, although they are expensive. Emergency Essentials (ad on page 15), Ready Reserve Foods, and Maple Leaf are among suppliers of #10 size cans of food intended for long-term storage. Their huge selection of foods would allow tasty, complete meals that could be stored for years.

Other emergency supplies should include a first aid kit, battery-operated radio, flashlight with extra batteries, non-electric can opener, matches, lantern, portable cooking stove and fuel, fire extinguisher, hand tools for repairs and to turn off household water and gas, a good knife, and, of course, the recommended plastic sheeting and duct tape to seal doors and vents.

Remember to include toilet paper, towelettes, soap, toothpaste, personal hygiene items, disinfectant, household chlorine bleach to purify water, and other sanitation items. These things will normally be in your home, but make sure you have a supply that will last at least two weeks. Don't forget formula and diapers for infants, prescription medications, contact lenses and supplies, extra glasses, and pet food.

Be prepared

The world is a new place. Terrorists today have the means, power, and desire to attack civilian populations with no hesitation. Who would have believed that we would be facing weapons of mass destruction on our own soil?

Terrorist attacks using weapons of mass destruction could be minor, causing fear and a few injuries, or could be devastating, killing hundreds of thousands and crippling our country. Whatever the case, there will be widespread panic and chaos. Now is the time to become informed about the possible threats, develop a plan for each threat, and prepare by storing the food, water, and emergency supplies that would be needed.

While future terrorist attacks are almost certain, it is possible to protect yourself against chemical, biological, and nuclear terrorism. Δ

For more information

American Red Cross
www.redcross.org

Department of Homeland Security
www.whitehouse.gov/deptofhomeland/

Federal Emergency Management Agency
www.fema.gov

Centers for Disease Control
www.bt.cdc.gov

National Library of Medicine
www.Sis.nlm.nih.gov/Tox/biologicalwarfare.htm

DARK WINTER

A simulated terrorist attack on three American cities using weaponized smallpox

By Dave Duffy

Historically smallpox has been the most deadly of all diseases for humans, killing between 300 and 500 million in the last century alone, far more than the 111 million people killed in all that century's wars combined. It is easily spread, kills 30% of those infected, and terribly scars and sometimes blinds those who survive. It was declared eradicated from Earth in 1980, but the Soviet Union has acknowledged maintaining a secret biological weapons program since then that employed 60,000 technicians and scientists. One fear is that some of the smallpox the Soviets worked with has gotten into terrorist hands, or that unemployed Soviet scientists desperate for money have been hired by Iraq, Al Qaida, or other terrorists.

June 22-23, 2001, nearly three months before the attack that toppled New York's World Trade towers, the United States conducted a major simulation of a terrorist smallpox attack against three American cities. It was named *Dark Winter*, and it lived up to its name. Within seven weeks, one million Americans were dead and the disease had spread to 25 states and 13 foreign countries. In the face of the out of control epidemic, panic had spread across America, interrupting vital services such as food deliveries to supermarkets, and our Government considered the possibility of a nuclear response, although against whom it was not clear.

Following is a reenactment of that exercise, edited for brevity but containing all the essential elements. The exercise took place at Andrews Air Force Base in Maryland, and was attended by many senior level government officials. Participating institutions included the *Johns Hopkins Center for Civilian Biodefense Strategies, the Center for Strategic and International Studies, the Oklahoma National Memorial Institute for the Prevention of Terrorism,* and the *Analytic Services Institute for Homeland Security.*

Former U.S. Senator Sam Nunn of Georgia played the President of the United States, Governor Frank Keating of Oklahoma played himself, five senior journalists who worked for major news organizations participated in mock news briefings, and a number of other participants played various key government positions ranging from the Director of Central Intelligence to key Government health advisors.

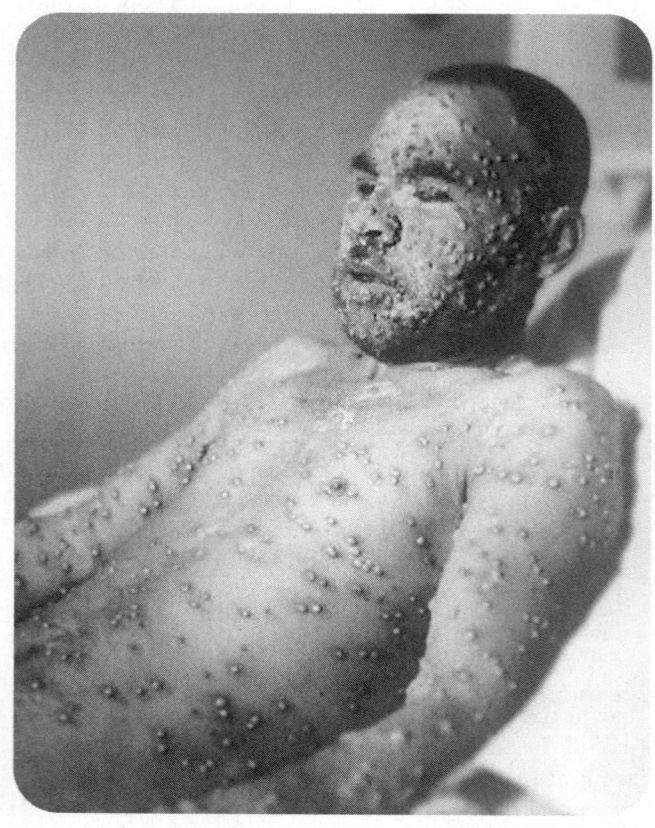

An Iranian citizen with smallpox in 1962

Fifty people connected with U.S. bioterrorism policy preparedness observed the exercise.

The goal of the exercise was to increase awareness among Government officials of the danger of such an attack, and to examine the decision challenges the highest levels of Government would face if confronted with a biological attack. The ultimate aim was to improve strategies of response.

Smallpox was chosen as the disease because historically it has been the most feared and deadly of diseases, and one of the more likely choices for terrorists. It is not only easily spread from one person to another, but there is no effective medical treatment. It may also be unstoppable in an unvaccinated population, and since the United States' mandatory vaccination program was stopped in 1972, the U.S. population is very susceptible to smallpox. Even that part of the population that was vaccinated as late as 1972 may have little or no protection against the disease.

Although smallpox was declared eradicated in 1980, two official repositories of the variola virus were kept: one at the *Centers for Disease Control and Prevention* in Atlanta, and the other at the *Russian State Research Center for Virology and Biotechnology* in Koltsovo, Novosibirsk in central Siberia. Those supplies were to be used for scientific research and vaccine development, but it is now known that both countries maintained secret biological weapons programs since 1980. By 1990 the Soviet Union had a facility capable of producing 80 to 100 tons of smallpox a year, and it typically warehoused 20 tons. Although Russia and the United States have since abandoned their biological weapons programs, other countries still have them. It is thought that several rogue states like North Korea and Iraq and possibly terrorists have obtained samples of the smallpox virus.

Although the exercise took only two days, it simulated a time span of two weeks occurring between December 9-22, 2002. The exercise involved three *National Security Council (NSC)* meetings taking place on Dec. 9, 15, and 22, with the participants being made aware of evolving details of the attack and being required to establish strategies and make policy decisions to deal with it.

Exercise controllers acted as special assistants and deputies, providing facts and suggesting policy options to deal with the smallpox outbreak. Simulated newspaper coverage and TV video clips of the ensuing epidemic were also shown to participants, and various simulated memoranda, intelligence updates, and top level assessments of the spread of the epidemic were provided to key players whose jobs would normally require such information.

Each of the three NSC meetings began with controllers giving the NSC players briefings on the progress of the attack, an assessment of who the perpetrators might be, the response of the public, the comments of foreign governments, and any other information they would normally receive in such an emergency.

Assumptions

Several assumptions were made for this exercise, based on historical evidence and a variety of data related to susceptibility to smallpox:

- *Assumption 1: It was assumed that the initial attack was from "weaponized smallpox," similar to what the former Soviet Union would have developed in its secret bioweapons program.*

This would be a far more efficient way of attacking the U.S. than with, say, infected jihad volunteers walking among the U.S. population. Weaponized smallpox can be aerosolized and dispersed in a variety of ways, such as attaching an aerosol device filled with weaponized smallpox, complete with a timer, to the wall of a shopping mall, airport, or ventilation system of an enclosed stadium, or attaching a spraying device to an unmanned drone (UAV) that has been programmed with global positioning (GPS) maps and flying it over a populated area.

- *Assumption 2: The U.S. population's "herd immunity" to smallpox was 20%, so that 228 million of its citizens were highly susceptible to infection.*

This is a matter of debate. It is known that 42% of the population has never received a smallpox vaccination, and the remainder have declining immunity from vaccinations about 30 years ago. No one knows for sure, but epidemiologic data suggest that initial vaccination gives protection for 5 to 10 years, while revaccination gives even greater protection, possibly more than 10 years. Those who have been vaccinated twice, then, say as a child and while in the military, should have the greatest immunity.

- *Assumption 3: The transmission rate of the disease was 10 to 1, that is, each infected person infected 10 others.*

Although transmission rates have varied widely historically depending on susceptibility of a population, the strain of disease, and various social, demographic, political, and economic factors, the simulation designers considered a 10 to 1 transmission rate a conservative estimate. The U.S. population, they pointed out, is highly susceptible because vaccinations stopped in this country 30 years ago. Also, we are a highly mobile society. By the time the first victims are diagnosed with smallpox (9-17 day incubation period), the disease will have already begun spreading to a second generation of victims. Some of the initial victims and the second generation of victims will have travelled to other cities by that time. Since few American doctors have ever seen a case of smallpox, and since the initial symptoms resemble flu, diagnosis is liable to be slow.

For this simulation, the 10 to 1 estimate was based on 34 smallpox outbreaks in the past involving cases of smallpox being accidentally imported into a country that no longer had endemic smallpox. Twenty four of the outbreaks occurred in winter, which is the time when smallpox spreads most readily and which is the time within which the simulated attack occurs. Of these 24, 6 outbreaks most closed paralleled the conditions of the *Dark Winter* exercise, and they were used to make the 10 to 1 estimate. The number of second generation cases in those 6 outbreaks ranged from 10 to 19.

One reason the 10 to 1 estimate is thought to be on the conservative side is because of the 1972 outbreak in

Yugoslavia, which encompassed many of the aspects one finds today in American society, namely, a great number of susceptible people and a wide geographic dispersion of cases. In that outbreak a man on a religious pilgrimage to Mecca and Medina was infected with smallpox while in Iraq, then brought it back to Yugoslavia. His infection was not diagnosed, nor were the 11 people he infected suspected of having smallpox. Not until 140 new cases developed was the epidemic recognized as smallpox. Some 35 people died from this single initial infection.

- *Assumption 4: The U.S. Centers for Disease Control and Prevention (CDC) had 12 million doses of vaccine available at the time of the exercise.*

The CDC actually had 15.4 million doses, but practical experience from the 1960s and 70s smallpox eradication programs showed that it was common to lose 20% of a vial's vaccine due to inefficiencies and waste.

- *Assumption 5: In the initial attack at three shopping malls in Oklahoma City, Philadelphia, and Atlanta, 3,000 people were infected.*

This is considered a plausible scenario scientifically since it would take only 30 grams of weaponized smallpox to infect 3,000 people via an aerosol attack.

The 1st NSC meeting, Dec. 9, 2002
The initial attack:

On December 9, 2002, during the first of three NSC meetings that will take place in this simulation, the 12 NSC members are told that a smallpox outbreak has occurred in the U.S. In Oklahoma, 12 cases of smallpox have been confirmed, with 14 more suspected. There are also suspected cases of smallpox in Georgia and Pennsylvania.

The governor of Oklahoma, Frank Keating, who is in town to make a speech, attends the meeting. NSC members are briefed on the disease, its lethality, its contagion, and the availability of smallpox vaccine.

All this takes place against a backdrop of the following geopolitical situation:

- Iraq is again threatening to invade Kuwait, and leaders of Kuwait, the United Arab Emirates, and Bahrain have requested the U.S., Britain, and France deploy troops to the region. The NSC meeting has been called to consider deploying forces.
- Since sanctions against Iraq had been lifted six months prior, it has been discovered that Saddam Hussein is aggressively pursuing a bioweapons program.
- Several top scientists from the former Soviet secret bioweapons program are believed to have been working in Iraq and Iran for the past year.
- An Al Qaida terrorist was recently caught trying to buy plutonium and biological pathogens from Russia.

President Nunn informs the NSC members that the agenda of the meeting has changed, that the U.S. has been subjected to a suspected smallpox attack, and that it could be related to their anticipated decision to deploy troops to the Mideast. No one has yet taken credit for the attack.

He introduces Governor Keating, who says hospital emergency rooms in Oklahoma City hospitals are very crowded and that many in the hospital staff have failed to show up for work, fearing a smallpox infection they might bring home to their families. The media is broadcasting nonstop news about the smallpox outbreak, and the Governor is already considering calling out the National Guard if fear continues to grow among the populace. He has already declared a state of emergency and requests the President do the same. He goes before the news cameras in a few hours, he says, and he'd like to be able to tell the people of Oklahoma that all 3.5 million of them will get the smallpox vaccine within 72 hours.

The NSC is then briefed on smallpox, using various slides of actual smallpox cases and statistics relating to the progression, spread, and lethality of the disease: U.S. doctors have no experience with smallpox and there is no rapid diagnosis or treatment. Isolation or vaccination are the only defenses. Only 12 million doses of vaccine are available, and a CDC contract for an additional 40 million doses will not be filled until 2004. The worldwide supply of vaccine is 60 million doses, but some of it is believed worthless due to inadequate storage by some countries.

The NSC members are told that the CDC has sent 100,000 doses of smallpox vaccine to Oklahoma, with vaccinations restricted to infected people, their close contacts, and investigators.

Council members are also told that the attack most likely occurred about Dec. 1, due to at least a 7-day incubation period for the disease. The second generation of cases, then, would be about Dec. 20, 11 days away. Urgent action is needed to halt the spread of the disease, but a modern, urban, mobile population, coupled with a limited supply of vaccine, does not offer encouraging prospects for controlling the outbreak.

The FBI tells the Council they will have 200 agents vaccinated and sent to Oklahoma within 24 hours, but they have no leads as yet. Several possible culprits are named: Iraq, Iran, North Korea, China, Russia all have the capability. But anyone who has obtained samples of smallpox, possibly from an unemployed Soviet scientist, could grow smallpox and launch an attack.

The Fourteenth Year

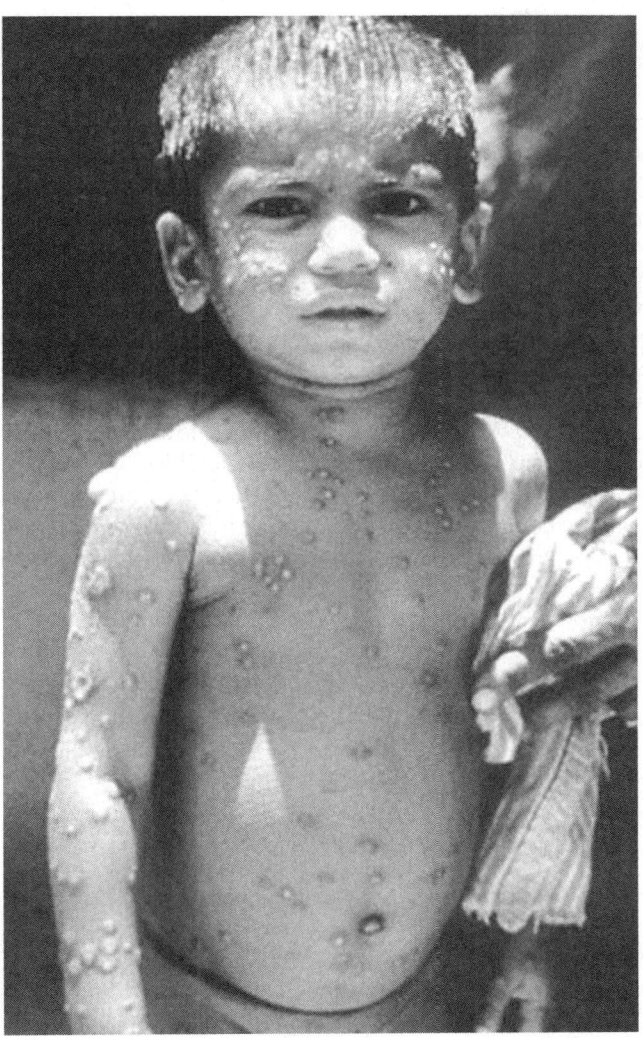

Child with full-body distribution of smallpox eruptions, Pakistan, 1955

Council members consider their options. The CDC and local authorities would already be isolating victims and their closest contacts. Should public gatherings be curtailed and schools closed? How should the available vaccine be distributed? Should the National Guard be activated, and should it be under state or federal control? Should there be mandatory or voluntary vaccinations? What should the public be told? What should be done about the deployment of troops to the Mideast?

They agree to inform the public quickly and completely to ensure cooperation with disease control measures. They decide to use the "ring method" of vaccination, which worked so successfully in eradicating the disease in the 1960s and 70s. With the ring method, all first contacts with the victim are vaccinated, then a second ring of secondary contacts are vaccinated. The NSC decides the ring method should also be used in other states, should the virus break out there. For strategic purposes they reserve 1 million doses of vaccine for Department of Defense (DOD) needs, and instruct the DOD to determine its priorities. They also decide to deploy an additional aircraft carrier battle group to the Persian Gulf to join the one already there.

The final action of the NSC is to prepare a presidential statement for the news media, which the President delivers to a nationwide audience from the press room.

The 2nd NSC meeting, Dec. 15, 2002
The outbreak spreads:

The second NSC meeting opens with a review of the following *news video clips*:

- 300 people are dead and 2000 are infected in 15 states. Hospitals are overwhelmed as tens of thousand of sick or fearful people seek medical help. Many hospital employees are not showing up for work.
- The epidemic has spread to Canada, Mexico, and the United Kingdom, with Canada and Mexico asking the U.S. for vaccine.
- Violence has broken out in some areas, with riots around a vaccination site in Philadelphia leaving two dead. Police and the National Guard are trying to control the crowds.
- Many countries have closed their borders to people travelling from the U.S. unless they can show proof of recent smallpox vaccination.
- Governor Keating is considering closing all stores to try and halt the spread of the disease. Malls across the country are already virtually deserted. The Governor has closed all schools and universities and cancelled all sporting events.
- The federal government is being widely criticized from all quarters for failure to have an adequate smallpox vaccine on hand. The lone pharmaceutical company capable of making smallpox vaccine says that at most it can produce 4 million doses per month, even if all FDA regulations are waived. Russia has offered to provide 4 million doses of vaccine.
- Panic buying is beginning to occur in some cities as food deliveries are slowed by the reluctance of truckers to go into areas with smallpox. There are sporadic reports of people of Arab appearance being assaulted on the street.

A *memo* is given to the Attorney General. It clarifies the *Stafford Act, the Posse Comitatus Act, the Federal Quarantine Law,* the *Insurrection Act,* and *Martial Law,* all laws designed to invoke federal authority in a national emergency. Among other things, the laws would allow the President to declare a national emergency and use military troops to quell civil disturbances, authorize the forced inoculation and isolation of people who could spread a communicable disease, restrict travel, dispose of bodies in ways contrary to personal beliefs, suspend habeas corpus (that is, arrest without due process), and curtail other liberties as needed.

Another **memo** to the FBI Director and Attorney General states there is a high probability that the attack came from another state or a state-sponsored terrorist group, and that an initial analysis of the smallpox used indicates it came from Soviet Union stocks or North Korea. The memo notes that as little as two years ago North Korean Special Forces were still receiving smallpox vaccine.

The President is handed a **memo** suggesting it may be problematic going forward with a war in the Persian Gulf, given the severity of the domestic crisis. He addresses the council members, announcing that the Secretary of State is ill and hospitalized. He says the lack of vaccine and the tactics of some states to stop the epidemic has led to serious economic disruption and civil unrest in some areas.

The Chair of the Deputies Committee, Dr. Tara O'Toole, outlines the progress of the epidemic and says all cases appear related to three initial attacks in Oklahoma, Georgia, and Pennsylvania. Vaccine, unfortunately, is running out amid growing political pressure to vaccinate more broadly. One million doses of vaccine are still being held for military personnel facing the potential war in the Persian Gulf. With all the vaccine that has been distributed, 1.25 million doses remain.

Dr. O'Toole further states that there is growing public demand for the forcible relocation of infected people to isolated facilities. She says contacts of infected people are not complying sufficiently with voluntary home isolation. There is also dangerous misinformation in some media about good vaccine and bad vaccine, advice to flee cities, claims that poor neighborhoods are being denied vaccine, and hate speech directed at certain ethnic groups.

The FEMA Director delivers his remarks: Health care facilities have become nonfunctional in some communities due to overcrowding and workers staying away from their jobs. At least 20 hospitals have closed their doors in Oklahoma. In many states National Guard troops are providing security at hospitals, even delivering food and critical supplies. Many states have prohibited public gatherings, stopped transportation, and closed airports.

Once again the NSC considers its options. Members decide to leave the National Guard, as well as quarantine and isolation issues, in the hands of the states. They will accept the vaccine from Russia, and proceed with a crash program to manufacture vaccine even though liability issues have not been resolved. They opt for mandatory isolation of all smallpox victims in dedicated facilities. They will encourage voluntary isolation of contacts using National Guard and Defense Department resources to supply food. Federal travel restrictions will be established, and penalties will be imposed for the promulgation of dangerous information.

An intelligence memo is given to NSC members: It indicates that a new exclusionary zone has been established by Iraq around a suspected bioresearch facility near Samarra. Activity at the facility appears normal but villages for a 10-mile radius around it appear to have been abandoned.

In a memo delivered to the Attorney General, there are reports of increasing incidents of violence, mainly against people with dark skin or who appear Arab-American. Two mosques have been defaced and one burned in the last 24 hours. In downtown Chicago, three dark skinned youths were shot dead, apparently because they looked Middle Eastern. The ACLU has sued Pennsylvania over the issues of mandatory vaccination and curtailment of transportation.

The NSC watches a newsclip in which the Governor of Texas announces the suspension of all travel between Texas and Oklahoma. He urges other governors to do the same, and he strongly criticizes the federal government for being "unable or unwilling to prevent the spread of the smallpox virus."

President Nunn addresses the nation on national TV. He relates the gravity of the crisis and appeals for Americans to remain calm and work together to defeat the virus, and to heed the advice of their elected leaders and health officials.

The 3rd NSC meeting, Dec. 22, 2002
A crisis out of control:

The third and final NSC meeting opens with a review of **news video clips**:

- The number of smallpox cases has reached 16,000, with 1,000 people now dead. The epidemic has spread to 25 states and 10 other countries. Although investigation suggests all cases are related to the initial attack in three states, the evidence does not rule out additional or ongoing attacks.
- The U.S. is suffering severe economic damage. In Atlanta and Philadelphia, most businesses are closed and massive traffic jams are occurring across the state as people try to flee the disease.
- A New York Times poll indicates that most Americans think that the state and federal governments have lost control of the epidemic. A CNN/Gallup poll says nearly half of Americans think the President should use nuclear weapons against any nation proven responsible for the smallpox attack.
- Violence is spreading across the nation as individuals try to keep others suspected of having smallpox at a distance. In New York, two police officers and three family members were killed when

the police tried to escort two family members with smallpox to an isolation area.

Then Dr. O'Toole once again outlines the progress of the epidemic for the NSC:

- In the past 48 hours there have been 14,000 new cases. Of the 1,000 dead, 200 have been from reactions to vaccination. It is estimated that 5,000 more will die within the next two weeks.
- The vaccine has now been depleted, and the U.S. can produce only 12 million unlicensed doses a month, beginning in four weeks.
- A major impact on the U.S. economy continues and there are shortages of many types of food across the nation. People are fleeing cities after the announcement of new smallpox cases.

The NSC asks for a worst case scenario. It is stark:

- By the end of the second generation of smallpox cases (about Jan. 3), 30,000 will be infected and 10,000 dead.
- By the end of Generation 3 (Jan. 20), 300,000 will be infected and 100,000 dead.
- By the end of Generation 4 (Feb. 6, which is 7 weeks after the start of the epidemic), 3 million will be infected and 1 million dead.

A *memo* is given to the Secretary of State:
- Russia, France, and Nigeria are demanding the U.S. share any vaccine it has to help fight the overseas spread of the epidemic.
- Cuba has offered to sell smallpox vaccine to the U.S. Cuba claims it has the know-how to produce the vaccine quickly.

Another *memo* is handed to the Director of the FBI and the Director of Central Intelligence (DCI):
- A credible Iraqi defector claims Iraq is behind the smallpox attack. Iraq has previously denied involvement, but has also warned the U.S. that it will retaliate against any U.S. attack in "highly damaging ways."

Finally, a *printed message* is handed to all members of the NSC. It states that the *New York Times, Washington Post,* and *USA Today* have received anonymous letters demanding the U.S. withdraw its forces from the Persian Gulf and Saudi Arabia. The letter claims responsibility for the smallpox attack and contains a generic fingerprint of the smallpox strain matching the fingerprint of the strain causing the current epidemic. Unless the U.S. forces withdraw in one week, it warns of renewed attacks using smallpox, anthrax, and plague.

The *Dark Winter* exercise ends with the NSC discussing how to respond. If the American people demand they use nuclear weapons, against who? Should they withdraw U.S. troops from the Persian Gulf? And finally, with no vaccine remaining and the epidemic out of control, how do they control the current spread of smallpox and any new attacks with disease?

End of *Dark Winter* exercise

Astonishing! The United States had been brought to its knees by a virus delivered covertly by terrorists who lurk in the dark recesses of the world. Few thought it remotely possible before the exercise, but afterwards many inside and outside of Government became alarmed at the possibility.

The *Dark Winter* exercise was no trivial undertaking. It was carefully planned and orchestrated, primarily by the prestigious John Hopkins University in Baltimore, Maryland, to answer one question: Could America withstand an attack of human-inflicted disease. The answer was a resounding No! — at least in the case of smallpox. We flunked the exercise on a catastrophic scale.

Three months after the exercise the U.S. was subjected to the September 11 attacks against the World Trade Centers in New York City and the subsequent anthrax mail attacks in Washington, D.C. Suddenly the attacks of terrorists were not just the stuff of "what if" simulations like *Dark Winter*. Our Government began working on defense strategies against such attacks, and it started evaluating its stocks of smallpox vaccine.

The vaccine situation is different today than it was in June of 2001 when the *Dark Winter* exercise took place. The U.S. has found more vaccine than we thought we had, and we have diluted other vaccine to make it stretch far enough to cover the American population. There are still questions about the effectiveness of this diluted vaccine after so many years in storage, but new vaccine to cover the entire population is being manufactured and will be ready in early 2004.

Risks associated with the vaccine are another serious consideration not discussed in the *Dark Winter* simulation. I've covered that in another article on page 28 of this issue. ∆

How safe is smallpox vaccine?

By Dave Duffy

At the start of 2003 the United States began the vaccination against smallpox of half a million health care workers so America can respond to a possible terrorist smallpox attack. It is only the beginning of a plan to vaccinate millions of Americans, beginning with health care workers and the military. The fear is that terrorists, and possibly Iraq, have acquired the deadly and disfiguring smallpox virus and intend to use it against us.

Many people may think no sane human being would consider using a disease like smallpox as a weapon. After all, even the diabolical Nazis of World War II possessed nerve agents and biological weapons but refrained from using them, even as they were bombed into obliteration during the last months of the war. But think again. According to many muslim terrorists, it is God's will that America the Infidel be destroyed.

It is not an unheard of rationale. In at least one documented case during the conquest of the Americas, a British colonel deliberately distributed smallpox infected blankets to Indians, which led to an epidemic among them. And during the Spanish conquest of the Aztecs, which coincided with another smallpox epidemic among the Indians, a Spanish priest wrote in his diary: "Thank you heavenly Father for sending this plague to destroy our enemies." There is even some evidence that the British tried to spread smallpox among the Colonists, and during America's own Civil War, there is an undocumented report of a Confederate supplying unsuspecting Union soldiers with smallpox infected blankets.

Man, historically, has always justified his most reprehensible actions, and muslim crusaders will have no problem justifying a smallpox attack against us.

What is smallpox?

Smallpox is a highly contagious disease caused by the variola virus, which is an orthopox virus in the same family as monkeypox, mousepox, camelpox, rabbitpox, and cowpox. Cowpox is used to make smallpox vaccine, called vaccinia.

Smallpox no longer exists as a naturally occurring disease, having been wiped out by the World Health Organization's (WHO) worldwide smallpox eradication program in the 1960s and 70s. But for thousands of years, since it first appeared about 12,000 years ago in settlements in northeast Africa, smallpox had been one of the most feared of

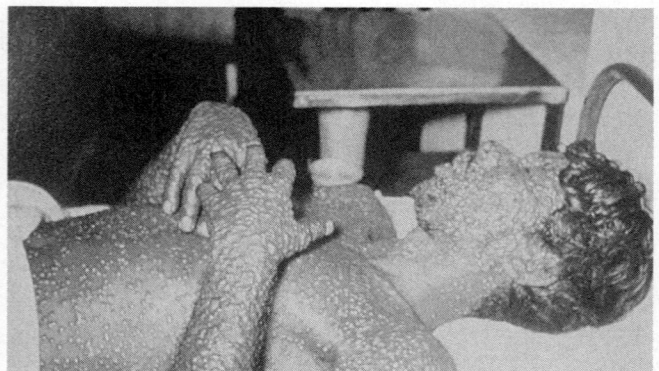

Man with smallpox. Smallpox has been eliminated thanks to vaccines.

plagues, killing hundreds of millions of people, decimating whole civilizations, and not even sparing kings. The mummy of the great Egyptian pharaoh Ramses V, who died in 1156 BC, bears the distinctive smallpox scarring on his face, and the Roman Emperor Marcus Aurelius was killed by smallpox in a plague that killed millions in the Roman Empire about 180 AD. In the last decades of the 18th century smallpox killed 400,000 Europeans a year, including four reigning monarchs, and in the 20th century the disease killed an estimated 300-500 million people. By comparison, wars in the 20th century, which was history's bloodiest century for warfare, killed 111 million people.

Historically smallpox has killed 30% of its victims, although that number has been higher in very susceptible populations. The New World populations of Indians had never experienced smallpox so were very susceptible. Between 1580 and 1620 smallpox reduced the Aztec population of Mexico from about 20 million to less than 2 million, after Spanish conquistadors had inadvertently introduced it there, and smallpox is the main suspect in reducing the overall North American Indian population from about 100 million at the time of Columbus's arrival to about 10 million a mere 50 years later.

How is it spread?

Smallpox is normally spread through direct contact with an infected person, and transmission of the virus occurs when a person inhales a virus-containing airborne droplet of an infected person's saliva. But it can also spread from contact with an infected person's fluids, clothing, and bedding. It is not spread by animals or insects.

The virus is very stable and will survive for months in an infected person's clothing and bedding, even dried in the dust in his sick room, in the form of viral material from the smallpox pustules or from the pustules' crusted scabs. These are much less infectious than the airborne droplets, but infected clothing and bed linens have historically been a source of smallpox outbreaks in Europe.

Smallpox victims are infectious with the onset of rash, which occurs 2-4 days after the onset of fever, which occurs 10-14 days after initial exposure to the disease. Victims are most infectious during the initial week (after development of rash) when they develop lesions in the mucous membranes of the mouth, tongue, larynx, pharynx, and upper part of the esophagus. The victim sheds part of the lesions in airborne water droplets during this period. As the lesions develop on the skin, the person remains infectious to a declining degree until the lesions turn to scabs and the scabs fall off.

Types of smallpox

There are three types of smallpox, **ordinary, flat, and hemorrhagic**, that can occur in unvaccinated persons, plus a fourth type, **modified**, that can occur in previously vaccinated people.

1) Ordinary smallpox (Variola major): This is by far the most common type. Once exposed to **ordinary** smallpox, it takes from 7-17 days for symptoms to appear. (The average incubation time is 12-14 days.) Then symptoms are flu-like, progressing from a high fever, cough, and fatigue to headache, backache, and other body aches with occasional vomiting and disorientation. After two to four days of these symptoms, the fever peaks and begins to decline, ushering in a rash that develops into hard painful lesions. The lesions appear first on the mucous membranes and pharynx, then on the face, forearms, and hands. Within a day or two, the trunk and lower limbs, including the palms of the hands and soles of the feet, also become involved with the rash. The rash lasts for about two weeks and becomes most pronounced on the face, forearms, and lower legs. At the end of 14 days the lesions, which by now have developed into hard raised painful sores called pustules, begin to dry up and crust over. By about day 19 the scabs begin falling off, with the scabs on the palms and soles falling off last. The resulting scars, which are most pronounced on the face, are the result of the destruction of the underlying sebaceous glands.

Thirty percent of victims will die, usually from toxemia leading to respiratory or heart failure. Death, if it occurs, is usually in the second week. Some victims will also become blind, generally as a result of opportunistic bacterial infections.

Ordinary smallpox can sometimes be confused with chickenpox. With chickenpox, however, the rash is more uniformly distributed on the body, with no rash on the palms or soles.

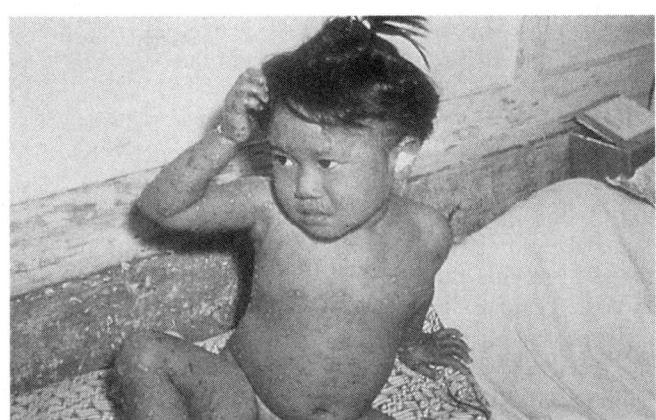

Smallpox lesions at day 17 of rash on a 5-year-old convalescing

2) Flat type smallpox: This is very rare and is believed associated with a deficient immune system. It occurs more frequently in children and is characterized by intense toxemia. The lesions remain soft and velvety, and never progress to the pustular stage. Although the majority of cases are fatal, survivors typically are not scarred.

3) Hemorrhagic smallpox: This is also rare and associated with people with a compromised immune system. It occurs more frequently in adults. The virus multiplies in the spleen and bone marrow and leads to the inability of the blood to clot, resulting in spontaneous bleeding from spots on the skin and from the mucous membranes. The illness includes a shortened incubation period followed by severe high fever, headache, and stomach pain. These victims are highly infectious, and death occurs in the fifth or sixth day after incubation, before lesions typical of **ordinary smallpox** have a chance to develop.

4) Modified type smallpox: This type usually appears in previously vaccinated people. The incubation period, followed by headache and body pains, are similar to **ordinary smallpox**. The rash, however, develops without the presence of fever, and lesions are fewer, more superficial, and progress more quickly, with crusting accomplished within 10 days. These victims are infectious, but not nearly as infectious as victims with **ordinary smallpox**.

History of smallpox vaccine

The decision by President Bush to resume smallpox vaccination marks the first time in U.S. history that a nationwide public health preventive measure has been put into operation to defend against attack with disease.

The vaccine for smallpox is called vaccinia. It is a live virus derived from cowpox, a relative of smallpox but much milder.

The earliest form of smallpox inoculation was developed in China and India about 1000 B.C. Called variolation, it consisted of taking the pus from the pox of an infected person and inoculating a healthy person with it. A mild form of the virus developed and granted the person lifelong immunity. The practice spread to Europe and the New World in the 1700s.

In Britain in the mid 1700s, cowpox was a disease that primarily affected milkmaids, and it was noticed that they became resistant to smallpox after they recovered. In 1774, a British farmer from Dorset inoculated his family with material taken from the udders of a cow with cowpox, thereby granting his family immunity from smallpox. And in 1796 a British surgeon extracted fluid from the pustule of a cowpox victim and injected it into a healthy child, conferring smallpox protection on him. By 1800 smallpox vaccination campaigns using cowpox began throughout Europe.

Modern science has now learned that cowpox is a virus that primarily infects rodents and only occasionally infects cows. It exists primarily in Europe.

The World Health Organization's (WHO) worldwide smallpox vaccination program, designed to eradicate the disease, began in 1967 and ended in 1980 when smallpox was officially declared eradicated, making it the only human disease ever eradicated. The last reported case of smallpox was in Somalia in 1971, and in the United States the last reported case was in 1949. Vaccinations for U.S. civilians stopped in 1972, and U.S. military smallpox vaccinations stopped in 1990. Vaccine production discontinued in the U.S. in 1982.

When eradicated, the world community agreed to keep two samples of the disease in laboratory repositories in the United States at the CDC in Atlanta, and in the Soviet Union at the Russian State Research Center of Virology and Biotechnology in Koltsovo, Novosibirsk, which is in central Siberia.

Vaccination has begun again under a renewed threat of the return of the disease. It is feared that hostile states such as Iraq and North Korea, and possibly terrorists like Al Qaida, now have the smallpox virus and may use it against us. The threat has become more credible since the terrorist attacks in New York on Sept. 11, 2001 and the subsequent anthrax attack by an unknown person or persons shortly thereafter.

Types of vaccines and availability

There is currently enough smallpox vaccine to vaccinate all 288.6 million residents of the U.S. This includes about 75 million doses of the 1970s era Dryvax vaccine and about 300 million doses of the 1950s era Wetvax vaccine. The old vaccine has been stored cold and has been tested every two or three years to test its potency. Some of the vaccine has been diluted up to five times to make it go further, but tests indicate it is still potent.

The U.S. has ordered 209 million more doses of a more modern smallpox vaccine from Acambis Inc., a Cambridge, Massachusetts based company, and it should be ready for use in early 2004. It hasn't been fully tested but initial tests indicate it will be safe and effective. The FDA has not yet licensed enough of any of the vaccine for general public use, but it will be made available to the public without licensing in the event of a smallpox epidemic emergency. There is no definitive way to test the potency and safety of the new vaccine in the absence of an outbreak of smallpox.

Protection

Successful vaccination produces total immunity to smallpox. Once vaccinated, it takes approximately 7-10 days to achieve protection. However, if you are vaccinated within 3-4 days of initial exposure to smallpox, you may receive total protection from the disease, or at least protection against severe illness. The vaccine is then good for about 5-10 years (no one knows for sure). If you are later revaccinated it is believed immunity from smallpox lasts even longer, although how long no one knows. There is no danger in being vaccinated multiple times. Dr. D.A. Henderson, the director for the Center for Civilian Bio-Defense Studies at Johns Hopkins University, who in 1966 was the WHO director overseeing the global eradication of smallpox, says he has been vaccinated between 25 and 100 times. The live vaccinia virus vaccine, he says, must grow in your skin to produce immunity to smallpox. If you are already sufficiently immune, the vaccine simply does not grow in the skin.

The severity of lesions from smallpox can vary greatly, either naturally or because vaccination years before has given a person partial, but not complete, protection. With nearly complete protection from vaccine, few lesions will appear, but even

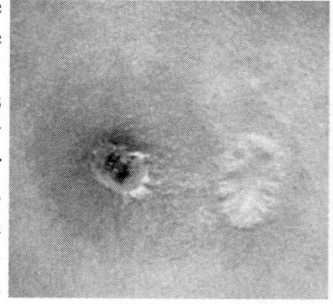

Close-up of the skin reaction at a smallpox vaccination site

The ring method of stopping a smallpox outbreak

At present the Centers for Disease Control's (CDC) plan to contain a smallpox attack includes widespread *voluntary* vaccination but, if necessary, *forced* quarantine of infected individuals and *mandatory* tracing and vaccination of anyone who may have come in contact with them.

They will employ the "ring" method to control an epidemic, namely vaccinate everyone who has had contact with an infected person, then vaccinate the ring of people who have had contact with the first set of contacts. It's the method used so successfully in the 1960s and '70s to finally eradicate smallpox.

Keep in mind that for up to four days after exposure to smallpox, vaccination will either keep a person from catching the disease or lessen its severity.

> **Vaccinia Immune Globulin**
>
> A major difficulty in treating adverse reactions to the vaccine is that in past years bad reactions were treated with vaccinia immune globulin (VIG), which is serum derived from people who recovered from infection with the vaccine virus. Due to the absence of smallpox vaccinations for 30 plus years, the supply of VIG is now about 700 doses, which is enough for anticipated adverse reactions if only 6 million people get vaccinated. Additional doses of VIG are being produced.

if a person was vaccinated many years before, lesions may be far less and more superficial than for a person who was never vaccinated. In this case a person could get a mild case of smallpox, with an accompanying mild rash. He will not die and may not even get very sick, but he may be contagious, capable of passing along fullblown smallpox to another person.

Adverse reactions to vaccine

Smallpox vaccine has a higher adverse reaction rate than any of the modern vaccines generally given. Based on the statistics of the 1960s and 70s smallpox eradication program, as many as 50% of people being vaccinated will have some sort of reaction from the vaccine, ranging from a sore, swollen arm and swollen glands to flu-like symptoms. In a study of adult primary vaccinees, it was determined that 36% became sufficiently ill to miss school, work, or a recreational activity, or to have trouble sleeping. In another study 17% had fever of at least 100 degrees Fahrenheit within two weeks of vaccination, 7% had a fever of 100 degrees or more, and 1.4% had a fever of 102 degrees or more.

One or two of every million people who get the vaccine for the first time will die from it, 15 to 50 will have life threatening reactions including eczema vaccinatum, progressive vaccinia (vaccinia necrosum), and post vaccinal encephalitis, and approximately 1,000 will have serious reactions including a toxic or allergic reaction at the vaccine site and spread of the vaccinia virus to other parts of the body. If all 130 million Americans never vaccinated got vaccinated, about 250 would die and 2,000 would have life-threatening reactions. This does not include people with AIDS, who could be very severely affected.

The data showed that the death rate and adverse reaction rate for those being revaccinated was cut by two-thirds, but still if all 158 million Americans who were previously vaccinated were to get revaccinated, it is expected that 40 would die and 800 would have life threatening reactions. Again, this does not take into account people with AIDS or other immune system problems.

Compare these adverse reaction rates with a more modern vaccine such as the measles/mumps/rubella vaccine, which has experienced 11 adverse reactions and no deaths among the 30 million people vaccinated in the last 12 years. The newer smallpox vaccine, the 209 million doses still under final testing, is expected to have fewer adverse reactions than the older smallpox vaccine.

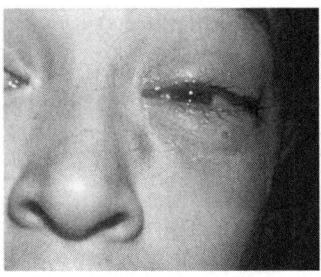

Secondary infection of the cornea in a 12-year-old male

The death rate and adverse reaction rate may be much higher today because the U.S. population, or any modern population, is highly susceptible to smallpox because it has been so long (1949) since the disease has been present in the U.S. and because it has been so long (1972) since vaccinations were discontinued. Health officials expect the death and adverse reaction rate to be much lower among that older 58% of our population that has been vaccinated in the past, even though for most of them it has been the distant past, and they expect the adverse reactions in the younger 42% of the population never vaccinated at all to be significantly higher.

The most frequent complications of smallpox vaccination

From previous data, adverse reactions from vaccination occurred most often in people receiving their first dose of the vaccine, and among children under the age of 5. Following are the most frequent complications.

Inadvertent inoculation at other sites. This accounted for half of all complications of vaccination. Occurring in 1 of every 2,000 primary inoculations, it generally resulted from the hand touching the vaccination site, then touching another part of the body, thereby transferring the vaccination. The most frequent inadvertent inoculations occurred on the mouth, eyelid, rectum, genitals, nose, and face. It generally resolves itself.

Generalized vaccinia. This occurred in 1 of every 5,000 primary vaccinations, and it is the result of blood-borne dissemination of vaccinia virus. It generally resolves itself unless there is an underlying condition involving an immune deficiency. Vaccinia Immune Globulin (VIG) (See Sidebar) can be used to successfully treat cases involving the eye.

Eczema vaccinatum. This occurred in 1 out of every 26,000 primary vaccinations, and it occurred in people who had current or healed eczema or other chronic skin problems. It typically covers the area affected by the skin condition, and it is usually mild and resolves itself. But on occasion it can be severe or fatal. VIG is used to successfully treat serious cases.

Progressive vaccinia (vaccinia necrosum). This is rare, severe, and often fatal, and it is caused by the vaccine site's

> ## People who should not get vaccinated
>
> **Eczema, dermatitis.** People who have had or now have atopic dermatitis or eczema should not get the vaccine unless they are exposed to smallpox. As many as 40 million Americans, or up to 15% of the population, have had or currently have eczema, which puts them at higher risk for a potentially fatal skin infection called eczema vaccinatum. The risk is particularly great for children, who have experienced a threefold increase in eczema since smallpox vaccination ended three decades ago. In a study from the 1970s, 123 people out of one million vaccinated people got eczema vaccinatum, most of them children. In another study in Europe, 6 percent of people infected with eczema vaccinatum died from it. Running the numbers, if the 40 million Americans suspected of having had or currently having eczema were to get the vaccine, the death toll among them would be 295.
>
> **AIDS, other immune deficiency disorders.** People who have a suppressed immune system, such as people who have had transplants or who have cancer, leukemia, lymphoma, or people with HIV and AIDS, are high risk groups. AIDS was not a known disease when vaccinations were given 30 years ago, so the severity of reaction for people with AIDS is not clear. Side effects can include brain swelling and extensive toxicity. Of particular concern to health authorities are the 100,000 to 350,000 Americans who have AIDS but who don't know it. Also, if you are taking immune suppressive medications such as corticosteroids, or if you are undergoing radiation, you should not be vaccinated.
>
> **Pregnant women, children.** Pregnant women should not be vaccinated, nor should they be vaccinated if they plan to get pregnant within one month of vaccination. Infants should also not get the vaccine.
>
> The current recommendation that infants not be vaccinated is in sharp contrast to the smallpox vaccination programs of the 1960s and 70s, when most of the vaccinations were given to children under the age of 1. Now, children under the age of one year are considered at increased risk for vaccine-caused brain infection. Children have been omitted from all of the current studies involving smallpox vaccines. Because children are more prone to touching the vaccination site, then touching other parts of their bodies such as their eyes, or even touching other children, the vaccination site should be covered with a special extra sticky bandage.
>
> Also, if you have any of the following conditions you should not get the vaccine until you have completely healed: burns, shingles, impetigo, herpes, severe acne or psoriasis, and chickenpox.
>
> Since the vaccinia vaccine is a live virus and can accidentally spread to others causing inadvertent vaccination, those people living with any of the above at-risk people should not be vaccinated. A vaccinated person is infectious until the vaccination site scabs over. A vaccinated person could spread the vaccinia virus by touching the vaccination site, then touching another person. In the 60s and 70s it was common for this to happen among young siblings.
>
> In all, about 50 million Americans should not get the vaccine, either because they have one of the conditions mentioned above or because they live with someone who does.

failure to heal. It occurs in people with underlying immune disorders and can occur after primary vaccination or revaccination. VIG is used to treat it, but with varying success.

Post-vaccination encephalitis. Also rare, this occurred in 1 out of 300,000 cases of primary vaccinations, with most occurring in children under the age of one year. It is characterized by fever, headache, vomiting, and sometimes convulsions, paralysis, or coma. Symptoms manifest themselves 8-15 days after vaccination. About 15-25% of cases died and another 25% had permanent neurological damage. VIG is not effective.

Sufficient voluntary vaccination means high U.S. "herd immunity"

A survey of Americans in late 2002 indicated that more than half of Americans would be willing to get vaccinated. But the survey was taken before there was widespread understanding of the risks involved.

At present the vaccine is being made available only to the military and the 10 million or so emergency health care "first responders" such as police, firefighters, ambulance crews, EMTs, hospital emergency care workers, etc. When the vaccine is made available to the public, it will be on a voluntary basis. People will simply have to weigh the risk of having an adverse reaction against the risk that we will be attacked with smallpox. The idea of making it widely available on a volunteer basis is to build up "herd immunity." Since a certain number of people will opt for the vaccine, the nation's "herd immunity" will increase. Then if we are attacked with smallpox, the increased herd immunity will lessen the severity of any resulting epidemic.

In the event of a smallpox epidemic, the Centers for Disease Control and Prevention (CDC) recommends everyone get vaccinated, even if you have AIDS. The risk of getting smallpox far outweighs the risk of having an adverse reaction from the vaccine. The vaccine can be taken for up

The Fourteenth Year

> **How vaccine is given**
>
> The vaccine is given by dipping a bifurcated (two-pronged) needle into the vaccine, then puncturing the skin of the upper arm 15 times in a few seconds. The puncturing of the skin is not deep. If the vaccination is successful, within three to four days a red, itchy bump will form, then develop into a large blister that fills with pus and drains. In two weeks the blister dries up and a scab forms. The scab falls off in the third week and leaves a small scar. To prevent the vaccinia virus in the vaccine from spreading to other people or other parts of your body, the vaccine site should be covered with a bandage. Children especially should be watched so they do not touch the site, then inadvertently touch, say, their eye.

to four days after exposure to smallpox and still be effective in either preventing the disease or greatly lessening its effects.

Although the CDC says smallpox vaccination will be on a voluntary basis, it is anticipated that in the event of an attack and subsequent smallpox epidemic, smallpox vaccinations will likely become mandatory in affected areas. Quarantines and isolation will definitely be mandatory. Based on historical experience, there is no other way to contain an epidemic.

You won't be able to sue

If you are one of the unlucky ones who does get an adverse reaction to the vaccine, you won't be able to sue anyone. The *Homeland Security Act* has a provision protecting vaccine makers and healthcare providers from such suits. People injured may sue in federal court, but they will have to prove negligence, which will be just about impossible because the vaccine is advertised as coming with risks. The liability protection for vaccine makers was deemed necessary in light of the fact the U.S. needed a new vaccine fast and no company was willing to make one unless they got liability protection.

Genetically-altered smallpox

All of the above may become moot if we are attacked with a genetically-altered form of of the smallpox virus. No one knows if such a virus exists, but Soviet defector Dr. Ken Alibek, the former chief scientist and first deputy director of Biopreparat, the former Soviet Union's secret offensive bioweapons program, says the Soviet Union was working on such a virus when he left their program in 1992. Dr Alibek is now a U.S. citizen and chief scientist at a private company in the U.S. that specializes in researching and developing medical defenses against biological weapons.

Also, both *NBC News* and the *New York Times* have reported that another former Russian virologist, the late Dr. Nelja Maltseva, may have given the genetically-altered strain of smallpox to Iraq.

Researchers have tested their ability to alter a related orthopox virus. They inserted the gene interleukin-4 into the mousepox virus, then exposed mice previously vaccinated against mousepox to the genetically altered virus. As they feared, many of the mice died. They are not sure if a genetically altered smallpox virus would defeat the smallpox vaccine, but it is definitely a fear.

The Iraq connection

Before they were thrown out in 1998, U.N. inspectors had discovered that Iraq had experimented with camelpox, another relative of smallpox, and one fear is that camelpox, which ordinarily does not harm humans, might be modified and used as a biological weapon. The smallpox vaccine, however, protects against all orthopox viruses, including camelpox. During their inspections in Iraq, U.N. inspectors found a freeze-drier labeled smallpox. Also, after the first Gulf War, 69 Iraqi prisoners of war were blood tested and were found to have built up immunity to smallpox, indicating prior vaccination against the disease. The obvious question is why?

Genetically engineered vaccines and anti-viral agents

U.S. scientists meanwhile are working on a genetically engineered vaccine that will be more effective with fewer side effects than old vaccines. They are also working on anti-viral agents that could, for the first time in history, effectively treat a person already infected with smallpox. No one knows if these efforts will be successful any time soon, but early laboratory studies suggest the drug cidofovir may be effective. Tests with animals are ongoing and being monitored by the CDC and NIH. There are 3500 doses of cidofovir on hand at present, which is enough to handle anticipated reactions if 15 million people are vaccinated. It will be administered under an investigational new drug protocol. Otherwise, there is no treatment beyond intravenous fluids and medicines to control pain and secondary infections.

Resources

For up to date information on the vaccine situation, you can call the CDC hotline: English: 888-246-2675; Spanish: 888-246-2857 or send them an email: cdcresponse@ashastd.org. On the internet you can find lots of information on smallpox and the smallpox vaccine, as well as on other biological and chemical threats, at the following sites: CDC.gov, WedMD.org, Cato.org, pbs.org, hopkinsbiodefense.org, mipt.org, fas.org. Δ

Think of it this way...
By John Silveira

Biological and chemical weapons through history

John Silveira

The weather here on the coast of Oregon is nice almost all year-round, and there almost always seems to be some kind of fishing—salmon or winter steelhead running on the Rogue, or rock cod, ling cod, halibut, cabezon, and more out in the ocean. So I wasn't surprised when I arrived at the magazine one morning, and parked at the curb in front of the office was the truck belonging to O.E. MacDougal, our poker playing friend from southern California.

I paused to look in the passenger's side window of his truck. There was a tackle box on the seat along with a bottle of Tabasco Sauce that looked as though it had been opened, and a few unopened cans of sardines.

"Mac here?" I asked Muriel as I went in the front door.

"No, but his truck is. I think he went that way on foot," she replied pointing north toward town.

A while later Dave Duffy came in. Dave's the guy who publishes this magazine.

"That's Mac's truck out front, isn't it?" he asked.

"Yeah," I said.

"Is he here?"

"I don't know where he is," I said. "Muriel thought she saw him walking downtown.

"Want to go for coffee?" Dave asked. "Maybe we'll catch him. There aren't that many places he goes to breakfast when he's up here."

Just then Mac walked into the office.

"Hey, Mac," Dave said. "We were just going to head out and see if we could find you."

Mac looked around, then sat in the stuffed chair near my desk. We made some desultory small talk about Mac's trip, about the weather, and the fishing prospects, while Dave and I got ready for our workday.

Dave's wife Ilene, the business manager for the magazine, came in and stood there a second staring at Mac.

"You're here!" she exclaimed. "When did you show up?"

"About an hour and a half ago. I went downtown, ate, then took a walk."

"Well, you'll have to come up for supper tonight," she said. "We're having salmon patties."

With that, she went to her office.

Dave started going through his mail and I was looking through the in-basket of submissions. Mac looked as though he was about to nod off.

"Hey, Mac, what do you think of all this terrorist stuff?" Dave suddenly asked.

Mac acted startled for just a second. He must have driven through most of the night. "Well, it's certainly something to be concerned about," he replied.

He sat there gathering his thoughts for a moment. "The 9/11 thing they pulled off was spectacular," he said. "But it's hard to tell whether they'll be able to pull off anything that dramatic again."

"What about the possibility of biological warfare or a chemical attack?" Dave asked as he still sorted through the envelopes on his desk.

Mac looked in Dave's direction. "Well, you know what people keep saying, 'We didn't expect them to use airliners as flying bombs, so we can't predict what they may come up with next.' There's a whole lot of truth in that statement."

"So, do you think they'll do something again? Something that involves biologicals or chemical weapons?" Dave asked.

Mac shrugged. "I think they will *if* they can figure out how to do it, and *then* if the opportunity presents itself. I think flying planes into buildings was easier to plan and execute than committing an attack with biological or chemical weapons is going to be. But I don't think they're likely to be

The Fourteenth Year

able to repeat their success with airliners again."

"What makes the chemical and biological weapons difficult?" I asked.

"Consider the difficulties the Aum Shinrikyo sect, in Japan, had with their sarin gas attack on a Tokyo subway. It wasn't their first try. They'd bungled some previous attempts. Some that included botulism and anthrax attacks. But even when they released sarin gas, a deadly nerve gas, in the confines of a subway, though they injured almost 6,000 people, they only killed a dozen.

"Their attacks did cause some damage, but the sect had recruited bright young scientists and engineers to poison people in a densely populated country, and they had less than impressive results. Certainly not even close to the scale that Al Quaida would have with airliners on September 11th. I can't see how it's going to be easy for Muslim terrorists to do a whole lot better than Aum Shinrikyo did. But they're certainly going to try. And I'll bet they've learned from Aum Shinrikyo's mistakes."

"What kinds of attacks might they stage using biological and chemical weapons?" I asked.

Mac thought a moment. "Let's start with biologicals," he began. "There are two types. The first involves diseases like anthrax and botulism where victims must come into direct contact with the stuff to be affected. Botulism, for example, can't be passed from person to person, and anthrax only does so rarely.

"The second type, however, and the kind we should fear most involves the use of pathogens like smallpox or the ebola virus. What you're trying to do when you use these biologicals is start a self-sustaining epidemic." He thought another moment. "A pandemic."

"What's the difference between an epidemic and a pandemic?" I asked.

"It's really a matter of magnitude. When you think of an epidemic, think of some kind of disease spreading. When you hear pandemic, think 'epidemic spread out over a *huge* geographical area—even worldwide. It's also used sometimes when describing an epidemic that affects most of a very large population.

> *"The defeat of the Persian armies, led by King Xerxes, that invaded Greece was due more to the hundreds of thousands of Persian soldiers who succumbed to disease along the way than it was to Greek military might. By some accounts, Xerxes brought an army numbering approximately 800,000, but some 300,000 of them died en route of plague.*

"So, if there's an outbreak of ringworm at the local elementary schools, someone may call it an epidemic. You might even call an outbreak of the ebola virus in Africa an epidemic as it spreads from person to person through several villages. In contrast, each year one or another of a strain of flu sweeps the world. That's an epidemic, but because of how widespread it is, it would be more appropriate to call it a pandemic."

"Have we always had epidemics?" I asked.

"They're not new to mankind. They've been with us at least since the first cities in the Old World. We know little about any of those early ones, today, but they were a greater part of human history than is usually taught in school.

"Before the rise of civilization, when humans lived in small isolated groups, there was little chance of epidemics spreading. If a disease leaped from animals to humans in a small village, the whole village may have been wiped out, but it's unlikely that any of them spread far or became pandemics."

"So most of them would have been localized," Dave said.

"That's right.

"But when we started building cities, diseases took on a new face. In cities, with their concentrations of people, there were more social interactions, both within and between groups, and diseases had greater chances to spread. With their large concentrated populations, epidemics became self-sustaining because there were more people to infect. Epidemics could spread because of the sharing of communal water supplies and food, and there was also the infestation of rodents who, along with their parasites, often harbored diseases like plague. Other diseases, such as smallpox, seem to spread only because of social contacts, and cities offered lots of chances for multiple social contacts."

"But how far back in history do we know about epidemics?" Dave asked.

"We know there have been plagues since at least the beginning of recorded history. There are accounts of plagues and epidemics in the Bible. We know from his mummified body that Ramses V, one of the Pharaohs of ancient Egypt, suffered the ravages of smallpox.

"And, though most of the history we learned in school was about battles, kings, and—lately—the social issues that changed the course of history, what we're not told is that many of the great battles that made the world what it is today were determined not by great generals, novel military strategy and tactics, or advanced weapons, but by diseases—epidemics. We are also not told that many of the sweeping social changes that took place in the past, from the end of feudalism to the settling of the New World, were not the result of grand social ideas, but the aftermath of deadly epidemics."

"Any examples?" Dave asked.

"The defeat of the Persian armies, led by King Xerxes, that invaded

Greece was due more to the hundreds of thousands of Persian soldiers who succumbed to disease along the way than it was to Greek military might. By some accounts, Xerxes brought an army numbering approximately 800,000, but some 300,000 of them died en route of plague.

"And what we are often not told is that in 430 BC, when Athens fell to the Spartans who had laid siege to the city, the fall was the result of an epidemic that swept through the city, not Spartan military prowess. Historical records aren't clear as to what the disease was. It may have been smallpox or typhus. Some modern epidemiologists have even raised the possibility that it was the ebola virus or another of the hemorrhagic fevers that cause massive internal bleeding.

"Alexander the Great's conquests were ended with his death at age 32 of pneumonia, most likely brought on because he was suffering from a bout of influenza or malaria. And for the years he marched through Europe, Asia, and Africa, disease was a constant companion of his troops. One of them just finally got him.

"Another good example is the decline of the Roman Empire. Historians have attempted to attribute it to a decline in values and to corruption, but the fact is that epidemics had decimated the Roman Army as well as the civilian population from which it was drawn. This not only led to having to staff the army with foreign mercenaries instead of Roman citizens, but their European enemies, who were largely unaffected by the epidemics sweeping the Empire, were emboldened to carry their wars to the weakened Romans. Some historians speculate that bubonic plague may have been the prime cause of the fall of the Roman Empire, not decadence.

"And the epidemics that spread back then were more brutal than we can imagine. In the sixth-century writings of John of Ephesus we find accounts of the Plague of Justinian that would boggle the modern mind. There were cases of ships that floated at sea for weeks, their entire crews dead from plague, until they washed ashore. And although we can't be sure of the accuracy of his numbers, he also reported the death toll in Constantinople, modern day Istanbul, was 5,000 to 16,000 a day and that the guards at the city's gates stopped counting the dead when the number of corpses passing out of the city for disposal had reached some 230,000.

"Today's scholars and demographers estimate that about one third of Constantinople's population died in the four months the plague reigned.

"Later, the Crusaders who marched out of Europe and into the Holy Land fell in greater numbers to microbes than they ever did to Saracen swords. One Crusade saw 100,000 people leave Europe and only 5,000 return. The overwhelming majority died of diseases either en route to, or when they reached the Holy Land.

"And when the feudal system came to an end in the 14th century, it wasn't because of economic theory, it was because of the shortage of available labor due to deaths brought about by the Black Death, a plague that caught most of Europe by surprise. At least a quarter, and as much as one third, of the population of Europe died in just a few years, and feudal lords, who once all but owned the serfs, suddenly found they had to pay laborers to keep them from fleeing to the cities."

"That many died? As much as a third of Europe? That must have been the epidemic to end all epidemics," I said.

"Not quite. There was at least one greater one. But to have an epidemic of comparable proportions to the Black Death today in the United States today, we would have to have an epidemic that killed roughly thirty million people each year for two years," he said. "Yet, there may have been an epidemic even greater than the Black Death—in the Americas, among the Indians."

"Yikes," I said. "This isn't the history I learned in school."

"No, it isn't," Mac said. "We also learned that Napoleon's defeat in Russia was due to the Russian winter, and though it can in part be attributed to starvation and cold, the main culprit was the scourge of all armies until the middle of the 20th century—disease.

"There have been thousands and thousands of other epidemics, many that could be classified as pandemics, that have occurred since mankind first moved into cities. And we've never heard of them. Some were local and confined to single cities, and whatever written records there may have been of them were lost.

New World epidemics

"It is because of the lack of written records that the great pestilences that devastated the Indians of the New World went unrecognized for so long."

"This must be the one that exceeded the Black Death," Dave said.

"That's right," continued Mac.

"Early European explorers had encountered numerous Indian villages in North America. So numerous they thought it too crowded to begin new settlemenrts. However, later, when English explorers landed on the coast of North America, there were very few Indians, but the bleached bones of human remains seemed to litter the landscape everywhere they went. The English settled on what they thought was relatively unoccupied land, and historians ignored the reports by the earlier explorers that the areas had once had large Indian populations.

"It's only been recently that historians have realized what had happened. Diseases, inadvertently introduced by the Spanish conquerors to the Indian populations of Central and South America a hundred years before the

English settled North America, had spread north and nearly obliterated the Indians. The Indians had almost no resistance to them and died by the millions.

"The entire New World, North and South America, may have been without epidemics of the sort that ravished the Old World until the first Europeans came and brought with them measles, diphtheria, influenza, mumps, smallpox, malaria, etc., and later cholera. These were diseases

> *And when the feudal system came to an end in the 14th century, it wasn't because of economic theory, it was because of the shortage of available labor due to deaths brought about by the Black Death, a plague that caught most of Europe by surprise. At least a quarter, and as much as one third, of the population of Europe died in just a few years...*

unknown to the Indians from Alaska to Tierra del Feugo until 1492, when the white man arrived from Europe and later brought his slaves from Africa.

"And the introduction of these diseases was catastrophic. Modern estimates place the population of the Americas as high as 118 million before 1492. A few centuries later there were fewer than 10 million."

"One epidemic after another attacked the Native Americans. Smallpox, for one, spread so fast across the continent, and ahead of the whites. It was carried by Indians themselves, from one tribe to another so that by the time the white man reached many areas, the disease had already wiped out most of the native population."

"Indians just disappeared?" I asked.

"When the Spanish explorer, de Soto, traveled along the Mississippi his journals say he encountered some 50 towns and villages along one 200-mile stretch of the Mississippi. But 150 years later, French explorers exploring the same stretch of the river didn't find even one.

"By the 1790s, when the English explorer, George Vancouver, arrived on the coast of what are now the states of Oregon and Washington, there were Indian charnel houses loaded with the corpses of smallpox victims. The disease had apparently made its way across the continent through contacts the tribes had with one another.

"In the meantime, the diseases the Europeans brought infected them as well as the Indians, though because of the way these diseases had swept through Europe, generation after generation, the whites had developed some resistance to them. Death rates among whites were much lower, for all of these diseases, than they were for the Indians who had almost no resistance.

"Still, among the settlements founded by the Europeans, there was epidemic after epidemic. In what was to become the United States, from colonial times on, it was not uncommon to have an epidemic of smallpox followed in a few years by an epidemic of diphtheria, then measles, then smallpox again, then yellow fever, typhus, influenza, diphtheria again, then polio... For example, colonial Boston saw an epidemic of smallpox in 1677, measles in 1687, scarlet fever in 1702, measles again in 1713 and 1729, and so on. Fortunately, the epidemics were usually localized.

"Time and again Boston, New York, Philadelphia, Charleston, and other cities were battered by disease both before and after the Revolution.

"And as the country grew and there was more contact among citizens in the various cites and states—hence, more opportunity to transmit disease—epidemics rose more often, then disappeared. No one knew why.

"And every now and then a local epidemic became a pandemic and affected most, if not all, of the country. Sometimes they spread around the world.

"One of the most notable epidemics to originate in the modern United States was one that came to be called

> *Modern estimates place the population of the Americas as high as 118 million before 1492. A few centuries later there were fewer than 10 million.*

the Spanish flu. It actually began at Camp Funston in Kansas and, from 1918 to 1919, it would kill more than half a million Americans and another 25 million people worldwide. By this time, of course, we knew that epidemic diseases were caused by microbes. But that did little to stop it.

Disease in war

"Then there were the epidemics that attended our wars. Disease during war is of interest because, throughout world history, and until recently, disease was almost always responsible for more deaths among the combatants than was actual battle. For every single battle-caused death among Northern troops during the Civil War, two other Yankee soldiers died of typhus, typhoid, smallpox, yellow fever, and other diseases.

"In our war with Mexico there were seven deaths from disease for every battlefield death. And in the Spanish-American War there were almost six disease-related deaths for each battlefield death.

"Even as late as World War I, disease killed seven men for every five who died in battle.

"The reasons for death by disease among the combatants, who were otherwise young and healthy, was the appalling lack of sanitation and pest control and the close quarters in the camps occupied by the troops."

"Worse yet were the living conditions of prisoner of war camps.

During its 14 months of existence, Andersonville Prison, in which Confederate forces held Union POWs, saw 45,000 Union troops imprisoned there, and 13,000 of them died of diseases related to malnutrition, overcrowding, or exposure.

"It wasn't until World War II, with the recognition of the importance of sanitary measures, pest control, and mass inoculations against typhoid, smallpox, and other diseases, that America was involved in its first war in which the number of Americans who died in battle exceeded the number who died from disease. It's been that way ever since.

"World War II may well be the first major war in all of history in which a country's battle deaths, among its troops, outnumbered deaths suffered from diseases.

Disease as a weapon

"Had anyone ever tried to use disease as a weapon during their wars?" I asked.

"Yes. But the problem was that, until recently..." He paused.

And Dave said, "...no one knew what disease was or the role bacteria and viruses play in them."

> When the Spanish explorer, de Soto, traveled along the Mississippi his journals say he encountered some 50 towns and villages along one 200-mile stretch of the Mississippi. But 150 years later, French explorers exploring the same stretch of the river didn't find even one.

"That's right," Mac said. "Until just a few centuries ago, no one had even seen a bacteria, and until the invention of the electron microscope almost all but a few of the biggest viruses were invisible to even the best optical microscopes. Even after bacteria were known to exist, it was at least another 200 years before anyone made the connection between microbes and disease.

"However, that didn't stop combatants, with a flair of novelty, from trying to employ disease as a weapon. Even centuries ago, they knew that some diseases, such as smallpox, could be spread by contact with the ooze that emanated from the pustules that formed on the bodies of its victims, and they knew that sewage and filth, as well as rotting cadavers, were related to or apparently caused at least a few diseases such as typhoid. And so biological warfare was born."

"Without having to know microbes existed," I said.

"That's right.

"The polluting of wells and water supplies with corpses of both men and animals is as old as history. Romans were known to throw dead animals into the water supplies of their enemies with the intent of weakening and demoralizing them. Often, it worked.

"Centuries later, right here in the United States, Confederate troops similarly led animals to ponds where they shot them and left their bodies to rot in the water so as to deny Sherman's advancing army any potable water supplies as it made its way to the sea.

"Sherman was less than amused by it and thought the southerners were barbaric as his troops burned farms, villages, and towns, one after another, and plundered the countryside wholesale to keep his army fed and moving.

"In 1340, during the siege of the castle of Thun L'Eveque in Hainault, in what is now northern France, attackers catapulted bodies of dead animals, including horses, over the walls with the idea of spreading disease. And though, as I've said, there was no germ theory of disease back then, they just knew that those who died of disease could often still spread it. They also knew that rotting bodies themselves could cause various other diseases. After a while, and after enough bodies had been lobbed into the castle, the attackers forced a truce.

"In 1346, while conducting a siege of Caffa—now Feodossia, Ukraine—a port on the Crimean peninsula in the Black Sea, an outbreak of plague, the Black Death, swept through the ranks of the Tartars who besieged the city. The siege failed, but before they called it off, they catapulted the bodies of their comrades who had died of

> *One of the most notable epidemics to originate in the modern United States was one that came to be called the Spanish flu. It actually began at Camp Funston in Kansas and, from 1918 to 1919, it would kill more than half a million Americans and another 25 million people worldwide.*

the disease over the city walls and into the city itself. Terrified residents fled Caffa, but some of those fleeing were *already* infected and they carried the disease with them to Italy, starting the second major epidemic of the Black Death to sweep through Europe.

"In 1422, forces attacking Karlstein, in Bohemia, catapulted animal manure—roughly 2,000 cartloads of it, if you can imagine it—along with the decaying cadavers of men killed in battle, over the castle walls with the intention of spreading illness. But the attackers gave up after five months and that siege failed."

"But it hadn't been from lack of trying," Dave said, and Mac laughed.

"Two thousand cartloads of the stuff," he said to himself, and he started laughing, too.

"In the New World," Mac continued, "the Spanish, Portuguese, and English had no reservations when it came to using whatever means and tactics they could employ to subdue or obliterate the native populations.

The Fourteenth Year

"Pizarro is said to have made gifts of smallpox infected blankets to Indians in South America, and General Jeffery Amherst, in whose honor Amherst, Massachusetts and Amherst College are both named, wrote a letter to one of his officers, Colonel Henry Bouquet, rendering advice on making gifts of smallpox infected blankets, handkerchiefs, and clothing that had come from smallpox victims in their infirmary, to the Delaware Indians, to hasten the spread of the disease which was particularly deadly among the native peoples. This started an epidemic of smallpox that decimated the Delaware and other tribes who came into contact with them. In fact, decimate isn't a strong enough word, since its literal meaning is 'one in ten.' It nearly obliterated them.

"Amherst also made favorable comments concerning Bouquet's plans to hunt Indians down using war dogs. And later he would bemoan that the English didn't have enough war dogs to effectively pursue what he referred to as the 'Spanish Method' of killing Indians.

"But it wasn't only Indians against whom the English used smallpox as a weapon. During the siege at Boston, just prior to the Revolutionary War, the British could have defeated the colonists by landing troops behind the Colonial position where they waited before the Battle of Bunker Hill. But they considered it an ungentlemanly tactic to do so. Thus, they lost the battle. But before departing by ships for New York, they had no reservations about introducing smallpox among the citizens, hoping to infect the forces of the Continental Army. However, this tactic failed because the Americans, upon reentering the city, saw the disease for what it was and immediately quarantined those who had it and stopped its spread."

"So *ungentlemanly* tactics were frowned upon at the time, but biological warfare inflicted on the citizens was not," Dave said.

"That's right," Mac said. "What's acceptable is often just what's acceptable at the time. Another thing the British objected to was the way American snipers picked off the British officers. It was okay for the troops to die, but..."

"I get the picture," Dave said.

"And the British may have used the same tactic, again, during the American siege of Quebec where smallpox spread through the ranks of the Continental soldiers and was a major contribution in the American defeat there."

"Weren't the British afraid of contracting the disease themselves?" I asked.

"Well, even though Edward Jenner hadn't yet invented his smallpox vaccine, which was made from the pustules of cattle infected with cowpox, it was understood that if you exposed people to the pus from mild cases of smallpox, you could confer a certain amount of immunity on the recipients. The British Army had already made it a common practice to inoculate their troops in this way."

"Oh, and it worked?" I asked.

"Yeah, it worked pretty well, though sometimes those inoculated this way developed deadly cases of the disease."

"And this too was done without realizing that it was microbes causing the disease," Dave said.

"That's right," Mac said. "And if we fast-forward to the 20th century, when the role of viral and bacterial pathogens in the spread of many diseases was understood, it wasn't long before someone used this knowledge to create biological weapons.

"During World War I the Germans attempted to spread livestock diseases, such as glanders and anthrax, among horses, mules, sheep, and cattle to upset the Allies food supplies. And, you've got to realize, even as late as World War II horses and mules were still used to transport supplies along the battle fronts. So anything that killed or maimed the animals offered a tactical advantage. However, the attempt had little success."

"In the meantime, the Germans brought a new type of weapon to the battlefield. This was the chemical weapon. Specifically, mustard gas."

"Is this the first use of chemical weapons in history?" I asked.

"Not at all. The first *recorded* use of chemical weapons was in 600 BC when Solon, the legislator of Athens, used hellebores—hellebore is a toxic plant—to contaminate the River Pleithenes. Drinking from the river gave the defenders of Kirrha explosive diarrhea making them unable to fight. The Athenians kicked their butts."

"Later, during the Peloponnesian War, the Spartans created sulphur dioxide, a toxic gas, by burning wood saturated with pitch, naphtha, and sulphur. They used it during the siege of Platea, Pelium, and other cites that were allies to the Athenians.

"Then, around 200 BC, the Carthaginians did poorly in a battle and before their retreat, they left behind wine they had poisoned with mandragora, a root that contains a narcotic. Their enemy drank the wine, the narcotic took affect, they fell into

> *General Jeffery Amherst, in whose honor Amherst, Massachusetts and Amherst College are both named, wrote a letter to one of his officers, Colonel Henry Bouquet, rendering advice on making gifts of smallpox infected blankets, handkerchiefs, and clothing that had come from smallpox victims in their infirmary, to the Delaware Indians, to hasten the spread of the disease which was particularly deadly among the native peoples.*

a sleep, and the Carthaginians came back and slaughtered them all while they were unconscious.

"By the way, the very first recorded use of chemical warfare in North America took place in 1623 when the Jamestown colonists invited an Indian leader named Chiskiak, along with his family and some two-hundred members of his tribe, for treaty talks and a feast. The colonists offered toasts of eternal friendship and fed

> ...*the very first recorded use of chemical warfare in North America took place in 1623 when the Jamestown colonists invited an Indian leader named Chiskiak, along with his family and some two-hundred members of his tribe, for treaty talks and a feast. The colonists offered toasts of eternal friendship and fed their guests. But, what they had done was to poison the food and drink they served to the Indians.*

their guests. But, what they had done was to poison the food and drink they served to the Indians. And before the 'feast' was over Chiskiak, his family, and two-hundred others from his tribe were dead.

"And this wasn't an isolated case. Some territorial newspapers in the Old West advised settlers on how to leave strychnine-laced food near Indian trails so that Indians could be exterminated. One newspaper boasted of the manner in which Minnesota settlers had poisoned over 100 Indians. The article described the efficiency and lower cost of the poison as compared to the cost of gunpowder and lead."

"Why did we finally decide to outlaw the use of these weapons?" Dave asked.

"It came about as a result of their use in World War I. There were 1.3 million battlefield casualties from them including 90,000 deaths. The Geneva Protocol of 1925 prohibited the use of bacteriological and chemical weapons, but not the research and development of them."

"Sounds like a Catch-22 clause," Dave said.

"That's right. So, despite the fact that everyone agreed they wouldn't use them again, many countries still engaged in research and development of them."

"But no one used them in World War II," I said.

"That's not true," Mac responded. "In WW II the Japanese, who were not signatories to the Geneva Protocol, killed as many as 10,000 people in Manchuria while developing various disease agents, including anthrax, cholera, typhoid, and plague. Later, during the war in China, hundreds of thousands of Chinese civilians fell victim to these diseases as Japanese aircraft dropped paper bags filled with plague-infested fleas over the cities of Ningbo and Quzhou in Zhejiang province.

"In other attacks they contaminated wells and, echoing what the English and Americans did to Indians, they distributed poisoned foods.

"One of the little known weapons used by the Japanese during World War II were balloon bombs. The balloons, which were launched from Japan, carried explosives and incendiaries. Over a 17-month period these bombs fell as far north as Canada and south as far as Mexico, and from California to points east of the Mississippi River.

"Their intent was to cause damage and to demoralize the Americans on the home front.

"The Japanese figured that, because the United States is an open society, the bombs would be newsworthy stories and, by eavesdropping on radio transmissions, they could learn how effective they were. But that didn't happen because whenever an American reported one, the FBI or some other agency showed up and threatened the citizen with treason and arrest if they talked about it. The result was that there was a virtual news blackout of the incidents.

"But what the Americans feared most wasn't the explosives and incendieries the balloons carried; we feared that the Japanese would use them to launch biological and chemical attacks against us. But not only were the Japanese never sure the balloons were actually reaching us, they also never succeeded in producing more effective biological munitions they could deploy for battlefield use. So the threat never materialized.

"After that war, despite an announced intention of not using them during the Cold War, both the United States and the Soviet Union researched the use of hundreds of different bacteria, viruses, and biological toxins and both countries developed sophisticated delivery systems to disperse them as fine-mist aerosols, packages that were to be included as part of bombs, or to be carried inside missiles.

"In 1969, we, the United States, conducted war games on ships loaded with animals and proved to ourselves that the weapons would work very well, even in a naval environment. In the meantime, Soviet ships lurked in the background and collected samples of the pathogens we used in that exercise.

"Then, in 1979, the United States ended its biological weapons program and we destroyed—or, at least said we destroyed—our stocks of pathogens.

Outlawing biological and chemical weapons

"Was it really for humanitarian reasons that we've outlawed these weapons?" Dave asked.

"First of all, they aren't *outlawed*. What's outlawed is *first use* of them. We've maintained, as have other countries, that if they're used against us, we may strike back with them.

The Fourteenth Year

> *In WW II the Japanese, who were not signatories to the Geneva Protocol, killed as many as 10,000 people in Manchuria while developing various disease agents, including anthrax, cholera, typhoid, and plague. Later, during the war in China, hundreds of thousands of Chinese civilians fell victim to these diseases as Japanese aircraft dropped paper bags filled with plague-infested fleas over the cities of Ningbo and Quzhou in Zhejiang province.*

"As to the humanitarianism of it all: There may have been some humanitarian thought involved when the Geneva Protocol of 1925 was drawn up, but I'd say not much. Countries willing to fight wars with napalm, machine guns, high-yield blockbusters, and who have in reserve, as this and several other countries do, a stock of nuclear warheads, is not concerned with humane ways of killing."

"So you think these weapons were outlawed for other reasons," Dave said.

"Yes, there were more practical reasons for outlawing them, but we've cloaked our excuses in humanitarian wrapping to hide those reasons. It's something politicians love to do."

"So what are the reasons?" Dave asked.

"There are a few main reasons, and probably a bunch of ancillary reasons. But two very good reasons are, first: these weapons are unpredictable. If the wind changes, poison gases can come back on your own troops. This was something that happened to the Germans in World War I. Generals don't like that. Your own troops can panic if you misuse them.

"Biological weapons can have the same effect. You might spread a virus in a foreign country but, if it's a contagious disease like smallpox, you may find it spreads beyond that country's borders, the way influenza does, and spreads back to your own. You might even spread a genetically altered pathogen on a battlefield and not be able to protect your own troops from it. This alone may prevent you from occupying the land you've won."

He paused.

"So that's the unpredictable side," I said.

"Yes. Second: biological and chemical weapons are the poor man's atom bomb. Outlawing them forces Third World countries to fight wars with conventional weapons. Fighting a conventional war is vastly more expensive because the weapons we fight those with must be deployed in far larger numbers, and they require expensive delivery systems."

"Like field artillery, fighter bombers, and cruise weapons," Dave said.

"Yes. Plus, those delivery systems are much easier to find," Mac said. "A canister of some biological agent smuggled into the country of your enemy would be harder to detect than a B-52 bomber.

"Then there's the problem that the conventional weapons Third World countries can afford are considerably less effective than some of the high-tech biologicals and chemical weapons they could either develop or purchase on the world's weapons market.

"The Iraqis and the North Koreans, for instance, could do a whole lot more saber rattling with a few good canisters of weapons-grade smallpox than they could do with a transport-ship-load of conventional 500-pound bombs. In fact, it's conceivable that all of our high-tech weaponry could be countered with just one high-tech pathogen. And that's the fear we have. We have hundreds of billions of dollars in conventional arms that we can press on Iraq or anyone else. What if Saddam Hussein said he'd strike back with a dozen canisters of genetically altered smallpox that he had hidden in this country—and he proved he had already put them here? Suddenly, the world's greatest superpower has been trumped with a few thousand dollars."

"I get the picture," Dave said.

"So, we don't want any two-bit dictator to have anything like that."

"And hence the problem with terrorists. All of the things that make them attractive to Third World countries may make them the weapons of choice for terrorists."

"Would terrorists use nerve gas or smallpox to attack us?" I asked.

"Consider this: during the eight-year Iraq-Iran war the Iraqis used 'banned' chemical weapons on the Iranians. They also used them on the Kurds. And there was no hue and cry from Moslem countries—neither those with theocratic governments nor those with secular governments—to take Saddam Hussein to task for it. To them, and to many other countries, biological and chemical weapons are just...weapons. Just as napalm and smart bombs are 'just weapons' to us.

"So to believe they will not use them, or, more so, to think terrorists won't use them, we would have to believe they are our moral superiors.

> *...this isn't just a Muslim thing. Christians have done it, Americans have done it, our Founding Fathers had done it. It's a human thing. We really have something to fear here, because the terrorists are human, regardless of how we otherwise may wish to think of them. And that thought should leave us quaking in our boots.*

And there's no reason to think this. In fact, they show every indication of being just like us, that is, human. And given the record of how humans have treated each other throughout history, this isn't just a Muslim thing.

Christians have done it, Americans have done it, our Founding Fathers had done it. It's a human thing. We really have something to fear here, because the terrorists *are* human, regardless of how we otherwise may wish to think of them. And that thought should leave us quaking in our boots.

"However, there's still another thing to consider. Unlike kamikaze attacks or suicide bombings, one of the things today's Muslim terrorists are going to have to consider is: Is it worth releasing some kind of pathogen to infect us, their perceived enemy, even if it means the disease may spread back to their homelands and kill their own people wholesale? And, given today's rapid travel, it's entirely likely that that would happen."

"Do you think they would?" Dave asked.

"Yes, some would."

No one said anything for a minute or so.

"Would we be as susceptible to an epidemic, especially one with a genetically altered pathogen, as the Native Americans were?" I finally asked.

"Of course not. Today we know of things that neither the Indians nor their European contemporaries knew of. We know how pathogens are spread, we understand hygiene, quarantine, and medical strategies.

"Still, a man-made epidemic, especially one made with genetically-altered pathogens, for which there is currently no vaccine, could be devastating. It could kill a lot of people. Maybe millions. But we wouldn't be as helpless as the Indians of two or more centuries ago were.

"But there's still more to consider than casualty numbers. An attack like that would be devastating to us psychologically, even if it didn't kill that many."

"How?" I asked.

"One of my greatest fears is what we would do to ourselves to gain the illusion of security."

"What do you mean?" I asked.

"We're gradually divesting ourselves of our freedoms in the belief that by doing so we're going to make ourselves safer from violent criminals, drug dealers, school shootings, poverty, pornography, and now terrorism.

"Of course, the fact is we still have crime, drugs, shootings, poverty, etc., and we'll still have terrorism, no matter how many of our rights we surrender."

"What's the solution?" Dave asked.

"The solution?" Mac asked.

"Yes, what do we do about the threat of biological and chemical weapons being used against us? Also, what's the solution for the threat these weapons have on our rights?"

"The solution has several sides. One is that we shouldn't give up any of our rights for any reason. Giving them up hasn't worked before. If these guys in Washington, D.C., can't do their jobs and fight terrorism without trampling on the one thing that makes us unique among nations—our rights, then let's send them packing. Let them get jobs pumping gas or whatever it is they're good at, and let someone who can do the job right take over.

"Second, we should demand back the rights we've already surrendered under other protectionist schemes that have come out of Washington, the RICO Act, for example. I realize this doesn't exactly relate to the issue of biological and chemical weapons, but it's something we should be doing, anyway.

"The third thing is, get out of the Middle East. Stop playing the game that we're the world's policeman. We're not. We're going to make ourselves the target of more and more terrorists with causes if we insist on pushing our nose into everyone else's business.

"I've said it before. We should live up to the philosophy of 'Speak softly and carry a big stick.' If we stop meddling in the political affairs of the rest of the world, the terrorists will lose interest in us, just as they have no interest in the Danes, the Costa Ricans, or New Zealanders.

"But the corollary to this is: If we've been minding our business and someone strikes at us—I don't care if it's a terrorist organization or another country—we should strike back immediately and decisively. Let others on this planet know that minding our own business doesn't mean we'll be patsies for them. Forget getting United Nations permission. Forget the hand wringing. Just do it. The last thing this country needs, if someone threatens us, bombs us, or commits terrorist acts against us, is to get the permission of the French, the Germans, the Russians, or anyone else.

"Let the world know that no one has anything to fear from us—unless they give us a reason to come after them."

With that we just sort of sat there. Dave started going through the rest of his mail. I started going through more of the submissions.

Muriel walked in with a coffee cup. She handed it to Mac who smiled and thanked her as he took it.

Muriel left.

I looked at Dave. He looked at me. We both looked back at Mac.

"She never brings us coffee. How to you rate?" I asked.

Almost on cue, Muriel came back. She paused in the doorway and said, "He rates because he's more charming than you two."

Then she left, again.

Mac smiled. He sat back and sipped his coffee. Dave and I just shook our heads. Δ

The Fourteenth Year

Preparedness for travelers

By Brad Rohdenburg

When the subject of preparedness comes up, do you think of having a stock of supplies in your kitchen pantry in case of a storm? Maybe a backpack in your office or the trunk of your car with the things you'd need until you could return home?

If you travel for business or pleasure, the concept is likely to apply to an unfamiliar city thousands of miles from home. Being ready for the unexpected while traveling will give you options you wouldn't otherwise have. Sometimes what might have been overwhelming becomes merely an inconvenience, or even an adventure.

So what should we anticipate? Consider what has affected travelers before us: natural disasters, transportation strikes, civil unrest, crime, epidemics, quarantines, terrorism, war. Things as common as snow, traffic jams, flight cancellations, or car accidents. Things as local as a bridge hit by a barge, a derailed commuter train, or a power outage. Things of magnitudes beyond our comprehension like the 1985 Mexico City earthquake, Mount St. Helens, the Mississippi flood of 1993, Chernobyl, the New England blizzard of 1978, the hurricane that killed 6,000 in Galveston in 1900, wars that involved the entire world.

Anything your imagination can conceive of, and even more things that it can't. Being prepared might not always be enough for every circumstance, but anything that improves your odds is better than nothing.

I once spent three days in the Nashville airport during a snow storm. There were no hotel rooms available at any price. Airport personnel provided hundreds of cots, but there weren't nearly enough to go around. The junk food from the kiosks in the terminal was gone within hours.

Immediately after hurricane Andrew, I was holed up in a Miami hotel room with no running water, watching from the balcony as looters smashed windows below. I ended up using water from the toilet tank. (Relax—I said the tank, not the bowl.)

I have acquaintances who were stranded at a ski resort in Utah when an avalanche closed the only road out.

Some of the things in my car: Insulated ground pad, sleeping bag, jumper cables, tow strap, fire extinguisher, first aid kit, flashlight, candle and matches, ice scraper, shovel, a pot for melting snow or storing water, and MREs.

During the New England blizzard of 1978, hundreds of people spent days in their cars on Rt. 128 around Boston. A friend was in a grocery store during the San Francisco earthquake of 1989. The roads and bridges to her home were destroyed. Another friend was trapped by a revolution in Guinea-Bissau—anarchy that didn't even make the news in a country that no one's heard of.

Tens of thousands of airline passengers on 9/11 were diverted to places without accommodations for them, and deplaned without their luggage. (Hearing about the hospitality they experienced in places like Gander, Newfoundland, restored some of my jaded faith in the nature of people.)

My family physician volunteered for a U.N. humanitarian mission to Congo. Rebels paid the hospital a visit, and he was the sole Caucasian survivor. (Hearing about that jaded my faith again.) He survived because he was alert to what was happening around him and prepared to act. Something that extreme will probably never happen to you. He didn't think it would ever happen to him, either.

As a gentleman from the destroyed city of Sarajevo said "War is like bad weather. It just comes."

When I read about disasters in the news, or watch them unfolding in living color on TV, I think about what those people would want if they could magically go back in time for a "do-over." What needs seem common to most times and places? Water first, usually. Then appropriate clothes, and then shelter and food. Sometimes medical help and protection.

General preparedness

Clothing is your first layer of shelter. Pack for what's expected, of course, but anticipate more. A trip might start in Miami and end in Fairbanks. Dress appropriately, not only for your destination, but for possible diversions along the way, unnatural weather extremes, heating or air conditioning problems, and extended stays.

Synthetics are warm and they dry quickly, but will do skin damage if they melt. (I'm a little paranoid about this as I've seen it happen.) Natural fibers are a better choice if fire is a hazard—and it is in your car, mowing your lawn, starting a barbecue, or going to a nightclub.

Cotton is comfortable, but loses its insulating value if it gets wet, and it dries slowly. Wool provides some warmth even when wet, but gets heavy and some types are itchy. Silk combines the best attributes of both, and is my favorite first layer. It can be washed in a sink by hand at the end of a day, and will dry overnight—both you and your travel companions will appreciate that if your one-day trip becomes a five-day trip.

Impractical shoes are the biggest clothing mistake I see travelers making. I love the look of a woman in heels, for example, but the leggy girl of your dreams will wear on you pretty quickly when her feet start to hurt. Bring along something comfortable just in case there's walking to be done.

"Carry-on" preparedness

Airline travelers have the highest standard of resourcefulness to meet in order to be prepared. Not everything you'd like to have when things get difficult will fit in checked luggage, let alone in carry-on bags. The Transportation Security Administration (TSA), a government agency that helps terrorists by disarming the 282 million of us who *don't* want to go on a suicide ride (but that's another article), won't allow so much as a Swiss Army knife onboard. Before a recent international flight, even nail clippers and a book of matches were confiscated from me. An elderly woman behind me had her sewing needles taken. (Of course, if a weapon were ever needed by either a terrorist or a law-abiding citizen, one can always be improvised. So far, at least, a can of soup in a sock isn't illegal.)

Personally, I'm armed wherever it's legal for me to be so. Armed or not, don't attract attention to yourself by acting like easy prey. Behave confidently but inconspicuously. In third-world countries, don't be a loud, rich American wearing expensive jewelry. Keep your wallet in a button-down pocket, and some of your money in a money belt or an ankle pouch. Make a copy of things like your passport information and keep it in a separate place. Ask your hotel's concierge about neighborhoods to avoid, and have them choose a taxi for you. Ask for a room above the ground floor. Most problems can be avoided simply by being alert, but consider taking a self defense course.

When I fly somewhere, I feel naked without at least a pocket knife. It's permissible to take one in your checked baggage. If you have only carry-on luggage, an inexpensive one may be purchased at your destination. Use it while you're there, then make someone's day by giving it away when you leave. In any case, I take a small course-grit diamond sharpening stone. It's weight and bulk are negligible. If necessary, even a scrounged piece of metal or plastic could be sharpened.

Keep a bottle of water in your carry-on, and top it off it when opportunities arise. The collapsible kind takes up less space and won't slosh annoyingly if you squeeze the air out. I bring a water filter or iodine crystals, too. You might not always be able to get water out of a tap. Pack some lightweight, nutritious, compact food. You're still free to patronize restaurants if that's your choice, but you won't be forced to rely on them.

Ear plugs and an eye mask will help you get some sleep on a crowded bus or plane. Other essentials for my "carry-on survival kit" are a toothbrush and floss, sunscreen, sunglass-

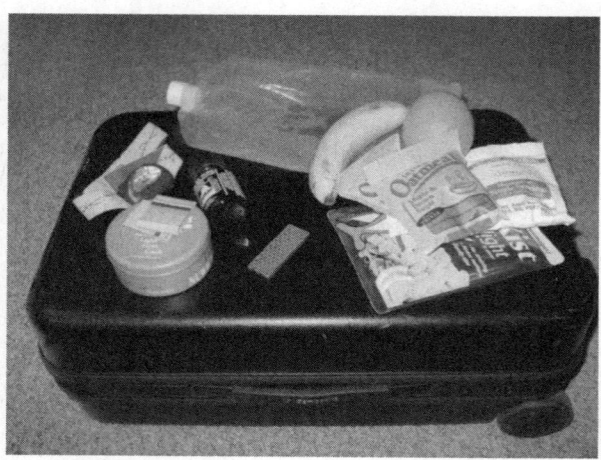

Some of the things in my carry-on bag: Water bottle, food, candle and matches, LED headlamp, course-grit knife sharpener, iodine crystals to disinfect water.

es, one of those candles-in-a-can, disposable lighter, a small first-aid kit (if you take medication, bring extra), a tiny LED flashlight or headlamp, and above all else: a good book. Something like, oh, say, a *Backwoods Home Anthology*.

Terrorism

Terrorism is making headlines these days, although it's probably less likely than weather or petty crime to disrupt your vacation or business trip. According to a recent news show, many people are buying gas masks. The odds of needing one, however, are miniscule. Unless you have sophisticated detection devices, the odds of knowing *when* you need one are even more miniscule. Visible clouds of biological or nerve agents don't roll down the street like in the movies.

Even if you do have a genuine need for a gas mask, and know when it's necessary to wear it and when it's safe to remove it, and even if you are trained in its use, it still must be instantly available, properly fitted, and with fresh filters of the proper type. For agents that can be absorbed through the skin, special suits are also necessary. Your money can be better spent.

I once read that the greatest risks to an airline pilot on the job are traffic accidents during the drive to the airport, and hotel fires during the layover. The same probably holds true for most passengers.

Automobile preparedness

Operate your car as if your life depends on it, because it does. Drive with common sense and at sane speeds. Make sure the next car you buy is crashworthy. (Common sense and sane speeds only count for so much if you're in a cat-food can.) Wear your seat belt. Have a fire extinguisher and a first aid kit. Know where they are and how to use them.

A duffel in my car also contains a sleeping bag, insulated ground pad, saw, jumper cables, tow strap, first aid kit, flashlight, a pot for cooking or melting snow, an ice scraper, and a couple of MREs (the militarly meals, ready-to-eat). I have used all of those things. I replace the MREs every year. (Want to make friends with the neighborhood kids? Give them your old MRE's. They'll be fascinated by them.)

Throw in whatever's appropriate for changing seasons, forecasts, or local conditions. In winter I add a hat, mittens, boots, shovel, and snowshoes. A candle or two will keep a stalled car reasonably warm. Be careful with fire, of course, so the solution doesn't become worse than the problem. A cell phone can summon help and reassure family. Keep your car's gas tank as full as is practical—it costs the same as leaving it empty, and again that phrase: It gives you more options.

A bicycle in the trunk, with an air pump and a spare inner tube, is my favorite automotive insurance. Walking a few miles with anything to carry is a time-consuming ordeal. On a bike, twice as far with twice the load is a pleasant outing.

Hotels

When you check into a hotel, make it a habit to look at the fire escape route posted on the inside of your room's door. Then open your door and look at the route the way you will look at it at 3 a.m. when you've been suddenly roused from a sound sleep. Count the number of doors and corners to get to it in case darkness or smoke prevent you from being able to see. (Do the same thing, while we're at it, when you board a plane, ship, or train: familiarize yourself with the way out. Count the rows of seats to it so you could get there in the dark, and look at how the doors or hatches operate.)

Don't use elevators during a fire because a power failure may immobilize them. Smoke tends to hug the ceiling. If it becomes a problem, stay close to the floor. (So why are the fire exit signs at the tops of the doors?)

If a fire alarm sounds while you're in your room, feel the door. If it isn't hot and you don't see smoke or flames through the peephole, evacuate. Remember to take your room key in case you must retreat to your room again. If you can't open the door, fill the bathtub with water and seal openings that smoke may come through with soaked towels. Breaking windows might create a draft that brings smoke in, so it's a last resort. Sit tight if you're more than a couple of stories above the ground. Most fires are confined to a few rooms or floors. We have a natural fear of fire, but smoke and panic are usually the greater threats.

I suspect that for most of the readers of this magazine, the concept of being prepared isn't new. But I hope this article has stimulated some thought and encouraged you to be alert and resourceful. Above all, being prepared is an attitude. ∆

Jackie Clay's basic "grab & git" emergency kits

When an emergency strikes that requires evacuation, that's not the time to start flinging items in the trunk of your car. Here are some suggestions for short and longer term evacuations. You'll want enough supplies to be comfortable, fed, and informed. **It is important for each member of the family, including babies to have his or her own emergency pack packed and readily available at all times in the event that you find yourselves having to flee separately.**

72-hour kit

This kit is contained in one large daypack. You can customize it for your family's individual needs.

Basic first aid kit for a family: Housed in a relatively small box or nylon pouch, this kit should include:
- 1 roll of 2-inch sterile gauze
- 1 roll of first aid tape
- a supply of any daily prescription medicine, kept fresh and current
- adhesive bandages, assorted sizes
- basic first aid pamphlet
- burn treatment, such as Burn Free
- small, sharp scissors
- tweezers and hypodermic needles to remove slivers or embedded glass
- iodine or tamed iodine
- pain and anti-inflammatory medication, such as aspirin, Tylenol III (with codeine), or children's pain, fever and anti-inflammatory medication, as needed

Clothing, food, water, sanitation (per person):
- 1 complete change of warm, sturdy clothes, including a set of lightweight thermal long johns
- 1 extra pair of sturdy socks
- space blanket
- stocking hat
- 2 large plastic garbage bags (can make a quick rain poncho, which also holds in body heat, as well as many other uses)
- pocket knife
- flashlight
- canteen with aluminum cup
- butane lighter
- half dozen MREs (military "meals ready to eat") in combination with TV dinners that do not require refrigeration
- 1 small Ziplock bag of dehydrated fruit
- 1 roll of toilet paper with center roll removed to save space; flatten the roll
- small bottle of dish soap (also used to wash up after exposure to potentially dangerous material)
- half dozen high energy food bars
- 1-liter sport bottle of drinking water
- 1 washcloth (fold & place them all in a zip-lock plastic baggie with dish soap)

(The rest are per family)
- fire starter blocks/sticks
- stainless steel mixing bowl (doubles as wash basin, water boiling vessel and cooking utensil to boil food)
- 9 volt radio with fresh battery
- compact, basic fishing gear (i.e. coil of line, a few hooks and universal lures (small), such as spinners, dry flies
- a few dollars in quarters and bills
- a small address book with phone numbers & other vital information
- a map of the local area

All of this can easily be packed into a large, soft-sided day pack. The heads of the family may also wish to include:
- a lightweight handgun and ammo for signaling and family protection
- a cell phone
- lightweight tent
- a small water filter

If at all possible, each member of the family should also include a very warm sleeping bag in their kit. It won't fit in the bag, but can be stuffed into a sack to carry and will be very welcome, especially in cold weather.

Adequate drinking and sanitation water is a must. It's best if you include at least five gallons of water, carried in the trunk of your vehicle; more is best for personal sanitation, especially after some sort of contamination (biological or other terrorist attack, chemical spill, etc.) This can be carried in a blue plastic water carrier or even several sturdy plastic jugs, such as milk comes in.

Above all, the family should have a PLAN for various scenarios:
- where they will meet
- who will do what
- bring what
- where they will go

People running around like chickens with their heads cut off are totally useless and likely to get into serious trouble.

Longer term evacuation needs

In addition to the above, have a secondary "grab and git" kit put together, should the situation look extremely serious, making a longer stay away from home necessary. I've found that this kit is most easily put together in large, inexpensive plastic coolers. It's based on a family of four.

Food cooler #1
- 1 large Ziplock bag of dehydrated vegetables
- 1 lb. potato flakes
- 1 small Ziplock bag of dehydrated onions
- include small Ziplock bags of other dehydrated vegetables your family may like: peas, carrots, etc.
- 1 dozen cans of canned ham, tuna, chicken, etc.
- 1 dozen dry "instant noodle & rice mixes"
- large Ziplock bag of dehydrated eggs
- small Ziplock bag margarine powder
- small Ziplock bag cheese powder
- small Ziplock bags of dehydrated fruit (raisins, apples, apricots)
- 1 lb. each of dehydrated beef & chicken soup bases
- 2 lbs. dry noodles
- 1 lb. dry beans
- 2 lbs. macaroni
- 10 lbs. flour
- 3 lbs. can shortening
- 1 small can baking powder
- small Ziplock bag of salt
- spices
- 1 lb. sugar
- 3 lbs. rice
- 6 boxes instant pudding mixes
- 3 pkgs. each of potato pancake mix, soup mix, and pancake mix
- instant coffee, tea, or beverage mixes
- sugar substitute for diabetics
- 1 lb. cornmeal
- 3 lb. dehydrated milk if you have kids, otherwise, 1 lb.
- powdered formula if you have babies

Kitchen box in cooler #2
- frying pan
- large and small saucepans
- metal spatula
- matches & lighter
- fire starter blocks/sticks in addition to the ones in the 72-hour pack
- mixing bowl
- green dish-scrubber pad
- paper towels with cardboard roll removed
- bowls for entire family
- silverware for entire family
- roll of lightweight wire
- hatchet
- small propane stove & fuel tanks
- several candles
- large bottle of good dish detergent (also for washing hair, bathing and washing clothes)

Other gear:
(This would go in a large heavyweight plastic storage box.)
- sleeping bags for each person
- Coleman lantern (for heat as well as light)
- extra mantles; sleeping bags protect lantern from breakage
- unopened gallon of Coleman fuel
- 10' x 12' plastic camo tarp
- medium-sized bow saw
- lightweight but family-sized tent
- warm jackets, gloves, and stocking hats for each person
- extra flashlight batteries (or a small solar charger and rechargeable batteries)
- small folding shovel or entrenching tool—the real military ones are best (for latrine duty, camp chores, digging out stuck vehicle)

Extended medical kit: (This would be packed in a large fishing tackle box) Along with the basic medical items listed above, you might want to add some of the following:
- antidiarrheal
- oral antibiotics
- oral electrolytes for stress and dehydration
- thermometer
- comprehensive first aid book
- cold medicines (cough, runny nose, sore throat)
- cotton roll
- hemostats
- suturing material, if you are trained enough to use it safely
- ointments for athletes foot, jock itch or vaginal yeast infections
- eye ointment or drops
- a dental kit to temporarily treat toothaches, replace fillings and mend broken dentures
- contraception, if appropriate

Your kit may include much more, depending on your needs and medical experience; ours includes casting material for broken limbs, scalpels, IV set and fluids and more.

A large new plastic garbage can is a great boon for water storage. They are not "food grade," meant to hold drinking water, but they will conveniently hold dish and bathing water and are lightweight and easy to carry. You can even put a sack of dog food in it, unopened, for your best friend, too. One or more white plastic food grade buckets are also indispensable to carry water and other necessities.

We have found that having a small, cheap travel trailer makes packing more than this very easy. I emphasize "small" as this trailer is cheap to pull, inconspicuous when backed into a hole in the forest, and does not scream "MONEY," as does a larger, nicer RV, especially during desperate times. Besides, it's nice to grab and git, if only to go fishing for the weekend—just for a practice run, of course. Δ

THE IRREVERENT JOKE PAGE

(Believing it is important for people to be able to laugh at themselves, this is a continuing feature in *Backwoods Home Magazine*. We invite readers to submit any jokes you'd like to share to *BHM*, P.O. Box 712, Gold Beach, OR 97444. There is no payment for jokes used.)

I went to the store the other day, and I was in there for only about 5 minutes. When I came out there was a motorcycle cop writing a parking ticket. So I went up to him and said, "Come on, buddy, how about giving a girl a break?" He ignored me and continued writing the ticket. So I called him a pencil-necked Nazi. He glared at me and started writing another ticket for having worn tires! So I called him a horse's patootie. He finished the second ticket and put it on the windshield with the first. Then he started writing a third ticket! This went on for about 20 minutes. The more I abused him, the more tickets he wrote. But I didn't care. My car was parked around the corner.

WIFE: The two things I cook best are meat loaf and apple pie.
HUSBAND: Which is this?

There was a married couple who were in a terrible accident. The woman's face was burned severely. The doctor told the husband they couldn't graft any skin from her body because she was so skinny. The husband then donated some of his skin...however, the only place suitable to the doctor was from his buttocks. The husband requested that no one be told of this because it was, after all, a very delicate matter!

After the surgery was completed, everyone was astounded at the woman's new beauty. She looked more beautiful than she ever did before! All her friends and relatives just ranted and raved at her youthful beauty!

She was alone with her husband one day and she wanted to thank him for what he did. She said, "Dear, I just want to thank you for everything you did for me! There is no way I could ever repay you!"

He replied, "Oh don't worry, Honey. I get plenty thanks enough every time your mother comes over and kisses you on the cheek!"

On the first day of college, the Dean addressed the students, pointing out some of the rules:

"The female dormitory will be out-of-bounds for all male students, and the male dormitory to the female students. Anybody caught breaking this rule will be fined $20 the first time."

He continued, "Anybody caught breaking this rule the second time will be fined $60. Being caught a third time will cost you a fine of $180. Are there any questions?"

At this point, a male student in the crowd inquired: "How much for a season pass?"

The contractor wrote on his clipboard, walked to the window, opened it and yelled out, "Green side up!" He then closed the window and continued following the woman to the next room. The woman looked confused, but proceeded with her tour. "In this room, I was thinking of an off blue," said the woman.

Again, the contractor wrote this down, went to the window, opened it and yelled out, "Green side up!"

This baffled the woman, but she was hesitant to say anything. In the next room, the woman said she would like it painted in a light rose color.

And once more, the contractor opened the window and yelled, "Green side up!"

Struck with curiosity, the woman mustered up the nerve to ask, "Why do you keep yelling 'Green side up' out my window every time I tell you the color I would like the room?"

The contractor replied, "Because I have a crew of blondes laying sod across the street."

Father O'Grady was saying his good-byes to the parishioners after his Sunday morning service as he always does when Mary Clancey came up to him in tears.

"What's bothering you so, dear?" inquired Father O'Grady.

"Oh, father, I've got terrible news," replied Mary.

"What is it, Mary?"

"Well, my husband, passed away last night, Father."

"Oh, Mary, that's terrible." he said, even though he knew her husband had not been easy to live with. "Tell me Mary, did he have any last requests?"

"Well, yes he did father," replied Mary.

"What did he ask, Mary?"

Mary replied, "He said, 'Please, Mary, put down the gun...'"

Ayoob on Firearms

IN TIME OF WAR: THE ISRAELI ANSWER TO TERRORISM

When war seems imminent, citizens think about protecting themselves. The war of the moment involves a declared enemy that has already used unconventional tactics to murder some three thousand innocent civilians within these borders. Closer to their own turf, they have a long and well-documented history of using terror tactics—mass shootings and suicide bombings—directed against innocent and unarmed women, children, and men rather than military targets.

We have seen the previews in Israel and Pakistan. We have seen them in captured Al-Qaeda training tapes. In one such tape, a carload of guerrillas is pulled over on what appears to be a four-lane highway. As a police officer approaches, the trunk lid pops open and he is sprayed with automatic weapons fire. One guerrilla walks up to the downed policeman's body and executes him with a head shot, then gets in the car and drives away with the rest of his band.

There are not a whole lot of four-lane highways in Afghanistan. It is clear that this is training for atrocities committed within the United States.

Early in the wake of September 11, 2001, the Israeli intelligence service Debka warned that Osama bin Laden had probably acquired at least four small, "dirty" nuclear devices, known as "suitcase nukes," from sources connected to the Russian Mafia. In a recent book, a researcher suggested that the Al-Qaeda arsenal of these devices might number more than 30. Given the history of other contraband brought into North America in ship containers and by other smuggling routes, there is ample reason to believe that nuclear bombs are already in place here, waiting to be triggered by the fanatics who control them.

The problem is clear. It's time to look at solutions.

When homeland security hits home

Since 9/11, a popular bumper sticker has circulated among gun owners. It reads, "The Second Amendment Is Homeland Security." This is more than just empty rhetoric.

In the last two years especially, street terrorist attacks in Israel have repeatedly been shortstopped by armed Israeli citizens. A terrorist opens fire at a crowded bus stop; a passing Israeli motorist draws his 9mm pistol and cuts him down. A late-arriving security man with an M-16 hoses the twitching terrorist just to make sure.

Another terrorist attempts to trigger an explosive device in a public place. An Israeli housewife draws her pistol and shoots him dead before he can detonate the bomb. The would-be martyr dies alone.

A third terrorist opens fire with an automatic weapon in an Israeli school. What could have been a mass murder on the scale of Columbine or greater is limited to a very short casualty list when Israeli parents and grandparents, who have provided volunteer armed security after receiving state training, open fire and kill him with their concealed pistols.

Note that in each of these episodes, it was an armed citizen who stopped

Massad Ayoob

the terror. Not a soldier. Not a security guard. Not a police officer. Just as wolves do not try to seize a lamb under the nose of the sheepdog, terrorists do not strike where armed protectors are known to be present. They scout the turf and select their victims more carefully than that.

Israel began the program of armed citizen guards in the schools after the Maalot massacre in the 1970s, when a large number of children were slain in a terrorist incident. The volunteer parents work in plain clothes, armed with concealed semi-automatic pistols, and are trained by Israel's home guard. It is significant that in the more than a quarter century between Maalot and the incident mentioned above when the citizen guards shot down the terrorist in the school in 2002, not a single child was murdered in an Israeli school!

With current terrorism alerts, readiness for many will include being constantly armed, if only with a small handgun like this light S&W Titanium .38.

The reason is that Israel wisely publicized the fact that the civilian volunteer guards, indistinguishable from the regular teaching and administrative staff, would be in place. It served as a tremendously effective deterrent. No Moslem fanatic who wants to go to Allah as a successful warrior who has slain many infidels visualizes himself making the trip after having been shot down by some geriatric with a gun before completing his mission. Any head trip as arrogant as that of a self-styled martyr cannot tolerate the thought of an ignominious death at the hands of an ordinary victim. It would be like a wolf picturing its own throat being torn out by a sheep: simply unthinkable, and therefore a natural deterrent.

Of course, the politically correct hand-wringers want nothing to do with this. Sadly, being helpless themselves, sheep tend to instinctively fear anything with canine teeth. Many of them cannot distinguish between the wolf and the sheepdog, and thus fear them both equally. We have seen this phenomenon in the knee-jerk reaction against arming pilots, for example, in the wake of 9/11. Never mind that it has worked remarkably well for the commercial air fleets of Israel and Russia in preventing hijackings. We have seen it in the adamant refusal of many to even think about armed protectors inside schools. Never mind that from Peru to the Philippines, as well as in Israel, institutional arming of school personnel or selected volunteers with appropriate training has put an end to murderous armed attacks on school grounds.

America's approach to its own fledgling Homeland Security program has been marked by some counterproductive decisions. I write this in Missouri, a couple of days after teaching a class to local police. I spent much of yesterday on the range, shooting with SWAT cops from the area.

Until 9/11, these officers had frequently trained at the Army's Fort Leonard Wood. They were grateful for the opportunity, and considered it some of the best Special Weapons and Tactics training they had ever received. "Your tax dollars in action" in a very effective way.

Alas, shortly after September 11, these services to local police were cut off and military facilities were dedicated strictly to training the military. Certainly, when America's response to Al-Qaeda ramped up, it was necessary to take maximum advantage of extant facilities for training designated personnel. At the same time, however, are not the domestic police the first line against terrorism in a homeland security program? It was law enforcement, not military, who captured those Al-Qaeda operatives who were arrested in the United States and are now in custody. It was an Oklahoma state trooper, not SEAL Team Six or Delta Force, who captured the most infamous of homegrown terrorists, Timothy McVeigh, after the bombing of the Federal building in Oklahoma City.

Shutting off US Government training to the cops, the front-line troops in the Homeland Security effort, is not a good thing. It also gives you an idea where Federal support for self-reliant American citizens stands on the current list of official priorities.

The 1911 .45 automatic remains the quintessential American combat handgun. This one is the excellent, affordable Kimber Custom II.

"By their nature": tools for the task

For decades, Israeli citizens in what Yanks would call "tough neighborhoods"—communes where there had been heavy terrorist activity—were allowed to check out Government-owned Uzi submachineguns. Are we going to see that in the United States? Not bloody likely. But, don't worry about it. You probably aren't going to need an Uzi.

The overwhelming majority of terrorist incidents in Israel that have been shortstopped by armed citizens have involved one particular type of defensive firearm: the 9mm semiautomatic pistol, usually with a high capacity magazine design. By its nature, the handgun is portable. It can always be with you when danger threatens without warning, and remember, by their nature terrorists strike without warning at times and in places where they know the attack will not be expected. By its nature, the handgun is concealable and invisible until deployed. Remember that by their nature, terrorists scope out their battleground before they initiate violence there, and make a point of avoiding attack sites that are conspicuously well-defended. It's that "wolf and sheepdog" thing again.

Fortunately, the last 15 years have seen a dramatic increase in the number of jurisdictions in which law-abiding private citizens in the United States can obtain a permit to carry a loaded and concealed handgun in public. The trend continues, with Missouri and some other states actively fielding legislation this year that would grant them the privilege. Given the profile of the threat, the timing is excellent.

A defensive firearm is a special purpose tool, and the selection of the tool must always be tailored to the task. The terrorists under discussion here seek target rich environments. Crowded schools. Crowded marketplaces. Crowded restaurants and nightclubs. This means that the private citizen engaging one in defense of himself and others will have a very narrow "firing corridor" through which the rescuing gunfire will have to be delivered without harming any of the many innocent bystanders who will predictably be at the scene.

Anyone carrying a firearm that might remotely be used for this purpose should spend plenty of time training in what is often

In use by counter-terrorist groups world wide, the Glock 17 holds 18 rounds of 9mm in pre-ban magazines. Author strongly recommends high speed hollow point ammo if 9mm is chosen.

called "surgical" shooting. The sights on the pistol should be true, that is, the gun should be perfectly sighted in to deliver the bullet's point of impact exactly to the handgun's point of aim.

We are talking about hitting very small body parts to instantly shut off the lethal danger which the target organism poses to a large group of innocent humans. A shot to the chest may not be enough. A man shot through the lung can stay up and running for a considerable period of time. If the brain is fully oxygenated, even a man whose cardiac function has been completely shut off by a bullet through the heart (and not every gunshot wound of the heart will shut that organ down completely) can continue purposeful, violent activity for as much as 14 or 15 seconds.

A shot to the upper central nervous system is more certain to stop violent activity immediately, but is also much more difficult to deliver. The spinal cord is only about as thick as its owner's little finger, and is encased in a serpentine column of bone. Even a shot to the brain is not 100% guaranteed to instantly shut off the action. The only certain "instant one shot stop" is a hit to the stem area of the brain, which destroys the medulla oblongata or pons. This is in line with the ears when aimed at from

More cops are carrying guns off duty than ever with current terrorism alerts. Here, author has been practicing "surgical" brain shots with a Kimber .45.

"Old-fashioned" service revolvers have the match-grade accuracy for surgical rescue shooting in capable hands. This is S&W's classic Combat Masterpiece .38 Special, with Remington +P 125 grain hollow points in a Safariland speedloader.

the side, and with the base of the skull when the shot must be fired from behind. The external anatomic landmark for a frontal shot will vary depending upon the position of the head.

If the head is erect in the normal posture, the deep brain target will lie directly behind the nose. If the head is forward in an aggressive posture, the level of the eye sockets will be in line with the primal brain target that must be hit. If the head is thrown back as in a triumphant shout, aiming through the mouth will guide the bullet to the brain stem.

The 9mm pistol has become virtually standard among civilians in Israel. However, that does not make it the best choice. Anecdotal reports of shootings of terrorists there by citizens and by police and soldiers (who have also standardized on the 9mm handgun) frequently show the bad guy to take many hits before he goes down. This is why the high capacity gun has become the 9mm of choice there. The most common brands are the old classic Browning, the Beretta, the Glock, and the Jericho (an Israeli-made clone of the Czech CZ75 design). One cannot help but notice a corollary fact: the high performance hollow point bullets that brought the 9mm Luger cartridge up off its knees and made it an acceptable fighting round are thin on the ground in Israel. Many citizens and police are likely to carry military style full metal jacket ("ball") ammunition. This stuff tends to just punch through the body, making little dimpled holes like ice-pick wounds and endangering those behind the target with exiting bullets.

Recent events in Afghanistan have shown the relative impotence of 9mm ball compared to the same style of .45 caliber ammunition that has been in historical evidence since before WWI. GIs in Afghanistan report that Al-Qaeda fighters are absorbing multiple 9mm ball rounds from the issue Berettas before going down, but tend to drop to one or two solid hits with .45 ball fired from the old 1911 style guns still in use by Delta Force.

The medium-caliber handgun cartridge such as the 9mm (.355" bullet diameter) or the .38 Special (.357" bullet diameter) requires an expanding bullet to best do its job of stopping human assault, while the .45 (.452" bullet diameter) has a long history of shutting off attacks with ball type ammo. Take a quick look at three US shootouts reported in the *Armed Citizen* column of the National Rifle Association's new magazine, *Women's Outlook*.

Case One: Finding a home invader in the bedroom of his 18-month-old son, Ronald Dixon "pulled a 9mm handgun out of his closet and confronted the stranger in the child's room. When the interloper advanced on him, Dixon fired his gun, hitting the man twice. The intruder, later identified by police as Ivan Thompson, then fell down the stairs and ran out of the house, but collapsed outside. According to police, Thompson has a record of 19 arrests, mostly for burglary. He was critically wounded in the chest and groin." (*New York Daily News*, 12/15/02.)

Case Two: US Marine Corps Sgt. James Lowery was at the drive-in window of a McDonalds in Gardendale, Alabama, while home on leave. "That's when a man with a .38-cal. handgun ordered him out of his customized Chevy suburban. Lowery complied and got out of his SUV, but the man then shot the Marine in the face. Lowery reached back into his vehicle, drew a .45-cal. pistol and shot his assailant several times. The robber, Thaddeus Antone, was pronounced dead at the scene. Lowery was listed in fair condition at a local hospital." (*Birmingham News*, 12/19/02.)

Case Three: Medgar Flowers was home alone with his wife when two armed home invaders entered shooting. Flowers struggled with one of them and finally the homeowner got close enough to the coffee table where he kept his own 9mm automatic. "Flowers was able to retrieve his

In every caliber, author recommends hollow point bullets for safety to bystanders.

gun and fired several times at the intruder. 'I didn't even know if I had hit him,' he said. 'There was no blood, and he never fell. It was like I hadn't shot him.' The struggle ended when Flowers' tormentor stumbled out of the house and died a short time later. The second gunman was not found." (*Baton Rouge Morning Advocate*, 01/04/03.)

Note that the Marine's .45 decisively ended the encounter in his favor. Note that the man shot in the face with a .38 responded by killing the man who shot him, and that two criminals shot with 9mms were able to perform considerable physical activity before collapsing of their wounds. Cowardly predators surprised at being shot in self-defense, they chose flight instead of fight. A committed, fanatical terrorist would be more likely to keep fighting and shoot innocent victims or trigger an explosive device before collapsing.

In a scenario where terrorism has struck the United States hard and ammunition is no longer readily available in stores, inexpensive "ball" ammunition, stocked in quantity for customers who practice with it extensively, will be the last to disappear from the shelves. Ball ammo in a .45 will probably get the job done; ball ammo in a .38 or 9mm often will not.

In any case, all such handguns should be loaded with expanding-bullet hollowpoint ammunition that is designed to stay in the body of the offender and not exit to strike an innocent bystander hidden from view behind him. While exotic high speed, low bullet weight, frangible projectiles can be had, they are too expensive to practice with, they often do not hit to point of aim, and quality control and accuracy are iffy with some brands.

Even a small .38 Special revolver is better than nothing when lethal danger threatens. Snub-nosed revolvers are harder to shoot than larger guns. With a full size service revolver, surgical accuracy is absolutely possible in trained and confident hands. With a small frame snub-nose, the shooter will often have to get closer to make an accurate precision shot. However, in some of our more tropical climates, it's carry a very small gun or carry nothing at all.

Bottom line

Our government has sent us a very clear message: Be Prepared. There is every reason to believe that more terrorist activity will take place in the American homeland. No, a pistol is no defense against a nuclear device that detonates downtown. But looking to the Israeli model tells us that the same monsters they have fought will be fighting us the same way.

Santayana was right. "Those who ignore history are doomed to repeat it." Δ

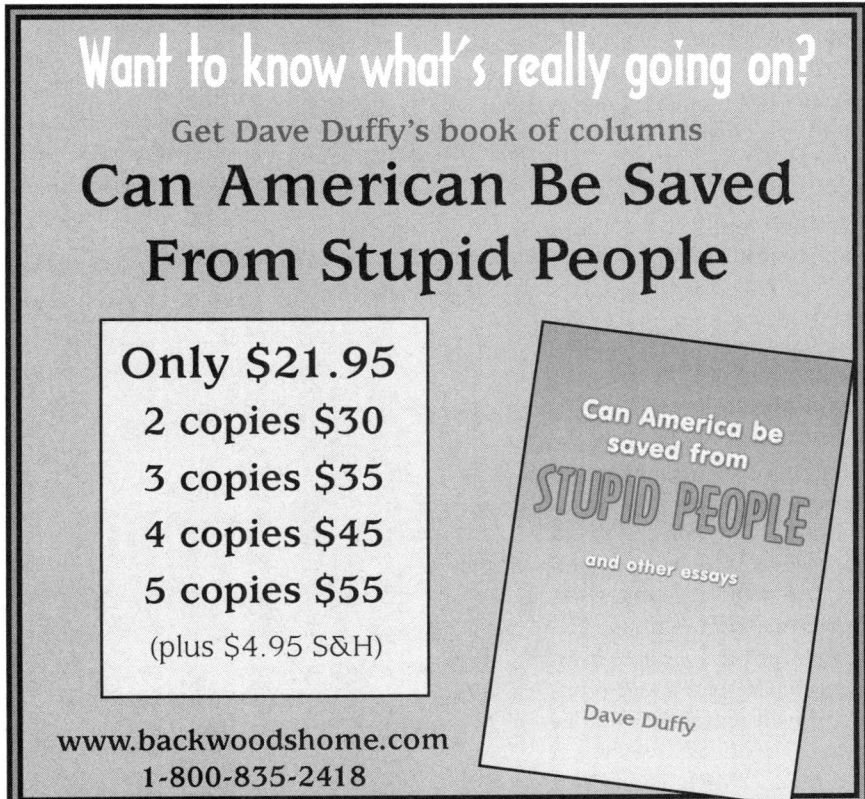

Traditional trail foods— transportable calories

By Brad Rohdenburg

Napoleon said that an army marches on its stomach. Frederick the Great defined an army as a group of men who demanded daily feeding. One can imagine the nutritional problems of a large group on the move. Armies through the ages have tried everything from bottling snails to bringing along herds of livestock. It's difficult to keep mess kits and cooking equipment adequately clean under rugged field conditions, so illnesses were rampant. In most campaigns, more troops have been lost to sickness than to the enemy. Sometimes it was impossible to deliver food to the front line troops who needed it most. Hunger has ended many ambitions. The search for transportable calories, the "research and product development" of earlier armies, has finally resulted in the MRE. "MRE" stands for "Meal, Ready to Eat." In accordance with the Office of the Surgeon General's nutritional requirements as identified in Army Regulation 4025, Nutritional Standards for Operational Rations, they will survive a 100 foot drop from a helicopter with no parachute, endure inclement weather and survive temperature extremes from minus 60 degrees Fahrenheit to 120 degrees Fahrenheit and have a minimum shelf life of three years at 80 degrees F and last for six months at 100 degrees F. Now people on the move can have a meal on demand by carrying it with them. Mess kits and pots and pans have been eliminated. MREs set the current standard for

Eating pemmican on the mountain

traveling rations, but they aren't magic. Those who use them are encumbered and inconvenienced by the weight and bulk of plastic utensils, condiments, heaters and a remarkable amount of packaging. Having to cook them to make them appealing wastes time. (I know, they're designed to be eaten cold if necessary. Have a few dozen that way and then come back and tell me about it.) And if you're buying your own MREs rather than having them issued by Uncle Sam, they're prohibitively expensive.

If you have a need for trail food—storable, transportable, convenient, affordable and palatable calories—maybe we can learn something from the old ways. Jerky, pemmican, hardtack, and parched corn are traditional travel rations that have passed the test of time. They are products that have been produced, relied on, and refined for centuries, even millennia. Just a touch of modern technology and convenience makes them even better today.

Jerky, pemmican, hardtack, and parched corn are ways to put game, livestock, wild berries, and garden produce by in times of plenty. Easily made, transported, and stored, they became frontier staples for travelers, hunters, and warriors. They are still excellent trail foods and emergency rations.

I take jerky, pemmican, hardtack, and parched corn along on wilderness trips. Supplemented by some tea, salt, and rice and whatever I can catch or gather, I can exist pretty comfortably and feel healthy doing it. Even if I take more modern foods along as well, the historical perspective is fun. They're comforting to have in reserve, too, in case the bush plane doesn't show up on time, or the wind keeps your canoe ashore for a couple extra days. (Their only drawback as emergency

The Fourteenth Year

Parched corn is easy to make, stores well, and makes a great trail food.

rations is that I'm tempted to eat them before I'm truly hungry).

Jerky

Jerky is said to keep for years, but it's so good that around my house it's shelf life is usually measured in minutes. Here's my favorite recipe:

> 1½ lbs. very lean ground meat—
> (Any meat that isn't fatty, including fish and birds. Avoid pork or bear.)
> ¼ cup soy
> ¼ cup Worcestershire sauce
> 1 tsp. Liquid Smoke
> ½ tsp. garlic powder
> 1 tsp. onion powder
> 1 tsp. black pepper

Combine all the marinade ingredients and pour over the meat. Refrigerate until the meat absorbs the solution. (Chilled meat is also firmer and easier to work with.) Roll the ground meat out and cut into strips about ¼-inch thick and an inch or two wide. The strips can then be dried either on plastic screens or in a food dehydrator. Our forebears often simply draped strips of meat over branches; they built a cool, smoky fire underneath to keep away flies if necessary.

Pemmican

At its simplest, pemmican is only powdered jerky bound together with melted fat. It tastes far better than it sounds. When you're working hard outdoors, especially in the cold, listen to your body. Pemmican will satisfy your craving for calories in ways that a candy bar won't. It's said to provide every essential but vitamin C. The concept of pemmican was borrowed from the American Indians. It begins with lean meat, traditionally of bison, moose, elk, or deer. It was dried over a fire or in the sun and wind. The dried meat was ground and shredded between stones. Sometimes ground dried berries, nuts, or honey were added. Finally, melted fat and/or bone marrow grease were mixed in. Pemmican could be eaten as is, or made into a soup or stew. When available, mint leaves or wild onions could be added for flavor.

The Hudson's Bay Company bought pemmican from the Indians and later the Metis as the staple food of their fur brigades and established a standard of quality. It paid a premium for "sweet pemmican" made solely from the best of lean meats—preferably from bison cows and young bulls—and only bone marrow grease. Pemmican production became the most important industry on the high plains next to the fur trade.

Pemmican was originally stored in the stomach or intestines of animals. Indians shaped it into small round cakes. The Hudson's Bay Company specified that it be stored in 45-kg. green bison skin bags called "parfleches," sealed with tallow. As the parfleches dried they shrank, in effect vacuum-sealing themselves. They would keep for years. During the fur trade, it was reckoned that pemmican was nutritionally worth four times its weight in meat. Hudson's Bay Company pemmican consisted of 50% dried meat and 50% fat/marrow.

"Modern" pemmican

> Very dry jerky. Use deer, moose, caribou, or beef (not pork or bear).
> Fresh beef suet. (the raw fat from around the kidneys and loins)
> Any seedless dried fruit not preserved with sulfites (optional)

Cut the suet into chunks and render (melt) it over low heat, until it becomes a rich golden-brown liquid. Continue to heat until all moisture is removed. It's important to remove all water from the fat to prevent it from going rancid. Strain it and throw away the solids. Allow it to cool—it will turn white. This is tallow. Rendering twice will make the tallow harder and give it better keeping qualities. Tallow, when cooled, resembles candle wax in color and consistency. In fact, if you have any left over, it can be made into candles. Lewis and Clark took cotton wicking along with them for that purpose, and wrote their journals by the smokey light of tallow candles. Add some beeswax or paraffin to make them burn better.

In a blender, grind the dried meat to a powder. Chop or grind the dried fruits and mix them with the dried meat powder. (Many who have acquired the taste for pemmican, myself included, prefer it without any fruit.)

Heat the tallow again. Make sure it is as hot as it can get without smoking. (Smoking means burning.) Pour the tallow into the dried meat mixture, adding **just enough** to moisten the particles. If it's too cool you will have to use a lot of it to stick the mixture together and the pemmican will be too rich and fatty. At this point, if the tallow is cooling down too quickly to allow it to soak in properly, you can microwave the whole mixture to warm it up.

Form the warm pemmican into blocks or bars or patties. Allow them to cool and wrap in waxed paper or store in plastic bags.

"Peanut butter" pemmican

If you can't quite bring yourself to eat the real thing yet, try this substitute:

| 1 part jerky
| 1 part peanuts or pecans, unroasted
| 1 part raisins
| 1 part any seedless dried fruit(s) not preserved with sulfites—apples, peaches, blueberries, etc.
| Peanut butter and honey, in a two-to-one ratio
| Cayenne pepper, to taste (optional, but contrasts nicely with the sweet fruits and honey.)

Powder the jerky in a blender. Add fruit and nuts. Microwave honey and peanut butter to soften them, then blend them into the mixture. (Use less than you think you'll need, just enough to bind everything together. If you get it wrong, it's easier to add more peanut butter and honey than to add more of everything else.) Add cayenne pepper, working it in thoroughly. Store in plastic bags.

Hardtack

Essentially a very hard cracker, hardtack was the standard traveling fare for soldiers, sailors, and pioneers up through WWI. Originally made from only salt, flour, and a little water, it was universally despised. It was traditionally either dipped in coffee, or soaked in hot water and then fried in bacon drippings. This updated version is far more healthy and tasty, and just as easy to store and transport.

| 2 cups fresh whole wheat flour (Best if you grind it yourself—wheat berries lose nutritional value rapidly once ground.)
| 2 cups fresh corn meal (Again, best if you grind it yourself right before baking.)
| ½ cup wheat germ
| ½ cup rolled oats
| 1 Tbsp. brown sugar
| 1 Tbsp. salt
| 1¾ cups water

Mix dry ingredients thoroughly. Add water. Knead until moistened but not sticky. Roll ¼ inch thick. Cut into 3-inch squares or rounds. Place on ungreased cookie sheets. Score with a knife to facilitate breaking later. Bake at 350 degrees for 30 minutes. Can be stored indefinitely in an airtight container.

Parched corn

Corn was the staple grain on the American frontier for pioneers and Indians alike, as it was (and is) relatively easy to grow, harvest, and process without machinery. There are four basic types: flour, dent, flint, and sweet. All may be dried on the cob, and may then be stored indefinitely. If you want to go modern, then just buy frozen whole kernel corn at the grocery store and dehydrate it.

Parching corn makes these hard kernels softer for your teeth and much more digestible. It's a lightweight, high energy food that was carried by Indian warriors and hunters. It was also considered a treat by pioneer children. It can be eaten as is, or ground and added to soups and stews. You'll be surprised at how it revitalizes you.

Heat a small amount of butter or lard or oil in a skillet on low. Wipe the skillet with a paper towel so that only a thin coat remains—just enough to prevent the corn from sticking. Pour in enough dry kernels to almost cover the bottom of the pan. Stir constantly to prevent burning. The kernels are done when they swell and turn light to medium brown and begin to pop. It takes from about one to five minutes. Dump the corn out onto a plate lined with a paper towel to soak up any remaining oil or grease, then re-oil your skillet and do some more. Enough for a day will fit in a plastic bag in your pocket.

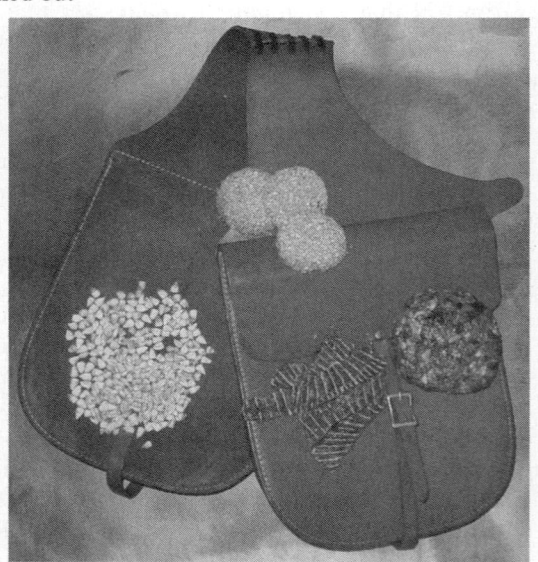

Four easy to make, easy to carry, and energy-packed trails foods, clockwise from left: parched corn, hardtack, pemmican, and jerky.

On your next outing, try traveling light. Jerky, pemmican, hardtack, and parched corn will keep you going all day, without utensils to clean, or trash to dispose of, or the need to stop and cook. For dinner, pemmican stewed with whatever greens or tubers you've foraged, thickened with parched corn and served with hardtack will give you a literal taste of days gone by. ∆

The home citrus orchard

By Anita Evangelista

It may seem like an impossible dream if you live outside of southern Florida, California, or Texas, but you can grow a home "backyard" orchard of oranges, lemons, limes, grapefruit, and exotic citrus even in the coldest climates. These attractive small trees provide a bounty of luscious fresh fruits, beautiful and intensely fragrant flowers, and lush glossy foliage. Best of all, growing these potted charmers is as easy as raising any houseplant.

I've grown various types of potted citrus trees for over 18 years, starting with a tiny twig of a lemon that had only five leaves on it. Today, that little tree has moved from California to Missouri, died back to the roots two times (when it was accidentally left out in the snow), and has produced in excess of 200 normal-sized lemons. We've had it so long, it seems like a member of the family. Over the years, we have added oranges, limes, kumquats, "Mandarinquats," and a little satsuma (a fragrant Japanese mandarin). The nice thing about citrus trees is that no matter which variety you choose, they have the same straightforward growth and care requirements. If you have ever raised a persnickety houseplant, you will be pleasantly surprised at how easy-going and tolerant citrus can be. The bounty, of course, is that they also provide you with fresh fruit loaded with vitamin-C during the deepest, darkest part of the winter.

Know your trees

Citrus trees are native to some of the world's warmest and most-pleasant climates, subtropical and tropical India and China. The fruit has been domesticated for thousands of years, and plantings have been made all over the warmer parts of the world, including Spain, Portugal, Brazil, the Caribbean, the Mediterranean, and Asia. It is grown as a houseplant on the rest of the globe. Even nurseries in England's non-tropical climate offer a wide assortment of varieties.

The familiar sweet orange is the most widely grown species of citrus. It was brought to the New World by Columbus in 1493, and planted for the first time in Hispaniola. By 1565, Spanish explorers had established orange orchards in Florida.

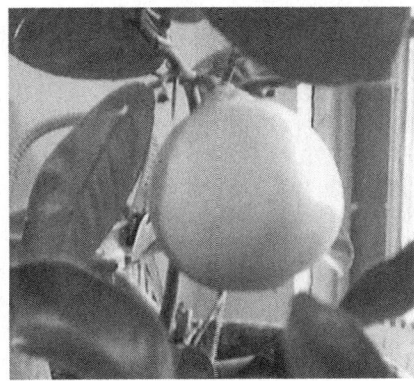

One of two yellow-fleshed grapefruit on a tiny 2-branch tree.

The most commonly-planted backyard variety of orange is the Valencia, a "juice-type" that may have a few seeds. The Navel orange, a seedless type that occurred as a "sport" or natural mutation, is also readily available as a potted plant. Navels are excellent for fresh eating and for juicing, although the juice can become bitter several hours after being squeezed. "Blood" oranges have bright red flesh and a tangy, sprightly flavor. Oranges grown in the constant warmth of a modern home will be thin-skinned and yellowish, while those that are exposed to cooler temperatures out-

Thin skinned Meyer lemons soaking up the sun in a south-facing window.

doors into the 40's, will form a thicker skin and brighter orange color. Blood oranges need cooler weather to develop their deep red flesh coloration. If kept in warmer conditions, the flesh may be merely speckled with red. Fruit matures from November to March and can be picked when they have developed some orange coloration, but will hold on the tree for months. Valencia fruit will "regreen" after winter is over, and can hold on the tree until early summer. Some orange varieties drop their fruit when they have over-ripened. Most potted oranges (and many other citrus varieties) are grafted onto "sour orange" rootstock, the hardiest type.

Lemons are the most productive of the planter-grown citrus. Some varieties grow extra-large on small bush-like trees, others produce flowers and fruit simultaneously. Eureka lemons are the familiar supermarket type, while Meyers are larger and have thinner skins. Lemons hold fairly well on the tree, and ripen over a long enough period of time that you can have fresh fruit through most of the spring and early summer for those ice teas and meringue pies.

Limes are commonly found in two varieties: "Key" (or "Mexican") and "Persian." Key limes are the ones made famous by the summer Key lime pie. The limes are small 1" fruit with an intense limey flavor and powerful aroma. They are picked while still green, although when they ripen to yellow, they still retain the wonderful lime taste and scent. Persian limes are shaped like small, flattened oranges. The flavor is less intense and somewhat smoother than Key limes, and they produce more juice than Keys for drinks or marinades. Like Key limes, they are used when still green, but will ripen through fall and winter to a pretty orange shade, though they still taste like mellow limes.

Grapefruit can be found as yellow-fleshed or red-fleshed varieties. Yellow-fleshed have a stronger, more bitter flavor and more juice, while the red-fleshed types are mildly sweeter and less acidic. Fruit grow very large, even on tiny spindly trees, and branches may need to be propped up to prevent cracking. Ripening is in fall through early spring.

Kumquats and their variants such as "Mandarinquats" are fast-growing highly productive trees. The fruit is tiny, about 1" across and bright orange colored. The flesh is also orange. Each fruit will have several seeds. Interestingly, kumquats have a sweet, tangy skin and somewhat sharp and bitter flavored flesh. The best way to enjoy these unusual fruits is directly off the tree. Just pop one in your mouth for an intense and juicy treat! These trees are able to bear almost year-around, and will often be covered with small, fragrant blossoms and fruit at the same time. It's not unusual for our 4' tall tree to have over 100 fruits ripening on it.

Mandarins are similar to oranges in coloration, and the fruit "sections" and peels easily. Supermarkets carry these 2", flattened specialty fruit around winter holidays, and offer them as "Clementines." Aside from their fresh-eating qualities, Mandarins can be used as an unusual decoration. Cut the fruit in half at the equator and remove the sections carefully so that the central white pith is left behind. Gently apply a few drops of cooking oil to the inside of the peel and smooth up along the pith. The pith can then be lit like a candle wick and will burn slowly due to the oil, releasing a gentle fruity scent. Mandarins ripen in the fall and winter months. They are more cold sensitive than oranges.

Growth and care

Potted citrus typically won't grow more than four or five feet high, though most remain less than 24" tall. Kumquats form a straight, upright trunk, while oranges, lemons, and grapefruit tend to be bushy, and a single plant can spread three feet wide in a lush canopy of glossy leaves. Plants can come to you bareroot, in small planters, or in standard planters. Most of my trees are in 5-gallon black plastic planters. This seems to be a good size that is large enough for healthy roots, and small enough to be moved around when needed. Larger pots, 7-10-gallon size, will allow your trees to grow a little bigger, but might make moving the plants a real ordeal.

Citrus trees require lots of sunlight. During the warm months when there is no risk of frost, trees can be moved to the outdoors on the south side of your home. They will soak up the sun, and after the dark indoor months, they will burst forth with sudden new growth. In the cold months, the trees will do well in a greenhouse, in a south-facing window, or under a "grow lamp." Your trees will do better if you prepare them for the trip indoors by shading them during part

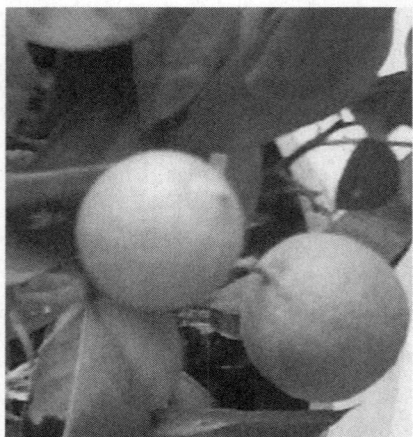

Persian limes ripen to a bright orange shade.

of the day in the autumn. The sudden change from outdoors to indoors may cause some leaf-drop. Typical indoor temperatures are fine for these trees during the winter. In the early spring, the trees appreciate being gradually hardened off to the outside weather by daily trips outdoors during the daylight hours. Bring them in at night if there is a chance of frost.

All citrus are frost-sensitive to some degree. Leaves and stems can tolerate temperatures into the high 20s, but fruit will be damaged by freezing. The potted lemon tree that we forgot out in the snow died all the way back to the soil surface. We thought it was a goner! We trimmed the dead-looking plant back to the central stem, and just waited. Lo and behold, it started to grow again two months later in the spring. Now, 10 years later, it has 14 fat lemons ripening on its healthy branches.

Citrus trees don't require any pruning, except perhaps for a little shaping and trimming of any dead or cold-killed wood. The natural form is compact and attractive. It is not necessary to mulch container-grown trees and might actually contribute to "foot rot," a type of root rot that eventually kills trees. These plants all prefer a planting mix of equal parts sand, peat, and bark (or perlite/vermiculite). This forms a firm but loose planting medium that will permit good drainage. Drainage holes of the container should be covered with screen mesh to prevent loss of the medium, then coarse gravel laid over the screen. The planting medium should then be placed in the pot to about one fourth the depth of the pot followed by the tree. Trim any crowded roots. Fill the pot with medium to about 2" from the pot rim, making sure any stem graft is above the soil level. Water thoroughly by filling the pot to the rim once a week, and let the planting surface dry between waterings. Snap off any twigs that grow from beneath the graft.

Citrus trees need good fertilizer. That is one of my two "secrets" to container-growing these trees. Different sources will give varying instructions on what to feed your potted trees. The most common is "fertilize with fruit tree food." While the plants will grow with an average fertilizer such as a 10-10-10 product, they don't seem to glow with good health under that diet. Citrus prefer a high-nitrogen diet, such as a 3-1-1 formulation. My first "secret" is simple—a bag of Bandini Citrus Food which I guard like a hoard of gold. This is a formulation of 12-8-4 fertilizer plus minor nutrients, and really does make a difference in the tree's growth and productivity. A 10-pound bag costs about $7, and I still have half of my jealously-protected supply left. I fertilize on the first day of every month, giving larger trees three tablespoons of the dry pelleted fertilizer, and smaller ones a single tablespoon. I have never tried to grow them by "organic" methods, but if I were going to experiment, I'd used blood meal or fish meal for the nitrogen component, plus bone meal and potash as the basic formula.

It's not unusual for me to meet someone who has grown a citrus tree for many years that flowers beautifully, but bears no fruit. Sometimes, it will be a tree that was grown from a seed. My second "secret," which answers this and ensures my citrus trees all produce fruit, is simple but often overlooked: cross-fertilization of the flowers. A single tree may be self-infertile, that is, unable to pollinate its own flowers. Others may be fully self-fertile, but rely on insects to carry the pollen from flower to flower. With two citrus trees, preferably of different varieties that flower at the same time, placed outdoors so bees can work on them, you can guarantee that good pollination has taken place. If the weather doesn't support pollinating insects when the flowers are blooming, you can be the pollinator. Just dust flowers gently with a soft craft paintbrush or cotton swab, first on one tree, then on the other. Your pollination rate and fruit formation will be even more assured if you have several different varieties of citrus trees.

Getting seed-grown trees to bear fruit may be an entirely different problem. It can take up to 15 years for a tree to become mature enough to fruit. Furthermore, even if the original seed came from a known variety (such as a Valencia orange), there is no guarantee that both of its parents were of the same type. It could be a first-generation hybrid of some kind. These trees can still be very attractive and produce fragrant flowers, but may never be able to give you fruit.

Insect pests are rarely a problem in backyard citrus grown outside of the main citrus-producing states (Florida, California, Arizona, and Texas). We've had occasional minor damage from munching grasshoppers, and the Key lime seems susceptible to a red-scale insect. Ants occasionally build nests in the pots during the summer months. Otherwise, the plants grow without interference from the usual troublemakers.

Tree sources

Citrus trees for home gardeners are much more common than they were two decades ago when I ordered my little twig lemon from a seed catalog. Many seed catalogs now carry citrus in 4" pots for $5 each or less, advertised in the "house plants" section. These are baby trees, and it will take them 3 years or longer to be able to begin fruit production.

Major department stores, including Wal-Mart and K-Mart carry citrus trees seasonally. Typically these run $4 each in 4-6" pots. In the summer and autumn, our local Lowe's had several varieties of citrus (including satsuma, blood orange, kumquats, and lemons) in 8" pots for $10 each.

There are on-line sources if you are anxious to begin growing these attractive and fragrant plants, located in the major citrus-producing states. Prices vary from $16 per 1-gallon tree (plus $8 shipping) to $44 (plus $15 shipping), depending on size and variety. Citrus cannot be shipped INTO Arizona, California, Florida, or Texas, even from other citrus-growing states, but can be shipped OUT of each of them.

Other websites can be accessed by keying "citrus trees" into your search engine. Both Florida and Texas agricultural agencies maintain extensive on-line information about growing citrus in their areas and are good sources for detailed data about these productive and pretty plants. ∆

Online nurseries

- Garden of Delights, 14560 SW 14th St., Davie, FL 33325. Many varieties. http://www.gardenofdelights.com
- Four Winds Growers, California. No street-mail address on the website, but many nice citrus pictures. http://fourwindsgrowers.com
- James F. McCann, Inc, PO Box 561652, Orland, FL 32856. Family operation. http://mccanninc.home.mindspring.com

Companion planting

By Beverly Mettot

Companion planting is nothing new, and yet in recent years it has made an extraordinary comeback, not only in fooling those pesky pests who thrive on fruits and vegetables in the vast majority of home gardens, but also in providing healthier, tastier foods.

The welter of odors, colors, and textures of heavily interplanted plant companions can confuse, deter, and even stop pests altogether. But plant companion methods can also confuse the home gardener in deciding which plants go where, with which other plants, and for what reason. Equally confusing are the ideal planting crops: why certain plants belong while others don't, which plants fool even the most persistent of pests, and which ones are better left out of the garden.

There are virtually hundreds of examples of plant companions recorded in garden lore, and modern research substantiates their effectiveness. For instance strawberries, cabbage, and tomatoes can be planted in and around sage to benefit one another in the garden. But plant cucumbers with that same sage and you'll have a disaster on your hands.

While everyone loves the idea of seed turning to vegetable, things can (and do) go wrong during the growing season, namely pests. As Jack Kramer pointed out in *The Natural Way To Pest-Free Gardening,* "Insects are a highly trained, well-ordered society. So well ordered they can quickly destroy valuable plants in the garden."

That's where companion planting comes in. By intermixing certain aromatic herbs, or pungent French marigolds, or any number of beneficial plants and flowers, the home gardener finds a natural deterrent which helps repel insects and better protects his crop.

The need for companion plants

I began experimenting with this method four years ago when I encountered my first tomato hornworm, and I'll be the first to attest that the combination of sweet basil and French marigolds really do keep these pesky little (or not so little) caterpillars at bay.

Much of today's companion planting is based on the combination of both fact and folklore, but scientists have enough evidence to convince them of the following:

• Plants with strong odors do confuse, deter, and oftentimes stop certain pests.

The interplanting of vegetables

The following table should act as a guide to help you eliminate certain problems in your garden.

Plant	Companion	Benefit
Anise	Coriander	Aids the growth and flavor of Anise.
Asparagus	Parsley or basil	Controls Asparagus beetles.
Basil, Sweet	throughout garden	Enhances the flavor and growth of everything around it.
Carrots	Sage	Deters carrot (rust) flies.
Chamomile	throughout garden	Brings overall health to the garden. Attracts good insects.
Chervil	Radishes	One plant requires heavy nutrients while the other requires very little.
Chives	Carrots, grapes, roses, and tomatoes	Curb Japanese Beetles, and black spot.
Corn	Snap beans or soybeans	Enhances growth of corn.
Cosmos	throughout garden	Bad insects won't come near it, but it will attract pollinating wasps.
French Marigolds	throughout garden	Strong odor confuses pests looking for their favorite plant.
Garlic	throughout garden	Repels aphids and beetles.
Mustard	Beans	One plant requires heavy nutrients while the other requires very little.
Mints	Cabbage, strawberries	Deters aphids and other aphid pests, as well as ants who invade strawberries.
Nasturtiums	throughout garden	Repels aphids and white flies.
Onions	Carrots	The two combined help to control rust flies and some nematodes.
Peanuts	Corn	Increases yields of both crops.
Peas	Lettuce, spinach, and Chinese cabbage	Benefit from the shade and wind protection peas provide.
Potatoes	Horseradish and/or tansy	Plant plenty for maximum benefits in attempt to ward off Colorado Potato Beetles.
Radishes	Squash, cucumbers, and/or Carrots	Great deterrent against Cucumber Beetles and Rust flies. Also eliminates diseases spread by these plants.
Rue	throughout garden	Disagreeable taste and bad odor sends even persistent pests on their way.
Sage	Strawberries, Cabbage, and/or Tomatoes	Deters unwanted pests and benefits each other in garden.
Savory	throughout garden	Ideal planting crop. Attracts good insects.
Spinach	Beans or tomatoes	Benefits from the shade both plants provide.
Strawberries	Borage or sage	Enhances flavor of fruit and strengthens plant's resistance to insects and diseases.
Tansy	Cabbage and/or potatoes	Deters Cutworms, Cabbage Worms, and Colorado Potato Beetles.
Thyme	Tomatoes and/or cabbage	All three together control Flea Beetles, Cabbage Maggot, White Cabbage Butterflies, Colorado Potato Beetles, and imported Cabbage Worms.

• Certain plants hide other certain plants we don't want detected.

• Certain plants, and especially herbs, are considered nursery plants for the good insects providing shelter, nectar, pollen, and even dark, cool moist spots for lacewings, lady beetles, parasitic flies, and wasps.

• Certain plants serve as a "trap" crop, which pushes insects away from other essential plants (rue's bad odor and disagreeable taste will keep even the most persistent of pests away).

• Certain plants create habitats which attract more beneficial insects (such as lady beetles, praying mantis, and ambush bugs).

Ideal planting crops are plants whose odors ward off unwanted insects. French marigolds are the best example. Not only does its strong odor literally confuse pests looking for their favorite plants, but their roots give off a substance which repels nematodes. The more you have planted in the garden, the better its effectiveness.

Among the most popular of repellent plants are garlic and chives because of their powerful ability to repel aphids and beetles. Similarly, savory,

THE DON'TS OF COMPANION PLANTING

Don't plant French marigolds with beans.
Don't plant tansy with collards.
Don't plant cucumbers with sage.
Don't plant chrysanthemums with lettuce.
Don't plant wormwood with peas or beans (wormwood in other areas of the garden will deter slugs).
Don't plant peppers with tomatoes, potatoes, eggplant, or where peppers were planted in the last three years.
Don't plant tomatoes with fennel or potatoes.
Don't plant families that are closely related, and attract the same pests.
Don't plant allelopathic plants too close to your garden.

chamomile, and thyme are ideal planting crops. These three herbs will attract more beneficial insects than any bright, pretty flower will. So when you're planning your summer garden, include plenty of each.

Virtually all herbs benefit the garden in some way, whether to attract good insects, enhance the flavor of nearby plants, or to confuse those insects we simply don't want around.

Certain flowers also attract beneficial insects: asters, zinnia, and sunflowers all work together to keep the good company coming to our yards. When I put in our sidewalk, I wanted plenty of flowers to line it. Many of the plants I included led me to my first encounters with lacewings and ambush bugs. Thank goodness I looked them up before plucking them off.

The don'ts

Sometimes, the toxins of one plant totally destroy the health or growth of certain other plants. A Black Walnut tree, planted within 60 feet of your garden, can inhibit the growth and/or development of vegetables, azaleas, rhododendrons, blackberries, lilacs, peonies, and apple trees. It gives off a toxin called juglone which can do some serious damage to other plants. This chemical reaction is known as allelopathy. Sunflowers also have allelopathic properties.

If you see a plant failing, but can't see any visible reason why, it might be its neighbor. (See "The don'ts of companion planting.") Δ

Want self-reliance?
www.backwoodshome.com

GET IN THAT KITCHEN AND RATTLE THOSE POTS AND PANS!

- breads • casseroles • beverages
- canning • jams, jellies & preserves
- salads • soups • vegetables • appetizers
- pasta, rice & beans

GET BACKWOODS HOME COOKING

Only $21.95
(plus $4.95 S&H)
Send a check or money order to
BHM, P.O. Box 712, Gold Beach, OR 97444.
Or order online at www.backwoodshome.com

Call 1-800-835-2418 to order.

the gee-whiz! page
By O.E. MacDougal

The Confederados

In the late 1860s, right after the War Between the States, some Southerners, dissatisfied with the outcome of the War and fearful of Union reprisals, migrated to Brazil. No one knows for sure how many left, but estimates run from 9,000 to 40,000. Whatever the numbers, it is the largest emigration from the United States in our history.

Why Brazil? Dom Pedro II, then Emperor of Brazil, was a supporter of the Confederacy. But more importantly, he realized that Brazil needed the agrarian, textile and educational expertise Southern planters could bring with them. He placed ads for immigrants all over the South and as far north as Baltimore and New York City.

For the Southerners who took the offer, it was a chance to build a new life for themselves and to preserve important elements of their Old South heritage. They came from every state in the South, though most were from Alabama and Texas.

At the time, slavery was still legal in Brazil and this has led to speculation that the Confederados went there in a futile attempt to perpetuate it. But the slave system in Brazil was in decline and was peacefully abolished in 1888. And, as it turned out, almost none of the Confederados engaged in slavery once they settled in their new country.

The most important of the American "colonies" founded was Vila Americana (American Town) in southeastern Brazil. It was founded by William Hutchinson Norris, a retired colonel born in Georgia who later became a lawyer in Alabama.

While most immigrants from other countries were quickly absorbed by the surrounding culture, the Confederados, though they numbered but a few thousand and appeared earlier than most of the other groups, retained distinctive traits of the Confederate South they left behind. And after 135 years, many of their descendants still speak English—English with a southern accent—as a first language.

Four times a year, under fluttering Confederate flags, women and girls in hoop skirts and men and boys wearing rebel gray dance reels, eat fried chicken and other southern dishes, and sing Dixie—in Portuguese. They are members of the Fraternidade Descendencia Americana, founded in 1954 to preserve ties to U.S. culture among the 100,000 to 150,000 heirs of the original emigrants.

Within a few generations of arriving in Brazil, Confederados were intermarrying with Germans, Italians, Arabs, Indians, and, of all people, blacks, so that today many of the "southern belles" and "rebel" soldiers dancing and singing Dixie would, if they were still in America, be considered mulatto or black.

This creates an irony in that the Confederacy and its flag, now symbols of racism to many in the United States, are devoid of that meaning among today's Confederados, many of whom are part black.

Also, many of the descendants of the Confederados—both men and women—have "Lee," as in Robert E. Lee, as part of their names. And Vila Americana (pop. 200,000) is the only city in Brazil that has had a coat of arms that includes a Confederate flag as its centerpiece.

Dom Pedro's gamble of attracting these immigrants from the American South has paid off. Among the contributions the Confederados brought to the parts of Brazil they settled were the plow, spade, harrow, and rake, and other tools virtually unknown to many Brazilian peasants of the time. But the Brazilians were quick to see the advantages of these tools and, just as quickly, adopted them. The Confederados also built their houses as they built them in the South, with chimneys, gutters, and window sashes. To their fellow Brazilians these became known as English houses.

Today, Vila Americana has the highest per capita income and educational levels of any city in Brazil, in part because the Confederados set up schools which are still among the best in Brazil. They also stressed education, started businesses, and many of the railroads and public works that now exist in that country were built by companies owned or run by the Confederados.

Postage stamps

There was a time when a person mailing a letter in the United States had the choice of either paying the postage or having it paid by the person receiving the letter. However, when letters were refused or undeliverable the loss had to be absorbed by the Post Office.

It was to stem these losses that, in 1847, postal laws were changed and it was decreed that, henceforth, the sender *had* to pay the postage. Evidence of this was a stamp that was affixed to the letter. Thus the birth of American postage stamps.

Ask Jackie

"Rescuing" sugar, making beet sugar, is pigweed poisonous?, "big" animals when they die, and growing "spelt"

Jackie Clay

Help! I stored sugar, both white and brown, for the the Y2K and now I have 2 and 10-pound rock hard lumps, instead of usable sugar. Should I just feed the sugar to the goats, or would it hurt them? Gee, I hate to waste all that sugar and money. Is there any saving it?

**Donna Beckman
Cascade, MT**

Whoa! Save that sugar. Unfortunately, sometimes stored sugar does get hard, due to humidity or other moisture. But all is not lost. For the brown sugar, which I assume is still in plastic bags, wrap two heavy paper bags around the plastic bags and rap the lump a few times with a good hammer. That will break up the huge lump into smaller lumps. Pour them out into a gallon glass jar. Now take a sheet of paper towel or a wash cloth and wet it, squeezing out all excess moisture. Place this on top of the lumpy sugar and screw down the lid. In a few days the entire jar will be soft and nice again. I use this all the time. An apple, sliced in half, will also work, but I've noticed an apple flavor in the brown sugar that is not always appreciated, depending on what you're using it for. I prefer the damp paper towel or washcloth. (Do not use a washcloth if you use dryer sheets or scented fabric softener, though.)

As for the 10-pound rock sugar, likewise place the sugar sack into two heavy paper bags and roll the top shut. Then take your trusty hammer and whack the lump a few times. White sugar frees up much quicker and better than brown. Now take a rolling pin and work the lumps still in the bag, 'til it is mostly free-flowing. Run the sugar through a sieve catching any remaining lumps. Put those back into the paper sack and roll them a bit more with the rolling pin. Voilà! You've saved an entire sack of rock hard sugar and a bunch of money.

By the way, this will also work for rock hard salt, too.

Jackie

Better late than never! Back in the Jan/Feb (2002) issue of BHM, you answered a reader's question about processing sugar beets into sugar in the negative, saying, in effect, that it is a factory only process, and can't be done at home.

Enclosed is a copy of a process to extract sugar from sugar beets at home. As you can see, we got this from R.H. Shumway, the catalog seed people. They sent it on request if you bought sugar beet seeds from them. To be honest, we have never run the process to the point of crystal sugar, although I see no reason why it wouldn't work.

I always wonder why Shumway is not mentioned more as a supplier by gardening authors. Maybe they're too down to earth.

**Michael E. Rapp
Reading, PA**

No, Shumway is definitely not "too down to earth" for me. It's simply that there are *so* many good seed companies out there that we can't mention them all. (Although that might be a good idea.) The reason I don't buy too many seeds from Shumway is that many of their seeds require a longer growing season than I have. They are a great company, with lots of good old time seeds at reasonable prices.

Now, as to the sugar refining process, I should have said that refining sugar at home is not feasible to most people as it requires much, much "dinking around," and the end results are not much crystalized sugar for a whole lot of work. My older kids did this one year as a family project. They used sugar beets that they found on the roadside that had dumped off of sugar beet trucks being hauled to the sugar plant. They didn't get enough crystalized sugar to sweeten a batch of Kool-Aid.

If any readers have lots of sugar beets which are very productive in the garden and lots of time, you can refine sugar at home. But don't expect it to be like "store sugar."

Jackie

I have been enjoying your magazine for some time now and I do not normally write unless I have deep concerns about articles I have read. I guess this is one of those times. "Harvesting the wild greens" at first seemed like a harmless article on an assortment of greens that I might be willing to try. I decided to look up some of the weeds on the Internet (Redroot Pigweed) and come to find out that that particular plant was very toxic and your article made no mention of that. I do hope that the person that wrote the article is still alive. I would think that you would do your homework and check validity of a story before publishing it.

Jason Meyer
Jason.Meyer@ci.hayward.ca.us

Gee Jason, I am certainly very alive, and so is my entire family. And we've been eating pigweed for years and years. Among experienced wild foragers, including centuries of Native Americans, pigweed is considered an excellent food source. And very tasty. I do not write about things I research or have just "heard about." I only write about how our family lives. I do not experiment on my family's health. Everything we eat is well researched and documented. Let me quote one recent source, *Edible and Medicinal Plants of Minnesota and Wisconsin*, by noted herbalist and author, Matthew Alfs, M.H. Under the heading of Pigweed (Green Amaranth; Red Amaranth; Rough Pigweed; Redroot Pigweed; Wild Beet) (Amaranthus retroflexus) you will find the following quote follows his description of the various foods pigweed provides (leaves, seeds): "Although pigweed is revered as a wild food, its medicinal applications have been little known. These, however are many and mighty."

Many survival books speak highly of amaranth or pigweed, including *Outdoor Survival Skills* by Larry Dean Olsen. And then Native Seeds/SEARCH says the following in their catalog: "All amaranth leaves can be eaten as raw or cooked greens when small, but some are more palatable. Cleaned seeds can be cooked whole as a hot cereal or ground finely in a mill or blender and added to your favorite recipe."

This does not sound like a "very toxic" plant. One caution, however, is appropriate with pigweed and many other greens including some we grow in our own garden such as spinach. One should not harvest loads of the plant in areas where there is heavy agricultural use, as it will accumulate potentially dangerous amounts of nitrates, in the same way many domestic plants do. Now eating one meal of even this pigweed will likely do no harm, but I certainly would not advise eating bushels of it, nor would I recommend eating a diet solely of pigweed from agricultural lands either. (Many water wells in such land have been contaminated with heavy nitrate deposits as well. One would certainly not advise a wholesale caution on drinking water because of it.)

Jackie

I would like to keep a couple horses and cows, but have never had large animals before. What do you do when they die? Is there an established way to remove the carcass? Do you just pick a quiet corner of your property and bring in a bulldozer? I have heard vaguely that some people will call canning factories for dog food or some such.

Rose K.
Albuquerque, NM

Death is a fact of life for us all. Fortunately, very few animals die on the farm. Usually one sells an older cow, or a person sells an older horse to buy a younger one before they are beyond use. Of course, some of us old softies keep favorite animals until they die. We just recently lost our old Morgan stallion at age 25. While in many places, you can simply call a rendering plant which renders dead livestock down into fertilizer and soap fat among other things, we feel that our big "pets" deserve better. A friend brought over a backhoe, and in ten minutes dug a nice deep grave for our old friend and that was that. He even put up the wood cross that our son, David, made for the horse that taught him to ride.

Farmers with large acreages and living in areas free of restrictions usually just drag dead livestock out into the woods and let nature take its course. (Assuming that the animal did not die of a disease that could be contagious.)

Jackie

I have been newly introduced to an old grain—spelt. Because of a wheat allergy, I am finding this grain of great interest. Do you have any ideas on how to grow spelt or any good recipes that come to mind? Thank you for your kindness.

Vince Williams
jacind@swbell.net

I'd be cautious in using spelt, as it is an old variety of wheat that was primarily used for livestock feed and it is a bit hard to thresh out effectively. It is grown and used almost like wheat, but it will be coarser when ground as there will often be bits of chaff that do not winnow out when it is cleaned. One of the first grains I helped plant was spelt. I thought they said "smelt" and wondered why anyone would plant fish all over a 40 acre field.

Have you tried some of the alternative flour grains? I use a lot of cornmeal, masa (corn flour), rice flour, amaranth, oat, quinoa, and others for fun, taste, and variety. We like flat breads made of these grains just about as much as we do a nicely browned loaf of fresh wheat bread. And we have no wheat allergies.

Jackie

Want more Jackie?
Go to:
www.backwoodshome.com

A Backwoods Home Anthology

The last word

Is television still a wasteland?

"...sit down in front of your television set when your station goes on the air...and keep your eyes glued to that set until the station signs off. I can assure you that you will observe a vast wasteland." Newton Minnow, former Chairman of the FCC in a speech to the National Association of Broadcasters, May 9, 1961.

I own a TV. But, other than to watch an occasional rented movie, I hadn't turned it on in years. I mean many years. There was no reason to. I didn't have cable, or a satellite dish, or even a TV antenna. (Do antennas even work anymore?) It wasn't that I was too broke to afford cable. I just agreed with Newton Minnow, that television is a wasteland—though I didn't think it was a government function to make it "better." Some friends told me I was better off without it. But there were a few others who said I was missing stuff—good stuff.

Good stuff on TV? No way. I'd seen it and it stunk.

Then I moved into a new place and the landlord mentioned there was still a live cable hookup. And because it was the minimum set up—no box or anything, there was no telling when they'd get around to turning it off, so I had cable until they did. Thus it was that one fateful night I decided to hook it up and...

...the first thing I noticed, after many years away, is that many of the commercials are actually pretty good. I know I never felt that way before. But now, I realized, a lot of thought goes into making them. More, it seems, than goes into most of the programs. I guess it makes sense when you think about it. They've got to grab your attention when you want to head for the refrigerator or take a bathroom break, and they've got to keep your attention even though you're going to see them again and again. That's what makes them both effective and irritating, their relentless repetition.

The next thing I noticed was the number of channels. I'd heard talk about them. There are hundreds. And that's where it gets interesting. I still thought of TV as ABC, NBC, CBS, and PBS, with a few local stations thrown in.

Not now. Suddenly, there's the *History Channel*, *History International*, the *Science Channel*, *Discovery Wings*...The list goes on. The first two weeks I found myself, night after night, sitting slack-jawed in front of the TV. There are things on TV I didn't even know existed.

I saw a program about the history of advertising, a documentary on Henry Ford, the history of concrete (that's right, concrete, and I'll bet you didn't know how important that bland grey stuff is to civilization), the arch—from ancient times to the present, the history and construction of forts, levers (another discovery civilization couldn't exist without), chain gangs (they're coming back), Ivan the Terrible (he deserved the moniker), the Boer War, the Roman Empire, Greek civilization, a detailed explanation of the Seven Wonders of the Ancient World—what they were, where they were, who built them, their fates, etc.

On the *XY Factor* I watched a documentary on the treatment of French women, following the liberation of France during WWII, who were suspected of "consorting" with the Germans. It bothered me because I hate to see women mistreated for any reason. Then I reminded myself these were the French, the same people who beheaded Lavoisier, arguably the greatest chemist of all time, only because he was a landlord. I shrugged.

I find I have to filter out propagandist points of view, both left and right, from some programs. Still, the information and analysis are priceless and it's often prompted me to go out on the Net to pursue subjects further, and I've even ordered books to follow up on some subjects.

And *Animal Planet*, did I tell you about *Animal Planet*? One program after another on animals: bats (did you know that until the advent of man, bats were the *only* mammals indigenous to New Zealand?), tarantulas (did you know there are tarantulas big enough to feed on mice?), Arctic wildlife (do you know how polar bears catch seals?).

Other than watching the Super Bowl and one episode of *The Simpsons* I haven't watched network television. I've never seen a "reality" show (the true reality shows are on the *History Channel, Discovery Wings*, et al.). ABC, CBS, and NBC are, as near as I can tell, still the wasteland Minnow spoke of. I don't know what he thinks of television today, but anyone with access to cable who can't get an education—that's entertaining—is spending too much time watching sitcoms, sports shows, game shows, etc. Best of all, there's no tuition—other than cable costs, and no homework, no exams. You just have to endure the ads.

Where do they come from? A lot of these programs are produced here while others are from the UK, Canada, New Zealand, and Australia. Otherwise, I don't know who funds them or what inspires (or possesses) someone to make them. But I'm ever so grateful. PBS cries for government funding lest educational TV go away, but these channels don't need government funding. And PBS isn't nearly as good as the *History Channel*.

It's a huge, fascinating planet—it's a marvelous universe—and someone's out there shooting it with a camera and adding narration to it.

Anyone who says television is a wasteland today either doesn't have cable or is simply too lazy to surf through the channels to where the real excitement and the interesting stories are. Not getting an education from it is like spending four years at a college boozing, partying, and sleeping late, then wondering why you never learned anything. ∆

— John Silveira

Backwoods Home magazine

July/August 2003
No 82
$4.95 US
$6.50 CAN

practical ideas for self-reliant living

Choosing the right backup generator

Making dandelions palatable
Successful cold storage
Defeating debt
Cooking with cornmeal
Grow and store herbs
Making healthy yogurt
Healthy homemade meals
Supercharge your AM radio

www.backwoodshome.com

My view

Gulf War II opened the eyes of Americans to the UN and the media

How many of you were tightly tuned to the TV like I was during Gulf War II. I hope a lot because it was a great education. Not just about the war, but about politics and the mass media.

The UN debate preceding the war was the most instructive view yet for the American public about where the UN stands when it comes to U.S. interests. Prior to this strident display of anti-Americanism, it was just a handful of malcontents like me saying that the UN was nothing but a collection of 3rd world countries working actively against America at every turn. Now most Americans know it.

France's participation in the debate was particularly edifying. This has-been nation that was freed with American blood from the Nazis in World War II frantically flew its diplomats around the world in an effort to garner UN Security Council votes that would defeat any American proposal about Iraq. America's diplomats have watched France work against U.S. interests for years, so it's about time that their anti-Americanism was put on public display for the entire American public to see.

Throughout the UN debate, America's mass media—with notable exceptions like *Fox TV News* and *U.S. News & World Report* magazine—featured "the fact" that "most of the world" was against President Bush's desire to go to war against Iraq. *CNN* et al highlighted the anti-American views of all the third world countries in the UN like they really mattered when it came to American strategic interests.

Just before the war commenced, *Newsweek* magazine featured a cover that screamed: *"Why America Scares the World"* and displayed a giant 21,500-pound MOAB bomb next to it. Inside the issue, the main article was titled: *"The Arrogant Empire"* with an introductory paragraph that read, *"America's unprecedented power scares the world, and the Bush Administration has only made it worse."* At the same time, *U.S. News & World Report's* cover featured an American soldier under the headline *"Ready to Go,"* and its inside articles gave an in-depth account of America's preparations to topple a brutal dictatorship that may be a threat to America. *U.S. News* was engaged in reporting the news while *Newsweek* was engaged in anti-Americanism.

When President Bush finally went to war over UN objections, the UN faded into the background but the mass media kicked into high gear. I was glued to the TV with my 20-year-old daughter, Annie, whose Marine Corps husband was on the front lines, so I had a keen interest in what was going on. But even I was unprepared for the distorted view of the war that *CNN* gave.

Dave Duffy

If you watched *CNN*, you'd have thought America's war plan was thrown into disarray by the "unexpected Iraqi defense." There was no cheering in the streets to welcome the Americans as liberators, as President Bush had promised. Something must have gone terribly wrong!

But all you had to do was switch to *Fox TV News* to learn that the war plan was on track. It seems that *Fox* had no axe to grind, and no anti-Americanism to vent, so they reported the news as it unfolded. The first week of war was just that, *Fox* reported—the first week of war. It was not anticipated there would be an instant victory, and the Iraqi people needed assurances they would not be executed by Saddam's Fedayeen before they cheered for the liberating American troops.

I channel surfed my way through the war, switching among all the news channels—*CNN, CNN Headline News, CNNfn, Fox, MSNBC*. The *CNN* channels had America's "shock and awe" campaign failing, but showed Iraqi civilians, especially Iraqi children, being maimed and killed. *Fox News* had America's battle planning "stunningly successful" with little collateral damage and few civilian casualties.

At the beginning of the war, *MSNBC* seemed to follow the *CNN* line with much negative reporting about America's war efforts, but as the war went into its second week, for some reason *MSNBC* began reporting the war like *Fox News*. They simply dropped their anti-American bias. *Newsweek* magazine, meanwhile, during the second week of the war, ran a special report issue with a cover featuring a bloodied American solder in obvious agony under the headline, *"How Bloody?"* while *U.S. News's* cover ran a photo of an in-control Marine firing his M-16 under the headline, *"Taking Baghdad."*

The difference in the war coverage was obvious for all Americans to see. *CNN* and its affiliates, along with news outlets like *Newsweek*, paraded what they perceived as American setbacks throughout the war, while *Fox* and news outlets like *U.S. News* paraded American success.

Guess who was telling the truth? — *Dave Duffy*

The Fourteenth Year

Making dandelions palatable

By John Kallas, Ph.D.

Dandelions growing in dense cut grass tend to be more bitter because of less shading and more root competition for water and nutrients.

We've heard stories about how good dandelions are. What one usually hears from enthusiastic wild food promoters is, "All you need to do is find very young dandelion leaves in the early spring, before the flower stalks appear. If you do this they won't be bitter. They'll be the most delicious and nutritious fresh greens you will ever eat."

Well my friends, that was not reflected in my early or continuing experiences with the plant. Was I doing something wrong? Why is it that you hear and read such good things about a plant that, even in its youth, is often excruciatingly bitter?

What I'm going to do is explain to you why I think that dandelions are indeed mostly bitter in the raw form—at almost any age—and share with you the secrets of transforming those same dandelions into the genuinely delicious food that so many rave about. We'll also dispel some misconceptions and old folk tales so you can get some practical use out of this abundant food source.

When I was first learning primitive living skills, I was intrigued by the thought of surviving off of what nature provides. Of all the plants talked about in the few survival books I had collected, dandelions were familiar and they were right under foot. So being the adventurous testosterone-ridden young male that I was, I tried them. Yacht, pituey, spit-spit-spit, blah! Well, so much for machismo. The bitterness was overwhelming. This did not help my interest in plants. I phased into animals and other survival skills for a while so that my taste buds could grow back.

On occasion while I was still living at home, my mom, trying to emulate a tradition of our Greek ancestors, would prepare dandelions gathered in a nearby vacant lot. She would serve them and we would all be in agony. Of course my parents, trying to be good role models, would hide their pain in an effort to convince us that these greens were, in fact, good. Can any of you explain to me the psychology of this? I'm still baffled to this day.

Once I got to college I became a more serious student of wild foods. By more serious, I mean that I began reading beyond the "this plant is edible" statement to the "this is how you prepare it" section. To this day, this progression to the "how" section is difficult for many eager wannabe primitive technologists. Many people just want to know what's edible and do not have the patience to learn details. Knowing the details results in the understanding that allows you to be more successful and *enjoy* what you are eating.

According to the books I read, preparing dandelions basically involved boiling the leaves in one or more changes of water. You add more

185

Young dandelions growing from seed. These small leaves are bitter from birth unless totally shaded from all light.

boilings for greens that are more bitter. Authors varied greatly on how many boilings you should do. Most centered on two. I tried two. Done properly, the bitterness will be poured off with the water, leaving the wonderfully rich flavor of the dandelion greens behind. They become quite delicious. If boiled too long, the greens begin to disintegrate.

But some things I was reading and hearing did not add up. I was continually reading in books and hearing from certain individuals that dandelions were not bitter if you got them early enough in the spring. I cannot tell you how many times I tested this theory. The overwhelming mass of my experience was that even the youngest, tiniest leaves were bitter—too bitter, in the raw, for my tastes. Picking them in the early spring before the flower stalks appear is very difficult. The flower stalks appear almost at the same time as the leaves on the earliest dandelions. The early dandelions grow rapidly directly from nutrient providing taproots. Consequently, the small emerging spring leaves are not really required to generate food for the growing flower stalk. The stalk can grow directly from the food provided by the taproot.

Even young dandelions growing directly from seed were bitter. Their lower stalks, totally growing by food generated from the leaves, would not develop until later in the spring.

While working on my Ph.D. about 20 year ago, I designed a survey-driven research project of senior citizens in a rural Michigan farming community. Many of these people were born between 1890 and 1910. Most had grown up in an era where there was no electricity, no cars, no supermarkets. They lived off canned, bagged, and bottled food they bought from the general store, whatever agricultural food they could produce or trade for, and wild foods they gathered from the surrounding area. The wild foods helped to spice up and add diversity to their diets. Dandelions were one of the most commonly eaten foods.

Dandelion leaves growing in tall grass that is well watered tend to be less bitter due to rapid growth, shading, and loose soil. Be careful not to gather in areas sprayed with herbicides, other chemicals, near roadsides, or railroad tracks.

This dandelion plant has gone to flower and seed, but the leaves are still workably bitter due to good shade, plenty of moisture, and rich soil, all of which promote continually growing new leaves.

When I asked these people if they experienced dandelions and dandelion salads to be bitter, almost everyone interviewed said no, dandelions were not bitter. I was wondering what planet I was visiting. Had all these farmers been replaced by alien pod people? What was I missing here? At some point, I began asking, "How did you prepare your salad?" This is what they told me: "You take a big mess of fresh dandelion greens, you cook up some bacon, you pour the hot grease over the dandelions, you chop up the bacon and sprinkle that over the greens, you cook up a couple of hard boiled eggs, chop them up and disperse them over the greens, you add salt and occasionally vinegar, and there you have it—dandelion salad (also known as wilted greens).

The gears in my brain now had something to work with. It was becoming more and more clear to me that anytime experienced dandelion eaters discussed flavor, it was within the context of how it was served, not the fresh plant straight from the ground. Hardly anyone actually eats dandelions that way.

There are also psychological issues here that hide the fact that most people find the raw greens bitter.

First, people who like the "prepared" dandelions they've eaten all their lives tend to sing their praises. So even though dandelions are quite changed by the time most people are eating them, they praise the plant. People who consume the leaves fresh hear these praises and wonder what they are missing.

Second, when the inexperienced sample the much-hyped fresh dandelion leaves for the first time and don't like them, they imagine that they are not picking them early enough or otherwise doing something wrong. How could all these dandelion lovers be wrong about the flavor of such a hallowed plant? Some folks are afraid to admit that they cannot stand the flavor.

Third, there are many people today that believe that bitter is good for the liver and proper digestion and that dandelions are a healing food. So they learn over time to tolerate much more bitter than the rest of us. For many of these people bitter becomes an enjoyable flavor. They often describe dandelions as not being bitter. What they really mean is that, to them, the dandelions they eat are not so bitter that they cannot enjoy them. Enjoying bitter is not the same as something not being bitter.

Okay, so enough about what I've seen and experienced, let's get on to the basic principles I've come up with that will help you enjoy dandelion greens.

Understanding the "bitter"

Dandelions are bitter because of a class of water soluble chemicals called sesquiterpenes. The key to enjoying dandelions is understanding how to work with these chemicals to minimize their impact on your taste buds.

Sesquiterpenes are part of the milky juice that runs throughout the dandelion plant. They are everywhere except for the non-green flower parts. Sesquiterpenes are less concentrated in rapidly growing leaves, hence the thinking that young leaves are not bitter. Well, in fact they are bitter, just less bitter than they could be.

Here are my best theories on what increase the bitterness of dandelions. First, after the spring rains cease, the ground begins to dry. That drying slows the growth of the leaves allowing leaf bitterness to concentrate. Areas kept relatively wet allow dandelions to continue growing rapidly all year long. Second, the more direct sunlight that bakes a leaf, the more sesquiterpenes develop, even in fast growing leaves. Plants growing in shaded areas or deep grass tend to be less bitter. The early spring sun maintains a lower arc across the sky than the summer sun. So less shaded summer leaves will be more bitter. In moist rich shaded soil, I have found optimal fresh dandelion leaves all year long. Note that they are still bitter to most normal humans, but not unworkable.

A "mess" of cooked dandelion greens drizzled in olive oil and sprinkled with dandelion flower petals. Mmmm... wonderful flavor with no bitterness. These greens were cooked for five minutes in only one pot of water because the least bitter greens were selected for use.

The author holding a wild salad.

There are great differences in people regarding the sensation of bitter. People like me, endowed with lots of extra taste buds in the bitter sensitive zones of the tongue, are super tasters for bitter. We can taste bitter a mile away and that taste lingers miserably for some time after the food has been swallowed. Other people have almost no bitter taste buds. These are the people who look at us in disbelief as we agonizingly wince like babies over bitter greens. About one in every 25 of my students cannot taste bitter very well.

Managing the bitterness away

As a result of my extensive experience preparing dandelions and the little I know about the science of taste, here are some conclusions I've drawn to bring out the flavor of dandelion greens while limiting the bitter sensation.

1. Dilution: This is where you mix your dandelions with something that dilutes the bitterness. This could include mixing it with milder greens (like miner's lettuce or chickweed) or putting in some dish with other ingredients so that the proportion of dandelion leaf is reduced relative to the overall food. One of the best ways to use fresh dandelions in a salad is to chop them into small pieces and sprinkle them over a mixed salad. The bitterness of the dandelions is lost, but the overall flavor of the salad is enhanced. The key to this is not making dandelions more than one-fifth the mass of the total salad and having the pieces be small enough so that they do not overwhelm the taste buds.

2. Masking: This is a taste bud thing. Fat is the main ingredient for doing this. This is why many of the old-timers (like the farmers mentioned earlier) poured bacon grease over their dandelions. My understanding is that fat, in the form of oils, butter, bacon grease, etc., cover taste bud receptors and reduce their sensitivity to the harshest forms of the bitterness. Fat also enhances the flavor of the greens.

3. Distracting: Adding sugar, vinegar, or other impactful flavor to a salad causes your brain to have competing taste sensations to the bitter one. This makes the bitterness less prominent and sometimes lost in the other flavors.

4. Leaching: This is the process mentioned earlier of boiling out the water soluble sesquiterpenes, leaving a wonderfully rich flavor. In my experience, using fresh, rapidly growing greens, you only have to boil them once for three to five minutes for them to release most of their bitterness. I typically just adorn them with a little olive oil and I'm a happy camper. The technique of leaching goes like this: Start a pot of rapidly boiling water, chop up the greens to about one inch pieces, put them in the water, stir to keep them submerged. After 3 minutes, sample a small piece. If not bitter, remove the greens from the water and serve hot. If still bitter, leave the greens in the boiling water. Sample again after five minutes. If still bitter, consider transferring them into a second pot of boiling water for three to five minutes. In my opinion, if they need more cooking than that, they are too bitter.

Some people prefer diluting, masking, and distracting to leaching because they can still eat fresh uncooked leaves. Others prefer cooked greens. Of course nobody uses these labels outside of my students. Normal humans like the farmers mentioned earlier just prepare their foods so they taste good. They do not think of bacon grease, bacon bits, shredded hard boiled eggs, and vinegar as diluting, masking and distracting them from bitterness. They just like their salad dressing.

You are now armed with the kinds of information that will help you get more satisfaction out of your dandelion greens. For me, a melted cheese and dandelion sandwich sounds great right now.

(Dr. John Kallas is the owner of Wild Food Adventures, Institute for the Study of Edible Wild Plants and Other Foragables. He has been researching, teaching, and writing about wild foods for more than 25 years. For more information go to: www.wildfoodadventures.com, (503) 775-3828, Wild Food Adventures, 5036 SE Mitchell St, Portland, OR 98206.) ∆

Get The Whole Sheebang!
www.backwoodshome.com

GET IN THAT KITCHEN AND RATTLE THOSE POTS AND PANS!

- breads • casseroles
- beverages • canning
- jams, jellies & preserves
- salads • soups
- vegetables • appetizers
- pasta, rice & beans

GET BACKWOODS HOME COOKING

Only $21.95
(plus $4.95 S&H)

1-800-835-2418
www.backwoodshome.com

Send a check or money order to
BHM, P.O. Box 712, Gold Beach, OR 97444

The Fourteenth Year

Dandelion facts and history

By Tom and Joanne O'Toole

Easily recognized by its bright, golden-yellow flower, the dandelion has deeply-indented ground-hugging leaves, and a hollow stem containing a harmless, bitter, milky juice. The weed usually spuds out in early spring as soon as the leaves appear, but controlling it seems to be an endless battle—with the dandelion often winning.

Those who crave the unblemished lawn have little chance once the dandelion has taken hold. They just seem to pop up overnight every spring, and the plant stays around until the frost hits in the fall.

A European import by the settlers to the New World, the hearty perennial is generally found throughout North America and reproduces through abundant spreading seeds. In the United States it is plentiful on the Pacific coast, in the north central states, and throughout the northeast. In Canada it is most prevalent in the eastern provinces.

This weed is resilient for a number of reasons. Its long, thick, tough, carrot-like taproot can burrow up to three feet underground—making it difficult to eradicate. The Chinese call it "earth nail."

The flower head is not one bloom, but a composite of hundreds of mini-flowers, each independent of one another. These sunburst blossoms at the end of the stem turn into white, fluffy seedballs. They then blow off in all directions, spreading their seeds and finding root for the next year. The seeds are conceived without pollination or fertilization.

The leaves grow in a flat, rosette arrangement and only the hollow stalk shoots up to present what appears to be a single blossom. The weed's built-in clock is controlled by light, telling the flower to close each evening and to open again at sunrise.

The name dandelion dates back to medieval France. Noting the jagged edges of the plant's leaves, the French called it "dent-de-lion," meaning tooth of the lion.

The resilient pest grows just about everywhere, and is extremely adaptable. You'll find it in meadows, pastures, along roadsides, in highway medians, in public parks, and grasslands. If you're in the mood for picking, it shouldn't be difficult to find.

Dandelion leaves are sold commercially in the northeast, but their popularity is not widespread. Yet, the weed offers a little something for everyone.

While the leaves can be plucked anytime, they are best in the early spring before the flower blooms and the leaves turn too bitter. The spring roots are also tender.

The best salads are made with fresh-picked leaves, and are seasoned like any other. They will be somewhat tangy and chewy. Some people even dip the leaves in batter and make dandelion fritters.

Some people serve dandelion salad because it is chic, and perhaps force it down no matter how bad it might taste. The young leaves are also cooked like spinach and served with the main course. Obviously, if it doesn't agree with you, don't eat it, and under these circumstances don't serve it to guests. Old-timers have probably acquired the taste more than the current generation. After all, during the Depression years people ate what they could get, and dandelions were plentiful.

As the season progresses, the fall roots are much stronger. If you wash and dry the root, then shred it in a blender, you can make dandelion tea. Some claim the tea helps people relax. If you roast the ground roots, you can make your own gourmet coffee substitute, or mix it with chocolate or coffee.

Dandelion wine became popular because it was inexpensive to make. It's still made, with the bloom making the best wine. With some families the process has been handed down, and the new generation continues to make it more as a tradition than anything else. It seems old habits die hard. Not a big seller as a commercial product, you'll likely find only a wine recipe—then you're on your own.

Medicinal? The dandelion has long been on the list of home remedies for whatever ails you. American colonists found its broth eased digestion and worked as a mild laxative. Perhaps the bitterness had something to do with thinking it was helpful. Like taking cod liver oil, if it tastes bad it must be good for you.

The dandelion was one of the more than 2,000 herbs used when the settlers came from England. The roots have been used in tonics and liver cures, as well as to stem infections, skin diseases, dropsy, and to settle the digestive tract.

The medical virtues of the dandelion are inscribed in its scientific name (Taraxacum Officinale) which means "official remedy for disorders."

Chinese prescribed the dandelion to treat appendicitis, abscesses, swellings, and snake bites. In Europe it was the herb of choice for illnesses of the spleen, kidney, heart, diabetes, high blood pressure, constipation, mononucleosis, and an aid to spring fever.

Dandelion juice was credited with removing warts, blisters, freckles, and growing hair on bald pates and eyebrows.

Packing four times the iron of spinach, dandelions are sold throughout the northeast region of North America, and are frequently found at roadside markets.

Dandelions are an excellent source of vitamin A, some B, and contain protein, calcium, iron, sodium, phosphorus, and a decent amount of vitamin C, magnesium, and potassium. Best of all, they are very low in calories.

Culinary respect? The dandelion leaves you find at markets are probably commercially grown, and it is a big business in some areas. The commercial product is grown under sheets of plastic to bring it to an early harvest, and it is less bitter than what you'd pick in your yard. Some supermarkets even stock leaves of the common weed.

Vineland, New Jersey, lays claim to being the "Dandelion Capital of the World" and contends more dandelions are grown here as salad greens than anywhere else in North America. ∆

Are you prepared?
Emergency Preparedness and Survival Guide
www.backwoodshome.com

Tomato canning tips

By Tom R. Kovach

When it comes to canning tomatoes, the USDA advises to increase both the acidity and processing time that was formerly recommended. The reason: today's fleshier tomatoes require these changes in ensuring a safe product.

Begin the process of canning by filling a boiling water bath canner half full of water. Place it on the stove and heat. Have enough quart-sized canning jars to fill the canner rack and wash the cans with hot, soapy water. Rinse well and place them in the canner until needed. Also wash the canning jar lids and bands and rinse well. Put these closures in a saucepan, adding water and bringing to a simmer. Remove the pan from the heat, leaving the closures in the hot water.

Make sure you choose tomatoes that are red-ripe, firm, and free of blemishes. Rinse and drain them. Put the tomatoes in a wire basket and lower them into a large sauce pot of boiling water. Blanch for 30 seconds or until the skins begin to crack. Remove and submerge the tomatoes into cold water.

Now core the tomatoes and peel them. The tomatoes can be left whole or cut in half. Put them in a large sauce pot with water to cover. Bring the water to a boil, then reduce heat and boil for 5 minutes.

Remove one jar at a time from the canner. Place 2 tablespoons of lemon juice or ½ teaspoon of citric acid in the jar (sugar can be added to offset the acid taste).

Using a canning funnel, add the hot tomatoes to the jar, leaving a ½-inch space at the top. Ladle the hot cooking liquid over the tomatoes, again leaving ½-inch of space. One teaspoon of canning or coarse salt may be added, if desired.

Run a nonmetallic spatula between the tomatoes and jar to release any trapped air bubbles. Wipe the jar threads with a clean, damp cloth.

Using tongs, remove a lid from the saucepan and place it flat on top, with the sealing compound against the jar. Add the band and screw it down firmly.

Stand the filled jars back in the canner. When all the jars are filled, check that there are 2 inches of water over the jars and at least 2 more inches of head space in the canner above the water level. Cover the canner and bring the water to a boil. Begin counting the processing time when the water boils. Process 45 minutes at a gentle but steady boil.

Remove the jars from the canner and put them on a wooden or cloth surface, several inches apart and away from drafts.

Let the jars cool 12 hours, then remove the bands and test the seals. Properly sealed jars should be stored in a dark, dry, cool area and should be used within one year. If jars don't seal properly, reprocess with new seals, or refrigerate and use within a few days. ∆

Dandelion recipes

By Tom and Joanne O'Toole

For dandelion gourmets there are many ways to prepare this amazing weed, and to include it in soups, salads, main courses, desserts, and wine. Here are a few recipes you might want to try.

Dandelion soup

2 quarts dandelion greens, loosely packed
2 quarts chicken soup
1 lb. mixed ground beef, veal, and pork
1 egg
2 Tbsp. bread crumbs
2 Tbsp. minced parsley
1 Tbsp. minced onions (extra fine)
¼ tsp. salt
1/8 tsp. seasoned pepper
Dash nutmeg
3 Tbsp. grated parmesan cheese
2 Tbsp. sour cream

Bring chicken soup to a boil. Add dandelion. Cook gently. If desired, ½ cup rice or 1 cup fine egg noodles can be added. Make very tiny meatballs out of remaining ingredients. When greens are tender, add meatballs and cook gently 10 minutes or until meatballs are thoroughly cooked. Serve hot with Italian or French bread.

Dandelion salad with eggs

2 quarts cleaned dandelion (cut into ½-inch pieces)
½ medium-sized onion, minced very fine
oil (olive or as desired)
vinegar (wine or as desired)
(Proportion of oil to vinegar is 3:1)

Season with ½ tsp. salt and 1/8 tsp. garlic salt. Dry the cleaned dandelion carefully. Mix all of the ingredients together gently. Then taste and add more seasonings as needed.

Boil enough hard boiled eggs to allow at least 2 per person. Eggs may be sliced into the salad. However, many prefer to serve the eggs separately, letting each person help himself.

Italian dandelion casserole

1 lb. ground beef (or beef and pork mixed)
1 cup bread crumbs
2 Tbsp. chopped parsley
2 Tbsp. finely chopped onion
1 tsp. salt
1 egg
¼ cup milk
6-8 cups dandelion greens
1 15 oz. can tomatoes, drained
1 cup chicken stock or bouillon
salt and pepper to taste

Mix together meat, bread crumbs, parsley, onion, salt, egg, and milk. Form 40 to 45 small meatballs about 1 inch in diameter. Brown them in oil. Drain and set aside. Wash dandelion greens. In a buttered casserole alternate layers of dandelions, browned meatballs, and tomatoes. Add the chicken stock or bouillon. Season with salt and pepper and simmer 20-30 minutes. Yields 6-8 servings. When serving the casserole, have hot pepper flakes and Parmesan cheese available on the table.

Variations:
1. Add a layer of onions.
2. Season the meatballs with garlic salt or add finely chopped garlic to the casserole.
3. Add other herbs—oregano, basil, or marjoram.

Dandelion wine

1 gallon flower heads
3 lbs. sugar
1 ounce yeast
1 gallon water
2 lemons

Remove petals by gathering them between the fingers while holding the base of the flower head. Put petals in the fermenting vessel and pour on three quarts of boiling water. Leave to soak for seven days, well covered. Stir daily and cover again at once. Strain and wring out fairly tightly and return the liquor to the fermenting vessel. Boil half the sugar in a pint of water and when cool add to the liquor, then add the yeast and the juice of two lemons.

Cover as directed and ferment for seven days. Then pour carefully into a gallon jar, leaving as much deposit behind as you can. Boil the rest of the sugar in the remaining pint of water and when cool add to the rest. Cover as directed or fit fermentation lock and leave until all fermentation has ceased.

For more ways to satisfy your palate, you can purchase *Dandelion and Regional Favorites Recipe Book*, with 16 recipes for dandelion specialties, from the Greater Vineland Chamber of Commerce for $4.50. Write to 18 North East Avenue, P.O. Box 489, Vineland, New Jersey 08360-0489. (800) 309-0019. Δ

How to select the right backup generator

By Jeffrey R. Yago, P.E., CEM

Now that the threat of terrorist sabotage to our utility infrastructure has been added to our basic concerns about storm related power outages, this may be the final straw in your decision to purchase a generator. If you are considering buying a generator for your home or farm, the first step is deciding what you want to operate when the power goes out. This will help determine the kilowatt (kW) capacity of the generator, the engine type (gasoline, propane, natural gas, or diesel), and installation wiring (plug-in or permanently connected).

You also need to consider how often you will need a generator. If you live near a large city served by multiple power lines, power outages will be rare and last hours, not days. The more rural your area, the fewer the utility customers affected when a utility line goes down, and that means a long wait since utility crews will address those lines serving the most customers first.

Some parts of the United States historically have more storm related power outages than others. Northern states have more winter snowstorms, Eastern states have more ice storms, Southern states have more hurricanes and Western states have more tornadoes, earthquakes, and rainstorms. California has recently demonstrated that utility grid interruptions and brownouts are not always winter storm related. Do you live in an area that has a history of extended power outages? If so, then maybe it is time you did something about it and purchase a generator.

There are generally three categories of generators for the residential market, and each have very different capabilities.

Portable generator

This is the typical portable 1-kW to 3-kW generator you find in most outdoor equipment and discount warehouse outlets. With few exceptions, these will have a small gasoline tank providing limited operating hours, a manual pull-starter, a handle for one person lifting, and a plug-in outlet panel to connect your electrical loads using extension cords. These generators have small lawnmower style mufflers which can be loud, and their lightweight construction and high 3,600 RPM engine speed limits their life to only a few seasons. Their main advantages are low cost ($400 to $600) and portability.

The portable generators in the smaller kW sizes are more suitable for camping, since they can only power a few lights, a small television, and several small appliances. The larger kW sizes have enough capacity to power a kitchen size refrigerator or well pump. These generators are not designed to be hard wired into your house wiring, and their higher noise levels and need for constant refueling reduces their desirability for a permanent back-up power system.

Contractor grade generator

Although still considered a portable gasoline generator, most of these generators use heavier cast iron engines that will provide much longer life. These generators are in the 4-kW to 6-kW capacity range, which is only slightly larger than the portable gen-

6.5 kW contractor grade Yamaha generator

*1-kW lightweight
Honda portable generator*

erators above, but are designed for much heavier use. Most of these generators have a protective tubular steel cage with a top mounted oversized fuel tank for longer run times between fill-ups. Units above 6-kW usually have two-cylinder engines and electric starters. Expect to pay $1,200 base price for this size generator and over $2,000 for a larger electric start model. This is the minimum size and quality generator I would recommend for anyone wanting a do-it-yourself back-up power system for their home.

Residential backup generator

There is no pretense here; these generators are designed to be permanently mounted on an outside pad and hard wired into your home's electrical circuit breaker panel. Although these are available with a standard gasoline engine, most are designed to run on propane or natural gas to eliminate the need to refill a fuel tank. These generators are also sold with long life diesel engines, but this will require keeping a fresh supply of diesel fuel available which may not be practical for some homeowners, although diesel fuel is safer to handle and more economical than gasoline.

These generators are available in any size you could imagine; however, 8-kW to 10-kW is considered the minimum size range for permanent residential back-up power applications. Expect to pay $4,000 to $6,000 for this size generator depending on quality and safety options, and more for a longer life diesel engine version. Once you make it past the initial price shock for a generator this size, you will be pleasantly surprised to find that the larger 12-kW to 16-kW residential models are not that much more expensive. If you need to power more loads at the same time like an air conditioner, central heating system, or electric hot water tank, then you may need a generator in this larger size range.

These permanently installed generators are much better suited for residential emergency back-up power systems than portable generators, since they include a sound absorbing weather-proof housing, a very good noise reduction muffler, and a slower 1800 RPM engine which greatly extends engine life. You will need a plumber to safely connect the unit to an existing natural gas or propane supply line, and an electrician to wire the generator to an electrical transfer switch which will be wired into your home's main circuit breaker panel.

Transfer switches

Of course you can drag your generator out of the garage during the next power outage and string multiple extension cords through an open window to your television, table lamps, and refrigerator. This can be very enlightening, especially during a rainstorm, as you trip over the kids and dog in the dark while stringing wet extension cords from one end to the other.

Up until a few years ago most transfer switches were large and costly, and only found on large commercial back-up generators serving hospitals, schools, and airports. These large devices are designed to constantly monitor the utility grid for a power outage, automatically start the generator, and safely transfer the emergency loads over from the grid to the generator. These automatic transfer switches also have a programmable timer to start and exercise the generator several times each month to keep everything operational, and provide operator warning alarms if the generator fails to start or has a service problem.

With the recent trend in more and more owner's of upscale homes and home-based businesses demanding their own reliable backup power system, manufacturers are now offering a much less expensive manual version of these transfer switches. Although manually operated transfer switches do not include the automatic generator start capability, they can be easily added to your home's electric panel. Since it is not practical to install a generator large enough to power everything in your home at the same time, these smaller manual transfer switches have multiple three-way switches to allow transferring individual electrical loads between the generator and utility grid, depending on which loads are the most critical at a given time. This allows using a much smaller generator, without the danger of overloading that would occur if all of the appliances were connected at the same time.

Most manual transfer switch panels are sold with an extra long heavy duty cable and plug that allows connecting the transfer switch directly into the generator's power receptacle without the need for hard wiring or generator modifications. Although a manual transfer switch may add $200 to $400 to your generator installation cost, depending on size and quality, it is well worth the price if you are serious about a back-up power system. When the next power outage occurs, you still may need to manually start the generator, but switching your critical loads over is now safe and easy. No more extension cords and open

Kohler automatic transfer switch

windows with exposed wires running outside in the rain. Some transfer switches are available with dual meters to help balance the loads on each output leg of your generator.

I am reluctant to mention the cheap version of connecting a generator to a home's power wiring without a transfer switch, but I feel it is necessary to highlight the danger of this technique. Almost everyone will have a brother-in-law who thinks they are an electrician, who wants to make a double ended dryer outlet extension cord for your portable generator to save money. My advice is do not ever think about it. This old trick uses an electric cable with a male plug on both ends that connect the generator's 240-volt outlet with your three-bladed electrical dryer receptacle.

This routes all of the generator's output directly into the electric buss bars inside the main circuit breaker panel of your home. However, your electric meter, all other electric loads, and the utility grid are also connected to this same electric buss. Since most people have a limited understanding of how their electrical service operates, they will not recognize the need to turn off the circuit breakers to all larger appliances like electric stoves and air conditioners, which almost guarantees they will overload the generator which is "back-feeding" their electrical panel through the dryer outlet.

They will also forget to switch off their service disconnect, guaranteeing the utility power will feed back into the generator as soon as the grid is re-energized. Every year there are hundreds of portable home generators that become fireworks displays in the backyard when the utility grid comes back on, not to mention the potential to also burn down the house. Since both the generator and the clothes dryer have "female" 240-volt receptacles, this requires both ends of this homemade cable to be "male," with electrically energized exposed blades that you could accidentally come in contact with prior to plug in.

Do not take the risk. Purchase a manual transfer switch with any 3-kW to 6-kW portable generator, and an automatic transfer switch for all larger pad-mounted generator installations.

New generator technology

One of the main problems with using a generator today is all the new electronic and computer equipment we all own which require a very stable voltage source that is free of electrical line "noise." Older and lower-cost generators cannot always provide this clean electricity, since their supply voltage will keep changing as the generator's engine adjusts to meet the switching load demands. Appliances in the United States are designed to operate on 60-cycle pure sinewave 120-volt AC power.

If you could view this on an electronic scope, you would see the utility grid voltage rise smoothly up to a peak, then reverse to peak again in the opposite direction, 60 times every second, rising and falling smoothly like waves on a pond. The 120-volt measurement is the average of this constantly changing voltage wave form, and the maximum peak-to-peak voltage is actually closer to 169 volts.

Some lower-cost generators use voltage controls to increase their advertised peak load capacity by reducing this peak voltage as the load increases. You would still measure 120-volts AC with a volt meter when this happens, and most lights and small appliances would not notice the difference, but some types of motors may run slower, and almost all battery chargers will experience a significance loss in performance since these devices need the full peak voltage to operate properly.

Generator manufacturers have started to address these power quality issues by offering models that include a true sinewave inverter added to the generator's output circuit. These inverter generators or "I" models, provide grid quality sinewave output with a rock stable voltage throughout the full capacity range of the generator. Although this feature adds signifi-

8.5-kW propane-fueled Kohler generator

The Fourteenth Year

cantly to any generator's base price without increasing its total kW capacity, this generator feature is desirable if you are planning to charge a back-up battery bank or power electronically sensitive computer or audio video equipment.

Generator load estimating

As mentioned earlier, it is not practical to install a generator that can equal the capacity of the utility grid supplying your home. This is not even done for commercial or institutional back-up power systems, which have only critical loads powered by their generator. These large emergency generators are normally only used to power emergency lighting, phone and fire alarm systems, and the pumps and controls needed to keep the heating system functioning normally. These generators are rarely sized to also power large central air conditioning systems, except for hospital operating rooms, micro-electronic clean rooms, and critical computer rooms. Just like the large system designer, you need to decide what electrical loads are absolutely necessary to remain operational in your home during an extended power outage, which will determine your generator size.

Most engine driven generators have a "stepped" linear relationship between their loading and their fuel consumption. Most lightly loaded generators will consume the same fuel from no load up to about 25 percent loading. Above this point, the fuel consumption will increase at the same percentage as the load up to about 75 percent of full load. Above this generator loading, the fuel consumption will increase at a higher rate than the load. The 50 to 75 percent load range appears to be the most fuel efficient operating range for most generators, and it should be clear that it is not fuel efficient to operate an 8-kW generator just to power one table lamp. This load-fuel relationship should be considered when selecting the loads that will be supplied by your generator, and when selecting the generator size matching this operating range.

GenTran manual transfer switch with individual load controls

Using the table of appliance wattage estimates, make two lists. Keep in mind that these are average values and you should verify the nameplate data on your own appliances if in doubt. Your first list will be the total wattage of all lights and appliances that must operate at the same time. Your second list will identify all larger electrical loads you may also like to supply, but are not required to operate while these more critical loads are on. This will help determine how many separately switched circuits you will need on any transfer switch, since these loads must remain off until they can be operated when all other loads are off.

An example of these less critical electrical loads would be a clothes washer, an electric hot water heater, a small window air conditioner, or a dishwasher. Although these loads could easily require all of the output of a smaller generator, you may be able to heat up the water tank from the generator and operate a washer

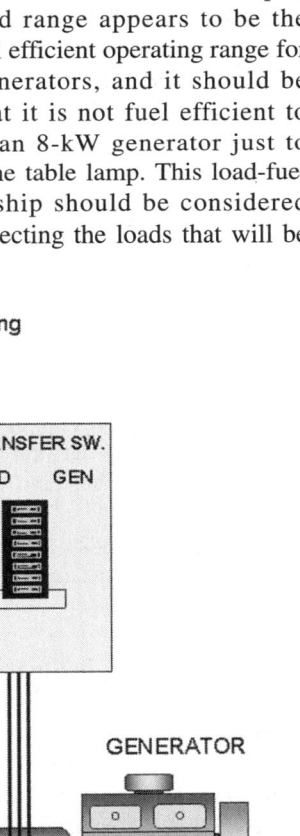

Schematic wiring diagram with only power wiring shown. Grounding and neutral wiring also required. All wiring must be per National Electric code and all equipment must be UL labeled.

195

later at night when all other loads are turned off. Remember that a water heater and well pump are usually 240-volt loads, and will require different switching and wiring than your 120-volt loads.

Generator load balance

Most generator nameplate ratings are their maximum peak capacity, which must be de-rated if the loads are continuous or consist of many separate appliance motor loads that will be randomly starting and stopping. Be sure to take this into consideration when making your final generator selection. Also note that most back-up generator capacity ratings are based on a balanced loading of their dual leg 120/240-volt output. This means that each 120-volt side of any 240-volt generator output is designed to supply half of the total nameplate wattage. A 4-kW rated generator may only have 2-kW capacity supplying each of its two 120-volt circuits. If all of your connected loads are 120-volt, then these loads should be equally divided between these two separate branch receptacles. If all of your electrical loads are connected to the generator with a single two conductor extension cord, your generator may only be able to supply half of its nameplate rating through this single cord.

Most generator panels have multiple receptacles on separate "legs" of the generator's windings. Be sure to take advantage of these multiple outlets by using two or more extension cords to supply your loads which will help balance the generator's dual voltage output. I have noticed that some portable generators now include a 120/240-volt load switch on the generator's receptacle panel to do this load balancing for you. When you will not be powering any 240-volt loads, this switch will combine the separate generator windings so almost all of the nameplate rating capacity will be available to the dual 120-volt duplex outlets.

Larger generators have a two-pole 240-volt circuit breaker instead of a receptacle panel to allow hard wiring the generator's output directly to your home's electrical service panel. If you will be using this type of wiring connection, try to make sure the individual load circuit breakers are divided equally to each side of this dual pole circuit breaker. All 240-volt generators need a fairly balanced loading on each 120-volt output leg to achieve their nameplate rating.

Electrical loads

Fixture/appliance	Run wattage
Incandescent bulbs	Bulb wattage
Fluorescent lamps	Bulb wattage x 1.2
Kitchen Microwave	1,260
Toaster	1,055
Drip coffee maker	850
Dishwasher*	1,150
20 cu. ft. refrigerator*	700
19" color TV	75
50" projection screen TV	180
DSS satellite receiver	15
Stereo VCR	22
Stereo amplifier	75
CD player	5
Tape deck	6
Circular saw*	1,400
Deep well pump*	1,000
Heating hot water loop pump*	98
Aquarium pump, heater, and light	145
Desktop computer and monitor	210
Inkjet printer	17
Fax machine	20
Cordless phone	2
60-gallon hot water heater	4,500
Clothes washer*	500
Furnace blower fan*	700

Electrical loads that include a motor or compressor noted with an asterisk (*) will have a momentary startup in-rush of electrical current almost double the normal run time wattage shown in the table, which could easily exceed your generator's peak capacity. Double the run time wattage estimates shown for all motor loads to make sure your generator can handle this initial start-up surge. Also note that all fluorescent lights have a ballast load that is accounted for by using the indicated 1.2 multiplier.

Conclusions

The purpose for buying an emergency generator is to have electricity during an emergency. I know that may sound obvious, but every year I hear about the guy who ran out and bought the first generator he could find when a snow storm was forecast, only to find out days later that it would not run without gasoline. Gasoline stored in a container or fuel tank will go "stale" after a few months, and your local gas station will also most likely not have power when you are without power. This means your generator will only run a few hours on the gas remaining in its tank if you have not planned ahead.

In order for this to be a truly reliable emergency power system, you need to have the fuel on hand to operate your generator for several days. You should rotate your gasoline or diesel fuel every few months, and make sure it is stored in a safe place. It is also much easier to store, rotate, carry, and refill the generator's tank from several smaller fuel storage containers than one large one. For example, my generator has a five-gallon fuel tank, so I keep four full five-gallon fuel storage containers on hand, but keep the generator's tank empty to avoid its fuel going bad which would require draining and re-filling before it could be operated.

Using the same size fuel storage container as the generator's tank capacity makes for smoother re-fill operations, especially when standing in the rain or snow. I use the oldest fuel first to fill other motorized yard equipment and rotate the numbered containers as they are refilled. You should consider adding a fuel additive to all standby gasoline and diesel fuel storage containers to extend their shelf life, but this still only adds months, not years to their useful life.

Buying a propane or natural gas fueled generator will eliminate these problems since these fuels do not go stale. However, all generators need to be started and run once or twice each month to circulate their lubricants, drive off damaging moisture, and charge their starter batteries. Do not expect a generator that has been stored in the garage for over a year to start on the first pull, and don't expect it to run with two-year-old fuel in the tank.

Regular monthly testing and running your generator, annual oil and filter maintenance, and keeping insects and rodents from building nests in the air intake is an integral part of keeping your generator ready for an emergency.

Having a portable generator and the fuel to operate can be a real life saver during a week-long power outage, but having an automatic start generator and hard wired automatic transfer switch can be downright decadent.

(Jeff Yago's latest text titled, *Achieving Energy Independence - One Step At A Time*, provides a very good introduction to off-grid living and back-up generator power systems. It is available from the *Backwoods Home* bookstore or by calling 804-784-0063.) Δ

Useful websites

Diesel Generators
Tuban Industrial Products
    www.eGens.com
Imperial Diesel
    www.imperialdiesel.com

Gasoline/Propane Generators
Generac Power Systems
    www.generac.com
Yamaha Generators
    www.yamahagenerators.com
Honda Generators
    www.generators-direct.com
Onan Generators
    www.coloradostandby.com
Kohler Generators
    www.kraftpower.com

**Transfer Switches
and Accessories**
Northern Tool and Equipment
    ww.northerntool.com
Reliance Controls
    www.reliancecontrols.com
Northwest Power Tools
    www.northwestpowertools.com
CVF Supply
    www.cvfsupplycompany.com
Mayberry Sales & Service
    www.mayberrys.com
Norwall power Systems
    www.norwall.com

A Backwoods Home Anthology

The informed juror

How an informed jury helps safeguard liberty

By Dr. Gary F. Arnet

"You are hereby summoned to appear for jury trial service. Failure to respond will subject you to punishment for contempt, including a $1,000 fine, imprisonment for five days, or both."

I understand that jury duty is my civic responsibility, but still when I got this jury duty notice my first thought was, "What a waste of time. How can I get out of this?" The thought of sitting all day in the jury box while lawyers argued back and forth manipulating facts in order to win their case just did not appeal to me. "There must be an excuse I can use to get out of this," I thought.

Then I thought of several newspaper articles I had recently read. In one, a man in our city was sentenced to 42 years to life in prison under California's "three-strikes" law, a law passed by voters to imprison violent criminals for life. Was this man's third strike murder, rape, or assault? No, it was stealing a pair of tennis shoes. "That's not right," I thought, "Nor, is it the intent of the law."

In another case, our local district attorney was quoted in the newspaper as saying he had asked a suspect to voluntarily come in to his office for questioning or else "We will kick your door in and drag you into the street." Wait a minute. If the crime this person is accused of committing is so minor that he can drive himself to the office, why can't the district attorney come to his house and knock on the door? Why would they have to drag him into the street? "That sounds like an abuse of power," I thought.

Then I read about a local 16-year-old high school girl at a large party of high school friends. She apparently took off her clothes, ran around naked, yelled *"What's a girl have to do to get sex around here,"* and then started having sex with multiple young boys at the party. Later, she began drinking liquor she brought to the party, continued with other boys, and passed out from the alcohol. Several boys under age 18 were charged with sexually assaulting her after she passed out. There is no question the boys are at fault and, if guilty, the boys do deserve punishment. Also, there is no question that her actions caused her own problems. It was the actions of the district attorney that got my attention, however.

The boys were given the choice to "voluntarily" plead guilty within five days and attend a "diversionary program" without jail time or else they would be charged as adults, facing eight years in prison and being required to register as sex offenders for the rest of their lives. Not much of a choice.

"Wait a minute," I thought, "Either the crime they are accused of warrants a diversionary program or prison as an adult. Which is it"? Also, "What happened to their constitutional right to a fair trial?" Is the district attorney worried he cannot get a conviction if the jurors consider the girl's actions that night.

Now I knew why I needed to comply with the summons for jury duty. I needed to be there to determine innocence or guilt, but even more so I needed to be there to make sure the defendant received a fair trial and was not "railroaded" by the district attorney.

This was not normal thinking for me. I am an average American citizen who supports my government and police and who is fed up with increasing crime. I believe the police and courts are trying to protect us from criminals. However, more and more, I am disturbed by the loss of our freedoms and our rights, and their attempt to win convictions at all costs.

My "day in court"

On the day of jury duty, I was one of more than 100 people called as prospective jurors for a particular trial. All had taken off work or stopped their daily lives in order to do their civic responsibility. Either that, or the threat of five days in jail for not showing up got their attention. I figured it must be an important trial to need so many prospective jurors.

When we were in the courtroom, I could see a clean-cut young man at the defendant's table. The judge began. "The defendant is accused of spray painting the front door of a business. The charge is vandalism under $400, a misdemeanor."

My first thought was, "What! You took all of us away from our work and lives for this?" My next was, "Wait a minute. This is so minor that I'm sure he could have plea-bargained this charge away if he was guilty. I'll bet the guy is innocent and he wants his day in court." Now I really wanted to be on the jury.

The judge continued. "As jurors, you are required to enforce the law even if you disagree with it. You must use the evidence presented and what you are told the law is as you deliberate this case. You cannot consider anything else. You cannot judge based on your beliefs about the law being right or wrong."

This did not sound right to me. I always believed that a juror has the right and responsibility to use their conscience in making a decision. The instructions given by the judge seemed like a way to manipulate outcome of the trial.

Then I remembered another case. Bryan Epis was charged in Sacramento Federal Court with a four-count federal indictment for "conspiring to manufacture 1000 marijuana plants," a crime which carries a mandatory 10-year prison sentence.

While a federal crime, he was co-founder of Medical Marijuana Caregivers and was operating legally in accordance with California's medical marijuana law established in 1996 by Proposition 215. Under this law, he was allowed to provide marijuana to seriously ill patients who had a doctor's prescription.

Whether or not one believes that the law or the use of marijuana is right, it was the actions of the federal prosecutors and the court that bothered me. The first federal attorney involved in this case offered Mr. Epis four months of house arrest in exchange for a guilty plea without a trial. Wanting the trial he is guaranteed by the *Constitution*, he refused.

A new federal attorney took over the case and offered him four years in prison in exchange for a guilty plea. When Mr. Epis again refused, the federal prosecutor filed charges that carried a mandatory 10-year prison term.

Now I was really confused. Was the crime so minor that four months of house arrest is appropriate, or was it so serious that he deserves 10 years in prison? Or, is the government trying to deny him his right to a trial by threatening a long prison term if he does not plead guilty "voluntarily?" "No problem, he will receive a fair trial and the jurors will decide," I thought.

Suppressing evidence

Unfortunately, that is not how it works anymore. The information the jury is told is severely restricted. They are given just what government (the judge and prosecutors) decide is appropriate, rather than all the facts needed to make an informed decision.

In this case, jurors were not allowed to hear about California medical marijuana laws or the reasons he grew the marijuana. The prosecutor even sought a gag order so the case would not be reported in the newspaper. "If the jurors see that there is a mandatory 10-year sentence, I don't see how the government can receive a fair trial," argued the federal prosecutor.

"Wait a minute," I thought, "Isn't it the defendant who has a right to a fair trial? Where does it say the government has such a right?"

Bryan Epis was convicted and sentenced to the mandatory 10 years in prison. A juror said afterwards that he would not have convicted him if he had known the sentence. So much for a defendant receiving a fair trial.

Today, there are many obstacles to a defendant receiving a fair trial, including bad laws, inappropriate application of laws, and manipulating the information juries can hear.

Bad laws come from many directions. Elected legislators at all levels of our government have swamped us with a tremendous number of laws, many valid and many not. Even good laws are applied inappropriately, as in the case of the man sentenced to 42 to life for stealing a pair of tennis shoes. It was a good law intended to remove violent criminals from society, but wrongly applied to an act of petty theft.

Unelected bureaucrats increasingly have the power to write and enforce regulations that have the effect and consequences of law, often without the right to a trial. Federal and state tax, environmental protection, and occupational safety agencies are all prime examples of such regulatory bodies.

Even the U.S. *Constitution* is constantly under attack. Unbelievably, in a case that is certain to be appealed to the U.S. Supreme Court, the Federal Appeals Court in San Francisco recently ruled that Americans do not have the right to own firearms as individuals, only the state-run militia can own guns. This is a surprising decision even for this notoriously liberal court.

Prosecutors also charge defendants with as many laws as they can find that remotely apply in order to overwhelm the defendant, often bending the laws to try to make them fit. They want a jury to think that with so many charges, the defendant must be guilty of something.

A children's dentist in Pasadena, California, was unfortunate enough to have a patient die in her dental office during treatment, despite following standard care. She was arrested on felony child endangerment, her own children were taken from her, and she was charged with violating 81 laws by the district attorney. At trial, all 81 charges were either dropped or she was found not guilty. Some of the charges were clearly lies and there was no reason she should have been charged in the first place. Jurors stated the trial was a huge waste of taxpayer money. The district attorney and the State Board of Dental Examiners ruined her life without having a case.

Trials without juries

The *Sixth Amendment* to the *Constitution of the United States* gives the accused in criminal prosecutions the right to "a speedy and public trial, by an impartial jury of the State and district wherein the crime shall have been committed." More and more, however, individuals are denied a trial at all.

In family court and cases by the IRS, jury trials are not allowed. Federal law and some state laws deny a trial in cases where the sentence that can be imposed is six months or less. They can charge a defendant with multiple crimes, each with a 6-month penalty that can run consecutively. Therefore, in an end-run around the *Sixth Amendment*, an accused can be sentenced to years in prison without a jury trial. The government tries to avoid a trial whenever possible, knowing that many cases would be thrown out if the juries realized how the laws were being applied.

Stacking juries

Our jury system is certainly not impartial. There are problems with how the jury is selected and the instructions they are given.

"Failure to respond will subject you to punishment for contempt, including $1,000 fine, imprisonment for five days, of both," was the statement that made me show up for jury duty. I wondered how many individuals don't even bother to respond to the summons for jury duty. I asked the court clerk, and, while avoiding directly answering the question, he said, "We send them a summons to see the judge, and if they ignore that a warrant is issued for their arrest." Forcing people to serve on juries is not a way to find impartial jurors.

Of the 100 or so of us summoned for the "graffiti trial," 16 names were randomly called. The judge informed them they were required to follow what they were told the law was, regardless of whether they agreed with it.

They were first questioned regarding whether they could be present the dates of the trial and a number were excused due to schedule conflicts. Sometimes, potential jurors are excused due to the length of the trial being a financial hardship. Often, these will be self-employed or other hard-working individuals who are not paid by their employers while they are on jury duty. This leaves government employees, welfare recipients, retired individuals, some workers of large corporations, and others with "time on their hands" as the main source of jurors.

The judge then excused some jurors because they had heard about the case or knew someone involved in the case. As potential jurors were excused, someone else from the group of 100 would randomly be called to fill their spot.

Next, both the prosecution and defense asked questions to each juror. They both have "peremptory challenges" in which they can remove a potential juror for no reason. This is where they "stack the deck" in their favor by trying to include those who may be sympathetic to their case while removing those who may not. Lawyers also use peremptory challenges to try to adjust the racial and gender make-up of the jury to favor their side.

One young man looked baffled and embarrassed as he was excused without an explanation. While no reason was given, I noted that he was an engineering student. Lawyers typically don't want engineers or others who are too analytical on a jury since they may think the case out rationally. Jurors with education, strong convictions, and knowledge are routinely excluded from juries. Defense lawyers I have spoken with said that prosecutors try to have a jury of impressionable people who have about a seventh grade education and who won't think about the case on their own. They want to be able to easily persuade them.

The problem with juries doesn't end with their selection. The judge and prosecutor control the testimony and the instructions that jurors are allowed to hear. The "whole truth and nothing but the truth" is not heard by the jury, only the information the judge decides should be heard. The judge determines the evidence that is admissible or inadmissible, the importance to be given to any evidence, and then requires jurors to consider only this information.

Many jurors have a problem with this. They want to be told the whole truth and then be allowed to decide the case. How can you judge the case unless you know all the facts?

Twelve jurors were finally selected for my case. Unfortunately, I was one of the many jurors not selected or even questioned. I left not knowing if this man was found innocent or guilty, but knowing that I needed to learn more about the rights of jurors.

What can a juror do?

Since it is pretty clear that it is hard, if not impossible, for a defendant to receive a fair trial today, what can a juror do? We all want criminals off the streets, but jurors are the only people who can make sure the defendant receives a fair trial.

The following is not something jurors will be told or something that the court wants them to know, but it has been so ever since the common law jury system was established almost 800 years ago.

On June 15, 1215, England's King John signed the *Magna Carta* (Great Charter) establishing liberties and rights of the population. Among other things, this established the principle of the right to a jury trial and the right and duty of the jurors to determine and judge the facts, to judge the justice of the law, and to declare the accused innocent. The intent of powers given to the jury was to protect citizens in case the government became too powerful and established laws violating the rights of the people.

The *Magna Carta* later became the basis of our liberties and *Constitution*. America's founding fathers also worried that the government they were creating could become powerful and corrupt, threatening the rights and liberties of Americans.

In the *Constitution* and the *Bill of Rights*, they provided the right to a trial by a jury of one's peers as a method to protect citizens from the power of an over-zealous government. A jury can refuse to convict a defendant who has clearly violated the letter of the law if they feel the law is unjust or unconstitutional, essentially vetoing the effect of the law.

In early America, jurors were told of this right and writings of our founding fathers show this was their intent. John Adams stated in 1771 "It is not only...[the juror's] right, but his duty ... to find the verdict according to his own best understanding, judgment, and conscience, though in direct opposition to the direction of the court."

In 1789, future President Thomas Jefferson stated, "I consider trial by jury as the only anchor yet devised by man by which a government can be held to the principles of its constitution."

Things changed as time went by. A Supreme Court ruling in 1895 found that judges were not at fault if they failed to remind jurors of this right. After that, judges not only stopped telling jurors they can judge the law, they now falsely tell jurors their only job is to decide if the evidence is sufficient to find the accused guilty. They are told they must do this even if they disagree with the law. Defense attorneys can be charged with contempt of court if they inform jurors that they may acquit if they feel the law is unconstitutional, unjust, or applied unfairly.

Jurors' real responsibilities

Throughout the history of America, juries have protected our freedoms by refusing to find an accused guilty of a law they felt was wrong. By refusing to convict an accused, they essentially have vetoed bad laws.

As early as 1735, a printer named John Peter Zenger was accused of seditious libel for publishing an article critical of colonial rule in violation of a law requiring government approval of anything critical of the government. Mr. Zenger admitted to publishing the article, stating that the facts justified publication. The judge stated that truth was no defense for violation of the law and the jury could not consider the truth. Disregarding the judge's instructions, the jury found Mr. Zenger not guilty.

When enough juries acquit defendants that have clearly violated a law, the government eventually stops trying to enforce the law. The Salem witch trials in 1693 were stopped after 50 defendants in a row were acquitted. Before the Civil War, Northern juries refused to convict individuals accused of assisting escaped slaves in violation of the *Fugitive Slave Act*, effectively stopping the law. During Prohibition in the 1930s, convictions of bootleggers and speakeasy owners became rare as jurors refused to convict the accused, despite the *18th Amendment* and the *Volstead Act*. Essentially, they vetoed the law and prosecutors eventually stopped bringing cases to trial. Subsequently, the law was overturned.

Over the years, most of these jurors probably just voted their conscience, not even realizing they had a legal right to judge the law. Many had been told by the judge to only deliberate on the facts presented and not question the fairness of the law.

Each juror has the power to affect change. There is nothing that requires a jury to reach a unanimous verdict. Under criminal law, only one juror must find the accused not guilty for him to be not convicted. When a jury decides to acquit a defendant, the decision is final and cannot be overturned. The judge cannot harass or punish jurors for voting their conscience and they may be asked, but not forced, to explain their verdicts.

If you are called for jury duty, it is an opportunity to protect the rights of the accused and, by doing so, your own rights and freedoms. Most of the time the law will probably be constitutional and, hopefully, applied justly. What can a juror do if it is not?

First of all, understand that nothing in the *Constitution* or Supreme Court decisions requires a juror to take an oath to follow the law as explained by the judge. As a juror, when you in good conscience believe that the law is wrong or unconstitutional, is being applied unfairly, the accused is being unjustly charged or made "an example of" by the government, you have the right and responsibility to find them not guilty, despite what the judge or your fellow jurors say. Remember, your one not guilty vote is all that it takes to prevent conviction. You will get the credit or blame for the results of the trial and will have to live with your decision.

The practice of a juror using their conscience to find a defendant not guilty because the law is unjust has been called jury independence, jury veto, jury discretion, jury referendum, or, commonly by the media, as jury nullification.

Jury nullification is essentially when an accused individual is acquitted of a crime that he clearly committed because the jury feels there are extenuating circumstances, feels the law is unjust or applied unfairly, or because the sentence is too harsh for the crime.

While historically a legal right, judges and prosecutors today fear an informed jury as a loss of their power. Sometimes, the only way the government can get convictions of bad laws is to tell jurors they are required to uphold the law and to bar them from the jury if they disagree. Judges have even told jurors that they may not consider the U.S. *Constitution* in their deliberations.

Prosecutors fear the jury that has all the information, for they may find the government's case or the punishment to be absurd. Do you think a jury would have convicted the man for stealing tennis shoes if they knew he would receive a life sentence? The jurors in Brian Epis' case said they would not have convicted him if they knew he faced a mandatory 10-year sentence.

Jurors will routinely be disqualified if they question the law, if they disagree with the law, or if they question the constitutionality of the law. They are also disqualified if they agree with the concept of an informed jury or of jury nullification. Judges who are hostile to jury nullification have even used their power of "contempt of court" to jail jurors, without a trial, if they believe in or discuss jury nullification with other jurors. An informed jury scares the court like nothing else.

To get more information

For more information on jury rights and what you can do, contact the Fully Informed Jury Association (FIJA), an organization started to inform jurors of their powers and rights, at www.fija.org or P.O. Box 5570, Helena, MT 59604. Also, inform others about jury rights by talking with your friends or writing letters to local newspapers. The more jurors that are aware of their rights, the better our justice system will be.

In America today, our individual rights and freedoms are under constant attack and it is the duty of all of us to defend them. Read the *Constitution* and know your rights as a citizen. If called as a juror, don't immediately look for an excuse to get out of jury duty. Rather, be happy that you can use your right to analyze the case and to vote your conscience to ensure a fair trial. An informed jury is the way we have to stand up to a powerful government. ∆

Restore the Bill of Rights
with
Fully Informed Juries

Find out how ordinary people, as trial jurors, can repair years of legislated special-interest damage to our rights, simply by saying *No* to bad laws!

Phone: 1-800-TEL-JURY
for a free
Jury Power Information Kit!

Want to know what's really going on?

Get Dave Duffy's book of columns

Can America Be Saved From Stupid People

Only $21.95
(plus $4.95 S&H)

www.backwoodshome.com
1-800-835-2418

Growing & storing herbs

By Tom R. Kovach

Herbs are chiefly grown for culinary purposes in seasoning foods, but their medicinal properties have also been used for centuries. They are not that difficult to grow. Here are some helpful tips:

Soil properties

The vast majority of herbs demand a well drained soil with a pH range of 6.0 to 7.5 for successful growth. (A measure of acidity and alkalinity of a solution that is a number on a scale on which a value of 7 represents neutrality and lower numbers indicate increasing acidity and higher numbers increasing alkalinity. Each unit of change represents a tenfold change in acidity or alkalinity). Outside, avoid planting in heavy clay soils as well as areas which are notorious for standing water. Containers used for growing herbs should always have holes in the bottom for proper drainage. Also, avoid using soils which have a high nutrient content. These rich soils may actually prove to be detrimental to the plant's development by promoting rapid, lush growth which is weak in volatile oils, the herb's important characteristic.

Light

Herbs, unless noted shade lovers, require at least 6 to 8 hours of direct sunlight in order to grow well. The more intense the light, the better the oils will develop within the glands of foliage and stems, creating stronger fragrances and seasonings. A southern or western exposure will meet the needs of most herbs, although some may do well in a very bright east-facing location. Inside, it is crucial to give herbs the best light available. During winter, when days are shorter and typically darker, fluorescent lights may be necessary to maintain healthy plants. Ten to twelve hours of artificial light daily is adequate for most indoor grown herbs. Inadequate light will result in spindly, thin growth.

Purchasing herbs

Plants can be obtained from local garden centers and nurseries beginning in early spring. Generally, these sources offer the more common herbs in six-packs or single pots. Speciality mail order catalogues offer more varieties of unusual herbs, but research your choices thoroughly. Northern gardeners have to be content with growing some herbs as annuals which would otherwise be grown as perennials in warmer regions of the country. Lemon verbena and sage are two such examples.

Propagation

It is important to check the specific propagation and planting requirements of each herb because some methods work better with certain herbs than others.

Typically, the herbs grown as annuals are best propagated by seeds or softwood cuttings. Other methods are usually used for hardy perennial herbs. For example, lovage and chives are successfully propagated by division in the spring.

Seeds can be started indoors under fluorescent lights during the late winter months. Lights should be set for 14 to 16 hours daily, placed approximately four to six inches above the seedlings, and raised as they grow.

Herbs should be transplanted outside once frost danger has passed and the soil has warmed and is firm enough to work. Space seedlings with the mature plant size in mind. Crowded conditions will result in tall, weak plants.

Watering

Garden bed plantings should be kept slightly moist between waterings. Water thoroughly by soaking the soil to a depth of approximately 6 to 8 inches to ensure that the root zone is receiving adequate moisture. Outdoors, container grown herbs usually dry out faster then those in beds, so they must be watered more frequently. Inside, water thoroughly when the soil feels dry a half inch or so below the surface, depending on pot size. Never allow the plants to wilt between waterings, but avoid constant soggy soil conditions. This is the cause of root rots which are the most common problem of herbs grown indoors, especially during dark winter months.

Fertilizer

Fertilize sparingly; herbs are not heavy feeders. In most cases, garden beds can benefit from using a 5-10-5 commercial fertilizer at the rate of 3 ounces per every 10 feet of row. Apply once or twice throughout the growing season. Use a liquid fertilizer at half the label-recommended strength once every 4 to 6 weeks or so for indoor plants and every 1 to 4 weeks for herbs in containers indoors.

Mulching

Mulching materials such as straw, marsh hay, and leaves provide good winter protection for hardy perennial herbs. Depending on the size of the plant, a mulch 2 to 5 inches thick will keep the temperatures around the plant more constant during late fall and early spring, keeping winter damage to a minimum. Mulching can also be beneficial during hot, dry periods of the summer by helping maintain moisture in the soil.

Problems

In general, herbs do not have serious problems with insect pests and diseases. If using pesticides, choose only those insecticides and fungicides which are labeled for use on herbs. Aphids and other insects can be somewhat controlled with forceful sprays of water or with insecticidal soaps if they are a constant problem. The most common problem with herbs, particularly those grown indoors, is root rot resulting from over watering and poor light conditions. The best precaution is to provide good soil drainage, bright light, and air circulation.

Harvesting

Culinary herbs can be harvested throughout the growing season by snipping sprigs and leaves as they are needed. Many will contain the best flavor if harvested just before the flowers are beginning to open. By making the cut a few inches down the stem and just above a set of leaves, new growth will constantly be encouraged and a bushier plant will result. This is especially important with annual herbs such as basil which would otherwise become quite woody and less productive if it were left to go to seed.

Herbs grown for their flowers are harvested by picking a few stems or whole bunches just before the flowers are fully opened. And those grown for seed, such as caraway, are best collected late in the season when the seed is ripe.

Regardless of the method used, the time of day is very important. Mid-morning hours are best to harvest as this is when oil content is highest. This is usually just after the dew has dried and before the heat of the day begins.

Once picked, herbs should be gathered quickly and kept out of bright light. Washing the herbs is not required but may be necessary if there is a lot of debris on the foliage. If this is the case, wash gently with warm water and pat dry or use a hair dryer on a low setting. Otherwise, excess water will slow the drying process.

Methods of preserving

Air drying: Gather 4 or 5 stems and tie the ends together. Hang them upside down in a dark, warm, well ventilated room. Label, using small tags, as dried herbs will look different than fresh and mix-ups can easily occur. The foliage should dry in 7 to 14 days depending on conditions. This method also works well for drying seed pods and collecting seeds. To collect seeds, simply place a paper bag around the hanging herb with holes in the side for air circulation.

As the drying process begins, the pods will open, the seeds will drop out and collect on the bottom of the bag.

Air drying can also be done under the same conditions using screen racks. Make sure the herbs are spread out only one layer deep. A cookie sheet or solid surface will not work as well, as only one surface will dry properly.

Oven drying: Again, using a screen type tray, spread the herbs evenly and set the oven no higher than 100°F or at its lowest temperature. Keep the door open and check every 30 seconds. The herbs will dry very quickly, within a minute to a minute and half.

Microwave: Microwave ovens provide the fastest means of drying herbs. But because of different wattages and models, specific settings would best be determined by experimenting with your own microwave. Start with using 15 second intervals and keep checking the herbs until they are thoroughly dried.

Freezing: Freeze small quantities of herbs at a time. A few leaves or sprigs placed in a labeled plastic bag works well. The material can also be chopped up and packed into ice cube tray compartments. Top it off with a little water and freeze. Avoid freezing large quantities as they can't be refrozen once thawed. Properly frozen herbs should be used within a year.

Storage: Once herbs are properly dried, strip the leaves from the stems. Do not keep stems as they tend to retain moisture long after the leaves have dried and may become moldy in storage. Store leaves whole, if possible, as the larger pieces have better flavor retention. However, if space is limited, crumbling or grinding the herbs can work; you'll just have to use more. Store in an airtight container. Herbs stored using these methods can usually last up to a year or a year and a half. Keep stored herbs away from bright light and heat sources and periodically check for any moisture buildup within the container. ∆

**Want a good garden?
Go to:
www.backwoodshome.com**

The amazing Yogurt

By Habeeb Salloum

"Not again!" I thought to myself as I angrily opened my lunch bag. Mother had this day, as she had for a whole week, made us children *arous bi laban* (a yogurt paste spread generously on paper thin bread, then rolled into a long cylinder shape). How I envied my schoolmates munching on neat white bread sandwiches. As I moved away to eat my lunch in a semi-hidden corner, I childishly resolved that when I grew up there would be no more *arous bi laban* for me.

Little did I know in those homesteading days, and in fact long thereafter, that the yogurt which I once detested is one of the healthiest foods known to mankind. My parents had brought with them from Syria a love for this delectable and nutritious dairy product, consumed in the Middle East since the dawn of civilization. Perhaps they did not know its many benefits, but they, as I do now, relished its taste. We ate it almost every day for breakfast and for snacks and I am now sure that this healthy food with a cultural and medical past was one of the reasons we children were rarely sick during our childhood years.

The ancient yogis of India mixed yogurt with honey and called it the "food of the gods." Cleopatra bathed in this milk product to give herself a clear and tender complexion and Genghis Khan fed it to his soldiers to give them courage. One of man's earliest prepared foods, yogurt can claim few equals in the folklore of the culinary arts.

Yet, even though it has been a cherished eatable in Middle Eastern and  Central Asian lands since the dawn of civilization, in the West, before the turn of the century, it was hardly known. Only recently has yogurt gained universal popularity and become a staple in the diet of many North Americans. Today, in the same fashion as in other parts of the world, especially in Asia and eastern Europe, its image as a life-extender has taken hold. Some label it "the miracle milk product," others "a mystery food," while the romantics call it "the elixir of life."

A milk curdled by the actions of cultures with the consistency of custard, yogurt was discovered about 5,000 years ago on the Mesopotamia plains. Later, the Turks, who carried it into eastern and central Europe, gave it the name we still use—yogurt. From the early days of its introduction in that part of the world, especially in Bulgaria, it caught on like wildfire and became known as a health food par excellence.

Modern nutritionists have established that its reputation as an almost medicinal food is justified. It has been found that yogurt contains a digestive enzyme which prolongs life. Humans naturally produce this enzyme in their childhood but it becomes deficient as they reach adulthood. It has also been proved that besides all the healthful elements found in milk, yogurt contains a teeming load of bacteria—about 100 million per gram. These multiply in the intestines and, by getting rid of the accumulated germs, relieve stomach ulcers, dysentery, and promote excellent digestion.

Much more easily digestible than milk, yogurt is ideal for the aged, pregnant women, children, and the sick. In addition, it is believed that regular eaters of this fermented milk tend to have clear skin and find no problem in enjoying a good night's sleep.

All types of milk, ranging from reindeer to cow, can be utilized in the making of yogurt. However, the fat and nutrient values vary depending on whether it is prepared from cream, whole milk, partly skimmed milk, or skimmed milk and if it has additives like fruits or syrups included. On the average, 100 grams of regular, plain yogurt contain 77 calories, 7.1 grams carbohydrates, 5.3 grams protein, 3 grams fat, 229 mg. potassium, 181 mg. calcium, 142 mg. phosphorus, 75.5 mg. sodium, and vitamins B1, B2, and B12.

For those wishing to cut down on the amount of fat, cholesterol, and calories in their diets, this near perfect food made from skimmed milk is a godsend. In preparing meals, brands labeled low-fat and low-cholesterol can be substituted for mayonnaise, sour cream, or similar products. This will constitute a tremendous improvement in their diets, at times working wonders.

Besides its nutritious value, yogurt is a marvelously versatile and adaptable food. It adds richness, flavor, and an appetizing aroma to a myriad of dishes. The possibilities of cooking with this tangy, cultured milk are infinite. It blends well with cheese, eggs, grains, meats, fruits, and vegetables and makes an excellent marinade. Delicious when flavored with syrups, nuts, herbs and spices, it enhances and is enhanced by other foods. The gastronomic repertoire of this so-called "milk of eternal life," which I had once shunned, is endless.

Basic yogurt

The following recipe can be made using all kinds and types of milk. If made from skim milk it is lower in fat and calories but somewhat weak in flavor.

```
2 qts. milk
4 Tbsp. plain yogurt
```

Place the milk in a pot and bring it to a boil, then lower the heat and simmer uncovered for three minutes. Remove it from the heat and transfer to a bowl. Allow to cool to a lukewarm temperature. (You will know that milk is cool enough if your finger in the milk can stand the count of 10.)

Thoroughly stir in yogurt and cover, then wrap with a heavy towel and allow to stand for eight hours.

Refrigerate overnight before serving or use in preparation of food.

Note: Always set aside part of the yogurt for the next batch.

Yogurt gazpacho

This recipe serves about eight. It's excellent on hot summer days.

```
4 cups plain yogurt
2 cups water
1 cucumber, about 8 inches long
2 cloves garlic, crushed
½ cup pulverized almonds
4 Tbsp. finely chopped green onions
2 Tbsp. finely chopped coriander leaves
2 hard boiled eggs, peeled and chopped into small pieces
1 tsp. salt
1 tsp. pepper
1/8 tsp. cayenne
croutons
```

Thoroughly combine yogurt and water in a serving bowl, then stir in remaining ingredients, except croutons. Chill, then serve with each diner adding croutons to taste. ∆

Are you prepared?
Emergency Preparedness and Survival Guide
www.backwoodshome.com

Get Cooking—
Backwoods Home Cooking, that is!

- breads • casseroles • beverages
- canning • jams, jellies & preserves
- salads • soups • vegetables
- appetizers • pasta, rice & beans

Only $21.95
(plus $4.95 S&H)

Call 1-800-835-2418 to order.

Send a check or money order to
BHM, P.O. Box 712, Gold Beach, OR 97444.
Or order online at www.backwoodshome.com

The Fourteenth Year

Successful Cold Storage
By Sylvia Gist

Crisp carrot sticks, fresh cabbage, and fried potatoes from my Montana garden in June? Yes, but only if I've kept them in cold storage from last summer's garden.

A garden is a wise investment and provides the freshest, most nutritious vegetables available during the summer. But I need it to supply vegetables year-round, and that can be a challenge here in northwest Montana. I lean toward self-sufficiency and eating a local, seasonal, sustainable diet; we try to grow what we eat and eat what we grow. We preserve, dehydrate, and freeze both fruits and vegetables, making a trip to the fruit room or freezer a real delight throughout the winter. But I also like to eat some fresh veggies and have succeeded in storing carrots, potatoes, cabbage, and onions until just about the time the next crop is ready. I manage to keep beets, pumpkins, squash, and apples into late winter.

Ideally, I would have a root cellar which maintained the correct temperature for the produce I would like to keep. Unfortunately, it's not that ideal, so I have to look for other places to store things. Fortunately, different vegetables like different temperatures, so everything doesn't have to go in the same place. Other storage options (depending upon the item) include in the ground, under a staircase, unheated rooms, outside stairwells, pits in the ground, or extra refrigerators, to name a few.

A storage method is only the last step to having successful cold storage and fresh vegetables in the winter. The first step begins with the seed catalog; it is extremely important to choose cultivars which store well. For example, not every type of carrot will

Heirloom Australian blue squash in mid-winter

still be edible the following May. Most seed catalogs are good at telling us which ones have good storage qualities. I have relied on their recommendations and have found particular cultivars of a number of vegetables that store very well for me.

Planting time and harvest time also affect the success of storage. Many storage vegetables are planted later and harvested after frost. In the following discussion, I will note what works best for me as I deal with a fairly short growing season and cool nights.

Carrots

The carrot named **Bolero**, a nantes-type hybrid, is a dual purpose carrot. It can be planted early for delicious sweet carrots, but when planted later (in June here), it will achieve a nice size of 6 to 7 inches in length with a 1-1½ inch diameter in time for fall storage. After storage, this carrot will still be crisp and sweet. Harvest as late as possible, after frost, but before the ground freezes. I snap off the green tops right where they join the carrot.

I choose nice straight healthy carrots of good size for storage and bag up the forked, broken, nicked, small, or oversized ones to put in the refrigerator for immediate use in canning, juicing, or munching. Then I take five-gallon plastic buckets, clean washed sand, and a pitcher of water to dampen it. Don't put too much water in the sand as it will pool in the bottom and make it too soggy. I try to dampen the sand in a different container and add the sand to my storage bucket as needed. First I put down a layer of sand and lay carrots side by side. I prefer the carrots don't touch. Then in goes another layer of sand to cover the first layer of carrots. I continue pressing carrots into the sand and adding sand until I am near the top of the bucket, where I put on an extra

207

Potatoes stored in a large basket on the floor of the fruit room

thick layer of sand and lay the lid on top.

This bucket is very heavy, so I put the carrots into it at the site it will spend the winter, which, for me, is at the bottom of a stairwell leading into the basement from the garage. When the weather gets really cold, I throw some rugs and blankets over the buckets to keep them from freezing. For ideal storage, carrots prefer 32° to 40° F and 90 to 95% humidity. If you don't have varmints underground looking for a free meal in winter, you can store them in the ground with a thick layer of mulch to prevent freezing.

Potatoes

Potatoes are a traditional fresh storage food, but all cultivars are not equal. The challenge is to have an edible supply year around.

Last fall I stored Red Norland, Sangre Red, Yukon Gold, and Kennebec potatoes of all sizes. Red Norland sprouted first, followed by Kennebec, Yukon Gold, and Sangre Red. **Sangre Red**, also called Sangre, is a round-to-oblong, white fleshed red potato with shallow eyes. It is a very good new potato as well as being great for storage. Digging them is easy, as they generally cluster very near the plant; it is also a heavy producer. Even though a local nursery lists them as so-so keepers, Sangre has been the last to sprout in storage, with the largest potatoes keeping the best. I will eventually have to pull the sprouts from them also, but I do not have ideal storage facilities—just a room in the basement where I keep my canned goods, where the temperature ranges between 50° and 60° F during the year. Potatoes prefer 40 degrees. Colder temperatures will turn them sugary. Much too crisp and juicy for hash browns in the fall, these Sangres reach the perfect condition for frying in June and July.

By planting these early season potatoes the end of May, I get large potatoes by the end of August, which I harvest in late September. Planting earlier, I can have new potatoes earlier, but for storage it works better to plant later here where frosts may kill the tops the first of June and potatoes grow well into summer as the nights are cool and the days moderate.

Cabbage

One of the greatest challenges in storing vegetables has been the cabbage. I tried a number of methods, but nothing worked until I started to grow cabbage especially bred for storage. So far my favorite is **Storage #4** (available from Johnny's Seeds). It will produce a large, very solid head, which is still nice and solid the following June.

While I start my early cabbages in March (eight weeks before the last expected spring frost), I start the storage cabbages the first week in May, about 100 to 120 days before the first expected frost in the fall, as it will make most of its head late in summer, but grow some and hold well into fall. I dig mine before the ground freezes or before the weather stays below freezing. I cut off the root, leaving 6 inches of the stalk, and trim off those loose outer leaves. I then wrap each very loosely in a plastic grocery bag and store them in the extra refrigerator or upside down in the stairwell next to the buckets I store the carrots in. During the cold months, they do best in the stairwell where ventilation is better. They prefer 32-40 degrees with 90% humidity. As the temperature rises outside, I have to move them to a refrigerator to last into summer. They can produce cabbagey fumes, which may make one reconsider keeping them in the house long term.

Onions

Perhaps my favorite vegetable in storage is the onion. The sweet ones have to be eaten in the summer and early fall, but the pungent ones can last until you have the next crop. A couple of long-day hybrids, **Copra** and **Norstar**, have worked well for me. I start the seed indoors in February, feed them fish fertilizer,

Cabbage after a winter in storage

and set tiny plants out in early May. Norstar matures sooner than Copra, but both are narrow necked hard onions of medium size. In August, I quit watering them.

When they mature, pull and dry them in the sun. If the weather isn't warm enough, it is necessary to push the tops over and then pull them and lay them out to dry for quite a while. When they have dried sufficiently, remove the dry tops (but not the skins) and put the onions in a basket or mesh bag and set or hang in a dry, cold (32° to 35° F.) place where they get ventilation. I don't have a perfect place, but these two cultivars do well even when ideal storage can't quite be met.

For those who prefer non-hybrids, the yellow potato onion, a multiplier onion, is terrific. They are smaller (up to 1½ inch), but store extremely well, being very hard well into summer. You plant this onion in early fall and mulch for winter. Remove the mulch in spring to find sprouts which can soon provide green scallions or grow (with liberal watering) into bunches of small onions which will dry down in July. Be sure to save some to plant for the next crop.

Squash and pumpkins

An easy crop to store is squash or pumpkins. Nearly all kinds labeled winter squash and even mature summer squash, such as the **Mid East cousa** type, can keep almost six months if they are picked at the right time and cured properly. At harvest, the skin should be so hard that a fingernail won't puncture it. Leave the stem on and cure both squash and pumpkin in the sun at 70° to 80° F for 10 to 14 days. If properly cured and later stored at 55° to 60° F with 60 to 70% humidity, they should hold through most of the winter. An unheated bedroom works well for me. Pies from fresh pumpkin taste delicious in March.

Beets

I hadn't even considered storing beets until a few that I had just thrown in a plastic bag in the refrigerator were in pretty good shape a couple of months later. Upon investigation, I discovered that, although the common Detroit Dark Red that I was planting can be stored if done properly, there are specific beets for winter storage. I purchased some **Lutz Greenleaf** seed and sowed it in the spring along with my other spring beets. It took a long time to germinate and then grew slowly, but in October, I dug some softball sized beets to store. Unless you are using a long season beet like Lutz, the seed should be sown in June or July for late harvest.

Beets tend to be more susceptible to frost damage (their shoulders often stick out of the ground), so they should be harvested before a killing frost. Harvest only mature beets and cut off the tops, leaving an inch of stem. Do not remove any of the root

Onions hanging in ventilated baskets in fruit room

Bolero carrots being removed from the bucket of sand in June following eight months in storage

tip. Brush off the dirt and pack in layers in damp sawdust, sand, or moss. Keep cold (near 32° F) and very moist at 90 to 85% humidity. As mentioned before, unwashed beets keep quite a while in bags in a refrigerator. Depending upon storage conditions, beets can last anywhere from two to five months in storage.

Winter radishes

If you like radishes, you can enjoy them throughout the winter if you plant the winter type. There are a number of cultivars which lend themselves to storage: **Miyashige** (fall harvest Daikon), **Long Black Spanish**, **Misato Rose Flesh**, **China Rose**, **Round Black Spanish**, and **Radish Sakwiajima Mammoth** to name a few. Generally, the planting date is July or early August, but each cultivar could be different, so pay attention to what the seed catalog tells you and adjust for your particular growing season. These radishes use more space; they not only may grow larger roots, but their tops are more leafy. Harvest in the fall and store only perfect roots. Trim off the leafy tops and treat like carrots, layered in moist sand, moss, or sawdust in your coldest above freezing storage place. They should last until February if stored properly.

Rutabagas/turnips

Rutabagas, known also as Swede turnips, are good candidates for storage. The turnip, however, gets mixed reviews. Johnny's Seeds doesn't recommend turnip storage, but some people have done it. Plant **Purple Top White Globe** in July or August and harvest three-inch maximum roots before heavy frost, cut off the tops, and treat them like carrots.

Laurentian and **Purple Top** (rutabaga, not turnip) are two common rutabaga cultivars recommended for winter storage. Plant in mid-June to mid-July or 90 days before intended harvest. Wait until there has been at least a couple of good frosts, usually October here, before digging for storage. If the roots are working their way out of the ground, I would hill some soil over them or mulch them when there may be a chance of freezing so the roots don't get damaged before I harvest. Cut off the tops and store like carrots. However, rutabagas shrivel easier than carrots, so you want to be sure to keep them moist. They can be waxed (sometimes you see them waxed in the supermarkets) to reduce dehydration; beeswax would be best if you choose this route. Rutabagas can be expected to last for two to four months in storage.

Celeriac

Celeriac, sometimes described as turnip-rooted celery, is an excellent keeper. **Monarch** and **Brilliant** are two good cultivars available. The trick with celeriac is the planting time. Start indoors (slow to germinate) in April but do not set out in the garden until June when the temperatures are averaging above 50° F. If the weather is too cold, the plant will think that it has passed through the first summer (in your house or greenhouse) and is in the winter cool down; when it warms up, the plant may bolt and go to seed.

Celeriac requires rich soil and plenty of moisture like celery, but is actually easier to grow. You don't want the plant to mature too early and get woody before you harvest. When you dig celeriac, break off the stocks, brush off the dirt, and remove long fine roots, if desired. It will keep a while on a shelf in the cellar; for the long haul, layer in moist sand, moss, or sawdust. Keep at 32° to 40° F with 90 to 95 % humidity.

Parsnips

Rated as the hardiest of all root vegetables, the parsnip could be awarded "best of show" when it comes to storage. **Harris Model** and related cultivars are popular. Since all parsnips are intended for storage, choose one that fits your needs (some are resistant to disease, etc.). Dig a deep bed and plant fresh seeds early in the spring, March through May (depending upon your season). Be patient as they may germinate slowly (up to 28 days). It takes a long season (100-120 days) and freezing weather to produce tasty parsnips. Frosty weather helps starch in the root turn to sugar so they taste sweeter. Then you can begin harvest.

You actually have four options. You can take advantage of all four. First, after a few moderate to heavy frosts, you can dig some to eat immediately. Because the roots can get very long, digging, not pulling, is recommended. Or to keep the ground from freezing, put down some mulch so you can dig later.

Even though the ground may not freeze under the mulch, you may not want to go out and dig in mid-winter; dig and store some in the cellar. These roots should have the leaves trimmed and be stored like carrots in damp sand, moss, or sawdust. Ideal conditions are 32-35 degrees and 90-95% humidity.

And for the final option, when the ground thaws in the spring, go out and dig the sweetest parsnips. They will be good until new leaves are formed; they get woody after they begin to grow. With parsnips, the last really could be the best.

Apples

Apples are the only fruit I have tried to store fresh through the winter. Since there are hundreds of cultivars, there should be quite a few that store well. The nursery catalogs will usually indicate that attribute. Usually, the storage apple will ripen late, so that it can be picked in cool weather. The apple I have had great success with is **Honeycrisp**. It has a sweet-tart flavor and is exceptionally crisp, features that were still noticeable after months in my extra refrigerator. Although a tad shriveled, they made excellent applesauce.

Some helpful pointers in harvesting apples: pick mature fruit, leave the stem on the apple, and cool fruit overnight before storing if the day is somewhat warm. Apples last best if stored near 32° F at 80 to 90% humidity; the warmer the temperatures, the faster they soften. They should be kept in shallow layers in baskets or slatted crates; they also need to be checked for spoilage occasionally. It is wonderful to have some homegrown fresh fruit to go with all those winter vegetables. They should be stored separately, though, as apples give off ethylene gas, which ages vegetables.

General harvesting tips

In cold storage, we are taking advantage of the plant's natural dormant stage between seasons. Success rates are also raised by following proven guidelines. Harvesting in dry, cool weather is helpful because cold weather encourages the vegetables to store sugars and starches rather than water in the roots. Brush off the dirt gently, but cleaning isn't necessary. Don't bruise the produce. Store only the best produce; bruised, broken, or nicked vegetables be used soon. Tops should be clipped immediately; if left on, they suck moisture from the root. Many tops are good to eat; chop some and dehydrate to add to soups later.

Folklore recommends that you pick apples and harvest root vegetables during the decrease of the moon, in the third and fourth quarters, because bruised spots will dry, not rot, and the food will keep better. If you follow the moon in planting and harvesting, you might want to keep this in mind also.

Two books which have been helpful for me to pursue my goal of providing the kitchen with year around vegetables from my garden are *Root Cellaring* by Mike and Nancy Bubel and *Four-Season Harvest* by Eliot Coleman. The first is about the natural cold storage of fruits and vegetables, with drawings for possible root cellars (and alternate hideaways) and details of how to store many different varieties of garden produce. Coleman's book is basically about ways to extend your gardening season, but includes a chapter on root cellars and indoor harvesting. Reading these books opened my eyes to the possibilities of having a larger variety of fresh vegetables from my own garden throughout the year.

Successful cold storage review

1. Select the best cultivar.
2. Plant at the right time.
3. Harvest at the right time.
4. Store properly.

I follow these steps, keep notes on planting and harvesting dates to determine the right time for my area, and store under the best conditions I have available. It can work for you too. Δ

HOPE FOR THE BEST PLAN FOR THE WORST

Backwoods Home Magazine has produced a book you may find useful in the coming months. It's a 300-page anthology of articles that addresses various aspects of preparedness.

Both for $27 (plus $4.95 S&H)

The articles have been gleaned from previous issues of *BHM* but have been edited to bring them up to date. Covered topics include fuel storage, food and water storage, cooking from food storage, maintaining electricity in a crisis, emergency medical kits, an emergency vehicle kit, a survival garden, and defensive firearms. We also have a companion CD-ROM containing the same articles, plus dozens more comprising hundreds of pages of information.

Book $21.95   CD-ROM $12.95

To order call 800-835-2418

or send check to *Backwoods Home Magazine*, PO Box 712, Gold Beach, OR 97444

Chokecherries

By Jackie Clay

Note chokecherries' leaf shape and clusters of berries

As chokecherries are found in nearly every state and climate, it's no wonder that Native Americans (who really lived self-reliance to the hilt!) of most tribes used them extensively. And, like ancient Indians, we also rely on these fruits of the wild orchard.

Finding and identifying chokecherries

Chokecherries grow along semi-open areas, often near water. They are usually a smallish shrub to small tree in shape, usually growing in groves. The leaf and bark resemble a sour domestic cherry. The chokecherries are easily spotted in the spring when their single white blossoms make them stand out dramatically. The blossoms hang in small, long bunches and perfume the air for weeks.

The cherries themselves begin as red, but you don't want to eat them then or you'll really know where they got their name! Yuck! They are puckering bitter. But as the weeks pass, keep an eye on those red, grape-like clusters, and you'll see them get darker and darker, finally turning a deep purple-black. When they are first dark, they are still a bit sour, but that's when you want to pick them for jelly, jam, and preserves.

As with every other native fruit, you do want to make sure what you are picking. About the only non-edible I can think of that you could possibly confuse the cherries with is nightshade. The berries are the same colors: red then black. But nightshade, which is poisonous, is a vine, not a tree or shrub and the leaves are not cherry-like.

Picking chokecherries

Chokecherries are usually abundant and easy to pick. Bob and I just picked three gallons in an hour. The one good thing about chokecherries is that you don't have to climb to pick 'em. I learned a lesson from an old black bear sow with cubs. There was a row of chokecherries along one of our pastures. I'd already picked a lot of them, leaving the big, plump bunches out of my reach. She strolled up to a bush, then right over it. As the branches bent under her weight, she just stood there pawing bunches of cherries into her mouth with great delicacy.

The cubs quickly learned her trick and simply snacked on the juicy cherries from ground level. I watched those three bears for an hour, learning much about pro-berry picking.

You can use her tricks, bending the bushes down to easy-picking level, but be careful not to snap them by over-doing the bending. We'll all need those bushes next year.

I generally pick into a small basket or pail of no more than a gallon in capacity. This is easy to handle and still light when full. When it's full, I dump it into a larger pail or basket, safely waiting in the truck. One reason that I pick into a small basket is because I've used larger baskets, then dumped the whole shooting match on the ground. Since then, I don't put all my cherries in one basket. This is especially important when your children go harvesting with you. They want to help, but can get a little excited. Spills are frequent.

I hold my basket directly under a bunch and strip the whole bunch into it (like milking a cow). Picking one cherry at a time is extremely time-consuming as they are smaller than wild grapes.

Extracting the juice

The most common use for chokecherries is jelly. This is followed by wine-making. As we are a family of non-drinkers, I don't do this, but I do make a lot of jelly. To do either, you will need to extract the juice from the chokecherries. Be advised that although the cherries are

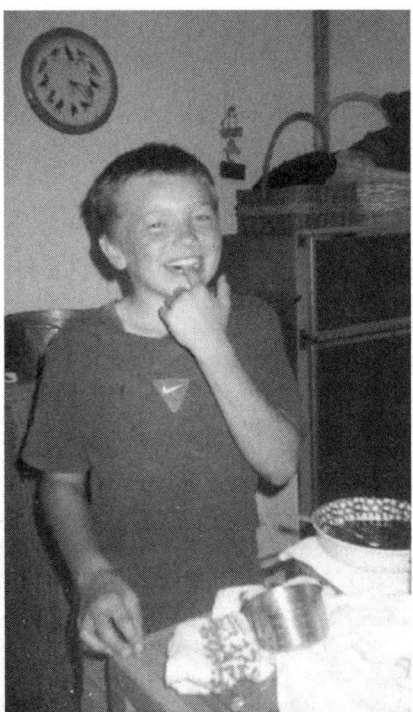

David, the official taste tester. I guess it passes.

juicy, they actually produce a small amount of juice. Three gallons of cherries will give about 4-5 cups of juice.

The usual procedure is to add ½ cup of water to the chokecherries in a large kettle and simmer for ten minutes. I help this out a bit by mooshing the cherries with my hands, squashing as many as I can to release more juice. The skin will hold a lot of juice in, even when simmered. As the cherries heat, I continue mooshing. Watch it, as the water/juice will get hot quickly and can burn you.

My son, David, loves this, as it is fun, and it turns your hands purple. (I tell folks watching me that if wine-makers can stomp grapes with bare feet, I can "moosh" chokecherries!)

When the batch is too hot to handle, stir constantly with a wood spoon. You don't want it to scorch, which it can quickly do, ruining the whole batch.

To extract the juice, dampen three layers of cheesecloth or a clean old

After "mooshing" and simmering, the mass is hung overnight in a jelly bag.

sheet about 20" square. Lay the dampened cloth in a colander, in a large bowl, then pour the cherries and juice out into it. Carefully tie up this improvised jelly bag with a strong cord, then hang it on a sturdy nail, just above the bowl. Remove the colander.

This must drip over night. In the morning, gently squeeze the bag and again let it drip for an hour. You can tweak it a bit more by placing a weight on top of the bag, in a colander over a bowl. This will result in slightly cloudy jelly, but you'll get more juice.

If you are making jelly or wine, your juice is now ready to proceed. If you're in a great hurry or want to harvest tons more chokecherries, you can simply can the juice. I do it all the time. We even use the juice, mixed with other juices, such as apple and pear and add some honey as a natural alternative to Kool-Aid. The chokecherry juice is strong, so a little goes a long way, and it tastes great.

When you want to get more "harvest" out of your chokecherries, you can squish the warm cherries through a sieve. This lets you make jam and preserves. It's also how some Indian tribes processed the cherries to make pemmican and other dried cakes to use for winter. Others ground whole cherries. I'm a little leery of this as the pits contain a toxin related to cyanide.

It takes quite a while to mash the cherries and juice through a sieve, but it's worth it, as you will get more to work with.

Here's a recipe for chokecherry jelly that is quite fool-proof.

Chokecherry jelly

5 cups juice
1 package Slim Set Fruit Pectin
3 cups sugar

You may add ½ cup water or apple juice to get exact measure (no more).

Add 1 package of Slim Set Fruit Pectin to juice in eight quart saucepan or pot, stirring well. Heat on high, stirring constantly, until it comes to a full boil. Stir in sugar, mixing well. Bring to full rolling boil, stirring constantly. Boil exactly one minute, stirring constantly. Remove from heat. Skim off foam, if desired. Fill hot, sterilized jars quickly, wipe off rims, and seal. Process immediately in hot water bath, which covers entire jars for five minutes. For altitudes above 1,000', check canning book for directions.

You can use the chokecherry pulp, which you have sieved, as above in any sour cherry recipe for jams or preserves. I use this native cherry jam as "plum sauce" for meats and an addition to many oriental dishes calling for that certain sweet-sour combination. I even plop a tablespoonful into a stir-fry with a teaspoon of chili paste for unique robust flavor.

Dehydrated chokecherry pulp

Chokecherry pulp dehydrates very well, making an "ugly" but useful fruit leather. I often mix sugar with it to taste, then dehydrate to harder-than-leather. When I want to use it, I can break off small pieces to rehydrate. One of our favorite uses is rehydrated tiny bits of chokecherry pulp in fresh, steaming homemade muffins. They also work well in pancakes, waffles, breakfast cakes, etc.

I shouldn't tell you David's secret, favorite snack, but I will. He likes to mix up a package of melted chocolate chips with pounded-to-flour dried chokecherries. He dips out spoonfuls of this mix onto a slightly buttered cookie sheet to dry. This turns out like large cherry-chocolate "kisses."

Indians and mountain men pounded dehydrated chokecherry pulp with smoked jerky and enough rendered fat to hold it together, making pemmican, the original "trail-mix," which was actually small, thin cakes. This provided a filling, high-energy food that kept well on the trail. This is a long way from so-called pemmican available today in plastic-wrapped strips—no fruit, no fat (calories for hard travelling in cold weather) and "mystery meat."

If you don't already make chokecherry gathering part of your family's wild harvesting, I hope you will next season. Remember to watch for those beautiful clusters of white blossoms in the springtime, calling you to enjoy their fall bounty. There's plenty for all of us. Ma bear, the robins, you.....and me! Δ

Jackie picks chokecherries along the river.

Alternative lifestyles

By Dorothy Ainsworth

My brother Leonard was a devoted but comically unconventional single father with two teenaged sons. He worked as a consultant for city and private water departments as a chemical engineer "on call" and traveled a lot.

On one such three-month assignment, the supervisor encouraged him to stay on the premises of the huge stock yard where he worked as a water-quality inspector by day and a watchman at night. The grounds had an office with bathroom facilities and a shower.

Since it was summer and the kids were out of school, Leonard thought of a brilliant idea for the housing situation and acted on it without hesitation.

He bought three little 16-foot self-contained travel trailers cheap ($300 apiece in the *Nickel WantAds*), towed them one by one into a shady corner of the yard and set them up "pow-wow" style—in a circle with all the doors facing the "campfire." Each brave had his own private realm of being, but the chief could keep an eye on things.

It worked unbelievably well. Son, Tim, 17, decorated his "bachelor pad" with rock star posters, and practiced his guitar constantly. Son, Dwain, 13, was into *Star Wars* and played hand-held video games that went "bleep bleep" incessantly. Now Dad could finally rest in peace in his own quiet capsule after a hard day's work.

The boys didn't feel a need to compete or rebel because they each had their own space. If they had a temporary grievance with Dad or a spontaneous outburst with each other they could take great pleasure in slamming their doors shut and locking themselves inside. Being able to run away without leaving home was the perfect solution for disgruntled teenagers.

When they were in the mood to socialize, which was often, they'd all prop their doors open, sit on their makeshift steps, and contemplate the universe, or affectionately banter and tease each other. When it came to the wit and humor department though, the boys were hard-pressed to ever get the best of their old man, who was a combination of Dave Barry, Gary Larson, and Einstein. I've never known a funnier man.

Almost every evening Leonard would bring out his acoustic guitar, and together with Tim on electric guitar and Dwain on harmonica, they'd enjoy a laughable jam session trading licks from Elvis to Aerosmith.

No matter what the mood-of-the-day was, one sure way to coax the boys out of their holes was by their noses. Leonard would cook up some aromatically enticing concoction, like hamburger and onions and fried potatoes, and pretty soon he'd hear two doors pop open. Then "sniff sniff," "knock knock": "Hey, Dad, we're hungry. What's for dinner?" right on cue.

Leonard saved a lot of money that summer. Before going on to the next job, he sold the trailers, got his investment back and moved to the big city—this time to a permanent position as superintendent of a water department in southern California. He rented a conventional house and tried to live a conventional life (Studebaker collection notwithstanding), but nothing ever quite compared to the fun, comraderie, and freedom of those good ole campout days. (Sadly, we lost Leonard in a plane crash in 1999.)

When I visited the "Tin Men" that summer and saw their communal arrangement first-hand, I was impressed and amused by such a creative idea and have since concluded that it would work in a variety of circumstances.

Instead of burying your teenagers between the ages of 13 and 17 and digging them up later (as the saying goes), just lovingly set them up in a travel trailer(s) in the backyard or carport. Ideally, they could work and save enough money to buy their own trailer of choice, thus earning their precious privacy, and valuing their "real estate purchase" to the max.

There are other practical applications for "disposable" trailers: If you are a family developing a piece of land and building a house, you could buy two, three, or more camp trailers and enjoy temporary "modular-living" for the fun and novelty of it, as well as saving money on rent. Search the want-ads for retro "Sputnik era" trailers—they're a dime a dozen and you can always recycle them.

Involving the whole family in the building process is an enlightening and bonding experience for all. Mom and Dad could set up the main (larger) trailer or RV, with communal electical hook-up and plumbing connected to the septic system, then stake out the kids here and there in the outpost camp trailers. After working together all day, each "party" would retire to their own cubbyhole to R&R. Not only teenagers crave the privacy of their own separate space. If they'd listen carefully they would hear an audible sigh of relief coming from Mom and Dad's trailer too.

Another use for a travel trailer is to convert it to a bathroom-on-wheels. Gut it out, build a painted-plywood shower, install a toilet and wash basin, hang a mirror and you're all set until the house is built. Of course you'll need electricity for the water heater (installed next to the shower stall), a water line, and septic hook-up, but that's it.

I know because I did just that while I was building my own house (which took years). When I was through using my "humble commode" I advertised it for sale in the *Nickel Want Ads* for $500 and got so many calls I could have sold 20 of them. Mobile is the way to go. You can get rid of anything with wheels and a trailer hitch. Δ

Want self-reliance?
www.backwoodshome.com

The Fourteenth Year

Homemade
cottage cheese, rhubarb pie, lemon custard pudding cake, pasties, beef stew, biscuits, butter, grouse breast

By Jackie Clay

We've all been there; we are striving toward a self-reliant lifestyle, growing, raising, and foraging much of our family's food. After all, we realize that not only does this give us control over what we eat (chemicals, ripening sprays, insecticides, bacteria, etc.), but home-raised foods taste terrific. Using these home-raised foods in quantity for daily meals allows us to eat cheaper, thus being able to put aside precious cash for other needs.

Our grandparents and some of our parents lived through the depression, and I know most of them say there was very little cash, but their family ate wonderful meals. By putting a little effort and imagination into it, meals using as many home-raised ingredients as possible can bestow untold riches on a family with a tight budget.

"Making your own" is not labor intensive and can be done in minutes.

Making cottage cheese

I've just set a big bowl of cottage cheese and I timed myself. Total time, so far, is 10 minutes. I'm working on this article now, and when I finish I'll spend another few minutes before it is set to drain, nearly finished. And this will provide our family with five pounds of cottage cheese. Wonderful cheezie cottage cheese with no chemicals. Five pounds of that watered down stuff in a cottage cheese carton at the store costs over $12. So who wants five pounds of cottage cheese? Legitimate question. Well, I'll pack two pounds in a freezer box and pop it into my freezer, we'll eat a pound fresh, and the other two pounds I'll press to make a basic cream cheese to use either with herbs on crackers, homemade bread, or in desserts such as cheesecake. I also use fresh cottage cheese in such things as lasagna.

The "hardest" part of making cottage cheese is first setting the starter. While you can inoculate milk for cheeses with commercial buttermilk, you will have some failures as it is sometimes weak and old. You can purchase freeze-dried packets of all-purpose cultures or specialized cultures for such cheeses as cheddar or blue cheese, should your cheese making expand. (Be warned that once you try the super-simple cottage cheese, you'll immediately begin thinking of making all of your favorite cheeses.)

Making the cheese starter:

Have several ice cube trays on hand to hold 2 quarts. Check the cube sizes to see if they are 1 or 2 ounces, as you will need a measured amount of starter later on.

Sterilize a half-gallon canning jar and lid by boiling for 10 minutes. Set the jar to cool, upside down. Pour fresh, strained, warm-from-the-animal milk into the warm jar, then put the lid and ring on snugly. Place in a water bath canner full of hot water, totally immersing the jar. Bring to a boil, then reduce to a simmering boil for 30 minutes.

Remove jar from kettle and let it cool to room temperature. The milk will be about 72°. Inoculate the milk quickly, adding the starter, then put the cover back on and gently rotate the jar to dissolve the starter, mixing it thoroughly with the milk.

Wrap with a couple of towels and hold at 72° for about 16-30 hours. You can use a yogurt incubator or simply set it over the pilot of your gas stove or some other inventive place. When done, the milk will be firm, like yogurt. As you won't be making 100 pounds of cheese, and as the starter will only remain good for about 3 days, it's easiest to freeze the batch using ice cube trays. Cover the full trays with foil or plastic wrap and

The garden, woods, and farmyard feeds a family from a well stocked pantry.

freeze. When hard, dump all the trays out into double baggies and store in the freezer. You can use all these cubes in the future for making cheeses, sour cream and other dairy products requiring a starter. Needless to say, I choose one day to make the starter (which only requires about an hour, all totaled) and another day to set my first batch of cheese.

Large curd cottage cheese:

> 1 gallon whole goat or cow milk
> 4 oz. of cheese starter (see recipe above)
> 1 tsp. rennet solution (4 drops liquid animal rennet mixed in 1/3 cup warm, boiled water)
> (makes about 1½ pounds)

1. Fill sink with very hot water. Pour the milk into a stainless steel kettle or deep glass container. Place a dairy thermometer in the milk, and wait until it reaches 72°.

2. Add the cheese starter and 1 tsp. of the rennet solution. Stir well. Cover the container and allow to ripen at 72° for 24 hours or more until it sets into a thick, custard-like curd.

3. Line a colander with a damp cheesecloth and pour in the curd. Catch the whey and feed it to the pigs or chickens, or save for other uses.

4. Gather up the cheesecloth, tie it closed with sturdy clean cord, and hang up the bag of curds over a bowl to drain over night.

5. Turn the cottage cheese out and serve cold or use it in any recipe.

You may save some, pressing it very firmly in any innovative mold (tin can with holes, PVC mold, etc.), which will result in a cream cheese type texture, used as a spread or even in cheese cakes. We add fresh herbs, fruits, and even ground nuts to our cottage cheese and pseudo-cream cheese, and never have leftovers. Total cost of a pound and a half of cream cheese, if you have your own milk, is about 12 cents.

Want it even cheaper and quicker? I often use this method.

Heat one gallon of fresh, warm milk to 180° and remove from heat. Add ¼ cup cider vinegar to the milk. The curd will form immediately. Drain in cheesecloth for several hours. Now it is cottage cheese. Or you can further press it into a semi-soft, cream cheese type product. Total cost is about three cents.

Desserts

When you have your own chickens, you can discover hundreds of ways to use eggs in meals without resorting to plain old eggs all the time. Some of the "sneakiest" ways of disposing of a bounty of eggs is to crank out the desserts.

Grandma's rhubarb pie:

One of my family's favorite non-egg use of eggs is Grandma's rhubarb pie. As we have abundant rhubarb both in the spring and in the pantry, we enjoy this special treat year-round. And because of the added eggs, this rhubarb pie recipe is not sour or bitter.

> 9" pie pastry
> fresh rhubarb to fill pie tin
> 1½ cups sugar
> 1 heaping Tbsp. flour
> ½ tsp. salt
> 1 Tbsp. butter
> 3 eggs, separated
> cold water
> 3 Tbsp. sugar
> pinch salt

Line a 9" pie tin with single pie pastry, fluting edge. Cut up enough fresh rhubarb to fill pie tin. In mixing bowl, combine 1½ cups of sugar, 1 heaping Tbsp. flour, ½ tsp. salt, 1 Tbsp. butter. Add 3 slightly beaten egg yolks, reserving the whites, and enough cold water to make a batter thin enough to pour from a spoon. Put rhubarb in unbaked pie shell and pour on batter. Bake at 350° until rhubarb is tender. While it is nearing this stage, make a meringue using 3 beaten egg whites, 3 Tbsp. sugar, and a pinch of salt. Beat until it holds peaks, then top the hot pie, sealing meringue to all the edges and peaking the top decoratively. Bake at 375° until meringue is golden brown. Serve cold. If I have lots of eggs, I sometimes double the meringue recipe, making a "mile-high-pie." Impressive!

Lemon custard pudding cake:

Another favorite of ours is lemon custard pudding cake. It only takes a few minutes to mix and is really a treat. (Besides it uses 4 eggs and 6 tablespoons of homemade butter.)

> 6 Tbsp. flour
> 6 Tbsp. butter, melted
> 2 cups sugar, divided
> 4 eggs, separated
> 1½ cups milk
> Grated peel of 1 lemon
> 2 Tbsp. fresh lemon juice
> Confectioner's sugar

In large mixing bowl, combine flour, butter, and 1½ cups sugar. Separate eggs; beat yolks and add to mixing bowl along with milk and lemon peel. Mix well. Add lemon juice. In another bowl, beat egg whites until stiff, slowly adding remaining ½ cup of sugar. Fold this into batter. Pour into a greased 2-quart baking dish. Place in a shallow pan of hot water and bake at 350° for one hour or until lightly browned. Serve warm or cold with powered sugar dusted on top. Makes six servings.

As you examine the above recipes you'll see that they contain ingredients found in my garden, canned or dried by me, or in our storage pantry. Our cow gives the milk/butter, the chickens give the eggs, the lemon I buy on sale. The rest is in the dry goods pantry. You can see I don't have to go to the store a whole lot.

Entrees

How about entrees? These are even less of a problem when we are trying to save money. With hunting or home raised meat supplying nearly all the meat, and the garden supplying the vegetables, take a look at these cheap, scrumptious meals:

Pasties:

> 4 8" pie pastry crusts, unbaked
> 1 lb. lean stewing beef/venison, cut into ½" chunks
> ½" mushroom slices (we use wild, foraged safe varieties)
> 8 med. raw carrots, sliced
> 1 med. raw rutabaga, diced
> 1 large raw onion, sliced
> 2 med. potatoes, diced into ½" cubes
> ½ lb. butter
> salt and pepper (or herbs) to taste

Place 1 pie crust on greased baking sheet and place ¼ of meat/vegetable mix on half of round. Add ¼ of the butter on top, then salt and pepper. Moisten the entire outer edge of the circle of pastry, then fold in half, over the filling. Crimp the edges well. You can use your fingers, pinching the pastry together, or use a fork to seal the edge. Repeat until you have four pasties, ready to bake. You may need two baking sheets. Prick vent holes on top to allow some steam to escape. I don't cut vents, as it allows too much steam to escape, resulting in rather dry filling.

Bake at 375° until golden brown. When you remove from the oven, brush butter on top. I use these a lot when canoeing or on a wilderness trek. Sort of old-fashioned MREs. And when you've eaten a pasty, you are full. Besides, they're really good. At home, you might serve them with leftover brown gravy. Just poke a hole in top, and drizzle the gravy inside to moisten up things a bit. Of course, this can be tough on the trail so I usually eat them dry. But you can rehydrate one of those cheap packs of instant brown gravy in about two minutes.

One tip, should you want to carry them on a trip. I wrap hot pasties in several thicknesses of newspaper, then with tin foil. They will keep hot for hours this way. Welsh and Scandinavian miners used pasties as a hot, homemade lunch. And they needed something that would stick to their ribs the rest of the exhausting work day.

Beef stew:

Another of our old-fashioned favorites is good old beef stew, served with hot, homemade biscuits. Of course, I've made it as frequently with venison, elk, or moose as I have with beef. The taste of this stew never changes. It's always stupendous.

> 1 lb. good, lean stew meat, cut into 1" chunks, no fat, no grizzle
> 3 large potatoes, cut into 1" chunks
> 2 large onions, quartered
> 4 carrots, sliced thickly
> 1 quart of tomato sauce
> 1 rib of celery, sliced

Place 2 Tbsp. butter into 2-quart cast iron Dutch oven and heat over medium flame. Sear meat on all sides. Add tomato sauce, 1 cup of water, then all vegetables. Mix well. Season to your family's taste. We use salt, pepper, and 1 Tbsp. of mild chili powder, plus 2 Tbsp. brown sugar. Cover and cook at a low heat until meat is very tender. If you must, add a bit of water as cooking progresses to avoid scorching. But at the last, I take off the cover to make it less like soup and more like a thick stew. Serve hot with biscuits.

Jackie's biscuits:

> 2 cups flour
> 2 tsp. baking powder
> 1 tsp. salt
> ⅓ cup shortening
> ½ cup dry milk
> warm water

In medium mixing bowl, combine first five ingredients, mixing well but not over-doing it. Add warm water until dough is quite soft but not so sticky you can't pat it out on a floured board. (If you get it too sticky, just add a bit of flour and knead it in lightly.) Pat it out on a floured board, then roll it flat, leaving it about ¾" thick. Grease a cookie sheet, then cut out biscuits with a biscuit cutter. I use a regular canning jar ring. It makes them just right. As you carry each one to the baking sheet, pat it in a little to "fluff it up," making it slightly thicker.

Arrange all biscuits so they are touching one another. Bake at 375° until they are just getting golden. Don't over-bake. Brush tops with butter and serve hot with honey and a good bowl of stew. They are great for breakfast, too. A nice touch is to sprinkle sesame or poppy seeds, even sugar and cinnamon, on top before serving.

Of course you can use fresh milk in place of dry milk. Just use warm milk in place of the dry milk and water. The warm liquid, I've found, makes the biscuits rise higher and become more tender. Also, you can use warm buttermilk in place of fresh milk for a different taste and texture. Just use cultured-buttermilk, not fresh buttermilk, left over from butter making.

I often make a double or even triple batch, then use these fluffy, satisfying delights for such things as chicken a la king, strawberry shortcake, or sausage patty, egg, and cheese breakfast biscuits.

Tasty butter:

And, of course, you'll want plenty of fresh butter to go with those hot biscuits. Here's a simple, quick way to turn your cow's cream into the most tasty butter you've ever eaten. I know words such as butter and eggs are not politically correct today, but if you work at feeding the cow and chickens, shoveling manure and chasing these critters in and out, you'll get the exercise necessary to burn up all that fat and cholesterol.

Skim off a quart of fresh, heavy cream. Pour into a sterilized churn. Never fill the churn or it will take for-

A Backwoods Home Anthology

Teach your children to fish for many hours of fun and lots of good eating.

ever to get the butter to "come." You need room for it to slosh. Lacking a churn, don't give up. I've found a super fast method. Dump 2/3 of a blender full of heavy cream and turn on a slow setting. You want it to churn, not whip.

Keep a careful watch of the churning cream. As the butter begins to come, you'll first notice the cream, now whipped cream, begin to separate. Flakes of solid will begin to appear, along with watery whey. Quite quickly, the flakes will clump into pea-sized pieces of butter. At this point, when using a blender, you might want to dump the contents out into a half-gallon canning jar (sterilized, of course). Finish the butter by simply shaking or rolling the jar back and forth until the butter clumps together in one or more large chunks. When using the churn, just churn until the butter comes.

Drain off the buttermilk, saving it to drink if you wish, then rinse the butter well with icy cold water, again churning or sloshing thoroughly.

Rinse the butter well, working it thoroughly afterward with a butter paddle or wooden spoon. You want as much water out of the butter as possible. As the butter seems free of water, add ½ tsp. salt into the pat, working it in well. For goat cream or cow cream when the cow is not on pasture, the cream is white. You may finely grate a carrot, then squeeze out the orange juice, adding it to the cream. This will give a pretty color to the butter, as well as making it extra sweet-tasting.

I like to use a decorative butter mold, which presses out ¼ lb. pats of butter, each with acorns and leaves stamped on top. When using any such wooden tools, dip them first in ice water or the butter will stick. Refrigerate the butter in well sealed containers, as butter very quickly picks up refrigerator odors. I often stack cooled patties of butter carefully, in wide mouth pint canning jars, closing firmly with a regular canning lid. You may freeze this butter, right in the jar, to use later.

Marinated grouse breast:

One of our favorite treats is marinated grouse breast, sauteed in butter, vegetables, and sprinkled with toasted almond slices. Sound good? You bet! Complicated? Not at all, taking only 15 minutes from start to finish, including time to dress the birds. Nuts, you say. You say you've taken twice that length of time to dress one bird. Check out this dressing tip my oldest son, Bill, discovered: Hold the dead bird by the feet. Place on a solid walkway or path, with the bird's tail toward your feet, belly up. Stand on the wings. Now pull firmly-hard on the legs. There will be a ripping sound, and suddenly you will be shocked to find a skinless, pink breast, entrails in one portion, leaving only the drumsticks to pluck.

---

4 boneless, skinless grouse
   breasts, halved
1 cup Italian Dressing
2 Tbsp. butter
1 cup mixed vegetables (carrot,
   broccoli, onion, mushroom)
4 cups thinly sliced almonds

Marinate the grouse breast halves in Italian dressing overnight in fridge. When ready to cook, remove breasts from dressing, draining. In a heavy skillet, melt butter, then sauté the breasts, adding the vegetables as they begin to brown a bit. Stir frequently; add a bit of water if necessary to prevent scorching. When meat and vegetables are tender, add almonds. Continue cooking until almonds are toasted. Serve over rice or homemade noodles. This is another wild game meal that draws rave reviews from even the most critical diner.

You'll quickly see that most of our meals cost pennies per serving. A lady once asked me if it was possible to feed a family of four for $50 a week. She was thinking of oatmeal and macaroni, I guess. I showed her how she could feed her family well on half of that. It does take some work and thought, but you'd be surprised at how quickly one develops patterns of thought. For instance, I learned years ago that simply adding some wild blueberries or chopped apples to pancakes or muffins made them a delight instead of a cheap same-old.

Encourage your children to go fishing. My oldest children brought home a constant supply of fresh fish, while having many hours of exciting adventure to boot. Those fish not only provide fresh, fried fish for the family, but fish patties, cakes, loaf, and smoked fish. Even the lowly sucker, which made abundant runs in the spring, was transformed into the most wonderful smoked fish and fish cakes. One only has to study possibilities, not mourn deprivation, in order to succeed in plain old good meals. Let your children always remember the meals that Mom or Dad cooked. Δ

For more great recipes get
Backwoods
Home Cooking
www.backwoodshome.com

THE IRREVERENT JOKE PAGE

The Fourteenth Year

(Believing it is important for people to be able to laugh at themselves, this is a continuing feature in *Backwoods Home Magazine*. We invite readers to submit any jokes you'd like to share to *BHM*, P.O. Box 712, Gold Beach, OR 97444. There is no payment for jokes used.)

A young man asked an old rich man how he made his money.

The old guy fingered his worsted wool vest and said, "Well, son, it was 1932. The depth of the Great Depression. I was down to my last nickel.

I invested that nickel in an apple. I spent the entire day polishing the apple and, at the end of the day, I sold the apple for ten cents. The next morning, I invested those ten cents in two apples. I spent the entire day polishing them and sold them at 5:00 pm for 20 cents. I continued this system for a month, by the end of which I'd accumulated a fortune of $1.37.

Then my wife's father died and left us two million dollars..."

Two confirmed bachelors sat talking. Their conversation drifted from politics to cooking.

"I got a cookbook once," said one, "but I could never do anything with it."

"Too much fancy work in it, eh?" asked the other.

"You said it. Every one of the recipes began the same way, 'Take a clean dish...'"

A motorist, driving by a Texas ranch, hit and killed a calf that was crossing the road. The driver went to the owner of the calf and explained what had happened. He then asked what the animal was worth.

"Oh, about $200 today," said the rancher. "But in six years it would have been worth $900. So $900 is what I'm out."

The motorist sat down, wrote out a check, and handing it to the farmer he said, "Here is the check for $900. It's post-dated six years from now."

Coming out of church, Mrs. Smith asked her husband, "Do you think that Johnson girl is tinting her hair?"

"I didn't even see her," admitted Mr. Smith.

"And that dress Mrs. Davis was wearing," continued Mrs. Smith, "Really, don't tell me you think that's the proper outfit for a mother of two."

"I'm afraid I didn't notice that either," said Mr. Smith.

"Oh, for heaven's sake," snapped Mrs. Smith. "A lot of good it does you to go to church."

A New York lawyer went duck hunting in rural Down East Maine. He shot and dropped a bird, but it fell into a farmer's field on the other side of a fence. As the lawyer climbed over the fence, an elderly farmer drove up on his tractor and asked him what he was doing.

The litigator responded, "I shot a duck and it fell in this field, and now I'm going to retrieve it."

The old farmer replied, "This is my property and you are not coming over here."

The indignant lawyer said, "I am one of the best trial attorneys in the United States and, if you don't let me get that duck, I'll sue you and take everything you own."

The old farmer smiled and said, "Apparently, you don't know how we settle disputes Down East. We settle small disagreements like this with the Down East Three Kick Rule."

The lawyer asked, "What is the Down East Three Kick Rule?"

The Farmer replied, "Well, because the dispute occurs on my land, first I kick you three times and then you kick me three times and so on back and forth until someone gives up."

The attorney quickly thought about the proposed contest and decided that he could easily take the old codger. He agreed to abide by the local custom.

The old farmer slowly climbed down from the tractor and walked up to the attorney. His first kick planted the toe of his heavy steel toed work boot into the lawyer's groin and dropped him to his knees. His second kick to the midriff sent the lawyer's last meal gushing from his mouth. The barrister was on all fours when the farmer's third kick to his rear end sent him face-first into a fresh cow pie.

The lawyer summoned every bit of his will and managed to get to his feet. Wiping his face with the arm of his jacket, he said, "Okay, you old coot. Now it's my turn."

The old farmer smiled and said, "Naw, I give up. You can have the duck."

On a wall in a ladies room ... "My husband follows me everywhere."

Written just below it ... "I do not."

A husband said to his wife, "No, I don't hate your relatives. In fact, I like your mother-in-law better than I like mine."

A simple backwoods hay baler

By Rev. J. D. Hooker

During the winter months, Steve and his wife Tandy feed between 120 and 150 bales of hay to a herd of pretty high-quality dairy goats on their northern Indiana farm. This couple's major source of income is derived from selling these goats. Once their initial investment in breeding stock was recouped, they hardly incurred any further expenses except for minor veterinary bills. By themselves they produce all of the hay their animals require, but the way their property is laid out makes it pretty well impossible to use any standard sort of tractor-drawn mowers, balers, or other equipment. Yet, wanting to become entirely self-sufficient in this area, they improvised and came up with their own system for mowing and baling.

First, for the mowing, they searched around for nearly an entire summer until they located a front-mounting, sickle-bar attachment for the older, two-wheeled Gravely tractor that they use for nearly every purpose on their small acreage. Any other brand of walk-behind, sickle-bar mower would work just as nicely. Steve and Tandy like the idea of owning a single machine they can use for nearly all of their equipment needs by simply switching attachments. Of course this has always been one of the strongest points of those older Gravely tractors.

The first winter they merely forked their dried grass into haystacks. Well covered with weighted-down sheets of plastic, and left right out in the open, this hay kept well enough. Still, Steve and Tandy were certain that regular bales would be much easier to handle and store. Which was why the next spring found Steve designing and putting together his own readily-portable, simple-to-use, human-powered, wooden hay baler. Once we'd seen his simple improvisation in use, my wife and I realized just how valuable it would be in our own operation. That same week I put together a duplicate for our own use.

The entire "baler" can be put together in just a couple of hours, using only a single 4x8 sheet of ¾" plywood, a couple of six-foot 2x4s, some 1½" wood screws, and a tube of construction adhesive. If you keep it painted or varnished for protection from the elements, it should hold up to at least a lifetime of use.

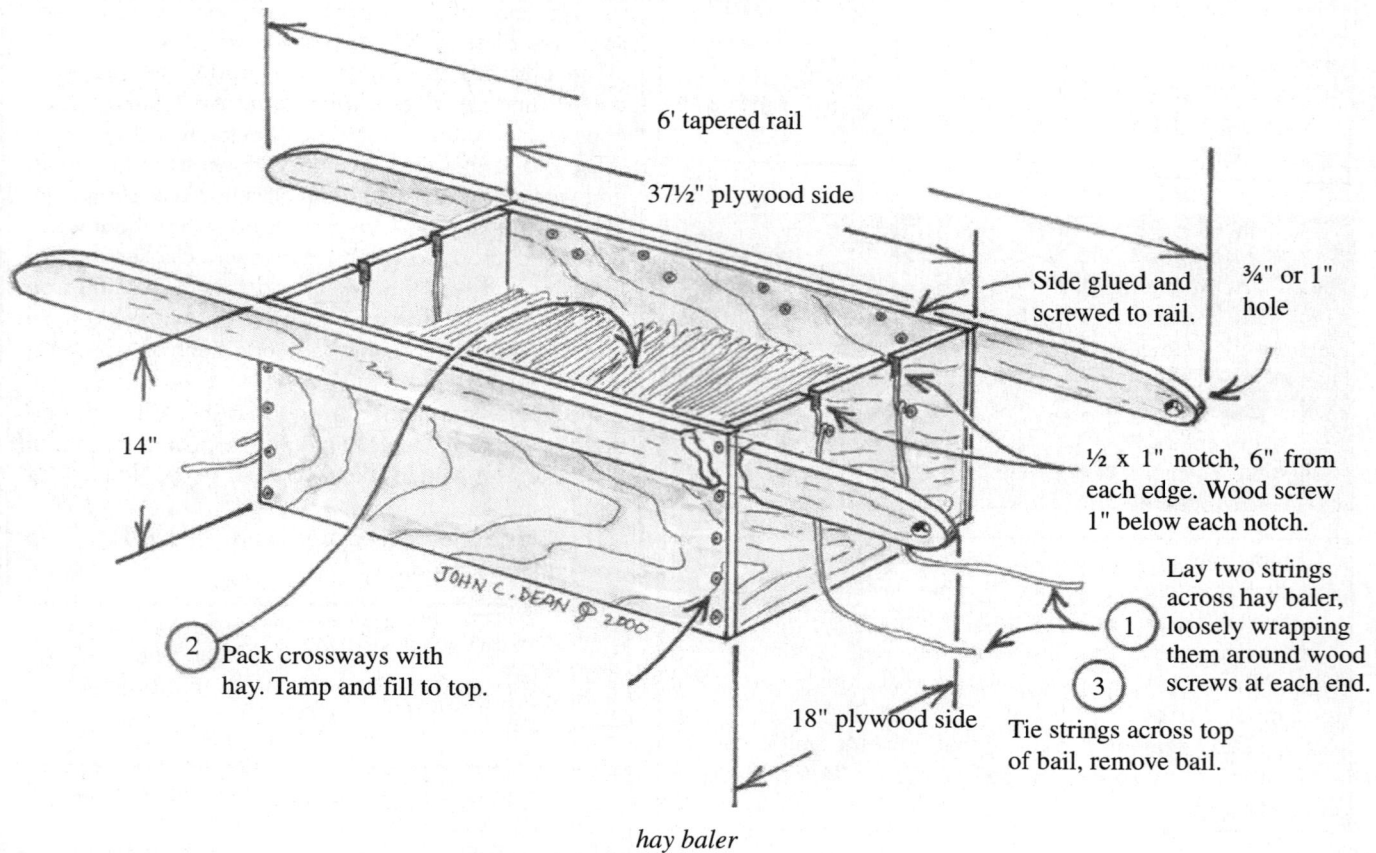

hay baler

If you're interested in producing your own simple, wooden baler, your first step will be to cut two 37½"x14" pieces from the sheet of ¾" plywood. Then cut two more pieces measuring 18"x14" each, from the remainder. Now, simply use some of the wood screws and construction adhesive to assemble the box-like body of the baler, as shown in the illustration.

Next, both ends of the six-foot lengths of 2x4 are rounded off, using a saber-saw or similar tool, as shown. Again, use both construction adhesive and wood screws to attach these handles to the top edge of the box as illustrated.

Along the upper edge of each of the narrower ends of the box, cut roughly ½"x1" notches about 6" from each side. Then, on the outside of the box and just about an inch below each of these notches, drive in a single screw about half way. Finally, drill ¾" to 1" diameter tow-rope holes through the rounded-off ends of each of the 2x4 pieces.

Steve simply flips the baler upside down, using the 2x4 handles as sled runners, then tows the baler behind their Gravely's riding surrey to where he'll be using it.

To use the baler, cut two pieces of baling twine, each roughly 8½' or 9' long. Fashion a loop in one end of each piece of twine, and slip it over one of the protruding screw heads. Then you can sort of drape each length of twine loosely in place in the baler, with a couple of wraps around each of the opposite screw heads to keep them in place.

Once the baler has been packed as full as possible with hay, using your feet to stomp it in tightly, remove the twine from the screws, slip each of the loose ends through its corresponding loop, pull it tight, and knot it securely. Now you can grasp the strings, lift the completed bale from the baler, and you're all ready to start over and produce your next bale.

Steve and Tandy have found that it's not a difficult task to bale about a third of an acre on a pleasant summer afternoon. That's with the aid of their children, who think bouncing up and down to pack the hay tightly inside the baler is great fun. Δ

www.backwoodshome.com

Chat with other self-reliant people at Backwoods Home Magazine's popular website.

Diagnosing appendicitis

By Dr. Bill Glade

It is Saturday afternoon, you are trying to get some work done and your child has a tummy ache. It has only hurt for a few hours and they are still playing, but the complaints continue. Lunch didn't go well, but there isn't a fever.

Should you wait and watch? Would it be better to drive to the Emergency Room and have the child examined?

Insurance will cover most of the medical costs but what about the time lost waiting for the exam? On the other hand you don't want to miss appendicitis if that is the problem.

Tummy aches are common and most are not appendicitis, but how do you decide when you should worry?

Appendicitis is the most common acute surgical disease in the abdomen. Uncommon under five years of age, its incidence peaks in the second and third decades of life. From around age 15 to 25 boys are affected more than girls, but at other ages both sexes are affected equally.

The appendix is usually a useful structure which assists our bowel in defending itself from the variety of substances and bacteria we ingest. Unfortunately it can become obstructed from thickened stool particles, enlarged lymph nodes, or ingested items such as seeds or intestinal worms. Following blockage the appendix swells with fluid and trapped bacteria begin to multiply. The resulting infection causes more swelling and the stretched appendix begins causing abdominal pain. With typical progression the pain becomes worse, the appetite is disturbed, and low grade fever may appear.

Surgical removal of the appendix at this time is curative and rapidly returns a sick person to healthy status. Untreated the infection and increasing pressure cause the organ to leak and the person can become quite ill. Surgery and recovery become more difficult and the chance of complications is significantly higher.

What signs and symptoms are useful in order to avoid these complications?

From years of treating appendicitis I've found three questions that have proven to be very helpful in arousing my suspicions that someone has acute appendicitis.

How long has it hurt and is it getting worse? Appendicitis doesn't happen; it evolves. The abdominal pain frequently begins in an innocuous fashion and the patient often feels that he has the "flu." Over several hours (typically 4-8) the discomfort increases and may be felt more in one part of the abdomen than others. The pain becomes more than an annoyance and frequently begins to interfere with activities such as play. Movement may cause an increase in the abdominal symptoms and sleep may be disturbed. The pain, initially a nuisance, now can no longer be ignored.

Does it hurt all over the abdomen or mostly in one place? Acute appendicitis tends to follow a common pattern. It is initially a diffuse discomfort that may center on the umbilical area. With time the pain increases and will usually localize to one place in the abdomen. This is most frequently the lower right side. However, because of variations in the anatomic position or length of the appendix, it can be almost anywhere. Other places where you might feel the pain include the lower left side, the back on the right or above the pubic bone. If you can gently push on your child's abdomen and one area hurts more than the rest, appendicitis is a concern.

Is the appetite normal? It is unusual for someone with appendicitis to have a normal appetite. For over 95 percent of patients, loss of appetite is the first symptom and pain occurs later. Vomiting happens three quarters of the time, usually after the abdominal pain has started. Most often it occurs once or twice. Diarrhea can happen; however, a more frequent complaint is the desire to pass gas or have a bowel movement. Unfortunately successful passage of either one doesn't relieve the increasing discomfort.

Diagnosing appendicitis is fairly easy if the appendix is located in the "usual" position. Unfortunately it frequently is not and acute appendicitis has been mistaken for many other illnesses including abdominal flu, kidney stones, ovarian problems, and an inflamed colon. This is a particularly difficult problem in the very young and in older adults. Their bodies do not react quite the same and as a consequence, the rupture rate is typically 50 percent or more. Most older teens and adults have a more typical course but many times specialized testing such as a CT scan is needed to confirm the diagnosis and rule out other possible causes for the pain.

A ruptured appendix occurs when the pressure in the blocked appendix becomes so high that the circulation is disturbed and gangrene ensues. The appendix leaks pus and bacteria into the abdominal cavity. If the leaking appendix can be contained by the body and the infection controlled, recovery can occur on its own. However if the containment process is ineffective the pus spreads and the person becomes dramatically ill with abdominal pain, fever, chills, and dehydration. Treatment consists of removing the appendix, draining the pus, and using antibiotics to prevent further spread of the infection. The person is usually sick for quite awhile and recovery is slow.

A word about examining someone with abdominal pain. Perform your exam with the person laying down, preferably with their legs drawn up slightly to relax the abdominal muscles. Make sure that your hands are warm and that you push *gently* using the flat part of your hand, not your fingertips. Don't prolong the exam. If it hurts, try to get an idea where it is localized and then quit. Their belly hurts enough; don't make it worse.

If the initial symptoms don't suggest appendicitis I would recommend keeping the person on clear liquids for a few hours. These are essentially flavored water and are represented by jello, broth, clear fruit juice, and sodas. Given frequently, in small amounts, they help prevent dehydration which will make any illness feel worse. From a surgeon's perspective they keep the stomach free of solid food in the event that an operation is necessary.

Acetaminophen (Tylenol) or ibuprofen can be given to relieve discomfort. A few hours of observation should help you determine if the symptoms change and suggest that appendicitis is a possibility.

If it is Saturday afternoon and your child is complaining, remember the following guidelines. If they have (a) a history of abdominal pain which is getting worse, (b) pain which is localized to one particular area of the abdomen, and (c) an appetite disturbance, particularly loss of appetite, appendicitis is a real possibility and further evaluation is indicated. A professional physical exam accompanied by a determination of the white blood count and urine exam should help to confirm or deny your concern. If the diagnosis is difficult, expect that further tests may be done including a CT scan or other specialized studies. Δ

Are you prepared?
Emergency Preparedness and Survival Guide
www.backwoodshome.com

Want more info?

Chat with other self-reliant people at *Backwoods Home Magazine's* popular website.

www.backwoodshome.com

the gee-whiz! page
By O.E. MacDougal

Art and invention

Today, inventors are considered technical wizards. But in the 19th century, inventors such as Thomas Edison and Guglielmo Marconi were considered "artists." This was based on their creative solutions to problems.

Oftentimes, the solutions inventors arrived at seemed simple and obvious—once they were demonstrated.

Though Edison's formal education ended at about the third grade, and he was almost without mathematical skills for most of his life, he had a way of approaching problems and a method of seizing chance discoveries that made him more than the equal of better educated men.

One story about him involves a new hire, a college graduate in engineering. He asked the new hire if he could figure out the volume of a light bulb. The young man left Edison's office and returned about an hour later. Using the mathematics he had learned at the university, he had calculated the bulb's volume and reported back to Edison with it.

Edison immediately told the young man his calculations were off by 10 percent. The man didn't see how that was possible after all the time he had spent doing calculations.

Edison took the bulb to a sink, broke off the end, filled it with water, then poured the water into a graduated beaker. And that, he told the young scientist was the easiest way to find the volume of the bulb. An obvious and direct solution, but one that eluded someone "trapped" by his education.

When painting and sculpting were one

Ever wonder why so many of the ancient Greek and Roman statues have that "vacant" look in their eyes—eyes that stare without pupils? They look downright eerie. But that's not the way the Greeks and Romans saw them, because they didn't look that way back then. This is because the Greeks and Romans painted their statuary. They painted the skin, they painted the sculpted clothes the figures wore, and they painted in the eyes—pupils and all.

Even the beautiful friezes and columns of the Parthenon, now stark marble, were ornately painted in their heyday. But paint doesn't last. It weathers, it flakes off and, over the centuries, the statues, the temples, the friezes were denuded and all that's left is the solid marble beneath. Now and then, statuary is found with remnants of paint still on them. But by the time of the Renaissance, when the "Classical" statuary of the ancient Greeks and Romans were rediscovered—first, by the Italians—most of the statues were already bare. (This has permanently influenced the way sculpture has been done ever since. Sculptures nowadays are never painted.)

Today, we can only imagine what these relics must have looked like when they had paint on them. Given the realistic details we now see in the naked marble, we must assume that they looked absolutely life-like when the Greeks and Romans painted them.

Abbreviations

It's got to strike at least a few people as odd that the abbreviation for *pound* is *lb.*, when there isn't an "L" or a "B" in the word pound, and that the abbreviation for *ounce* is *oz.*, when there is no "Z" in ounce.

The abbreviation for pound comes from the Latin word for scale, *libra*, and libra was also the term for an ancient Roman unit of weight equivalent to approximately 11½ of our modern ounces. Libra was also the traditional unit of weight in Italian, Spanish, and Portuguese speaking countries before the adoption of the metric system. Libra is also a zodiacal sign whose symbol is—the balance scale.

So, where did the word "pound" come from? It comes from another Latin word, *pendere*, which means "to weigh."

The word ounce comes from the Italian word *onza*, which was 1/12 of the old Italian unit of weight, the libra, hence the "Z" in oz., while the word onza came from the Latin term *uncia* which was 1/12 of the Roman libra, and although our standard (*avoirdupois*) pound is made up of 16 avoirdupois ounces, a jeweler's pound, by which precious metals are measured, is called a *troy* pound and, like the Roman pound, is made up of 12 troy ounces.

How do avoirdupois pounds compare to troy pounds? An avoirdupois pound can be broken up into smaller units of measure called grains and an avoirdupois pound is 7,000 grains while a troy pound is 5760 grains. Thus an avoirdupois ounce is 437½ grains while the jeweler's troy ounce weighs 480 grains.

Ayoob on Firearms

Shooting left-handed

In the Letters page of the January/February 2003 issue of *Backwoods Home Magazine*, Denton Warn writes, "Mr. Ayoob's four-page advertisement for the Glock pistol leaves out one important point. I have handled Glocks at gunshows, and found that they are unsuitable for left-handed use. Ten percent of the population is left-handed, and there are occasions when a right-handed shooter may have to fire with the left hand. There are very few autopistols suitable for left-handed use and almost none of significant caliber have a grip comfortable for smaller hands. Fortunately, I can use my right hand pretty well, so if I felt the need to carry an autopistol, I could get by. Till then, I'll stick with revolvers."

Cousin Warn, I feel your pain. Seriously. I've been teaching left-handed people to shoot for more than 30 years now, and a couple of weeks a year I carry, qualify, and compete left-handed to stay sharp for teaching that segment of my students, which by the way tends to run a little higher than 10 percent. As you insightfully noted, any right-handed shooter may suffer an injury that forces them to become a temporary southpaw, and that makes the topic of left-handed shooting a worthwhile one for any gun owner.

Semiautomatic pistols

Since semiautomatic pistols in general and the Glock in particular were the focus of reader Warn's letter, we'll start there. The "autopistols are made for right-handers" thing goes back to the first 60 years of the 20th Century, in which such classic pistols as the Luger of 1908, the Browning-designed Colt of 1911, the Walther double action beginning in the late 20s, the Browning Hi-Power of 1935, and the Smith & Wesson Model 39 of 1954 all had their safety or safety-decocking levers mounted on the left side of the gun to be accessible to the thumb of a right-handed shooter. Not until the 1960s did we see the ambidextrous manual safety for the 1911 pistol, pioneered by the great gunsmith Armand Swenson, come to the public's awareness. Smith & Wesson had gone through four-fifths of the 20th Century before they produced a semiautomatic pistol with an ambidextrous safety/decocking lever.

Today, the ambidextrous "fire control system" is commonly available, either standard issue or as an option at slightly extra cost. Moreover, we have a generation of "KISS Principle" (Keep It Simple, Stupid) auto pistols, with double action only firing mechanisms and "slick slides" devoid of safety catches or decocking levers. These are truly ambidextrous. The Glock is a classic example of this.

Each of these guns comes from the box with the slide-lock lever and the magazine release situated on the left side of the frame, positioned for a "righty" to manipulate with the right thumb. Does this mean they are unsuitable for left-handers? No! It only means that the southpaw needs to do what he or she has been doing all their life, and cleverly adapt to a right-handed world.

Instead of hitting the magazine release button with the left thumb, the

Massad Ayoob

southpaw's dominant hand is now positioned to come back and hit it with the index finger. This generally requires less of a shift of the hand on the gun than does the thumb-manipulation when done by a right-hander as the guns' designers intended. It is actually faster for the lefty! If the release button is located at an angle where your particular index finger doesn't reach it naturally when firing left-handed, use the middle finger instead.

The slide-lock lever can also be faster for the southpaw. Many righties have thumbs too short to reach that lever mounted on the left side of the gun without shifting their hands, and have to use the left hand to do it. But the lefty has three strong options for releasing the slide-lock lever to complete a speed reload.

The southpaw can use the left index finger to release the lever on every

227

This shooter has no problem expertly manipulating a .45 caliber SIG P220 left-handed.

such gun but the SIG, where the lever is located too far back to allow that. This is the high-speed technique that southpaw Bob Houzenga has used to win six national champion titles in practical handgun shooting. The lefty can do what I do when shooting with that hand, and use the fingertips of the right hand in a karate "spear hand" movement to reach up and pull down the lever after the palm has slapped the fresh magazine into place. The magazine insertion movement positions the support hand ideally for this maneuver. Finally, the left-handed shooter can simply use the whole (right) support hand to tug the slide to the rear to release it from the locked position. While slower than using the release lever, this is widely taught to right- and left-handed shooters alike as a gross motor skill that will better survive loss of dexterity under stress, and is thus truly ambidextrous.

There are certain semiautomatic pistols, the Beretta and the SIG-Sauer to name two, which in several models have an interchangeable magazine release button that can be swapped to the right side of the gun to put them in reach of the southpaw's left thumb. However, I truly believe that they are slower than using the first two techniques described above. This is why some of the right-handed handgun cognoscenti switch their Beretta and SIG mag release buttons to the right side of the frame. They can now use their trigger fingers to dump the magazine instead of their thumbs, and thus share the speed advantage the lefty already has with the standard pistol!

The aforementioned southpaw champion Houzenga carries a .40 caliber Glock 23 on duty as a chief of police. He does not feel handicapped by his choice of gun. Neither does left-handed gun expert Mike Boyle, who wears a .357 caliber Glock at work every day.

Double action revolvers

Reader Warn follows a long line of left-hand-dominant handgunners who found the revolver more ambidextrous in shooting. It certainly is that. I suspect he has already discovered that the double action revolver with swing-out cylinder is actually faster to reload for the southpaw than it is for the righty. The reason is, revolver cylinders all swing out to the left, and once the cylinder is open it is presented directly to the left hand. The southpaw can hold the open revolver in the right hand and use the more dextrous fingers of his left hand to insert the cartridges directly from belt pouch or pocket to the loading chambers. The righty, by contrast, must reach up and over the whole gun to get at the cylinder with his dominant hand.

It frustrated me back in the early '70s to see police instructors teach left handed officers to change hands and do a right-handed reload of the service revolver, because they didn't know any other way to do it. The southpaw should be able to reload a revolver faster than a righty of equal dexterity. The key is in knowing how to open the cylinder. Instead of changing hands, simply bring the left thumb up over the hammer area to the cylinder release latch and then thrust the thumb forward, while the thumb of the right hand pushes the cylinder out of the left side of the frame. Then use the left hand, which is ideally placed for the task at this moment, to palm-slap the ejector rod and punch the spent casings out and clear. Now the southpaw's dextrous left hand can grab the speedloader or the loose cartridges and feed the fresh rounds into the cylinder. When this is done, the fingertips of the right hand will be ideally placed to close the cylinder as the left hand returns to a firing grasp on the grip frame.

One small point: you want to use the left thumb to push the cylinder latch forward for release on the Smith & Wesson, the Taurus, and the Rossi, and to punch the latch straight inward toward the frame on the Ruger. If you

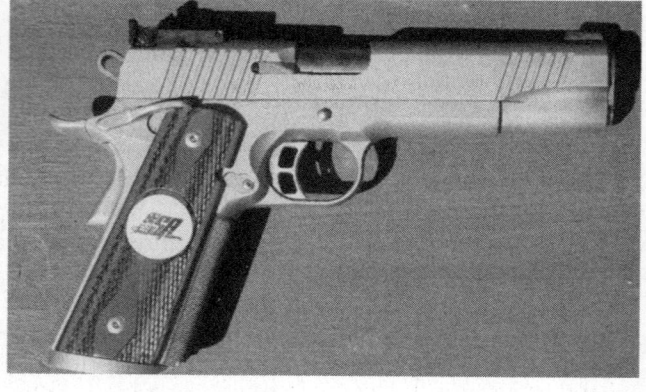

This Kimber Team Match .45 auto has an ambidextrous safety, placed for a southpaw's thumb at the right rear of the frame.

have a Colt revolver, whose latch moves backward to release, it will be faster—indeed, amazingly fast—for the southpaw to use the tip of the left index finger to draw the latch rearward. This requires much less movement of the hand, creating the speed advantage. The Colt is the fastest-opening double action revolver a southpaw can use.

Single action revolvers

All single action revolvers are characterized by the need to thumb the hammer back to full-cock position before the trigger can be successfully pulled to fire a shot. In this respect they are totally ambidextrous. Most follow the pattern of the Colt Model P (Single Action Army, or "Peacemaker," model of 1873) in that they must be unloaded of empty shell casings and reloaded with live cartridges one round at a time, through a loading gate located at the right rear of the cylinder on the revolver's frame.

Gun experts for many decades have theorized that Samuel Colt must have been left-handed to design the "Peacemaker" this way. The southpaw shooter's thumb is ideally positioned to flip open the loading gate of this revolver, or the Ruger Single Six or Blackhawk or whichever of the countless clones of that popular handgun that have followed. As a competitor in the popular "Cowboy Action" shooting sport, I can tell you that on the rare occasions when the course of fire requires us to reload a single action revolver, I have learned that the fastest way I can do it is to switch the sixgun to my left hand and handle the task like a southpaw.

Shotguns

For more than a century, "hammerless" double barrel shotguns—whether the barrels were arrayed "side by side" or "stacked" to "over and under" positions—have had the most ergonomic of safety catches. Located on the tang (the portion of the frame or receiver that extends into the butt stock), this lever is simply pushed forward when you want to fire and kept in the rearward position when you want the gun to be "on safe." An identical system has been seen on most "hammerless" single barrel/single shot scatterguns.

Most slide action and semiautomatic shotguns that use a cross-bolt manual safety (that is, a push-button mounted at the trigger guard area) can be reversed for left-handed use or ordered from the factory as a brand-new "southpaw shotgun." The lefty who has to use such a gun borrowed from a right hander can adapt simply enough by taking a firing hold on the gun, and reaching the left middle finger under the trigger guard, pushing the button to the left. This will release the cross-bolt safety to the "fire" position. A press to the right with the left index finger (trigger finger) will "on safe" the gun again. When the gun is set up for your dominant hand, of course, it will be more efficient to use the index finger to press the crossbolt safety laterally to the "fire" position, and the middle finger to reach to the opposite side to push it back to the "safe" condition.

A handful of pump and auto shotguns, notably the Mossberg brand, use a sliding safety on the rear of the rifle. Adapted from earlier double barrel shotguns, the sliding safety is operated by the thumb: forward is "fire," and back is "safe." This is the most ergonomic of safety catches. It has been adapted to such bolt action rifles as the Savage Model 110 and the early production versions of the Ruger Model 77, and is seen today on

Southpaws are among our most successful shooters. This is Jaskiel McDowell, 12, National Junior Handgun Champion in Sub-Junior class. A lefty, he won with this .22 caliber SIG/Hammerli Trailside .22 auto pistol.

the sophisticated Steyr-Mannlicher. There is simply no manual safety for a bolt action rifle that is more ambidextrous than this type.

Old-fashioned double barrel shotguns with exposed hammers are making a comeback among those gun buyers who tend toward nostalgia, and exposed hammer single shot/single barrel shotguns which must be thumb-cocked to fire are totally ambidextrous in function. The shooter simply needs to know that whichever hand is performing the manipulation, the lever that opens the action needs to be pushed to the right.

Rifles

Rifles tend to be single shot, lever action, bolt action, slide action, or semiautomatic in design. Let's take them one by one.

Single Shot rifles which have exposed hammers are totally ambidextrous. So are traditional style hammerless single shot rifles such as the Ruger.

Lever action rifles are for the most part ambidextrous. The Winchester

94 and Marlin 336 are the most common paradigm. They have outside hammers that must be either thumb-cocked if there is a round in the chamber, or levered with the whole hand to get a round into the chamber of a gun carried with only the magazine loaded with cartridges. Many experts now believe these rifles were originally intended to be carried with loaded magazines but empty chambers. The most recent versions have frame-mounted cross-bolt safeties which go across the firing pin area. Whether you are a righty or a lefty will determine whether you off-safe with your index finger and on-safe with your thumb, or vice versa. In either case, it is the shooter's responsibility to familiarize himself with the "manual of arms," that is, the protocols of properly manipulating the firearm.

One famous southpaw shooter who favored the lever action, at least early in his career, was Charles Askins, Jr. Whether he was hunting animals or hunting men as a Border Patrolman, he was partial to the Savage Model 99 lever action rifle, and found that in caliber .250 Savage it was quite effective at killing man-size creatures.

For most of the 20th Century, the hunter who fired a rifle from the left shoulder and wanted a bolt action either had to pay big bucks to a custom gunsmith for a left-hand conversion, or go through some pretty awkward gyrations to get the next cartridge into the firing chamber. Savage was the first company to offer a factory-produced left-handed bolt action rifle, way back when cars had tailfins. The Savage was followed by Weatherby, Remington, and the other big makers, and today it's no problem for the left-handed shooter to find a "mirror image" bolt action rifle.

The slide action rifle, if you're buying a new gun today, is typified by the Remington 7600 series. Its cross-bolt safety is "switchable" to south-

(1st of 2) Right hand holster confirms that Police Chief Russ Lary isn't a southpaw, but like all his officers he stays in practice shooting lefty, both two-handed as shown...

paw configuration. Everthing else is "even Steven" as far as workability between righties and lefties.

The semiautomatic rifle covers a broader range of manipulation options. Rifles like the popular Remington 7400 can be had in left-handed models. Some auto rifles, the M1 Garand, the M14 and its civilian clone, the Springfield Armory M1A, and the Ruger Mini-14 and Mini-30, have push/pull safety levers at the front of their trigger guards. Forward is "fire," back is "safe." The Garand, the M14, and the M1A place that lever in a cut in the front center of the trigger guard, making the operation truly ambidextrous. On the Ruger rifle, the lever is located at the left front of the guard. This makes the device actually easier to operate for the shooter who fires from the left shoulder.

The M16/AR15 type rifle is probably the most popular today for home defense and "action shooting" competition. In its original form, the fire control lever was situated on the left side of the frame to be accessible to the right thumb when the right hand was on the pistol grip and controlling the rifle's trigger. Many guns of this type today have mirror image "ambidextrous" fire control levers. If you are a lefty and you have an AR with only the right-hand lever, don't despair. Simply learn to keep your left thumb to the left side of the pistol grip as you fire the gun. There is no particular need for the firing hand thumb to wrap around to the opposite side on an AR. With the lefty's thumb to the left, it should be perfectly placed to push the lever on its 90 degree arc from "safe" to "fire," and another 90 degrees to "full auto" if the southpaw is in legal possession of the selective fire/fully automatic version.

A righty speaks to the southpaws

This writer is very strongly right-hand dominant. However, being an "honorary southpaw" a couple of weeks per year has "raised my consciousness" in this regard. Having picked the brains of countless straight-shooting lefties over the last three decades, I would offer this advice to Denton Warn and other left-handed readers.

Yes, the right-handed majority got you again. They designed the guns the same way they designed can openers and cursive script handwriting and all the other things to which you have so successfully adapted. The lifelong challenge that has been dumped on you continues.

However, your ability to overcome a world that is subtly prejudiced

(2nd of 2) ... and left hand only, in case of injury. Pistol is lightweight Ruger P97 .45.

against you mirrors what law abiding gun owners go through, and adapt to. You have to do it twice over. I'm sorry about that, but I can't change it.

On the other hand (no pun intended), as we have noted above there is no significant disadvantage to the southpaw shooter that comes from the world of right-handed gun designers that can't be corrected for in an altered "manual of arms." Moreover, there are several design characteristics in the firearms world, as noted above, that actually give the southpaw an advantage over the "northpaw."

We Americans, accustomed to driving on the right side of the road in cars whose steering wheels are on the left, take a while to adapt in England and South Africa, where we must sit in the right front seat to drive cars on the left side of the road. It feels weird and unnatural at first, but we adapt.

So it is with the southpaw shooter. And, being used to adapting in a right-hander's world, the southpaw learns what black people have learned in white-dominated countries and what women have learned in male-dominated cultures.

They learn to, in the words of Clint Eastwood, "Improvise, Adapt, and Overcome." Δ

Want more Ayoob?
www.backwoodshome.com

Get The Whole Sheebang!
www.backwoodshome.com

Ask Jackie

Castrating cattle, moving to a cabin, propane refrigeration, cleaning the grease out of range hoods, tipi living, using a pressure cooker as a canner, "recanning," and low-yield tomato plants

Jackie Clay

We raise a few livestock, mainly for home use. We have a bull calf that we are keeping for beef. We were told to wait to castrate him when he was about 500 pounds, which he is now. I don't know whether that was a wise decision. I need your advice. What is the best method to castrate and since we don't have a chute, how is the best way to restrain the animal? I was told you had written a book on home vet work. If so, please let me know how to get it and how to castrate our bull.

**Larry Estep
Gate City, VA**

Whew! I'd get the guy who advised you to wait till your calf weighed 500 pounds to come over and hold him while you castrate him. (I mean the bull, now!) I usually castrate our bull calves, meant for beef, at about 150 pounds, where I can handle them nearly single-handed without a chute or cowboy.

I revised *A Veterinary Guide for Animal Owners*, which my late husband and I wrote 20 years ago. You can get this book from any bookstore. In it are described several methods of castration. The one I much prefer is the use of a "clamp" which pinches the blood vessels and effectively castrates the calf with no blood or cutting involved. It is not the "band" method, where a strong rubber band is slipped up over the scrotum, cutting off all circulation. This can be dangerous, as tetanus and infections following this method of castration are all too common.

What I would recommend is that you have a veterinarian who has a portable chute come out and do the deed. These chutes tow behind a truck like a trailer. The bull calf is corralled, roped, or herded into the chute where he can be safely handled and castrated.

If this is impossible, I'm afraid I'd make young beef out of your bull before he gets too big for his britches, escaping from home and causing neighbor trouble, as they will often do. Next time, "pinch" that bull calf when he is much smaller and easier handled.

I have castrated such large bulls by roping them, haltering the animal with a stout halter, tying him to a fence post of a plank or pipe corral, then closing a strong gate up on his free side. With several helpers, one to hold the gate tight against the bull's side by using a rope behind his butt tied to the center of the gate, then run to a fence post on the other side for leverage, and another strong, fearless helper to hold the base of the bull's tail straight up over his back with as much power as he can muster. This immobilizes his hind legs to a great extent. Then he may be castrated with the Burdizzo clamps. **Never clamp both** testicles at once. You must never clamp across the center division between the testicles. Do one at a time instead.

Again, this is *not* a safe procedure, and carries risk of injury. But I have done it several times when there was no other alternative available. I'd call the vet, myself. Good luck.

Jackie

My husband and I would like to know how to move to a cabin and is this a pipe dream or can it be done?

**Judy Cheney
bluebird49@utahweb.com**

You're darned right you can move to that cabin. While it is a dream, it certainly is *not* a pipe dream. I don't usually "sell" things, but I would suggest buying the *Jackie Clay CD* from *BHM*. On it are dozens of articles I've written, many of which pertain to moving to a backwoods home and living skills necessary to make your life there comfortable and enjoyable. It's $12.95.

As you know, telling you the complete how-tos of moving to a cabin would take more than this whole magazine, but I can offer some useful suggestions:

- Work together, forming a realistic goal for your family.
- Pay off as many debts as possible, and contract for even fewer in the future.
- Rip up your credit cards.
- Plan well, considering the fact that *everything* takes longer and costs more than you expect it to.
- Of course constructive, creative thinking can certainly cut costs for everything.
- Buy what you can afford, rather than what you "want." You can usually remodel your less than perfect piece of heaven into a wonderland—with work.
- Consider that anywhere you go, you will need at least a modest form of income and plan for it.
- Keep an open mind to the suggestions and help offered by locals who have lived in the area for some time; some are truly helpful and some are "know it alls." What is *their* place like? Would you like your place to look or work like theirs?
- Plan on working hard for your dream; harder than you would work for others. It takes commitment. And endurance. And patience.
- Know that it *can* be done, and that hundreds of common folks are out there doing it. Right now. You are not "weird" or "nuts."
- Pick up a copy of *Countryside Magazine* at the newsstand. It's full of letters from just such people every month, telling what they're doing, mistakes they made, and success stories of their triumphs.

Good luck in your dream. If you have specific questions regarding this move, please feel free to write.

Jackie

I would like to know when you make your move to the wilderness, how are you going to use your propane refrigerator? Are you going to use small tanks that you can bring in yourself? Do you plan for not using the gas refrigerator, and if so, what is it? I use a propane refrigerator and I do love it. But I would like to phase it out and be more self sufficient in the future. Any ideas?

Kathy Lupole
nikita@citlink.net

Yes, we do plan on using our propane refrigerator, at least during the summer months, when we make our move to the wilderness. We use it, and love it, right here in our almost-wilderness, here in Montana. We will use 100-gallon tanks, which can be hauled in via snowmobile or whatever transportation mode we are using at the time. But you're right, using *any* fuel of this sort is not completely self-reliant. We could use an efficient electric fridge, powered by solar panels, but we are trying to be as economical as we can as well. The propane fridge and lights use about two 100-gallon tanks worth of propane a year.

In the winter in the north, a simple, insulated wooden cupboard fastened in a window will provide pretty dependable cooling until it gets warm outside. We've had pretty good luck sinking a large barrel in the ground, cooling it from a black plastic water line wrapped around it, which led from our spring to the house; the water was usually at about 40° or less, and kept food in the covered barrel nicely cold—sort of a poor person's spring house. We did worry about a bear finding our outdoor fridge, however.

One seldom-thought-of idea is not to have a fridge at all. I know of people who have done this and been very happy with the arrangement. Cook only fresh food, and cook only enough to eat up or keep till supper in a cold cellar. Use only fresh milk, held briefly in that cold cellar, making butter every few days so it doesn't need to be refrigerated. Pick salad vegetables in the cool of the morning, and hold them until dinner in the cold cellar, then rinse well with ice water from the well or spring to "crisp" up. Only have home canned meats or small carcass meats during the warmer months so no meat must be held cold in the fridge. Chickens, rabbits, and fish are easy. Butcher larger animals in the cold fall and early winter months, when natural cooling is simple. It was the old way, and makes a lot of sense.

Jackie

I have a question that maybe you can help me with. What can be done about that miserable greasy junk that builds up on the range hood. I HATE the range hood, but it is needed. Nothing short of pure acid seems to clean the inside of the hood. Any environmentally safe suggestions? I have been at this hood for days with everything I have in the house. I am afraid I am now a toxic site!

Used one of your bread recipes from a back issue and it was the best. I added sunflower and pumpkin seeds to it!

Kelley Jane
bambis_revenge@yahoo.com

You can try this. It works quite well for range hoods and is a more natural approach. First of all, heat a big kettle of water on the stove. A canning kettle with the lid off is good. Really steam up the place, with the vent fan on to suck that steam upward. Then, with good ventilation, use straight ammonia and a steel wool pad without chlorine to scrub the hood. (Ammonia mixed with chlorine creates a poisonous gas.) If you still need help, mix a heavy ammonia concentrate with water that is as hot as you can stand working with. The hot water will help soften the grease crud. But this is never an easy, fun job. Make sure you change those filter pads regularly, as much grease will collect on them and plug them up, making more grease collect on the hood itself. Also try to use a spatter screen while frying, as it will trap a large amount of grease before it drifts up into your hood.

Jackie

Have you ever heard of anyone selling everything to go live in a tipi on a piece of property while they build a cabin. We are considering doing exactly that.

When we were building our house here in Kentucky we lived in tents for four months. We survived ticks crawling all over the tents trying to get at us, a downburst (small tornado) right over us (destroyed our cook tent & popped open all our coolers) and an abnormal heat wave starting in June. I said I'd never do it again but... It's that homesteaders' adventure itch!

**Kathy Baker
Breeding, KY**

Sure, Kathy, I've heard of many people doing just that. Some of them made a great success of their adventure, and a few failed. But, because you have already had a taste of such an adventure, I'll bet your chances of succeeding are high. A tipi is actually quite an efficient means of housing year-round. But it does require picking a good tipi pattern and material. And you definitely will want an ozan, or liner, which keeps condensation from dripping, and improves circulation and heat in the winter. A very good book on tipi living is *The Indian Tipi, Its History, Construction and Use* by Reginald and Gladys Laubin. It gives hundreds of tips on how-tos and problems some people have encountered (usually due to defects in the tipi manufacturing or the lack of experience of the tipi dwellers).

After all, generations of Native Americans lived comfortably in tipis. But a tipi is not a house and you must adapt your lifestyle to the tipi while living in one. (Not much room for the TV, VCR, and Game Boy.) But tipi living is a grand adventure, and the first time you come in from the dark, after seeing your tipi glowing like a huge lantern in the dark, still woods, you will know you are *home*.

Jackie

My wife and I bought an 8-quart pressure cooker/canner from Presto. The regulator weight has one setting: for 15 pounds. Of course the unit comes with an instruction booklet, but it is not terribly detailed. All the recipes in the Ball Blue Book *and* Putting Food By *use 10 pounds as a reference for most foods. Is there a way to adjust the time to process, or do you know of any way we can adjust the cooker to 10 pounds? Using a different regulator weight?*

My next question concerns recanning foods. I know that you can't refreeze food, but are there any health risks of re-canning? I have recently used tomatoes that we canned earlier this summer to make a batch of spaghetti sauce and then I canned about 15 quarts of that.

We had some huge tomato plants, over 8 feet high. There was a lot of foliage, but I think the yield was relatively small. We had 5 containers of tomatoes, one pepper and one cucumber. Should I have pruned the plants? How do you do this? I did pinch off the suckers all season. The soil was quite a bit of manure and good dirt. We also took vegetable waste that we pureed up in a blender to feed the tomatoes about once a week. We had a ton of green tomatoes at the end of the season and made 15 pints of chow chow (a relish condiment made with green tomatoes).

But I really would have liked more ripe tomatoes.

**Chuck and Denise Cline
twopatriots@peoplepc.com**

You know, I think I would call the Presto Customer Service Department (number on your instruction booklet). The pressure cooker/canner that I think you bought is meant to be used primarily for a pressure cooker, but they advertise it as a canner, also. A larger unit is primarily a canner, meant for that purpose. Perhaps you could use a 10-pound weight, sold with the larger canner. But I wouldn't do it until talking to the Presto folks. Just in case.

No problem in recanning food other than a slight loss of nutrients. And I think that home canning fresh foods quickly and then recanning them would be about equal to the store cans of foods that have been picked over or underripe, hauled and mauled, stored for lengthy times, *then* canned. I recan foods all the time, as time allows. I, too, can tomato sauce, then later recan it, adding meat, making spaghetti sauce, soups, stews, chili, etc. I even have bought #10 cans very cheaply and recanned smaller jars of the store canned food. For instance, I bought #10 cans of pie cherries at a discount grocery for 99¢ a can, and recanned them into pint jars. They turned out just fine. As for the tomatoes from Jack and the Beanstalk-land, I'd guess that you might have a combination of a fairly late variety of tomato and a heavily fertilized plot. Using a very fertile, manured garden plot, heavy with nitrogen will make for huge plants, lots of leaves, but little fruit. I'd wager a guess that by the time your plant used up the excess nitrogen and "got down to business," the season was just about over. Ditto for the one cucumber and single pepper. Sounds awfully suspicious, to me.

This year, I'd work the soil up well, and not fertilize it at all until you have tomatoes beginning to set well. Then as they grow, fertilize accordingly. And you might try a less tall, earlier variety, such as Goliath, Oregon Spring, or Early Cascade.

Jackie

Making wild nuts
into nut oil, nut meal, and nut butter

By Rev. J.D. Hooker

Come the last days of August, I start spending even more time out in the woods than usual, because this is when squirrel season opens up around here. The Good Lord never provided any more succulent tablefare for a man to enjoy than the meat from these tasty little creatures.

But, there's more to this time in the woods than that. Those tall hickory, black walnut, and pecan trees that feed those tiny squirrels also offer plenty of tasty and highly nutritious food for us humans. I always take along an old burlap feed sack on each hunt to stuff with walnuts and hickory nuts.

When ripe, the outer hulls of hickory nuts are naturally segmented and readily pull off in four separate pieces. The outer hulls of the walnuts come in a single solid piece, but are soft and easily mashed under foot. Unless you don't mind running around with deep-brown stained hands, I recommend wearing gloves as you remove the walnuts from their hulls.

We've found that just about every type of nut will keep for a long time inside of its uncracked hull, yet once opened, most go rancid, turn moldy, or develop a stale taste quickly. We only crack open roughly the quantity we'll be needing at one time, leaving the rest in the shell until needed.

The best method we've found for removing hickory nuts and black walnuts from their shells is to stand the nut on end and deliver a sharp rap with a hammer. An awl, ice-pick, crochet hook, knitting needle, or a regular nut-pick can be used to remove the meats. For us, this is usually an evening project. My wife puts a movie in the VCR for the kids and grandkids to watch while we work.

Of course the largest pieces you manage to pick out can be used up according to any use you might have for regular store-bought walnuts or pecans. You should try dipping some in honey, sprinkling with a little salt, and roasting them in a hot oven. Or, try stirring together ½ cup of melted butter, 1 cup of corn syrup, 1 cup of sugar, ¼ tsp. of salt, ½ cup of dark rum, and 4 beaten eggs. Pour this into an unbaked pie shell, top with 1½ of hickory or black walnuts mix of the two, and bake for 55 to 60 minutes at 325 degrees. This is even better than pecan pie.

Eaten straight out of their shells, used in cookies and baking, oven roasted (with or without a dusting of salt), or enjoyed in any other manner, nuts pack a mighty big nutritional wallop inside their small packages. Over the years we've made a point of learning about several other valuable uses for these free forest gleanings.

With a few exceptions (chestnuts, hazelnuts, and a few others are nearly fat-free, and this won't work with them) an exceptional cholesterol-free oil that's ideal for baking and frying is pretty simple to extract from nuts.

Start by simply using a hammer or running them through a food chopper to coarsely crush a gallon of nut meats. Place these chopped nuts into a large pot of boiling water, and cook at a low boil for 5 or 6 hours (add more water as needed). Set aside in a cool place for several hours or overnight.

Once thoroughly cooled, the layer of oil and chopped nuts floating on top of the water is easily spooned off. Strain through a couple layers of cheesecloth and reserve the oil for any purpose where you might normally employ any type of vegetable or cooking oil.

Don't discard the remnants of the crushed nuts you've strained out. Lightly toasted in the oven, and run through a grain mill, they'll provide you with an exceptional substitute for corn meal. Very finely ground, this can be substituted for up to 50 percent of the white flour called for in any recipe. Aside from using this meal in muffins, breads, cakes, piecrusts, and so forth, this "nut meal" makes the tastiest crispy coating I've ever sunk a tooth into, when my wife fries up chicken, fish, or similar fare.

We also use a method very similar to this oil extraction process to produce our grandchildren's favorite food staple, nut butter.

The nut meats are spread on cookie sheets and toasted for 20 to 30 minutes in a 450-degree oven. Once cooled, they're fed through our hand-cranked grain mill and ground to a floury consistency. This "nut flour" is then boiled following the same procedure used for oil extraction, and set aside to cool. Once cooled and left to set for several hours or overnight, the residue floating on top of the water is again spooned off, but rather than straining to remove the oil, we blend the stuff together. Our grandkids especially like "nut-butter" and homemade jelly sandwiches. If you or your kids like peanut butter, you're really going to love hickory, pecan, almond, or walnut butter. Don't just take my word on that though, try this for yourself. Δ

A Backwoods Home Anthology

The last word

The "curse" of oil

To many, the oil beneath the sands of the Middle East is a kind of godsend for them. My take on it is that it's illusionary wealth in the same way that the mining of gold and silver in the New World by the Spanish ultimately proved to be more bane than boon for them, and the way stealing technology became economic suicide for the Soviets during the Cold War.

What the Arabs have achieved is tantamount to what a student cheating in high school achieves. Both "easy wealth" and cheating provide an instant reward, but neither provide a foundation. And like cheating in high school, once you get locked into easy wealth, you discover you need more and more of it just to keep going.

So, here's my thesis: the oil the Arabs are selling isn't a blessing at all; it's a curse.

Historical examples

From the 16th to the early 19th centuries, the Spanish sent shipload after shipload of mineral wealth back to their country from the New World. But instead of using it for capital investment, the gold, silver, and gems soon left Spain to be spent in other countries to buy the goods those countries produced. In the meantime, those "resource-poor" countries like England, France, and Germany, who hadn't found gold mines in their colonies or at home, had to depend on developing technology, building factories, and creating trade routes to build wealth. Gradually, Spain, while keeping the facade of being rich, became a country without an economic base, trying to keep up with its resource-poor neighbors who had built industrial bases that sustain them to this day.

Something similar happened with the Soviet Union during the Cold War. They stole technology from the West, rather than develop their own. But in the long run their thievery benefitted the West, not the Soviet Union. Like the cheating high schooler, the Soviets discovered that the more complicated technology became, the less capable they were of doing original work because they hadn't built a foundation. The result was that, although they did make huge strides in a few fields, such as metallurgy and mathematics, they fell way behind in numerous others. What comes to mind is computers. Rather than getting in a race with the United States, as the Japanese did, to develop the tools of the Information Age, the Soviets were content to sit back and just take what they could steal.

The difference in the two economies, the Japanese and the present day Russians, is testament to the rewards of making sacrifices in costly R&D and hard work versus the fleeting rewards of theft. So, technologically and economically, the Soviets/Russians fell further and further behind. Today the Japanese are an economic world power while the Russians are an economic basket case.

It should be noted that the Soviet refusal to understand what it takes to be a major economic power goes back years before the Cold War. As an example, when Henry Ford went to the Soviet Union as a guest of Stalin in the 1930s, Stalin reputedly asked him how the Soviets could build a trucking industry, something required for a modern industrial country. Ford said, "Build cars." If you create a nation of drivers, trucks and a trucking industry would naturally follow. Ford didn't believe you could build a trucking industry in a country where the populace rode in mule carts. And he was right. The automobile would have created the foundation for what Stalin wanted. But he couldn't see it, so the cars weren't built, trucks never became much of a factor, and the Soviet Union suffered.

There are even earlier examples in prehistory of how "easy wealth" destroys. In prehistoric times, wealth did not go to those societies that hunted and gathered best, it went to those which domesticated cattle and planted gardens.

Now it's the Arabs who will never really get anywhere until they realize that wealth doesn't come easy—or, in their case—from a hole in the ground. It comes from hard work, working smart, and original research and development.

If they were smart, there would be programs in the Arab world to use the petroleum revenues, which aren't going to last forever, to build high-tech industries. They would be building factories—instead of palaces and buying luxuries from the West. And the beauty is, they could afford to fail at it for awhile. For example, they could start making computer chips and, if they don't make 'em right at first, no problem. Keep using that oil money to perfect it. And not just computer chips. Use the money to start making machinery, build factories, and make cars. Use it to create ship building equipment. If they worked at it the way the Americans, English, Germans, and Japanese did, eventually they'd get it right.

They should also invest in education—real education, not sociology and psychology majors, but engineering and the sciences, things on which civilizations are really built. Then, to keep those who receive the education in their countries, instead of being lured to the West as so many are, they should give *those people* grants to start factories, perform research, etc. Then they'd have the best of two worlds: one of today in which they live off the ephemeral wealth coming out of holes in the ground, and the other, a world of wealth they could build that would sustain them today, as well as generations to come.

Otherwise, when the oil runs out, or if the West finds energy alternatives, or if more accessible oil is found elsewhere in the world, the Arabs are going to discover what Spain and the Soviet Union discovered. ∆

— **John Silveira**

Sept/Oct 2003
No 83
$4.95 US
$6.50 CAN

Backwoods Home magazine

practical ideas for self-reliant living

Battery powered retreat

A baby quilt to remember
Creating your own job
Solar battery charging
A chicken coop home
Wild flower buds
Lyme disease
Firewood

www.backwoodshome.com

Publisher's Note

Mousers and cat loonies

I must really be old fashioned. I live in the country and have plenty of rodents running around, just like many of you, so I need a few mousers to keep things under control. It's a great life for a cat. They've got so many things to hunt they hardly bother with their cat food. But the cats themselves sometimes get picked off by a bobcat, owl, or mountain lion, so you have to replace them now and then.

That's the situation I was in recently, so I looked around for a cat at an obvious place—the nearest animal shelter. After picking out a couple of nice kitties that I knew would love my barn and its inhabitants, the smiling lady cat attendant handed me a piece of paper and said I had to read and sign it. It was a contract promising not to abuse the cats. No problem; I like cats. But above where I was to sign was a statement giving them permission for one year to come into my house any time, without warning, so they could inspect it to make sure the cats had a good environment.

I looked at the attendant with more than a little surprise on my face and read that part of the contract to her and said, "That's just a joke right?"

"No it's not," she said firmly. "We need to know that these cats are going to a good home."

I half smiled and half laughed at her. "But you're talking about me giving you the right to come into my home, at any time, unannounced. Into my personal home?"

"That's right," she said with an authority that made me think of an old East German matron from the days when East German women athletes all looked like brick layers.

By the stern look on her face I knew she would not be receptive to me expounding on the importance of privacy and the sanctity of one's home, so I said as politely as I could that I would try and find cats elsewhere.

A day or so later I answered an ad in the paper by a lady who was selling cats, and subsequently went to a house where at least 15 cats were crawling all over the furniture and a meekish looking husband. She wanted $10 per cat and told me the cats were accustomed to being indoors and under no circumstances were they to be allowed outside at night. Then she produced the same piece of paper that the cat lady Gestapo matron had asked me to sign.

What the hell is going on? All I want is a couple of mousers. My daughter finally dropped off a couple of cats on a visit, and they worked out just fine, until one was taken by an owl and the other by a bobcat. But they had a great life while it lasted. Of course that's probably at least part of what's behind these cat contracts; no one wants to put the kitties at risk of being eaten by cat predators. Plus the cat loony activists out there are probably sincerely on the lookout for people like me who insist their cats live outdoors *all the time*.

Here's the way I see it: Cats are predators of mice, rats, moles, gophers, and other little things that are troublesome to a country dweller like me. In exchange for their service at controlling pests, I give my cats the best cat food I can find, a nice home in my barn, and lots of pets and scratches on the head. I've had lots of cats and the outdoor ones have always, without exception, been healthier than the indoor ones.

My old cat, Champagne, was 14 when I had to have him put down because he could no longer eat or walk. But those 14 years were full of great hunting and adventure; I couldn't begin to count the number of mice he left at my front door. He wouldn't think of sleeping indoors at night, because he owned the night, prowling and stalking like the practiced feline he was born to be.

Sure, some of my other cats became a midnight snack for an owl or a roving bobcat, but that's part of the country calculation for pets. Sometimes dogs get taken by mountain lions too. But the life these pets have while it lasts is great, surely a lot better than that of housebound city cats where they are not allowed to practice most of their instinctive hunting and stalking behavior.

These cat loonies are dooming a lot of unwanted cats with their contracts to inspect people's homes. I want cats, and so do most country folks. But the only contract we want is the traditional unspoken one whereby the cat catches pests in exchange for room and board. That's a great contract, a perfect symbiotic relationship. The cat gets to live a *natural life* with its occasional perils of owls and bobcats, plus they get the added benefit of contact with a caring human, which is an especially handy thing when a vet is required.

Cat loony activists need to get a life.

U.S. Marines, a CD-ROM, and Fox News

Last issue I mentioned a CD-ROM we were producing that chronicled the activities of the *3rd LAR Battalion* of the *U.S. Marines* during *Operation Iraqi Freedom*. The CD-ROM is finished, but unfortunately we can't give it to the marines because *Fox News* won't give us permission to use their video clips. It had never occurred to me that *Fox* might object to what is essentially a public service on our part, but they have. I got a letter from their top lawyer specifically denying me permission. Sorry Marines. Fox still did a great job covering the war.

Meanwhile my son-in-law, Marine LCpl Erik Tuttle, has returned home from Iraq with some great stories. One of the best was about how his battalion hadn't taken a shower in two months. He said, "We knew we were smelling bad when the Iraqis would come up to us and spray us with cologne."

— *Dave*

My view

"I stink!" but that's okay

There are valuable life lessons to be learned from realizing you're not very good at a lot of things, even at things you think are important to be good at.

My lessons began in 1959, when I was 15. As a third string quarterback for Cathedral High School in Boston, I really wanted to be a great football player, but as I sat in the half time locker room of Franklin Field, with our team being massacred by powerful Matignon 50-something to nothing, things seemed bleak. Coach Tatter, who would never recognize my talents, looked down at our silent, sullen faces for only a few seconds before he bellowed, "We stink!" I can't remember the rest of the pep talk, but it was brief.

I knew he was right, and if "we stank," I must really have stunk because I was third string. Matignon, lead by future pro quarterback Jack Concannon, continued to pound us the second half, and we lost by the score of 90 to 6. The coach did not speak to us after the game, and I quit the team next year because I couldn't endure the embarrassment of being third string on a lousy team in my senior year. I wasn't convinced then that I stunk, but I had my suspicions.

Now that I am 59, and having spent a lifetime testing myself at various sports without success, I have taken up my final sport, golf, on the theory that it will reduce stress and improve my health. I had played golf years before, poorly, but this time around I took lessons from a teaching pro. It became apparent to me immediately that I was better than I had been years before. In fact, I thought I was so good that I forgot all about my stress and told my wife I would master the game, then join the *Pro Senior Tour* and make my retirement living that way. She believed me and bought me a set of "professionally fitted" golf clubs for Christmas.

It's been a year now, with several sets of lessons from the pro having been diligently digested and practiced, and the stress that led me to the game has been forgotten as I continue to immerse myself in the joy of playing. But my game has not reached the pro level. In fact, I am not very good at all. Progress comes slowly, almost imperceptibly, and despite my ardent practice, some days my golf absolutely stinks. At my local course, called *Salmon Run*, which admittedly is a tough Oregon woods and ferns-lined course where the slightest deviation from the fairway means a lost ball, I lose an average of 30 balls per round. Luckily I've found a place to buy good used balls for 33 cents each.

Dave Duffy

A few months ago I began to suspect I would never get very good at golf. And in the last few weeks I have begun to accept what last year was the unthinkable: I stink at golf too.

But unlike high school football where my personal esteem was founded upon youthful pursuits, I've decided it's okay that I stink at golf, and I plan to increase my participation in this enjoyable, relaxing sport.

I generally take my three young sons with me, and I pay them whenever they do well: a dollar for bogey, $2 for par, and $5 for birdie. Only one, Robby, has ever collected on a birdie as they show signs of having talents similar to mine.

But golf got me to thinking. I've stunk at a lot of things like golf, but I've succeeded at other, more mundane things, like being a good father and a good husband.

In the sometimes difficult transition from failed high school quarterback through failed golf pro, I've finally come to understand that failure is only a rudder that steers you towards success. Each failure turned me towards something else. When I failed at football, I turned to track in college. When I failed at both track and college, I turned to U.S. Army enlistment, and when I failed at that (I at least got an honorable discharge), I became a newspaper reporter, where I finally found moderate success. Then I became a Defense Department technical writer, with a little more success, and finally this magazine's publisher, which is a total success. I just had to be patient, I realize, not get down on myself, not blame others for my failures, and keep trying.

Mr. Tatter was right when he told us high school athletes that we stank, but he probably should have added the caveat: "But don't worry about it. Life's going to be full of these shellackings. Just go out the second half and give it all you can."

I've been examining my life with its failures and successes lately, in part because I have partially retired from the magazine so I have more time to engage in such retirement pastimes as reflection. I think it was Shakespeare who said, "It is far better to have stunk at golf, than to have failed at life."

Or was that Homer? *— Dave Duffy*

Battery powered weekend retreat

By Jeffrey R. Yago, P.E., CEM

Blake McKinney owned several acres of beautiful deep forest wilderness along a fast-moving year-round fishing stream that was perfect for a planned weekend retreat. Mr. McKinney, an attorney in western Virginia, had purchased this property located along the Virginia-Tennessee border with the hope of building a small weekend cabin his family and friends could use away from the city.

He found the perfect plans for a 900-square foot, two-story lodge with a large open deck that would extend right up to the water's edge. The cathedral ceiling living room with large wood-burning fireplace would become their entertainment center. Although the kitchen, dining area, two bathrooms, and three bedrooms were kept relatively small to stay within the small building footprint, they would still provide separation and privacy for friends and family wanting to "rough it."

Building on a rocky valley floor along this ancient creek bed would not allow digging a basement, but the desire to keep above the level of lowland flooding resulted in building the first floor above a five-foot high crawl space. Although not high enough to stand up in, the added concrete floor and access door provide a good dry storage area for all that fishing gear.

The McKinney family wanted to keep the rustic feel of the original forest, so the house site was selected to avoid cutting any large trees, and the undisturbed heavy ground cover of pine needles assured that Blake would not be doing any yard work. As all good intentions go, however, there was a very big problem with this plan, which is what got me involved in the story.

Their property was one of the many old homesteads that became "land islands" years ago when the National Forests were created around them, so now the thousands of acres of

The Fourteenth Year

Rear deck steps lead down to the water's edge.

restricted public land use has effectively blocked all utility line access. This would mean no all-electric kitchen, no central HVAC system, no major appliances, and no video games. When I first met Blake, the cabin was almost completed on the outside, but the electrician had stopped all work since there was no utility power for him to connect.

Selecting a system

Anything can be powered by the sun in my work, but when I visited the site for the first time it was obvious the location at the base of a high mountain range blocking the south exposure and nestled among extremely tall pine trees told me any serious solar power system was out of the question. It was determined that a generator would be required, but nobody wanted to hear one operating constantly all weekend.

We decided the best solution would be a hybrid power system, having all 120-Volt AC appliances powered from a Trace 4 kW sine wave inverter, with the inverter connected to 12 industrial L-16 size batteries wired in series-parallel to provide a 24-volt DC output.

An insulated plywood battery enclosure was built around the battery bank in the crawl space that includes an outside vent pipe to exhaust any battery gasses generated during the charging process. We selected an 8.5 kW Kohler 1,800-RPM propane fueled generator to charge the batteries, and a large underground propane tank would provide months of maintenance free fuel. It was possible to use a smaller generator, but the higher amperage capacity of this generator provides faster battery charging and longer quiet time between charging.

The south-facing roof only had enough unshaded area for a small 150-watt solar array, barely enough to offset the battery bank's self-discharging during weeks of un-occupancy. The limited sun hours each day would be partially offset by the many days between cabin occupancy.

Blake and I agreed that for this concept to work, he must purchase the most energy saving lights, appliances, and HVAC systems available; otherwise, his generator would need to run continuously. Although I designed the home's power system and supplied all of this equipment, a local electrician provided the actual equipment installation and wiring. After the installation was finished, we provided the system startup service and programmed the inverter to maximize the generator powered battery charging process.

Selecting appliances

All lighting installed was compact fluorescent and T-8 tube high efficiency fixtures with full-color spectrum lamps. Realizing that the inverter would shut down anytime the battery voltage dropped too low during these long unattended periods, we decided to install a few 24-volt DC

Inverter power system mounted on the back wall of the battery box

241

lighting fixtures at key locations including stairwells, corridors, and over the system control panel. This would provide basic lighting until the generator was restarted to bring the cabin back to life. Nobody wanted to have television or video equipment during these get-away weekends, and the cool deep woods guaranteed air conditioning would not be needed. The large fireplace would provide all required heating, but hot showers and a fully functioning kitchen would be mandatory.

We decided the long unoccupied periods would make a conventional hot water heater impractical even if it was supplied from the large underground propane tank for the genera-

AquaStar instantaneous domestic hot water

tor, so we installed an AquaStar instantaneous propane hot water heater. This 125,000 BTU hot water heater can heat a continuous 2 gal/min flow of 50-degree ground water without any storage tank instantly up to 140 degrees for as long as you keep the faucet open, and will still shut-off the instant the water flow stops. I have seen this same unit supplying scalding water for two simultaneous showers in the dead of winter.

We had intended to utilize this water heater to also heat a small piping loop of baseboard hot water radiation around the perimeter walls of the ground floor rooms, but decided the potential for pipe freezing during long periods of unoccupancy was too risky. Since the large fireplace would provide the serious heating during occupancy, it was decided to install a small in-wall forced air propane heater which included a small supply duct down under the floor to also heat the water piping and storage battery areas.

Although intended to operate only long enough to take the initial chill off the cabin until a fire could be started in the fireplace, a low limit thermostat allows the heater to restart if near freezing temperatures are reached inside the cabin or around the heavily insulated battery box in the crawl space.

Now that these lighting, heating, and hot water issues had been resolved, it was time to tackle the kitchen. A modern four-burner gas stove and oven was ordered with older design pilot lights instead of complex electronic controls and high-energy usage electric glow plugs. This would solve the cooking issue

Now for the refrigerator. Since they will bring the refrigerated foods and drinks needed each weekend, keeping lots of foods cold for long periods was not necessary. We also realized the refrigerator would be the largest energy using appliance in the cabin

Pad-mounted Electric Start Kohler 8.5 kW propane generator

and we didn't want to operate the generator during weeks of un-occupancy just to keep a few things cold. We decided to install a 24-volt DC Sunfrost 12 cu. ft. refrigerator freezer.

This is the most energy efficient refrigerator made and its heavily insulated walls insure the small dual compressors will operate much less

Sunfrost 24-volt DC refrigerator

The Fourteenth Year

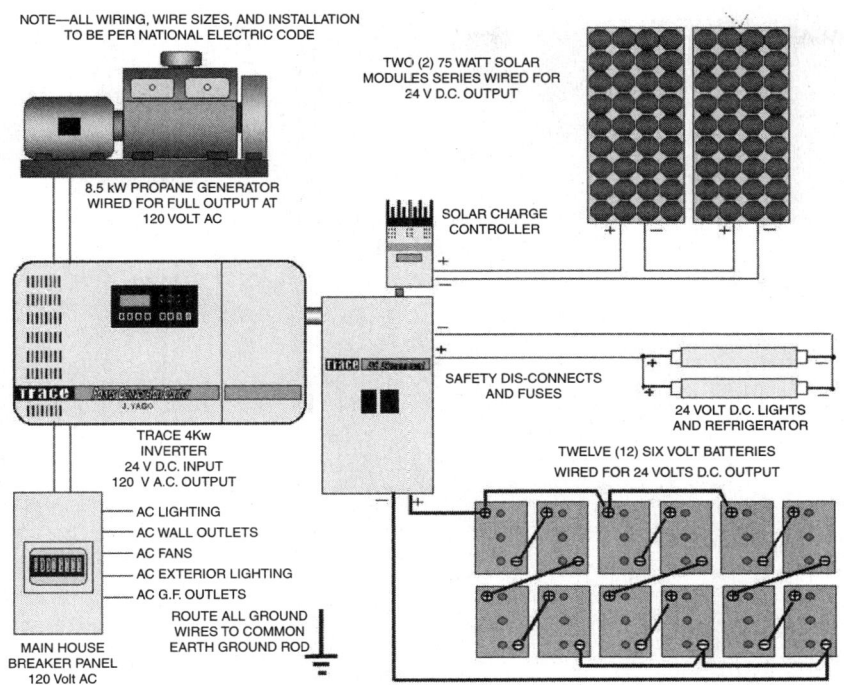

Wiring diagram

than a conventional refrigerator. We chose this DC model since it could be powered directly from the 24-volt battery bank, avoiding the need to operate the inverter with its associated standby losses during long periods of unoccupancy.

Controlling the system

The final issue was to decide how this system would be controlled, since the intent was to provide a home away from home without spending the weekend servicing complex electrical equipment. A remote system monitor and inverter control panel were installed near the front door. This control system is capable of fully automatic operation of the generator and the battery charging process; however, it was decided to not operate the generator in automatic mode when the cabin is not occupied since any generator starting problem would not be observed and could damage the generator.

Upon first arrival, a check of the display panel may show the solar maintained batteries are still low and in need of charging. By manually pressing a button on this display panel, the generator is started and the inverter comes to life putting as much charge as possible back into the batteries. Since it will take this generator about three hours to fully recharge the batteries, this is the best time to operate any high-energy usage appliances like the warm up gas furnace, kitchen appliances, or power tools directly from the generator. By nightfall the batteries will be recharged and the inverter will shut down the generator for a nice quiet evening.

Depending on how long the cabin was unoccupied and the current weather conditions, it may be possible to go through the entire weekend without restarting the generator. However, it is a good practice to bring the batteries back to full charge just before "check out" time. Hopefully, with enough sun, the small solar array will offset the standby battery losses and the electrical usage of the DC refrigerator until the next weekend or holiday visit.

More and more people are buying rural property to have a retreat from city life, but still want the comfort and labor saving conveniences of modern appliances. If you are buying property in an area not served by utility lines, perhaps a hybrid solar-generator-battery power system will fit your needs too. Δ

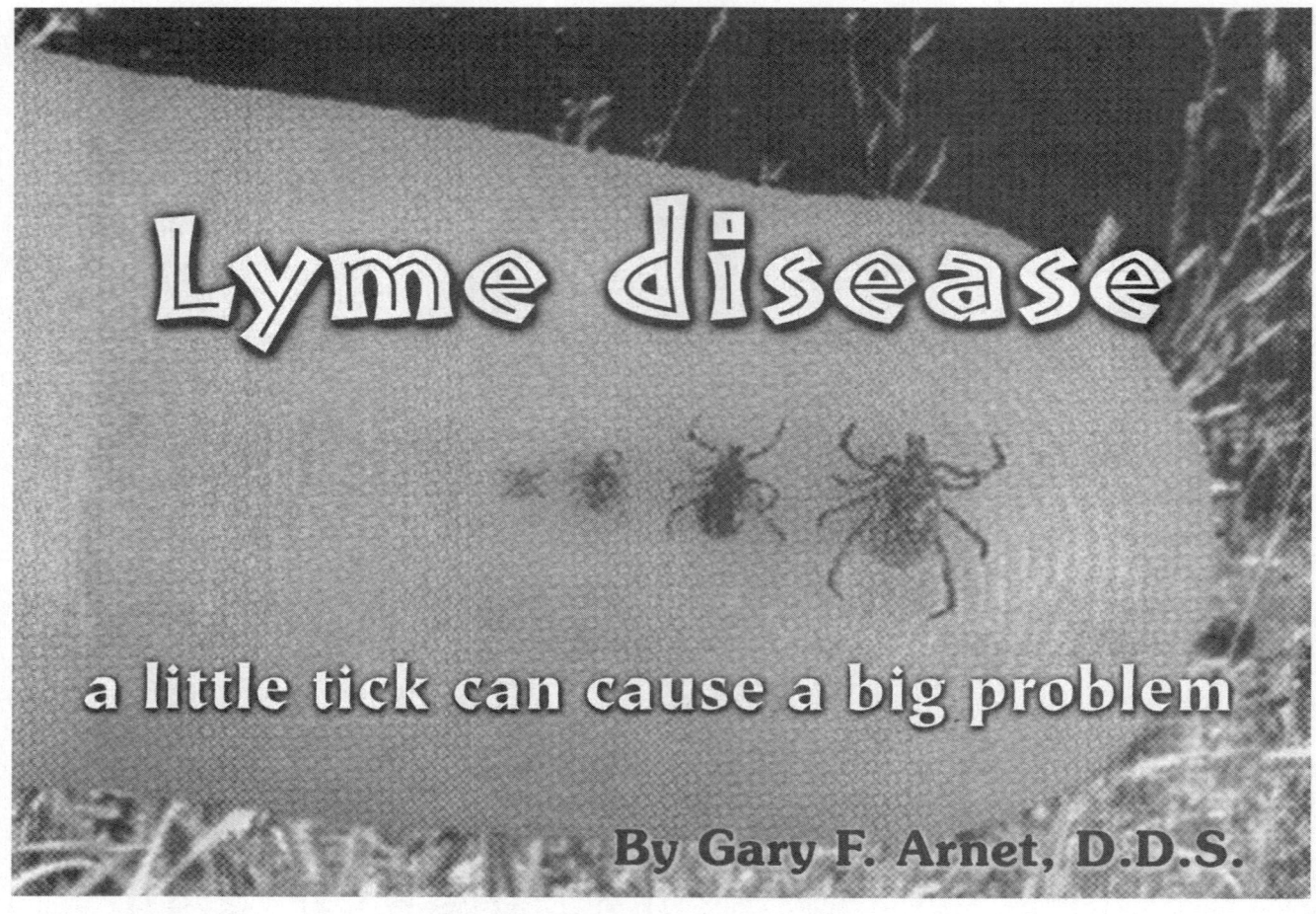

Lyme disease
a little tick can cause a big problem

By Gary F. Arnet, D.D.S.

Ticks that cause Lyme disease are smaller than more common ticks. Juvenile ticks, called nymphs, are only the size of a poppy seed, while adult females are the size of a sesame seed. From left to right, larva, nymph, adult male, and adult female stages are shown on a finger. (Courtesy of California Department of Health Services)

Kyle was an active 12-year-old boy who spent summers hiking, fishing, and enjoying the outdoors when he lived in a rural area of Butte County in northern California. That was until he developed a form of juvenile arthritis that was so severe he couldn't go outside. Doctor after doctor couldn't determine what was wrong, until one finally made the diagnosis. Kyle had an advanced stage of Lyme disease.

Lyme disease is a serious bacterial infection transmitted by certain infected ticks. The 1,990 people who lived in Lyme, Connecticut, in 1975 were seeing a dramatic number of children with arthritic swelling of joints that would come and go. Physicians said the children had juvenile arthritis, but mothers disagreed, insisting it must be infectious because so many children were affected.

They were right. Further research determined this was a bacterial infection transmitted by deer ticks, which was subsequently named Lyme disease after the town.

Ticks are parasites that feed on another animal host. They belong to the arachnid family and are related to scorpions and spiders, not insects. In addition to Lyme disease, ticks cause at least nine other human diseases in the United States.

The deer tick (*Ixodes scapularis*) in the northeast and north central states, and the Western black-legged tick (*Ixodes pacificus*) in the western states, are the carriers for *Borrelia burgdorferi*, a type of spirochete bacterium that causes Lyme disease. Smaller than the common cattle or dog tick, these ticks need to host on the blood of birds, reptiles, or mammals, including humans, to grow and reproduce. They transfer the bacterium between host animals.

Over 145,000 cases of Lyme disease have been reported in the United States since 1982, with 17,730 reported to the Centers for Disease Control (CDC) in 2000. Each year the number of new cases increase and Lyme disease has now been reported in 48 states and the District of Columbia.

The Fourteenth Year

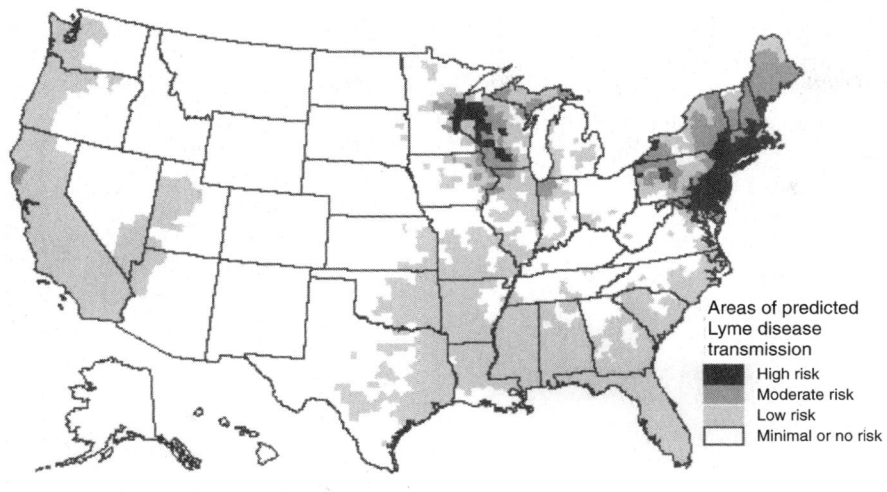

Map of the geographical distribution of Lyme disease in the United States (Courtesy of the U.S. Centers for Disease Control)

Most of the cases are concentrated along the East Coast, the Great Lakes, and the Pacific Northwest. Ninety percent of the cases are in 10 states, the vast majority being found in New York, Connecticut, Pennsylvania, and New Jersey. Northern California and Oregon account for the majority of cases on the West Coast. The geographical location of the disease is slowly increasing from current locations.

Since it was discovered, Lyme disease has increased dramatically and is a major health concern in certain areas of the United States. It is a multi-system inflammatory disease that affects the skin in early stages and spreads to the joints, nervous system, and organs in later stages. It can be readily cured if treated with antibiotics early, but can be crippling and linger for months or years if it becomes chronic. The best treatment for Lyme disease is to avoid catching it in the first place.

Symptoms

Many people do not remember being bitten by an infected tick. The first symptom in 80% to 90% of people is an expanding rash that develops from 3 to 30 days after the bite. Called erythema migrans in medical terms, it appears either as a solid red rash or as a central red spot surrounded by normal skin which itself is surrounded by another ring of red rash. Sometimes called a bull's eye rash, it is usually about five to six inches in diameter, although it may be larger. It is not itchy or painful and may last for three to five weeks.

Other symptoms such as fever, chills, joint pain, swollen lymph nodes, and fatigue are common about the time the rash appears. They are often mild and brief, not seeming serious enough to warrant medical care. Antibiotic treatment with doxycycline or amoxicillin for three to four weeks is generally effective in curing the disease at this early stage.

Many other serious symptoms develop as Lyme disease progresses. These potentially debilitating symptoms may occur weeks, months, or occasionally years after the bite. They may include severe fatigue, numbness or tingling of the extremities, facial paralysis, severe headaches, painful arthritis, joint swelling, mental disorders, and cardiac abnormalities. Intravenous antibiotics may be required for four weeks or more, although this treatment may still fail to cure the disease.

The best way to prevent Lyme disease is to understand the deer tick and Western black-legged tick and to avoid them. If you cannot avoid their habitat, take precautions to prevent ticks from attaching to your skin.

Tick ecology

Ticks have four life stages over a period of two years and must feed on blood from a host at three times in their life cycle in order to develop. In late summer, very young ticks, called larvae, hatch from eggs and pick up the *Borrelia burgdorferi* bacteria by biting infected animals. They then drop from the host and find a protected site under leaves to pass the winter. Larvae are a light tan, translucent color about the size of the period at the end of this sentence.

Late the next spring or summer, juvenile ticks, called nymphs, rise

Hikers, campers, fishermen, and anyone else who works, lives, or vacations in many areas of the United States are at risk for contracting Lyme disease unless they take precautions.

from the ground to search for a suitable feeding site. Blackish in color and about the size of a poppy seed, they wait on vegetation from ground level to 18 inches high. They attach to passing animals, especially white-footed mice in the east and western fence lizards in the west. After feeding for five to six days, they drop to the ground to find shelter under leaves or other vegetation. Nymphs account for most cases of Lyme disease and actively feed from April to August.

By late summer, nymphs molt into adult ticks. Females are brick-red and about the size of a sesame seed, while males are smaller and are black. Adult ticks occur in the fall and spring and again search for a blood meal in order for the eggs of the female to mature. For this blood meal they favor larger mammals such as deer and humans. They feed for 8-10 days, swelling to the size of a small pea. Female ticks drop off the animal after mating and lay eggs on the ground that take about two weeks to hatch.

Adult ticks may pass on Lyme disease to the host, but their size and longer feeding period makes them easier to detect and remove. They are active from October to November and again during April to May when the temperature is above 35° to 40° F.

The large incidence of Lyme disease in the east is due to the large numbers of white-footed mice and deer, the preferred hosts of the deer tick, and the proximity of humans who live and play in the same area. Nymphs feed on the white-footed mice which are the principal "reservoir" of the infection, while adults favor deer and other large mammals.

On the west coast, *Borrelia burgdorferi* is transmitted by the western black-legged tick. The mechanism of transmission of the disease from animal to animal is the same with the exception of one important fact. The favorite host of the tick in the nymph stage is the western fence lizard. This lizard has been found to contain a substance in its blood that kills the Lyme disease spirochete. It renders the tick incapable of infecting its next host. For that reason, only 5% of adult western black-legged ticks carry the disease, while 50% of the adult deer ticks found in the east are infected. This is why the incidence of Lyme disease is lower in the west, where western fence lizards are common.

Ticks crawl to the tips of grasses and plants waiting for animals or humans to brush against the vegetation. They then attach themselves to the passing animal. They do not jump or fly.

Once on the host, they attach to skin and insert their barbed mouth through the skin to feed on blood while their bodies slowly enlarge. While they can attach anywhere, they most often attach to hidden, hairy areas such as the groin, armpits, back of the knee, nape of the neck, or scalp. If they first contact clothing, they will crawl upward in search of exposed skin. Ticks on the scalp have usually crawled there from other parts of the body.

A tick must be attached for at least 24 hours to transmit Lyme disease. Some studies report it requires 36 to 48 hours of attachment to pass on the disease, although health departments in some high-risk areas use 12 hours as a guide. Generally, a tick has not been on the host long enough to transmit Lyme disease if it is not yet swollen with blood. Therefore, promptly locating and removing the tick will reduce your chance of being infected.

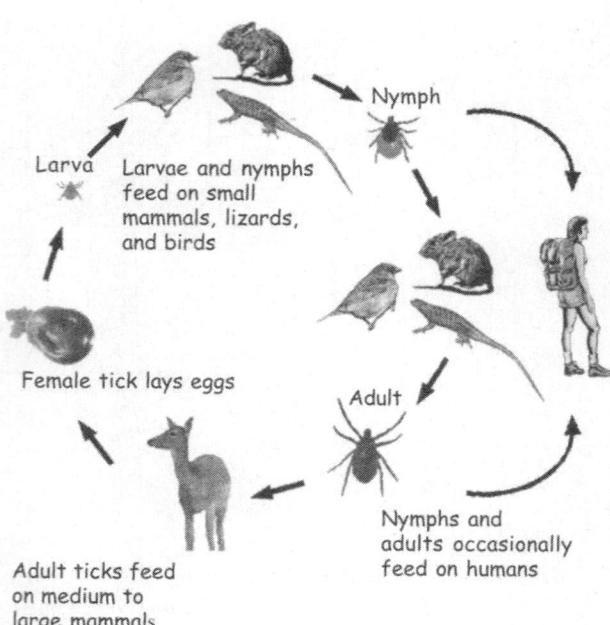

Life cycle of the western black-legged tick (Courtesy of California Department of Health Services)

Tick habitat

Hikers, campers, hunters, fishermen, outdoor workers, and others who frequent grassy or wooded outdoor areas are frequently exposed to ticks. Homeowners living in rural wooded areas are also commonly infected. Even people living in urban areas can be exposed in their yard if, for example, their dog brings home an infected tick that drops on their lawn. Playing in the yard or other contact with vegetation can result in exposure to ticks. Others at risk include travelers passing through an area and not being aware of the possibility of encountering infected ticks.

Ticks have been found from sea level to 7,000 feet. They are prevalent where there are abundant deer and rodent hosts, favoring a shaded, moist environment. Overgrown grassy areas, leaf litter, and low vegetation in brush or wooded areas are favorite habitats. Around a house, fallen leaves, debris, and woodpiles (often

Areas that attract deer, such as the edges of meadows, trails, and grassy areas, are the prime habitat to find adult ticks.

frequented by mice and other small mammals) are common places to find ticks. Likewise, stone walls attract small mammals and increase the chance of encountering ticks, especially in some areas of the northeast.

Leaf litter, such as oak leaf debris, is the prime location to encounter nymph-stage ticks from April to July. Seventy percent of the cases of Lyme disease occur during these months due to exposure to nymphs. Be careful in this habitat and avoid it if possible.

Deer habitat is another area to expect ticks which lie in wait for passing animals. Deer frequent ecotomes, the junction of two ecology zones. They will often be found traveling near the edge of a grassy meadow surrounded by heavy brush, ready to hide in the protected brush at the first sign of a predator. Ticks also will be found in this area with the highest concentration being within an area about 10 feet from the edge.

Other common areas to find ticks are slopes that face south and slopes where there is difference in soil and vegetation. Along human or game trails, 80% to 90% of the ticks can be found on the uphill side of the trail.

Protecting yourself

The only way to completely prevent the chance of Lyme disease or other tick-borne diseases is to avoid exposure to ticks. Understanding their life cycle and habitat is a start; however, other precautions are needed to avoid being bitten by a tick since it is not always possible to avoid their habitat.

Don't walk barelegged in woods, tall grasses, or dunes where ticks may live. Wear light-colored long pants and a long-sleeved shirt made of a tight weave material so that you can spot ticks easily. Wear enclosed shoes or boots and consider tucking your pants into your socks in high-risk areas. Stay on well-traveled, cleared trails, remembering that 80% to 90% of the ticks will be found on the uphill side of the trail. Avoid sitting on rock walls or on leaf littered ground. Check your clothes and exposed skin throughout the day for

Protect yourself from ticks that carry Lyme disease by wearing light-colored long pants, long-sleeved shirts, and enclosed shoes or boots. In high-risk areas, consider tucking your pants into your socks when walking through brush.

Things to remember about Lyme disease

- Lyme disease is transmitted by infected deer ticks in the east and western black-legged ticks in the west.
- Not all deer ticks or western black-legged ticks carry Lyme disease.
- Ticks must be attached to the host for at least 24 hours to pass on the disease.
- Nymph stage ticks are smaller and more likely to transmit the Lyme disease than adult ticks.
- Know the habitat where you can expect to find ticks.
- Use precautions when in "tick country" including proper clothing and repellants.
- Check yourself daily for ticks and remove any that are attached to decrease your chance of being infected with Lyme disease.

ticks, remembering that they climb upward in an attempt to find exposed skin. A final full-body check for ticks should be done at the end of each day. Remember, their favorite locations are hidden, hairy areas, such as the groin, armpits, back of the knee, nape of the neck, or scalp. Be sure to also check children and pets.

Insect repellants will also stop ticks from attaching to your skin. Clothes may be sprayed with insect repellants that contain diethyl-meta-toluamide (DEET) or Permethrin.

DEET may be used on clothes or skin in concentrations no greater than 10% to 15% on children and no greater than 30% to 35% on adults. Use just enough to cover exposed skin or clothes, but do not apply to skin that is covered by clothing. DEET may be applied every four to eight hours.

Permethrin repellants are for use on clothes only. Do not apply them to the skin. They should be applied to the outside of clothing before putting them on and allowed to dry outdoors for at least four hours before wearing. The clothes should not be treated more than once every two weeks.

Read the labels of any insect repellant carefully and follow the manufacturer's recommendations. Serious reactions to repellants may rarely occur. When used improperly with children, DEET products may cause slurred speech, confusion, seizures, and even coma.

When you return home, clothes can be spun for 20 minutes in the dryer for the heat to kill any ticks that were not noticed and a full-body check for ticks should again be performed.

If you live in a tick-infested environment, you can reduce the tick population around your home by clearing leaf litter, brush, and tall grass from around your house, rock walls, piles of wood, and the edges of gardens. Lawns should be kept mowed and edged. Any debris that could attract rodents and small mammals should be cleared. Woodpiles should be stacked neatly in a dry location off the ground.

A licensed professional can spray residential areas with an insecticide in late May to control nymphs and in September to control adults.

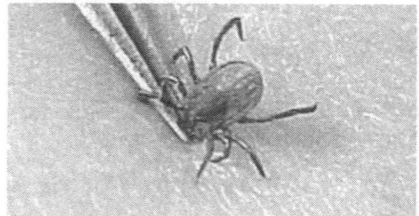

Remove a tick by grasping the mouth parts where they enter the skin with pointed tweezers and pulling outward with a steady motion until the tick is pulled out. Never grab the body. (Courtesy of California Department of Health Services)

Insect repellants in aerosol or lotion form will stop ticks from attaching to your skin. Repellants used on the skin should be no greater than 15% DEET for children and 35% DEET for adults. Aerosol Cutter Insect Repellant contains 9.5% DEET and would be good to use with children.

In the late 1990s, a vaccine called LYMErix was developed to prevent Lyme disease. The CDC Committee on Immunization Practices recommended the vaccine for persons age 15 to 70 who lived, worked, or vacationed in areas of high tick-infested habitat. In February 2002, the manufacturer removed it from the market citing poor sales. A complicating factor was that up to one-third of the population has a specific blood trait that put them at risk for developing an untreatable autoimmune arthritis from the vaccine.

Removing ticks

Don't panic if you find a tick attached to your skin, as not all ticks are infected and they usually need to be attached for at least 24 hours to transmit Lyme disease.

Remove the tick using pointed tweezers. Grasp the tick by the head or mouth parts where they enter the skin and pull the tick outward with a steady motion. Gradually increase the force until it is pulled out. Never grab the body, as the contents of the tick can be forced into the bite, increasing the chances of the tick transmitting the disease. For the same reason, do not use a hot match, petroleum jelly, nail polish, alcohol, or any other irritant.

It is not a problem if part of the tick's mouth remains embedded in the skin, since the bacteria that cause Lyme disease are contained in the tick's body. Remove remaining mouth parts as you would remove a splinter by using a sterilized needle.

The tick can be taken to your local health department to identify the type of tick and to determine if it is infected with *Borrelia burgdorfer*. The tick should be placed in a sealed container or a sealed plastic bag along with a moist cotton ball or moist Kleenex. It must not be allowed to dry out or it cannot be tested. Contrary to what is often said, do not place the tick in alcohol if you plan to have it tested, as this will dry out the tick and make testing impossible. Take the tick to the health department in a timely manner.

The health department can examine the tick to determine if it is a deer tick in the east or western black-legged tick in the west. If it is, it can be sent for fluorescent antibody testing to determine if the *Borrelia burgdorferi* bacterium is present. This test is about 95% accurate in determining if the tick is infected.

Just because *Borrelia* is present in the tick doesn't mean it was transmitted to the person to whom it was attached. The health department will want to know how long you estimate it had been attached and the geographical location where you may have acquired it. Within a county, cer-

---

For additional information on Lyme disease

Center for Disease Control:
www.cdc.gov

American Lyme Disease Foundation, Inc.:
http://aldf.com

tain tick populations are infected at higher rates than other areas.

Monitor the site of the bite for the next 3 to 30 days to watch for the appearance of a rash. Be aware of any other early symptoms such as fever, chills, joint pain, swollen lymph nodes, and fatigue. These may be mild and seem unimportant. See a physician immediately if any rash or other symptoms occur.

Lyme disease is certainly something you don't want. Knowledge and proper precautions can limit your risk. Know if the area you are in has ticks infected with Lyme disease, wear proper clothes, and use insect repellants. Check yourself, your children, and your pets regularly for ticks, and clear the area around your house and yard. Be aware of the early symptoms of Lyme disease and seek medical attention early if there is even the slightest chance you have been infected. Enjoy the outdoors, but take precautions to avoid being a victim of this disease. ∆

Piccalilli — a late summer bonus

By Marcia E. Brown

Popularity of the movie *Fried Green Tomatoes* has sparked new interest the last few years in those ubiquitous green tomatoes that many gardeners have in plenty near the end of the growing season.

My grandmother, respected as both gardener and cook, welcomed those end-of-season hard, green fruits as more than a bonus. To her, they were jewels of the season.

Beyond frying them in batter for supper treats, each year she turned a peck of them into a large batch of piccalilli, one of our favorite relishes. By late August, jars of emerald piccalilli stood ready in her pantry not only to serve at family meals but also to be given as much welcomed gifts to friends at Christmas.

Grandma has been gone for nearly 50 years, but her special recipes continue to please. Written in her Victorian style handwriting, in faded pencil and in ink long browned by age, they fill a notebook that is one of my treasures. The piccalilli "receipts" are scribbled on a sheet of brittle paper, a bridge over time.

The results are as tasty today as they were when the tomatoes came from Grandma's own garden.

Grandma Emma's piccalilli

- 1 peck (8 quarts) green tomatoes, stemmed
- ¼ peck green bell peppers, stemmed
- 1 cup white onions, papery part peeled
- 3 lbs. cabbage
- 1 cup salt
- 1 cup white mustard seed
- 3 cups brown sugar
- 4 oz. stick cinnamon
- 3 oz. whole cloves
- 1 oz. allspice
- vinegar

Put the tomatoes, peppers, onions, and cabbage through a food chopper or chop coarsely in a food processor. Mix the vegetables thoroughly.

In a large container of crockery or glass, spread the vegetable mix in layers, sprinkling each layer with some of the salt until it is all used.

Let the mixture stand overnight. Drain it the next day.

Tie the spices and mustard seed into a cheesecloth "bag." Place this with the drained vegetables into a large canning kettle. Cover with vinegar. Cook slowly over low heat for two hours, stirring frequently to prevent burning and sticking.

Fill sterilized canning jars with the mixture and seal according to the jar manufacturer's directions.

If she had enough green tomatoes, Grandma might also make a version without the cabbage.

Sliced tomato and onion pickle

- 1 peck green tomatoes, stem ends removed
- 2 qts. peeled white medium onions
- 1 cup salt
- 3 qts. vinegar
- 1 oz. stick cinnamon
- 1 oz. whole cloves
- 3 lbs. light brown sugar

Slice the green tomatoes, discarding the stem ends. Slice onions. Mix together with the salt in a large pickling crock. Let stand overnight. Drain. In a large canning kettle, place the tomatoes and onions. Add two quarts of vinegar and two quarts of water. Bring to boil and simmer for 15 minutes. Drain again. In the same kettle, place one quart of vinegar and add the cinnamon, cloves, and light brown sugar and simmer for 20 minutes, stirring frequently. Add the tomato and onion mixture and bring to a boil. When this is thoroughly scalded, remove from heat.

Place the mixture in scalded quart canning jars and seal according to manufacturer's instructions.

In the cold of winter, a taste of tomato relish brings back the smells and color of the last days of summer, and memories of Grandma cherishing late August's bounty. ∆

The Fourteenth Year

Ayoob on Firearms

1911: The classic homeland security pistol

If you've read American firearms history at all, you know the lore of the .45 automatic. How during the Philippine insurrection, the newly issued .38 revolver failed miserably against psyched-up Moro warriors, and ancient .45 revolvers were dragged out of mothballs and re-issued to embattled American troops in the Pacific. How this led to the Thompson/LaGarde study of handgun ammunition effectiveness in 1907 that indicated nothing of less than .45 caliber should be issued as a sidearm to US troops. And how John Browning's brilliant design of a semiautomatic pistol in that caliber, as manufactured by Colt, was subsequently adopted as "Pistol, US, calibre .45, Model of 1911."

In the trenches of WWI, for the first and the last time in American military history, it was determined that every single one of America's troops needed to carry a .45 caliber handgun at the front. Though the ".45 automatic" was the first choice, the industry couldn't make enough of them and both Colt and Smith & Wesson pressed their revolver lines into production for the classic Model 1917 double action revolvers. These used ingenious half-moon clips developed by S&W to hold three of the "rimless" .45 auto cartridges together for fast reloading of these "revolvers using autoloader ammo." Not until the last quarter of the 20th century would shooters figure out that a full moon clip could hold six such cartridges at once. This allowed the fastest possible revolver reload…right about the time all the cops decided they wanted semiautomatic pistols, which were faster still to reload.

With modern techniques, even the lightest, hardest kicking 1911 .45s are controllable. Here Ayoob fires the tiny Springfield Micro Compact. Spent .45 case is in mid-air above gun, but recoil has barely lifted the muzzle from the centerline of the target.

Time marched on. In the early 1920s, a US military board convened to determine what had been learned in the Great War that could improve the design of the nation's military small arms. It was determined that about half the soldiers thought the 1911 pistol had too long a trigger, too short a grip tang safety, and sights that were just about useless. Before 1930, this advice coalesced into the improved Model 1911A1. Its trigger was much shorter and easier to reach, and this was aided by new scalloping around the trigger guard area of the frame. Bigger sights that were easier to see were added. The hammer was reconfigured and the grip safety's tang lengthened in hopes of preventing the pinch at the web of the hand that many doughboys had reported when the gun was cycling. The 1911A1 would remain the classic shape of this classic pistol for the remainder of the century.

"Legendary Manstopper"

The bolt-action 1903 Springfield and 1917 Enfield .30/06 battle rifles had proven themselves splendidly rugged and accurate when sniping at enemy soldiers across the battlefield. But, when the enemy was right there in the trenches with you, ready to spear you with the blood-stained bayonet of his Mauser, these long, heavy rifles that needed a four-step process to hand-cycle another cartridge into the firing chamber were not the optimum defensive tools. The 1911 pistol, on the other hand, proved to be in its element there. Eight quick flicks of the index finger unleashed eight

A "snubby" with 3-inch barrel, the Springfield Armory Micro Compact 1911 .45 shot this impressive group in a police-style qualification.

heavy 230-grain bullets, almost half an inch in diameter and traveling some 830 feet per second. At close range, when a single .45 slug struck the enemy in the wishbone, he tended to be immediately rendered hors de combat. To hell with bayoneted rifles, said the doughboys; this Colt .45 automatic was the ticket to getting out of the trenches alive once the enemy hordes had flowed into those trenches with you.

Countless tales of up close and personal pistol fighting emerged from WWI. The bottom line was that when Americans shot Germans with Colt .45 automatics, the Germans tended to fall down and die. When Germans shot Americans with their 9mm Luger pistols, the Americans tended to become indignant and kill the German who shot them, and then walk to an aid station to either die a lingering death or recover completely. Thus was born the reputation of the .45 automatic as a "legendary manstopper," and the long-standing American conviction that the 9mm automatic was an impotent wimp thing that would make your wife a widow if you trusted your life to it.

Then came WWII. The .45 automatic was the standard military weapon then as well. Used heavily in both theaters of the war, it was particularly valued in the Pacific, where Japanese sappers tended to infiltrate through the wires and be on top of the Yank soldier with knife in hand when the American woke up to deal with it. And the legend of the .45 as the "one shot, one kill" weapon was reinforced. It did not hurt that reputation that the average target in the Pacific was a rice-fed, half-starved biped who weighed about 130 pounds.

Then came Korea, and then Vietnam. Nothing happened to change the image of the .45 automatic as a deadly manstopper. In the mid-1980s, several trends converged upon the one firearm that had served the American military the longest. NATO was pushing the USA for complete compatibility in small arms ammo, and every other nation carried 9mm pistols. Except for target pistols for the pistol teams, the US government had not purchased new 1911s

For those who don't like cocked and locked, ParaOrdnance offers their LDA series in double action only. This is one of their concealed-carry models.

since before the Korean War, and the old guns were getting pretty clapped out. Finally, it is said, the Pentagon wanted cruise missiles in Italy and Italy wanted a lucrative US military contract in return. In any case, it was at that time that the United States armed services adopted the Italian Beretta Model 92F, caliber 9mm, as the official US service handgun that would be designated the M9 and would replace the 1911.

Fast forward to the present. When the War Against Terrorism went into the caves of Afghanistan, pistols became the weapons of choice for soldiers working on point in very close quarters. It became apparent that the 9mm with full metal jacket Geneva Convention ammo was as impotent as it was in WWI, with Al-Queda fanatics soaking up several rounds before they gave up the ghost. Those Yanks fortunate enough to have .45s—Army Delta Force, who purchase their own 1911s out of a stipend provided, and all the Special Operations Command elite who have access to the HK SOCOM pistol in that caliber—found that one or two full metal jacket .45 hardball rounds were all it took to drop a terrorist in his tracks. The call went out again: "We need .45s."

What goes around comes around. Santayana was right. Those who ignore history are doomed to repeat it.

Contemporary perspective

Back to the present: the United States in the time of the long-foretold terrorism. The time of Homeland Security.

It is simple common sense to tailor the tool to the predictable task. If we start getting what Israel got, suicide bombers and cowards who open fire in public on what they think are a herd of helpless victims, all you can expect to have with you to interdict the threat is a concealable pistol. It will have to deliver a powerful blow that will stop the recipient in his tracks, a factor we've already discussed, and it will have to deliver that shot unerringly in a close time frame, which is a 1911 design advantage we'll discuss shortly.

With modern American ammunition, the 9mm is perfectly adequate. This means a 115-grain hollow point bullet in the 1300 foot second velocity range, or a 124 to 127-grain hollow point bullet in the 1250 feet per second range. The former is readily available to police as the Winchester "Illinois State Police Load," the Remington equivalent that was long standard with the Secret Service, or the Federal 9BPLE round that was favored by the Border Patrol when that agency allowed the 9mm as an optional sidearm. The latter is available to police as the Winchester SXT Ranger +P+ 127-grain, or the CCI Gold Dot 124-grain +P+.

Sadly, most of this high performance ammo is sold only to police. Remington offers the public a 115-grain +P 9mm hollowpoint at 1250 fps. CCI will sell you the +P+ 124-grain Gold Dot 9mm they sell to police. Pro-Load will sell you their Tactical 115-grain hollow point 9mm at 1300 fps that actually out-performs most of the police loads. The problem is, in times of crisis the exact brand of ammo you want is often unavailable, and it's not wise to buy a gun that only performs at its best with one specific type of ammunition.

The cheapest, most widely available 230-grain full metal jacket .45 hardball will still probably solve your anti-personnel needs. No ball round is ideal for self-defense, because it tends to overpenetrate excessively. A .45 ball round can go through the bad guy, through and through the poor sucker behind him, and lodge in the body of an unseen innocent bystander who is third in the row. Hollow point ammo, designed to open up and stay in the body of the intended target while at the same time dumping all its energy into that designated target, remains the ammo of choice.

Training is the best way to master the .45. Here, 1911s jump on the indoor firing line of the "Dark House" at Firearms Academy of Seattle as master instructor Marty Hayes, left, observes.

The good news with the .45 Auto caliber is that the better hollow points will do exactly that: stay in the bad guy and not exit with enough power to kill a good guy behind him. We're talking for the most part something between a 185-grain hollow point at 935 to 1150 feet per second, a 200-grain hollow point at somewhere between 900 and 1050 feet per second, or a 230-grain hollow point at a velocity range from 830 to 950 feet per second.

My police department issues .45 automatics. Black Hills makes our ammo at their factory on special contract, guaranteeing 850 to 880 feet per second velocity with a 230-grain Gold Dot bonded-jacket hollow point. Whether in gelatin or in flesh, the bullets expand impressively, stopping at an optimum penetration depth. The ammunition is accurate and feeds reliably.

Analogous loads are available as (in alphabetical order) CCI's Gold Dot, Federal's Hydra-Shok, PMC's StarFire, Remington's Golden Saber, and Winchester's SXT series. Since these 230 grain "standard pressure" loads effectively duplicate the recoil and trajectory of inexpensive 230 grain full metal jacket training ammo, they shoot to the same point of aim/point of impact coordinates. This means that once you've put a couple of hundred hollow points through the gun and know it will feed, you can save a bunch of money by practicing with inexpensive "generic hardball" of the same bullet weight and velocity, and have totally relevant practice.

Specific 1911 advantages

The 1911 pistol is testimony to John Browning's engineering genius, written in steel. It is slimmer and flatter than any of the more "modern" .45s. When you tuck it into your waistband, it doesn't dig on the side toward you nor bulge on the side away. It's grip-to-barrel angle is natural for most people, meaning that if you close your eyes and point your

1911 .45s come in all shapes and sizes. This is one of the author's favorites, the Colt CCO, with 4¼-inch barrel of the Colt Commander and the short grip frame of the Colt Officers.

hand at the target, when you open your eyes you'll see that your 1911 pistol is pretty much aligned to hit that target. If you buy into the "point-shooting" theory of handgun self-defense, a gun that points where you look is absolutely essential. If, like me, you believe that the gun should be visually aligned with its target, a gun that points "automatically" where you look gets you to line of sight quicker. It's a win-win situation.

The handgun is a defensive weapon, meaning that it is reactive rather than offensive. The great trainer of fighter pilots Col. John Boyd defined the OODA Loop: Observe, Orient, Decide, Act. When you Observe danger and Orient yourself to the fact that only gunfire can save you, and then Decide to respond and Act out that response, you want a quick, reactive handgun. Since the 1911 is best carried fully loaded with a round in the chamber and "cocked and locked"—the hammer cocked on the live round, and the thumb safety "on safe"—you want to learn to wipe that safety lever into the "fire" position as you bring the gun up on target.

With a pre-cocked, single action trigger pull, the 1911 now puts only a short, easy trigger press between you and the necessary hit. Repeat as necessary: the same easy pull will follow for each subsequent shot.

One big advantage of cocked and locked carry is that it mandates the gun be "on safe." If the wrong person gets the gun away from you, he has to figure out which of those little levers "turns on the gun." This will buy you time to either rectify the situation up close and personal or run a considerable distance, either of which beats hell out of the bad guy holding a "point gun, pull trigger" weapon on you at contact distance.

In the hands of such seasoned, well-trained lawmen as the LAPD SWAT team, the 1911 .45 pistol has historically delivered an extremely high percentage of hits for the shots fired in life-threatening close combat. The pistol is simply easy to use well when in the grip of hand-shaking, gut-clenching "fight or flight response." Browning built it to perform exactly that way. The design succeeded.

For those who like everything about the 1911 design except the cocked and locked part, ParaOrdnance makes their excellent LDA .45 in sizes small, medium, and large. The hammer rests in the down position, and a double action only trigger requires a long but light and silky smooth trigger pull for each shot.

Selecting the 1911

There are more good brands of 1911 pistol than ever. Being a pessimist, and a police supervisor, I like guns that are SNAFU-proof and drop-safe. That means pistols with a design that physically prevents the gun from discharging if it is dropped

With frame rail for InSight M3 light, Springfield Armory TRP Operator is ideal for home defense. This is one of the most highly evolved of today's 1911s.

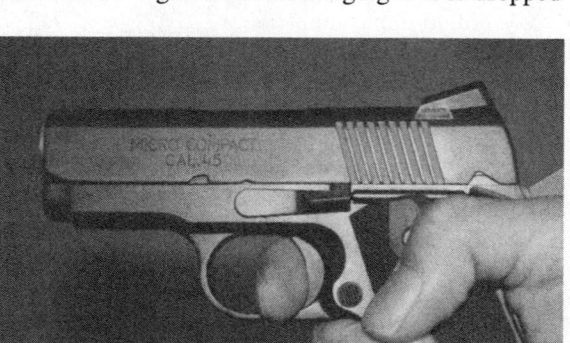

Good ergonomics in action. Short 1911A1 trigger of Springfield Armory Micro Compact allows deep finger placement for good leverage.

to the ground or struck sharply while in the officer's holster.

This brings you, basically, to four commercially available 1911 handguns. There is the Colt Series '80, which uses a trigger-activated firing pin block. There is the Para-Ordnance series of pistols made in Canada, which licenses the exact same design from Colt. There is the Kimber II series, which uses the grip safety activated Swartz principle from the 1930s as reworked by modern handgun design genius Nehemiah Sirkis. Finally, there are Springfield Armory 1911 pistols as produced circa 2001 and later which use a combination of a lightweight titanium firing pin and an extra-strong firing pin spring to make unintended "inertia discharge" physically impossible.

Within these four brands, you can get everything from literally pocket-sized subcompact .45 1911s that hold six rounds in the magazine and a seventh in the chamber, to the "wide-body" Para-Ordnance P14, which with "grandfathered pre-ban" magazines can hold a total of 14 .45 ACP rounds.

The 1911 in the backwoods

Backwoods folk have been using the 1911 pistol to good advantage since WWI, when that quintessential backwoodsman Alvin York fired six or seven shots from his Colt .45 auto and killed as many charging enemy infantrymen. He was awarded the Congressional Medal of Honor for that feat.

Generations of worn-out guns made of GI parts just thrown together, coupled with training that was deemed "good enough for Government work," has given the 1911 pistol a reputation for poor accuracy. By and large, that reputation is not deserved. Your better 1911s, as manufactured today, will stay in 2½ inches or better at 25 yards with ammunition of top quality.

I have two custom Colt 1911A1 .45 pistols, one crafted by Mark Morris and the other by Dave Lauck, that will each put 5 shots in an inch or better at 25 yards when loaded with Federal Match hardball or Federal 230-grain Hydra-Shok. Nor do you need the attentions of a custom pistolsmith to achieve that kind of accuracy. My Springfield Operator TRP (Tactical Response Pistol) cut a one-inch group at 25 yards out of its factory box with 5 rounds of Winchester 185-grain Mid-Range Match ammunition. My Kimber Custom stainless (the least expensive pistol that company makes) put 5 rounds of Winchester Ranger 230-grain +P police ammunition into an inch and a quarter at the same distance. Both of my Colt CCO pistols will do about 2 inches at 25 yards with the ammo they like best. CCO stands for "Concealed Carry Officers" model and comprises the short 4¼-inch barrel/slide assembly of the Commander pistol on the even shorter frame of the little Officers ACP. Finally, I've had several Para-Ordnance pistols that would hit the one-inch mark for a 5 shot group from 25 paces.

When I first visited hunting ranches in Texas, I had expected to see the hands and the guides carrying Colt Peacemakers and Magnum revolvers. Not hardly; almost every man-jack among these working cowboys wore a 1911 .45 auto tucked in the waistband of their jeans or on the front seat of the pickup truck beside them.

The woodsman has to consider the long range shot. An accurate 1911 .45 can deliver the goods here; the secret is to know how much that slow, heavy bullet drops as the range extends. As one observer put it, "The standard 230-grain .45 slug has the trajectory of a basketball." Save yourself some computation and do what I do. In the woods as opposed to on the street, I load my .45 auto with Remington's deliciously accurate 185-grain +P .45 jacketed hollow point. I discovered long ago that if my .45 was sighted in spot on at 25 yards with standard 230-grain ammo, it would put the shot where the sights were at 75 to 100 yards. The 1140 foot-second muzzle velocity of that 185-grain Remington .45 +P really flattens the trajectory.

Because of its short trigger pull and cocked n' locked condition of readiness, the 1911 .45 auto is better suited to the skilled and dedicated practitioner than to the amateur. That said, nearly a century of history has made the 1911 .45 automatic the quintessential "homeland security" pistol, from the rural game fields to house to house combat, and nothing is going to change that. Δ

Creating your own JOB

By Gary F. Arnet

"I lost my job today," my friend John told me recently. "I have been with the university for five years and with the state budget crisis they just cut my position. I don't know what to do."

As we talked, he said, "You know, I never really liked that job. I was just filling a spot in their bureaucracy and doing it to make a living."

John is not alone. In this tough economy, many in all walks of life are losing their jobs as the national unemployment rate hovers around 6 percent. While personal bankruptcies are on the rise, statistics show that 80% of the people who declare bankruptcy could have prevented it if they had only another $500 a month more. Besides those losing their jobs, millions more are bored with what they do every day. Many of those fell into their job because they needed to make money, not because it was their passion.

A job is something you do for a paycheck and quit when the wage stops. A career requires deeper personal investment and marks achievements with money, prestige, or power. A calling, on the other hand, is a passionate commitment to work for its own sake. It is something you love to do and people with callings are happier and more successful than those with jobs or careers.

There are many creative ways to make money and live without a job.

That's not to say without working. No, it does take work to make money. It is just that you are not working at a job you don't like.

What made America prosperous and the envy of the world is the American dream of being able to start a business and become successful. To do so, you need the determination to work as hard as it takes to become successful. Most people who are broke have only themselves to blame because they have not done what they need to in order to succeed.

So, whether you lose your job, need more money to make ends meet, hate your job, or just want the money to improve your lifestyle, there are ways besides working for someone else that will allow you to do so.

There are endless creative ways to make a living without a job. One of the best ways is to find something you love to do and then figure out how to make money doing it. This may require opening your mind to look beyond what you have done in the past, your current skills, and what others say. Think about what you would really like to do and then figure out a way to get there.

Multiple incomes

Having multiple sources of income is one way to secure financial freedom. Just as it is important to diversify stocks you hold in an investment portfolio, it is important to diversify your income.

You don't want "all your eggs in one basket" when it comes to income. For most people, most of their eggs come from their job, which is at the mercy of their employer and the economy. Lose that and they have lost everything.

Diversify an income by finding multiple sources of income. It is surprising how quick a few dollars adds up. Doing something to earn only $200 a week will create an additional $10,400 a year. Five hundred dollars a week adds up to $26,000. Who couldn't use that?

Let's say that someone loses a job that pays $48,000 a year. It certainly could be hard to find another job at that rate or to start a business that would earn that much. It may be easi-

The Fourteenth Year

Work in the service industry is one way to easily start a business. There is demand for reliable individuals who will wash windows, clean houses, do yard work, and take care of pets.

er to replace that income by finding four smaller sources of $1,000 a month each. They would only need to earn $250 a week from each of these income sources to earn $48,000 a year. Now, that is more achievable.

Sources of income include any ways you can earn money, not just working at a job. Renting out a room in a house, renting storage space in a garage, basement, or for a boat are ways people earn additional income. Some people rent an unused portion of their yard or property to someone who needs space to grow a garden or raise animals. Others rent their house or yard for a movie shoot or for weddings. Buying and renting houses or duplexes can add income.

Small farmers are traditionally masters of making money from every possible source. They have to be if they are going to survive. For example, a family that raises almonds on a small amount of land may not only sell the almond nuts as a crop, they might also sell the almond husks for animal feed, and cut up dead trees to sell as firewood. Most of the nuts might be sold to a distributor, but they may save some to make flavored nuts and almond butter to be sold at farmer's markets and craft fairs.

They might use land around their barn to rent out space for horses, selling the horse manure for compost, and also have a large garden from which they raise herbs, vegetables, and flowers to sell at a farmer's market.

Chickens may be raised to sell their eggs. The chicken manure, along with the horse manure, may be used to raise earthworms for sale, selling the manure as compost afterwards. They might even rent a nice shaded area by a creek for weddings or giving farm tours to "city folks" for a fee. Sure this is a lot of work, but every little bit helps.

Your niche may not be in agriculture, but this example shows how you can find every possible way to make money off your main product or service.

Cut spending

One of the easiest ways to make money is to not spend it. For every $100 a person spends, they need to earn at least $125 to $150 to pay all the payroll, income, and sales taxes. While the last thing most of us want to do is to cut spending, it really can make a huge difference in the amount you need to earn in the first place.

A bankruptcy court recently sent me a notice about someone who owed me money. Attached was a 10-page list of about 150 businesses and individuals to whom this lady was in debt. There were a few major debts for a house and car, but, by far, most of the $100,000 debt owed was for small amounts under $200. She lived an expensive lifestyle, denying herself nothing, while not even trying to live within her means. She could have very easily avoided bankruptcy by just managing her spending.

If it seems that the money always seems to run out before the end of the month, it may be wise to look for ways to cut back on expenses. Large fixed expenses, such as mortgage, auto, and insurance payments are hard to cut back unless you decide to reduce your lifestyle; however, other expenses can be controlled relatively easily.

Analyze every expense as to whether it is an absolute necessity, important but can be delayed, or simply a luxury or convenience, and decide where to make changes. Nothing says you shouldn't include luxury or convenience expenses, but maybe less expensive ones could be used or items purchased less often.

Financial advisor Ray Martin who writes for CBS MarketWatch.com estimates a family of four in the northeast could save over $8,000 a year without much pain or effort if they saved small amounts in a few areas of their life. He gives the following suggestions.

A couple could save $150 a month by dining out once a month instead of weekly. At least another $100 a month per person could be saved by bringing lunch to work or school instead of buying food and beverage. A pack-a-day smoker would be healthier and could save $120 a month by quitting smoking, more if medical costs associated with smoking are considered.

Bank fees add up tremendously. Avoiding ATM transaction fees, annual credit card fees, and credit card interest and late fees can save quite a bit. Paying bills online can save the cost of postage and checks. Martin estimates most people could save $800 a year by managing bank fees.

Gasoline is an increasing cost for consumers, especially in some states. Since only high-performance cars, such as BMWs or Mercedes, need high-octane gas, using regular will provide savings. Avoiding unneces-

The Internet has become a $900 billion industry. Using your computer at home, there are unlimited ways to make money now that it is easy to reach a worldwide audience.

sary driving and consolidating errands into one trip can also save on gas costs.

Using energy efficient appliances, lowering the thermostat in the winter and raising it in the summer, insulating water heaters, turning off lights, and other energy saving ideas can save utility costs at least $500 a year or more.

Consumer technology is great, but expensive. Cell phone, additional phone lines, pagers, phone services such as call-waiting, call-forwarding, and answering services, cable or satellite TV subscription service, DSL service, and web service subscriptions can add up to $100 to $200 per month. Decreasing or eliminating unnecessary or minimally used services can add up to large savings.

Consumers can save a considerable amount by buying food in bulk at discount warehouse stores. Individually prepared meals, such as frozen dinners, are expensive. Sodas, chips, cookies, and other "junk foods" are fine on occasion, but limiting them to occasional instead of daily use can improve the diet while saving money. Having a plan for meals and bringing a shopping list to the market limits impulse buying and, therefore, cost.

Evaluate insurance to see if raising deductibles or changing companies can lower costs. Buying auto and homeowner's insurance through the same company can reduce insurance costs by 10 to 15 percent.

There are many other "little" things that don't seem to cost much, but taken together add up. A few hundred here and there and soon you are saving thousands of dollars a year without much sacrifice.

Creating income

When I was talking to John about his job loss, we kept discussing friends we knew who make a living without a job. That is when it struck me how many people do this and what opportunities exist.

While there are hundreds, if not thousands, of ways to make an income doing something you enjoy, sometimes you need to look "outside the box." Instead of looking at established job descriptions, look at what you love to do and then figure out a way to make money at it. Be creative.

Like history? Start a tour business showing people the local historical sites in your town. Like to fish? Become a fishing guide. Like to bake? Make custom-ordered cakes. Like shopping? Become a personal shopper. Like the Internet? Make a commission selling things for others over Ebay or other auctions.

Your income can even vary by the season. One friend I know makes a living for his family as a ski instructor and by owning a snow removal company in the winter, while being a water ski instructor and handyman in the summer.

While there are many sources of income out there, most fall into a few broad categories. The stories of the following people are all real, although I have changed their names to protect their privacy.

Service industry

When David left the Army Special Forces he found there was not much of a civilian job market for snipers. Having no other training, he fell into something others don't want to do—washing windows. He has developed a large clientele of businesses and homeowners that allow him to make a good living, while giving him the freedom to travel and go hunting when he wants. This has been his sole source of income for more than 12 years.

His secret? He discovered that many people don't have the time or interest to do routine work around the house and are more than willing to pay to have it done. In fact, it can be hard to find reliable, trustworthy people to do work around your house. Dave does a good job at a fair price and is not afraid of doing other work.

Many people supplement their income by selling products of crafts or hobbies that they enjoy, such as woodworking, stained glass, or quilting. A few people even turn this into their full-time income.

Need your gutters cleaned out? Sure, he'll do that. Need a plant moved? Some debris hauled? He'll do that also.

Jan has made a living for 15 years cleaning people's homes. She works full-time and accepts only clients that she likes. She is reliable, thorough, and has a waiting list of people who want her to clean their houses. It is surprisingly hard to find quality and trustworthy cleaners. How did she start? Word-of-mouth. Her first client told their friends about Jan and word spread fast until she was so busy she had to turn business away.

People will pay others to clean their house, clean gutters, rake leaves, shovel snow, do shopping, wash and detail cars, organize closets or garages, take care of their animals, house-sit when they are gone, mow their lawn, clean their pool, manage their flower gardens, and even scoop up dog droppings from their yards. Many people have more money than they have time, making a perfect opportunity for someone looking for work.

Hobbies and crafts

After retiring from a career as a cardiovascular nurse, Ben was looking for a way to spend his time. He took up woodworking on a lathe, making beautiful bowl and lamps from wood he finds near his mountain home. Finding he loved lathe work, he soon had given away bowls to all his friends and still had a garage full of finished products.

He started traveling around to craft and art fairs to sell his extra work. He found in some urban areas he could sell a bowl for several hundred dollars, and, all of a sudden, he was earning several thousand dollars a weekend.

Lisa is 16 years old and makes gorgeous fused glass and silver jewelry. She sells about $1,800 of jewelry a month at art fairs, stained glass stores, and through her web site. Not a bad high school income for doing something she loves to do.

Don, a dentist, carves custom gunstocks out of black walnut as a hobby. His work is very elaborate, detailed, and in demand. He works only when he feels like it and customers gladly wait and pay any price since his work is unparalleled.

Homemade crafts of all types are in demand when you find the right market. Judy, a receptionist at an office by day, makes cute, elaborate cookie dough Christmas ornaments while watching television at night. She can sell $1,000 worth of ornaments in a weekend at a craft fair. Not a bad income from a part-time hobby.

Hobby and craft products are certainly a way many people make some extra income while having fun. Some even make a full-time living. Those interested in more information should read *Handmade for Profit: Hundreds of Secrets To Success in Selling Arts and Crafts* by Barbara Barbec.

Teaching a skill

Local community colleges and adult education programs have community education classes that teach everything from bicycle repair, wilderness survival, traveling on a budget, gardening, tamale making, and genealogy to getting out of debt, planning your retirement, and computers.

Classes are taught by instructors who know their topic and not by professional teachers. Most instructors teach because they love their topic and want to pass along their knowledge. Some teach to meet people interested in their field or hobby and others teach to attract future customers in their regular business or to sell books they have written. Instructors are paid to teach the course by the college, making it another small income source.

Parents gladly pay to find qualified teachers in music and art. Tutors are in demand to help students learn mathematics, reading, and science. People pay to learn woodworking, ceramics, stained glass, and other hobbies. Surprisingly, there is even a business in teaching ballroom dancing to couples needing to learn to dance for their wedding. There is demand for just about anything you can teach.

Farming and gardening

Maisie Jane Bertagna was in high school when she started preparing and selling seasoned almonds as a FFA project at school. Her product was a hit and she started Maisie Jane's California Sunshine Products. Now in her 20s, Maisie now employs a number of people and her products are distributed in stores nationwide.

Matt is an almond farmer, but has raised and sold fresh fruits and vegetables at a local farmers market since he was 10 years old. He enjoys spending Saturdays seeing old friends at the market while he supplements his income. Others with small gardens grow specialty vegetables in their yards for sale to local restaurants and organic food stores. There are many ways to make money from your love of growing or raising foods.

Love flowers? How about selling potted or cut flowers? One person set up a business where she grows flowers and has contracted with small businesses to provide them with an arrangement of fresh flowers for their reception room or office every week. Specialty nurseries can be set up on as little as 1000 square feet of land.

Dog breeding can be a profitable and fun way to make some extra money, as can raising other animals. There is a market for almost anything you can raise.

Internet

The Internet is a $900 billion industry that has truly revolutionized the way an individual can do business. Anyone can launch a web site and open an online store to sell almost any product or service, reaching a worldwide market that was once only available to large corporations.

Some of the opportunities available include web sites to sell products, selling over E-bay and other auctions, self-publishing, starting E-zines (electronic magazines), and writing online newsletters on topics that interest you.

Considerable other work is also being done over the Internet. For example, a draftsman I know works from his house receiving jobs from companies over the Internet. He does the work in his free time at night and weekends and returns it via the Internet. Work is so good he is thinking of making this his full-time job.

One nice thing about many Internet businesses is that they do not require you to be available by the phone at all times. Your Internet business is still working while you are at work, play, or even sleeping.

A number of books are available on making income on the Internet, including *Multiple Streams of Internet Income* by Robert Allen.

So much more

Opportunities to earn money are limited only by one's imagination. If you love to travel, why not make money at the same time. Travel income sources include freelance writing for travel magazines, being a photographer, leading group tours, and buying or selling for an import/export business. If you want to travel abroad and know a foreign language you are in even more demand.

People earn money with freelance photography, videotaping weddings, baking, decorating cakes, leading local historical tours, researching family histories, and cutting and selling firewood. Other home businesses include mail order businesses and information products such as audiotapes, videotapes, or computer software. Those with a passion for writing earn money self-publishing books, writing for magazines, and creating newsletters.

The possibilities are literally unlimited. Finding your passion is the first step in making an income without a job. If you follow your love, the money will follow. For other ideas read *Careers for Non-Conformists* by Sandra Gurvis or *Making a Living Without a Job* by Barbara J. Winter.

You can keep trudging along complaining about your life and waiting for something to magically change or you can do something about it. Find your calling and take the steps to follow your dreams. Whether you are trying to earn some extra income or looking for a new career, the possibilities are endless. ∆

Venison burger chow mein

By Tom R. Kovach

With both my parents born in Hungary, I grew up enjoying a number of delicious Hungarian dishes. Some were kind of spicey and many were heavily accented with paprika, that favorite old Hungarian standby. My mother, who passed away when I was young, was a great cook. So was my father. But as I grew up and went off into the military, I traveled around the world and became quite fond of a number of different ethnic foods. I really enjoy south of the border fares such as tacos and burritos. And I could eat Italian spaghetti on a regular basis.

And I also developed a special liking for Chinese food, from noodles to rice, to chow mein and sweet and sour dishes. I also like game meat like venison and grouse. So I sometimes try to combine the wild game meat with some of my ethnic dishes. For example, venison burger works well in tacos and it makes for good meat in any spaghetti sauces. But I've also found that venison goes quite well with some of my favorite Chinese foods. Here's one recipe I enjoy which doesn't take very long to prepare:

Venison burger chow mein

    1 lb. of venison burger (Actually, a pound or so of chopped venison steak will work too).
    1 stalk of celery diced
    1 medium carrot diced
    1 small onion diced
    1 can vegetable beef soup (10 ¾ oz.)
    1 can cream of mushroom soup (10 ¾ oz.)
    1½ soup cans of water
    1 can water chestnuts (8 oz)
    1 can bean sprouts (14 oz.)
    chow mein noodles

Brown venison burger, onions, carrots, celery and drain excess juice. Use low heat. Add the soups, water, chestnuts and bean sprouts. Simmer for 15-20 minutes so that all the ingredients can blend well together. Serve over chow mein noodles or over hot, cooked rice. Dash on a little bit of black pepper and some soy sauce for a little more oriental flavor. This should make 4 to 5 servings (depending upon how hungry everyone is). ∆

Harvest your own firewood

By Pete Earl

Harvesting firewood has many rewards: exercise, satisfaction, saving money, and the security of having your own fuel supply for winter warmth. Here are some pointers in the art of cutting your own with maximum safety and minimal effort.

Instead of just cutting green wood and letting it dry over the summer, consider going after aged hardwood, those dead trees that are losing their bark. I call this "vintage firewood" because it has aged like fine wine. If you love a blazing hot fire, this is your ultimate fuel.

Gear to get

A big part of your success will depend on your gear. You'll need lots of it, but after the initial outlay, your heating costs go way down.

Chain saw. Go as big as you can afford. I struggled for years with a little 1.8 cu. in. engine saw. Now I have a 3.5 cu. in. model that can really cut! I suggest at least a 3 cu. in. saw. Test start it outside the showroom and check for easy starting, smooth idling, and a working bar oiler. Rev the engine, then dip the bar tip near the ground. You should see some sign of oil flying off the chain if the oiler is an automatic one. Don't get a saw so heavy you'll have trouble using it. I consider a chain saw very dangerous. Remember that this tool can cut your leg or your head off in two seconds. I took a waterproof marker and marked a long line on the side of the saw 20 inches from the bar tip. Now I have a built-in log measure.

Gas. Get regular gas and add gas stabilizer (such as STA-BIL) to it as soon as you get home. This keeps the gas from gunking up. You'll also need two cycle oil to add to the gas.

Bar oil. Get a good quality brand by the gallon to save $$.

Gear bag. Every time you head into the woods be prepared to spend the night. All sorts of accidents can happen, so your gear bag could save your life. I use a small canvas bag covered on the outside with a plastic grocery bag. A sharp hatchet and six-inch long wedge are essential for freeing your saw from being pinched in a bad cut. Include a large space blanket, a bunch of hard candy, water bottle, matches, and a signal whistle. You'll need your bar adjusting wrench occasionally. A spare wool hat and pair of thick gloves are a good idea. If you're alone, a walkie talkie or cell phone would be great to have. Add a small first aid kit or a war surplus combat bandage in case you suffer a deep cut. I also bring two 12 oz. dry gas bottles, one filled with bar oil and the other with gas mixture. Wrap them tightly in a thick plastic bag to contain any spillage.

Clothes. Dress warmly, even in warm weather. A hard hat is a good idea; use a chin strap. Under the hard hat wear a wool hat. Most of your body's heat loss is through your head.

Safety goggles are a must and ear protectors are good if you have a loud saw. Wear tight-fitting clothes with no scarves or necklaces that can get caught in the chain. Thick gloves and boots complete your wardrobe. Don't forget an orange vest or jacket if it's hunting season.

Selecting trees

With your fueled and oiled-up saw in one hand and gear bag in the other, you're ready to hit the woods. I cut almost all oak and maple, avoiding pine and spruce. Even dried, these last two produce a fair amount of creosote, which can cause devastating stove pipe and chimney fires. With the exception of oak, aged wood needs to be found before it hits the ground and rapidly rots away.

Dead trees can be tricky to spot at a distance. Crumbling top branches and peeling bark are good signs. I've developed the habit of peeling off a big section of bark at eye level on my walks through the woods. This trick really helps spot trees when cutting time arrives. Since I have to haul my logs out by hand, I try not to cut anything larger than nine inches in diameter. Even aged oak is heavy. Avoid badly rotted trees that fall apart in your hands.

Cutting down

Once you've found a suitable dead tree, make sure there is a felling line. A tree hemmed in by others close by isn't worth bothering with. Clear away the base area and any eyepoker branches near the tree. Make sure you have good footing, especially in snowy and wet weather. Drop your gear bag and saw 10 feet away, out of the felling line. If the tree is thin enough to be shakable, put on all your protective gear and shake the trunk as hard as you can, **looking up** at the top all the while. This whipping action often cracks off any "widowmaker" branches just waiting to snap off and stab you in the neck! If any break off, run—do not walk—several yards away. Next, plan the exact felling line. A tree that's already leaning more than a few degrees in one direction will usually fall that way.

Now comes the big question: to notch or not? Someone could write a small book on the art of notching, but it won't be me. I almost never bother, unless I'm cutting a large tree. The notch advantage here is that it helps make a clean cut with minimal splintering of the trunk as it falls over. Most trees come down smoothly with just one 20 or 30-degree cut at the base. Make sure any cutting companions are at least 50 feet away, to one side of the felling line. Rev your saw to full speed before cutting and use the teeth at the bar's base to bite into the wood to help prevent kickback. **Always** keep all parts of your body out of the saw's cutting plane. Putting your head over even an idling saw could be dangerous. One slip and your face will meet some sharp teeth when you hit the ground.

Once the tree starts definitely falling, release the throttle and quickly retreat at least 20 feet away **at a right angle** to the felling direction. Standing behind that tree can be fatal. Either springy top branches or your tree landing on a smaller, springy one can cause the trunk to break free from the cut and slam back like a battering ram faster than you can duck.

Debranching

Debranching is routine so it's very easy here to get careless and cut toward your leg or in line with your

For hauling from the woods during the winter, the author's homemade sled, complete with metal runners, does the trick of removing logs from the forest. The sled should never be overloaded. It makes going uphill more difficult and it can make going downhill treacherous.

An old bike can be converted to a tool for hauling heavy logs from the woods, but you should not overload it and you must always be mindful of the kind of terrain you're taking it over.

head. Don't let your guard down. I like to cut off all the branches before sectioning up the tree. Toss them well out of your way and you're ready to start sectioning. Begin at the top so that the bottom half will be lighter and easier to handle. Using your saw's measuring mark, make shallow cuts to mark two logs then cut through at the third mark. If your log length is less than 16 inches, add another log length to make your sections about five feet long. As I approach the base of a thick tree, those marks get several inches closer together. This makes the last few sections much lighter and the logs easier to split. Watch for embedded nails, fence wire, and small rocks in the wood. They can damage your chain and cause kickback. When cutting sections flat on the ground, you should cut three quarters of the way through. Do this until you can cut a section with air under it, then roll the trunk a half turn and finish the cuts.

Hauling out

Now comes the hardest part, getting those heavy logs home. Cutting, splitting, and stacking in place is fine if you plan to use a pickup or ATV to haul the wood out soon. I want to get those logs back to my woodpile ASAP for two reasons. A sudden ice or snow storm could cut you off from your wood or someone might come along and take a strong liking to your beautiful logs.

I've built two log haulers that make the job much easier. My bike and the wood for my sled both came from a landfill dump. For the bike find one with a straight frame and wheels, take off all the gear, fenders, and seat. Make a new log seat out of a 16-inch long piece of 2 by 6-inch lumber. Support that piece with a base built around the seat post. Add boat cleats or large steel rings at each end and tie a 3-foot long piece of thin rope to the far cleat. Turn the handlebars up enough to create a carrying bracket up front. Put on wide tires with rugged tread. Use the bike only in dry weather. Wet leaves or ice or snow make this hauler unsteady because the tires can slip and push the load onto you.

For snowy winter conditions my beefy sled is perfect. It's made from two 1¾ by 6-inch boards that are 60 inches long. The top three 2 by 4 connectors are each 18 inches long. The lower connectors are several inches off ground level and angled forward to plane the sled up over light snow. Secure all connectors with 4-inch long screws (and a monster screwdriver). Cut some smooth curves on the front ends, then stain all the wood. Drill 4 holes about 2 inches deep at the corners and drop in some 12-inch long bolts to keep the logs in the sled. You'll need metal runners or the sled won't slide much. I used sheet aluminum. Take your bottom, curved length measurement and your runner width to a sheet metal shop. Have them cut the length and triple the runner width to allow for side overlaps, then ask them to bend each piece to form a U-shape the exact runner width. Once home, put some shallow notches in the front curve area and nail the metal to each side of each runner with galvanized nails. Drill two rope holes in front and put in a 27-foot length of ³⁄₈ inch rope. I prefer manila because it stays warm and flexible in cold weather. By doubling the rope you reduce its bite into your waist or shoulders.

If you'll be pulling up steep hills, don't overload the sled and overexert yourself. Watch out going down slopes, also. Don't let the sled pick up a lot of speed and run you down. Logs in motion pack a punch.

Splitting

Once you've bucked your logs into stove-size pieces, splitting the giant ones can be a chore. I recently moved up from using a splitting maul to a hydraulic splitter. It's a 4-foot long steel "I" beam with a wedge at one end and a 10-ton jack at the other. Pumping two long handle levers moves the jack and rams a log against the wedge to split it. This beauty requires no gas or electricity and really saves your back. Check tool catalogs such as Harbor Freight Tools for one. It costs about $150.

Store your split logs under some sort of solid roof. Tarps tend to load up with snow and ice, then rip and leak like crazy. Completely dry wood is important for maximum heat output.

Yes, cutting your own firewood is a lot of work, but think of it as a free gym workout. You'll find that the satisfaction and security of having those hunks of superb fuel stacked out back is fantastic. Of course, saving hundreds or thousands of dollars a year on heating costs is the big reward.

It's real hard to have too much firewood, so keep on cutting. Δ

the gee-whiz! page
By O.E. MacDougal

Warm blood

What is it that actually makes an animal, such as a mammal or a bird, warm blooded while all other organisms in the animal kingdom, reptiles, fish, insects, etc., are cold blooded?

Unique to birds and mammals is that the cells in their muscles are always "vibrating." The vibrations are miniscule and unnoticeable to the eye. In the human body these vibrations occur at anywhere from 6 to 12 times a second. To vibrate like this, the cells have to consume food energy and the main by-product is heat, which makes us warm blooded.

Reptiles derive only a little of their body heat from the food they consume; the rest comes from ambient air and sunshine and this is the main reason why we often see snakes and lizards sunning themselves on rocks and on road surfaces when the sun is out.

The advantage of warm bloodedness is that warm muscles operate much more effectively than cold muscles so warm-blooded animals can operate more efficiently on cold days and in cold climates making the pursuit of mates and food, as well as the escape from potential predators, more likely. (There are no arctic reptiles nor do they exist above the timberline of high mountains.) But warm-bloodedness comes at a cost. To maintain this high level of energy consumption, mammals and birds must consume greater quantities of food. It is one of the reasons we find proportionally fewer mammals than reptiles and insects in areas where food sources are scarce, such as deserts.

The obvious advantage of being cold blooded is that cold-blooded organisms, such as lizards and snakes, don't have to consume nearly as much food to survive as mammals and birds do. However, cold-blooded animals usually have to raise their body temperature to mate, pursue quarry, and to escape their predators—particularly when those predators are mammals and birds.

There are "exceptions" in the warm-blooded/cold-blooded classification of animals. Most warm-blooded mammals, for instance, keep a more-or-less constant body temperature, but some don't. Conspicuous among these are bears, bats, gophers, and groundhogs whose body temperatures can fall by as much as 50° F when they hibernate. Bats, in fact, have a problem maintaining a constant temperature whenever they're inactive, and their body temperatures fall dramatically just nesting or sleeping.

And there are fish, such as tuna and mackerel sharks (see *gee-whiz!* in Issue 74, March/April 2002 of *BHM*), whose body temperature is higher than their environment because of an unusual arrangement of blood vessels in their circulatory systems that allow their bodies to retain heat produced in their bodies' muscles before it is lost through their gills to their environment. They aren't really warm-blooded in the sense we think of mammals and birds being warm-blooded, but they are unique in the world of the so-called cold-blooded animals. Then there are also certain insects, such as bees and hawk moths, that can raise their body temperatures to those well above their environment by flapping their wings.

Writing

Writing was apparently invented by, of all people, accountants and tax collectors. Its origins, around 7500 BC, began with an attempt to keep records of farm production, commercial transactions, and taxation.

Archaeological evidence indicates that the earliest method for keeping track of crop harvests, animals, and other things originated in the Middle East. At first they used tokens made of clay. One token, shaped like a cone, stood for some measure of grain, perhaps a basketful or a cartload. Another, shaped like a cylinder, stood for a head of a certain type of livestock. And there were disks, spheres, ovoids, and at least 300 others, each designating a certain product like honey, wine, or metals.

One token for one cow was fine, but what if you had 90 cattle? They began using hollow clay spheres to hold the tokens. On the outside of the spheres were impressions of cones, spheres, etc., so one knew what the container held. Inside were 90 "cattle" tokens.

After several millennia of this, it became simpler to dispense with the tokens and just inscribe the symbols directly to tablets with a stylus. And instead of making 100 cylinders to represent 100 cattle, new symbols to represent *numbers* were invented.

But they didn't stop here. Eventually, names of people were recorded. Symbols were invented to stand for sounds, just as the letters we use today stand for sounds. By 2700 BC, other spoken words were written using these sound symbols and by 2400 BC whole narratives—histories, stories, poetry—were recorded. Such was the first written language, Sumerian.

So, today everything from the writing in the *Bible* to *Harry Potter* owes its existence to accountants.

The Fourteenth Year

The art of Wood splitting

By Phil Nichols

There is nothing nastier to clean up after, more labor intensive to use, remotely close to as backbreaking, as dangerous to life and limb (I personally know one man who was trapped by a falling tree and severely injured, another whose leg was completely shattered when a limb he was cutting in a dozed up pile of timber snapped forward unexpectedly, and a good friend experienced in every aspect of wood who died when he failed to outrun a relatively small tree that fell the wrong way), or as generally disagreeable as wood. Yet for all that, I still love cutting and splitting our yearly wood supply.

In this age of never ending stress and high speed mechanization, few moments can compare with those spent drinking in the sour earthy aroma of a freshly split and stacked woodpile that you've worked up with the pure clean sweat from your own brow.

It's also extremely satisfying to bask in the warm luxurious heat of your own fire while the fierce beasts of winter batter at your door, content in the knowledge that Mother Nature can do her worst and you'll still be just fine.

Having wood heat not only provides a sense of security but can also save hundreds of dollars per year in fuel bills when you do the work yourself.

I've often said, "Next to a full belly there is nothing more gratifying than a full woodpile." The obvious question of course is how to fill it up (the woodpile that is).

You have two options for getting started: find a woodlot where you can cut down trees yourself or pay someone to deliver split firewood or unsplit rounds. If you're going to work the wood up yourself you'll have to decide whether to buy a woodsplitter, rent one, or tackle the chore the old fashioned way with maul and wedge.

For the past 30 years or so (a number of which were spent selling firewood as a side business) I've been doing it the old fashioned way. However, unlike my good neighbors in our local Amish community I do opt for a chain saw rather than their two-man bucksaws and handheld bow saws for felling and cutting. But once my wood is ready to split I still pursue the same self-reliant course as my great-grandfather before me.

With each passing season, as the pains of old age intensify, I reevaluate the wisdom of my position and consider laying down my maul and wedges in favor of a hydraulic alternative. But each year I say to myself, "Maybe next year."

Now would be a good time to state my cardinal rule: if you have a choice, *never* cut or split wood when it's hot outside, as this is an open invitation to heat exhaustion or much worse. Late fall, winter, and early spring, when temperatures are below 40° F, are the times to work wood. You can always tell when fall has returned to the Ozarks as the buzz of working saws once again echoes through the timber.

If you've opted to cut trees yourself you've got some decisions to make once your wood is down and blocked up (cut to the desired lengths). Should you split it where it lies, load it, transport it, and stack it or load the unsplit rounds, transport them, unload them, split them, and then stack them? This of course is a matter of preference, logistics (if you can't get your pickup close to your wood and don't have a farm tractor and trailer the only option sometimes is to hump it out and rounds are a lot easier to carry than split wood), time (not all of us have the luxury of leaving our wood in the timber to cure), security (there is nothing more disheartening than to leave after spending several backbreaking hours laboring over a pile of wood only to discover that someone else has enjoyed the fruits of your labor when you return), and physical ability (loading really big rounds can be extremely arduous).

I always try to handle wood as few times as possible. Count the steps in the first scenario I presented and you'll find that there are four: split, load, transport, and stack. Now count the steps involved in the second strategy. That's right, an extra hands-on activity (unload) snuck in there. These are the terms that you have to think in, as it's your back that's going to be taking the beating.

If you decide to try swinging a maul or sledge you'll soon discover that hand-splitting is about equal parts of *brute strength*, *finesse*, and *art*.

Generally speaking, seasoned wood tends to split a lot easier than green wood if you're doing it by hand. So anytime I'm cutting green wood I like to stack my rounds near where I've felled the tree (using two trees 20 to 25 feet apart as bookends works well) and let them season for several months before splitting. Frequently, I'll cut and stack one winter and split the next. This does involve more handling initially but it evens out in less wear and tear on me.

Some folks favor cutting green wood in the fall and then splitting it that winter after a hard freeze. When the sap and fibers are frozen the wood tends to split easier.

In my later 20s and early 30s I could stand for eight hours in sub-freezing temperatures with my insulated coveralls stripped down to my waist as I wielded my favorite ax, sledge, and wedge. Now in my mid 50s that's no longer the case. I have a lifetime of conditioning to this sort of hard labor, I still lift weights twice a week, do aerobic/stretching several times a week, and I'm lucky to get in an hour's actual splitting nowadays. I've adapted to this turn of events by learning to split awhile, stack awhile, and sit awhile. Point being, don't overestimate your physical ability. If there is any doubt as to your physical condition, go and get a complete checkup before you even think about picking up a splitter. This is most definitely not an endeavor for the faint of heart.

I wear eyeglasses which protect me to a degree but I would strongly suggest that you invest in a good pair of safety goggles. Kickboxing or catchers shin pads are another good idea until you get hang of what you're doing and a pair of steel-toed working boots. A flying wedge or deflected ax or maul stroke can lead to major misery to your shins or feet. I speak from bloodied experience. You'll also need the toughest pair of "Mule Hide" leather gloves you can find. I don't recommend thick insulated gloves as their bulkiness makes it difficult to firmly grip the handle of your splitter. If you're working in extreme cold it's better to wear a pair of plain "Jersey" gloves under your leather ones. This combination makes for better flexibility with added warmth.

The first step in the actual splitting process is determining which tools you'll be the most comfortable with while attempting to exploit the weaknesses in a given piece of wood and subsequently learning how to use them.

In my youth I used a single-bitted ax and sixteen-pound sledge exclusively. Both wooden handled. The problem with wood handles is durability. All it takes is one overshot to shatter the handle across the top of a wedge or over the edge of a round. I used to use multiple wraps of duct tape to good effect in an effort to get more mileage out of a given handle.

It was the advent of fiberglass composite handles which really increased the amount of use I could get out of a given implement. I strongly advocate their acquisition.

Through the years I've tried about every variety of maul and handle

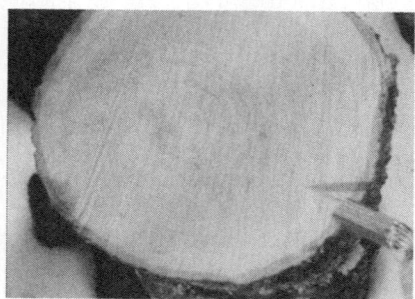

Figure 1

style and have settled on a #8 (I suspect this is indicative of 8 pounds as that's the weight of the tool) "sledge-eye" (the type of handle socket) wood splitter head, outfitted with a standard fiberglass sledge handle (see Figure 4). I favor this combination because it serves double duty as splitting device and sledge, is fairly lightweight, easy to handle, highly effective, and nigh on to indestructible.

Contrary to popular myth it isn't necessary to keep your maul or ax honed to a razor's edge. You're not attempting to cut the wood, only to wedge it apart. The sharpened beveled edge serves only to create an entrance for the upper tapered portion of the splitter, be it maul or ax.

If you find that you prefer an ax to a maul I advise against attempting to use this tool to drive your wedges, though I have done so in a pinch. It's better to keep a sledge around for that chore. Axes do not have the weight necessary to effectively drive a wedge and their striking surface is too narrow to make for safe hammering.

The art of swinging

Speaking of hammering, swinging a maul or ax is part of the *art* of wood splitting. Done well it actually makes the work look easy. Done poorly it can be down right dangerous as well as overly exhausting. Control, control, control is the name of the game, with a bit of technique thrown in for good measure.

Face the intended target with your feet shoulder width or a little better apart. Hold the splitter with your right hand just ahead of the knob at the butt of the handle and your left a few inches below the splitting head. (This is, of course, reversed for you lefties out there, and this lefty position is, in fact, the right hand position for *BHM*'s publisher, Dave Duffy, who is also an avid wood cutter.) As I swing up and back the arc carries the splitter behind my right shoulder, through the center of my back and up over my head. At the apex of the swing the splitter handle is merely cradled in the open crook of the thumb and forefinger of my right hand. This is the point where you apply force to the heretofore centrifugal motion of the splitter. The right hand closes and slides down the handle as the splitter passes its apex and begins to descend on the target. At the moment of impact both hands are touching at the butt end of the handle.

Just as my maul makes contact with wood or wedge I flex my knees which reduces the strain on my lower back. To further lessen the strain I select one of the largest and flattest of my rounds to use as a table for the pieces to be split. (This platform also acts as an anvil, so to speak). This way the wood you're working on is about waist height, which tends to

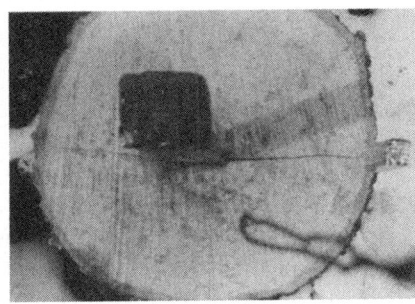

Figure 2

keep your back in a more upright position at impact. As my maul meets the wood and my knees flex I exhale with force. It may sound a little Zen but you actually learn to explode through the wood. (I don't pretend to be a modern Ergonomics expert. I've just discovered through 30 years of trial and error what works and what doesn't.)

Often the hardest part of the program on hamstrings and back muscles is wrestling around to get some of the larger pieces up on the table.

The only real way to perfect your swing is to get out there and start swinging.

As you begin to gain a feel for the follow through and rhythm of this activity you'll soon learn to place your blows in the same spot each time. Unless you're working with really small pieces (five to six inches in diameter) you will seldom succeed in splitting with the first blow. Therefore it is usually necessary to strike your target along the same fracture point on multiple occasions, the wedged portion of your splitter being driven deeper into the block at each stroke. It's a matter of concentration and control. The wasted effort in having to pump-handle your splitter out of the wood after missing your mark multiple times is a miraculously efficient teacher.

Reading wood

Once you've mastered the tools of the trade the second step involves learning to "read the wood." You accomplish this with your body and mind as well as your eyes.

I mentioned earlier that seasoned wood is generally easier split than green. This is due in part to the presence of "visible" cracks and checks that develop as the wood dries. These sign posts tell you where the wood is most vulnerable to penetration. However, even when the wood seems to be saying, "split me here" you'll still often encounter unseen internal knots, branches, and anomalies even in dried wood which say, "Oh, no you don't."

Let's explore when and how to apply a maul and wedge. If you look closely at Figure 1 you'll see the tiny fissure that I've chosen as my point of attack emanating away from the blade of my pocket knife. In Figure 2 I've tapped my wedge into this crack and as you can see the wood is already starting to split along this pathway. In Figure 3 I'm demonstrating how *not* to drive a wedge. If you happen to strike your wedge a glancing blow rather than squarely on top it will frequently shoot out of the wood (a very common occurrence when splitting green or frozen wood) with extreme velocity.

As you can see in Figure 4 a steel wedge has a tapered side and a flat side. It's been my experience that a wedge will invariably fly out in the direction that the taper is pointing. Moral: if you're not facing either side of the taper your chances of avoiding injury are enhanced considerably. Figure 4 also shows me facing and striking the flat side of the wedge.

Figure 3

You'll notice that the piece of wood in Figure 1 is smooth, round, and easy. This is the kind of wood you want to learn on before taking on problem wood which require more *finesse*.

Normally the only time you'll need wedges is when you're tackling really large rounds or some of the tougher woods such as blackjack oak, elm, ironwood, or hickory. This is part of the "body" reading-wood equation. Any time you give a particular round several of your best licks and the wood does not begin to split, it's time to consider using a wedge. Though it's not a bad idea to rotate the round 90 degrees and try it again before bringing on the steel. Frequently the

Figure 4

grain of the wood will split more ready in one direction than the other. If that doesn't work start driving a wedge.

I believe the worst wood I ever encountered was basswood (also known as Linden). You could hit this stuff with everything you had and the ax would just bounce off. I either had to nibble my way around the outside edge knocking off a little slab at a time (this is also a good strategy when working with really stringy woods such as elm but it's much harder to maintain the control necessary to prevent a glancing blow from jeopardizing your feet and shins) or sink my ax in the heart to create an opening and then try to drive a wedge home that wanted to squirt out with every blow.

Figure 5

Another concern about wedges is mushrooming. After you've used a wedge for some time the repeated blows tend to cause the steel at the top to push out over the sides: see Figure 3. Eventually these mushroomed edges begin to split apart creating potential shrapnel when struck just right. The cure is to periodically grind the edges smooth or to discard the wedge.

The inherent dangers in the use of wedges is why I do not allow onlookers while I'm splitting.

Figure 5 shows what I refer to as a "problem piece." Normally this is exactly the type of guy you want to use a wedge on because the convergence of two limbs is always tough and difficult to split. But with the right approach the job can be done quickly using nothing but your maul. If you had started by attacking this block lengthwise, through both limbs, I can just about guarantee that you would have beat yourself senseless

Figure 6

with little result. Instead, in Figure 6, I've gone after the one clear piece in the block, which split off fairly easily. Next in Figure 7 I've flipped the remaining block over where its surface is less angled and provides an easier target. Figure 8 shows the final product which was achieved in three or four blows.

When dealing with problem pieces always bear in mind the Law of Diminishing Returns. Loosely paraphrased—if you increase the amount of time and labor required to split one

Figure 7

piece of wood then your overall production for that session will decline.

If you're stubborn like me, dealing with some of the worst cases can actually degenerate into a contest of wills, "me against the wood." If you get to this point *stop* and ask yourself if the effort required to triumph over that one bad hombre might be better spent working on the whole. If you can't break down a round into something useable, without extreme measures, then just set it off to one side with others of its kind and move on. This is reading wood with your "mind."

I traditionally use this collection of rejects to fuel the fire ring anytime we've got a mess of folks over for a good ole fashioned country weeny roast. These gnarly toughies burn hot and long while I still get the satisfaction of seeing them go up in smoke.

It's not unusual when I sink my maul into one of the tougher specimens that it will not easily work free for the next blow. In which case I employ the "brute force" part of the equation. Depending on the size of the block in question I reverse my grip (with my left hand at the butt end of my splitter and my right directly beneath the head), heave the block straight up over my head in one motion, and slam the flat side of the maul down on my table log. This maneuver drives the block down onto the wedge-shaped maul and almost always achieves a split. The risk here is that your splitting tool isn't stuck as tight as you thought it was. I've gouged out a chunk or two of hide when my splitter pulled out of a large piece (50 to 75-pounders), just as I applied downward pressure, dropping it straight down my back.

A safer option is to bring out your wedge and drive it in next to the stuck tool with a spare ax, sledge, or maul. This generally widens the gap enough to free the encumbered splitter.

If you routinely work with large rounds (24 inches or more in diameter) it's a good idea to keep a couple of 3' x 5/8" or 3/4" round bars flattened or tapered on one end around to separate split halves (rebar works really well for this purpose). Sometimes when you drive a wedge in as far as you can the given round still won't split all the way through. You just insert the bars into the crack on each side of the wedge and push with one arm while pulling with the other (scissor fashion) to finish split-

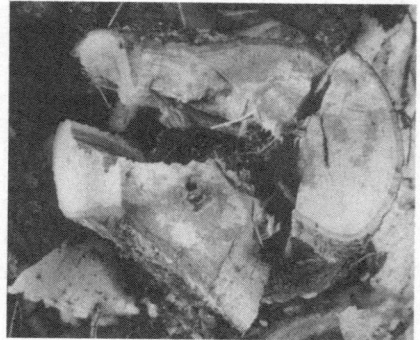

Figure 8

ting the piece. Else you have to push the round over on its side and drive another wedge in at the bottom to finish the split.

This concludes my outline of the methods and cautions I employ when tackling the age old job of getting in the wood.

I believe that I've made it pretty clear that this activity isn't for everyone. But for those of you who really embrace the satisfaction of accomplishment through good old fashioned physical exertion, hand-splitting can be a really worthwhile endeavor. Not to mention the fact that it's some of the best therapy I can think of in this stressed out world of ours.

If I remember correctly Former President Ronald Reagan used to periodically repair to his California ranch just to spend some time swinging away with his favorite ax. I'll wager that he understood the soul refreshing quality of simple physical labor.

Always remember, "Nothing warms you more times than wood." Δ

Standby battery charging techniques can ensure engine startups

By Jeffrey Yago, P.E., CEM

Those of us living beyond the suburbs own various sizes and types of yard and garden machinery. From the mandatory riding lawnmower for those weekend warriors with one-acre yards up to 4-wheel drive diesel tractors for working farms, everywhere you look there are engine-driven machines to make rural life easier. Many of us now also own RVs, ATVs, log splitters, garden tillers, leaf vacuums, chipper-shredders, portable generators, and garden tractors, and each may use some type of battery that must stay charged.

Larger farms have motorized hay balers, planters, plows, and an endless array of other specialized types of crop machinery. If you are like me, your little stable of power machinery sits weeks or seasons between uses and rarely start when needed due to discharged or dead batteries. The pull cord starter is now a rare exception, not the rule, so you are left with few options. A typical **flooded lead acid battery** will lose up to one percent of its charge per day while idle. In just over two months, this would mean a drop to almost half the original amp-hour capacity.

The solution for most homeowners would start with a search for that rarely used $10 battery charger and tangled cables buried somewhere in the back of the garage. Since tractor batteries never fail when parked next to a wall outlet, the next task is locating a 100-foot extension cord. After finally figuring out which cable goes to which battery terminal and in which order, the deceased battery is

A small solar module, attached to the roof of this tractor, ensures that the starter will still turn over, even after a long period of idleness.

brought slowly back to life. There must be a better way, and new battery charging technologies are providing several good solutions to this age-old problem.

Battery Design 101

Before going into more detail on how you can keep all of your idle equipment batteries fully charged, let us briefly review some battery design basics. Battery technology has undergone major changes during the past few years as manufacturers search for higher amp-hour capacities in smaller packages, lower weights, and zero maintenance.

There are many new battery design features that lower weight and increase charge density, but most have been accomplished through very exotic materials and chemicals that are difficult or impossible to recycle, not to mention having a much higher cost. On the other end of the scale, the old technology and fully recyclable flooded lead acid battery has also undergone some major changes. To eliminate periodic water refilling, most flooded-type car, truck, and marine batteries now include gas re-combiner caps that take the venting battery gases and convert them back to a liquid, which then drains back into the battery cells. These special caps are usually permanently attached as the liquid electrolyte is intended to last the life of the battery.

To reduce maintenance even further, battery manufacturers now offer **valve regulated lead acid (VRLA) batteries** in both gel cell and **absorbed glass mat** (AGM) designs. Unlike the maintenance-free flooded liquid electrolyte batteries, VRLA batteries are completely sealed and

270

Comparison of battery charging voltages

12-Volt Battery Type	Bulk Charge Volts	Float Charge Volts
Open flooded (lead antimony)	14.5	13.4
Sealed flooded RV/Marine	14.4	13.4
Sealed AGM lead acid	14.4	13.6
Sealed gel lead acid	14.1	13.5

pressurized and can be mounted in any position, including upside down.

The valve regulated gel cell is still technically a lead acid battery, but the acid and water electrolyte have been converted into a jelly or paste, which is injected into all internal spaces around the lead plates just before the battery is permanently sealed. The valve regulated AGM batteries have porous fiberglass pads pressed against each side of the lead plates, which are then soaked with liquid electrolyte prior to battery sealing. These valve regulated sealed batteries do not have any filler caps and do not require any maintenance.

Although more and more mowers and garden tractors are now being sold with sealed gel or AGM batteries, there are still many conventional flooded lead acid batteries in service due to their much lower replacement costs.

Conventional battery charging

When planning an alternative method of maintaining the charge for your occasional-use motorized equipment batteries, it is very important to identify which battery type you have, since different battery types require different charging voltages. This also means that many older style battery chargers are not suitable for charging many of the newer battery types.

Most published battery charging data tables are based on a standardized ambient temperature of 77° F. Higher or lower battery temperatures will require adjusting the manufacturer's recommended charging voltages to achieve the same level of charge. As a rough guideline to determine which voltages to use, it is recommended to subtract 0.1 volt from the table values above 85° F ambient. Below 55° F ambient, it is recommended to add 0.4 volt. When charging below 35° F ambient, it is recommended to add 0.7 volt to the table values. Many of today's newer battery chargers include a temperature sensor that takes care of this adjustment for you.

When referring to the following battery charging comparison table, note how a higher charging voltage is used during the initial bulk charging period than used for final float charging. This provides a shorter overall recharge time, while reducing the chance for overcharging at the end of the charging cycle. Be sure the battery charger you use has the appropriate output voltage for the battery type to be charged; if in doubt, check the manufacturer's charging information that came with your battery.

Low-cost battery chargers usually do not have automatic cycle or timer controls, and provide the same charging voltage, regardless of how discharged or over-charged your battery may be. If left connected for an extended period, these inexpensive chargers can easily damage a battery by "boiling" all of the electrolyte out of the battery. If the battery is sealed, this overcharging could actually destroy the battery.

More expensive battery chargers include automatic controls that constantly take sample measurements of the battery's present voltage through the charging cables, and adjust the charging process accordingly. These newer chargers start the charging process with a high bulk charge voltage and amperage to minimize charging time, then automatically switch to a lower absorption charge rate as the battery reaches a fully-charged state.

Finally, after fully recharging the battery, these more sophisticated chargers switch to a very low float or trickle charge, which is just enough current to offset the normal charge loss for a battery in a standby or idle state. These chargers usually have a battery selector switch or jumper to modify all charging voltage and current setpoints as required by each battery type.

Even a small riding mower can benefit from the installation of a solar panel that ensures its battery is always ready.

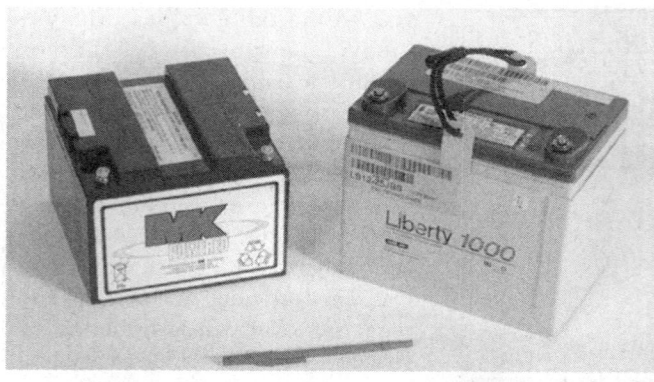

VRLA batteries are completely sealed and pressurized and can be mounted in any position, including upside down.

Standby battery charging

We are going to assume the charging systems on your mowers and tractors are providing adequate bulk charging to keep the batteries fully charged while in use, but you need some way to provide a float charge for those long periods when your equipment is not being operated and the batteries are slowly discharging.

This means any battery float-type charger we install to hold a battery at full charge does not need to have a high charging amperage. However, it will need to have battery monitoring technology to prevent over-charging and boiling all of the electrolyte out of the battery. I have found two very reliable products to do this, and both can be installed with minimum wiring skills and tools.

Most solar module manufacturers now offer a small self-regulating version of their larger solar photovoltaic panels. These modules are usually 5 to 10-watts in size which is 1 to 2 square feet in surface area. Some manufacturers make their solar modules using non-glass covered solar cells bonded onto the surface of a metal sheet, as shown in the accompanying photos of actual installations. Several manufacturers offer a module made of an unbreakable plastic laminate solar material mounted in an aluminum frame, which is ideal for more rugged applications.

One manufacturer even offers a flexible solar sheet having an adhesive backing that can be bonded directly onto metal roofing or a metal engine enclosure. All of these self-regulating modules include an internal diode or a reverse flow protection circuit to keep the battery from discharging back through the connected solar module when the sun is not shining. If you choose to use a larger non-regulated solar module, you will need to add a charge controller to regulate the battery charging process. Without a reverse flow protection diode or a charge controller, your solar charging system may discharge more of the battery charge at night than it will make up during a sunny day.

Connecting a self-regulating type solar module to any battery is simple. These modules are usually shipped with several feet of pre-wired cable ready for direct battery connection. No fuses, switches, or other electrical equipment are needed due to the very low voltages and currents produced. These modules can be mounted directly to the roof or motor housing of the mobile equipment by screws or bolts. Of course the obvious downside for any solar powered battery charger is the solar module must receive sunlight to work, which is not possible if the equipment is sitting in a garage or not facing the sun.

For equipment normally kept inside a shed out of the weather, your best charging solution is an electronic battery float type charger such as this 120-volt VAC battery float charger.

If you have engine driven equipment that are normally kept inside a shed out of the weather, but you still need to keep the battery charged during weeks or months of non-use, your best charging solution is an electronic battery float type charge. These units are approximately the size of a small box of tea, and can be permanently mounted directly under the hood or engine cover of your motorized equipment. Instead of the usual alligator clamp type battery connecters, these battery wires terminate with large diameter ring terminals held in place by the battery terminal bolts. The 120-volt power cord can be left plugged in continuously, since these chargers will not overcharge or over-

Inexpensive solar modules, 5 to 10 watts in size and 1 to 2 square feet in surface area, are adequate for maintaining a charge on an idle battery.

Useful websites

Battery maintained chargers

BatteryTender Chargers
www.batterystuff.com

Schumacher Chargers
www.batterychargers.com

BatteryMinder Chargers
www.batteryweb.com

Accupro Chargers
www.dry-it-out.com

ChargeTek Chargers
www.chargetek.com

Solar battery chargers:

www.batterystuff.com
www.baproducts.com
www.rvsupplywarehouse.com

Solar chargers for commercial and industrial applications:

www.pvforyou.com

---

heat a battery even if never disconnected.

Since they are only providing a very tiny trickle charge to maintain an already fully charged battery, they use only a minimal amount of electricity. I like to use these on all standby electric generator installations since generator starter batteries are notorious for reaching their fully discharged state just in time for the next power outage.

Regardless of which standby battery charging method you use, the next time you drag that riding mower out of the garage after a long winter, it should start right up. Unless of course the gasoline you accidentally left in the tank has now turned into paint thinner.

(Jeff Yago's latest book titled, *Achieving Energy Independence—One Step At A Time*, provides a very good introduction to solar power systems and alternative battery charging techniques. It is available from the *Backwoods Home Magazine's Bookstore*—see the oder form on page 88—or by calling 804-784-0063.) Δ

Keeping cats out of the garden

By Tom R. Kovach

If you own a cat or cats, or if your neighbors do, remember, cats do not belong in gardens—any kind of gardens, whether they be herb, vegetable, or flower gardens.

Cats can carry parasites that pose a health hazard to humans. And if a cat starts using your garden as a litter box, it could cause you health problems. Produce that has direct contact with the soil should always be thoroughly washed before storage and then washed and peeled before being used.

As a gardener, you can pick up any parasites that might exist in the soil through any cuts or openings in your hands when you work the soil. Wear gloves and wash your hands very well each time you work in the garden. Do not go into the garden with bare feet. Some folks say that mothballs will repel cats. I'm not sure about that, except that some people also don't like the smell of mothballs.

The experts tell me that the best way to keep cats out of your garden is by using chicken-wire fencing or spray repellents. If you plant in rows, lay the chicken wire in long strips between the rows of vegetables (or other items, flowers, herbs, etc.).

Before you use repellents, check with your doctor or your local poison control office to make sure that the product is safe for children playing nearby. And the repellent must be applied regularly.

If you want to spend a few bucks, there is another item that is said to work. It is the Scarecrow Motion Activated Sprinkler, produced by Contech Electronics Inc. It's a battery powered, motion-detecting lawn sprinkler that squirts water from its pulsating sprinkler head. Cats (who aren't that wild about water to begin with) are startled by the noise and the spray of water, and will hopefully avoid that area in the future. The company, located in Canada, claims that 86% of its customers say the product repells cats. It covers up to 1,000 sq. ft., and costs $79. It's available online at: http://www.scatmat.com/Products/. Or call: 1-800-767-8658. Δ

Want to know all about energy?

Get our energy CD-ROM with 152 articles.

only $12.95

(plus $4.95 S&H)

1-800-835-2418
www.backwoodshome.com

For health, pleasure, and relaxation Gardening rules!

By Alice B. Yeager
Photos by James O. Yeager

When planning your garden, don't overlook dwarf fruit trees. Many varieties of Japanese persimmons are a delight to eat even before they are fully ripe as they are not mouth-puckering.

There's something about a garden, from spring start to fall finish, that is invigorating. I'll admit that the first few digs in the spring can lead to some sore muscles and second thoughts, but, after that, everything falls into place and gardening becomes not just a pleasant experience, but a healthy exercise and a relaxing time. Plus the end products of gardening are a bounty of healthy food.

Gardens don't have to be large and capable of producing enough food for a family of 10. They can be any size your space and spare time will allow. A nice amount of produce may be harvested from a small garden if you stick to plants that are not large and rambling like watermelons and winter squash. Space given to early maturing vegetables (spinach, lettuce, radishes, and others) may be used for summer plants and then fall greens thus making threefold use of the garden.

There is no denying that there is healthy exercise connected with gardening whether you're growing vegetables, herbs, berries, or whatever. Soil has to be loosened up in the spring, as winter rains and snow are not known to leave dirt in a ready-to-use condition. If plenty of organic matter (leaves, grass clippings, pine needles, etc.) was heaped on the soil during early fall, it should be friable and a pleasure to work. If it was left bare to the elements, you can count on putting out more effort to cultivate it. Fall preparation definitely makes a garden easier to deal with in the spring.

In our garden we have gone entirely to raised beds (4-feet by 8-feet each). This makes it easier to confine mulch to the beds and to water when necessary. Between them we have a mixture of white clover and native grasses. We mow the aisles and put the clippings in an enclosed composter with vents for air circulation and rain seepage. Also added to the composter are kitchen scraps such as fruit and vegetable peelings, egg shells, etc. No meat products or grease are used. Nothing is added that will require a long time to decompose, i.e., sticks, shrubbery trimmings, etc.

Every garden should have a composter or a wire enclosed spot where compost may be produced. Keep it fairly moist and make it easily accessible to stirring and removing the finished product. You'll wonder how you ever managed without this boon to the garden. Not only is one's own compost supply convenient to have, but you'll never get such lush results from a bag of chemicals. Plants fed with decomposed organic material have a longer life span, are more pro-

Fresh young garden lettuce combined with other spring greens, including green onions, makes a delicious side dish or salad.

ductive, and are more able to cope with hot summers than the ones dependent on poor soil and chemicals to see them through.

Mowing between our beds creates a pleasant, relaxing walking situation. No dirt clings to our shoes and there's the sensation of walking on a carpet. A fringe benefit comes when we step on small runners of aromatic plants such as peppermint and pennyroyal that have crept into the aisles. Brushing against a bed of sweet basil fills the air with another delightful odor.

Gardening can begin as early in the spring as the climate will allow. However if a gardener is not interested in early crops such as English peas and carrots, he or she may prefer to wait until all danger of frost has passed and go for summer vegetables—squash, tomatoes, beans, etc. My advice has always been to plant what you actually like and will use. There's no point in planting rutabagas if you hate them with a purple passion.

While deciding between likes and dislikes, give some thought to the vitamin and mineral content of what you want to plant. For instance, spinach is high in Vitamin A and potassium, with a goodly amount of calcium. Beet greens (especially tops of red beets) are even richer than spinach in these benefits. Garlic, that wonderful seasoning for all kinds of cooked foods, salads, etc., is not only easy to grow, but it is said to be very beneficial for the digestive system and is helpful in high blood pressure cases.

Folks who suffer from a lack of iron should definitely lean toward planting beans, as they contain a number of vitamins and minerals including iron. Beans may be served in so many ways that it's hard to become tired of them. Our ever popular tomato gives us Vitamin C, phosphorus, and potassium among other health benefits. Ways of preparing tomatoes are countless.

Another wonderful vegetable is the sweet potato. It's chock full of vitamins and minerals, is easily digestible, and is a good body maintainer for persons engaged in physical labor. The Irish potato is also a fine body-building food.

If you have room in your garden for some berries and fruit trees, check out the vitamins and minerals contained in figs, peaches, blackberries, strawberries, apricots, or anything that will grow in your area. If you are particularly interested in the healthful side of what you raise, it might be well to invest in a book listing the vitamin and mineral contents of food plants. It's good knowledge to have at hand.

Moreover, plant with a view to preserving your excess harvest for future use. Some great soups may be made from summer vegetables, tucked away in the freezer and thawed out on cold days for truly tasty and nourishing meals. "Soup's on" has a pleasant and inviting ring to it.

There's quite a time span between planting and harvesting, and unexpected spring cold spells can stunt plants put out too early. We take the precaution of not transplanting tender plants to our garden until after Easter. There is a period known as blackberry winter that occurs right around Easter when blackberry patches are in bloom. This happens whether Easter occurs early or late. Temperatures plunge at night and often go into the thirties. The blackberry plants seem to come through all right, but tender plants can be given a severe setback if not protected. Waiting until after blackberry winter to set out transplants saves us a considerable amount of time and worry. Of course, one can always cover the plants, uncover them during the day, and cover again in late afternoon. Why go to this bother when the plants can be set out at a warmer time and left uncovered?

Once the transplants are in the soil, there is the matter of defending them against predators—cutworms, flea beetles, tomato hornworms, snails, slugs, and sow bugs. These are the worst culprits for us. Unfortunately, these pests, as well as many others, are widespread. It seems there's

Tomatoes and peppers, like many other vegetables, should be eaten raw to derive the most health benefits from them. However they are so good used other ways—spaghetti sauce, soups, casseroles, and on and on.

always something that seeks out garden plants for a tasty meal.

Cutworms have become a thing of the past in our garden. Although I don't like to use 10 Sevin Dust, I have found that a tiny bit at the base of cutworm-prone plants will do in the cutworms. Sevin Dust is not friendly to earthworms, and earthworms are important to your garden, so use it very sparingly.

Eggplants look great when first transplanted and usually get off to a healthy start. It never fails that tiny holes like pinpricks begin to appear in the soft velvety leaves. This is the beginning of an onslaught by **flea beetles**. They are little and they jump just like the fleas on animals, so hand-picking them is out of the question. I have found the quickest way to get rid of flea beetles is to lightly dust the leaves with Sevin Dust. I always try to pick a time when there is no breeze blowing so that the dust will be confined as much as possible to the plants with the problem. (Flea beetles also attack the leaves of numerous other garden plants, but they seem fondest of eggplant, tomato, and pepper plants.)

Tomato hornworms are another matter. These voracious eaters do considerable damage overnight stripping leaves and tender stems as they go. They will also ruin the green tomatoes and young peppers. Fortunately, the worms are large and easily seen ranging from two to four-inches in length. They are light green with white side stripes and a black horn on their tail end. They do not sting and, if you are not squeamish about picking up a worm, you can rid your plants of hornworms by hand-picking, thus avoiding dusting or spraying. If you can't locate the hornworm in the midst of the damage, try looking for fresh droppings. If you see a large hornworm with what appears to be small white cocoons on his back, you are seeing the work of braconid wasps that lay eggs on the worms. Young larvae feed off of their hosts. In the meantime, the hornworms continue to dine on your plants. Interesting things go on in a garden.

Snails and **slugs** also zero in on garden plants. They like to feed at night and, therefore, are less noticeable during daylight hours. However, the damage to plants can be extensive. I used to have problems with marigolds literally being stripped of foliage by tiny slugs until I remembered that I had at one time wiped out quite a number of slugs by using small amounts of table salt where they congregated. I extended the same idea to the garden, putting a tiny bit of salt around the base of the marigolds. That got the slugs along with their undesirable cousins, the snails. Old boards or trash make excellent hiding places for these fellows. Diatomaceous earth is also a remedy for getting rid of soft bodied pests, but once dampened by rain or heavy dew it is no longer effective and you have to put out a fresh supply.

Low on iron? Raise and enjoy beans fresh from the garden. Dried beans are also noted for their iron content.

Sow bugs used to be prominent around our garden area. They hid under flower pots, bricks, and any other place likely to be moist. Sevin Dust is deadly to them and it doesn't take much of it to eradicate them. Just sprinkle the dust where they hang out. Sow bugs feed on the roots of plants and sometimes plants are almost spent before one realizes the cause of the trouble.

There's a certain satisfaction that only a gardener knows when pests have been dealt with and plants are showing their first blossoms. Then tiny fruits appear and everything looks promising. A sigh of relief is in order and, barring a natural disaster such as a hailstorm, one can be pretty certain of some fresh vegetables being in the offing.

A good book on preserving food comes in handy when a garden produces an overabundance of good things to eat. Bookstores have a number of such books. Just be sure instructions apply to whatever you are going to harvest from your garden. You don't need a book that concentrates on how to preserve things grown in New England if you live in the South. Some companies specializ-

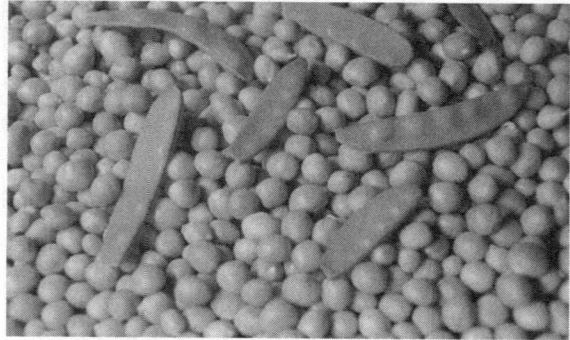
English peas are one of spring's star vegetables. A few hulls cooked with the peas, and later discarded, help to enhance the flavor of the peas.

The Fourteenth Year

Sweet basil is only one of many herbs that change ordinary foods into gourmet delights. Gardens should always have a spot for a variety of kitchen herbs.

ing in canning supplies offer their expertise in books written from their test kitchens. You can get addresses and prices of those books from new cartons of jar lids and seals for sale on your grocer's shelves. Order early as it sometimes takes a couple of months to receive the books.

I have been gardening forever it seems and I have found that working with a garden not only promotes good nutrition, but it is a great way to relax, enjoy life, and relieve stress. Stress used to be known as worry. Now it is big business as evidenced by the drugs used to deal with it.

Stress can build up until people actually come down with ailments that are hard to define. Many folks end up taking medications that they don't need just because stress is taking its toll. Some individuals with a bent toward physical exercise head for the gym or take up jogging. None of this has ever appealed to me. I'd rather carry a basket of fresh produce from the garden into the kitchen and enjoy the fruits of my labor.

Anyone interested in healthy living and having something substantial to show for time spent, can actually start gardening in the winter when all of those intriguing seed and nursery catalogs make their way into the U.S. Postal system. There's something about the planning stage that at least takes one's mind off of the dreary weather making it possible to project thoughts toward greener times. Arm chair gardening helps to lift spirits and deal stress a blow.

Isn't it great that most of us have three seasonal choices for gardening—spring, summer and fall? Maybe all three, depending on where you live.

Recipes

Chicken stock:

| 1 medium size fryer or young hen cut in pieces |
| 2 large celery stalks cut in 3-4 inch pieces |
| 1 large carrot cut in 3-4 pieces |
| 1 medium size onion, quartered |
| 1 clove garlic, halved |
| 2 dried bay leaves |
| 10 cups water |

Put all of the above into a large covered stockpot, bring to a boil, and reduce to simmer. Cook for about 2 hours or until chicken is tender and about to fall off the bones. Strain the stock. If you want fat-free stock, let the stock chill until the fat rises to the top where it may be easily removed. In the meantime, remove the chicken meat from the bones and save it for a later use (chicken salad, chicken, and spaghetti, etc.).

This stock is a must if you want something on hand that you can turn to when time is short. It makes a great base for soups, gravies, and other dishes and may be frozen or canned. The quick way is to let it cool down and put it in airtight freezer

Okra is cultivated extensively in the South and other places where summers are fairly long and warm weather prevails during the period. It is reported that okra's mucilaginous nature makes it suitable for treatment of stomach ulcers.

Any gardener with enough room for a few blueberry bushes should plant some. Not only are blueberries "good for you," but they can be used in many ways—jams, muffins, pies, etc. They're easy to pick—no thorns.

containers allowing a half inch at the top for expansion. Date and label containers and put them in the freezer. If you prefer to can the stock, pour the hot stock into hot, sterilized jars leaving about one-inch headspace. Adjust two-piece caps and process at 10-pounds pressure in a steam-pressure canner—20 minutes for pints and 25 minutes for quarts.

Chicken vegetable soup:

8 cups chicken stock
2 cups water (optional)
3 cups cooked chicken, cubed
2 cups green beans, snapped
2 cups okra cut in ¼-inch slices
1 cup sweet basil leaves, loosely packed
2 cups onions, chopped
4 cups tomatoes, chopped*
2 cups whole kernel corn
1 cup bell peppers, diced
1 cup carrots, diced
salt and black pepper to taste

*Before the tomatoes are chopped, the whole tomatoes should be immersed in boiling water about a minute so skins may be easily removed.

Bring the stock and water to a boil. Gradually add rest of ingredients and simmer until the vegetables are tender but not overdone. If you would like a thicker type soup, when the simmering begins add a half cup of rice or some of your favorite pasta—broken spaghetti pieces, macaroni, etc. Cover the pot, but stir occasionally to keep anything from sticking to the bottom.

This is a very versatile recipe. Other vegetables, herbs, and seasonings may be added. For instance, you may have some mild hot peppers that can take the place of the black pepper. If basil leaves are not available, try a couple of dried bay leaves.

Leftover soup may be frozen in airtight freezer containers. Be sure to leave about ½-inch airspace to allow for expansion. Otherwise, you may find tops pushed off of containers or worse.

English pea soup:

3 slices cured bacon
1 qt. water
3 cups English peas, shelled (reserve some clean hulls)
½ cup green onions, chopped
1 cup new potatoes, diced (scrape off thin skins and discard)
2 sprigs fresh mint
salt and pepper to taste

Fry bacon and set aside. Cut in small pieces. Put a quart of water in a good size covered pot and add about three tablespoons of bacon drippings. Put in all the other ingredients including a few clean pea hulls. Bring to a boil and then cut back heat to simmer. When vegetables are tender, discard the hulls and mint. Scoop out about a cup of the potatoes, onions, and peas and set them aside. Puree the rest of the soup in a blender or mash with a fork until mushy. Return to the pot and stir in the reserved potatoes, onions, and peas. Reheat and serve with your favorite crackers or hot bread.

There are a number of variations to this soup. Some folks like to thicken it with heavy cream while it's hot. (Don't boil or simmer after adding any cream.) Others add a bit of flour and water beaten smooth. Thickened versions can be garnished with chopped chives or parsley.

Wilted spring greens:

About a gallon of fresh garden lettuce (Oak Leaf, Bibb, Green Ice, etc.), tender radish leaves, and any other tender, mild-tasting garden greens
4 green onions
3 slices cured bacon
3 Tbsp. cider vinegar
2 Tbsp. water
½ tsp. salt
1 tsp. sugar
¼ tsp. black pepper

Cut off the roots from the lettuce and greens and discard any blemished leaves. Peel off the tough outside parts of onions and cut off the roots. Thoroughly wash all the lettuce, other greens, and onions to remove dirt, dust, or insects. Put in a colander and drain off as much water as possible. Tear all the greens into pieces. Cut the onions into ¼-inch slices and combine with the greens.

In a heavy large skillet or sauce pan, fry the bacon until crisp. Set the bacon aside and cut it into small pieces. Let the bacon drippings cool a bit before adding the vinegar, water, and seasonings; otherwise, there will be a tendency for the liquid to pop all over the place. Reheat. Put in a sizable amount of the greens, quickly adding more and tossing with the liquid until all greens are coated. Do not let greens wilt down too much or they may become mushy. Let them keep a good degree of crispness. Remove them to a serving dish and sprinkle with the bacon pieces.

This makes a delicious side dish or it can be simply enjoyed with some hot crusty bread of your choice. ∆

Get Backwoods Home Cooking

$21.95 plus $4.95 S&H

Send a check or money order to
BHM, P.O. Box 712
Gold Beach, OR 97444
1-800-835-2418
www.backwoodshome.com

Harvesting the wild: Flower buds

By Jackie Clay

When you've had a long day out in the fields, you deserve a break. And a bud. No, I don't mean a beer. I mean a good meal, featuring, of all things, flower buds. Now before you toss this down, think about it. You are probably very familiar with several flower buds, commonly eaten in most homes: broccoli, cauliflower, and artichokes. I don't know how many times I've gotten busy with other things, only to go out in the garden to pick one of these, only to find that I was too late. The buds were in full flower, past their prime as a vegetable.

In the wild, there are many, many flowers and flower buds that are not only *edible*, but actually choice fare for the table. Native Americans regularly dined on these tender, seasonal delights. If you've been following the *Harvesting the Wild* series, you've already learned about dandelion and cholla buds. Let's take a look at several other common buds and tasty flowers available to us. While they are most often thought of as "survival" foods, they form an extended garden for our family, and many other backwoods dwellers.

Milkweed

Nearly everyone is familiar with the common milkweed, with its large oval leaves and seed pods that pop open in the fall, sending fluffy parachutes sailing through the air. As these dry seed pods remain on the dead plant through the winter, it's usually easy to identify the next spring's milkweed patch. As with all wild plants, the wild forager should make sure the plant is the common milkweed before consuming any part.

As the milkweed gains mature height, clusters of buds form and begin to open. These flat clusters of buds open to lavender flowers. The best time to harvest milkweed buds is when they are tightly closed. Snip these buds from the plant and gather a nice bowlful. To eat, simply bring a pan of water to a boil, adding a pinch of salt. Then boil for four minutes. Drain and discard the water. Boil briefly in two more changes of water, then drain and enjoy with butter and a squeeze of lemon, if you desire. Milkweed buds are very good. The reason for the three boilings is to remove any trace of bitterness from the milky sap.

Also very good are the very young milkweed pods. These are best eaten when only an inch or an inch and a half long. Simply pluck these immature pods, then boil for four minutes, draining and discarding the water. As with the buds, boil again for a minute, twice, discarding each water. Then boil for about 10 minutes in fresh, salted water until tender. You will think you're eating okra. And like okra, you can also slice and bread the pre-boiled pods and deep fry them. They taste like okra, but are not as "slimy."

Immature milkweed pods are a valuable addition to meat stews and soups.

Yucca

The common yucca is found just about nationwide. It's tough, pointed, strap-like leaves make it look pretty dry and useless. But you should taste the small, tender flower buds that form along the tall flower stalk in the late spring. Pick the buds when they are quite small and tight and you will think you are eating fresh garden peas. They are very succulent and tender.

Simply pick these buds as you would peas, then boil just enough to make them tender, not mushy. I like them either with a pat of butter and sprinkle of salt, or in a light cream sauce.

Another favorite of mine is to harvest the just-opened yucca flowers on a cool morning. Dip them in your favorite vegetable dip and eat raw or

The buds and flowers from the yucca are very tasty.

*Male flower—note no bulge below flower.
Succulent squash and pumpkin flowers are a "new" traditional vegetable.*

take them home for lunch. While they are still very fresh, you can also dip them in deep frying batter (such as tempura), then deep fry briefly until just crisp and golden brown. They are also excellent served with a sweet and sour dip.

The amateur wild forager would do well to harvest milkweed from plants showing dried pods from previous years' growth to avoid confusing edible common milkweed from toxic dogbane (smaller leaves, banded stems, and no pink flowers). As with any new wild food, sample a small amount first to avoid upsets due to sensitivity to a certain food.

Wild daylily

How about the common wild daylily. This large, showy orange flower forms on a tall stem, accompanied by many other buds, as each flower only stays open for a day, hence its name. The plant is a shaggy bunch of drooping, strap-like leaves. In many areas, the wild daylily fills ditches and roadsides for miles. Not only is the daylily gorgeous, but tasty, as well.

Yes, you can eat the domestic daylily, but with so many new colors and variations it seems almost a shame to eat the flower buds. But if you get tempted, just remember that the flower would only last a single day anyway, and there will be many more very soon.

Daylily buds are best harvested when fairly long, but before they show any sign of opening. I like them dipped in batter and fried, but my very favorite is to make egg foo yung with them. Simply whip up the whites of two eggs per person, add a pinch of salt, and a sprinkle of hot chile, if you like. Then chop several daylily buds, along with one small onion.

Gently fold in beaten egg yolks and vegetables. Fry four-inch wide patties in vegetable oil until done. Serve warm, topped with sweet and sour sauce or traditional egg foo yung sauce, which is 1½ cups chicken broth blended into 1½ Tbsp. cornstarch in a small pan. Stir in 1 tsp. soy sauce, ½ tsp. salt, a dash of black pepper, and a ½ tsp. sugar. Cook over medium heat, stirring constantly. When thickened, serve hot over egg patties. These are very good, and nearly everyone loves them. (Just don't tell folks they're dining on flower foo yung.)

And if these aren't good enough, you must try batter-fried whole, open daylily flowers. I especially like the new hybrid domestic daylilies that have a thicker, ruffled petal. They have more substance than their wild cousins, but the wild daylilies are pretty darned good, as well.

Violet

There are many violet species which grow throughout North America, ranging from white, yellow, and, of course, violet including bi-colored flowers. All are edible. While the leaves can be eaten as one would spinach, as a child my very favorite was violet flowers. The new flowers

Pink or common milkweed provides many tasty foods throughout the season.

Wild violets make an interesting addition to a wild spring salad.

are crunchy and slightly sweet. You can toss a handful on top of a salad to beautify it. Or throw some in a light-colored Jello dessert after it has cooled a bit. Pioneer children thrilled to violet candy, which was simply moist violets dipped in precious white sugar, then allowed to dry. This creates a delicate shell around the sparkling flower. A very pretty "candy."

Pumpkin and squash blossoms

While not "wild" in the true sense, you will think the pumpkin and squash vines have run wild by the time they bloom. If you pick the male flowers (the ones that do not have a slight bulb at the base), you will not damage your future crop at all. These flowers are excellent when slightly stir fried with mild chiles and onions. Or you can dip them in tempura batter and deep fry them until golden brown. Serve with your favorite dip. I like them with a bowl of chili and sour cream. Dip them first in the chili, then just a bit of sour cream. They are *so good*.

You can also stuff pumpkin and squash blossoms that are open, nearly all the way. Simply mix up your favorite meatloaf recipe, including bread crumbs, then gently stuff each blossom. Tuck the ends of the petals in and repeat until the baking dish is full. Bake at 350° until almost done, then sprinkle with grated cheese and drizzle catsup over the top. Bake until done. Be ready for raves.

Why don't you try some of these delectable buds and flowers this year? They are so easy and fun to pick, and even easier to prepare and serve. Have a bud....on me. Δ

Black walnut warning

By Tom R. Kovach

The toxin in the roots of black walnut trees can cause problems with other plants near those roots.

Black walnut trees produce juglone, which is a substance that is toxic to certain other plants. Tomatoes are very sensitive to juglone, as are other members of the tomato family. These include eggplants, peppers, and potatoes. Other plants sensitive to juglone include blueberries, blackberries, apple trees, white pines, azaleas, and rhododendrons.

Plants or trees affected by juglone can be killed or injured within one to two months after they have come in contact with the root zone of black walnuts. The toxic zone occurs on average in a 50 to 60-foot radius around the trunk of a mature tree, but can be up to 80 feet. The area affected extends outward each year as a tree gets bigger. Young trees two to eight feet high can have a root diameter twice the height of the tree, with susceptible plants dead within the root zone and dying at the margins.

Garden plants that are not sensitive to juglone include onions, corn, beets, and beans. There are a number of trees, vines shrubs, ground covers, annuals, and perennials that will grow in close proximity to walnut trees.

Because juglone breaks down when exposed to air, water, and bacteria, walnut leaves can be composted. The toxic effect can be degraded in two to four weeks. In soil, breakdown may take up to two months. Black walnut leaves may be composted separately and the finished compost tested for toxicity by planting tomato seedlings in it. Sawdust mulch, fresh sawdust, or chips from black walnut are not suggested for plants which are sensitive to juglone. But the composting of the bark or walnut chips for at least six months provides a safe mulch even for plants sensitive to the toxin.

For more information you can check with your local agriculture agent. Or get the publication: *Toxicity of Black Walnuts towards other Plants*. Go to http://www.extension.umn.edu. Click on *Publications* and then *Briefs* to search for the publication. Δ

Sew a baby quilt in two days...
for a lifetime of memories

By Ilene Duffy

During my last year of teaching school, I was pregnant with Jacob. I'll always remember receiving a beautifully crocheted baby blanket that one of my student's mothers made for me. So when I heard that middle son, Robby's teacher was going to have her first baby this past school year, I immediately imagined her delight in receiving a baby blanket made, in part, by her adoring class.

Most mother's days are filled with activity and not a whole lot of time to sit around and stitch, and I'm no different in that department, so when planning this quilt I knew that I needed to come up with a design that would be simple enough for me to complete the project in just a few days. (Besides, the end of the school year crept up and I needed the students' art work for this project.) Here's how my novice sewing abilities turned this idea into a completed baby quilt.

I knew that I wanted each student to take a square of fabric and draw a design using fabric pens. My friend, Rhoda, was the substitute for the class for the last month of the year. So when she and I were going to buy the fabric for the top layer of the quilt, she said, "Since there are 27 kids in the class, let's have each student pick a letter of the alphabet and draw pictures that go with their letter." With only 26 letters to go around, we thought that one student with good handwriting could write out "To Mrs. Margolis, from your 4th grade class."

In order to plan out the pieces to be cut for the quilt, I used graph paper and sketched out a simple log cabin design using squares and rectangles. During the planning stages, I didn't know the sex of the baby, so yellow, green, and a baby hand-print fabric were the prominent colors for the borders of each square rather than blue or pink. Each log cabin square consists of a 6" square of fabric with a 6" x 3½" rectangle sewn to the bottom of the square and a 3½" x 8½" rectangle sewn to the right of the previous two pieces. Here, it's important to note that I used a ½" seam allowance for all seams for the top layer of the quilt. The finished design has 5 log cabin squares across and 6 going down the quilt for a total of 30. The students used 27 of the squares and the remaining 3 were designed by the 2 substitutes for the class and me.

Mrs. Margolis' 4th grade class with the completed quilt

Photo: John Silveira

The Fourteenth Year

The following is a list of the materials I used to make the quilt:

- 30 6" squares of fabric
  (9 pink, 9 blue, 6 yellow, and 6 green)
- 1⅓ yards of 45" fabric for the back of the quilt (I had loads of a baby hand-print fabric on hand that I had previously purchased)
- 25 rectangles of fabric, 6" wide by 3½" high
  (13 baby print, 6 yellow, and 6 green)
- 4 rectangles of fabric, 3½" wide by 6" high
  (2 baby print, 1 yellow, and 1 green)
- 20 rectangles of fabric, 3½" wide by 8½" high
  (10 baby print, 5 yellow, and 5 green)
- enough quilt batting to fill a 40" by 44" blanket
- enough of the baby print fabric to cut 4 strips of fabric, each 2" wide for the binding of the quilt (2 strips 45" long, 2 strips 41" long)

Being a novice seamstress, the procedure for putting it all together was quite simple. I measured and carefully cut all the squares and rectangles. After all the artwork was completed on the fabric squares, it was time to stitch. Using my design on graph paper as a guide, I sewed the bottom of the first square to its corresponding 6" wide by 3½" high rectangle, then ironed the seams open. In fact, I was diligent about ironing all the seams open right after sewing them. A long rectangle (3½" wide by 8½" high) was sewn to the right of the previously sewn pieces to form the first log cabin square. Again, I referred to my graph paper guide to make sure I had the correct color for each rectangle before sewing. I sewed together all 30 log cabin squares and placed them in order in a stack.

The next step was to sew the top 5 log cabin squares together, then the second row, etc., until I had all 6 rows sewn together. Of course, the last step in the piecing of the quilt was to sew the 6 strips of rows together, from the top of the quilt to the bottom. In one evening I had the whole top layer pieced.

My next step was to get Dave to take the boys to school the next morning so I could play hookie from my magazine duties in order to have time to complete the quilt during daylight hours. First I cut the fabric for the bottom layer of the quilt. I cut it so it was about two inches larger on all four sides than the top layer. I cut the batting so that it would also have about two more inches on all four sides than the top layer.

I cleaned off my kitchen table to use as a nice flat surface in order to baste all three layers together. I layed out the bottom layer, right side of the fabric facing the table, then the batting, then the pieced, top layer

Thirty log cabin squares formed this simple, quick-to-make quilt.

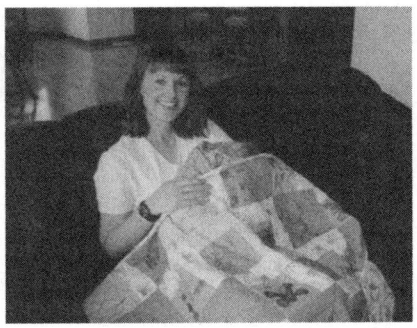

Mama Kelly, baby Marisa, and her new quilt

with the right side facing up. I used a needle and long pieces of thread to hand baste all three layers together. I had read in a quilting book that it's a good idea to leave the extra margin of the batting and bottom layer of fabric before quilting, as the process of quilting the three layers together has a tendency to cause the top layer to be slightly different in size after stitching.

I decided to do all the quilting using my sewing machine, rather than by hand. I also knew I wanted to avoid quilting on the students' artwork, so I kept all the quilting stitches on the border pieces.

After all three layers were completely quilted together, I cut the batting and bottom layer to be the same size as the top layer. Then I took out all the threads from the basting.

The last step was to attach the binding around all four edges. I cut the four 2" strips of fabric for the binding, then sewed the corners together on the diagonal to form what looked like a picture frame the same size as the quilt, then pressed the seams open. I pressed under the raw edges of the binding strips ⅜" on each side and machine-stitched the binding to the top of the quilt, right sides together. I folded the binding to the back side of the quilt and hand-stitched the ironed down edge in place.

The finished project just needed to be washed before delivery to baby Marisa. ∆

Grouse hunting
...the ultimate joy of autumn

By Linda Gabris

Nothing instills such excitement or makes my heart flutter louder than the sudden whir of a flushed out grouse. No matter how many times I've heard it, the whoosh of wings always comes as a thrilling surprise that startles the daylights out of me, like an electrical shock that I just can't seem to get enough of.

I've been grouse hunting since I was old enough to tote a gun and, as much as I enjoy the pursuit of big game and waterfowl, I have to admit that grouse hunting ranks number one on my list of autumn outings, for not only is it a challenging sport but also a super long season. And best of all is the fact that having a stash of grouse in the freezer means great eating all winter long.

Although opinions will forever vary over what gun and ammo is the best pick for grouse, I think the number one thing for any upland bird hunter to consider is to make sure their choice is powerful enough to deliver a quick, clean kill—but not so powerful that there's nothin' left of the prize but a mess of feathers.

Learning to hunt years ago with my dad in the hardwood stands behind our back stoop, I used an old 20-gauge shotgun which was handed down to me from my father. I lugged the trusty thing for years before retiring it as a keepsake of cherished memories of my younger days spent in the woodlands. I've been fortunate enough to try out a fair range of makes and models of shotguns over the past number of years, and I must say a 20-gauge is still a favorite pick.

Before I retrieve a gun from my vault for a day's hunt, I consider the state of the woodlands I intend to

Author with a grouse

trudge through. Early in the season when trees and shrubs are still heavily branched in leaves, I find that my 20-gauge with modified choke delivers plenty of spread, and No. 6 shot gives me the penetration for cutting through obstructions. Although it doesn't take a ton of bricks to bring down a grouse, one has to consider the brush factor when hunting in early season and choose a shot that throws a wide pattern. In late season, when the trees are bare and I can keep my eye on the bird for further distances, I find No. 4 shot works well.

One of the trickiest things about grouse hunting is training your eyes to pick up the perfectly camouflaged forms of these plump birds. I remember when I was a kid how dad would tease me because I couldn't distinguish a grouse up ahead on the trail from a clump of mud. Learning to spot them is like training your eyes to see stereoscopic images without using 3-D glasses. But once you develop the skill, the image seems to register quickly without strain or over-focusing. Being able to spot the birds on the ground before they burst into air gives a little more time for planning action.

The best woodlands to hunt grouse are those that offer feed. There are numerous species of birds belonging to the grouse family, and although they are similar in character and habit they thrive on food that is available in their regions. The crops or 'berry bags' of downed birds will reveal their diet trends. Studying the contents carefully will help make future hunts more successful.

Those shot in hardwoods will contain berries and plants familiar on hardwood forest floors. Crops of prairie chickens will be filled with such delights as grain, goldenrod, sunflower, and other common seeds.

Harvesting wild hazelnuts
...getting two birds with one stone

While out in the grouse woods hoping for supper why not keep your eyes peeled for the second tastiest treat in the woodlands—wild hazelnuts. Also known as wild filberts, these little gems resemble commercial filberts except that they are somewhat smaller, their shells are a bit thicker, and their meat is so much sweeter. But best of all they're free for the pickin' and nothin' compliments a grouse dinner more than an elegant coating of these delicious nuts.

Hazelnuts in the wild

American or beaked hazels are native shrubs which grow up to about 12 feet and can be found in abundance across North America growing in sunny spots of mixed hardwood stands. Hazelnut shrubs are often spotted hugging fences or hemming meadows.

The bark of mature plants is smooth and bright brown while immature twigs are lighter in color and covered in fuzz. The oval, double-toothed leaves have deep, well-spaced veins and are covered in silky hairs giving them a velvety feel. Immature twigs are lighter in color and covered in fuzz.

The shrubs have both male and female flowers that are separate but on the same bush. Male flowers are born in catkins that develop in fall and mature in spring. They dangle from bare branches shedding a shower of pollen on the female flowers that are tiny rusty clusters. In mid autumn the nuts ripen in sets of twos, sometimes threes, snuggled in fuzzy husks that turn from green to brown as they ripen.

One of the trickiest things about harvesting wild hazelnuts is to beat squirrels to the ready nuts. If you pick them too early the nut will not be developed and you'll end up with a heap of empty shells. But if you wait too long, squirrels, who seem to know exactly when the nuts are ready, will hoard them up right under your nose. Best thing to do is hunt down a patch and keep a close eye on it. Cracking a nut with a stone will tell when they are fleshed out and prime for picking.

Make sure you throw a pair of gloves in your pack for gathering the nuts as the silvery husks are picky on the fingers.

Once home with your pickings, the nuts must be husked. If you want to use a handful of nuts immediately, peel off the husks using gloved hands. If you can wait a day or two before using, the sheaths will wilt and become easier to loosen and peel away. If you've found a good stash of nuts, they can be buried in mud for a week or two and the husks will rot off.

A basket of wild hazelnuts

Hazelnuts can be cracked and eaten fresh or the kernels can be extracted from the shells and roasted in a moderate oven for about 8 minutes or until slightly brown. This gives them a sweeter, nuttier taste.

Shelled nuts should be stored in an airtight container. Unshelled nuts can be stored in a cool, dry place for years although they are so good I can't imagine a stash ever lasting that long.

If you're a huntin' nut who likes to stash away a few treats for winter then you'll love the addition of these tasty little nuts to your pantry.

Birds hunted in or near bogs will have telltale signs of cranberries or blueberries in their bags. Studies show that grouse eat buds and needles of evergreens in wintertime which is believed to help them digest food in place of stones that might be hard to obtain from frozen or snow covered ground. Since they need to fill their gizzards with stones in order to digest food, grouse are often spotted alongside gravelly paths or streams 'mining' in early morning and evening.

Deciduous stands and willowy scrubland, burned and logged areas that are rich in seedy growth, old orchards, clearings, and edges of forests are prospective places to tramp grouse hunting trails. I have found that any trek that winds through bunchberry, clover patches, or wild rose brushes laden with bright fleshy hips offers good chances of flushing out a plump ruffie or two.

Grouse hidden in the colorful depths of autumn are often scared up by the rustle of crispy foliage under the hunter's foot. Drumming and a sudden whir are thrilling sounds that the grouse hunter must be ready to quickly react to. This reaction is known as "swinging-through" and consists of getting the gun moving faster than the bird. One's instincts must work all at the same time—hearing, then seeing, or vice versa—the bird, swinging the gun, aiming while panning, then pulling the trigger at the precise moment. Grouse are fast flyers and can instantly burst into flight, skimming trees in a cunning, dodging manner, making a calculated shot the ultimate challenge.

Some grouse hunters enjoy the companionship and aid of a good bird dog which can stir up flocks of birds and are great at retrieving. If you've got a well trained grouser with a begging face that you just can't refuse, then by all means let the devoted critter tag along. Or rather you tag along with him! Sometimes I adopt faithful Old Barney from my hunting buddy to take along on a stroll. Other times I go solo preferring a slower, more relaxed pace.

Next best thing to hunting grouse is eatin' them. One thing that puzzles me is hearing tell of a grouse that was too tough to chew. I've never come across one yet that didn't cut it as a great meal. Especially one dressed in a golden jacket of sweet wild hazelnuts picked from the same woods from whence the bird was harvested. Now this is the crowning glory of a great hunt.

Grouse breasts, coated with the hazelnut breading

The finished dish

Breast of grouse in hazelnut jackets

This is a very elegant dish to serve when you want to impress your hunting partner or a special dinner guest. The grouse breast is tender and succulent on the inside and crispy coated with distinctive sweet hazelnuts on the outside. This recipe serves two, but you can double it as long as you don't crowd the pan.

> 1 grouse breast, de-boned (to de-bone a grouse breast, run a sharp knife down each side of the breastbone, working the meat away with your free hand. Slice each half into two thin fillets. Save bones for another day's soup.)
> ¼ cup of ground wild hazelnuts. A few more if doing two birds. (You can substitute commercial filberts if you haven't had a successful nut hunt)
> ½ cup of flour seasoned with pinch of salt, pepper, thyme, and a bit of sweet basil
> 1 egg
> 4 Tbsp. buttermilk or heavy cream butter

Flatten grouse pieces by pounding gently with a mallet. Combine ground nuts and seasoned flour in a paper bag. Blend egg and buttermilk together. Dip grouse into egg mixture, then drop into paper bag and shake until coated. Place on a sheet of waxed paper and allow to dry for about 8 minutes or until nuts are adhered to the meat.

Melt butter and sauté the pieces until golden on both sides. Sprinkle with a few drops of fresh squeezed lemon juice. One breast serves two.

Goes great with a few fried mushrooms dipped and coated in any leftover batter and crumbs. Serve with a crisp green salad. Add wine and you've got it made. ∆

(This article was previously published, in part, in *BC Hunting and Shooting Magazine*.)

For more give and take with the readers of *BHM*, go to the readers' forum:
www.backwoodshome.com

Life in a chicken coop

By Chuck Davis

Living in a chicken coop for four years was a much better experience than it sounds. The chickens were long gone, the pack rats evicted. That was a start but it took a whole lot of imagination to think we could live in that filthy, decrepit structure and like it. But when the work was done, we were in a cozy, warm cabin reminiscent of an early settler's lifestyle. I felt that both the cabin and I were chronologically misplaced in history.

Life in the 12 by 17-foot coop-turned-cabin was a big change into a small space from our four bedroom, two-story farm styled house that had burned to the ground. Significantly inadequate fire insurance left us without sufficient money to rebuild.

Abhorring debt, a building loan was not an option. We stayed temporarily in a small house we had in town, but town life was intolerable, where privacy required curtains and closed doors, shutting off light and air. Incessant city noise bashed our senses. Sleep was difficult and peace foreign.

For happiness we had to go where our horses and dogs were, where bugling elk are heard and moose meander. Tall pines mantled the mountains behind us, a defunct gold mine over the hill one way, Georgetown Lake the other, and to the south a several-hundred-acre mountain meadow stage, the rugged Pintlar Wilderness Area. It was a grand, idyllic location, where I could pee off the porch if so inclined and not offend neighbors or get crossways with the law.

After the house fire, only four buildings remained on our few acres: two framed garages suitable for small Model T Fords, a deteriorating barn, and the 60-year-old, recycled-log chicken coop in serious disrepair.

The coop had no foundation. Bottom logs sat on large flat stone and some showed ominous signs of rot. Chinking was cement mortar, mostly crumbled away. The roof, a layer of asphalt roofing over 2 by 12-inch boards, kept the rough-sawn ceiling boards intact. A foot-deep layer of chicken dung covered the dirt floor. Rags and cardboard nailed to some interior walls gave pause to steady mountain winds.

When I broached the idea of remodeling the coop into our home my wife, Trisha, was surprised but saw the possibilities and was actively involved in the clean-up and build-up. She is now a registered nurse but had worked as a drywall finisher and tile setter when younger. I was an electrician and now claim to be a chainsaw carpenter.

Work began on the coop in October and we moved into a cozy cabin in February. First the roof was rebuilt. A frame of 2 x 6-inch boards on 24-inch centers was built over the existing roof so 6-inch fiberglass insulation could be installed. That frame was sheathed with half-inch plywood, a layer of rolled asphalt roofing, then metal Delta Rib roofing. It is leak proof.

Next, the chicken waste and a foot or so of dirt and rocks were removed to make room for the insulated wood floor. The joists are 2 x 8-inch boards on 16-inch centers. Working from above, wood strips were nailed to the joists 6 inches below the subfloor level. Quarter-inch plywood was cut to size and laid between the joists, with 6-inch insulation on top of that. The rot in base logs was superficial and chiseled away before pouring the concrete foundation. A portable electric cement mixer was used to mix the wheelbarrow-sized batches.

The "before" of the kitchen area

Trisha Davis sits in the finished kitchen.

The subfloor is 5/8-inch plywood. Six-inch tongue and groove pine flooring, salvaged from the burned house, finishes the floor. The wood had been protected by water-soaked wool carpets and Congoleum linoleum. All areas with synthetic textile carpet burned through to the ground, wet or not.

Interior log walls had 60 years of accumulated grime, the rear wall being the worst. Between tacked up cardboard and the logs, pack rats had nested for decades. The excrement and urine had so fouled the logs they were beyond cleaning and an eyesore. Decontaminated with a strong bleach solution the wall was framed out, insulated, plastic sheeting vapor barrier put in place, and sheet-rocked. Painted white, the wall brightens the cabin. With sponge, rags, brush, and a solution of household cleaner, Trisha tackled the walls, scrubbing them into like-new beauty. And then she did the chinking.

To seal the cabin logs we opted for a commercial chinking system rather than mortar, which crumbles as log walls settle. Romex wiring was run between logs prior to chinking. Outlet and switch boxes were fitted into chiseled out openings in the logs. To begin, strips of closed-cell foam were snuggly fitted between logs as an insulating filler, reducing the amount of chinking needed. The strips we used are called backer rod and resemble black, oversized, soft spaghetti. We bought 100-foot rolls in diameters of ¼ and ½-inch and so on to correspond to the size of the space to be filled.

The original 60-year-old, 12' x 17' chicken coop

Log Jam is the brand of chinking we used. It is a gritty textured latex compound sold in five-gallon buckets. A bucket is about $110 in Bozeman, Montana. The stuff is flexible and won't pull apart with minor log movement and is available in several earth tone colors. It is applied with what resembles a large caulking gun and is smoothed with a wet sponge.

Our water line is buried six feet deep as winter cold can freeze the ground for several feet. We dislike the spider web of overhead power lines, so we buried our electric and phone service in two-foot deep trenches. Utility ditches and foundation excavations were dug after spring thaw. Until then water was carried 50 feet from an existing frost-free hydrant. Kitchen waste water was collected and hauled in five-gallon buckets. We learned a lot about water conservation. A Porta-Potty was in a nearby tool shed.

We kept the original hen house door, but added a barn latch. We call it a Davis door as it is barely more than 5½ feet high, just about right for the stubby Davis clan. Picture windows are double glazed while the small kitchen and a crank-open window are single panes of glass.

The finished cabin is heated by electric baseboards. A wood heater in that small space would have kept us unbearably hot. As it is, the big south facing windows deliver enough solar heat that the door and windows are open even on the coldest of days.

The following year a log-walled 12 by 18-foot addition was built for a bathroom and bedroom. Logs came from a friend's property, all of which were dead-standing Lodgepole pine. The largest was 22 inches at the butt. I used a draw knife to peel the bark, then felled the trees and handled them with the aid of an A-frame boom I built for my pick-up truck. A front-mounted electric winch provided the lift to place the logs into walls.

We don't live in that little cabin anymore and I sorely miss it. It opened the door to a new way of living. We now have 20 acres, 2 creeks, no electricity or running water, and a stack of logs that will soon be a log-walled, straw bale-insulated home we will build with the aid of the boom and the cement mixer. But we'll always be able to say we once lived in a chicken coop. ∆

Chuck stands before the not-yet-finished coop at a point when the windows were in.

The Fourteenth Year

How to make money from storage building auctions

By Bill Wilson

Buying and selling is a time honored way of making a living. However, like any profession, success in merchandising requires following some fundamental rules. The most basic of these is to obtain items of good quality that people will actually want to purchase, and to acquire them at a low enough cost to ensure adequate profit. Once this challenge is met, the entrepreneur's success is largely assured.

Fortunately, across the United States a huge supply of desirable products exists for low prices. Furniture, electronics, appliances, clothing, books, art, toys, tools, and a plethora of other goodies can be had for a fraction of their true value. The purchaser can use these items themselves, or resell them for a generous markup. Startup costs are minimal: a van or pickup truck (a trailer towed by a car will do) and a few hundred dollars are all that is required to begin your own business.

Finding merchandise

I am not talking about raiding dumpsters, joining wholesale clubs, or fencing stolen merchandise. I am discussing public storage buildings, which you can find in virtually any community coast to coast. Millions of individuals and businesses use these facilities to store all sorts of goods. Many of them eventually fall behind on their monthly rental bills. After an extended period of non-payment the storage building owner can legally claim the items. He or she will often hold periodic public auctions to sell off the goods in order to recoup a portion of their lost rent.

It is important to remember that the USA has become a nation of pack rats. Consumers acquire all sorts of things that they will never need or even use. Impulse purchases, seasonal items, unwanted gifts—all these and more end up under lock and key for extended periods. Seniors selling a large home and moving to a smaller one realize they have tons of unwanted possessions. Singles or couples buy a new sofa, DVD player, or television and store the old one. Children grow up and leave home, and the parents hold on to their clothing, old musical instruments, books, and clothing for sentimental reasons. Businesses upgrade their computer systems frequently, and the original PCs are seen as obsolete; they are put "on ice." Ours is truly a throw away society.

The result of all this financial fickleness is that large quantities of perfectly good things end up in rented storage buildings. Then death, financial hardship, or just plain apathy or forgetfulness kick in, and the items are forgotten. This is where the real opportunities for you come in. The units range in size from twenty five square feet up to several hundred. Some are even climate controlled, and may contain freezers full of fresh meat or other perishable goods. Chances are, there is such a place near you right now, packed with all sorts of treasures waiting for you to claim them.

The first step in taking advantage of this opportunity is learning when the auctions in your area take place. Get a copy of the local *Yellow Pages* directory and look under "storage facilities." Contact the offices. Make sure you do not call storage building dealers, the people who actually sell the little sheds you see in back yards nationwide. You want the businesses that rent their own units on their own property.

Ask for the owner or manager, and tell them you want to know when the next auction is going to be. Some places hold them on a regular basis, and can give you the exact date and time. Others hold them "as need aris-

Flea markets, newspaper ads, local radio stations, your own yard, and the internet are all great places to sell.

es," but do not currently have one planned. Put these on a call back list, and check with them once a month or so. Still others put a notice in the newspaper when the time for the auction approaches. Learn what paper they use and watch its classifieds.

On the day of the auction, show up a few minutes before it begins, ready to do some heavy lifting. A pickup or other large truck is ideal. A van is great, but there might be some head room problems. A bigger car can work if you use a utility trailer as well. You will also need work gloves, tarps, or blankets to cover the items in case of rain, and, if possible, hand trucks and/or a partner. Of course you will also need a place to store your purchases for a while until you sell them.

Bidding at auctions

Bidding at auctions is an art form unto itself. You may wish to just watch others at the first two or three you attend, just to get a feel for how much items go for. Keep in mind that your primary goal is resale. Don't bid $300 on a building full of goods that you can only make 50 bucks on. A good idea is to check local flea markets, yard sales, classifieds, salvage stores, E-bay, etc., to see what different items go for.

The auctioneer will open the buildings one at a time to let the bidders see what they contain. If most or all of the goods are in boxes, then he or she will break these open and display their contents to the crowd. Bring a pad and pen and try to estimate the approximate resale value of the merchandise. Then place your highest bid at no more than 50 percent of that amount. If in doubt about the profitability of the contents, then don't bid; there is always another day, and you don't want to get stuck with tons of unwanted junk filling up your storage area.

A typical storage unit, this one yielded camping equipment, a wooden rocking chair, BBQ grill, and other treasures.

As discussed before, the variety of things you can find at these auctions is astounding. Appliances, furniture, electronics, books, clothes, toys, pet supplies, CDs, records and cassettes, VHS/DVD movies, and boxes filled with knickknacks are common finds. Cash, jewelry, gold and silver coins, even automobiles have been found. You want to look the stuff over as thoroughly as possible to make sure that rain has not leaked in and destroyed things. If you smell mildew or see evidence of water damage, then pass that building up. Mice and other rodents sometimes get in, but they rarely do much damage, except to clothing and stored food. (Speaking of clothing, check the pockets and linings of any you get. Old people hide money in them. Wads of cash have been found stuffed in shoes and mattresses). Storage buildings with shingle roofs and heavy, tight-fitting doors do the best job of preserving stored items.

Sorting, repairing

Okay, the auction is over, and you were the high bidder on one or more lots. You can usually claim your merchandise on the spot. Start going through your acquisitions immediately. You want to separate the good stuff from the absolute junk, which you will haul to the dump. One strategy is to break open the boxes and hold up nice finds while other bidders are still milling about. Quite often they will make purchases from you right there.

Sometimes you will obtain things that need a little work. This is where a working knowledge of electronics, appliance repair, and/or woodworking comes in handy. You may locate a color television that only needs an inexpensive part to get it working again. Lawn mowers, garden tillers, and the like are often cast aside as "broke," when all they need is a spark plug or other minor repair. A clothes dryer may only require a new lint filter to run like new. Scuffed or dirty furniture can be cleaned and polished. Learn to see past the dust and dents to discern an item's true value. Many people have furnished their own homes this way, and saved hundreds if not thousands of dollars doing so.

Store your stuff carefully. Stack it neatly, cover it with tarps or blankets, make sure the weather will not get in, and lay out some poison in case vermin get in. Write down your inventory, noting general condition and what you think you can get for each item.

Re-selling

Now you can look at selling your goods. The venues for doing this are numerous. Newspaper ads are a good bet for larger or pricier items. People scan the classifieds every day looking for bargains. In addition, many local radio stations have weekly "swap shops," usually on weekend mornings where you can call in, tell what you have for sale, and leave your phone number for interested parties. Call nearby broadcasters to find out about these. Sometimes television stations offer the same service.

Flea markets, also called "swap meets," are great places to sell things.

Check your local area for them. *The Official Guide To U.S. Flea Markets* by Kitty Werner is a nationwide listing of markets. The office will rent you one or more tables to display your merchandise on; fees range from three or four dollars a day per table up to fifteen or twenty for one inside a building with climate control. Check with the manager for prices and procedures for dealers. At some markets you can just show up the day of the sale and claim your own space; others require you to pay a few days in advance. Visit the market on a sale day before you bring your goods out; make sure there is good customer flow.

Be sure and bring plenty of change, bags for the purchases (available at any grocery store; just offer them a few bucks for 40 or 50 of their sacks), a comfortable chair to sit in, and a cooler with drinks and some food. A beach umbrella can keep you cool in warm months. Bring a book or portable radio to help the time pass. Covering your tables with tarps, blankets, or heavy paper makes your display more appealing to the eye. Wide varieties of rather colorful folks both sell and buy at the markets, and you should meet some interesting people. For more information, check out *How To Make Cash Money Selling At Swap Meets, Flea Markets, Etc.* by Jordan Cooper, available from Loompanics Unlimited (www.loompanics.com).

Yard or garage sales are another way to rake in the dough. If you have a home with a good sized yard or a carport or garage, this option can work for you. Make sure you have plenty of change for your customers, as well as bags for their purchases. Advertise the upcoming sale in your local paper, put up signs in the neighborhood stating the day and address of the sale, and be outside early, ready to do business—yard sale fans are early risers. The old pros at this business set their merchandise out the night before, and cover it with tarps, so they do not have to set up the morning of the sale.

In many rural areas and small towns, retail auctions are a favorite form of entertainment. Dealers bring truck loads of products they have bought wholesale elsewhere and put them up for bid one at a time. Forget any images you may have of rich people wearing fancy clothing and buying rare antiques or Kennedy memorabilia. These sales are frequented by working class and country folk, the same types you will see at the flea market.

You can make a hefty profit by selling at these auctions, but you need to know what you are doing. Find out when and where they are held by checking your *Yellow Pages*, local papers, or just asking around. Go several times before you decide to sell. Watch the bidders and the auctioneer. Talk to the manager and find out what the terms are; usually the house will get a portion of whatever money you make. Retail auctions can be great fun as well as lucrative.

In many parts of the country it is legal to set up an impromptu store front along the roadside, in front of abandoned stores or in the hinterlands of large parking lots. Cops will not hassle you as long as no one complains. In the south it is common to see people selling produce, clothing, decorator rugs, stuffed animals, or other goods right off the back of their trucks or out of a van. The northeastern states seem much less tolerant of this form of free enterprise, however. The rule of thumb is this: if you see others doing it without being persecuted, then you can do it too. Gas stations and convenience stores that have gone out of business are great locales. Bring your stuff and set it out for customers to see. Leave plenty of parking room, and expect many people to drive past your setup while checking out the goods.

Other venues include pawn shops, web pages, and collectors. It is amazing what people will collect. Campaign buttons, old books, walking sticks, teddy bears, shaving razors, beer mugs, and even prepaid calling cards have their enthusiasts. Read a few books on antiques and collectibles to become conversant on the subject. Internet sites like E-bay are great as well.

No matter how great a sales person you are, you will eventually end up with some goods that just will not move. You can often sell these in bulk to other dealers at a low price. Charities like the Salvation Army and Goodwill will give you a receipt for donated items that you can use to reduce your taxes.

America is a fantastic place to live, with wealth literally overflowing its containers. It is quite possible to live off the fat of the land, even in these days. Storage building auctions offer fantastic opportunities for the entrepreneur. I should know; I have been benefiting from them for years. Now you can too. ∆

Restore the Bill of Rights with Fully Informed Juries

Find out how ordinary people, as trial jurors, can repair years of legislated special-interest damage to our rights, simply by saying No to bad laws!

Phone: 1-800-TEL-JURY for a *free* Jury Power Information Kit!

A *Backwoods Home* Anthology

Living the outlaw life:

Credit card monte:
Finance flim-flam and how to foil it
by Claire Wolfe

It was the strangest thing. Month after month, I charged nothing on my credit card. Month after month, I paid nearly double the minimum payment. I was such a good girl. Yet each month, my balance didn't drop as much as I thought it should.

Maybe I wasn't really such a good girl, after all. I spent way too long muttering, "Hm, isn't that funny?" (and then forgetting about it) before I finally examined the statements. And there it was—one big subtotal relentlessly going up-up-up $30-something each month, despite all my efforts to bring it down-down-down. No, it wasn't a mistake. Belatedly, I'd discovered a fine example of typical credit card policies—aka, financial flim-flam.

I'll tell you in a moment what was going on; it's something that may be happening to you right now. I'll also share some other tricks you can expect from your helpful, friendly banker.

First, though, let me take a second to explain where I'm coming from. I don't use credit cards these days, though I did for many years. I distrust big corporations, but rejoice in free enterprise. I believe the best form of "consumer protection" is generally to read the fine print, and not to blame business people or scream for new laws when our own carelessness gets us into trouble. I know that independent people like the readers of *Backwoods Home* often have to do a balancing act between stubborn self-sufficiency and using credit to help them achieve their backwoods dreams.

That said, however, the bald-faced fact is that credit card issuers, compared with nearly all other businesses, are skunks of the stinkiest order. They have less respect for their customers than carnies do for marks. Their morality is right down there with that of a hooker lifting the wallet of a drunken john.

Credit card issuers operate like pickpockets. They create a complex screen of misdirection so you won't know how neatly they've set you up to lose.

They're like the slimy character who sweet talks the girl into bed—and then doesn't respect her in the morning, because he never respected her in the first place. She was never more to him than something to...

Ahem.

In short, credit card issuers are scum. But they're attractive scum. They lure us with the prospect of "free" goods and services (after all, you only have to worry about the payment later). They encourage our lust for every gorgeous thing. They're our companions in every indulgence, every wild whim.

And sometimes they're useful. Unless you've dropped out of the world of banking and credit altogether, you probably have a credit card in your wallet. If you ever need to rent a car or a trailer, make a purchase over the Internet, get your truck repaired while stranded in a strange town, or tide your family over during a time of illness or unemployment, chances are you'll use that credit card and be glad you have it. Cards offer benefits for those who use them properly. And when you're financially desperate, that little piece of plastic can look like your best friend.

So most people won't want to avoid credit cards. But we should keep open eyes and a tight hand on our wallets, given the tactics and (lack of) ethics in the credit card industry.

292

Speaking of ethics, let's take a close look at that letter you've just received from the nice folks at the First Bank of Mordor.

"You have been pre-approved for a credit card with a rate starting as low as 2.9 percent!" You've seen this statement on countless envelopes. Let's take it apart. "You have been pre-approved." Nonsense. You have not. That's just a lie to encourage you to send back the application. (Try sending it back without your social security number on it and find out how "approved" you actually are.) Now look at the phrase "a rate starting." "Starting" is the operative word. For three, four, or five months, you may indeed pay a low interest rate on purchases you make with the card. Then whammo!—the cost of those already-purchased goodies becomes an immovable lump of lead. Suddenly, your purchases are accruing finance charges at a much, much higher annual percentage rate (APR).

Finally, we come to the famous phrase, "as low as." This phrase means that the 2.9 percent "promise" on the envelope may not actually apply to you at all—not even for the first friendly months. Read the fine print and you'll see that the actual rate you have to pay may be two, three, or more times higher than the one on the envelope. It depends on your credit history. Fine. But the really bad thing is, you won't know your rate until the card is in your hands.

Can you spell BAIT-AND-SWITCH?

"Transfer your existing credit card balances to our Titanium Card and pay just 5.9 percent interest!" Boy, this one can be tempting. But don't bite that apple. There are two tricks in this short statement. Let's say you're now paying an 11.99 percent interest rate for $1,000 worth of purchases. Cutting that rate in half sounds great. Only thing is, exactly as we saw above, a few months after you transfer that $1,000 balance, the introductory offer runs out—and suddenly your rate goes up. That's zinger number one. But you can usually discover that one easily by reading the fine print.

Zinger number two is harder. Credit cards commonly carry two separate interest rates—a low one for purchases, a much higher one (which can be double or more) for so-called "cash advances." Well, guess what? When you transferred the purchase balance from your old card, it became a cash advance balance on your shiny new card! And now instead of the 11.99 percent you were happy to get rid of, you're paying 18.99, or even 22.99 percent on those same purchases.

"Use these free 'convenience checks' and pay only 3.9 percent until March!" Every few months, your credit card company sends you "free" checks and offers some incentive to use them. Here's what they don't tell you—at least not in print that can be detected without an electron microscope: Everything you put on those checks is a cash advance. Buy a sweater? It's "cash," not a purchase. Pay your electric bill? It's "cash." Purchase a pizza? That pizza is a "cash advance," too. Once the low promotional rate runs out...zing! You pay the maximum finance charge your account can bear. You may also have to pay cash-advance fees, which can be in the vicinity of $10 per transaction. That makes for a pretty expensive pizza. And one more catch; unlike purchases, which usually have a grace period, cash advances begin accruing interest from the moment you make them.

In most cases, only someone desperately broke or ignorant would use a "convenience check." And that's exactly what the card issuer is hoping you'll be. Nice attitude, eh?

"We have updated your agreement." When you apply for a card, you're presumed to be making an agreement with the card issuer to meet specified terms. Okay. The only thing is, this "agreement" is a lot like the one you have with the IRS. The bank can change the rules any time it wants. And you can't. If you don't like the new terms, your only recourse is to cut up your card immediately, without ever using it again (that's important), and send a written notice closing the account. Nothing so one-sided deserves to be called an "agreement." But to this point, you really did agree.

Once again, though, the sheer imbalance of power isn't the worst part. Your friendly banker manipulates the fine print in ways that are designed to buffalo you. Multiple, seemingly innocuous, changes over a period of months can add up to one zinger. You have no way to connect the dots unless you're not only reading, but compiling and studying, all the related changes to the fine print. And we're talking some big zingers, too. Like a multi-step change in late-fee policies that causes your interest rate to jump from 10.99 percent to 23.99 percent when the post office loses your next payment.

And if you call the card issuer's 1-800 number to protest, the representative will blandly inform you that you "agreed" to such punishment—simply because you didn't close the account after they changed the fine print on you.

Finance-charge folly. The nominal interest rate on any loan understates the total finance charges you pay in the long run. That isn't deception. It's just mathematics, a function of compounding.

Nevertheless, the cost of running up credit cards is much higher than the lenders want us to know. Mafia accountant Nuncio "Numbers" Goldberg demonstrated that fact in his article "Four-Card Monte: How banks are charging 80% interest."* Numbers was generous enough to let me borrow both his figures and part of his title for this article. Here's Numbers' tally of a $20,000 cash balance on a credit card

---

*The article can be found at http://www.notruth.com/content/hcredit0002.htm. This is a humor site, "The World Association of Liars, Thieves, Slavers, and Murderers." But there's nothing funny about the figures—or about the other credit-card tricks that faux Mafia accountant "Numbers" Goldberg describes.

Table 1: Month 1		
	Fixed loan	**Cash advance on credit card**
Rate	10.00%	19.99%
Amount borrowed	$20,000	$20,000
Payment *Note: the loan payment is fixed by agreement; the credit-card payment is calculated at a standard 2% of the balance.*	$424.94	$400.00
Interest paid, month 1	$166.67	$332.98
Principal paid, month 1	$258.27	$67.02
Interest as a % of payment	39.20%	83.20%

Table 2: Month 58		
	Fixed loan	**Cash advance on credit card**
Rate	10.00%	19.99%
Amount borrowed	$20,000	$20,000
Payment	$424.94	$330.35
Interest paid, month 58	$10.45	$275.00
Principal paid, month 58	$414.49	$55.35
Interest as a % of payment	2.50%	83.20%

compared with a $20,000 fixed-rate loan from a bank. Table 1 shows where things stand after payment #1. But compare it to the situation at month 58, in Table 2, when the fixed loan is nearly paid off.

The fixed loan takes five years to pay off, and the interest averages 21.6 percent of your payments. The credit card cash advance takes *90.5* years to pay off and interest averages 80.3 percent of payments. Your total payback amount is...well, why bother to tally it? You're not going to live that long.

All this scarcely begins to touch on the various fees and finagles that arrive with your credit card—fees becoming steeper and finagles becoming more complex by the year.

Credit card companies claim that these ploys for sneakily squeezing money out of customers are a necessity. Ever since the dot-com bomb and 9-11 tanked the economy, they're losing their shirts. Or so they loudly wail. But they've brought the worst of their trouble on themselves. During the booming 1990s, card issuers "went bottom fishing for new customers" (as one industry watcher charmingly put it). They began aggressively promoting credit cards to folks who previously didn't qualify for them. At that time, credit cards were far and away the most profitable segment of the banking industry, and every lender wanted in. Now, losses in the so-called "sub-prime" credit card market (the "bottom fishing" market) have risen from 5 percent to nearly 20 percent. Some issuers have gone out of business and others are scrambling to stay alive.

Well, pardon us for not weeping for the poor, abused lenders. Look at the tactics described above. These companies are trolling for exactly the kind of customers they're attracting. Approach a prospect with the intent to deceive and manipulate, and you really can't be shocked—simply shocked!—if your customer turns out to be so dumb, so crooked, or so fed up with you that he doesn't pay his bills.

Yes, we can indeed "read the fine print." That's a fine idea. And it's nice to have the convenience and security of a credit card. Nevertheless, when dealing with such bounders and cads, you need what you might call "plastic explosives" to defend yourself.

For instance:

1. **Avoid credit cards if possible.** Deal in cash, or if you have a bank account, get a debit card and use that instead. See my article "Bye Bye Banking" in the January 2002 Web issue of *Backwoods Home* for more on living without banking. Of course, that's not practical for everybody or every transaction (like renting a car). So ...

2. **Get a secured credit card.** Many banks offer cards that require you to put up a deposit. To get a credit line of $1,500, you might put up $1,000, which the bank holds as security. Millions of people go this route to establish credit or rebuild damaged credit. It can also be useful if you don't like credit but want to have a card for emergency use.

3. **Get an American Express card.** Businesses treat it like a credit card, but you're required to pay the full balance each month. Thus you avoid credit blues and many credit temptations. (Just don't sign up for their extended payments option.) The downside—as you've heard in competitors' commercials—is that the American Express card isn't accepted everywhere. No...wait a minute. That's a point in its favor.

4. **Be a math whiz or make friends with one.** When you're contemplating credit, a quick glance at annual fees vs. annual percentage rates doesn't begin to tell you which card will be least painful to own. Here's an example. At the Credit Card Guide (http://www.creditcardguide.org/), you'll find a table that shows finance charges for four sample credit cards. Each card has APR of 18 percent and its holder carries an identical small balance of around $300. But the monthly finance charge ranges from $1.50 to $7.50—solely because of different ways the card issuer calculates the balance. Now think about how that affects your wallet if your balance is $3,000. Or $30,000. Visit Web sites like the Credit Card Guide and learn in serious detail the terms and terminology of credit.

5. **Be careful when you use dual-rate cards to make purchases.** If the card you use has a higher finance charge for cash advances, and if you have any remaining cash-advance balance on your statement, don't—ever, ever, never!—use that card to make purchases. Banks will pay the least profitable (for them) items down first. And meanwhile, the finance charges will keep growing—and compounding—atop the cash-advance. (This is what happened to me in the incident I described at the top of this article. I had made a single cash purchase months earlier. Until it was paid off, that lone, forgotten purchase prevented my cash-advance balance from ever going down, no matter how much I paid each month.)

6. **Make a payment every two weeks instead of once a month.** Take a look at the current minimum payment on your card. Split it in two. Instead of sending it as one payment, send half of it now and half of it two weeks from today. (Make sure both halves arrive before the due date so you don't incur late charges.) Then keep paying the same amount every two weeks, no matter how low your minimum payment drops. The math is complicated, but the effect is simple; your balance will go down as fast as possible—assuming you don't run it back up again.

7. **Call the bank's 1-800 number and ask for a rate reduction.** You can't lose. According to the consumer-rights project, The Truth About Credit, 56 percent who call come away with a reduced rate. (This may not work if you've recently been hit with punitive finance charges. In that case, they'll make you wait and sweat.)

8. **Don't use your credit card for anything your bank might consider a "quasi-cash" transaction.** These include lottery tickets and betting chips at a casino. And of course those "convenience checks" your bank keeps shoving at you. You'll be charged the cash-advance rate, even if you think you're making a purchase.

9. **Don't get too excited about cards with no annual fee.** They almost always carry higher finance rates than cards that charge a yearly fee. Usually, they'll benefit you only if you religiously pay off your entire balance every month.

10. **If you can't avoid temptation...**Call 1-888-5-OPTOUT (1-888-567-8688). Assuming you have the patience to get past the frequent busy signal, you can use this number to tell all three of the big credit-reporting agencies that you don't want solicitations from credit card companies. Also, fill out your bank's opt-out form to keep them from selling information on you to other vendors.

11. **Don't feel you need to be honorable to those who treat you dishonorably.** You may go on paying punitive rates because you don't want to ruin your credit. But don't feel you have to do it because it's the "right" thing to do. There may be honor among thieves. But there is none between credit card vendors and their marks. ∆

Ask Jackie

Chokecherries, chicken runs, keeping lard, canning potatoes, "moving out," root cellaring potatoes, fried dry pea patties, canning chicken on the bone, pressure canning on electric stoves, canning milk, short season planting tips, canning eggplant, mush, & tomato preserves

Jackie Clay

Is there anything suitable to substitute for chokecherries? They are hard to find commercially, but I would like to try some recipes. What would you recommend for a substitute?

Kay Olson
Mankato, MN

There really isn't a decent substitute for chokecherries in many recipes. A neat idea would be to go up north on a weekend in the fall, and pick some wild ones. We used to live up out of Sturgeon Lake, and the wooded back roads all over the north are good places to find these glistening black beauties.

Jackie

I keep my four laying hens in a fenced in area. It is about a 100-square foot-space. Besides regular raking and general cleaning, is there more I should do to maintain their run, considering the amount of time they spend there?

Greg Scully
scully4@mtaonline.net

Most chickens don't even get so large a run, or any cleaning or raking of their run, so yours are way ahead of most. However, I like to have more than one yard so that they can be alternated. Then you can change the hens to a new yard, till, and plant the old run. This works fertilizer from the chickens into the soil and prevents intestinal parasites from becoming a problem in your birds. It also loosens the chicken-tromped soil. After tilling an old yard, you can either plant it with a chicken crop, such as rye grass or rape (canola) for them to harvest later on, or you can use it as a garden spot for yourself as that chicken manure is great stuff for corn, cabbage family crops, and beans. I wouldn't plant potatoes (overly fertile soil causes scab), tomatoes, or peppers (too much fertilizer will cause them to run to huge plants, but little fruit).

Jackie

I really enjoy your articles and am awed by the amount of canning you manage to do. I'm interested in starting to use lard more and get rid of hydrogenated and other processed oils and have been reading about the benefits of using lard. I would like to render my own and am mainly wondering about storing it.

I've read from many sources that it keeps well in a cool dark place, but what I need to know are some better specifics, like about how long will it keep and how cool? And last, how will I know it's gone bad? Smell? Color?

Also, If you happen to have any expertise on rendering lard, I'd love to know some tips on it.

Mary
mary@jsteng.com

When the bulk of my children (between five and eight kiddos) were home, we always butchered two hogs in the fall to help provide not only our meat, but also lard for cooking. To us, lard is more flavorful than shortening and gives the food a special taste that is lacking in food cooked with oil or shortening. I simply kept my lard in covered two-gallon crocks in the basement (cool and dark). When I needed to fill my smaller two-quart crock in the kitchen, I just went down and scooped out enough from the larger crocks. This lard kept very well until we butchered again in the late fall. (Of course, very little was left.)

As the family grew older and my children left home to begin their own families, we butchered only one hog and the lard kept much longer, as I cooked and baked less, of course. So to keep the lard fresh longer, I filled sterile wide-mouthed canning jars with hot lard, right from rendering, then made absolutely sure the rim of the jar was clean and free of grease, placed a hot, previously boiled lid on the jars, screwed the ring down firmly tight and set the jars aside on a dry towel until they were cool.

In this way, the jars are sealed and the lard will keep fresh much longer. In unsealed crocks, "old" lard will eventually become rancid. You can tell by the smell. It won't kill you, but no one will want to eat your cooking.

How cool? Fifty or fifty-five is fine. Cooler is better. The cooler you keep the lard, the longer it usually lasts. I've had two-year-old lard in crocks in the basement that was fine. In sealed canning jars, it seems to keep nearly forever.

If you have a freezer, you can also freeze lard with good results. Just be sure it is in airtight containers so it will not "freezer burn," which also imparts a nasty taste.

Lard is easy to render. Just cut up chunks of pure pork fat; no meat, bone, or skin. Place them in a heavy pot and turn the heat on low. Plan on staying near the pot. Hot lard is dangerous, especially to children and pets who might get curious. As the fat melts, stir it occasionally, then skim off any browning bits. These are cracklin's and are a tasty treat. We like them crumbled up in corn bread. They are very rich, so you won't want to gobble up a handful.

I've rendered smaller batches of lard by simply placing chunks of fat in my turkey roaster, and putting it in the oven at 225° F until the lard is melted. Skim off the cracklin's and you're ready to strain your lard.

When the fat is all melted and the cracklin's taken off, strain the liquid lard through several thicknesses of cheesecloth into the crock or jar you will be storing the lard in. For smaller batches, you may carefully pour the hot liquid lard; dip the lard for larger batches, keeping the pot very warm. Partially solidified lard will not strain well. You want to get out all the small brown bits on the bottom of the kettle for the best appearance and flavor.

Jackie

We can't wait to try your home canned bologna. But it would be nice to have a recipe for canned potatoes to go with it.

**Lanney and Laurie Lavoy
Bredenbury, Saskatchewan**

I can potatoes almost every year. Mostly because a few jars of them come in so handy, from time to time. I can whole, smaller potatoes and those little guys that I just can't throw away at harvest time. The whole tiny potatoes, the size of your thumb, I can scrubbed, with the skins on. When you get ready to use them, you can either use them with the skins on, or simply squeeze them like a grape, and they will pop out of them, leaving a perfect whole potato.

Potatoes are very simple to can. But I've learned to can them in pint jars, for the reason that if you can them in quart or larger (potatoes only, not stews or mixes), the potatoes will become mushy. They get overcooked, due to the longer time you must process quart or larger jars. Pints can be processed quicker, thus are cooked for a shorter time.

Here's how to can potatoes: Wash and sort potatoes, rejecting any with rotten spots, damage, or scars. Peel larger potatoes, cutting into convenient chunks. I leave the smaller ones whole, with the skins on, but scrub them well. Boil for 10 minutes, then pack hot in pint canning jars. Wide mouth works best. Fill to within one inch of the top, then pour boiling water in to fill within 1 inch of top of jar. Add ½ tsp. salt, if desired. Remove any air bubbles by running a wooden spoon handle down next to the potatoes. Wipe the rim of the jar clean, then place a hot, previously boiled lid on jar and screw down the lid firmly tight. Process pints 35 minutes in a pressure canner. You **must** use a pressure canner when canning any vegetables or meat.

These potatoes may be used later in potato salad, in stews, soups, potato casseroles, etc. And, because they are already cooked, they make handy, speedy, satisfying meals.

Jackie

I have 40 acres paid for (Yes!) that is 40 miles east of where I work. The problem is, I am self-employed, dependent on people (they are my patients) and even though I am further south than NW MT, it does get snowy/icy here.

There is a small town between the land and where I work and I have thought about buying a fixer-upper house there as it would be possible to get to work in 30 minutes from there, and I could be out at the land in about 20 minutes on the weekends for building some kind of alternative home.

Of course I am single. Please give me some advice and or a pep talk! I have a very bad neck, with 3 bulging discs, so heavy lifting is out of the question for me. Am able to do almost anything else if I don't overdo it.

*Julia
drjrader@nwaisp.com*

Having 40 acres, debt free is a major accomplishment. Congratulations! I can't advise you on whether or not to buy the half-way fixer-upper house. I can only tell you what I would do under the same situation. Personally, I would get out on the land as soon as you can. I realize that a 50 minute or so commute is a long one. Many of my friends here drive as far each day to work. And, as you said, roads do get icy and snow covered at times. If you bought the house, you would be saving 20 minutes each day in driving. But your trade off would be putting your extra cash and energy into the new house, not your homestead.

It's hard during the winter, as you will leave for work in the dark and get home in the dark for several weeks. But there are many more months where you will have several hours after you get home each day to work (or just plan and *enjoy*) your new homestead.

What can you do in only an hour? Well, let's take a look at my day, today. In an hour's time... and I did not kill myself, either... I planted a young cherry tree, changed the nest box straw in the chicken coop, planted a pound of onion sets and four rows of peas while watching a gorgeous wild turkey tom strutting down in our valley. I saw the first tiny sprouts of new grass and alfalfa prickle the worked earth of our renovated horse pasture, heard two bluebirds singing, and smelled the fresh garden earth, newly mowed lawn, and apple blossoms. All in one hour. Now multiply that by five days a week, add the weekend, and rest on the Sabbath. I think it comes out to a whole lot, don't you?

And in four hours, you could frame in a chicken coop or your first cabin's one wall.

At "over the half-century mark," I am well acquainted with having to work around bad body parts. But with practice, you develop ways to do just that. There's no way I can lift a 400-pound log up on a wall. (Thank God for tractors with front end loaders or a good quiet team of horses!) I can't carry a heavy fruit tree, complete with a root ball that weighs 50 pounds, up and down hill to where I want to plant it. So I tip the garden cart down on its nose, slide the root ball into it, then tip it upright. And off we go. You get the picture.

And for that longer drive, get some good tapes and CDs. You might even take classes in gardening, cheese making, or yoga. And *dream* while you drive. You're on the way. The best of luck.

Jackie

I am planning on having a great crop of potatoes this year from my garden. I don't have a root cellar or basement. I do have some land and can dig a hole if needed. What is the best way to store potatoes??? I have even thought of putting them in a 55-gallon drum and placing it in a hole. Not sure. Any help?

**Dan Dickerson
Water Valley, Mississippi**

There are a lot of ways to successfully store potatoes without a root cellar. I home can many of mine, a few pecks at a time. But you sure can't make French fries out of canned potatoes, so you will want to store them as long as you can. Yes, you can store potatoes and other root crops in a 55-gallon drum, although a wood barrel would be better, as it wouldn't be as apt to sweat through condensation.

When your potatoes have been dug and sorted (be very careful to reject any damaged ones, as they'll rot), spread them in a dry, shaded area to cure for at least 24 hours. **Do not** wash them. Dig a hole large enough that three-quarters of the barrel will be buried in the ground, on an angle (which allows access to the potatoes without standing on your head). Gently fill the barrel with the dry, cured potatoes, not just dumping them in, which may bruise them. Don't fill the barrel any more full than ground level. Punch at least two half inch holes on the sides of the barrel for ventilation.

Now stuff the rest of the barrel with clean, very dry straw or even crumpled newspaper. This acts as insulation and helps absorb small traces of condensation before it causes rotting problems.

Close the barrel and heap dirt over the entire excavation site to act as insulation. Then stack bales of straw over the whole works.

Your potatoes should keep well until late spring. Only open the barrel on warmish sunny days. Potatoes are very sensitive to cold, quickly chilling, turning black spotted, and rotting.

This method will work in most climates, except where there is extreme winter cold for prolonged periods of time.

Jackie

I was reading back issues of BHM and came across an article about long-term food storage (Jan/Feb 2002). In the article, you mentioned you made something called "fried dry pea patties." These sound interesting. How do you make them?

Also, I would like to know if I could can chicken with bones (like drumsticks, thighs, etc.) I usually freeze it, but recently we suffered a power outage and I had to throw out a lot of food from my freezer. P.S. I am writing by candlelight. Our power is still off! This makes day #4.

**Sarah Funk
Looneyville, WV**

You are experiencing one of the "emergencies" that most of us, sooner or later, experience. Maybe it's not as dramatic as terrorists and smallpox, but to you, when it's happening, it's pretty much an emergency. Which is just why I've preached preparedness for a long, long time.

I too, lost a good part of my huge freezer-full due to a lengthy power outage, which is why I don't have one now. I can or dry most everything including chicken and other poultry, complete with the bones. This is really a time saver when we are butchering chickens, as it allows me to can many more birds in a day than I could possibly do if I deboned them all. And, as a bonus, you can debone the canned chicken at a later date, saving the bones to boil up with some of the lesser parts, such as the backs, wings, and skin, to make a dynamite soup stock with the same jars of chicken that your stir fried dish or barbecued chicken came from.

The fried dry pea patties are unusual, and I got the recipe from my mother, who got it from her mother, etc., etc. It tastes good, too, and gives you just another option for using some of those foods in your long-term storage pantry. Here it is:

Fried dry pea patties:

> 2 cups cooked split peas (just tender, not mushy), mashed
> 1 chopped onion or 1 Tbsp. dehydrated onion flakes
> a little dehydrated parsley
> 2 beaten egg yolks
> 2 Tbsp. cream or heavy mixture of dehydrated milk & water
> salt, pepper, and spices, to taste

Shape into patties. Dip in flour. Chill one hour or more. Fry slowly in lard. Serve with catsup or barbecue sauce.

Here's another "different" pea recipe you might like. You may use fresh garden peas or dehydrated, rehydrated peas.

Pea patties: Line muffin tins with pie pastry and bake. Make cream sauce of 2 Tbsp. butter, melted with 2 Tbsp. flour stirred in well. Add 1 cup milk, salt, and pepper to taste. Cook 1 to 1½ cup of peas gently until just tender. Add to the cream sauce. Put a spoonful in each baked shell. You may also grate a bit of cheese on top. Serve hot.

Jackie

I've been canning for years, usually with a boiling water bath canner, occasionally with a pressure canner. Lately, because of the shape our country is in and because of your catching enthusiasm for canning, I have been doing a lot of pressure canning. My canner is about 6-years-old but hasn't been used much until recently. It is a weighted gauge type and looks like new. My problem is that I cook on an electric stove. We don't have natural gas where I live in Maine. We can't afford a new gas stove with the propane hook up, so I am stuck with electricity. It is VERY difficult to keep steady pressure with an electric stove. While I rarely let the pressure drop below 10 pounds, it often fluctuates from 10 pounds to higher, and then back down to 10 again, no matter now careful I am. Because of this, I often lose liquid from my jars, and a lot of that liquid is grease, since I'm canning many meat dishes. The jars all seal fine. But I worry about their contents. I've been told as long as they're sealed, the contents are fine even if they are unattractive. I wonder though if the seals will last. I just canned 16 jars of barbecued ribs and I'd hate to lose them six months down the line. Do you have problems with jars losing liquids? Do you obtain a seal if they do, and how long does your seal last?

Melanie
RVNDGN@aol.com

I sympathize with your problems regulating your electric stove for canning. When I first started canning, it was on an electric stove, and I too had trouble. I solved it by switching to using my wood burning kitchen range. But for you, perhaps an easier fix would be to buy a two-burner propane stove. These are available at most discount tool catalogs, such as Harbor Freight and Northern Tool, or your local propane dealer. They cost about $20. (They are used for "camping" and are not a typical kitchen stove, only a basic countertop, two burner unit.) Then you will just need a 40-pound or even a 100-pound propane tank with a hose and regulator and you are in business. Many propane companies simply sell you the propane and furnish the bottle at no cost. The hose and regulator are very inexpensive.

With this set-up you can home can, regulating the heat with precision. Voilà, no more boiled out liquids! And you can cook if there's a power outage, as well.

Yes, I've had liquids boiled partially out of jars I've canned. Usually when I get interrupted by something while I can and the pressure rises, then falls, as I discover the problem. It is unattractive, but I've never had any problem with the seals failing. As with all home canned food, always examine each jar before opening it to be sure the seal is tight; look at the food and smell it after opening it. Just to be sure.

Jackie

My son has been reading BHM for about a year and the very first thing he does is read "ASK JACKIE". He thinks you have all the answers to everything. So he wanted me to ask you if goats' milk can be canned at home in glass jars. We are wanting to buy some dairy goats and wanted to know if we could can the excess milk to be used at a later date.

Nancy Lynch
Nancy_LynchSurveyingCo@msn.com

Boy, do I *wish* I had all the answers. But those I do manage to have, I'll happily share. You're off on a great adventure and lots of fun with your new dairy goats. They're so versatile and easy to handle and house. Yes, you can home can milk (goat or cow), and I have done it with success. But you have to know that the end result does not taste like fresh milk, rather more like condensed milk. For that reason, it is really better to have your "girls" freshen, or give birth and come into milk, at different times of the year. This ensures that you have a constant supply of fresh milk.

The process of home canning milk is simple. You can either pressure can it by simply filling the clean jars to within ½ inch of the top with freshly strained milk. Wipe the jar rims clean and dry with a clean cloth. Place hot, previously boiled lids on the jars and tighten down the ring firmly-tight. Process in a pressure canner at 15 pounds for 10 minutes. Start timing only when the canner reaches 15 pounds.

Pressure canned milk will be a tanish-cream color and taste "cooked," but will be fine in all cooking or mixing with chocolate milk mix.

To water bath can your milk, fill jars in the same manner. Then place in water bath canner, on rack, and cover with hot water to an inch over the jars. Bring canner to a boil. Begin timing once canner reaches a full boil, and boil for one hour. Remove jars and place on dry folded towel to cool out of drafts for 24 hours.

This milk will be a bit creamy looking and also taste "cooked," but it will be fine in all cooking or flavored drinks, such as chocolate or malted milk.

Remember that on the homestead there is no such thing as "excess" milk. Milk is only the beginning. There is ice cream, yogurts, cottage cheese, simple soft cheeses, hard cheeses, and cream cheese. Then there are the pig and calf you can raise on goat milk to butcher later for very tasty meat. And the wethers from your does that you can raise for the best chevron ever. Not to mention goat milk soap. How much fun you folks have in store for you. I'm excited, as we have a doe, due to kid in two weeks, and I can't wait to get started.

Jackie

I read in the article (A Comfortable Base Camp) that you had done about the same thing I did and sold everything before moving to Montana. Everyone I have talked to goes on about the short growing season here. From the articles you do, I don't see you having any trouble with the growing season. What is your growing season like?

What part of Montana do you live in? Do you have any more tips for someone looking to go completely off grid and start with a piece of land with a creek running through it?
**Greg
Northwest Montana**

I have to smile when you say that everyone goes on about the short growing season. For that's what everyone did, everywhere we have moved (Minnesota, northern New Mexico at 6,000 feet, and, of course, Montana). "You can't grow anything here! We tried and everything froze" is about the gist of the comments. My polite reply? "Ha! Wait and see." And those same folks came out and gorged themselves on our fresh peas, corn on the cob, and tomatoes.

No, we don't just pick a good spot. We have learned to work with the climate, not try to fight it. When you fight Nature, you cannot win.

Our homestead is in west central Montana, about halfway between Helena and Great Falls, up in the Big Belt Mountains, at 4,000 feet, above the tiny fishing town of Craig and the Missouri River. Never heard of the area? That's why we're here; it's not a popular tourist area and we love it.

Yes we have a "short" growing season...compared to Mississippi or California. But we successfully gardened at 7,400 feet (above the Continental Divide in Montana) with a growing season of less than 75 days. And we had snow every month of the year. But we had a good garden.

Some tips for short growing season are use Wallo'Waters to gain at least a month, possibly twice that, in growing season. I recently did an article for *BHM* on these very effective season extenders. They are basically a circle of plastic tubes which you fill with water and place around the plant (or seeds, such as melons). The Walls protect the tender plants down to 16°. I've had tomatoes in Wallo'Waters when we received a foot of snow and temperatures much below freezing for two days. The tomatoes not only lived, but thrived and grew. It is April 27th, and I have had 20 tomato plants in the ground with these beauties for nearly two weeks. I can't plant unprotected tomatoes until the second week in June.

I also use mulch and clear plastic, where needed, for plant protection and growth booster.

By planting only short season, productive varieties (not just the varieties available in local stores), along with the season extenders, keeping the soil loose, fertile, and happy we manage to keep our pantry full, eat well, and enjoy our garden. No matter where we live.

Tips? Briefly: avoid debt, work hard, but enjoy life, research each project before you start it, go slowly enough to enjoy yourself, live simply, learn from your mistakes (you will make them, as we all have), and give thanks for your successes, no matter how small they seem at the time. Keep reading *BHM*, the anthologies, and back issues for help with your new projects. Good luck and happiness.

Jackie

Can eggplant be home canned? Does it need to be blanched or anything? All the canning references I have are for freezing, and I don't have a lot of freezer space.
**Jim Strokotter
Monroe, MI**

Yes, Jim, you can home can eggplant, but I'm not sure you'll like the results. Basically, it is canned like you would summer squash or zucchini. And the results are about the same: not so hot. It tends to get mushy and flavorless. One way to beat that is to can slices of eggplant in spaghetti sauce. It still is a bit soft, but much more flavorful than otherwise. Remember, when canning any combination, such as meat and vegetables, or tomato sauce and squash, to process for the longest time for any ingredient, and also if any ingredient, such as meat or a vegetable, must be pressure canned, you must pressure can the combination.

With the tomato sauce/eggplant mixture, heat tomato sauce to boiling, add slices of eggplant and simmer five minutes. Dip out eggplant into clean widemouth jars. Fill to within one inch of the top, adding tomato sauce to cover to within one inch of the top. Adjust lids. Process in pressure canner for 30 minutes at 10 lbs. pressure (adjusting pressure for altitude, if necessary. See your canning manual).

Jackie

I am looking for a recipe for making tomato preserves. I used to make them all the time and had a recipe from the Sure-Jell box, but I don't find it there anymore.

Sel Corley
sjc34@totalzone.com

Yes, I do have several recipes for making tomato preserves, all slightly different. But here's a basic one. In the others, the spice amounts seem to differ, not much else.

Tomato preserves:

- 1½ qts. small, firm ripe, peeled tomatoes
- 4 cups sugar
- ¾ cup water
- 1 thumb-sized piece ginger root
- 1 Tbsp. mixed pickling spices
- 1 cup thinly sliced lemon without the seeds

Add the water, sugar, lemon, and spices (tied in a spice bag) to a large sauce pan. Simmer 15 minutes. Add the tomatoes and cook gently until the tomatoes become transparent. Stir often to keep from sticking. Cover and let stand overnight in cool place. Remove the spice bag. Drain, reserving the syrup. Set the tomatoes and lemon aside. Boil the syrup until hot and it starts to thicken. Add the tomatoes and lemon back in. Boil one minute. Pour hot into hot half pint jars, leaving a quarter inch of head space. Wipe jar rims clean. Place hot, previously boiled lid on jar and screw down ring firmly tight. Process 20 minutes in boiling water bath.

Jackie

Back in the 1920s when I was a kid, we used to have something called graham mush for breakfast occasionally. It was made from ground wheat which was sold in bulk in five-pound amounts and packaged in a plain brown paper sack which was sealed shut. This mush was highly flavorful and delicious. When I purchased my grain grinder to grind wheat for bread, I anticipated making mush also with some of the meal but was disappointed to find it absolutely tasteless!

Thinking that perhaps the trouble was caused by using hard wheat, I bought a few pounds of soft wheat, but the results were the same. Help!

Genevieve Gray
South Elgin, IL

Graham mush is one of the easiest and most basic uses for home ground wheat. (Graham simply means "coarse" flour.) Mix 1 cup of graham flour with ½ tsp. salt and mix with enough cold water to make a paste. Then slowly add to 2 cups rapidly boiling water, stirring constantly. This is most easily done in the top of a double boiler to prevent scorching. Cook until it tastes done, perhaps 20 minutes or more. Place hot into a bowl, adding cream and sugar or perhaps fruit. It is really good, much better than Cream of Whatchamacallit! Perhaps you forgot to add salt or to cook it enough to bring out the flavor? Or did you add sweetening? It is pretty bland, without cream and sugar. Better luck next grinding.

Jackie

The last word

Gun control, race, and rotten politicians

Is gun control really about guns? Sounds like an odd question on the surface, but it's really right on target. In fact, the answer is: No, gun control is not really about guns. It's about failed social programs, the destruction of the black family in America, and the rotten politicians who are responsible.

The "welfare handouts in exchange for votes" schemes began in the 1930s with Roosevelt's New Deal, and they coincided with the beginning of the dissolution of the American black family. Although discriminated against back then, blacks had about the same percentage of intact family units as white families, and as a race black crime was about the same as white crime. Today, thanks to decades of accelerating "welfare for votes" social engineering, the black family unit in the ghetto is history (welfare checks have replaced fathers) and the black crime rate is manyfold that of whites.

The welfare checks not only destroyed the black head of household in the ghetto, but also the black family's self respect and its ability to be self-reliant. As it does with most poor, dependent, fractured families, it lead to an increase in crime. But rather than admit their horrible mistakes in making people dependent on handouts rather than on themselves, the politicians have claimed that guns are responsible for the high crime rate in America.

The test is put to that lie by simply subtracting out minority crime statistics in America, and America is left with a crime rate that is lower than most Western European countries. This despite the fact that gun ownership among American whites is the highest in the world. The low rate of violent crimes is not just a white phenomenon either; gun crimes among middle and upper-class blacks is comparable to that of whites.

But politicians don't want to admit they have cynically destroyed a race to take advantage of their votes, so they (and you know the politicians I'm talking about) perpetuate the myth that guns cause crime.

The original intent of the social welfare programs *may* have been good: create a huge welfare state that would save the poor, particularly the black poor, but I believe the real motive was to buy a huge block of votes for liberals—read that as the Democratic Party. The latter half of the plan worked fine: most poor now vote Democratic, and 95 percent of blacks do. But, as many predicted, the welfare state brought ruin to the very people it was supposed to benefit. It resulted in:
- welfare dependency that now spans generations
- the dissolution of the family
- skyrocketing crime

Rather than admit their mistake, politicians set out to make it taboo to point out that this nation's bloated violent crime rate has become mostly an ethnic phenomenon. Rather than questioning their failed social programs they have chosen to blame guns. Their new mantra became, "If the guns go away, the social programs will succeed." Never mind that the cities that have the most restrictive gun control have the highest crime rates, and that states that have loosened the requirements for concealed carry permits have seen a subsequent drop in their own crime rates.

In the meantime, the liberal media distorts the issue. If a gang of black youths do a driveby shooting in L.A. and kill several children, it's treated as local news, but if a white high schooler shoots a fellow student in Nebraska, Iowa, or New Hampshire, it becomes national news. Why? Because the mainstream media (which is overwhelmingly liberal and anti-gun) seizes on the unusual to promote the lie that guns cause crime.

But the truth is that black youths kill more other blacks in one year than whites killed by lynching in the South in the 20 years when lynching was most common, from 1920 to 1940. After Columbine one black mother asked what all the fuss was about, saying these things happen everyday with black kids. Speaking before blacks, Rev. Jessie Jackson once said that when he's walking alone in a city and hears footsteps coming up behind him, he hopes that, when he turns around, he'll find a gang of white kids rather than a gang of black kids.

Here's the truth: Guns don't cause crime, and poverty doesn't cause crime. But the nanny state with its destruction of the individual and the family does because this skyrocketing crime all began with the welfare state and the destruction of poor black families.

Quite simply, our troublesome crime rate is driven by destructive social policies that are now kept in place to buy votes, and gun control is an attempt to deflect criticism from these liberal failures and to pretend the cause of all these failures is an inanimate object—the gun. In truth, liberals don't really care about guns except as a scapegoat. I wouldn't be surprised if they really don't even want guns to go away because as long as they're around they can blame the inanimate object and remove the focus from the real cause.

For all of his faults, Louis Farrakhan sees the truth behind the dependency of blacks on white liberals. His message: Turn your backs on them, and go home and take control of your families and neighborhoods. What could be scarier to a white liberal, for whom the black vote has become like a narcotic, than for blacks to discover they should become as self-reliant as most of their white neighbors? Δ

— **John Silveira**

Nov/Dec 2003
No 84
$4.95 US
$6.50 CAN

Backwoods Home magazine

practical ideas for self-reliant living

Small town America

Making jelly
Irreverent jokes
Treating snake bite
Quick woolen mittens
Wild animal neighbors
Portable solar charger
Homemade pumpkin pie
Making money with birds

www.backwoodshome.com

My view

Animal rights loonies save the chickens but ruin the County Fair

We had our County Fair between issues.

It was a small Fair with just a few thousand in attendance, but no one in our town of 1500 would miss it for the world. There's the parade into the fairgrounds with pretty cowgirls on horses, fire engines sounding their bells and sirens, local businesses in hokey homemade floats, and all sorts of candy thrown to the children lining the one-mile route through town.

Then there's the Fair itself with its homegrown bands, immaculately groomed goats and sheep, and mouth watering blue ribbon pies. And, of course, there's midway, with its "characters" heralding the local children onto fantastic rides that come to this town only once a year. But the most popular part of our Fair is rodeo, not just because it has the real life drama of cowboy battling gravity as he rides a bronk or bull, but because at the end of rodeo comes the event that sums up the sheer delight of a small country Fair—*Barnyard Scramble*!

After the last bull has been ridden and the scores given out, there is a long pause before the gravel-voiced announcer suddenly bellows:

"Here it is folks, the event we've all been waiting for! Baaarnyaaaard Scraaaamble!!!"

Anticipating the announcement, dozens of children and their Moms have already made their way down the grandstand and are crowded together at a big gate at one end of the arena.

In *Barnyard Scramble*, the entire rodeo arena is used to free all manner of animals, from chickens and rabbits to goats and sheep, so that first the young kids (up to age 6), then the older kids (12 & under), can chase after them and catch them. They get to keep what they catch. All the animals have been donated by local folk.

It's the real young kids that cause much of the excitement. When they are released into the arena, the cameras flash and the crowd roars with laughter as they try to catch chickens and ducks and rabbits. Mom (Dads usually stays in the stands) often has to help her youngest catch a chicken, as these birds are real tricky runners. But in the end most of the youngsters catch something.

During the second wave, the older kids run and dive and roll around in the dirt as they try to corral everything from chickens to sheep. A fast sheep is not that easy to catch, especially when you can only use your bare hands. It is really fun to watch, and, according to my three young boys, even more fun to take part in.

Barnyard Scramble is one of those events that sets apart a small country Fair from a bigger city Fair.

But this year at the end of rodeo, the much anticipated announcement about *Barnyard Scramble* did not occur. The event our kids had waited all year for had been cancelled. Why? Animal rights activists in our town had simply gone to the Fair Board and convinced them that *Barnyard Scramble* constituted "cruelty to animals." No public debate, no sampling the opinion of the community, no testing of this "cruelty" hypothesis to see if it was true—just cancellation of *Barnyard Scramble*. Most Fairgoers learned of the cancellation only after they got to the Fair.

My neighbor, who is the father of two young children, summed up the general feeling in our community: *"Barnyard Scramble wasn't hurtin nuthin. Pretty soon they'll make it so the kids can't have any fun."*

It was another solid victory for the animal rights loonies, and another loss to a small community. I suppose this victory will be repeated again and again throughout America in a self righteous effort to protect chickens and other innocent animals throughout the land.

What a shame! We are becoming a nation of sheep as animal rights tyrants and other fringe groups among us tell us how to live. I expect little protest in our community. This little writeup may be all there is. More and more, people are just accepting these arbitrary decisions forced on us by self-proclaimed do-gooders who claim to be speaking for defenseless animals. There's no science behind their claims, no give and take argument about what's best for both animals and the community. A disgruntled, sourpussed organized fringe group just puts up a fuss, and a community—at least the Fair Board that's supposed to speak for the community—caves in.

I wonder if they'll cancel midway next year because some group will claim our children are somehow being exploited by the "characters" who run the rides. Got to protect the children, you know, no matter how miserable you make them. Perhaps they'll forbid all Fair food entries because that blue ribbon apple pie *might* get cooked by someone who doesn't wash their hands thoroughly. Eating poison pie is no laughing matter, after all. Rodeo is a no brainer. We had a young cowboy ambulanced out of the arena this year. He was okay, this time, but maybe next time he'll end up dead. Better cancel the event now while he's still alive.

You know what I think. I think we should round up all the do-gooder loonies who insist on telling us how to live our lives and put them in a cage. Let them out only on Halloween when their once-a-year expression of their ideas will fit in nicely with all the other scary, crazy stuff, then put them back in their cage for another year so we can get on with our normal lives.

Of course, I delude myself. We can't do that. These loonies have rights. I just wish the rest of us would start sticking up for ours.

— *Dave Duffy*

Your wild neighbors

By Jackie Clay

Photo by Dave Thompson

One of the definite bonuses of living in the backwoods is having only wildlife for neighbors. Here at our Montana mountain homestead, we see more wild animals than people, and we really like it that way. We've gotten so used to the comings and goings of our wild neighbors that I sometimes forget that others are not so familiar with the wildlife in the woods and meadows around their homes. Let me introduce you to some of your neighbors.

Bears

There are only a few areas throughout the United States that do not have bears living in the backwoods. Nearly all of these bears are **black bears** (even though many are not black at all). The "typical" black bear is a little bigger than a Newfoundland dog. Adults weigh between 250 and 500 lbs., with some a bit smaller, and some fat, older males heavier. At a distance, they can be told by their round rump, which is higher than their shoulders when walking on all fours. The face profile is a bit Roman nosed or straight. The fur is a glistening black, with an occasional white marking on the chest or throat. Often the coloring around the muzzle and eyes is a rusty brown.

But black bears, especially in the west, are frequently brown, cinnamon, or even blondish. I saw a beautiful bear in our yard several years ago that was a shining reddish gold, like a red-haired girl. It was absolutely stunning in the morning sun. So gorgeous that I grabbed my camera and chased after it for half an hour in my underwear. In coastal British Columbia another unique coloration of the black bear occurs: a white black bear.

It is this color variation that sometimes gets the black bear into trouble in areas where the grizzly bear also roams. I've had dozens of people tell me that a grizzly was in their yard or spotted down the road. But on checking out the tracks, it's a "brown" blackie 99% of the time. In years past, the other-than-black color phase was called a "Cinnamon Bear," as if it was another species. But now it is commonly known that a cinnamon colored bear is just a rust-colored black bear.

Tracks and signs. As bears are seldom seen during the daylight hours, you will more often see bear signs than a bear. Bear scat looks like a large dog pile, often a very large dog pile. In the spring there will be much greenish black coloring, as the bears

305

will be eating tender new growth. During the summer, you will see more traces of deer hair (bears often scavenge dead animals), berry seeds, and vegetation. In the autumn, bear scat is usually full of wild plum and chokecherry pits. Here, during chokecherry season, you'll all of a sudden see great black cow plops in the road. On closer inspection, they are bear plops, full of chokecherry pits.

You'll know a bear is in the neighborhood when wild apple, cherry, chokecherry, and hazelnut bushes are broken and their fruit harvested enmasse, often overnight. Or when your garbage can has been neatly opened and the contents strewn about on the lawn. Or when the birdfeeders have been emptied and rummaged through.

The tracks of a big adult are a little larger than the average human hand. The front paw shows a pad, five toes and claw marks quite close to the toes. The back foot leaves a nearly human foot shaped track with claws, again, close to the toe prints.

Considerations for the homesteader. The black bear is usually quite shy around humans. But there are a couple of exceptions. A female with cubs is very protective. Those cubs are adorable, but NEVER try to get close for a photograph or, worse yet, to "catch" a cub. Mama will object strenuously. People have been mauled and even killed by protective females.

Black bears can become a nusiance around the homestead if you've left any type of food about. This is especially bad if you're in the camping mode while building a new home. They've learned, in many areas, that humans mean food sources and can come snooping around with their very good sense of smell. And they love garbage, livestock and pet food, beer, soda, hummingbird food (sugar water), butchering scraps, and honey—fresh from the bee hives. But

Black bear

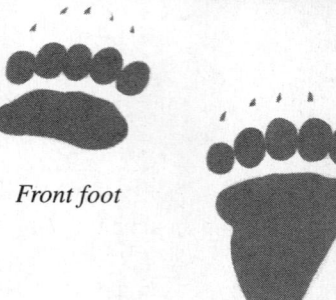

Grizzly bear prints

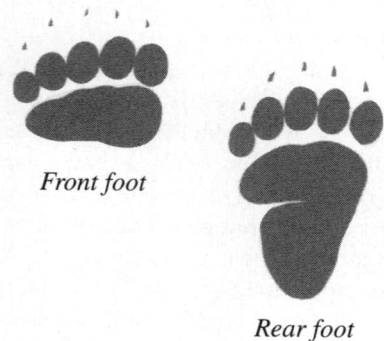

Black bear prints

Grizzly bear

the good news is that if you keep a very clean camp, leaving nothing out to attract bruin, he'll give the area a quick sniff and pad away for better pickings.

On occasion, a blackie will prey on livestock, usually small, young animals such as tethered goats or newborn calves lying far from their mother. For this reason, it's always a good idea to have your livestock in a barn or otherwise close to home at night.

Although a black bear has occasionally looked upon man as prey, the truth is that blackies are not lurking in the woods, ready to pounce on you. I've lived around them for most of my life, and have never had the remotest bit of "bear trouble."

The **grizzly bear** is neighbor to a few homesteaders, living primarily in northwestern Wyoming, scattered

The Fourteenth Year

Mountain lion

mountain areas throughout western Montana, western Canada, and in Alaska.

The grizzly is usually larger than the black bear, although there can be some confusion here, as a large black bear weighing 400 lbs. is bigger than a small female grizzly weighing only 250 lbs. The body profile is definitely different. A grizzly's rump is usually at or lower than the shoulder, which is humped. The face is dished, making the nose appear higher. There is also a shaggy appearance to the fur about the face and neck. The grizzly can be many colors, but never shiny black.

Being more of a predator than the blackie, the grizzly supplements its grass, root, seed, and fruit diet with fish, deer, elk, and moose—often the young of the larger prey. But, like the black bear, it also loves carrion, garbage, and human food.

The chances of ever seeing a grizzly in the wild in the lower 48 states are very remote. We run the remote woods and mountains a lot, and have only seen a small number "in person." But it's a good idea to keep this fellow in mind when hiking, camping, and living in the wilds, as he (or she) is more aggressive than the black bear, and has the equipment to do quite a bit of damage to a foolish human.

Never approach a grizzly with young (even large young; they're still her babies) or when it is near a food source, such as a carcass or garbage can. Nor should you surprise a bear, especially in dense brush or at close quarters. As with the blackie, keep all food sources out of camp and unavailable to the bear. This includes feed, coolers, drinks, and garbage. And never put out bait to attract bears to your area. As the old saying goes, "A fed bear is a dead bear," meaning that bears that learn that humans provide food become problem bears and must be shot.

Tracks and signs. The grizzly leaves a distinct track because of the length of its claws, which are usually two or more inches longer than those of a black bear. These sharp "fingers" show as dots well away from the pad in the tracks. A black bear's claws are little longer than a big dog, and the indentations show quite close to the pad marks. While there can be quite a difference in the size of the individual bears, most adult grizzly tracks are quite a bit larger than those of black bears. And because of the sheer size and weight of an adult grizzly, often only the heel and front pad show in a hind paw print.

The scat is similar to that of a black bear, but usually larger and containing more animal hair.

While the grizzly can be an aggressive predator, there is little to fear living in grizzly country if one takes the normal "bear precautions" mentioned above.

Remember that no matter what you see in the movies, a grizzly is *not*

Front foot

Rear foot

Mountain lion prints

Mountain lion

307

likely to peer in your window at night or crash down your door in an effort to gobble up your family. In reality you stand a much better chance of being struck by a meteor.

Mountain lions

Mountain lions or cougars are king cats, found scattered throughout much of the United States and Canada. And cat-like they are; they act much like a very large (over 100 pounds) edition of your house cat. They play with toys (bits of hide or a dead rabbit), their family, and even chase their tails. They effectively stalk and kill game in scope with their size: often rabbits or deer. Cougars purr and even "meow" with a little kitten voice at times.

Mountain lions are becoming a bit too common in some areas, especially northern California, where they are not hunted and have learned to stroll into the edges of suburbia to snatch pet dogs and other small animals for easy meals.

There have been some attacks on humans, especially small children. Does this mean that we should live in terror of these critters? Not by a long shot. For every attack on humans by a cougar, there have been dozens of attacks by seemingly harmless pet dogs, such as poodles and cocker spaniels.

We have lived in cougar country for years, and have been careful to instruct our youngest son, David, in what to do if he should be approached by a cougar while he is alone. As I've said, cougars are very cat-like, and they are really timid and shy animals. Normally, all one has to do is to speak to a cougar to let it identify you as a human, and it bounds away in terror. If not, we've told David to grab up a stout club and "look big" by pulling his shirt or jacket up over his shoulders and holding his arms upright and out from his body. And stand still. As with any other predatory animal, running away often initiates an immediate and very active chase response. If the cougar does not leave and stalks or approaches, we suggest adopting an aggressive stance: shout, stamp feet, and swing the club like he means business. Few cougars will stand in the face of such threatening behavior.

I knew of a fisherman who was attacked by a young (but large) cougar, who "fought" it off with a fly rod.

David also usually runs our mountains with his dog. While cougars do prey on dogs, a large fearless dog usually strikes terror into the heart of a lion. Here cougars are often hunted with hounds and they know that dogs plus humans often equals rifle shots.

Bobcat

While mountain lions are fairly common, chances are you will never even get a glimpse of one, even if you live in their backyard. I've been lucky enough to get a distant look at three in all the years I've lived in lion country. They definitely won't break down your door to attack you.

Tracks and signs. A cougar track is quite large, wider than the average hand. In snow, it looks huge. You can tell it from a bear track, as the hind foot leaves a track just about like the front paw—no bare-footed human foot look. And, because a cougar has retractable claws like your cat, you won't see any claw indentations in the track. A dog or wolf leaves claw marks as well as paw prints.

In deep snow, you will get occasional light drag marks where the tip of the lion's tail brushes the top of the snow here and there.

Considerations for the homesteader. Lions will occasionally take young calves, lambs, and goats, usually when they are quite a way from the buildings and activity of the family. Therefore, it's best to bring the stock in to the barn or corrals at night, just to be sure. In nearly 40 years, I've never lost an animal to a cougar or had any type of close encounter. Having one or more large dogs about the place that *stays home* is a definite plus, in my opinion.

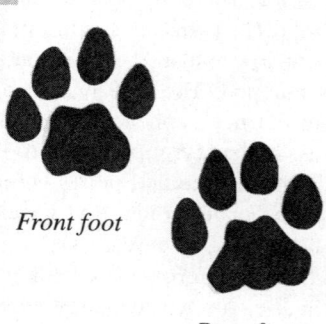
Front foot

Rear foot

Bobcat prints

Bobcats and lynx

These short tailed cats are the smaller cousins of the cougar, and are more apt to be seen. The bobcat is quite common throughout much of the United States and Canada. This cat is a little bigger and huskier than the average big house cat, weighing in at between 15 and 25 pounds. He is reddish brown with black spots and white highlights under the chin and

The Fourteenth Year

Lynx

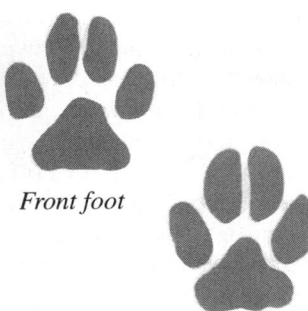

Front foot

Rear foot

Lynx prints

tail. His rump is higher than his shoulders and his tail is stumpy and only a few inches long. His feet are large for his size. Like his bigger cousin, the lynx, the bobcat has ear tufts, but they are shorter and less luxuriant.

The easiest way to tell a bobcat from a lynx is to first determine if lynx are known to live in your area. Where bobcats are found nearly everywhere with a bit of woods, the lynx is found almost exclusively in the north, in scattered populations.

Then consider the sheer size of the lynx, which is quite a bit taller and his paws and face are broader, as well. During the fall and winter, the lynx becomes quite greyish, where the bobcat stays more reddish brown in color.

Both the bobcat and lynx prey on rabbits, mice, voles, and birds.

Tracks and signs. The bobcat leaves a track that is cat-like, but larger. His claws leave no trace, as they are retractable. And in light snow or mud, you can notice the "fuzzy" marks of his large paws, rimming the large-cat track. In deep snow, you'll just see large cat tracks that you know no housecat made.

The lynx, being a considerably larger cat, makes larger, deeper tracks than the bobcat. He also has built-in snowshoes in those huge, plush feet of his, enabling him to run after rabbits and other game on top of the snow during the winter.

Like the house cat, the bobcat and lynx will usually scrape dirt and litter over their scat and scratch at dead wood to sharpen their claws.

Considerations for the homesteader. Because the bobcat and lynx prey on small mammals and birds, they occasionally get into trouble by snatching poultry from the chicken yard. This is usually done at night, so the best prevention is to close the poultry inside a snug coop at night. We also close the small chicken door, as a bobcat could climb the wire fence and enter the coop. It's an easy job to open the doors in the morning and it lets us sleep soundly, knowing our poultry is safe.

I've never known of a bobcat or lynx to attack a human that wasn't seriously bothering it. In fact, David stalked to within 15 feet of a bobcat down in our valley, just for the fun of it. The bobcat was mousing, and engrossed in the hunt, allowing David to carefully crawl quite close. But the wind changed and the cat was gone in a flash. We were watching and David was thrilled.

Wolves

I think people are afraid of bears and wolves in wild areas more than anything else. Because we have lived much of our lives among these animals, folks are always asking us whether we have had "trouble" with them. The honest answer is a definite NO. Especially with wolves. These maligned canines are so shy and naturally wary of humans that we consid-

Wolf

309

er it a huge gift to even hear their howls or catch a fleeting long distance glimpse of one. I've studied wolves nearly all my life, and I know of not one substantiated attack on a human by a non-rabid wolf. (And I've been bitten by several dogs, from poodles to border collies.)

I guess it's all the stories and movies that have people so spooked by wolves. And their bright piercing yellow and black eyes that seem to look right through you.

Where wolves once roamed the entire United States and Canada, today you will only find them in northern Minnesota, parts of Wyoming and Montana, along with a few scattered, isolated populations in other states. There is a healthy wolf population in Alaska, along with much of the Canadian wilderness.

Despite the movies, wolves do not stalk and eat people. They much prefer rabbits, deer, caribou, and moose. They also eat thousands of mice, frogs, grasshoppers, and other small prey.

The grey wolf is about the size of a big German shepherd dog. His legs and body are long. His tail does not "wag," but is carried out from his body, being raised a bit while hunting or playing, drooping down when at ease. It never curls up over his back, like a husky.

While grey wolves can come in any color, from pure black to silvery white, most are shades of brown, black, silver, and tan.

You can tell a coyote from a wolf by looking at the coyote's slim, pointed muzzle and sharply pointed ears. A wolf's muzzle is strong and heavier, his ears broader. And the wolf weighs from 60 to 100 lbs. or more, where the little coyote only weighs in at about 35 lbs. The coyote's howl is a yammering of yelps and howls—a single animal sounds like a pack at times. But the wolf howl is unmistakable. Full and rich, it is a sound that no movie can duplicate.

Tracks and signs. The wolf leaves a huge track. Not only are his feet

Wolf

large, enabling him to run across snow, but his toes spread out, creating an even larger foot that does not sink deeply while he runs. An adult wolf's track is nearly as wide as a human hand, and about as long as the palm. The nails show plainly. In deep, fluffy snow, you will occasionally see wisps where the tip of his tail brushes the surface.

Wolves leave droppings that appear dog-like, but nearly always contain a good portion of hair, feathers, and bone. The wolf is an efficient consumer. He not only eats the muscle meat, as do humans, but the guts, the contents of the stomach and intestines, the skin and much hair or feathers, and even completely eats most of the bones. Because of this, you will find the lesser-digestible ingredients of his diet in his scat.

Considerations for the homesteader. As with living with any other wild predatory neighbors, it's a good idea to keep small and young livestock near the homestead buildings and human activity. Keeping young sheep or calves half a mile from home can be too much temptation at

Front foot *Rear foot*
Wolf prints

times. It's best to bring such easy prey in at night.

I have homesteaded with wolves in the area for a long time, and have never lost a chicken or animal to a

Coyote

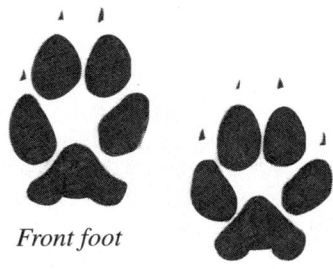
Front foot   *Rear foot*

Coyote prints

wolf—though I've lost a lot of poultry to the cute raccoon.

I don't believe that wolves present any threat to human beings, including children. Of course one wouldn't turn their two-year-old loose in the forest to wander alone, but a wild, healthy (i.e. not rabid) wolf certainly won't snatch Junior out of his playpen in the backyard. And as far as I know, there have been extremely few, if any, modern cases of rabid wolves in the U.S.

Coyotes

The coyote is common in much of the United States and Canada. He is the wolf's smaller cousin, much as the bobcat is to the lynx. Because of his furry coat, he looks larger than he actually is. Few coyotes weigh much more than 35-45 pounds. The coyote is also known as the brush wolf in some areas.

Where the grey wolf is extremely retiring, never living in areas of dense human population, the coyote has been highly adaptable. There are coyotes living within the Los Angles city limits. There they pick through garbage cans, steal dog food left outside, and even snatch occasional pets, stray cats, and small dogs.

Unfortunately, because these urban coyotes have lost their fear of man and are seldom hunted, they have become quite brazen, coming into yards during the day even when humans are present. There have been a few cases of small children being attacked.

But in the backwoods, the situation is far different. Coyotes are often hunted and shot at, and they are quite human-shy.

The coyote is long legged, grizzled greyish tan, with pointed ears and a slim, pointed muzzle. His bushy tail usually hangs down and out from his body and is the same color as his body. There is no black or white tip.

In the wild, the coyote eats many things, from wild fruit and mushrooms to mice, birds, rabbits, and occasional deer. He also eats many hundreds of grasshoppers, frogs, snakes, and bird eggs.

Tracks and signs. The coyote's track is very similar to that of a medium sized dog. In fact, it is very difficult to tell them apart. The track is about two inches long and an inch and a half wide. The nail prints are always visible.

In the snow, you can often distinguish a coyote track from a dog by following the track line. The coyote often pauses to mouse in the grass, digging and leaping up and pouncing down on a mouse beneath the snow. A dog seldom does this.

The coyote's scat is like the droppings of a medium sized dog, but nearly always contain hair, feathers, egg shells, or bone, and sometimes tin foil or other remains from garbage foraging.

Considerations for the homesteader. The coyote has gotten a bad name with homesteaders, as he sometimes becomes bold and snatches lambs, poultry, and other small animals from the barnyard. Last year, despite two good dogs, a coyote sneaked in and grabbed a setting hen out of a bush, not 10 feet from our cow yard.

But this is an occasional happening, and with decent prevention, that's all it will ever be. Like all predators, most coyotes are most active at night. So by bringing poultry and small livestock inside their shelters at night (and having these buildings sturdily built), you will avoid much coyote trouble. Likewise, it's best to keep your small stock and poultry reasonably close to home.

A coyote is not likely to come near human habitation, especially if you have one or more large dogs guarding the area. But they will occasionally pick off a bird or small animal straying (or staked out) far from home.

We about lost a huge hen turkey to a coyote. The turkey was ranging too far from home, way down our valley. A coyote grabbed Turk Turk, but our milk cow (who *hates* dogs) attacked the coyote and made it drop the heavy turkey. The dogs ran the coyote off when they heard the commotion. And the turkey survived.

In rare instances, coyotes have attacked young children. But this is *rare*, and nearly always it's an urban coyote involved. I've never felt that my children were in any way unsafe, playing in coyote country. But then again, we live in the way-backwoods where coyotes are shy because most ranchers carry a loaded rifle in the back window of their trucks. But even in northern Minnesota, where we had many, many coyotes, I never heard of a single coyote-human conflict.

Next issue, I'll introduce you to some more of your wild neighbors so you can better get to know the ones that frequent *your* backwoods. Δ

Ayoob on Firearms

ON A QUIET HOLIDAY, A COP GIVES THANKS

Massad Ayoob wrote this article in November 2002. We run it now as a holiday tribute to firefighting, emergency medical, and law enforcement agencies and their personnel everywhere. — Editors

It's the early morning hours of the day after Thanksgiving 2002 as I write this. I'm still wide awake from patrol and won't be ready to sleep for a while anyway. Constant alert status does that to you. Adrenaline doesn't just go away when you're done with it.

The same people who work those midnight shifts when most are sleeping tend to work the holidays when most are relaxing. It bonds those folks with one another: hospital personnel, 24-hour store and restaurant workers, and particularly the men and women of the emergency services world: fire, ambulance, and police.

Do not shake your head and "tsk, tsk" for us. It's something we accepted when we took the job. If we work near where we live, we can get home for at least part of the holiday. If you're on evening shift, you try to stay moderate as you partake of the Thanksgiving feast at mid-day, then maybe get in a short nap, and you're ready for "second watch." Workin' midnights? Feel free to take that second helping, and a longer nap before you suit up for the graveyard shift, knowing that on this of all nights you probably won't get too hungry at work.

Even day shift is manageable. Long ago, as a young patrolman, I recall a Thanksgiving when I got off work at 1600 hours (4:00 PM) on the dot, then drove—still in uniform—in my private car to join my young wife at her parents' for the family gathering. I peeled off the uniform shirt and jacket and the duty belt and locked them in the car. I chowed down on still-warm turkey while wearing blue uniform pants, shiny black patrol shoes, a white T-shirt, and a backup .38 in an ankle holster. It was the "immediately after work dress code" that LAPD's famed police trainer Rich Wemmer jokingly called "the Metro Tuxedo."

Quiet streets, quiet thoughts

Thanksgiving isn't just a day for scarfing poultry and pie and watching football. It's a day to give thanks. The best job can be turned into the worst torture by a bad boss, and the worst job can be made enjoyable by a good leader. I have a great boss, and that makes a satisfying job even more so. Recently divorced, I've volunteered to work a double shift on the holiday so the married folks can be home with their families. My chief makes a point of pulling the first half of day shift to ease the load for me. This is the kind of person you want to work for. Everyone under his command would follow him on a raid through the gates of Hell, and one or two suspect he might be able to figure out a way to get the warrant. Good bosses are something to give thanks for.

So are good working conditions. We have the best equipment, with redundant capability, something particularly important to emergency services personnel in rural areas like this, who work far from available backup.

Massad Ayoob

The guns are almost all Rugers. Each of us is issued the rugged Ruger P90 .45 automatic as a primary sidearm, along with the most street-proven snatch-resistant holster ever made, the Safariland 070/SS-III designed by ex-FBI agent Bill Rogers. For backup, each of us is issued a Ruger SP101 .357 Magnum snub-nose revolver and an Alessi concealment holster. Each patrol vehicle contains a Ruger Mini-14 .223 semiautomatic rifle with multiple high capacity magazines. All are made of stainless steel, the better to withstand the condensation that plagues equipment in an intensely four-season environment. (Today, temperatures in the low single digits will chill the rifle when the cruiser is parked unattended, and the heater will be on full blast when the vehicle is rolling. It's the reverse in summer heat, with triple-digit heat factors vis-à-vis air conditioning.) Finally, each vehicle also contains a Mossberg Jungle Gun, the semiautomatic 12-gauge shotgun that was designed to Crane Arsenal specs for DEA to issue to indigenous support personnel in South American operations. While I prefer a rifle for most long gun needs in police work, the short barrel and folding stock of the Mossberg police shotgun make it faster to deploy out of the vehicle in a fast-breaking, close-range emergency.

A firearm is only as good as its ammunition. We have Federal full-power Express double-ought buckshot in the 12 gauges, and Black Hills ammo in everything else. In the .45s, it's the 230-grain Gold Dot bullet, running at 850 feet per second, the same load chosen for his personal defense by gun expert Peter Kokalis (Small Arms Review, Soldier of Fortune). In the .357s, it's the 125-grain Magnum hollow-point that is legendary for stopping power. In the .223, we use the 52-grain "Moly-coated" bullet at 3200 feet per second; massive stopping power, deadly accuracy, and penetration that is not excessive for the police patrol mission. We've never had a misfire in countless thousands of these rounds, and our department has won the last two state championships in a row shooting Black Hills. The combination of reliable guns and reliable ammo is comforting when you're out there alone. It's a combination you can go to the edge with, when the job description includes going to that very edge.

It's the same with the vehicles. While most of our patrol fleet is the last surviving full-size rear wheel drive four door sedan with separate heavy-duty frame, the Ford Crown Victoria, we also have the option of a four-wheel drive Chevy Tahoe. It's a "country cousin, city cousin" thing. True, with the Police Interceptor package (healthy engine, beefed up suspension and electrical system) the Crown Vic is a responsive machine that's a pleasure to drive, especially when you have to drive fast. But in the boondocks, the leviathan Chevy SUV has much to recommend it. For one thing, it sits you up high, where you can look out over the traffic and spot things you wouldn't see in a low-slung sedan. Not for nothing do lifeguards sit on elevated chairs at the beach. This ain't a beach, but the lifeguard analogy remains in effect. Then, there's the weather to consider.

Yesterday was snowy and slushy, with auto accidents all over the state. Today has dawned clear, if bitter cold, and already our road crews—"seasoned" in more ways than one—have cleared the public ways. Their plows and their salt have taken the roads down to clear, dry asphalt. The interstate highway is like a race-ready track, and the secondary roads are almost as good.

But the dirt roads are still greasy with ice. Forecasts call for more snow tonight, and the shifts I've volunteered for extend 'til then. Besides, it's a holiday. City folk visiting their country cousins may take a dog for a walk in those beautiful snowy woods they read about in Robert Frost poems and get lost. Hunting season is in full swing, and a deerstalker may not return on time and require a search party. In such moments, big machines with four-wheel drive make a whole lot of sense. For today, I choose the Tahoe.

The best equipment. One more thing to be thankful for. The thanks are duly given.

The job is people

I enjoy this. I'm a full time trainer and a part-time cop, and most of my time for the police department is spent in plainclothes: training, admin, public relations, the occasional investigation. It's a treat to be back in uniform doing patrol, the very heart of police work whether your practice is located in the inner city or, like mine, in the kind of community *Backwoods Home* subscribers buy the magazine to read about.

It's a beautiful place. The patrol tour takes me past breathtaking vistas of valley and of mountain, past the sort of winter wonderland scenes that many people only get to see on Christmas cards. At one point, I park at roadside. On the left, I'm monitoring traffic...but on the right, I'm gazing at the crystal-clear water of a brook, black in the winter light, as it cuts between two snowy banks filled with birch trees. A small pleasure for which to give thanks? No, a large pleasure. I've been on patrol on "busman's holidays" with New York City cops in parts of the Bronx that looked like bombed-out Dresden, with Kentucky State Troopers whose sectors encompassed the very depths of Appalachian poverty, and with South African Police in the heart of Soweto. People who read *Backwoods Home* make huge economic sacrifices to move to such places as where I am now, in the name of one of the few good catch-phrases the Yuppies ever came up with: Quality of Life. I get to work here. You bet I give thanks for that.

But, in the end, it's not the equipment or the scenery for which I give the most thanks. It's the people. Back road or interstate highway, people see the uniformed cop in the patrol car and wave at me. They use all their fingers, as opposed to the one-finger salutes I've seen the police car draw in some other places. I am happy to wave back.

Today, I'm sitting alone in this car, responsible for the safety of about three thousand people if something bad happens. That hit me my first night on solo patrol when I was 23 years old, and now, as an ancient Coposaurus Rex, that realization still has not lost its impact. IACP, the International Association of Chiefs of Police, used to say that a community needed one full-time officer per thousand people to have proper police service. Crunch the numbers and figure out that there are only 40 hours of every 168-hour week worked per officer. Then factor in sick time, vacations, training time, paperwork time, court time, and all the rest, and understand why there is nowhere near one cop per thousand people really available for immediate response to needs for police service anywhere in America. In a perfect world, responsibility and power would be exactly commensurate, but this is not a perfect world. For cops, the responsibility always seems to outweigh the power.

But, particularly in a rural community, getting to know the people you serve makes up for a lot. You follow peoples' lives. You thrill at their triumphs. You hurt with them when they hurt.

I learn that this Thanksgiving morning, young Jeremiah has bagged a fine white-tail buck. It's his third in as many years. What makes this memorable is that Jeremiah is only 12 years old. The big deer fell to a single shot, just like his other two. This shot was a .223 Remington round, fired from a short-stocked Youth Model Ruger Model 77 bolt action rifle. That's a light load for deer, but it works if you have the patience and self-control to wait for the perfect moment and then deliver performance with unerring accuracy. Jeremiah does. Last year's buck, with his dad's .308, was also a clean and humane one-shot kill. So was the one the year before, when he was 10, with a muzzle-loader.

There are communities where a young man on a public way holding a rifle would elicit a call for the SWAT team. Up here, we know it's Jeremiah, and the cops I know will stop only to ask him if he's seen any deer sign today, and if he would like a ride back up the road to his father's truck. It's one of the good things about working in a place like this.

Sadly, not all our kids turn out like Jeremiah. The Tahoe carries me past the dwellings of two adult children of our community whom I've had to arrest and send to prison in years past. One has paid his debt to society. He served his sentence, got out, and started a small business. I hope he does OK. He was selling dope to young people. He did it for the quick buck. He found out in the state penitentiary that when you amortize your time behind bars, that quick buck isn't all that big. Another of life's lessons learned.

The other hasn't quite paid off his debt to society. It's still on mortgage, and in his case the mortgage is parole. He was a sexual predator when I put the handcuffs on him. It wasn't his first time. He has convinced the parole board that it was his last. We'll see. There are those in society who say that our approach to him should be "forgive and forget." That might have sounded good to me thirty-some years ago before I first donned a badge, but life experience has made me more cynical, as it does with almost all cops.

"Forgive and forget"? We are fully prepared to forgive. However, we have learned the hard way that forgiveness is contingent upon the certainty—not the well-intentioned assurance or fond hope, but the certainty—that the one who would be forgiven will do no further harm. Yes, cops can forgive. We just don't forget.

Part of our job is handling regular check-ins of parolees and probationers. Dispatch calls me to meet one such at the station. I do. He's a large young man, with a reticence about him that's hard to read. Embarrassment that he needs me to initial his "daily check?" I hope so. Being embarrassed by having done bad things is a good sign. This is why that place where we send the dangerous ones is called the "penitentiary." It is a place to be penitent, to admit your faults and hopefully make the commitment that you will "go forth and sin no more." Or is it just a sullen resentment at having been caught, at having to conform to society's rules? Frankly, I don't know yet. Time will tell.

This kid is the same age as the boy my younger daughter is dating. Her beau seems like a nice young man. I'm glad that neither of my kids has ever hooked up with the kind of youth with whom The Job brings us in contact so often. "Younger Brat" is a senior in high school, has just gotten back some kick-ass SAT scores, and is safe and sound with her mom and her extended family this Thanksgiving. "Elder Brat" is three thousand miles away, a successful elementary school teacher working on her graduate degree, spending her second Thanksgiving with a husband who is the kind of young man that parents of daughters pray their children will marry. I am reminded that, yes, I have much for which to give thanks this day.

I was a young patrolman when I was given wise advice by Col. Paul Doyon, then superintendent of the New Hampshire State Police. "The Job is not badges or guns or clubs," he told me. "The Job is people." I never forgot that. It's the right day to give thanks for that handful of mentors we are given in life, among a sea of mere instructors.

Reflections

Darkness has long since fallen. The radio is eerily silent. People are not doing stupid and dangerous things. Life is good. I've logged 75 miles of road patrol and seen not a single candidate for a drunk driving stop, nor a single motorist exceeding the speed limit sufficiently to warrant a stop.

Things have been equally good for the other emergency services. In the small town I serve, only the police department has sustained on-duty presence. Our crack fire department and our excellent emergency medical crew—the FAST squad, which stands for First Aid Support Team—are all volunteers. Today, most of them are on standby. These good men and women donate their time for both training and duty in a long-standing rural tradition of community members contributing to the safety of the place where they live. They're drinking apple cider instead of hard cider with their Thanksgiving turkey, checking the pagers on their belts, ready at a moment's notice to race to wherever they may be needed to quench flames or stabilize a life-threatening illness or injury. Their job is cheating death. They do it very well. They must be giving thanks that their services are not needed today and tonight, even as I am giving thanks for the exact same thing.

But death can't always be cheated, even in the quiet places. Last week in the small town of Red Bluff, California, a 31-year-old policeman named David Mobilio was murdered execution-style as he gassed up his patrol car. I was in nearby Sacramento consulting with a local agency in regard to an officer involved shooting case, and saw the helpless frustration in the faces of Mobilio's brother officers. Their badges wrapped in black, the universal symbol of mourning for a brother lost in the line of duty, they asked themselves what could motivate even the most vicious sociopath to murder a cop that way. On Tuesday morning, as I was about to fly home, the local radio stations came alive with reports that the suspect had been cornered in a hotel by police in Concord, New Hampshire.

I live in Concord, a short drive from the community I serve as a police officer. By the time I reached the Sacramento airport, the radio was reporting that the Concord PD special reaction team had taken the suspect into custody, alive. I arrived home in the wee hours of Wednesday, and the media seemed to be focusing on the fact that when he fought police while being booked, an existing wound on the cop-killer's head had re-opened, and required a bandage after he had been restrained. He had told reporters that he had murdered the young officer to make a statement about police brutality.

Now it was Thursday. It had been a quiet Thanksgiving. Just before I went 10-2, off duty, I typed out a letter to the local newspaper commending the Concord cops and the resident FBI agents for their professionalism, courage, and restraint in taking the suspected cop-killer alive. I could also give thanks for the fact that I've been able to go to other countries and see how things are done elsewhere. I've been to places where a man like this would have left the scene in a body bag whether or not he resisted. It was a day to give thanks for living in the best country with the best cops.

Driving home, I realized something. I had started the day feeling sorry for myself because I was spending my first whole Thanksgiving away from nuclear family. I had ended the day giving thanks that my kids and my ex were OK. And I had finished it with renewed pride in being a member of another family, the family of emergency service personnel who swear an oath to sacrifice their lives if they must, to protect the people they exist to serve.

I didn't feel sorry for myself anymore. I realized that I had just spent a Thanksgiving actually giving thanks instead of just eating and partying.

And I give thanks for that epiphany, too.

This column is respectfully dedicated to the memory of Officer David Mobilio of the Red Bluff, California, Police Department. Δ

Shaving with a straight razor

By Steve Gregg

I went to my grandfather one day and said, "Papaw, show me how to shave with a straight razor."

My grandfather was a kind, gentle man, and I was the apple of his eye. I could do no wrong. So I was somewhat taken aback when he looked at me as though I were an idiot and said, "They, great I am!" His catch phrase. "What do you want to know that for?"

"Well," I stammered, blinking and trying to think of an answer, "because a day could come when there aren't any razor blades."

"Why would that happen?" He asked, looking at me with that you-poor-dumb-boy look.

"I don't know. Just show me how."

That was more than 20 years ago; I've been shaving with a straight razor ever since. Why? Because I fell in love with it—from honing and stropping my razor, to whipping the lather, to the sensation of the steel gliding across my face. There's nothing like it.

I don't even own a safety razor anymore, or a can of that shake-it-and-squirt shaving cream for that matter. My only regret is not keeping all the money I've saved over the years by switching to a straight razor.

Want to give it a try? It's easy, fun, pleasurable, and cost effective. In all fairness, though, somebody living in Afghanistan might argue with me, but that's because they don't have a choice in the matter. They've probably never seen anything but a straight razor. Here in America it's nothing more than a novelty, a relic from a bygone era, but it's also a way to preserve a part of our past that every man used to take for granted.

Besides, what if a day really does come when there aren't any razor blades?

The first straight razor I ever bought cost $20 brand-new and was made in Germany by Robert Klaas. Despite what you may think, a brand new straight razor is not ready to shave with. It has to be sharpened first. This is done on a razor hone (I am fortunate enough to have located an antique razor hone at an antiques store) or a very fine sharpening stone.

You will also need a razor strop (not "strap" as most people think), strop dressing, a mug filled with a disk of Williams' mug soap (better than any I've tried), and a shaving brush. All are available on the Internet (www.shavingsupplies.com) and at some drug stores.

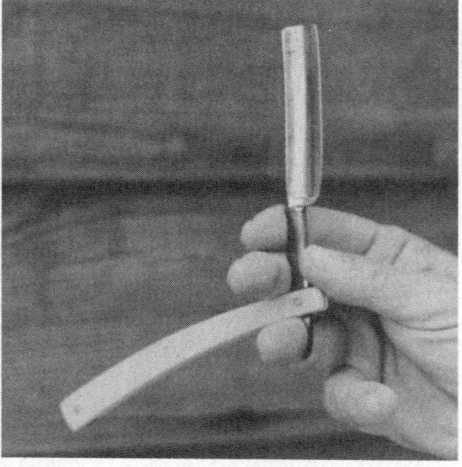

The proper way to hold a straight razor

Sharpening your razor

Place the razor perfectly flat on the stone with the edge turned away from you. Stroke it as if you're trying to slice a piece of the stone, as if you were whittling. Apply very little pressure, not much more than the weight of the razor. After a dozen or so strokes, flip it over. With the cutting edge facing you this time, draw it toward you. Take the same number of strokes.

All quality straight razors are "hollow ground" and made of high-carbon steel, meaning you don't have to worry about holding any kind of an angle while sharpening. It also means it will rust. Very easily, I might add.

After honing, the razor goes over to the razor strop. The strop consists of a thick piece of canvas on one side, a thick piece of leather on the other. The canvas side warms the steel and gets it ready for the leather side. You can't see it, but sharpening on the stone leaves a microscopic "burr" along the edge. Stropping removes the burr. Believe me, you can feel it when you shave.

Pull the strop tight and begin on the canvas side. Strop away from the cutting edge. If the strop bows when you begin stropping, you're either applying too much pressure or you're not holding the strop taught enough. Do it just the way they do it in a Western movie; i.e., drag the razor away from you, flip it over, and pull it back. Speed is not a factor. Take eight or ten strokes on each side of the blade.

Now go to the leather side. If you did not already apply strop dressing, do so now. (Strop dressing is a very fine honing compound of about 6,000 grit. It also preserves the leather.) Strop your razor just like you did on the canvas side.

You now have a sharpened straight razor.

Shaving

Drop a disk of soap into your mug, get your new brush (badger hair is best), add a few drops of hot water, and begin whipping. The lather should be just like the kind that comes from a can—thick and creamy. It takes some practice to learn how much water to add, but it isn't much.

Wet your face with hot water and apply the cream with the brush.

Grab up your razor. Hold it just like they do in the movies. Begin on a part of your face that's easy to get to and that you're comfortable with. Try going with the grain. If the razor pulls, it's not sharp enough. Clean your face off and begin again. A sharp razor will glide over your face just about like a safety razor.

Now go against the grain. Test the freshly shaved spot with the back of your hand. If you feel stubble, dip the razor into cold water and make another pass. Cold water lessens razor burn.

Some areas of the face are rather tricky. The only advice I can give you is to just keep trying till you find the most comfortable approach. It'll come to you. After all, your grandfather did it, didn't he?

Cleaning up

Now rinse the soap off your face with cold water. Rinse your razor off and dry it thoroughly. Place it on a shelf and pick up your brush. Rinse it off and hang it someplace to dry. Do not leave it in the mug. If you do, you'll eventually ruin it.

If you use aftershave lotion (I never do), splash some on and congratulate yourself for learning a new skill. Now go show your wife, but don't try to talk her into shaving her legs with your straight razor. You'll only be wasting your breath.

The more you use your razor, the easier it will be to sharpen and the sharper it will become. It will also begin to turn black with age. Don't be alarmed. High-carbon steel does that. It's a sign of the quality of the steel. Rust, on the other hand, will have an orange appearance—you can feel rust. Immediately remove any rust with a little mineral oil and a rag, and find a better place to store your razor.

Final thoughts on razors

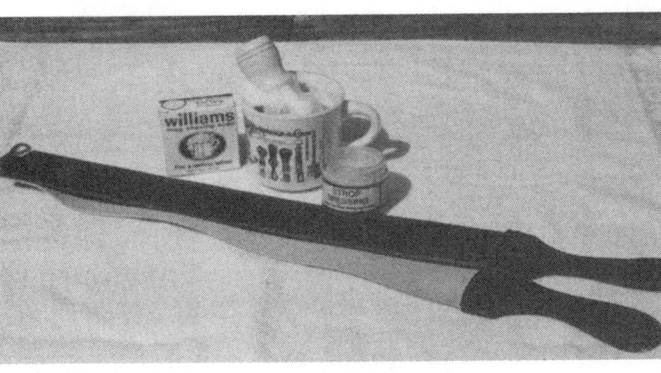
Williams' mug soap; mug & brush, lathered and ready to use; strop dressing; razor strop

Some antique straight razors are worth thousands of dollars, but most are worth nothing more than what you're willing to pay for them. Just because it's old doesn't mean it's worth anything.

I have two antique straight razors, but they're not valuable. One is made by The Torrey Razor Company of Massachusetts and has an ivory handle. It cost me $15 at a junk store. The other one is made in Sweden by Eskilstuna, also $15. Both are excellent razors.

My strop is made by the Illinois Razor Strop Company and is a number 127. Brand new, it cost me $20 — a lot of money 20-plus years ago. The company is still in business, and they do make good strops, but the new ones are not heavy enough to suit me. The red leather, Russian strops are much better. Purchase strop dressing along with the strop.

You will also see what's called a "paddle strop." Don't waste your money. They're great for something like a wood chisel, but not a straight razor.

A few tips for an old razor that you actually intend on using:

1. Stay away from one with excessive rust.
2. Check for nicks and cracks in the steel.
3. Check for cracks in the handle.
4. It should open and close with a very light touch—a straight razor should practically fall open when you pick it up.

Clockwise from bottom left: German-made, bought new 20-plus years ago (steel is starting to blacken); antique with ivory handle (USA); circa 1940 antique (Sweden); antique razor hone

Tips for a new razor:

1. Stay away from stainless steel. It's too hard to sharpen. Besides, all steel rusts eventually, even stainless. If it doesn't, it contains more alloys than steel.
2. Try to buy from a place where you can actually hold the razor, or at least be able to return it if you don't like it. Nearly all straight razors will have a different feel and balance to them.

Shaving with a straight razor does take some getting used to. If you're one of those men who wants a super close shave that feels like a baby's skin, forget it. Just stick with the triple blade, Teflon coated, $15 per pack sort of razor. But if you do Civil War reenactments or living history performances, or just like the old ways of doing things, a straight razor may be just what you need. Me? I just like shaving this way. If you put a new blade in your razor and make all the other preparations needed before shaving, I can mix my soap, hone my razor, shave, and be done just as quickly as you can—and I'll have a lot more fun doing it.

One final thought. My Papaw died years ago, but I know he's looking down from somewhere up above and shaking his head as I shave, wondering to this very day why his favorite grandson is so stupid. A straight razor. "They great I am!" ∆

THE IRREVERENT JOKE PAGE

(Believing it is important for people to be able to laugh at themselves, this is a continuing feature in *Backwoods Home Magazine*. We invite readers to submit any jokes you'd like to share to *BHM*, P.O. Box 712, Gold Beach, OR 97444. There is no payment for jokes used.)

In a big city at a crowded busy bus stop there was a beautiful young woman wearing a tight mini skirt. As the bus stopped and it was her turn to get on, she became aware that her skirt was too tight to allow her leg to come up to the height of the first step of the bus.

Slightly embarrassed and with a quick smile to the bus driver, she reached behind her to unzip her skirt a little, thinking that this would give her enough slack to raise her leg. Again, she tried to make the step only to discover she still couldn't. So, a little more embarrassed, she once again reached behind her to unzip her skirt a little more, and for the second time attempted the step. Still, much to her chagrin, she could not raise her leg. With a little smile at the driver, she again reached behind to unzip a little more and again was unable to make the step.

About this time, a large Texan who was standing behind her in line picked her up easily by the waist and placed her gently on the step of the bus. She went ballistic, turned to the would-be good Samaritan, and yelled, "How dare you touch my body! I don't even know who you are!"

The Texan smiled and drawled, "Well, ma'am, normally I would agree with you, but after you unzipped my fly three times, I kinda figured we was friends."

submitted by: Peter Martin, Euless, Texas

Out of the Mouths of Babes

After a church service on Sunday morning, a young boy suddenly announced to his mother, "Mom, I've decided to become a minister when I grow up." "That's okay with us, but what made you decide that?" "Well," said the little boy, "I have to go to church on Sunday anyway, and I figure it will be more fun to stand up and yell, than to sit and listen."

The Sunday School Teacher asks, "Now, Johnny, tell me frankly, do you say prayers before eating?" "No, sir," little Johnny replies, "I don't have to. My Mom is a good cook."

A man was walking along the beach when he stumbled upon a lamp. He picked it up and rubbed the sand off of it. All of a sudden a genie popped out. "I will grant you one wish, anything you want I will grant you. Just name it." The man pondered for a while and then asked the genie if he could build him a bridge to Hawaii. He told the genie he really wanted to go to Hawaii but couldn't stand planes or ships. He wanted to drive there. The genie asked the man if he was crazy. "Don't you know how impossible it would be to build a bridge all the way to Hawaii, why the cement pillars would be immense. No, you come up with another wish, this time make it a good one." The man thought for a minute, then said, "OK I would like to understand women." The genie thought for a little while, then asked the man how many lanes he wanted on his bridge.

Q: How do men sort their laundry?
A: "Filthy" and "Filthy but Wearable."

Q: How does a man show he's planning for the future?
A: He buys two cases of beer instead of one.

Church Bulletin Bloopers:

Sometimes, writers of church bulletins get in a hurry and do not proofread for content, just spelling, and the bulletins turn out items like the following:

This afternoon there will be a meeting in the south and north ends of this church. Children will be baptized at both ends.

The ladies of the church have cast off clothing of every kind and they can be seen in the church basement on Friday afternoon.

Tonight's sermon: "What is Hell?" Come early and listen to our choir practice.

After every flight, pilots fill out a form called a gripe sheet, which conveys to the mechanics problems encountered with the aircraft during the flight that need repair or correction. The mechanics read and correct the problem, and then respond in writing on the lower half of the form what remedial action was taken, and the pilot reviews the gripe sheets before the next flight. Never let it be said that ground crews and engineers lack a sense of humor.

Here are some actual logged maintenance complaints and problems as submitted by Qantas pilots and the solution recorded by maintenance engineers.

(P = The problem logged by the pilot.)
(S = The solution and action taken by the engineers.)

P: Left inside main tyre almost needs replacement.
S: Almost replaced left inside main tyre.

P: Test flight OK, except auto-land very rough.
S: Auto-land not installed on this aircraft.

P: Something loose in cockpit.
S: Something tightened in cockpit.

P: Dead bugs on windshield.
S: Live bugs on back-order.

P: Autopilot in altitude-hold mode produces a 200 feet per minute descent.
S: Cannot reproduce problem on ground.

P: Evidence of leak on right main landing gear.
S: Evidence removed.

P: DME volume unbelievably loud.
S: DME volume set to more believable level.

P: Friction locks cause throttle levers to stick.
S: That's what they're there for.

P: IFF inoperative.
S: IFF always inoperative in OFF mode.

P: Suspected crack in windshield.
S: Suspect you're right.

P: Number 3 engine missing.
S: Engine found on right wing after brief search.

P: Aircraft handles funny.
S: Aircraft warned to straighten up, fly right, and be serious.

P: Target radar hums.
S: Reprogrammed target radar with lyrics.

P: Mouse in cockpit.
S: Cat installed.

P: Noise coming from under instrument panel. Sounds like a midget pounding on something with a hammer.
S: Took hammer away from midget

There was this guy who went golfing every Saturday and Sunday. It didn't matter what kind of weather it was, he was hooked on a round of golf on his days off.

One Saturday he left the house early and headed for the golf course, but it was so bitter cold that he decided he wouldn't golf that day and went back home.

His wife was still in bed when he got there, so he took off his clothes and snuggled up to his wife's backside and said, "Terrible weather out there."

She replied, "Yeah, and can you believe my stupid husband went golfing."

A bum, who'd obviously seen more than his share of hard times, approached a well-dressed man on the street. "Hey, Buddy.....can you spare two dollars?"

The well-dressed man replied ....."You're not going to spend it on liquor are you?"

"No, sir, I don't drink," retorts the bum.

"You're not going to throw it away on fishing gear, are you?" ... the gentleman asked.

"No way! ... I don't fish either!" ... answered the bum.

"You wouldn't waste the money on a deer lease, would you?" asks the man.

"Never!" says the bum, "I don't hunt!"

So the man asked the bum if he'd like to come home with him for a home cooked meal. The bum accepted eagerly. While they were heading for the man's house, the bum's curiosity got the better of him ... "Isn't your wife going to be upset when you bring a guy like me to your house for dinner?"

"Probably," said the man, "but it'll be well worth it for her to see what happens to a man that doesn't drink, fish or hunt".

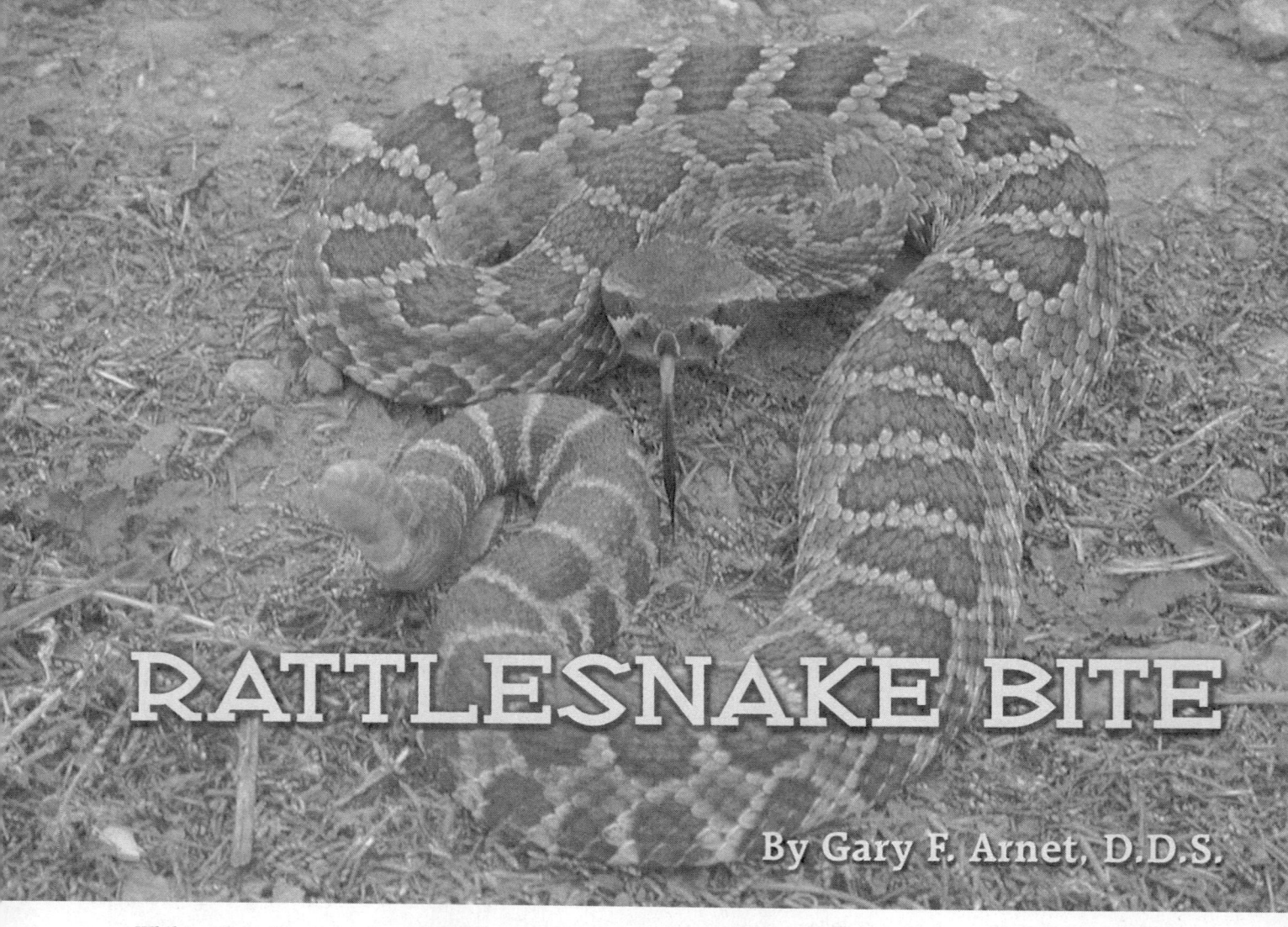

RATTLESNAKE BITE

By Gary F. Arnet, D.D.S.

While rattlesnakes are an important part of ecosystems and keep down the rodent populations, most people would still rather avoid an encounter. Shown is a Southern Pacific Rattlesnake (Crotalus viridis helleri). Photo courtesy of Dawn Wilson, PhD and Glen Lubcke, herpetologists at California State University, Chico.

At about 11:30 a.m. on May 16, 2003, 52-year-old Ron Cooke parked his work truck by the side of the road near Lytle Creek in southern California and walked about 500 yards away, stepping over rocks in a dry riverbed. Stepping on what he thought was a log, he was rapidly bitten twice in the lower leg by a thick-bodied rattlesnake.

Instead of calling 911 (a fire station was just a mile away) he called his employer on a cellular phone for help in locating a hospital. He then drove himself to a hospital 16 miles away and was later transferred to a major university hospital with expertise in snakebites. Alert and conscious when first admitted to the hospital, he developed neurological symptoms within a few hours and, despite modern medicines and technology, died shortly thereafter from a series of strokes caused by the venom. He left two sons, one who was to graduate from high school a few weeks later.

Although a very serious medical emergency, rattlesnake bites are rarely fatal. Every year, 8,000 poisonous snakebites occur in the United States, many by rattlesnake, with up to 12 deaths reported per year. Many victims recover with permanent damage or deformed extremities.

Rattlesnakes are one of four types of poisonous snakes in the United States, the others being water moccasins (cottonmouth), coral snakes, and copperheads. Rattlesnakes are found in all 48 continental states, Canada, and Mexico. No snakes are found in Alaska or Hawaii.

Thirty-two species of rattlesnakes, containing 70 subspecies, have been identified and categorized into two genera: Crotalus and Sistrurus. In many parts of the country, only one species exists, making identification easy.

In other areas, especially, California, Arizona, New Mexico, and Texas, several species co-exist in the same areas, making identification more important. In some desert areas of southern California where the Mojave rattlesnake that produces nerve-damaging venom exists with other rattlesnakes that produce hemolytic venom that damages tissue and blood, identification of the species of rattlesnake is important in the treatment. It would be a good idea to know the identification of the poisonous snakes in your area if you spend much time outdoors.

The odds of being bitten

Over 50% of the people bitten by rattlesnakes were trying to handle or kill the snake, and the vast majority of the cases involve the handler being under the influence of alcohol. Maybe not surprising, young men in their late teens and early twenties are most commonly involved with this type of bite.

The rest of the bites are true unexpected accidents that may or may not have been avoidable. Sometimes these bites could have been prevented by a little caution, and by knowing where snakes might be located and their habits.

If you live in the desert there is a good chance you will encounter a rattlesnake. If you live or travel in just about any rural area in the United States you may also run into one. They may be encountered in wild areas, but just as often they are found around homes, gardens, parks, and golf courses. They are everywhere, but are not often seen because they are so cryptic and shy.

Rattlesnakes live in many areas from the seashore to 11,000 feet elevation. They live in deserts, mountains, at the beach, and in forests, prairies, and swamps. And, with so many people moving into rural areas, they also live in our neighborhoods. With so many snakes around, it is amazing there are not more snake-human encounters or more bites. There are more fatalities from lightening strikes (another rare occurrence) in Florida each year than there are fatal snakebites nationwide.

What this also means is that of the thousands and thousands of doctors we have, only a few will have experience treating rattlesnake bites. Thousands may only treat one in a career and most will go an entire career without treating such a patient.

If you receive a rattlesnake bite, a very complex medical problem, the doctor treating you may have very little experience, or you may be the first patient he or she has ever seen. Once a rattlesnake bite occurs, time is of essence. You don't want to wait while your doctor reads up on what to do, or has to find a specialist to call for advice. Better to understand snakes and avoid being bitten in the first place.

Identifying rattlesnakes

Rattlesnakes come in different colors and sizes, yet all have several features that make them easy to identify. While the many species of rattlesnakes vary in location, their appearance, and in the type and severity of the venom they produce, they have some things in common.

The best way to identify a rattlesnake is by the shape of the head. Non-poisonous snakes have a head, neck, and body that are about the same diameter. They almost appear to be the shape that a child may make when rolling clay.

Rattlesnakes, on the other hand, have a muscular, powerful body, a thin neck, and a distinctive triangular-shaped or arrow-shaped head caused by well-developed poison glands on the side of their head. This applies to rattlesnakes, water moccasins, and copperheads. Other native poisonous snakes, such as coral snakes, and exotic poisonous snakes that have been imported may have thin heads, characteristic of non-poisonous snakes.

Color or patterns on the skin are not a good indicator, as some non-poisonous snakes such as the Pacific Gopher snake and Bull snake have similar rattlesnake-like markings as a defense against enemies. Pupils of

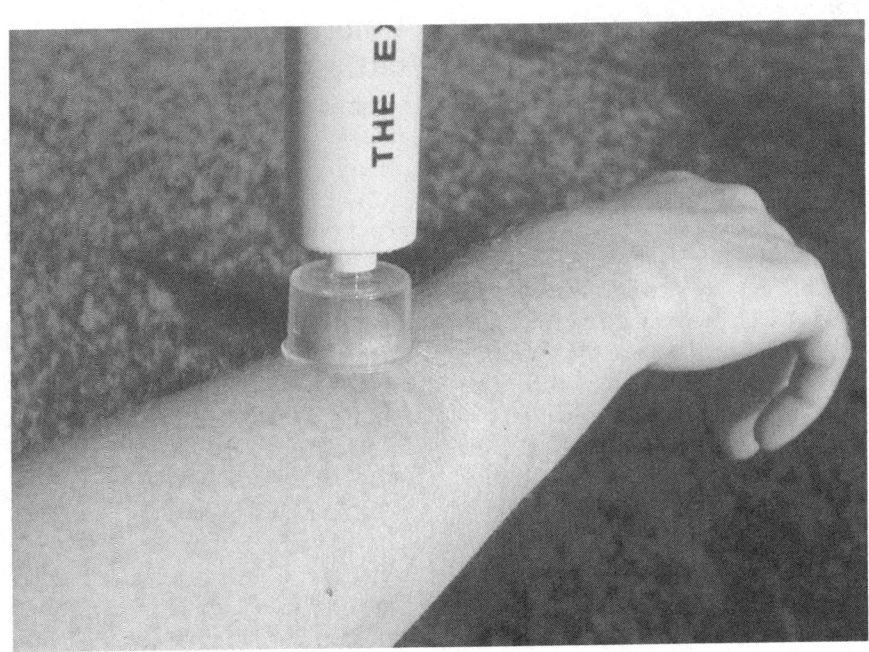

Note the amount of suction caused on the skin when the Sawyer Extractor is used on an arm.

Rattlesnakes, such as this Sidewinder (Crotalus cerastes) have triangular shaped heads and usually have rattles. Their skin pattern is camouflaged to blend in with their environment. Photo courtesy of Dawn Wilson, PhD and Glen Lubcke, herpetologists at California State University, Chico.

rattlesnakes eyes are oval like a cat, rather than round like non-poisonous snakes, but getting close enough to look into their pupils is a good way to get bit in the face.

Rattlesnakes, water moccasins, and copperheads are all pit vipers. That is they have a pit (loreal gland) below their eye used for finding food. Again, you don't want to be close enough to the snake to use this as a method of identification.

Most rattlesnakes have rattles on their tails (one species does not) which they may vibrate when nervous making a characteristic buzzing noise to warn off predators or those getting too close. If surprised, they will strike without first rattling a warning.

Rattles are not always a good indicator to identify a rattlesnake, as they may be absent. Born live (viviparous), rattlesnakes initially have a pre-button, or little knob where rattles will form. Rattles are formed with each successive shedding, which may be several times a year (therefore, you cannot tell the age of a snake by the number of rattles). A young rattlesnake may not have rattles, even though their bite is still dangerous. Note newborn rattlesnakes are very small and have been found in swimming pools, potted plants, and houses.

Where to expect rattlesnakes

Rattlesnakes may be found almost anywhere. Their value is that they control a large population of rodents, including mice, rats, and rabbits, which would rapidly overpopulate and possibly spread disease if left unchecked. Eighty percent of the diet of rattlesnakes is rodents, although they will also eat ground nesting birds, lizards, and other snakes. It is estimated that they may consume as much as 25% of a rodent population in a given area every year.

Rattlesnakes do not dig their own dens, rather hiding in preexisting structures. They are usually hidden, helped by the natural camouflage pattern on their skin, in areas such as rocks, logs, brush piles, woodpiles, and grass. Often these will be areas also frequented by their prey. They may also take over the burrows of other snakes or mammals. They are known to wait at one end of a fallen log across a river waiting for prey using the log to cross the river. These are the same logs hikers and backpackers may use to cross. Rattlesnakes may also be found basking in the open, warming in the sun on a rock or log any time of the year. Banks of rivers and edges of lakes are also areas to expect to find them.

As reptiles, rattlesnakes do not generate their own heat, so they need to use the environment to control body temperature. In warm temperatures, such as the desert, they are active from March through October, at first active during the day. As daytime temperatures become hot, they are active at night and spend the day in the shade of a rock, bush, or building. They have been found absolutely everywhere, including in cars and in the shade of tires around airplane wheels. On cool evenings, they are often found lying on concrete or asphalt roads and parking lots, enjoying the retained heat.

Around houses, walkways should be kept clear of brush, rocks, or other hiding places and brightly lit at night. Rattlesnakes are more visible on pavement or barren ground. Eliminate rodents with traps or poisons and fill in their holes, so rattlesnakes do not take them over. Clean up and be careful around woodpiles or junk piles. These are attractive places for rattlesnakes to live, providing shelter and food. Discarded metal sheeting or roofing material lying on the ground is a good spot to expect to find a snake.

> *The antivenin, which costs about $450 a vial (at least 10 vials are needed to treat a victim) is not available at every hospital and, at times, is hard for hospitals to obtain. Many hospitals are lucky if they have enough antivenin on hand to treat one snakebite patient.*

During cool weather, snakes become inactive. In winter, they will hibernate in protected dens. Some species are known to migrate some distance to return to the same den, with sometimes 50 to 100 snakes hibernating together. Be careful of that area in the spring.

Rattlesnake bites

Most rattlesnakes are very docile unless they are harassed. They will try not to strike, remaining hidden by their location and camouflage color. Given the chance, they will escape rather than strike. However, if harassed or surprised they will strike without warning. They often strike from a coiled position, but they may strike from any position and can strike a distance of one-half to two-thirds of their body length. A six-foot snake can potentially strike you four feet away.

Rattlesnakes locate the presence of warm-blooded prey by finding food with their loreal glands, pits located between their eyes and nostrils, and chemically receptive tongue. They are extremely accurate, even in the total darkness of night.

Venom is injected through two fangs that are thin, gradually tapering cones that are actually elongated and modified maxillary teeth. In larger snakes, they may be up to an inch long. They are attached to the upper jaw and fold back when the mouth is closed. Replacement fangs grow behind the primary fang. A fang will function in an adult rattlesnake for 6 to 10 weeks before being replaced by a reserve fang.

Venom glands located on the side of the jaws, and giving the triangular shape to the head, are pear-shaped and produce and store venom. The compressor glandulae muscle surrounds the gland and causes venom to be ejected through the fangs when needed. The snake will inject its prey with venom and back off until it has had a chance to work, proceeding to follow the wounded prey with its heat sensing ability before swallowing it whole.

As many as 60% of human bites are "dry bites" that contain no venom. The others inject venom that varies by species of rattlesnake. Venoms are often described as either hemotoxic (affecting tissue and blood clotting) or neurotoxic (affecting the nervous system), but most actually contain many different chemicals that effect blood clotting, interfere with transmissions of nerve impulses, dissolve tissue cells, and specifically target cells of the heart, kidneys, muscles, and other sites.

Non-poisonous snakes do not have rattles or the distinctive triangular head. Their color pattern may be different than a rattlesnake, as shown by this striped garter snake, or similar, as in the case of gopher or Bull snakes.

Non-poisonous snakes have a head, neck, and body that are about the same diameter. They almost appear to be the shape that a child may make when rolling clay.

Preventing bites

Hands, feet, and ankles are the most common locations for rattlesnake bites. Avoiding snakebites is a matter of following a few "do's and don'ts" when traveling in rattlesnake country.

Do:
- Always hike or camp with someone who can go for help if needed.
- Tell a responsible person where you will be and check in with them.
- Bring a portable phone or other method of communication.
- Carry a Sawyer Extractor if you are going into the wilderness.

A Backwoods Home Anthology

This Great Basin Rattlesnake (Crotalus viridis lutosus) is coiled and in strike position. Rattlesnakes can strike up to two-thirds of their body length, four feet for a six foot snake. Note how its coloring camouflages it into the background environment. Photo courtesy of Dawn Wilson, PhD and Glen Lubcke, herpetologists at California State University, Chico.

- Wear hiking boots and long pants.
- Stay on paths where you can see where you are stepping. Avoid heavy grass or underbrush. Make noise with your feet while walking to let snakes know you are around.
- Use a walking stick. A snake may strike it instead of you.
- When stepping over a downed tree, check the other side before stepping.
- Check around rocks, logs, stumps, or rock fences before sitting down.
- Look for concealed snakes before picking up rocks, branches, or firewood.
- Be careful moving boats left on shore for a few hours.
- Teach children to leave snakes alone. Curious children who pick up snakes are often bitten.
- Always leave snakes alone.

Don't:

- Try to pick up, play with, kill, or otherwise harass a rattlesnake.
- Tease a rattlesnake to see how far it can strike.
- Put your hands or feet in places you cannot see, such as reaching down around a log, rock, or bush or reaching up when climbing rocks. Snakes climb walls, rocks, trees and are often at high altitudes.
- Crawl under fences without first looking under them carefully.
- Sleep near piles of wood, brush, or trash, at the entrance to a cave, or near swampy areas.
- Gather firewood after dark.
- Pick up a stick while swimming; rattlesnakes are good swimmers.
- Underestimate a baby rattlesnake. Although small, they are still deadly.
- Walk at night in snake country without boots and a flashlight.
- Handle freshly killed rattlesnakes; you can still be bitten.
- Keep rattlesnakes as pets. (Why ask for trouble.)

Treatment of rattlesnake bites

A variety of symptoms may develop after a rattlesnake bite. The first are usually pain, swelling, and bleeding at the site and pain, followed by swelling extending up the limb. Nausea, vomiting, sweating, chills, dizziness, weakness, numbness, tingling of the mouth, and changes of pulse or blood pressure may occur, as well as excessive salivation, thirst, swollen eyelids, blurred vision, muscle spasms, bleeding disorders, difficulty breathing, and unconsciousness. Even "dry bites," ones in which no venom was injected, can become painful and infected.

The problem with rattlesnake bites is that, at best, they can cause massive tissue destruction, leaving per-

A Sawyer Extractor is a device available for about $10 at outdoor stores and is reported to suck some of the venom out of a snakebite wound. It can be easily carried in a first aid kit when hiking through "snake country."

manent disability, or at worst, cause death.

Every rattlesnake bite must be considered a medical emergency and the victim must be taken to a hospital immediately. If they are some distance from a hospital, it is appropriate to transport them by helicopter to a Level 1 Trauma Center. At the hospital, the main treatment will be the use of antivenin, which counteracts the effects of the tissue damaging enzymes in the venom.

The antivenin, which costs about $450 a vial (at least 10 vials are needed to treat a victim) is not available at every hospital and, at times, is hard for hospitals to obtain. Many hospitals are lucky if they have enough antivenin on hand to treat one snakebite patient.

While many physicians or hospitals are experienced or prepared to treat rattlesnake bites, many are not. If bitten, make sure you are taken to a hospital that does know what they are doing and has antivenin on hand. When you get there, ask the physician to contact physician consultants available at a poison control center, a university hospital, or other specialists in treating rattlesnake bites. I know this may sound like you are telling them what to do (and some physician's egos could get bruised), but often as not, the doctor may be in the back room trying to read up on what to do, and advice on where to obtain consultation would be helpful.

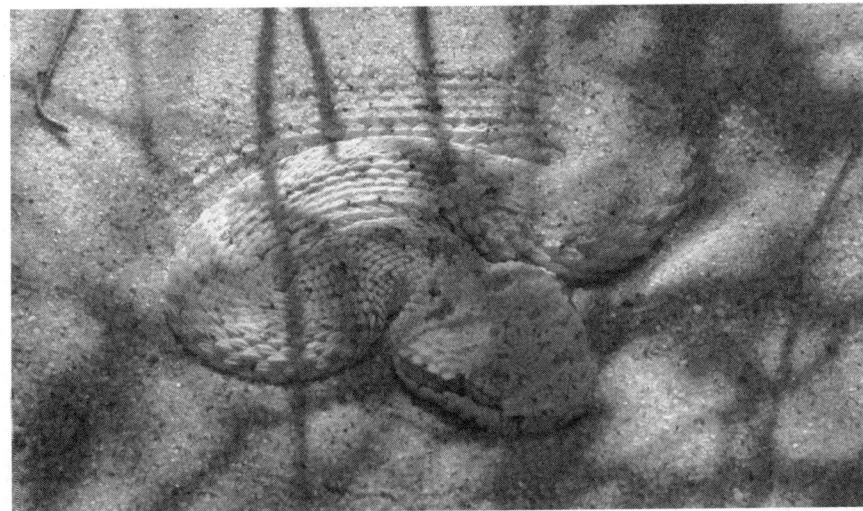

Some rattlesnakes protect themselves from the heat by burying their body in the sand under a bush in the desert during the day. This photo shows how hidden and camouflaged the snake is, and is a good example of the characteristic triangular head. Photo courtesy of Dawn Wilson, PhD and Glen Lubcke, herpetologists at California State University, Chico.

Trained herpetologist, Glen Lubcke, studies rattlesnakes, such as this Southern Pacific Rattlesnake, and advises people to never pick up or handle rattlesnakes. Most rattlesnake bites are caused when people "play" with snakes, often while intoxicated. Photo courtesy of Dawn Wilson, PhD and Glen Lubcke, herpetologists at California State University, Chico.

First aid

I am not a physician and have not treated rattlesnake bites. The following first aid information is given for general information only and is obtained from what appears to be the common standards listed in first aid books and medical websites, including the snakebite protocol for physicians by Terrance M. Davidson, M.D., Professor of Surgery, University of California, San Diego (www.surgery.ucsd.edu/ENT/Davidson/Snake/Crotalus.htm).

- Move away from the snake to avoid being bitten again. Avoid jumping or running blindly, as there may be other snakes around. Do not try to kill the snake for identification. This wastes time and risks other bites, and the antivenin is the same for all species of rattlesnakes.
- Immediately call for medical help while calming and reassuring the victim. Keep the victim from moving around and ask them to lie flat, preferably with the affected limb lower than the

This young Northern Pacific Rattlesnake (Crotalus viridis oreganos) has not yet developed rattles, but can be distinguished from a non-poisonous snake by its triangular head. It was found warming itself on an asphalt road at sunset, a common spot to find rattlesnakes. Photo by author.

level of the heart. Remove any rings, watches, or bracelets that could cut circulation if swelling occurs.
- If fang marks are present, apply a Sawyer Extractor with the largest cup available over the puncture site to try to remove some of the venom. Place it over at least one of the fang marks, and apply over both if more than one Extractor is available. Leave in place until there is no more drainage from the fang marks. A Sawyer Extractor is a negative pressure syringe reported to suck venom from the wound and widely available for around $10 at sporting goods and camping stores.
- Immediately wrap a constricting band on the limb just above the site of the bite, between the bite and the heart. This can be something like an elastic bandage and should be tight enough to block the lymph drainage, but not to constrict blood flow. It should be about the tightness that would be used to wrap a sprained ankle. This is not a tourniquet that is so tight it constricts blood flow and damages tissue. Leave the constricting band in place until the victim is at the hospital where it will be removed after administration of antivenin.
- Continue to reassure victim and treat for shock by having them lie down until medical help arrives.

What not to do

Some treatments for snakebites used in the past actually worsened the injury and are no longer advised. This includes cutting an "X" between the fang marks with a knife or scalpel and applying suction to the fang marks with your mouth. Don't apply hot, cold, or ice to the injured area or place a thin constricting band, such as rope, shoelace, or belt. Avoid strenuous physical activity and don't drink alcohol.

For the number of rattlesnakes in North America and the number of snake-human encounters, the number of rattlesnake bites to humans is low. The problem is that the effect can be catastrophic. Even with excellent, timely care, permanent disability or death can occur. And, given the low number of bites, it is hard to find a physician or hospital that has extensive experience in treating bites, and antivenin is not always available. Your best protection is to understand where to expect rattlesnakes and take precautions to avoid an encounter. Enjoy the outdoors, but be prepared. Δ

Get The Whole Sheebang!
www.backwoodshome.com

Visit the Backwoods Home Magazine CHAT ROOM at the BHM website:
www.backwoodshome.com

Keep those gadgets working after the
power goes out

By Jeffrey R. Yago, P.E., CEM

The recent 2003 northeast electric grid failure taught the residents of many large cities what most rural residents learned years ago: Lights, air conditioners, televisions, stereos, elevators, subways, computers, refrigerators, cash registers, money machines, gas pumps, and traffic lights do not work when the power goes out. They also learned very quickly that they could not recharge all of the dead batteries in their cell phones, pagers, personal digital assistants (PDAs), video cameras, laptop computers, digital cameras, and portable phones without electricity.

This lesson was not as obvious as you might think, as an interconnected utility grid tied to many different power plants surrounds all large cities. A failure of one power plant or a downed power line is easily bypassed or back-fed from other sources in minutes by system managers, with little or no power interruption. At least that's the way it is designed to work. Obviously, the system managers during the August 14, 2003 East coast power outage didn't get the memo.

Those of us living in smaller towns at the end of a single power line know what to expect when the power goes out and we have flashlights, battery-powered radios, and extra supplies at the ready, since we go through this with every major storm. Many rural residents have their own generators and backup power systems and do not worry when the grid goes down. We should keep in mind that most residents of large cities live in apartments or condos in multi-tenant buildings, and having their own generator, and a roof-mounted solar array is not possible.

Batteries

If you are in this situation, you may not be able to keep your major appliances operating during a power outage, but there is a way to keep all those important communication gadgets working, regardless of how long the power is out. The most obvious first step is having lots of extra batteries on hand. Newer alkaline batteries have extremely long shelf life if

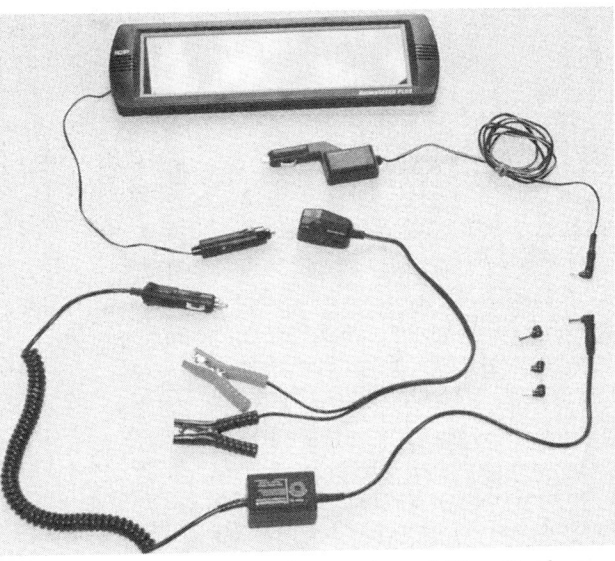

A solar module and an endless variety of 12-volt adapters are available to power portable electronic devices.

stored in a cool and dry location, and these are the batteries you should buy for emergency power needs even though they are more expensive. Since you may be in the dark when spare batteries are needed, I suggest selecting an easy-to-find central location in your home or apartment where you should have at least eight each of the most common battery sizes. In most cases this will be the smaller AAA, AA, and 9-volt batteries. Flashlights and desktop radios typically use the larger C or D-size cells and really use the power, so you may want to have even more of these larger sizes at the ready.

Most of today's cell phones, pagers, and laptop computers use larger built-in special voltage batteries, which are designed to be recharged only by an AC wall outlet while remaining in the device. If we could remove these batteries, you would find large heavy plastic blocks with odd shaped electrical contacts, having voltages well beyond our old familiar round flash-

Nickel cadmium and nickel metal hydride batteries in custom shapes

327

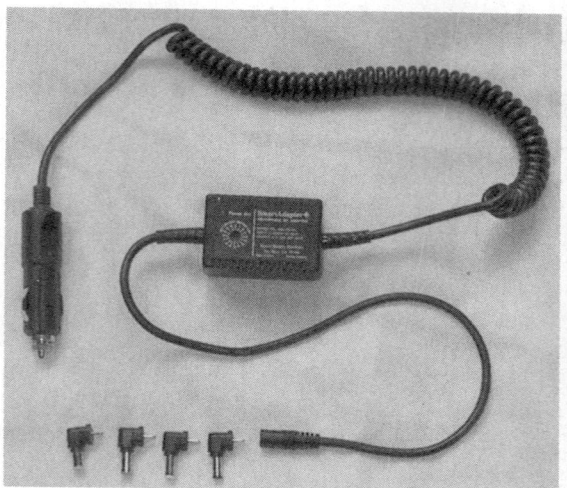

Versatile car adapter with adjustable voltage output for 6 to 21 volts and interchangeable tips (Nesco Battery Systems)

light batteries. To reduce battery weight while packing more and more operating time in as small a space as possible, most electronic device manufacturers first switched to nickel cadmium hydride (NiCad) batteries, then to more expensive nickel metal hydride (NiMH) batteries which have even more power density.

All NiCad batteries have a "memory" problem when recharged. If the battery is not completely discharged prior to recharging, the recharge will bring the battery back to full, but the battery will discharge down to the new low limit when it is discharged again and generate less operating time.

More power demanding electronic devices are turning to nickel metal hydride rechargeable batteries that hold twice the charge of an alkaline battery and can be recharged up to 500 times. NiMH self-discharge faster than NiCad batteries when not being used, but NiMH batteries do not have the memory problem of NiCad batteries. Newer battery chargers are designed to recharge both NiCad and NiMH batteries equally well, assuming you have a wall outlet and grid power. So how can you recharge these exotic internal batteries when the electric grid is down?

During any emergency or power outage you should already have a battery powered AM/FM radio, an LED or fluorescent battery room light, and a stock of spare disposable alkaline batteries that will keep these basic devices operational for several days. But, you will also want to keep your cell phone, pager, and your PDA or laptop computer operating, so you will need a different solution for these.

Adapters

I suggest buying a low cost 12-volt car adapter for each of your electronic gadgets. Since today's more complex portable electronic devices require lots of battery power, most manufacturers offer optional low cost cables and charging adapters that will allow powering them from a car's cigarette lighter socket. Some charging adapters include built-in circuits to convert the 12-volt DC car voltage into multiple voltages required by different electronic devices. For small electronic devices, this could be 3, 4½, 6, or 9 volts DC. However, some larger laptop computer batteries may require up to 21 volts DC, and a special higher cost adapter is needed to raise, not lower, the 12-volt car battery voltage. These more expensive 12-volt adapters include a small dial that allows you to select which output voltage your device requires, plus interchangeable output plugs which allow one device to fit almost any electronic device.

Since you may not want to idle your car for hours or risk a dead car battery just to recharge a cell phone, there are some really great new low cost products that will solve this charging problem without the need to connect to either a wall outlet or car battery.

Solar battery module

After you have selected which devices you need to keep operating, and you have purchased a 12-volt car adapter for each, you will need to purchase a solar battery charging module. Unlike the larger solar modules that you see along the highways to power signs and warning lights, these smaller solar modules are designed to be connected directly to the battery to be charged. Any required fuse or reverse current flow protection is built in, so all you need is a 12-volt female adapter which will accept the different car adapter plugs connected to your electronic devices. This allows using a single solar module to recharge all of your electronic gadgets that have a car adapter, and its small size can easily be stored in a briefcase, glove compartment, or utility drawer.

Since a cigarette lighter socket is a standard physical size and voltage for all vehicles, you do not need a sepa-

Larger 10-watt solar module and 12-volt car adapter to power laptop computer

rate charger for each device and vehicle. Do not purchase a solar module smaller than 2-watt output, as it will take longer than a single afternoon to recharge all but the smallest battery sizes. For large laptop computer batteries, I recommend a 10-watt solar module, which will provide approximately 1 amp of charge current. Remember that disposable alkaline batteries may have a very long life, but they cannot be recharged, so keep them separate from your rechargeable batteries and never connect them to any charger. Any battery you plan to recharge must be clearly labeled as "rechargeable." For any device that uses disposable batteries, you may want to replace them with rechargeable batteries and buy one of the desktop chargers that can recharge multiple batteries at the same time.

Car Charger Products	Supplier	Web Address
iSun Sport and Power Pack	ICP Global Technologies 514-270-5770	www.icpglobal.com
Solar Power Pak	Solar World Colorado Springs 800-246-7012	www.solar-world.com
Diogenes	Sundance Solar Warner, NV 603-456-2020	www.sundancesolar.com
PortaFlex and Accumanager 20	Creative Energy Technology 518-278-1428	www.cetsolar.com
#SPA	C. Crane Company 800-522-8863	www.ccrane.com
Solar Port and Solaris 25	Solardyne Corporation Portland, OR 503-830-8739	www.solardyne.com
Smart Laptop Adapter by Nesco Battery Systems	CompUSA computer stores	www.compusa.com
12-volt Adapters and Device Connectors		
#270-1561 #980-0692 #273-1827 #273-1817	Radio Shack stores	www.radioshack.com

Inexpensive 2-watt solar module and 12-volt car adapter will recharge most small electronic devices.

Solar chargers

I purchased the fold-up solar module and all of the adapter cables described in this article at a local Radio Shack store for under $50. If you need a more professionally assembled system, there are several excellent solar battery charger kits available that include everything in a compact fold up case.

Some solar chargers are similar to a typical desktop charger stand that holds multiple AAA, AA, C, and D-size rechargeable batteries, but this assumes they can be removed from the electronic device for recharging. The solar module is placed in a window facing the sun and connects to this charging station by a short cable. Some manufacturers offer a complete emergency power kit that includes a rechargeable light, fold-up solar module, and all required special adapters to fit most cell phones and laptop computers in an easy-to-store carry bag.

Uni-Solar makes solar modules in various sizes that have a flexible backing material that is almost unbreakable. I strongly recommend these flexible or hinged fold up modules for camping or mobile applications. The table lists some suppliers to help your battery charging needs.∆

Recycled bicycles

By Brad Rohdenburg

Good bicycles are wonderful things. As you exercise your way to the office or biology class without noise or pollution, they help you lose weight, feel healthier, look better, sleep more soundly, and perhaps live longer. They give you a sense of freedom and self-sufficiency. They might save you money by allowing you to do with one less car. In congested cities they bypass traffic jams, providing not just low-cost mobility but sometimes more mobility than a car.

Their technology is comprehensible to anyone who made it through junior high school. If they aren't left out in the rain too often, they can be maintained for generations with basic hand tools.

They connect you with a fascinating history. Evolving from Velocipedes—toys known as "bone-shakers" to those who rode them over cobblestones—through dangerous highwheels and "safety bicycles," they were finally made practical when a Scottish veterinarian named John Dunlop invented pneumatic tires.

By 1895, bicycles as we know them had arrived—ball bearings, chain drives, variable gears, cable controls, and air-filled tires on wheels with wire spokes. Mass production techniques made them affordable, and suddenly the working class had unprecedented mobility, their practical radius as pedestrians multiplied by a factor of about five. Bicycles were well on their way to supplanting horses as personal transportation before they were in turn superseded by the internal combustion engine. Bicycles didn't require pastures, barns or a winter supply of hay and oats. They didn't kick, bite, or run away. (They still don't kick or bite, but they seem to have learned to run away if you don't keep an eye on them.) Even after the advent of affordable automobiles, bicycles continued to be thought of as utilitarian transportation in much of the world, like the Netherlands and parts of Asia. In wealthy North America, though, they were once again relegated to toy status.

This aluminum-framed Raleigh showed almost no wear and needed only its rear wheel trued and the rear derailer adjusted. In many parts of the world it would have been a prized possession.

Then during the 1970s, the OPEC oil embargo hit us baby-boomers, and there was a second "bike boom." Millions of ten-speeds, more properly called road bikes, went into the garages of America. Many of them were of very high quality, and many of them were never ridden much as gas prices came back down and their owners aged.

Nowadays, road bikes are out of fashion and mountain bikes are trendy. But again in the American tradition, they tend to be thought of and designed for sport and recreation rather than as transportation. People put them on automobile roof racks and drive them places to play in the dirt. The features that make them fun off-road are disadvantages on pavement. Fat tires and knobby treads have greater rolling resistance than thin, slick tires. Upright handlebars permit only one body position, no matter how long the ride or what conditions or winds are encountered. Short wheelbases are uncomfortable and tiring. Shock absorbers and 21- or-more speeds add unnecessary weight to be propelled up hills. Fashionable or not, three-decade-old road bikes will dramatically outperform state-of-the-art mountain bikes on hard-surfaced roads. They are a superior choice for anything but bombing down debris-strewn dirt trails.

There are many other types of bicycles, too, serving many other purposes. The focus of this article will however be very specific: High end 10 and 12-speed road bikes from the

1970s and early 1980s. Such a bike will have drop handlebars and 27-inch wheels, a rear freewheel cluster with five or six sprockets, and will commonly weigh less than 20 pounds.

The basic geometry of these bikes had been established by the time of the first World War. Since then, millions of people have ridden billions of miles, all the while trying to figure out how to reduce weight and increase speed, efficiency, comfort, and reliability. Although the technology was mature well before the 1970s, incremental improvements and refinements have continued. Road bikes being manufactured today have freehubs, with cassettes of seven or more cogs, as opposed to freewheels with clusters of five or six sprockets. Shifters are now integrated with brake levers. Cables are routed more cleanly and aerodynamically. And rims have gone to the European standard, with metric sizing now being the norm.

Old road bikes are thus outdated as well as out of fashion. They have very little resale value, and dealers are reluctant to even take them in trade. Uncountable multitudes of them are therefore languishing in garages or basements, or being hauled to landfills. Yet, in some ways, those older bikes are superior to even the newest versions. They tend to have better frame clearance in case you'd like to add fenders or slightly wider, more comfortable tires. Their frames are more likely to have threaded eyelets with which to attach fenders and racks. They were made before liability concerns outweighed common sense and affected the form of things like front forks and bottom brackets. Today's bikes, in a sense, are designed by lawyers.

In 1979 my college graduation present to myself was a 12-speed. I still have it, and it was well-maintained until I was hit by a car fairly recently. (Okay, technically I hit the car, but the end result was the same.) Once my road-rash cleared up, I went to the local bike shop in need of new wheels, fork, brake, and crankset. The proprietor no longer stocked either 27-inch wheels or freewheels, but he let me in on a trade secret: The best place to get those parts is the local dump or at yard sales. He told me that he himself literally threw away about 50 bikes a year. Sure enough, I started looking over the scrap metal pile at the local recycling center on trash day, and within a few weeks I'd found everything I needed. And the quality was better than that of the originals. Since then I've assembled several more bikes for myself and friends, and one for my daughter to take to college this fall. I've upgraded our components when opportunities presented themselves, too, and collected a cache of spares.

If you're interested in the economic and ecologic sense of alternative transportation and don't already own a bike, this is a chance to experiment without a large investment. If you have an old bike with sentimental value in your attic—a friend that's carried you thousands of happy miles—maybe it's time to put it back in service with upgraded brakes, wheels or drive-train parts. If you already have a nice bike, you might also want a "beater" to ride in the rain, or where theft is a concern. The uglier the better, but it should still be in excellent mechanical order. Re-using is the ultimate form of recycling, and good for everyone concerned.

Now, back to the scrap metal pile: You might get lucky and find a complete bike in good order, but usually parts are missing or damaged—most

The serial number indicates that this Trek was built in 1983. It was missing pedals and a saddle.

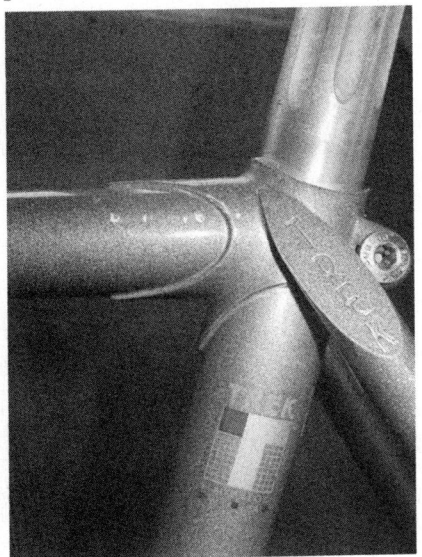

A lugged steel frame

often wheels, saddles, and pedals. Grab those whenever you see any worth grabbing. Frames will occasionally be of aluminum, but usually of steel. Avoid cheap welded frames with stamped components. While they can be made ridable, they will never be rewarding and aren't worthy of your time and effort. Good steel frames will be "lugged"—made with sockets that strengthen the joints between tubes, the areas of highest stress. Another quick way to recognize quality is to look at the right crank and "spider"—the starfish-shaped piece that the front chainwheels are bolted to. If they're cast as one piece, it's a decent bike. Look, too, for wheels with alloy rims and stainless spokes. Steel wheels are heavy and unresponsive. (Hey, I think I was married to one of those once ....) If a bike's frame is the wrong size for you, maybe it's the right size for someone you know. Or maybe the components are worth salvaging.

Give any older bike a thorough going-over. The bearings should be cleaned and repacked with grease. New brake pads are always a good idea. Even if they aren't worn, they harden with age. Replacing cables is usually worthwhile, too. Modern ones have stainless steel wires surrounded by a low-friction liner, conducive to clean, quick shifting and braking. The handlebars will likely need re-wrapping. Look in used book stores for a repair and maintenance manual with a copyright date in the appropriate date range. While you're at it, get a book or two about how to ride—there's more to it than you might think. The mysteries of adjusting derailers and servicing headsets will be solved once you sit down with a book and your bike and follow the procedures step by step. You may feel more comfortable if you dissect a junk bike first, just to see how things work, before you begin on your legitimate restoration project.

Throw away anything that adds useless weight. Those brake extension levers on some bikes, for example. At best, using them will teach you poor riding habits. At their worst, they can be dangerously inefficient. If you prefer straight handlebars and upright brake levers, you can create a hybrid.

If the front derailer is damaged, save yourself some weight and complexity and do without it. Remove it and one of the front chain rings, and you own a five-speed. Do you really need any more? If you don't have many hills to contend with, consider going all the way to a single speed. This will relieve you of the need for the rear derailer, all the rear sprockets but one, and the shift levers and cables. It will save a few additional ounces with a shorter chain, too. A singlespeed is noticeably more efficient than a multispeed in the same gain ratio because of its lighter weight and the lack of drag from derailer pulleys. There are several websites that will guide you through the process so that you'll end up with the requisite straight chainline.

Another option for a missing or damaged rear wheel is to replace it with one that has a more modern cassette-style freehub. This may involve spreading the stays of the frame to accommodate a wider axle, but it's not rocket science and again there's information on the web.

While I have a generally minimalist philosophy, there are some things that are worth adding to a bike. Locks are an unfortunate necessity. Flat tires are by far the most common mechanical malfunction, so a patch kit and tire levers should be in a small bag under your saddle, and a frame-fitting pump on the seat tube. On a long ride, your hands will appreciate rubber brake hoods. Toe clips are considered obsolete by some, and take some getting used to, but they'll convert the energy you use just to keep your feet on the pedals into forward motion. (Clipless pedals are even better, but require

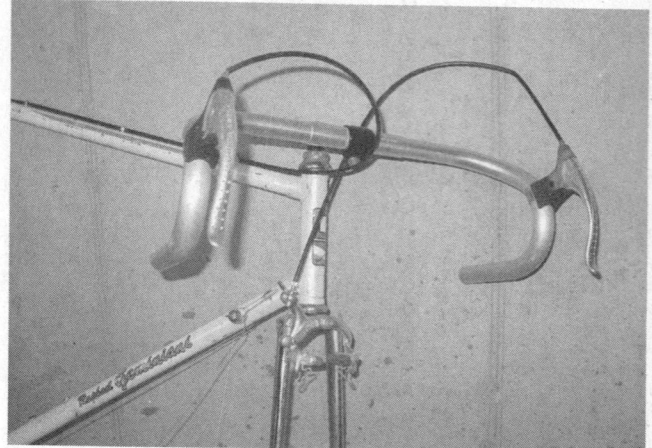

This Italian-made frame has very high quality lugged, double-butted tubing and Campagnolo components. It was top of the line in its day.

A quick way to recognize quality: If the right crank and "spider"—the starfish-shaped piece that the chainwheels are bolted to—are cast in one piece, it's a decent bike.

The Fourteenth Year

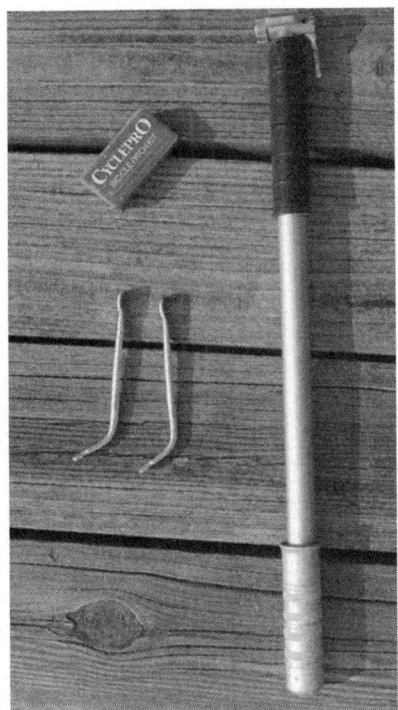

Since flat tires are the most common mechanical problem, carry a patch kit, tire levers and a frame-type pump on your bike.

special shoes that you won't want to walk around in at your destination.) A water bottle will fuel you so you can fuel your bike. Lights will keep you visible at night. Those with LED's are remarkably small and efficient. I'm ambivalent about fenders and racks—if they make sense for you, put them on. Small fenders are useless, but full ones will keep you drier and your bike cleaner if you're not just a fair-weather cyclist. If you carry paperwork or lunch or clothes, a rack will keep your center of gravity lower than a backpack will.

Cyclists tend to be friendly folks who will cheerfully help you. Chances are you already know someone who would be glad to advise you about refurbishing a bike and fitting it to you. ∆

"When I see an adult on a bicycle, I have hope for the human race."
— H.G. Wells

Skunks

By Tom Kovach

With no market for skunk hides, the population of these smelly little creatures has increased in many parts of the country. Skunk encounters by humans and their pets can be a rather unpleasant experience... to say nothing of the smell.

The U.S. Department of Agriculture has some tips on discouraging skunks from hanging around your place. They are:

- Do not leave pet food outside overnight.
- Make sure your garbage is stored in secure containers.
- Make sure all access holes to crawl spaces under your home (skunks love crawl spaces) are either sealed or covered with wire mesh.
- If your foundation is porous, bury 3-foot mesh fencing a foot from the foundation. Don't leave piles of fence posts, lumber, junk cars, etc, near your home. Skunks will use this sort of cover for den sites.

You can trap and remove skunks with single-door covered cage traps. Bait the trap with cat food (unless you have a cat). You can also use raw whole eggs or bread with butter.

If you or your pet do get sprayed, a good skunk deodorizer is a mixture of 1 quart hydrogen peroxide, ¼ cup baking soda and 1 teaspoon dishwashing liquid. Don't store this mixture in a sealed container. The hydrogen peroxide reacts with the baking soda, creating carbon dioxide gas which will build up pressure and the container could explode. ∆

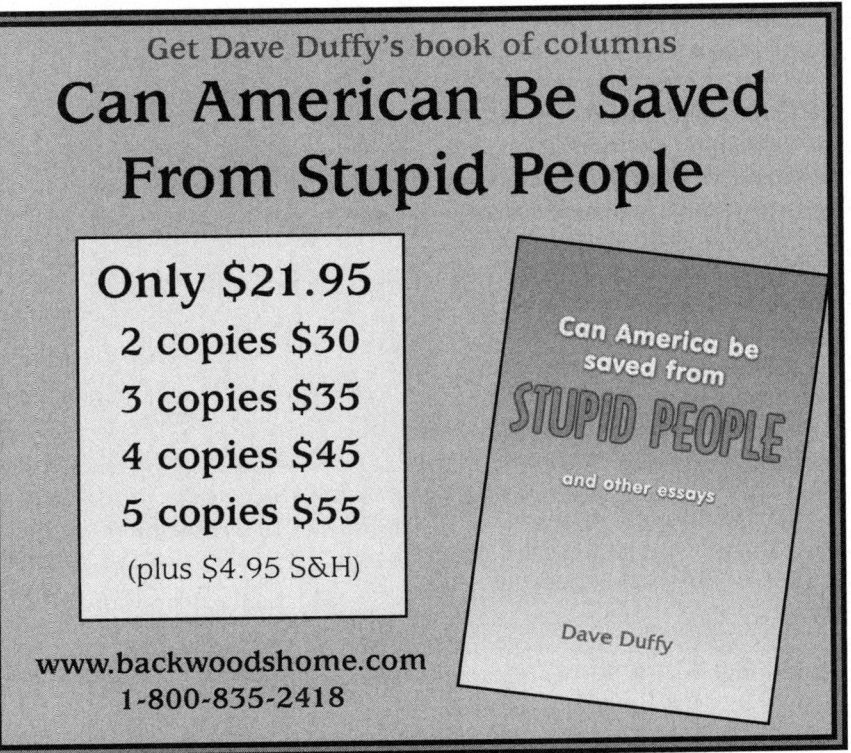

A *Backwoods Home* Anthology

Cultured milk

Food of centenarians

By Edna Manning

Cultured milk products have been enjoyed in the Middle East, Europe, and parts of Asia for centuries. The Greeks felt that yogurt had therapeutic qualities for diseases caused by intestinal disorders. Bulgarians attribute their good health and longevity in part to their daily intake of cultured milk products.

The most common of the cultured milk products are yogurt, kefir, piima, buttermilk, and quark or cottage cheese.

Yogurt is simply milk thickened to a custard consistency by certain acid-forming bacteria growing in it. The special bacteria that turn milk into yogurt are lactobacillus bulgaricus, lactobacillus acidophilus, and streptococcus thermophilus. The coagulation and the fermentation of milk sugar into lactic acid is caused by these bacteria. This action curdles the protein in yogurt and acts as a preservative.

The bacteria in yogurt have already begun to break down the protein molecules into lactic acid, making it easy for the body to assimilate. Thus yogurt is helpful for people who have lactose intolerance, because they lack an enzyme that helps to digest milk sugar in regular milk. Yogurt helps the digestion process to move along smoothly and quickly.

In the Near East, babies are frequently fed yogurt for two or three months after they are weaned. Breast fed babies receive bacillus bifidus, a bacteria similar to lactobacillus bulgaricus found in yogurt.

Some doctors prescribe yogurt to replace normal intestinal flora that are destroyed when oral antibiotics have been used for an extended period of time. Antibiotics destroy

Yogurt makes a light and tasty dessert with a few strawberries added for color and flavor.

"good" bacteria along with the "bad" bacteria.

Studies show that yogurt can be helpful in lowering the cholesterol levels in the blood by decreasing the amount of cholesterol the body produces.

Research would also indicate that the bacteria in yogurt can help guard the intestinal tract for carcinogens.

Yogurt has also been used to aid in the healing of ulcers, digestive disorders, yeast infections, and nervous fatigue.

Yogurt is also used in cosmetics such as face masks and body lotions.

Commercial yogurt can be purchased in any supermarket. It comes in a variety of flavors and brands, many with low butterfat content.

Yogurt can be made from any kind of milk, including soy milk. The flavor will vary with the type of milk used.

Yogurt is not complicated to make yourself. Only two ingredients are necessary: milk and a starter culture. Use fresh whole or skim milk, powdered milk, or a combination. Adding a third of a cup of dry milk to a quart of skim milk will produce a more firm, nutritious yogurt.

Starter cultures for cultured milk can be purchased at Health Food Stores. You can also purchase a container of plain yogurt for your starter.

Dried starter will keep for several months in a cool place. If you use yogurt as a starter, you will have to buy a fresh supply every once in a while, as the bacteria strain tends to weaken after a time. Whenever it begins to take longer to set, buy a fresh starter.

The next step in yogurt making is the heating and cooling of the milk.

First sterilize all the utensils you will use with boiling water. Then heat one quart of pasteurized milk to a temperature of 105 to 110 degrees F If you're using raw unpasteurized milk, heat it first to 180 degrees F, then allow to cool to 110 degrees F Stir in a couple of tablespoons of commercial yogurt into 1 cup of your prepared milk and add this to your remaining milk and mix well. If you use a powdered starter, follow the directions on the package.

Pour milk into sterilized jars or small plastic containers. (Use small containers as yogurt tends to separate and get watery on top once some of it has been used.) Cover the containers.

Incubation is the next step. This can be done by using a yogurt maker or any warm place where the temperature can be kept at 110-115 degrees F. My favorite method is to simply use the oven with only a 40 watt light bulb on.

Yogurt can take from six to ten hours to incubate. Check periodically to see if it has set to the proper consistency. It should be smooth, have a mild flavor, and be slightly tart. You can obtain either a mild or a more tangy yogurt by adjusting the incubation period. The longer it is incubated, the tangier the results.

Refrigerate immediately. It will keep for up to two weeks. If whey forms on the top, pour it off. Remember to save a few tablespoons for your next batch.

Kefir is similar to yogurt, but has yeast cells present causing fermentation, thus producing a drink that is slightly alcoholic and effervescent. The flavor is sweeter and milder.

To make kefir, simply add culture (kefir grains, the fermenting agent) to raw milk and incubate at room temperature for 12 to 24 hours. Pour through a sieve, reserving the kefir grains for the next batch. Serve chilled.

Blend with fresh fruit to make a delicious drink.

Piima is a Scandinavian cultured milk product. It is milder than either yogurt or kefir and very easy to make. Simply stir your culture into pasteurized milk at room temperature. Allow to incubate for 8 to 24 hours.

Buttermilk is really the liquid left from butter making. The "buttermilk" found in stores is a cultured milk made from pasteurized skim milk. Lactic acid bacteria is added to the milk and the mixture is left to clabber at room temperature.

Homemade buttermilk can be made by adding a culture to pasteurized milk or, if you make your own butter, from pasteurized real buttermilk.

Quark or **Cottage cheese** is also easy to make from raw, unpasteurized milk. The milk can be poured into a large cooking pot, covered and left to incubate in a warm place (about 80 degrees F—again, I use the oven with a light bulb on). After about 24 hours the milk has thickened. At this point, heat the clabbered milk slowly at a very low temperature, stirring gently on occasion to separate the curds from the whey. In about 40 minutes, the curds will have shrunk. Hold temperature at 120 degrees for about 15 minutes until the curds feel firm but not rubbery. You can now ladle the curds into a colander and drain the whey. The whey is rich in B vitamins and can be used in baking.

Beatrice Trum Hunter's, *Fact/Book on Yogurt, Kefir and Other Milk Cultures* is a practical, informative book on the benefits of cultured milk which includes a variety of easy to make recipes. Check your local library. ∆

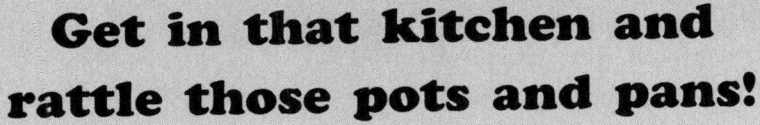

Small Town America

Thorne Bay, Alaska

(This is part of a series on *"Small Town America."* If you'd like to write about your small town, send your article to *Backwoods Home Magazine*, PO Box 712, Gold Beach, OR 97444.
— Editor)

By Jon Stram

Three weeks in Thorne Bay, Alaska, working on our cabin, relaxing with our friends, and just generally living life the way it was meant to be lived, were over for another six months. My wife, Juanita, my youngest daughter, Jamie, and I had been working on planing and grooving a load of red cedar boards in preparation for paneling the inside of our cozy 16 x 20 cabin. We wired for electricity, added on a carport/covered work area, and kept ourselves so busy that we only took one day out for salmon fishing. Still, catching a nice 12-pound silver salmon on your first cast of the day is not a bad way to remember your fishing time.

The sight of Jack, our young chocolate Labrador, chasing pink salmon through the shallows of Gravelly Creek and proudly presenting me with one live salmon after another is a picture I'll never forget. Of course, as soon as he'd head back out for another salmon, I'd toss the almost spawned-out salmon back into the creek to complete its journey. Pinks in the final stages of spawning aren't exactly gourmet fare.

The beauty and bounty of Alaska, after all these years, still overwhelms me. Hills are covered in hemlock, red

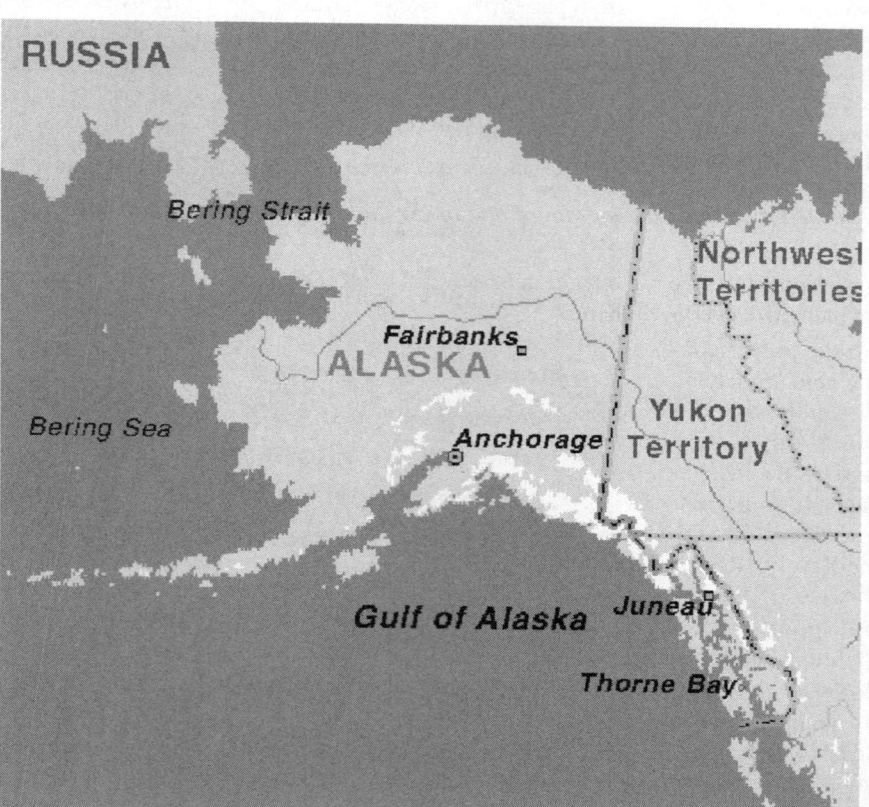

and yellow cedar, and spruce trees. Blueberries, huckleberries, salmonberries, and currants compete for every square inch of space. Streams so full of spawning salmon—pinks, silvers, chum, and sockeye—that at times you can't retrieve a lure through them without snagging one or more with every cast. Dungeness crab and clam for the taking, so numerous that you can fill a bucket in 10 to 15 minutes. Sitka blacktail deer seemingly around the corner of every bend in the road, and the numerous black bear, appearing and disappearing as they gorge on salmon and berries, preparing for the possibility of a long, cold winter.

The bittersweet thoughts of heading back home to the Lower 48 filled my mind as I lay on my sleeping bag and pad on the hard, plastic cots that the Alaska Ferry System so thoughtfully provides for us low-budget travelers. I was already missing my good friends, Ernie and Margie, Earl and Chris, Bill, Wally, Bud, and so many others. It's always so hard to leave, and this time was no different. The prospect of once again entering Civilization (a misnomer to put it gently) was none too inviting. It was the morning of September 11, 2001. Little did I know at the time how truly uninviting it would soon turn out to be.

The people

Wonderful as the environment is, the best part about Thorne Bay are the people and the sense of communi-

The Fourteenth Year

View of Thorne Bay, some float buildings, and the School District Office Floathouse from "The Port"

ty you get living here. You can't live here long before you recognize everyone by the vehicles they drive, and everyone you pass on the road gives you a wave. You can't walk down the road with a gas can in hand before the first person passing by will ask if you need a ride or some help. With only one grocery store, two gas stations, two sporting goods and general hardware stores it doesn't take long before you know every merchant in town personally, and yet you'll find that you rarely need to leave town to get a necessary service or supply. If you really want to get to know some of Thorne Bay's residents quickly, just stop by the *Thorne Bay Community Church* any Sunday morning about 10:30, and you'll be surrounded by a group of some of the friendliest people you'll ever meet, and you'll probably have an invitation for lunch, even if it isn't Potluck Sunday. If for some reason you don't get a lunch invite, just stop by *Dale's Pizza* or *Someplace to Go* for a homemade burger and fries. No *McDonald's* here.

Thorne Bay, Alaska, is located on the east side of Prince of Wales Island, in Southeast Alaska, near the town of Ketchikan. You can get to Ketchikan via Alaska Airlines, a one and a half hour flight from Seattle. From Ketchikan you can then hop aboard a float plane for the half hour flight to Prince of Wales Island, or you can take a two and a half hour ferry ride to Hollis, on Prince of Wales Island. You can also drive and ferry from Down South, either getting on the ferry at Bellingham, Washington, or Prince Rupert, British Columbia.

Prince of Wales Island is the third largest island in the United States, over 90 miles long, 40 miles wide, and with a 1,500+ mile road system. It is sparsely populated with under 5,000 people. Craig, Klawock, Hollis, Hydaburg, Kasaan, Coffman Cove, Whale Pass, Point Baker, Naukati, and Thorne Bay are the main towns on the island, with anywhere from 40 to 1,500 per town. In the recent past, most of the employment has been timber based, and with the current downturn in lumber prices and slowdown in logging activity, the overall island economy is quite depressed. Don't let that depress you, though. There's still plenty of opportunity for the innovative backwoods home person with a few skills and an active imagination.

Advantages

Let me just give you an idea of some of the advantages of life on Prince of Wales Island, especially in Thorne Bay. First off, Alaska has no state income tax, no state property tax, and no state sales tax. That's right. None. Vehicle registration fees will be under $100 per year for the average vehicle. To make the situation even better, Alaska has a unique thing called the *Permanent Fund Dividend*, where the state actually pays each individual in each family

"Some Place to Go," a small walk-up fast food restaurant in Thorne Bay

who lives there, just to live there. In 2001 the dividend was $1850.28, which meant a family of four received $7405.12. In 2002 the dividend was $1540.76 and a family of four received $6103.04 in about October or November of 2002. If you are careful and creative, you can stretch that out quite a ways.

Every Alaskan resident is also allowed up to 10,000 board feet of personal use wood that can be harvested off of National Forest lands with a free permit from the Forest Service. Eighty-five percent of Prince of Wales Island is National Forest, and there are numerous small mills around the island that will help you cut, haul, and mill your wood into lumber, and then deliver it to your building site. It doesn't take much to get all the lumber you'd need to build a house or cabin and all the outbuildings you could want. You'll have to see the quality of the raw lumber you'll get: red and yellow cedar, spruce, and hemlock. You'll never want to buy Down South lumber again.

If you haven't been to Southeast Alaska, you probably think about Alaska as the land of snow and ice. That's a common misconception.

There's a good reason for the fact that most of the residents of Prince of Wales come from Oregon, Washington, and Montana. The weather is not that much different from what they're used to. Prince of Wales is technically a rain forest, and being an island on the Inside Passage, it has a coastal climate. It has an average wintertime low of only 32° F, summertime highs into the 70s and low 80s, and average yearly rainfall in the 150 to 200 inch range. If you can't stand clouds and rain, don't come to Prince of Wales. Winters will range from mild, with very little snow and freezing weather, to mildly severe, with snow accumulations from November to March and freezing temperatures.

One difference you'll notice on Prince of Wales Island is the absence of small cars and sedans. Ninety-five percent of the vehicles on the island are pickups, Suburbans, and SUVs. While a decent two-wheel drive vehicle will get you around on any of the gravel roads on the island nine months out of the year, the roads do tend to be rough and a little hard on your suspension and spinal column. Be sure to stay on the roads, though, because if you get off into the muskeg, you'll need to be winched out. A good four-wheel drive vehicle and chains will get you around fine in all but the very worst winter weather. The state is currently paving the main roads from Hollis to Hydaburg to Craig, Thorne Bay, and Coffman Cove. Within a couple years or so, you'll be able to travel to most of the major destinations on the island without getting off of pavement, unless you take one of the numerous side rides to hunt, fish, explore, or cut firewood.

The topsoil on Prince of Wales is very shallow, as the island is basically a big rock with a huge network of caves underneath its surface. We have a growing season that usually starts in mid-April, running through September or October. You'll need to build up your soil, and a lot of residents either have tire gardens, raised beds, or greenhouses for their produce.

There is no pasture on the island, which explains why you'll see no horses or cattle on the island. You could probably raise poultry or goats, but you'll need to think about protection from both the elements and the local black bear and wolf population. Prince of Wales Island has no brown or grizzly bears and no moose or caribou population.

Hunting and fishing

However, if you're a hunter or fisherman, Prince of Wales Island is a paradise. Residents are allowed to

Jamie Stram works with a pocket knife, removing slivers of wood from the edges of cedar interior boards after grooving edges with the table saw.

harvest two black bear per year, with the black bear hunting season open 10 months out of the year, September through June.

Four deer are allowed per person per year, with deer hunting season running five months, August through September. There is no cost for either deer or black bear tags for residents.

Waterfowl season runs from September until the end of the year, and sometimes extends into January.

Fur trapping in the winter is also an option. For most of the big game hunting, there are very few weapons restrictions, and you can use archery gear, crossbow, shotgun, rifle, handgun, or muzzle loader. Separate seasons for bow hunters, rifle hunters, handgun hunters, or muzzle loader hunters just aren't a fact of life on Prince of Wales.

July is the only month of the year without a big game hunting season going on, and since most residents carry rifles, shotguns, or handguns in their vehicles most of the time, our *Second Amendment* right to "Keep and Bear Arms" is pretty much taken for granted. I've never been questioned for carrying any combination of firearms, bows, or fishing tackle.

Fishing is almost endless: winter steelhead for the hardy fisherman, with trout fishing starting up in the early spring. Chinook fishing starts up in May, quickly followed by sockeye, pink, chum, and silver salmon. Halibut, bottom fish, crab, and clam are available year-round, weather conditions permitting.

You'll definitely want a boat and motor if you live on Prince of Wales, but it doesn't have to be a big one to start out with. Thorne Bay is on the inside of the Inside Passage, and if the weather and wind isn't kicking up, the bay and ocean will often be as flat and calm as a farm pond.

Alternative energy

For the most part, if you live in any of the rural areas, you can use about any form of alternative energy you'd like, as alternative energy is a way of life in most of Alaska. Solar power isn't real popular on Prince of Wales though, since sometimes we don't see the sun for weeks on end.

In most of the towns on Prince of Wales, water, sewer, and electricity will be available if you live within town.

Outside of town is a different story, though. Electric lines are slowly spreading to some of the rural areas on the island, with South Side Thorne Bay only getting electricity within the past few years. In the populated rural areas on the island, the steady drone of generators is a common sound. Thorne Bay is gradually getting quieter as more and more people get on the electric power grid. The average electric bill for our cabin is only about $20 per month, but we still keep the generator for backup power, as do most of the local residents.

Utilities

Outhouses are much in evidence, as sewer lines are only available in

Jamie's friend, Sunshine, plays on the computer next to the refrigerator in the living room/kitchen/dining room in our cabin.

Juanita sharpens a chainsaw on the front porch of our cabin-in-progess.

town, and you will need to get a permit to put a septic system or drain field on your rural property. They do have regulations on that.

No one drills wells on the island, but freshwater springs are common on most pieces of property and most rural dwellings also use a rain catchment system, water storage tank, and filter system to take care of their water needs. With 150 to 200 inches of rain per year on the average, most people keep their storage tanks pretty full. You just need to match the size storage tank to your family size and expected water usage. You can still drain gray water directly into the soil, but you'll need to make other plans for your toilet facilities and black water, unless you live in town on an existing sewer line. Don't expect to ever be provided with a public sewer system if you live in a rural area on the island. Ain't gonna happen.

Most areas have phone service, either via land line, radio phones, or cell phones. Phone service is getting better year by year. Internet service is still pretty spotty, but I'm sure that will get better over time, as computers and the Internet are still the wave of the future, even in rural Alaska. And you can always get satellite internet service. However, there are still a lot of residents who don't have phones, often by choice, and Citizen Band Radio systems are still quite common in both residences and vehicles. Getting hold of some of the local residents can be quite interesting and involved at times.

Building

There are several common ways to obtain buildable property on Prince of Wales Island. You can check with one of the local realtors, such *Gateway City Realty* at (907) 826-3640, or *Prince of Wales Island Realty* at (907) 826-2927, or on the Internet at www.ktn.net/powr and email at powir@aptalaska.net. At times, you can still purchase land by sealed bid auction through either the *University of Alaska*, www.ualand.com or the *Alaska Mental Health Trust Fund*, www.dnr.state.ak.us/mhtlo. There are usually several houses and pieces of property available for sale by owner, and to find these you either need to know someone who lives there and is knowledgeable about property for sale, or you need to just start driving around looking for the "for sale" signs. There are bulletin boards at most of the grocery stores, gas stations, and other gathering places on the island, and that's where most of the local residents advertise and find out what is available and from whom. You can also look in the Classifieds in the *Island News*, the local newspaper. The address for the *Island News* is P. O. Box 19430, Thorne Bay, Alaska 99919; their phone number is (907) 828-3420; their email address is islnews@apta-laska.net.

You can reach the Prince of Wales Chamber of Commerce for a multitude of information. Their phone number is (907) 826-3870; fax number is (907) 826-5467; email is powcc@aptalaska.net; web site is www.princeofwalescoc.org; and their address is: P. O. Box 497, Craig, AK 99921. They should have Forest Service Road Maps available, too.

Currently, most of the island doesn't require building permits or inspections for private homes and cabins, and there is no building code to follow. If you want to live in a trailer initially and add on a wannigan, no problem. The drawback is, if you want to buy an existing home, you'll need to check it out carefully, and you'll probably have a more difficult time arranging any bank financing. Most likely, though, you'll probably just have to work out a deal with the owner on a private contract. Just be careful.

We've built our cabin with lumber milled locally, mostly red cedar, and most of the material was either given to us, bought used, or bartered for. We have less than $2,000 cash into the entire 16 by 20-foot cabin—2 bedrooms, loft area, bathroom, kitchen, living room, utility and storage room, front porch, and a carport/covered outside work area. We have all the comforts of home that we want: wood stove, washer, dryer, propane stove, refrigerator, freezer, smoker, etc. A green metal roof, red cedar board and bat exterior siding, and planed red cedar interior paneling pretty much finish off the cabin the way we like it. The 4.2 acres were paid for by trading some used vehicles, paying some cash over time, and assuming a small bank loan, for about $20,000 total. That's another story, for another time. Δ

(Jon Stram sells an informational CD about Prince of Wales Island for $12.50. Send payment to Jon Stram, 103 Foothills Dr., Newberg, OR 97132. Phone: (503) 538-5145. email:castaway@gte.net)

Using typical transportation for Thorne Bay, Jon Stram rides in his 17-foot boat with 6-horsepower motor.

Bill Ingles and Jon Stram, on the front porch of the cabin, plane 1"x 6"x 8' red cedar boards for the cabin's interior.

Chat with other self-reliant people. Go to *Backwoods Home Magazine's* popular website at: www.backwoodshome.com

The Fourteenth Year

Woolen winter mittens in minutes

By Anita Evangelista

There's nothing so comfy and warm in the snowy dead-of-winter as a pair of thick, soft woolen mittens. Many of us have fond childhood memories of a favorite pair that accompanied us out to play or to collect firewood. Wool makes one of the warmest and most sturdy winter fibers, is a renewable resource and, with basic care, can last literally for decades.

But really nice woolen mittens can set us back a significant sum or take quite a few nights to knit from scratch.

There's another way to acquire these beauties. It only calls for basic stitchery skills and a few cast-off garments. It takes less than an hour to put a pair together. And they can be attractive enough to be given as holiday gifts.

The first step is to locate a wool sweater—a favorite one that has gone past its prime, or one that accidentally went through a hot-water cycle in the washing machine. Our local small town has a thrift store which routinely carries wool sweaters in all colors and sizes, with lots of choices in style and texture. Your town probably does too. You can also find good buys at garage sales. Choose only pure wool sweaters for this project. These garments will have the famous overlapping circles "wool mark" on the label. Of course, you can make mittens from any fabric, although cotton ones simply will not keep your hands warm, and wool mixed with other fibers (such as polyester or Angora rabbit) won't be as durable.

The blue men's large-size wool sweater shown below ended up in the washer and super-hot dryer, which resulted in the garment shrinking, as wool will do, down to a child-size item. The arms of this sweater, however, had been stuffed with socks (don't ask!), so they retained their bulky shape throughout the process. The final outcome was very heavy, sturdy semi-felted wool on the trunk, and loose, airy wool on the arms.

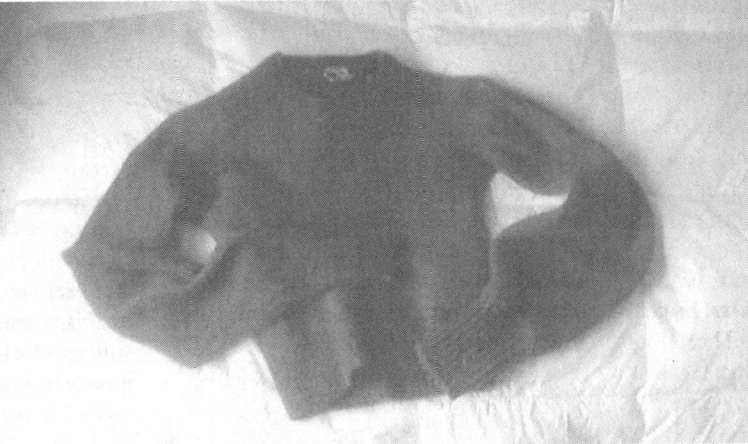

This formerly large men's sweater shrank and felted while being washed and dried. The torso area wool is thick and firm.

The thick, stiff fabric that occurs when wool is heated and agitated, such as in a washer or dryer, is actually a desirable product if you want the equivalent of "boiled wool." Boiled wool was used during the Middle Ages as a type of poor-man's armor: it was thick and durable enough to protect wearers against arrows and knife attacks. Today, the wool industry in France knits beautiful super-large berets and vests, then boils them until they felt and shrink into normal-sized hardy, warm, boiled wool garments.

So, although this favorite blue sweater is past the point where it can be used as a sweater again, it can still be converted into mittens, one "lightweight" pair from the sleeves, and one super heavy "boiled wool" pair from the body.

The second step is to make a pattern of your hand, or the hand of the person who will receive the mittens. Place your hand on a sheet of paper, fingers together and thumb extending to the side, with wrist extending straight (rather than angled to one side). Now, using a pencil, trace around your hand. Keep the pencil vertical (upright) as you trace. This will help keep the hem area consistent. When you're done, you'll have a pretty clear outline of your hand.

Next, soften the outline and round it out into a true "mitten" shape. Then add about ½ inch to the edge, all the way around. This will allow for the hem. Now, trim the pattern out of the paper, and make a duplicate pattern, so that you'll have one for each hand.

The third step is to lay the two patterns onto the sweater. Turn the

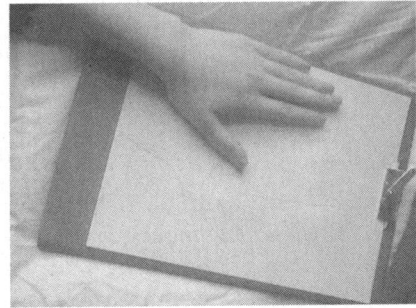

The drawn outline follows the form of the hand.

sweater inside-out first. You can use either the body portion of the sweater or the arms, or both, if you're making two pairs of mittens. Leave the cuff edges on to act as cuffs on your mittens-to-be. Pin the patterns in place temporarily, passing your pins through both thicknesses of the sweater. If you use the sweater's arms, lay the pattern so that the "pinky side" of your pattern is against the arm seam. This will reduce the amount of sewing you'll have to do.

The fourth step is to mark around the edge of the pattern, leaving a clear outline on the sweater. I used a black indelible marker pen to outline my patterns on this blue fabric, but chalk or a wax marker may work just as well. Carefully remove the pattern, and pin the two layers of fabric together again. Now, trim around the pattern mark line, leaving the side-seam intact. The trimmed fabric edges may have a tendency to unravel a little bit at this point. You may wish to use your marker to draw a "sewing line" about ½ inch in from the cut edge. That's where you'll sew the pieces together.

The fifth step is to sew the mitten seam, about ½ inch in from the cut edge. If you're handy or so inclined, you can use a running slip stitch to catch and hold the cut edge down (the same style as the arm seam on the sweater). Plain cotton-polyester thread works fine for this, but for more fancy mittens you could use a lightweight worsted wool yarn in a contrasting color. I've sewed mittens using dental floss and probably fishing line would work as well. The thread should just be sturdy enough to hold the weight of the fabric firmly together.

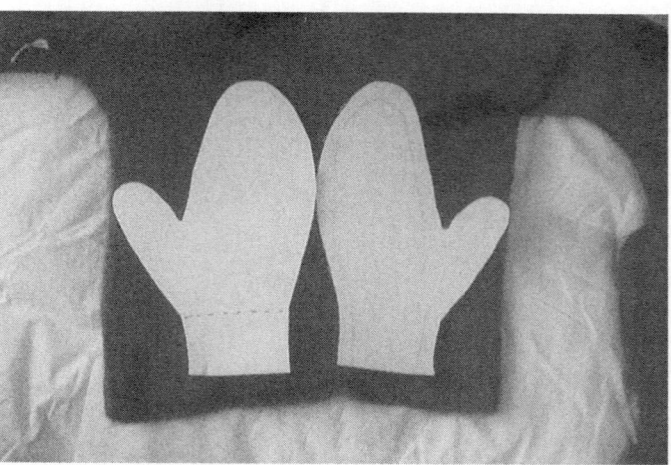

Mitten patterns laid on the sweater body. Notice that the edge of the cuff area has been marked with dotted lines on one pattern.

The final step is to turn the mitten right-side-out, and try it on. If it seems too loose, you can turn it inside-out again and sew a new seam portion to tighten up the floppy areas. You're done!

If you wish, you can sew additional designs, initials, or patterns in contrasting colors onto the back of the new mittens, or run a colored yarn around the cuff end. That will take a bit longer, but the result is a very personalized one-of-a-kind item.

Mitten care is simple: wash in lukewarm water using a mild shampoo or liquid dish detergent. Rinse in lukewarm water, carefully press out the excess liquid without twisting, and dry flat. Or, if you made your mittens extra-large to start with, just toss them in the washer, dry in a hot tumbling dryer, and take out a child-size pair of boiled mittens. Δ

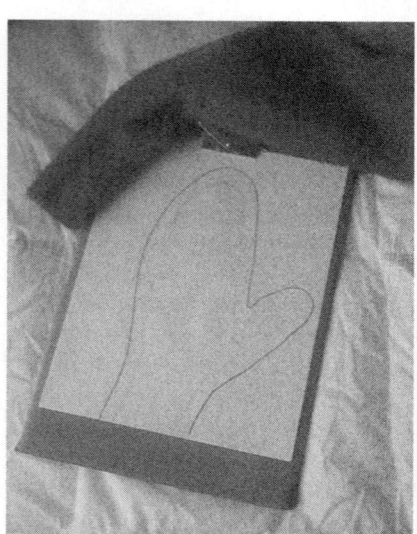

The drawn outline has been "enlarged" by adding a ½-inch wide strip which will allow for a seam area when the mitten is sewn together.

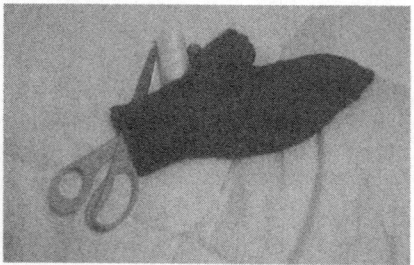

Edges lined up and stitching has begun.

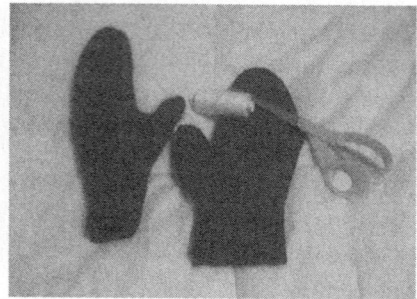

Mitten on the left has been sewn and turned right-side-out. Notice that it is smaller than the cut pieces on the right which haven't been sewn yet.

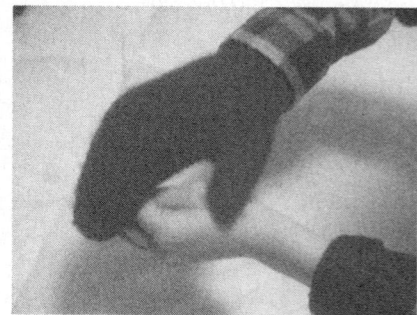

Mitten is done and it fits like a toasty warm glove.

The Fourteenth Year

Ask Jackie

Goats, homemade peanut butter, tipi liners, cleaning greasy messes, "old" storage food, pressure canners, using potato flakes, choosing batteries, canning with "real" cans, pickles, tie-dying, apple jelly from apple juice, and preserving roses

Jackie Clay

Here I am again! Now I am canning. Thanks to you and your answers to my questions on that. I have another one, on the matter of goats. I have 12 milk goats at the moment and going to expand as soon as we get moved to our new place in Missouri. It has fruit trees (already bearing). From reading your vet book I know peaches, plums, cherries and any fruit with a pit is poisonous to them, but what kind of plants and flowers are poisonous?

We will be moving, hopefully, in September or October.

**Ron and Bernice Knapp
Clearwater, KS**

I really wouldn't worry too much about your goats eating poisonous plants. Of course I wouldn't recommend a diet including them, but from my experience most animals can nibble on them without side effects and only get into trouble when there is little *but* poisonous plants to eat. You see this a lot when the animals are confined to a small pasture. They quickly eat up the good forage, then resort to eating the poisonous plants and become sick or die.

A few plants that you may watch out for include lupine, bracken fern, poison hemlock (along wet areas), chokecherries, and dock (which is edible in small doses, but can cause problems when consumed in a large amount). Talk to your County Extension Agent when you get moved to Missouri. He can tell you what toxic plants you may encounter in your county there.

As for the pit fruits most are toxic in the wilted state if green branches break off in a storm and land in the pasture. Animals can often nibble on the green branches and leaves with no ill effects; mine nibble on chokecherry leaves often. Notice, again, that I emphasize "nibble," as animals cannot make a steady diet of chokecherry without ill effects. Good luck on your new homestead.

Jackie

Jackie, do you happen to have a recipe for making homemade peanut butter?

**Scott Mancuso
Scott.Mancuso@nmcco.com**

Making homemade peanut butter is easy, not to mention very tasty. All you have to do is throw one cup of roasted peanuts into a blender with two Tbsp. of vegetable oil and as much salt as you want (probably ½ tsp.). Then whiz until it is peanut butter. You will want to refrigerate and use it, as it will go rancid easier because it is without chemicals to keep it fresh.

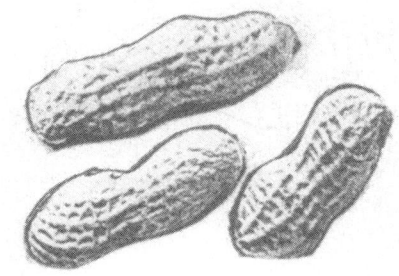

To make crunchy peanut butter, simply whiz a first batch to the "chopped" stage, dump them into a bowl, then do the next to "creamy." Mix the two and you have great crunchy peanut butter.

Taking it a step further, you can home-can your peanut butter to keep it from going rancid by packing it tightly into clean canning jars to within one inch of the top, wipe the

343

jar rim very clean, then place a previously boiled warm lid on the jar and screw the ring down firmly tight. Process the jars in a hot water bath for one hour.

Remember, this old fashioned peanut butter will need to be stirred before each use, as the oil will tend to rise to the surface when it stands. Great stuff, though.

        Jackie

In the the July/August issue, in your Ask Jackie column, you stated that the liner of the tipi is called an ozan. I have lived in a tipi on and off. I strongly recommend it. It is one of the finest nomadic constructions to date. However, the ozan is actually an overhead cover used as an adjunct to the liner to help in the retaining of heat in the winter. The liner is simply called a "liner." I mention this so that if the person who asked the question wants to buy a tipi they don't end up with an item they don't want when they go to purchase it and set it up.

Also...Another great environmentally friendly method of removing built up grease is to apply any cheap vegetable oil to the troublesome area and scrub with a green "scrubby" pad. This idea is most obvious in the notion that we use some form of fat to make soap. The fat acts as a suspension material for the grease you are trying to dissolve. This will break up the majority. Then use a mild cleaner such as vinegar or plain dish soap to clean off the surface. Baking soda, used out of the box like cleanser, works great for anything really stubborn. Oh, and plan to throw away the green scrubbies when you are through. They won't be fit for anything else.

       Robin Wood
       La Crescenta, CA

I'll try the vegetable oil scrubbie treatment for my next greasy mess. You're never too old to learn. I've used baking soda for many household cleaning jobs. It does work great.

The ozan is an extension of the lining, which can be left upright to provide more "drip" protection and insulation, or draped down over the bed or sitting area for rain or added ease of heating a smaller area. In the old days, the ozan was part of the lining, but you are right, today manufacturers sell the ozan separately from the lower liner. I would definitely recommend both. In the old days, where permanent camps were set up, the ozan, along with "stuffing" consisting of dry grass between the liner and tipi wall and additional windbreak outside, were used during the winter. In the summer, the liner/ozan were used to prevent dripping from rain and condensation running down tipi poles. I'm sorry I was not clear.

        Jackie

I love your column. It is one of my favorite parts of this magazine. My question concerns some storage food that I inherited.

The man used a wooden, uninsulated shed built in the '30s to store his home canned food and other storage food items. The food was subjected to temperatures as low as 20° and as high as 95°.

There is wheat which is nitrogen packed in mylar bags, inside plastic buckets. It has been in storage since the mid '90s. There is rice, packed into plastic buckets, using the dry ice method, with no mylar bags, also from the mid '90s. My guess is that these items are probably fine, but what should I look for before use, to be certain?

There was Jiff brand peanut butter from 1998. I opened a jar. It smelled fresh and tasted ok. There was no rancid smell about it, although I figure most of the nutrients are gone.

There were some Mountain House freeze dried meals from 1998. I cooked, smelled, tasted, then ate one of those meals. It seemed to be fine. But again, I suspect this too had lost a lot of its nutrition due to age and storage conditions.

I know not to use cans that are bulging, any food that smells or tastes bad. What about these items I have mentioned—wheat, rice, peanut butter and freeze dried meals?

      Kevin Childress
      Hickory, NC

Lucky you. If you decide to throw out these perfectly great foods, send 'em up here. I've actually eaten beans that were carbon dated 1,000 years old. They were dry beans, sealed in a pottery jar, sealed with wood and pine pitch, found in an Indian ruin in New Mexico. I also saved seeds from this batch, which went on to grow.

As to your inheritance; nearly all dry grains, such as rice, wheat, and corn keep for years and years unless attacked by insects or mold due to less than dry storage conditions. I would not be afraid to come to your house and eat any of these dry grains. If they look good, smell good and taste good, they should be fine. After the 1,000 year old beans, what's 10 years or so?

The peanut butter is fine. It goes rancid, but won't poison you. As long as the jars are sealed, you're fine. And I wouldn't worry too much about the loss of nutrients. Some do bid adios after a period of time, but many nutrients stay for years. Eat plenty of fresh foods from the garden or more recent pantry, and it'll be fine.

Same goes for the freeze dried foods. I have eaten plenty of "old" freeze dried food. As long as the food is dry, sealed, and free of any off flavors, mold or any other nasty, they should be fine. A lot of the "freshness date" stuff is bull__. But it does cause thousands of people to throw away perfectly good food. So they turn around and buy more. Now who would profit from this? Hmm. But folks buy it because someone says we'll be healthier for it. Please pass the 1,000 year old beans. At least they don't have ingredients I can't spell or pronounce, let alone recognize.

Jackie

I have hot water bath canned tomatoes and jams, froze veggies and meats for years. Due to old stories, though, I have been afraid to try my hand with a pressure canner. I have finally caved in and bought a 20-quart pressure canner and would like to know about canning salmon. We catch quite a bit of this fish and halibut, as well, living here in Alaska. I would like to preserve it in jars.

Lissa Ryan, Anchorage, AK

Congratulations. I'm so glad you gave in and are willing to conquer your fears of pressure canning. There's really nothing to it if you simply get a good canning manual and follow the directions, step by step. I can most of my fish "plain" and do the recipe thing after storage.

Salmon and other fish are easy to put up. And once you try it, I'm sure you'll go on to can meat and poultry, too. Living in Alaska, you need to try canning moose. It's our favorite meat.

Can only fish that is very fresh and has been promptly cleaned and held on ice until processing as fish is one of the foods that can be dangerous to improperly can, due to the danger of botulism. Only can fish in pint or smaller jars to ensure that the entire contents of the jar is heated thoroughly and sufficiently.

The basic process is simple. Clean and draw the fish thoroughly. Make a brine of one cup salt to one gallon of fresh, cold water. Cut the fish into jar length pieces (remembering that you must leave one inch of head room, that is, air space at the top of the jar). Let stand in the brine for one hour. Drain well. Pack fish into hot jars, skin side next to the glass. Wipe the jar rim well. Place hot, previously boiled lid on jar and screw down ring firmly tight. Process pints for 100 minutes at 10 pounds pressure, adjusting the pounds of pressure need if your altitude is greater than 2,000

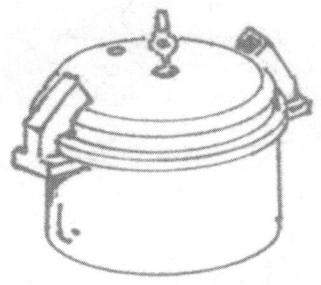

feet for a dial gauge or 1,000 feet for a weighted gauge. See your canning manual for altitude adjustments.

The Division of Fishery Industries, United States Department of Interior, Washington, D.C. can provide you with many seafood canning recipes. Good canning and write if you have any questions as you go along.

Jackie

Do you have a recipe for potato pancakes using potato flakes (instant mashed potatoes)? I wrote to those potato people (you know the ones in Idaho) and all they said was "buy our mix!"

This would be a good way to use up the potato flakes I have in storage.

**Judy Benevy
Springfield, WV**

There are lots of things you can do with those potato flakes, besides making mashed potatoes. (I must say potato flakes do better in some other things than mashed potatoes.)

Here's one recipe I use for potato pancakes from dry flakes. First grind or crush your flakes for a finer potato flour. You can even whiz them in your blender, if you have one. I add 1 cup potato flakes, ½ cup flour, 1 tsp. salt, 2 tsp. baking powder and enough milk (reconstituted dry or fresh) to make the batter almost thin enough to pour thickly off a spoon. Then add 1 large egg and 1 tsp. onion powder. Mix well until the batter is fairly thick, but will pour nicely. Heat 2 Tbsp. (more or less, depending on the size of your frying pan) shortening, then drop pancakes from a soup spoon onto the frying pan. Gently fry on one side until done, then turn with a spatula. Serve hot. They're great with ketchup, honey, preserves, or even apple sauce.

Other uses for the potato flakes are adding to canned tuna or ground meat to make patties to fry. We really like that one. Simply add a handful to a couple of cans of drained tuna and a pinch of salt. Mash together well and add an egg. Stir well and pat into patties. Now take a saucer or bowl and throw a handful of dry flakes into it. Carefully lay one patty at a time in the flakes and pat them on the top, as well, then place in frying pan with melted grease and fry on a medium heat.

Leftover roast or other meat may be ground in a meat grinder, along with the potato flakes. Mash together well, and add your egg, as with the tuna and proceed the same. The potato flakes add a nice taste and make the tuna or meat stretch further. The dry flakes make the outside of the shell nice and crispy.

You can also use the potato flakes in bread. Just add half a cup, in place of half a cup of flour. The starch in the potato flakes feeds the yeast and makes a nicely flavored bread.

Jackie

I would suggest that you change your list from "9-volt radio with fresh battery" to a "AA radio with fresh battery." Radios built to run on two AA batteries are common these days if you look for them, the batteries last 51 times longer, they are less expensive, and easier to store. 9-volt radios are generally older designs that consume far more power than is necessary using current technology. They are also prone to a reverse polarity connection which will quickly destroy the radio. Since AA batteries have many uses these days, it makes more sense to eliminate 9-volt batteries and store one backup type that can be utilized in a number of roles, should the need arise.

**Leonard Umina
El Dorado Hills, CA**

I didn't know that, Len. Very good information. But how about going one step further. We just added a crank/solar powered small radio to our grab and git box. No batteries to worry about, at all. As it is, our old 9-volt radio (which is our main travel radio) gets a new battery about once a year. It is listened to infrequently. In an emergency situation, you would probably only listen to a few minutes of news at a time, then shut it off, not spend hours listening to your favorite tunes. Our readers are so informed about so many subjects that it is absolutely amazing.

Jackie

I was wondering; I have done canning before and am doing it now again. I purchased some tin cans and the machine that goes with them. I have never done this before. Have never seen tin cans for canning, but it is in an old time book I have. Just wondered if you knew of anyone that has used them before?

**Judy
Priddyboythree@aol.com**

The only book that I've seen that has instructions for canning in tin cans is the older *Putting Foods By* by Ruth Hertzberg, Beatrice Vaughan, and Janet Greene. Many folks have put home-canned foods up in tin cans. One problem with canning foods at home with tin cans is that other than bulging cans and spoiled food, later during storage, there's no real way to know if the cans have indeed sealed properly. When home canning with the common, two-piece lids you can actually see the lid sucked tightly in when the seal is good, making this a safer method of canning at home. And then there is the cost of buying new cans for every batch of canning that you plan on doing. Canning jars and the rings are reusable; you only need to buy inexpensive new lids each year.

One hint in canning with tin cans is to "sacrifice" a couple of cans before you actually can. Partially fill them with water, seal the can with your sealer, then drop them into a kettle of boiling water. If there are air bubbles coming from around the sealed rim, your seal is not good and your can sealer must be adjusted again.

Be sure you use instructions meant for tin cans, as the canning process is definitely different than when you home-can with glass jars.

Jackie

Is there a safe to can garden vegetables without a pressure cooker?

**Virginia Cawthon
onelbc@hotmail.com**

No. The only safe to home-can vegetables, meat, seafood, and poultry, which are low acid foods, is with a pressure canner. The only way you can home-can vegetables without a pressure canner is to pickle them, which, using the right recipe, in effect makes them high acid vegetables because of the vinegar required to pickle them. I make pickled peppers of several types, an end of the garden pickle, which uses cauliflower, peppers, carrots, etc. And of course, there is sauerkraut, which is a way to put up cabbage without pressure canning.

Go ahead. Pick up a pressure canner (new on sale, used at a yard sale or the Goodwill) and start canning all those goodies.

Jackie

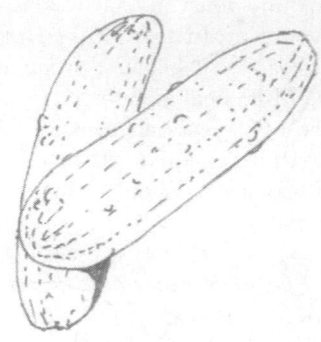

I am planning on canning pickles this year, my first canning endeavor. I appreciate your help with these questions. Do I have to use special canning cukes? I'm currently growing a Japanese variety. Can I cut my cukes into quarters? With "raw pack" should the water be at a rolling boil before lowering jars in?

Can I use honey instead of sugar? If so, do you have a conversion table? Can I have only 2 or 3 jars in the pot or does it have to be full?

**Jen French
jbfrench@mum.edu**

Good luck with your pickling. It's so easy and a lot of fun, actually. To answer your questions: No, you don't need special pickling cukes. I've even used zucchini. I would stay with the way the recipe calls for, such as sliced thinly, cut into chunks, cut into spears. I'm assuming you want to quarter your Japanese cukes because they're so long they won't fit into the jars right. In this case, you can quarter them, if making spears. It doesn't matter if the end is cut. Have the water at just below a rolling boil, simmering, when you put your jars in, or the steam may burn you. Until you have some pickling experience, I'd recommend that you stick with sugar. Then you can try recipes, switching honey for the sugar. Yes, you can put any number of jars in the hot water bath, even one. Again, great pickling.

Jackie

I am incarcerated in Gardner, Mass and am lucky enough to have a 15 by 2-foot garden plot to grow some veggies. I share the plot with four other guys and we do pretty well with what we have to work with. We have two types of hot peppers, lettuce, carrots, beets, wax and green beans, plum, cherry, & Big Boy tomatoes, Chinese cabbage, parsley, summer, and zucchini squash.

Is there a way to tie dye T-shirts with beets or other veggies?

As we are very limited in fertilizer, what else besides leaves, grass clippings, and coffee grounds could I possibly use? The area has a lot of clay and direct sun all day. We water with 2½-gallon water cans averaging 12 gallons daily.

**Tom Ford
Gardner, MA**

It sounds like you boys have a great little garden. A lot of people, with much greater resources, do not do as well. Yes, you can use beets to tie dye your T-shirts. You simply slice the beets thinly and simmer in enough water to cover them until the color has bled into your water. Likewise, you can get a yellow dye from onion skins. Maybe you can get some from the kitchen or grow a row next season.

Likewise, for fertilizer, you could get vegetable scraps from the kitchen, such as potato peelings, carrot peels, cabbage leaves, etc.? I realize that in some instances, health regulations may forbid this, but give it a try. Then dig these into the rows between the plants to prevent any possible odor or flies, which may hinder your gardening endeavor. This is called trench composting and works well. Working in any organic material, such as plants that are done bearing, is also a good idea. Don't use any that appear diseased, though, or you may spread something you'll wish you didn't.

Growing a wide row of a green manure crop, such as thickly sown peas (which you can pick and eat before turning in the vines), rye, or alfalfa, then spading it in does a fantastic job of improving garden soil. Good growing.

Jackie

I have tried making apple jelly from apple juice. I always follow the instructions exactly, but it always seems not to set up. Can you give me a good recipe for this or tell me what I am doing wrong? We love apple jelly and I love to can my own vegetables.

**Reneé Hoover
Hdixiechic@aol.com**

First of all, be sure your apple juice is 100% apple juice. I would guess that you perhaps got an apple juice drink, which includes sugar and water to "thin" it down. That would certainly account for batches that didn't turn out. I use the recipe that comes in the SureJel box. It's easy, quick, and has always worked for me.

Jackie

I just had a question regarding the roses that I received two weeks ago from my boyfriend. I kept them until

the petals were almost falling off and then went to remove them into a nice keepsake dish. When I was removing them, I noticed that they were sprouting all up the stems. I would like to know if I can plant them and how to get them to root. I trimmed off the dead stock at the top and put them all back in fresh water. Any help you could give me would be greatly appreciated.

**Tiara Halo
tiarahalo43@hotmail.com**

I'm sorry, but I doubt that your roses will root and become plants. Usually cut flowers will give all they have to sprout, then wither and die, despite your best wishes they would live. You can try cutting the bottom of the stem anew, then dipping them in a product called Rootone, available at most garden stores. Follow the package directions and give it a try. Maybe wondrous things may happen. Perhaps you will give your grandchildren a bouquet of roses from these dying stems. Stranger things have happened.

Jackie

**Get
The
Whole
Sheebang!**
www.backwoodshome.com

Hey! Sandwichman!
Selling sandwiches for an income

By Donn Rochlin

There's a saying in Sedona: "The surest way to make a million dollars in Sedona is to move there with a million dollars. Well according to my experience that turned out to be true with money in general, but the decision to move to the beautiful and seductive red rocks of Sedona, Arizona, turned out to be one of the greatest experiences of my life.

Not knowing quite what to expect in making the transition from the "hubbub" of Fresno, California, and having been born and raised in Los Angeles, I was about to embark on an entirely new and challenging life change. Imagine, a town with only one stop light, one movie theater, two markets, and a main street you could hear a pin drop on after 9 p.m.

Even in the light of this major downsizing now going on in my life, I remember thinking, "With my background in sales and marketing it shouldn't be any problem to get a well paying job."

Well, rude awakening #1: *No jobs*. With no savings or finances to fall back on, the financial realities of living in a small town started to set in. After months of scraping up odd jobs (hodding bricks, singing telegrams, landscape helper, housecleaning, and even washing dishes), I had had it.

I remember laying in my bed staring at the ceiling and thinking, "There's got to be something I can do to show this town and myself, I'm here to stay. I'm not going to be one of the financial casualties forced to abandon my dream of living where I want."

Interestingly enough, it happened to be the day after Thanksgiving and I started to think about all that leftover turkey and how for weeks after the feast my family would live on it (turkey soup, turkey sandwiches, etc.).

I started reminiscing back to years ago, in Los Angeles, when my wife came up with a great idea to deliver snacks to employees who worked the graveyard shift at several of the convalescent hospitals in our area. Having once worked at one of them, she knew that it was difficult for them to find anyplace to eat at that hour of the morning. She prepared some sandwiches and various snacks and hit the streets. Even though it provided a little extra income, the business was short lived, as she got weary of getting up at midnight every night.

So here it is, at least six years later, and as I'm laying there a light goes on: "That's it! I'll start a lunch delivery service."

I jumped out of bed and called a friend of mine who I thought of because of her culinary talents. I told her about my idea. The next morning we appraised the leftover turkey and agreed we could get 12 to 15 sandwiches out of it. I said "Let's do it. You make 'em and I'll sell 'em."

When I arrived at her apartment the next morning, I was amazed. She had worked her magic. I mean these where the most beautiful sandwiches in the world, three inches high with crispy lettuce, bright red fresh tomatoes, mayonnaise and spices, and everything a turkey sandwich is about. We decided to charge $3.75.

"People will go crazy," I predicted.

I loaded the beauties into my cooler and headed out into the winter frost at 9 a.m. I walked into any business showing signs of life and announced myself.

"Hi. I'm the Sandwichman. We're a new lunch delivery service in town. Would you like to be included on our daily route?"

From that day on, I rarely heard a no. I returned three hours later with nothing more than crumbs in my cooler.

Needless to say it was the beginning of a lot of fun, a profitable business, and a genuine service to the community. Each day we'd add a few more sandwiches to the cooler.

About four weeks into our enterprise, and with steady growth on the horizon, we decided we'd better get legal. We were definitely going to outgrow our apartment kitchen, not to mention the attention we'd soon draw from the health department.

Before securing the necessary permits we would need an approved commercial kitchen. It needed to be something affordable and available to us every morning at 5 a.m. I came up with the idea of contacting the local Elks Lodge. They only used their kitchen for special events and never early in the morning. It was perfect.

We struck a deal with them and set up production. With our permits in order, we now qualified to purchase all of our supplies through a wholesale food distributor. I remember how excited I was to watch those sandwiches run down our assembly line, each one being christened with the "Sandwichman" label and popped into the cooler.

By now we had hired our first employee to help build sandwiches, and within a couple of months we had to hire three more salesmen. Our route had grown over five times. We were really on the map now.

We expanded our menu to include not only turkey but tuna, chicken salad, pastrami, and seafood burritos. One of our most requested items was our homemade fudge brownies. In the summer months we offered salads and fruit kabobs.

We became so well known I remember people coming up to me in the parking lot on my day off, "Hey, Sandwichman, can I get a sandwich?"

So, in less than six months with the help of some good friends, a good product, the support of our community, and the desire to live in one of the most beautiful parts of the world, we were a success.

Even though we moved on to fulfill other dreams, I always look back on those two years as a testament to the human sprit and a constant reminder to go for the dream to live the way I want, trusting that I'll always have the resources I need when I need them. I think it always gets back to a basic success principal I learned years ago: No matter where you are, find out what people want, give it to them at a fair price, and count your blessings. Δ

The joys of making soap

By Grace Brockway

My initial enthusiasm for making my own soap was deflating with each book I read on the subject. They all warned of the dangers of lye, one of the key ingredients, to such an extent that I began to wonder if I would be risking my life to attempt making soap. Goggles? Rubber gloves? Lots of ventilation? No aluminum pots? And above all, don't let the lye touch you or it will burn holes in your skin.

Well, I'm happy to say my enthusiasm for the idea of making soap stayed strong enough that I decided to try it in spite of all the cautions. Being the skeptic that I am, I figured that the books were required to be extremely cautious to avoid lawsuits from individuals possessing less than a full ration of common sense. Making soap is really quite easy and lots of fun. I reasoned that if I proceeded with a sensible amount of caution things should be okay. I'm glad I did.

Cautions

Lye really is nasty stuff. It's corrosive, it gives off chocking fumes until it is all dissolved in the water and it can indeed burn your skin on contact. You need to be careful not to let the lye crystals touch your skin as you slowly pour them into the pitcher to dissolve. Stir gently with a wooden spoon when adding the water so as to avoid splashing. I learned that it is definitely a good idea to have a window open for ventilation when dissolving the crystals. I also tend to hold my breath until the lye is all dissolved just for good measure. The first few times I did this step I worked outdoors just to be safe. After a bit I decided this was overkill and reverted to just opening a window.

Wearing rubber gloves is also a good idea because the lye and the raw soap can burn. I definitely make sure to remember the gloves when cutting the day-old soap into bars and when setting the bars out to dry as they can bite. By the way, if you ever do splash lye on your skin pour a little white vinegar on the area. The vinegar will neutralize the lye and take away the sting.

One more caution: Lye will eat through aluminum pans. Use only glass, enameled pans with no nicks, plastic, or stainless steel containers. You can use wooden spoons as long as you are aware that they will deteriorate and splinter over time. Plastic or rubber spatulas work well and don't disintegrate.

Okay, so now the cautions are out of the way. Let's talk next about what you'll need to make your first batch of soap.

Utensils

You'll need one large cooking pot in which to melt the lard/oils, a glass or plastic pitcher in which to mix the lye and water, a glass or plastic measuring cup and a wooden or plastic spoon or spatula for stirring. You'll also need a mold, such as a rectangular plastic box, if you have one, or you can make one out of wood. I made a wooden one, using plywood for the base and 1 x 4 lumber for the sides. You'll also need a cover to put on top of the mold after you pour in your soap mixture. You can use another piece of plywood or heavy cardboard for this. A blanket will be needed to wrap it in, and some freezer paper to line the mold so the soap mixture doesn't leak out the cracks. If you'd like to do it the old-fashioned way wet an old towel and line the box with that. It will leave funny patterns on the bottom of the soap, but won't affect its quality. I have found that a little soap leaked through the towel when I tried this, however, so if you're worried about a bit of mess you may not want to do this.

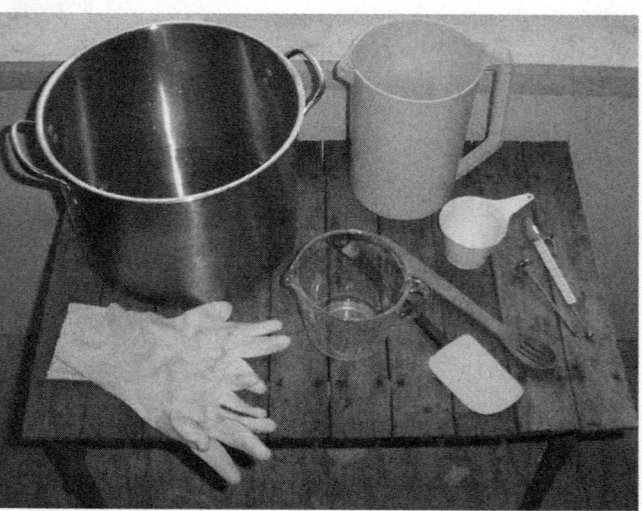

Among the tools you'll need are a large cooking pot, a measuring cup, rubber gloves, a glass or plastic pitcher, a thermometer, and a wooden or plastic spoon or spatula.

Ingredients

Now, what is soap actually made of? Soap is made by combining lye and fat. When heated and combined the mixture undergoes a chemical reaction and becomes an entirely new substance: soap. The type of fat you use is up to you. If you use beef fat (suet) your soap will be brown. If you use pig fat (lard) it will be white and vegetable oils will give you a creamy off-white bar. Soap made with vegetable oils will be softer than those made with beef or pig fat. My personal favorite is lard mixed with coconut oil. The coconut oil will create a richer lather. If you'd like scented soaps, you will also need to add some essential oil. Each type of fat requires a different ratio of lye water to fat so it will be a help to you to get your hands on a book with recipes suited to the type of soap you want to make. For a simple first-try batch, I have included a couple of my favorite recipes at the end of this article.

Most of the modern soap making books will try to convince you that you should buy a scale and weigh everything, including your water, rather than to measure it in cups. This approach will certainly give you more accurate ratios of lye to lard/oils. My interests in Colonial living led me to try making soaps with as few modern utensils as possible. Doing so taught me that using either weighed or measured ingredients will produce usable soap.

The same holds true for using thermometers and bringing your lye water and lard/oils to the correct temperatures. The goal is to get both mixtures to nearly the same temperature—somewhere around 95 degrees F. I used thermometers for a long time. Then came the day I was demonstrating soap making at a living history museum and couldn't use any modern utensils at all. I then had to rely on the old-fashioned method of feeling the outside of the containers to determine when they were the same lukewarm temperature. I was rather nervous about using this less than scientific method, but it worked just fine.

Step by step

Okay, so let's talk about how a batch of soap is actually made.

One: Pour the lye powder into a large glass or plastic pitcher. Now slowly add the four cups of **cold** water, stirring carefully so as not to spill or splash. (**Do not** use hot water, as this could cause the lye to bubble up or even explode.) As the lye dissolves the water will heat up drastically, to around 120°. It will take about 1½ to 2 hours for this mixture to cool down to the temperature range needed for mixing (anywhere between 79° and 98° works best). If you'd like to hasten this process you can stand the pitcher in a basin of cool water. The other approach is to mix the lye water the day before, but then you'll have to raise its temperature by standing it in warm water when it comes time to use it.

Two: Melt the oils/lard on the stove in a stainless steel pan. Keep the fire low—they only need to melt and if you get them too warm, then you have to cool them off again. It's easiest if you heat them just enough to melt them. Remember, the range we're looking for is between 79° and 98° F.

Three: When the lye and lard have reached the correct temperatures **slowly** pour the lye water into the lard/oils, stirring constantly and steadily. The mixture will turn an opaque peachy colour. Keep stirring until it begins to trace. Tracing occurs when a bit of the mixture drizzled off the spoon leaves a trace or track on the top of the mixture in the pot, rather like honey does. This step could take up to an hour to occur. But it could also happen as quickly as 10 minutes, but in my experience an hour is more likely. Don't be discouraged if you never do see tracing; I've had many, many batches that never

The old-fashioned way to mold soap was to use a wooden box lined with an old towel that had been wetted.

traced at all as far as I could tell and they still turned out fine. When you get tired of stirring and it still hasn't traced leave it alone for up to a half an hour and then come back and stir some more. If it still hasn't traced in a couple of hours, but it is showing signs of beginning to thicken, go ahead and stir in the essential oils and then pour it into the mold. It will probably be fine.

Four: Cover the mold with the plywood or cardboard and then cover the whole thing in a big blanket (wool works best) and let it sit for 24 hours. Be sure to keep it level while covering it and while it sits or you'll end up with thicker bars at one end of your mold. After the 24 hours are up, unwrap it, put on your rubber gloves, and cut it into bars. Set the bars somewhere clean to dry and cure. They'll need to sit for about two months so find a place where they'll stay clean, warm, and dry. I use an old screen, covered with a piece of muslin and set on blocks of wood for airflow. I turn the bars of soap on edge after a week or so to dry all sides.

Once they're thoroughly dry you may notice a light coating of powdery ash on the bars. This isn't harmful, but you might like to take a knife and scrape it off so the soap looks nicer. The longer the bars are stored the harder they become and will therefore last longer when used.

Five: Store them in a cool, dry place. As you make more batches, using different scents, you'll want to store them in separate boxes so the scents don't taint each other.

By now I hope you're convince that, with a little common sense and caution, soap making can be easy, fun and highly rewarding. If you'd like to do more reading on this subject I would recommend either of these two books: *The Soap Book* by Sandy Maine (Interweave Press) and *The Natural Soap Book* by Susan Miller Cavitch (Storey Communications).

Soap recipes

Here are two good beginner recipes, one using lard and one using vegetable oils. As you become more familiar with soap making you can adapt them to your own tastes. The number of bars and how thick they are will depend on the size of your mold.

Basic lard soap:

- 13 cups of lard
- 4 cups of cold water
- 1 can of Red Devil lye
- 4 ounces essential oil for scent (optional)

Basic vegetable oil soap:

- 3 cups coconut oil
- 10 cups vegetable shortening
- 4 cups cold water
- 1 can of Red Devil lye
- 4 ounces of essential oil for scent (optional)

Sources of supplies

Red Devil lye can be found in most grocery stores, in the household cleaner section. Lard is often with the vegetable oils, as is the solid vegetable shortening (such as Crisco). Essential oils can be found at health food stores, though to get the quantity needed for these recipes you may wish to order them from a company such as Attar Herbs & Spices located at 21 Playground Road, New Ipswich, New Hampshire 03071 (800-541-6900) or on the web at attarherbs.com. Unfortunately, essential oils are quite expensive and Attar's minimum order is $50.00, plus shipping and handling. Soap works just fine without any scent, so if the cost is off-putting, try making your first batches with no scent added. ∆

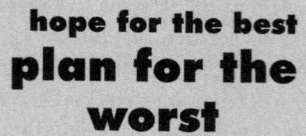

The Fourteenth Year

Wind chill factor makes it colder than you think

By Tom and Joanne O'Toole

Checking the temperature is not always a reliable indicator of how cold a person will feel outside. There are many other determinations. One important guideline is the wind chill factor.

After many years the U.S. National Weather Service has changed the wind chill temperature index, and the new formula is now being used throughout Canada and the United States. The old index calculated wind speed in terms of how quickly water freezes at 33 feet above ground (the typical height of an anemometer), while the new replacement index is based on readings at a height of five feet above ground (average face level) and determines freezing temperatures on people's faces.

Originally developed by Arctic explorers and the military, wind chill is nothing more than an "equivalent temperature." It describes the chilling effect of various combinations of moving air, at different temperatures, across exposed skin.

There are a number of definitions for the wind chill factor, but simply put, it combines air temperature and wind speed to come up with a reading of what it really feels like outside.

Wind moving past exposed skin during cold weather increases the body's heat loss. The body pumps warm blood to the extremities in an attempt to maintain the proper body temperature. However, if the temperature is low, and the wind is strong, the body often cannot keep up with heat loss and the skin temperature decreases. While the usual effect of the wind chill is just plain discomfort, freezing of exposed portions of the body can result.

A scientific definition to that elusive characteristic of the weather known as "cold" was first put forth by Antarctic explorer Paul A. Siple and his colleague Charles F. Passel in 1939. Some of the tests used water-filled plastic cylinders to measure the speed at which water freezes at dif-

ferent air temperatures and wind speeds.

Siple coined the term "wind chill" to describe their concept of the relative cooling power (or heat removal) of the human body with various combinations of wind speed and low temperatures.

Army researchers devised the basis for the wind chill index in the 1940s to help the military develop clothing for soldiers.

Wind chill has gained popular acceptance because it is easy to understand. Weather forecasters throughout Canada and across the northern tier of the United States routinely refer to the wind chill. The U.S. National Weather Service across the southern states computes the wind chill factor whenever temperatures dip below 40° F and wind speeds rise above 10 miles per hour (mph).

On a calm day (no wind) with a temperature of say 10° F, the temperature as it relates to the body is that same 10°. But when the wind starts blowing, the temperature affecting exposed skin drops dramatically. If the wind is a relatively slow 5 mph, the wind chill factor is already down to 1 degree F. If it's blowing at 15 mph, the wind chill plunges to 7° *below* zero.

The stronger the wind during a given temperature reading, the lower the wind chill factor. It's the relationship between wind speed and the actual temperature that produces the chilling effect. A further concern is for outdoor activists who create their own wind or increase the existing wind—skiing, snowmobiling, and running, for example. Their movement magnifies the air flow, so they should be especially aware of wind chill.

When someone says the wind is "penetrating," what actually happens is the air movement evaporates moisture from the exposed skin, decreasing the temperature. In the summer this feels great (a reason fans are so popular) because it has a cooling effect on an overheated person. Heat is lost in the evaporation process. However, this same experience can have serious consequences during cold weather when hunters, fishermen, backpackers, and other outdoor people want to retain as much heat as possible.

Through physical exertion the body heat production rises, perspiration begins, and heat is removed from the body by vaporization. Any part of the body touching a cold surface also takes away body heat (conduction), as does breathing cold air that results in the loss of heat from the lungs. So, the wind chill chart isn't strictly accurate because it doesn't take into account all the possibilities of heat loss, or the preventive measures against it.

Thus, the temperature of the air is rarely a reliable indicator of how cold a person will feel outdoors. Other elements of the weather such as wind speed, relative humidity, and sunshine (solar radiation) also exert an influence. The state of health and metabolism of a person, along with the type of clothing worn, will also affect how cold one feels.

Frostbite and hypothermia

Two serious wintertime afflictions of wind chill are frostbite and hypothermia. Both are dangerous to those who do not know how to handle them, or become unable to cope with their effects. While frostbite is seldom fatal, hypothermia can be life-threatening.

Frostbite is tissue damage caused by exposure to intense cold, and usually occurs when wind chill temperatures fall below -25° F.

The early stages of frostbite are a burning or stinging sensation in the affected parts. The skin will be bright pink at first as ice crystals begin to form under the surface. Numbness sets in as the skin turns to pale white, with a hint of gray or yellow spotting.

When actual frostbite occurs, parts of the body begin to freeze. It usually starts with the extremities—nose, ears, fingers, and toes—spreading to the cheeks of the face, and on to the hands and feet.

Medical attention is essential. Until help arrives, or the victim can be taken to the nearest treatment center, outdoor companions should give whatever aid they can and keep the affected parts as warm as possible. Fingers are usually frostbit first, and they can be slipped under the arm pits, inside the upper thighs, or in the mouth for warmth. You can also make the temperature rise by flexing fingers and toes. Without assistance—and sometimes even with it—the consequences are gangrene, severe infection, and possible amputation.

Another result of wind chill is hypothermia, the rapid cooling of the body's inner core to below its normal temperature of 98.6° F. Some of the symptoms are violent shivering, slurred speech, exhaustion, drowsiness, disorientation, and impaired judgment. (See the following article on hypothermia.)

Hypothermia is sneaky, gradually overcoming a person who has been chilled by wet clothing, low temperatures, or brisk winds. The important thing to remember is, temperatures do not have to drop below freezing for this condition to set in.

Few people consider that smoking, drinking, prescription drugs, and narcotics present added dangers in wind chill conditions. All of these dull your sensitivity to the circumstances, and have physical effects that will make you more susceptible to frostbite and hypothermia.

Alcohol dilates the capillaries of the skin, increasing the heat loss of the body. Nicotine smoke absorbed by the blood causes the capillaries to constrict, thus restricting the blood flow to the earlobes, fingertips, and other areas of the body. Medication can have side effects too, which might mean you shouldn't venture outside during extraordinary weather.

With winter always offering the possibilities of extremely low temperatures, those who enjoy the outdoors have a responsibility to be aware of the wind chill factor and what it can mean.

Wind chill charts for regular reference are available wherever outdoor equipment is sold.

When you venture out in winter, dress for both the weather and the wind, wearing loose-fitting, light-weight, warm clothing in several layers, which can be removed to prevent perspiration and subsequent chilling. Snug mittens are better protection than fingered gloves. Δ

Wind chill chart

Wind speed in mph	Equivalent wind chill temperatures at actual (calm) air temperature readings (F)												
calm	30	25	20	15	10	5	0	-5	-10	-15	-20	-25	-30
5	25	19	13	7	1	-5	-11	-16	-22	-28	-34	-40	-46
10	21	15	9	3	-4	-10	-16	-22	-28	-35	-41	-47	-53
15	19	13	6	0	-7	-13	-19	-26	-32	-39	-45	-51	-58
20	17	11	4	-2	-9	-15	-22	-29	-35	-42	-48	-55	-61
25	16	9	3	-4	-11	-17	-24	-31	-37	-44	-51	-58	-64
30	15	8	1	-5	-12	-19	-26	-33	-39	-46	-53	-60	-67
35	14	7	0	-7	-14	-21	-27	-34	-41	-48	-55	-62	-69
40*	13	6	-1	-8	-15	-22	-29	-36	-43	-50	-57	-64	-71

* Over 40 mph, little added effect

☐ Little Danger (for properly clothed person)

Danger of frostbite within 30 minutes

Danger of frostbite within 10 minutes

Danger of frostbite within 5 minutes

Hypothermia
a real winter danger

By Tom and Joanne O'Toole

Hypothermia is a deadly enemy. It steals body heat and kills more outdoor enthusiasts every year than anything else.

Hypothermia is the rapid and drastic chilling of the body's core temperature (normally 98.6 degrees F) during adverse conditions, and begins when the body loses heat faster than it can be replaced. As the body temperature drops because of exposure to cool air and cold water, things begin to happen in a predictable sequence. Left unchecked, it affects one's mental condition and physical reactions, and can result in unconsciousness. The ultimate result is death.

While cold rain or wet snow, combined with a brisk wind, create classic conditions, hypothermia is not exclusive to northern winter weather and bitter cold. When water temperatures are 50 degrees F or less, and air temperatures as high as 60-70 degrees F, hypothermia is possible. Given the right set of circumstances, it can (and does) occur anywhere.

Skin, surface fat, and superficial muscle layers act as insulation for the vital organs—heart, liver, kidneys, lungs, and the like. As hypothermia takes over, the internal temperature is dangerously lowered creating an extremely serious condition. It quickly leads to mental and physical collapse.

There are two types of this debilitating condition—chronic (long onset) and acute (rapid onset).

Chronic occurs when one is exposed to a cold environment for an extended time, and usually develops in air temperatures between 30 to 50 degrees F. It is commonly associated with winter hikers and backpackers, but can creep up on hunters, cross-country skiers, snowmobilers, and others.

Acute hypothermia happens from sudden immersion in cold water, and depending on the water temperature, can develop from within a few minutes to several hours. Boaters, ice fishermen, skaters, trappers, and those at or on water are often affected by this hazard.

Moisture is the worst enemy in the fight against hypothermia, and gets its start when victims become wet from their own perspiration, a sudden shower, or from an accidental plunge into water.

Protecting yourself

If you slip into cold water from a boat, it is best to get back in or cling to the craft. Staying as far out of the water as possible maintains more body heat, and postpones advanced symptoms. If getting out of the water is impossible, you should be wearing your Coast Guard-approved personal floatation device (PFD) that doubles your chances. A PFD not only helps insulate the body from cold water (reducing heat loss), but lessens the need to move in order to stay afloat.

You can also greatly extend your survival time by assuming the Heat Escape Lessening Posture (HELP) or fetal position—sometimes called the self-huddle. To do this, cross your ankles and bring your knees up toward your chest to protect the trunk of the body. Wrap your arms around your legs just below the knees, cross your wrists, and hold tight.

The greatest heat loss is from the head and neck, and these areas should be kept as high out of the water as possible. The other "hot spots" that lose heat most rapidly are the groin and the sides of the chest. These areas need to be protected the most.

Under hypothermic conditions, avoid the drown-proofing technique as it requires putting your head in the water, and causes you to cool faster than if floating with your head held high.

If there are several people in the water, use the "huddle" method to help each other preserve body heat. Lock your arms around one another and stay side-by-side in a circle.

Swimming to shore can be a deadly decision. The general advice is to stay with a disabled boat. Distances are deceptive, and rescuers can more easily spot a capsized boat than a lone paddler. Swimming burns up body heat, and in 50 degree F water even

> ## Progressive hypothermia
>
> There are degrees of hypothermia, and you can determine the state of the victim by recognizing the symptoms. If you want to categorize the stages, consider:
>
> **Mild Hypothermia (98.6-95 degrees F):** Conscious and alert; sensation of cold; pain and numbness; teeth chattering; vigorous shivering; normal speech; increased heart rate; and some loss of manual dexterity (fingers and toes).
>
> **Moderate Hypothermia (95-90 degrees F):** Conscious, but mentally cloudy; diminished shivering; stumbling; non-coordination; slurred speech; weak; confused; and drowsy.
>
> **Severe Hypothermia (90-85 degrees F):** No shivering; inability to follow instructions; mental confusion; staggering and frequent falling; unusual behavior; blurred vision; unintelligible speech; and possible unconsciousness.
>
> **Profound Hypothermia (85-80 degrees F):** Unconsciousness; rigid muscles; greatly lowered blood pressure; decreased heart rate; diminished respiration; dilated pupils; and appearance of death.

the best strokers could not make a mile.

Because cold water draws heat from an individual indefinitely, any activity drains the body's stored energy. Thrashing around creates swirling water, which steals heat from the body more rapidly than still water. Even treading water brings on complications faster. Remaining motionless just about doubles the time a person can endure.

You might be surprised to know hypothermia is the leading cause of death in boating accidents.

The historic sinking of the *Titanic* in 1912 is a dramatic example of hypothermia's effect. When the great ocean liner started sinking, passengers put on their PFDs and headed for the lifeboats. When rescue ships arrived two hours later, most of the people in the lifeboats were alive, but none of the almost 1,500 people floating in the 32 degree F water (still wearing those life jackets) lived.

The colder the water and air surrounding a victim, the more sudden and severe the hypothermia. While water will conduct heat away from the body 25 times faster than air of the same temperature, when it is choppy or there are swift currents, along with a blowing wind, the body's heat will be pulled away 35 times faster. Water chill is much greater than wind chill.

Everyone differs greatly in their ability to survive. Large people with ample body fat cool slower than small, thin people. Women cool more rapidly than men, and children cool the fastest. Of course, health, resistance, and the will to live are all contributing factors.

Treating hypothermia

Any person pulled from cold water or found on land when the classic conditions exist should be presumed to be in trouble. As one's temperature drops, the heart begins to slow, and the victim becomes weak and confused as less oxygen is delivered throughout the body.

Once the affliction begins, many people are unable to counteract the process by themselves. When the blood to the brain is slowed, the mind fails to function correctly. There are many symptoms, but it is usually the other person who recognizes them in someone having the reactions. Frequently the person experiencing the tell-tale signs becomes too disoriented to realize what is going on.

Ignore protests that everything is okay. Denial of being cold is common, and a hypothermic may truly believe nothing is wrong. Their judgment is impaired. They become drowsy, and usually want to drift off to sleep—but to sleep is to die.

Victims can range from appearing drunk or in a delirium, to acting desperate or combative.

Any of these reactions are probably a signal someone is suffering from hypothermia: difficulty with simple tasks (clumsy actions); dull eyes; listlessness; slurred speech; incoherency; confusion; forgetfulness; fatigue; an inability to control the hands, arms, or legs; stumbling; slow breathing; cold, stiff muscles; uncontrollable shivering or trembling; the stomach cold to the touch; apparent exhaustion; or someone dozing off and being hard to arouse.

Advanced stages of hypothermia render a person unconscious, the skin turns bluish-gray, muscles are rigid, breathing is shallow, and the pulse is weak. Rewarming is crucial, and medical assistance is necessary.

Do's and don'ts

What to do? Too often people try to help, and invariably do the wrong thing for someone who is hypothermic. There are certain "common sense" things you must **not** do:
- don't massage the arms or legs
- don't raise the legs
- don't put the person in hot water
- don't allow any type of exercise
- don't give alcohol or drugs
- don't administer hot drinks or hot food

What you should do is promptly get them out of the elements, cover the head and neck to prevent further body heat loss, remove wet or damp clothing and replace it with dry garments, keep the body warm to maintain the vital organs, and handle the person gently. Gentle handling is extremely important so as to not cause ventricular fibrillation—a condition when the heart quivers but does not pump blood.

Once it is determined a person is becoming hypothermic, it is essential others offer aid to prevent additional body heat loss. Skin-to-skin contact is an excellent way to transfer body heat. A field measure for rewarming is to remove all clothing and place the victim in a sleeping bag or in a blanket with one or two rescuers who have also removed their clothing.

If this is not possible, build two fires and put the person between them. Even better would be four fires, to surround them with heat.

If the victim appears dead, continue trying to restore body heat. Often hypothermics appear lifeless. Yet, their vital organs continue to function—but at a much lower rate—and they are alive. The medical adage is, "No one is dead until they are warm and dead."

Ever hear of "after drop?" This occurs with deeply hypothermics after they are moved to a sheltered spot. As a person is rewarmed, the stagnated and cold blood from the extremities returns to the core of the body, dropping the internal temperature even lower. Just as recirculation is started, death may occur.

When this happens, the official cause is frequently listed as something other than hypothermia. Those in cold water lose control of their arms and legs and drown, while those on land die of heart failure. Sometimes death is listed as "due to exposure," yet the real reason was hypothermia.

Prevention

Instead of hoping you'll be clear-headed enough to recognize the symptoms, know enough to prevent them. There are a number of things you can do.

When heading outdoors during questionable weather, dress properly. Several layers of loose clothing are better than tight clothes, and wool clothing traps body heat even when wet. Mittens are always warmer than gloves. Because much of the body's heat is lost through the head, a hat, cap, or stocking pullover will trap heat and allow your body to send more warm blood to your hands and feet. Most important, stay dry and change clothes if they become damp or wet.

One of the best safeguards against hypothermia is to eat hot meals and drink warm liquids before going out. This provides the nutrition and fuel your body needs to stay warm. In the field do not allow yourself to become dehydrated, and keep nibbling on high-energy snacks to help maintain body heat.

If weather conditions worsen, seek shelter wherever possible, and protect yourself from the wet, wind, and cold.

The best preventive maintenance against hypothermia is awareness. Everyone should put on rain gear before getting wet. For insurance, an extra set of clothing should be with you, in the camper, or at least nearby.

Outdoor enthusiasts—who frequently believe they are tougher than the other guy—should be able to recognize in advance the conditions that lead to the problem, and take the necessary precautions to avoid trouble. The savvy person also must be able to spot the warning signs in others in their group.

You don't have to be in the wilds of Hudson Bay, on the Alaskan tundra, or in a Montana blizzard to succumb to hypothermia. Given the right circumstances, you can become a victim in the Everglades of Florida, on the southwest deserts, or in (or out of) a rowboat on a favorite lake.

Hypothermia doesn't just happen to the other guy. We all need to know the danger signs. ∆

From weasels to chocolate bars — it all came to naught

Remembering ...

By Habeeb Salloum

The biting January wind savagely stung my body, as atop my old mare I made my way through the drifting south Saskatchewan snow. This day, my six mile long weasel trap line was a route of suffering and pain. I could feel the fierce-freezing wind stabbing through my many layers of clothing. My toes inside the sheepskin-lined boots gradually became colder and colder until I could feel that they were becoming numb.

Yet, I was happy. In my saddle bags were two large weasels whose hides I was sure would fetch 50 cents apiece from the fur and hide buyer who made, in late winter, by horse and sled or buggy, his yearly rounds. For me, in the 1930s, this was a fortune. I was just entering my teens and with our family living from hand to mouth, even a few cents were, in my small world, a fortune.

The few times that I had travelled by horse and buggy with my father to Neville, the closest town to our farm, some 16 kilometers (10 miles) to the north, I often drooled over the chocolate bars in the general store where we shopped for our groceries. Of course, a few times my father splurged and bought a bar to be divided among two or three of the accompanying children. This always made me yearn for more. As a child, chocolate was never far from my mind.

To pass the time, as I often did when inspecting my traps, I began to recite out loud the verses of Robert Service—even today, one of my favorite poets. I truly identified with the words of his poems such as *The Cremation of Sam Mcgee*. Over and over, I recited his verses as my mare ploughed through the drifting snow.

Still, the cold and poetry could not snuff out my yearning for chocolate bars. I remember my mouth watering, thinking of the endless bars the weasels in the saddle bags would buy. The drifting snow and piercing cold were momentarily forgotten as I dreamt of feasting on chocolates to my heart's content. My sweet tooth world of fantasy kept me company until I was back home warming my hands over the red-hot coal stove around which, during the freezing winter, our whole family slept at night and sat around during the day.

Warmed by the fire, I was content. Not every time when I made, atop my old

mare, my weekly round of the trap line was I lucky. Usually, if I even found one weasel, my spirits would reach dizzying heights. Most of the time, the traps were empty or closed shut by some sly coyote, an intelligent animal who often outwits the most experienced of hunters.

Nevertheless, this winter, in my mind, I had done well. From my weasel hides and the rabbits which I had shot—whose hides I sold from 5 to 10 cents each—I had saved $5 for that day in spring when I would accompany my father to town.

Early in April that year, along with my father and elder brother, we were on our way by horse and buggy to Neville for our spring shopping—to buy the essential foods and seeds needed for our usually large garden. However, my mind was elsewhere. The $5 in my pocket made me feel like a millionaire. I was excited, thinking that soon I would be gorging myself with chocolate bars.

My thoughts were deep in this dream world of sweets when we drove from a dirt country road onto the dirt main street of town, lined on both sides with mostly business establishments. Neville, at that time, a village of some 200 souls, was to me a glittering metropolis, full of exciting things to see and do.

From among its establishments were two gas stations with their garages and machinery dealerships, four towering grain elevators, a railway station, two general stores filled with goodies, a lumberyard/hardware, a post office, a busy restaurant, a hand-drawn fire fighting engine, and the Neville Hotel which incorporated a beer parlor. It was a night spot which, as a child, I often heard our visitors discuss—at times, not too kindly, especially when they talked about the bar room fights.

Today, Neville is a fast-fading prairie town. Some years ago, during a visit to western Canada, I travelled to my boyhood town. The fantasy metropolis of yesteryear had become almost a ghost town. Its population had dwindled to less than 50 and the main street, although now paved, was edged by empty spaces. Here and there a few homes and businesses barely clung to life and its inhabitants, in the main, were past their prime.

The Fourteenth Year

.... the old days

Qawarma
a food since antiquity

By Habeeb Salloum

During the 1930's Great Depression, the hot winds were fierce as they blew across the south Saskatchewan plains. No more than eight-years-old, I was struggling with a pail of water, half as large as myself, through a blinding sand storm. Every day my chore was to carry water from a well, half a mile down from our hilltop home, for two aged sheep we were fatting for the autumn kill. Exhausted, I reached the barn where my mother was feeding the sheep green vegetable leaves.

"Why do I have to bring water for these sheep? Why can't I take them down to the well to drink?" I was near to tears as I sat down by my mother's side.

She smiled at my childish tantrum, "It is essential that we do not tire these animals. They must be heavy with fat when we butcher them for qawarma in the autumn."

My parents, who emigrated from Syria in the early 1920s, had taken a homestead in southern Saskatchewan, but no sooner had they ploughed the land than it turned into desert. To survive they utilized the ingenuity they had inherited from their forefathers.

In their country of birth, farming had never been a life of luxury. Living with little wealth for thousands of years our ancestors, like most peasants in the lands of antiquity, had developed a variety of foods which have stood the test of centuries. As had our forbears, my parents, in their new land, even if they rarely had money, always had food for their numerous offspring.

Qawarma, one of the mainstays of these historic edibles, had been developed in the Middle East, perhaps since man first became civilized. In their new homeland, my parents kept up the tradition of making this time-honored type of preserved meat. All summer long, a few aged sheep or an old cow would be force-fed many times a day, and sometimes even at night, until they were loaded with fat.

In the autumn, after the animals were butchered, the fat was removed and melted. The meat was then cut into very small pieces and cooked in the fat. When the meat was well cooked, along with the fat, it was placed in earthenware utensils or glass jars. These were stored in a cool earthen cellar, becoming our meat supply for the following year. With no refrigeration of any kind, it was an ideal way to ensure we had meat for the whole year. Our neighbors during the summer months could only think of a roast or steak. As for our family, we always had tasty qawarma.

The railway station was no more; of two gas stations only one remained—a sad replica of its former self; the hotel had disappeared and what businesses remained appeared to be less than thriving. A relative accompanying me and who once lived in the area, surveying the town summed up the scene, "It's a town waiting to disappear."

Standing on the corner besides the remaining poorly-stocked general store, my mind went back to that day when I left my father and brother and hurried down the wooden sidewalk, edged by a dirt avenue filled with horses drawing wagons and buggies, to the nearby Towler General Store. My emotions became more and more aroused as I neared my goal. The thought of feasting on not one but a dozen chocolate bars sent shivers through my body which I still vividly remember.

Almost passing out in anticipation, I picked the bars, smiling all the time at the storekeeper. Sliding a hand in one pocket, then the other to draw out the money, I found them both empty. I was devastated. Bursting out into tears, I rushed out retracing my footsteps a half dozen times. Alas! My hard earned money was gone. My dreams had come to naught.

How my few dollars had disappeared in the short space between where we had stopped and the store haunted me for days. It was a mystery which I was never able to unravel—to me, one of the greatest misfortunes of my youth. In later years, I experienced many pitfalls, but the loss of my chocolate bar money left with me the most unforgettable mark. ∆

When we slaughtered our fattened animal, it was to us children the beginning of gourmet dining. In the ensuing days, we feasted on many succulent dishes prepared from the butchered animal.

My favorite treats were those prepared from the intestines and the stomach. Scrubbed with soap and water until they became spotless, the intestines and stomach were than stuffed with rice (if it was available) but usually with bulgur, spices, herbs, and chick peas. In the ensuing days, we feasted on dish after dish, each one more tasty than the next. Even after more than 78 years, I can still smell the enticing aroma of stuffed karsh (stomach) which I enjoyed so much in my boyhood years. However, in the subsequent days, it was the qawarma dishes to which we looked forward.

In the Greater Syria area, the farmers in the past universally utilized qawarma in their cooking. Today, except in the country homes, it is rarely employed in the kitchen. The modern city Arab scoffs at it as a peasant food, best forgotten. However, in the countryside, it is still a basic food for the hard-working farmers. In the same fashion as we utilized qawarma during our Depression years, they use it as a main ingredient in their many sapid stews and stuffed vegetable dishes.

Unlike in the past, today the making of qawarma in a modern kitchen is a simple task.

This recipe is a minuscule of our qawarma production in the years when it was the cornerstone of our daily menu:

Qawarma

> 2½ lbs. melted beef fat (not suet) or margarine
> 5 lbs. lean beef (any cut), cut into ¼-inch cubes (mutton may be substituted for beef)
> 5 tsp. salt
> 2½ tsp. pepper

Place the melted fat or margarine in a pot and heat, then stir in meat, salt and pepper.

Cook uncovered over medium heat, stirring once in a while to make sure the meat does not stick to the bottom of the pot, until the meat is well cooked—until meat sticks to a wooden spoon.

Allow to cool, then pour into earthenware utensil or glass jars, making sure the meat is covered with ½ inch of fat. Discard the remaining fat. Store the qawarma in a cool place and always return to a cool place after use.

Note: Melt as much qawarma as needed in a recipe, then discard the fat. There is no need to refrigerate the qawarma if it is well-cooked. If the utensils or jars are well sealed the qawarma will stay usable for at least a year.

The following are two of the qawarma dishes we enjoyed during the Depression years.

Eggs with qawarma (*Bayad maa qawarma*)

Eggs with qawarma is perhaps the most common breakfast food among the villagers of Syria and Lebanon. To me, the many modern breakfast foods cannot compare with this simple dish.

> 4 heaping Tbsp. qawarma, fat removed
> 4 large eggs
> ¼ tsp. salt
> ¼ tsp. pepper
> 2 Tbsp. butter

In a bowl, thoroughly combine qawarma, eggs, salt, and pepper.

Melt butter in a frying pan, then add the qawarma egg mixture. Stir-fry over low heat for a few moments, until the eggs are cooked. Serve immediately with toast and coffee. Serves four.

Parsley salad with qawarma
(*Salatat safoof maa qawarma*)

A unique salad, this dish is today rarely prepared in the Middle East. For a delightful treat, this recipe is a must.

> ½ cup chickpeas, soaked overnight, then drained
> ½ cup bulgur
> 3 cups finely chopped parsley
> 1 small bunch of green onions, finely chopped
> ¼ cup of finely chopped fresh mint
> 2 medium tomatoes, finely chopped
> 1 cup qawarma, fat removed
> 1 tsp. salt
> ½ tsp. pepper
> 2 Tbsp. olive oil
> 4 Tbsp. lemon juice
> half a dozen cabbage leaves, cut in half

With a rolling pin, break chickpeas in half, then pick out and discard the skins. Place in a saucepan and cover with water, then bring to boil. Cook for 20 minutes over medium heat, then remove from heat and set aside in their water.

In the meantime, soak bulgur in cold water for 15 minutes, then drain by placing in a strainer and pushing water out by hand. Place in a salad bowl, then set aside

Remove chickpeas from water and add to bulgur (do not discard water), then stir in remainder of ingredients, except cabbage leaves.

Place cabbage leaves in the chickpeas water, then boil for a few moments. Remove, then place on top of salad. Serve immediately while the cabbage leaves are still steaming. Each person should be served one or two cabbage leaves with their portion of the salad. Serves about 6. ∆

For more recipes go to www.backwoodshome.com